THE COMPLETE
Canadian Living
COOKBOOK

THE COMPLETE
Canadian Living
COOKBOOK

350 inspired recipes from

Elizabeth Baird and the kitchen

Canadians trust most

RANDOM HOUSE CANADA

The Complete Canadian Living Cookbook is dedicated to Beverley Renahan, the editing genius behind *Canadian Living*'s respected recipes.

© 2001 by Transcontinental Media Inc.

First published in Canada in 2001 by Random House Canada, a division of Random House of Canada Limited.

Random House Canada and colophon are trademarks.

National Library of Canada Cataloguing in Publication

Baird, Elizabeth, date—
   The complete Canadian living cookbook : 350 recipes / from Elizabeth Baird and the kitchen Canadians trust most.

At head of title: From the Canadian living test kitchen
Includes index.
ISBN 0-679-31117-3 (bound).—ISBN 0-679-31289-7 (pbk.)

   1. Cookery.   I. Title.

TX714.B345 2001   641.5   C2001-900849-X

First paperback edition

Cover photography: see page viii
Interior page design: Sharon Foster Design

Printed and bound in Canada

10 9 8 7 6 5 4 3 2

Contents

Acknowledgements   vii

Introduction   ix

Get Cooking with *Canadian Living*   1

Chapter 1 · Appetizers   16

Chapter 2 · Soups   42

Chapter 3 · Salads and Side Dishes   64

Chapter 4 · Poultry   94

Chapter 5 · Beef   124

Chapter 6 · Pork and Lamb   154

Chapter 7 · Fish and Seafood   184

Chapter 8 · Eggs, Cheese and Vegetarian   206

Chapter 9 · Pasta and Pizza   228

Chapter 10 · Quick Breads and Yeast Breads   252

Chapter 11 · Desserts   278

Chapter 12 · Cakes   300

Chapter 13 · Pies, Tarts and Pastry   324

Chapter 14 · Cookies, Bars and Squares   350

Chapter 15 · Preserves   376

Contributors   394

Glossary of Cooking Terms   395

Index   397

ACKNOWLEDGEMENTS

Thanking all the people who have contributed to *The Complete Canadian Living Cookbook* is a pleasure. Heartfelt thanks go to The Canadian Living Test Kitchen staff, present and past. Our test kitchen manager is Heather Howe, a professional home economist who first came to the Test Kitchen as a student in the late 1980s, soon after I became food editor. Heather graduated to full-fledged staff member, and before becoming chief of the kitchens, worked under all three of our previous managers: Patsy Jamieson, Daphna Rabinovitch and Donna Bartolini. Each in her own way helped build and maintain the excellent reputation of the food department through creativity, a fine palate, exacting standards of recipe development and team leadership. But everyone who has worked in The Canadian Living Test Kitchen, professional home economists and chefs alike, has played a part in this book: Susan Van Hezewijk, who toiled over compiling recipes and creating new delights for each chapter, Emily Richards, cohost of *Canadian Living Cooks*, Annabelle Waugh and Nicole Young make up the current brigade, with additional leadership from associate food editors Andrew Chase and Daphna Rabinovitch. All have stirred family and heritage recipes and new inspirations into the pots of these pages. The past roster of stellar staff in my time includes Claire Arfin, Vicki Burns, Toni Clark, Janet Cornish, Heather Epp, Kate Gammal, Jennifer MacKenzie, Dana McCauley, Lynn Patterson, Ruth Phelan, as well as those who have contributed for shorter periods: Carolyn Gall Casey, Lisa Marie De Rosa, Riki Dixon, Lesleigh Landry, Joanne Leese, Jan Main, Gail Gordon Oliver, Iris Raven and Adell Shneer. I also wish to acknowledge the food writers who have created recipes especially for *Canadian Living*: authors Anne Lindsay, Rose Murray and Bonnie Stern; founding food editor Carol Ferguson; former associate food editor Margaret Fraser; and teachers Pam Collacott, Linda Stephen and Joanne Yolles. To all of you, thanks for your tasty contributions to our tested-till-perfect reputation and philosophy.

Special thanks also go to the staff members who come to The Canadian Living Test Kitchen not to cook but to question, check and verify — our skilled senior editors who make sure recipes read accurately and consistently and that no ingredient has been forgotten or misrepresented. Senior editor Beverley Renahan is the force behind us all, and she has been helped over the years by colleagues Susan Lawrence, Donna Paris, Julia Armstrong and Jo Calvert. It is thanks to Julia Armstrong, project editor of *The Complete Canadian Living Cookbook*, that this volume exists. Heartfelt thanks go to her for her patient, solution-oriented, tireless and creative coordination; she is a true weaver of words and puzzle solver. Saviours to all of us who work in the magazine and book business are the copy editors; at *Canadian Living*, they are presently under the leadership of Tina Anson Mine. For their important work on this book, I wish to thank in particular Barbara Philps and Jennifer Lloyd. Thanks also to inputter Rosemary Hillary and indexer Laurie Coulter. Significant others include our managing editor, Susan Antonacci, and her team, including Olga Goncalves, Teresa Sousa and Jacqueline Holder, as well as business manager Nancy Baker. Deserving of kudos are the dietitians, notably Sharyn Joliat, at Info Access (1988), who provided nutrient analysis for our recipes.

But words alone are not enough. Photographs inspire, and making food look beautiful for the camera is an art. Credit here goes to *Canadian Living*'s creative director, Michael Erb, and the members of the art department, along with the photographers and food and props stylists listed on page viii, all of whom have worked their magic in studios to make the food on a page look spectacular.

I extend thanks to our colleagues and partners at Random House Canada: David Kent, former president, who has been part of *Canadian Living*'s cookbooks since 1991, editorial director Anne Collins, executive editor and guiding light Sarah Davies, talented designer Sharon Foster, art director Scott Richardson and production manager Janine Laporte. No book ever gets into the hands of cooks unless there is marketing and promotion input; thanks go to Sheila Kay, to the staff under director of sales and marketing Brad Martin, and to all the booksellers across Canada whose support all of us at *Canadian Living* warmly applaud.

Of course, I cannot forget the guidance and support behind the *Canadian Living* name, from publisher Debbie Gibson. I have enjoyed working on this cookbook with editor-in-chief Charlotte Empey, who has encouraged all of us involved in the project to do more and to do better in order to produce an outstanding reference volume and recipe collection Canadians will be proud to keep handy in the kitchen and to cook from for generations to come.

Thank you to all.

Elizabeth Baird
Food and Nutrition Editor
Canadian Living

PHOTOGRAPHY

Cover photography
Front cover and spine: Yvonne Duivenvoorden
Back cover: Yvonne Duivenvoorden (staff photograph and Peking Hamburger Dumplings); David Scott (Cedar-Planked Salmon)

Chapter openers: Yvonne Duivenvoorden

Food photography
David Scott: Baked Brie with Strawberry Mint Topping, Stuffed Jalapeño Peppers, Cuban Grilled Pork Sandwich, Bread Salad, Mediterranean Seafood Soup, Salsa Barbecued Beef Brisket, Lamb Moussaka, Pasta Puttanesca, Cedar-Planked Salmon, Orange Fennel Rack of Pork, Country Seed Bread with Raspberry and Red Currant Jelly, Classic Angel Food Cake, Bumbleberry Cobbler on the Barbecue, Brutti ma Buoni, Chocolate Caramel Macadamia Tart
Yvonne Duivenvoorden: Peking Hamburger Dumplings, Simply the Best Scalloped Potatoes, Roasted Roots Salad, Baby Spinach and Goat Cheese Salad, Roast Chicken with Lemon and Garlic, Strawberry Rhubarb Galette
Michael Kohn: Herbed Rösti, Dutch Meatball Soup
Kevin Hewitt: Quick Orange Buns
Ed O'Neil: Mandarin Sorbet

STYLING

Food styling
Olga Truchan: Baked Brie with Strawberry Mint Topping, Stuffed Jalapeño Peppers, Cuban Grilled Pork Sandwich, Bread Salad, Mediterranean Seafood Soup, Salsa Barbecued Beef Brisket, Lamb Moussaka, Pasta Puttanesca, Cedar-Planked Salmon, Orange Fennel Rack of Pork, Country Seed Bread with Raspberry and Red Currant Jelly, Classic Angel Food Cake, Bumbleberry Cobbler on the Barbecue, Chocolate Caramel Macadamia Tart
Julie Aldis: Spicy Thai Shrimp and Noodle Soup, Peking Hamburger Dumplings, Simply the Best Scalloped Potatoes, Roasted Roots Salad, Baby Spinach and Goat Cheese Salad, Roast Chicken with Lemon and Garlic
Sue Henderson: Herbed Rösti
Claire Stancer: Dutch Meatball Soup, Quick Orange Buns
Lucie Richard: Strawberry Rhubarb Galette
Ruth Gangbar: Mandarin Sorbet

Props styling
Catherine MacFadyen: Peking Hamburger Dumplings, Baked Brie with Strawberry Mint Topping, Stuffed Jalapeño Peppers, Cuban Grilled Pork Sandwich, Simply the Best Scalloped Potatoes, Roasted Roots Salad, Bread Salad, Mediterranean Seafood Soup, Roast Chicken with Lemon and Garlic, Salsa Barbecued Beef Brisket, Lamb Moussaka, Pasta Puttanesca, Cedar-Planked Salmon, Orange Fennel Rack of Pork, Country Seed Bread with Raspberry and Red Currant Jelly, Classic Angel Food Cake, Bumbleberry Cobbler on the Barbecue, Chocolate Caramel Macadamia Tart
Lara McGraw: Herbed Rösti, Baby Spinach and Goat Cheese Salad, Mandarin Sorbet
Shelly Tauber: Dutch Meatball Soup
Oksana Slavutych: Spicy Thai Shrimp and Noodle Soup, Quick Orange Buns, Strawberry Rhubarb Galette

INTRODUCTION

Whenever The Canadian Living Test Kitchen staff have a chance to visit personally with Canadians — teaching classes, meeting readers, demonstrating our favourite recipes at shows and special events — we're bombarded by questions, the most popular one being "What's it like to work in the Test Kitchen?"

And no wonder. The Canadian Living Test Kitchen enjoys an enviable reputation as the largest and most prestigious media test kitchen in the country. But more important, we're trusted as the kitchen that creates, tests and serves up delicious recipes for everyday and special occasions, showcasing Canadian produce, new food talent and our rich multicultural food heritage. For more than 25 years, Canadians have counted on our recipes and menus to make cooking a joy — and eating a pleasure.

Our food philosophy is simple: food, lovingly prepared and lovingly shared, encourages us to connect with each other, and to nurture and sustain our rituals, traditions and heritages. We're passionate about food — the historical, sociological and cultural aspects, the preparation, even the shopping — and, of course, the enjoyment of it. And we welcome every opportunity to show Canadians how to reap Canada's bounty, how to transform it into delicious everyday and special-occasion meals, and how to have a wonderful time doing it.

Our days are a celebration of peeling, chopping, slicing, simmering, roasting, steaming, folding, whipping, glazing and kneading as we develop and test recipes in our kitchen so that they'll turn out perfectly in yours. We test our recipes not once, not twice, not three times — we test them till they're perfect. And what does that mean? The food looks good, smells good, tastes good, and the methods incorporate good home-cooking techniques, the kind cooking Canadians really use to get food on the table. If a recipe doesn't meet our high standards, we know it won't meet yours, either, so it's back to the drawing board until we're satisfied that you and your family will be satisfied.

We constantly ask ourselves and each other (creating recipes in The Canadian Living Test Kitchen is a collaborative effort) whether a dish is as tasty, attractive and easy to make as possible. The truth is, our life is food, and we want everyone to enjoy cooking and eating as much as we do.

The Complete Canadian Living Cookbook is our latest gift to Canadian cooks, from beginners to old hands in the kitchen. We canvassed our readers and TV viewers to find out what they wanted in this latest addition to their cookbook shelf, and they told us: the very best recipes for mid-week dinners, parties and celebrations, with the tips and tricks we count on from *Canadian Living*, simply and beautifully packaged in one book — in short, the only cookbook they really need.

We think we've created just that, and more. Enjoy.

Elizabeth Baird
Food and Nutrition Editor
Canadian Living

Get Cooking with Canadian Living

INTERPRETING THE NUTRITIONAL ANALYSIS

- To meet nutrient needs each day, moderately active women aged 25 to 49 need about 1,900 calories, 51 g protein, 261 g carbohydrate, 25 to 35 g fibre and not more than 63 g total fat (21 g saturated fat). Canadian sodium intake of approximately 3,500 to 4,500 mg daily should be reduced. Men in the same age group require about 2,700 calories, 64 g protein, 371 g carbohydrate, 25 to 35 g fibre and not more than 90 g total fat (30 g saturated fat). Teenagers 13 to 18 generally need about 2,100 to 3,200 calories, 46 to 58 g protein (males at the higher end of the range and females at the lower end), and adequate fat intake to maintain growth and development; when teens stop growing, the guideline of consuming no more than 30 per cent total fat from calories daily starts to apply. Carbohydrate intake for teens should be 50 to 60 per cent of energy.

- The percentage of recommended daily intake (% RDI) for calcium, iron, and vitamins A, C and folate is based on the highest recommended intakes (excluding those for pregnant or lactating women).

- Figures have been rounded off. They are based on the first ingredient listed when there is a choice and do not include optional ingredients. Recipe variations have not been analysed.

- Abbreviations: cal = calories, pro = protein, carb = carbohydrate, sat. fat = saturated fat, chol = cholesterol.

CANADIAN LIVING RECIPE ASSUMPTIONS

Before cooking with *Canadian Living* recipes, it's essential to know our assumptions. For example, although the size of egg is not specified, we use large eggs. While this may not make much difference in a chocolate chip cookie, it will certainly have an impact for a soufflé, in which the difference between a large egg and an extra-large or medium one is substantial.

- Read the entire recipe, checking to make sure you have all the ingredients and equipment.

- Prepare and measure ingredients before starting to bake or cook.

- Because temperatures of ovens and burners differ slightly, we often provide a range in cooking times. Always check for doneness at the first specified time or before.

- For stock, use canned broth, with a one to one water ratio, or use good-quality powdered stock. You can reduce the ratio of condensed or powdered stock to water to avoid oversalting a dish.

- Use regular table salt and freshly ground pepper.

- Lemon and lime juices are always freshly squeezed.

- Unless otherwise specified, fruits and vegetables are medium in size, washed and peeled, seeded, pitted or hulled as necessary.

- Eggs are large. Let come to room temperature before using for any baking recipe.

- Butter is salted, unless specified otherwise.

- The oven is preheated.

- Milk and yogurt are 2%.

- Bake or roast in the centre of the oven, unless specified otherwise.

- Cook foods uncovered unless specified otherwise.

- If a choice of ingredient is offered (for example, fresh coriander or parsley), the first is preferred but the second offers a reasonable alternative. The taste will not always be the same.

MEASURING UP FOR SUCCESS

Accurate measuring of both dry and liquid ingredients is essential for success in baking and, to a lesser extent, in cooking. Even minute changes in the proportions of a recipe can cause problems in cakes and cookies. Whether using imperial or metric measures, it is imperative to follow one system throughout the recipe.

- There are basically two types of measuring cups: dry ingredient and liquid ingredient. Dry ingredient measures come in sets of graduated sizes in both imperial (¼, ⅓, ½ and 1 cup) and metric (50, 75, 125 and 250 mL). Liquid ingredient measuring cups have levels marked on the outside of the glass or plastic cup with enough space below the rim to prevent spills.

- Standard measuring spoons are used for both liquid and dry ingredients. They are also graduated with markings: ¼ tsp, ½ tsp, 1 tsp, 1 tbsp, or 1 mL, 2 mL, 5 mL, 15 mL.

- For dry ingredients, such as all-purpose or whole grain flours, granulated sugar or cornstarch, lightly spoon into a dry measure until heaping, without packing or tapping. Level it off with the straight edge of a knife. For brown sugar, pack it down lightly until it holds the shape of the measure when turned out.

- For liquid ingredients, place the liquid measure on a flat surface. Pour in liquid to the desired level and then bend down so that your eye is level with the measure to check for accuracy.

- For fat ingredients, such as butter, shortening and margarine, cut off desired amount according to convenient package markings. Or press firmly into a dry measure, levelling off the top with the straight edge of a knife. Use dry measures for sour cream, yogurt, cream cheese and grated or shredded cheese.

TABLE OF LIQUID AND DRY MEASURE EQUIVALENTS

- Pinch for dry ingredients or Dash for liquid = less than ¼ tsp (1 mL)
- 3 teaspoons = 1 tablespoon (15 mL)
- 2 tablespoons = 1 fluid ounce (25 mL)
- 4 tablespoons = ¼ cup (50 mL)
- 5 tablespoons and 1 tsp = ⅓ cup (75 mL)
- 8 tablespoons = ½ cup (125 mL)
- 10 tablespoons and 2 tsp = ⅔ cup (150 mL)
- 12 tablespoons = ¾ cup (175 mL)
- 16 tablespoons = 1 cup (250 mL)
- 1 cup = 8 fluid ounces (250 mL)
- 4 ounces = ¼ pound (125 g)
- 8 ounces = ½ pound (250 g)
- 16 ounces = 1 pound (500 g)

SUBSTITUTIONS: AN AT-A-GLANCE REFERENCE

There's nothing more frustrating than being ready to bake or cook only to discover you are missing that one essential ingredient. Here's a handy list of baking and cooking substitutions to save you a last-minute dash to the store.

Baking

- 1 cup (250 mL) sifted cake-and-pastry flour = 1 cup (250 mL) all-purpose flour less 2 tbsp (25 mL).

- 1 cup (250 mL) self-rising flour (flour already containing leavening, commonly found in British and Australian cookbooks) = 1 cup (250 mL) all-purpose flour plus 1 tsp (5 mL) baking powder and ¼ tsp (1 mL) salt. (Self-rising flour is now available in many Canadian supermarkets.)

- 1 cup (250 mL) granulated sugar = 1 cup (250 mL) packed brown sugar.

- Light and dark brown sugars are interchangeable for sweetening. Dark has a more pronounced molasses flavour.

- To make superfine or berry sugar, whirl granulated sugar in food processor until in smaller, finer crystals.

- 1 tsp (5 mL) baking powder = ¼ tsp (1 mL) baking soda plus ½ tsp (2 mL) cream of tartar.

- 1 oz (30 g) unsweetened chocolate = 3 tbsp (50 mL) cocoa powder plus 2½ tsp (12 mL) butter.

- Chocolate chips: equal amount of chopped chocolate. (However, you cannot always substitute chocolate chips for chocolate.)

- Bittersweet chocolate: equal amount of semi-sweet chocolate.

- Old-fashioned large-flake rolled oats: equal amount of quick-cooking rolled oats. Do not substitute instant oats.

- Corn syrup: equal amount of molasses or maple syrup.

- Currants: equal amount of raisins, dried cherries or dried cranberries.

- 1 cup (250 mL) buttermilk = 1 cup (250 mL) milk mixed with 1 tbsp (15 mL) vinegar or lemon juice. Let stand for 10 minutes to coagulate.

- 1 cup (250 mL) milk = ½ cup (125 mL) evaporated milk plus ½ cup (125 mL) water. Mix powdered milk according to package instructions; usually ⅓ cup (75 mL) powdered milk and enough water to fill measure to 1 cup (250 mL).

- 1 cup (250 mL) buttermilk or sour cream = 1 cup (250 mL) plain yogurt (in recipes such as muffins, loaves and pancakes; some adjustment may be necessary).

- 1 tsp (5 mL) lemon juice = ½ tsp (2 mL) vinegar.

- 1 cup (250 mL) cream cheese = 1 cup (250 mL) cottage cheese puréed until very smooth plus ¼ cup (50 mL) butter or margarine. This kind of substitution works satisfactorily for a simple cheesecake provided you purée the cottage cheese beforehand to smooth out the curds.

- Butter: equal amount of firm margarine. Do not substitute soft margarine in baking.

- Lemon rind and juice can replace lime; since lime is more sour, taste and adjust. Similarly, lime can replace lemon; add judiciously.

Other Handy Substitutions

- 1 tsp (5 mL) dry mustard = 1 tbsp (15 mL) Dijon mustard (for wet mixtures).

- 2 tbsp (25 mL) soy sauce = 1 tbsp (15 mL) Worcestershire sauce plus 2 tsp (10 mL) water plus pinch salt.

- 1 tbsp (15 mL) Worcestershire sauce = 1 tbsp (15 mL) soy sauce plus dash each hot pepper sauce and lemon juice plus pinch granulated sugar.

- 2 tbsp (25 mL) hoisin sauce = 2 tbsp (25 mL) oyster sauce or fish sauce (if hoisin called for is less than 2 tbsp/25 mL, it can be replaced or omitted; if more, flavour is too important to substitute).

- Curry powder: equal amount of curry paste.

- 1 clove garlic, minced = ¼ tsp (1 mL) garlic powder.

- 1 tbsp (15 mL) chopped fresh herbs = 1 tsp (5 mL) dried herbs. This is a general rule; it will not apply for very large amounts of chopped fresh herbs, such as those exceeding ¼ cup (50 mL) or for more assertive herbs, in which case the amount will be slightly less or specified in parentheses in the recipe.

- 1 tbsp (15 mL) minced fresh gingerroot = 1 tsp (5 mL) ground ginger.

- ½ cup (125 mL) wine = 7 tbsp (100 mL) stock and 1 tbsp (15 mL) vinegar (preferably wine vinegar) OR 7 tbsp (100 mL) apple juice and 1 tbsp (15 mL) wine or cider vinegar.

- 1 cup (250 mL) tomato juice = ½ cup (125 mL) tomato sauce and ½ cup (125 mL) water.

- 1 cup (250 mL) tomato sauce = ½ cup (125 mL) tomato paste and ½ cup (125 mL) water.

- Chopped leeks or shallots: equal amount of chopped onions.

- Chopped chives: equal amount of green part of green onions, chopped.

FOOD SAFETY IN THE HOME

Kitchen Savvy

- Before starting to cook, wash your hands thoroughly with hot water and soap for 20 seconds before rinsing. Wash your hands after using the toilet or blowing your nose.

- Keep a clean kitchen. Cleanliness is a cook's best friend. Bacteria from raw food can spread from the food item to a countertop or from the cutting board to utensils, sponges and dishcloths.

- Change your dishcloths and tea towels every day. Scour your sink and countertops every day.

- Invest in two different cutting boards: one for raw meat, seafood and poultry, and another for ready-to-eat foods such as breads, fruits and vegetables.

- After working with raw meat, seafood or poultry, always wash cutting boards and utensils with a mixture of 1 tbsp (15 mL) chlorine bleach to 4 cups (1 L) water, soaking them in the solution for 45 seconds before rinsing. Since bacteria can seep in and set up residence in cracks, always discard any old or scarred wooden or plastic cutting boards. Always wash your hands in hot, soapy water for 20 seconds after handling raw meat, seafood or poultry.

- Wash your can opener after every use.

- Rinse fresh fruits and vegetables before eating or cooking. For salad greens, use a salad spinner after washing to remove the rinse water.

- Cook meat, poultry and eggs to advised doneness (see Meat Doneness Chart, page 11).

- Keep hot foods hot, above 140°F (60°C), and cold foods cold, below 40°F (4°C).

- Refrigerate leftovers as soon as possible, never leaving cooked foods at room temperature for longer than two hours.

- To quick-chill make-ahead or leftover items, divide large amounts into small, shallow, uncovered containers. Refrigerate, leaving enough airspace around each container to allow circulation of cold air. Cover or top with lid when cold.

- Large quantities of very hot food should be cooled down for 30 minutes before refrigerating so as not to overburden the refrigerator's cooling system.

- Periodically check your refrigerator and freezer temperatures; refrigerators should be at 40°F (4°C) or below and freezers should be at 0°F (-18°C) or below.

- Store eggs in their cartons in the coldest part of your refrigerator, not in the door trays. Always discard cracked eggs. Respect the best-before date.

Cooking Savvy

- Don't put any cooked meat, seafood or poultry on a plate that has come in contact with raw meat, poultry or seafood. The same goes for any utensils that touched these ingredients when raw. Use clean tongs and lifters to turn and remove cooked food from skillet, oven or grill.

- Use a meat thermometer. Always check that the food in question is cooked to the right temperature (see Meat Doneness Chart, page 11).

- Completely thaw frozen meat, poultry or fish before cooking. Never thaw at room temperature. Thaw on a plate or tray on the bottom shelf of the refrigerator so that juices do not drip onto other foods. Calculate five hours per pound (500 g). To quick-thaw, immerse wrapped frozen item in cold water for one hour per pound (500 g), changing water often.

- Never refreeze partially thawed meat without cooking it first. Do not buy previously frozen food that has thawed.

- Don't attempt to cook food in stages as this encourages still-active bacteria to multiply.

- Buy all fish and shellfish from reputable sources with a high turnover.

- Never reuse grocery bags or meat trays that once carried any raw meat, seafood or poultry.

- Be aware that even acidic foods such as fruit juices are susceptible to cross-contamination if they have not been pasteurized. Pasteurization removes all doubt by killing all bacteria with high heat.

Picnics and Hot-Weather Awareness

- Keep serving times outdoors as short as possible.

- When enjoying a picnic, chill food before packing and always keep your food covered and chilled inside coolers well stocked with ice and ice packs.

- Place coolers in the shade for as long as possible.

- Plan amounts carefully to avoid leftovers; discard any uneaten meat, poultry, seafood, salads or dairy products.

HIGH-ALTITUDE BAKING

High altitude affects baking. If baking at high altitudes, follow these guidelines:

- At high altitudes, leavening agents such as baking powder, baking soda and yeast release more and larger gas bubbles, which expand very quickly and then, before the heat in the oven has firmed them, collapse, causing cakes and breads to fall. For cake batters, reduce the baking powder or soda by ⅛ tsp (0.5 mL) for each teaspoon (5 mL) called for in the recipe. Most cookie recipes need not be altered since less leavening is generally the rule.

- Since yeast doughs rise more quickly, rely more on visual cues than on suggested times to make sure the dough has risen until doubled in bulk only. If you let it rise longer, the bread may develop large air cells, causing it to fall during baking.

- Moisture evaporates at a lower temperature, which results in baked goods that are drier. Line your cake and baking pans with parchment paper or greased waxed paper.

- The internal temperature of a cake baking at high altitude is lower, which means it will take longer than the time specified. Increase time by a few minutes, but do not alter temperature.

- Since excessive sugar weakens a cake's structure, reduce the amount of sugar called for if the initial amount is more than half the quantity of flour called for. Reduce sugar by 1 tbsp (15 mL) for every cup (250 mL) called for.

Shopping Savvy

- Always examine the packaging at the store. Avoid swollen or dented cans or damaged packages; their contents may have been exposed to bacteria.

- Select perishable items (meat, poultry, seafood, produce, dairy products) last and put them away first.

- In hot weather, bring a cooler and ice packs to the store or market to transport perishables.

ESSENTIAL KITCHEN EQUIPMENT

The Right Knife

While all of the equipment listed below is considered essential to the kitchen, there is one indispensable tool: an excellent chef's knife. A good knife makes the difference between cooking as a chore and cooking as a pleasure. Here is a list of knives every kitchen needs, with the first two taking priority.

Chef's knife: available with 8-inch (20 cm), 10-inch (25 cm) and 12-inch (30 cm) blades.

Paring knife: a small knife used for cutting fruits and vegetables; it is useful to have two on hand.

Serrated knife: for cutting breads, cakes and tomatoes.

Slicing knife: differs slightly from a carving knife in that it has a rounded tip and a scalloped edge and is used for slicing hams and other cooked meats, raw fish, fruits and vegetables.

High-carbon stainless steel is the optimal material for a knife since it will stay sharp longer and not rust. Choose knives that feel heavy and well balanced. Choose a knife with a riveted wood or moulded plastic handle with a blade that extends through the handle to the butt. Wash knives by hand; do not put them in the dishwasher because that dulls the blade and may even damage the handle. Store knives in a wooden knife block or on a magnetic rack.

It is also worthwhile to invest in a 12-inch (30 cm) medium-grained sharpening steel with a protective guard at the top of the handle. Position your knife by grasping the steel firmly in one hand, pointing it upward and away from your body. Tuck your thumb safely behind the protective guard. Hold the knife in your other hand with the cutting edge facing you. Set the heel of the blade at the base of the steel, at a 20-degree angle to the steel. Draw the blade from its heel to its tip in one diagonal stroke, pressing lightly and moving the blade across the steel and away from you. Repeat for a total of five times under the steel and five times over so that both sides of the blade are equally aligned.

Measuring Equipment

Have a set of graduated dry measuring cups (metal or plastic), at least one set of graduated measuring spoons (slim metal spoons are preferred for ease of spooning out of bottles), and a set of graduated liquid measuring cups (usually glass). It's handy to have more than one set of each, in case you've used the 1 tbsp (15 mL) measure for something wet and then need it to measure something dry. A scale is also very useful.

Stove Top

Saucepans: The foundation of any kitchen, saucepans come in many different sizes. Don't feel obliged to buy a set. Buy the best quality you can afford as they are a lifetime investment. Choose those with a heavy base, a tight-fitting lid and oven-proof handles. Stainless steel is a good choice as long as the base encloses a thick pad of aluminum or copper for better heat distribution. Saucepans are usually sold by capacity, either in litres or quarts or both. You'll generally need two or three, ranging from 1 to 4 quarts (1 to 4 L), each about 4 inches (10 cm) deep.

Dutch oven: Used both on the stove top and in the oven, Dutch ovens are good for everything from preserving to stir-frying to braising. Choose a heavy-bottomed one with a 6-quart (6 L) capacity. Both stainless steel with an aluminum pad and enamelled cast iron are reliable choices.

Skillets: Having a few in different sizes, differentiated by diameter, is useful; they range from small (6 inches/15 cm) to large (10 or 12 inches/25 or 30 cm). Also, having them in a variety of materials is useful: cast iron, nonstick and heavy-bottomed stainless steel. For nonstick, use plastic or wooden spatulas to avoid scratching the coating. When The Canadian Living Test Kitchen calls for a large skillet, use a 12-inch (30 cm) skillet, measured across the top. A cast-iron skillet is perfect for searing steaks and chops and cooking small roasts, and it is the ideal skillet for a tarte tatin.

Stockpot: Use a large, narrow, tall pot for making stock, cooking pasta and boiling corn. An 8- to 10-quart (8 to 10 L) stockpot is recommended.

Saucepan with double boiler insert and steamer insert: If you don't have a double boiler insert, improvise by placing a stainless-steel bowl slightly larger in diameter on top of the saucepan.

Grill pan: A must-have for grilling inside year-round. Available in nonstick and cast-iron surfaces.

Wok: Choose a flat-bottomed wok with either one or two handles. Woks are now available in a variety of materials but the preferred is still carbon steel as stir-frying necessitates quick high heat. A high-sided skillet can always stand in for a wok. Try to buy one with a lid, which makes it ideal for braising and steaming. Many come with a curved metal wok spatula.

Ovenware

Casseroles: Round, oval, square or rectangular in a variety of materials; it's good to have at least one or two large ones and a medium and small one. Available in 6 cups (1.5 L), 8 cups (2 L), 10 cups (2.5 L), 12 cups (3 L) and 20 cups (5 L), all with tight-fitting lids.

Gratin dish: Usually wide and shallow, often oval, with either sloping or straight sides. Most often used for scalloped vegetable, baked pasta or potato dishes in 4-cup (1 L) or 6-cup (1.5 L) capacities.

Roasting pans: Typically made of stainless steel, enamelled steel or aluminum; a low one with a rack is the most useful to have on hand. Ideally a roasting pan has sides that are 2 inches (5 cm) high and a rack — both of which allow the heat to circulate freely around the meat. Choose a pan to suit the size of roasts or poultry you typically make. Too large a pan means the wonderful juices collecting on the bottom of the pan will burn; too small and air circulation is compromised. For an average-size chicken, select a pan that is 14 x 10 inches (35 x 25 cm), and for larger birds such as turkey or goose or larger roasts such as a brisket, we suggest 17 x 12 inches (42 x 30 cm).

Soufflé dishes: Straight-sided, round dishes made of porcelain or stoneware and traditionally fluted; sold in 6-cup (1.5 L) or 10-cup (2.5 L) capacities.

Bakeware

Baking dishes: Usually square or rectangular, in a variety of sizes, identified by their dimensions and capacity: 8-inch (2 L) square, 11- x 7-inch (2 L), 13- x 9-inch (3 L); made of glass, usually about 2 inches (5 cm) high.

Baking pans: Like baking dishes but made of metal. Sizes include 8-inch (2 L) square, 9-inch (2.5 L) square, 13- x 9-inch (3.5 L) rectangular and 8- or 9-inch (1.2 or 1.5 L) round.

Cake pans: An assortment of springform pans, a tube pan 10 inches (4 L), and a 6- or 10-inch (1.5 or 3 L) Bundt pan.

Loaf pans: Essential for quick breads, tea loaves and meat loaves, the most common sizes being either the 8- x 4-inch (1.5 L), which is best for a meat loaf that calls for 1 lb (500 g) ground meat, or the 9- x 5-inch (2 L). Available in glass and metal; also ones with built-in drainers for meat loaves.

Pie plates: Pies are made in 9-inch (23 cm) pie plates, but it's handy to have a 10-inch (25 cm) pie plate for deep-dish variations. Buy either glass or dark metal ones for crisp pie crusts.

Baking sheets: Invest in both rimless baking sheets for making cookies (the absence of sides lets heat circulate more easily and allows the cookies to slide right off when baked) and rimmed baking sheets (with sides to contain batter and perfect for roasting vegetables and wings). We don't recommend using dark baking sheets as food darkens more quickly.

Tart pans: Available in a variety of sizes (8-, 9-, 10-, 11-inch/20, 23, 25, 28 cm), as well as miniature, these metal pans have removable bottoms and fluted sides. Wash only in hot water to keep perfectly seasoned. Do not wash in dishwasher.

TEST KITCHEN TIPS

• To measure the size of a baking dish or pan, measure across the top of the dish from the inside edge to the other inside edge.

• If substituting a glass baking dish when a recipe calls for a metal one, reduce the baking temperature by 25°F (10°C) and check the item five minutes before the time noted.

More Baking Basics

- Baking weights or beans
- Cookie cutters
- Custard cups (the most useful is ¾ cup/175 mL)
- Metal cooling racks
- Mixing bowls in a variety of sizes (stainless steel or glass recommended)
- Muffin tins
- Offset spatula for icing cakes and pastries (its flat blade with a step next to the handle prevents the cook's hand from getting in the way when spreading batter or icing)

- Pastry brushes
- Piping bags and nozzles (pastry bags come in a variety of sizes, measured by length; it's actually easier to manipulate a larger one than a smaller one; purchase a bag at least 10 or 12 inches (24 or 30 cm) long and tips with a variety of openings; do not cut the opening of the pastry bag too large or the pastry tips will simply fall through)
- Rubber spatulas, including some high-heat-resistant ones
- Wooden rolling pin
- Wooden spatulas
- Wooden spoons

Other Handy Utensils and Machines

- Blender
- Bulb baster
- Colanders/sieves
- Cutting boards: wooden and plastic
- Food mill
- Food processor
- Grater
- Juicer
- Kitchen scissors
- Ladles
- Melon baller
- Metal or wooden skewers
- Microplane rasper
- Mixer: upright table model or hand-held
- Pastry blender
- Pepper grinder
- Potato masher
- Salad spinner
- Skimming spoon
- Slotted spoons
- Thermometers
- Timers
- Tongs
- Vegetable peelers
- Whisks
- Zester

MEAT COOKING CHART

Beef

CUT/TYPE	COOKING METHOD
Premium Oven Roasts: Prime Rib, Rib Eye, Tenderloin, Top Sirloin	• For all roasts except tenderloin: Roast at 325°F (160°C) for 20 minutes per lb (500 g) for rare, 25 minutes per lb (500 g) for medium, and 30 minutes per lb (500 g) for well done. • For tenderloin: Roast at 450°F (230°C) for 10 to 15 minutes per lb (500 g) for rare to medium-rare.
Oven Roasts: Inside Round, Outside Round, Eye of Round, Sirloin Tip, Rump Roast	Add water to roasting pan to depth of 1 inch (2.5 cm). Place 2- to 5-lb (1 to 2 kg) roast on rack over water in pan. Roast in 500°F (260°C) oven for 30 minutes. Reduce heat to 275°F (140°C); roast for 25 to 35 minutes per lb (500 g) for rare to medium-rare.
Pot Roasts: Cross Rib, Boneless Blade, Shoulder, Brisket, Short Rib	Brown on all sides in lightly oiled Dutch oven. Add 1 to 2 cups (250 to 500 mL) liquid, such as wine, juice or stock. Cover and simmer on stove top or in oven at 325°F (160°C) for about 3 hours or until tender.
Grilling Steaks: Rib, Rib Eye, T-Bone, Strip Loin, Top Sirloin, Tenderloin	• For ½- to ¾-inch (1 to 2 cm) steaks, grill or broil for 3 to 5 minutes for rare, 5 to 7 minutes for medium, and 7 to 9 minutes for well done. • For 1-inch (2.5 cm) steaks, grill or broil, 5 to 7 minutes, 7 to 9 minutes, 9 to 11 minutes accordingly.
Marinating Steaks: Inside Round, Outside Round, Eye of Round, Sirloin Tip, Flank	• For ½- to ¾-inch (1 to 2 cm) steaks, grill or broil for 3 to 5 minutes for rare, 5 to 7 minutes for medium. • For 1-inch (2.5 cm) steaks, grill or broil, 5 to 7 minutes, 7 to 9 minutes accordingly.
Simmering Steaks: Blade, Top Blade, Bottom Blade, Cross Rib	Brown on all sides in lightly oiled Dutch oven. Add ½ to 1 cup (125 to 250 mL) liquid, such as stock, juice, wine or canned tomatoes. Cover and simmer on stove top or in oven at 325°F (160°C) for about 1¼ hours or until tender.
Stewing Beef: Simmering Short Ribs, Boneless and Bone-In, Stewing Cubes	Brown in small amount of oil, adding onions and other seasonings as desired. Add 4 cups (1 L) liquid per lb (500 g) such as stock, tomato juice or wine to cover beef. Cover and simmer on stove or in 325°F (160°C) oven for 1½ to 2 hours.
Quick-Serve Beef: Stir-Fry Strips, Fast-Fry Minute Steak, Grilling Kabobs, Fondue Cubes	Season with pepper and other spices to taste. Do not add salt. Cook in lightly greased pan or wok over medium heat for 2 to 3 minutes for strips, or 2 to 4 minutes per side for steaks.

Pork

CUT	LB	KG	325°F (160°C) MIN/LB (500 G)
Loin: Centre Cut, Bone-In Rack of Pork	3–5	1.5–2.2	20–25
Tenderloin End, Boneless	3–4	1.5–2	25–30
Single Loin, Boneless	3–4	1.5–2	20–25
Rib End, Boneless	2–4	1.0–2	25–30
Crown Roast, Unstuffed	8+	3.5+	20–25
Double Loin, Boneless	3–5	1.5–2.2	30–35

continued on page 10

Pork continued

CUT	LB	KG	325°F (160°C) MIN/LB (500 G)
Leg: Inside and Outside, Boneless	3–4	1.5–2.0	20–25
Shoulder: Shoulder Butt or Picnic, Boneless Shoulder Butt or Picnic, Bone-In	3–6 5	1.5–2.7 2.2	30–35 25–30
Tenderloin	½–¾	250–375 g	roast at 375°F (190°C) 30–35 (total cooking time)
Pork Chops	For ¾-inch (2 cm) thick chops, grill or broil for 8 to 12 minutes.		

Lamb

CUT	LB	KG	325°F (160°C) MIN/LB (500 G)
Leg, Boneless Rolled	3–4	1.5–2.0	25–30 (rare) 30–35 (medium) 35–40 (well)
Leg, Bone-In	5–7	2.2–3.15	20–25 (rare) 25–30 (medium) 30–35 (well)
Leg, Bone-In	7–9	3.15–4	15–20 (rare) 20–25 (medium) 25–30 (well)
Rib Chops	For 1-inch (2.5 cm) chops, grill or broil for a total of 7 to 11 minutes.		
Loin Chops	For 1-inch (2.5 cm) chops, grill or broil for a total of 7 to 11 minutes. For 1½-inch (4 cm) chops, grill or broil for a total of 15 to 19 minutes.		

Chicken

CUT	LB	KG	325°F (160°C) ROASTING TIME
Whole Chicken (stuffed or unstuffed)	3	1.5	2 hours 20 minutes

Turkey

CUT	LB	KG	325°F (160°C) ROASTING TIME
Whole Turkey (stuffed)	14	6.3	4–4½ hours
Whole Turkey (unstuffed)	14	6.3	3¼–3½ hours

DETERMINING MEAT DONENESS

The best way to determine doneness is to use a meat thermometer. Invest in a reliable brand and always keep it handy. Insert into thickest part of roasts or into centre of meat loaves to determine doneness according to internal temperatures below. For stuffed chicken and turkey, insert thermometer into thigh, not stuffing. Always avoid touching bone as that will give a false reading.

In addition to checking for internal temperature in whole meats and poultry, check for the following:

Doneness of Chicken and Turkey
- Wings, thighs and whole chicken or turkey done when juices run clear.
- Breast pieces and kabobs done when no longer pink inside.

Doneness of Pork
- Juices run clear when pork is pierced and just a hint of pink remains inside.

Doneness of Ground Meat
- Must always be cooked until well done and no longer pink inside.

MEAT DONENESS CHART

MEAT	RARE	MEDIUM	WELL DONE
Pork		160°F (70°C) (just a hint of pink remains)	
Ground Pork			170°F (75°C)
Beef	140°F (60°C)	160°F (70°C)	170°F (75°C)
Ground Beef			170°F (75°C)
Lamb	140°F (60°C)	160°F (70°C)	170°F (75°C)
Veal	140°F (60°C)	160°F (70°C)	
Chicken Pieces			170°F (75°C)
Ground Chicken			175°F (80°C)
Whole Chicken (stuffed or unstuffed)			185°F (85°C)
Whole Turkey (stuffed or unstuffed)			180°F (82°C)

FRUITS AND VEGETABLES: A BUYING GUIDE

- The fruits and vegetables are based on commonly available sizes found at the supermarket. Where there is a range, we have based amounts on the first figure; for example, for 2 to 3 apples, we have used 2 apples.

- As well, for chopped or sliced fruits and vegetables, we assume that they have been trimmed, pitted, stemmed and peeled where appropriate, as in our recipes.

- The indicated peak times are for fresh Canadian produce, although some, like carrots, may be available year-round, while others, such as apples, are available from cold storage at other times during the year. Availability varies according to location and weather.

- For fruits and vegetables that are typically imported and often available year-round, lemons for example, wherever possible we have indicated peak times for these as well.

- Some vegetables and fruits are also available year-round frozen: cranberries, wild blueberries, strawberries, raspberries, rhubarb, peas, corn, beans and broccoli are examples of produce that freezes well.

- Canned fruits and vegetables are also options: peaches, pears, pineapple, apricots and applesauce are a handy staple, as are canned tomatoes, beets, corn and legumes.

Fruits

Apples	1 lb (500 g) = 2 to 3 apples 1 apple, grated or chopped = 1 cup (250 mL) 1 apple, sliced = 1½ cups (375 mL)	late August to April
Apricots	1 lb (500 g) = 5 to 7 apricots 1 apricot, sliced = ½ cup (125 mL)	July to August
Avocado	1 lb (500 g) = 2 avocados 1 avocado, sliced or cubed = 1 cup (250 mL) 1 avocado, mashed = ½ cup (125 mL)	April to August
Bananas	1 lb (500 g) = 4 bananas 1 banana, sliced = 1 cup (250 mL) 1 banana, mashed = ¾ cup (175 mL)	year-round
Blueberries	1 pint = 12 oz (375 g) = 2 cups (500 mL)	July to September
Cantaloupe	1 cantaloupe = 3 lb (1.5 kg) = 7 cups (1.75 L) chopped	July to September
Cherries	1 lb (500 g) = 50 cherries = 3 cups (750 mL) 1 lb (500 g) pitted = 2 cups (500 mL)	late June to early August
Cranberries	1 bag = 12 oz (375 g) = 3 cups (750 mL)	September to late December
Grapefruit	1 lb (500 g) = 1 to 3 grapefruit = 1 cup (250 mL) sections 1 grapefruit = ¾ cup (175 mL) juice	year-round; peak in winter
Grapes	1 lb (500 g) = 3 cups (750 mL) stemmed	August through early October

Honeydew	1 honeydew = 5½ lb (2.45 kg) 1 honeydew, chopped = 12 cups (3 L)	July to September
Kiwifruit	1 lb (500 g) = 4 to 6 kiwifruit 1 kiwifruit = ½ cup (125 mL) sliced/chopped	year-round; peak in fall and winter
Lemons	1 lb (500 g) = 2 to 3 lemons 1 lemon = 1 tbsp (15 mL) grated rind; ¼ cup (50 mL) juice	year-round; peak in winter
Limes	1 lb (500 g) = 4 limes 1 lime = 2 tsp (10 mL) grated rind; 3 tbsp (50 mL) juice	year-round; peak in fall
Mandarins	1 lb (500 g) = 3 to 4 mandarins 1 mandarin = 1 cup (250 mL) sections; 2 tsp (10 mL) grated rind; ⅓ cup (75 mL) juice	November to January
Nectarines	1 lb (500 g) = 4 nectarines 1 nectarine = 1 cup (250 mL) sliced or chopped	August to mid-September
Oranges	1 lb (500 g) = 2 to 3 oranges 1 orange = 1 tbsp (15 mL) grated rind; 1 cup (250 mL) sections; ⅓ cup (75 mL) juice	year-round; peak in winter
Peaches	1 lb (500 g) = 2 to 4 peaches 1 peach = 1 cup (250 mL) sliced 1 peach = 1 cup (250 mL) chopped or diced	mid-July to mid-September
Pears	1 lb (500 g) = 2 to 3 pears 1 pear = 1 cup (250 mL) sliced or chopped	August to late November
Pineapple	1 pineapple = 2½ lb (1.25 kg) 1 pineapple = 5 cups (1.25 L) chopped	year-round; peak in winter
Plums	1 lb (500 g) = 5 plums 1 plum = ½ cup (125 mL) chopped or sliced	mid-July to late September
Raspberries	1 pint = 12 oz (375 g) = 2 cups (500 mL) 2 cups (500 mL) = 1 cup (250 mL) puréed; ⅓ cup (75 mL) puréed and seeded	July (some available until September)
Rhubarb	1 lb (500 g) trimmed = 10 stalks 1 stalk, trimmed = ½ cup (125 mL) chopped	forced: January until April outdoor: early May to July
Strawberries	1 quart = 30 strawberries = 1½ lb (750 g) 1 quart = 4 cups (1 L) hulled 1 quart = 4 cups (1 L) sliced/chopped 4 cups (1 L) = 2½ cups (625 mL) puréed	early June to mid/late July (some available until September)
Watermelon	1 medium-large watermelon = 14 lb (6.25 kg) 1 lb (500 g) = 3½ cups (875 mL) cubed	August to end of September

Vegetables

Artichokes	1 large artichoke = 12 oz (375 g)	spring, fall
Asparagus	1 bunch = 1 lb (500 g) = 24 stalks 1 bunch chopped = 3 cups (750 mL)	April to late June
Beans (green/yellow wax)	1 lb (500 g) = 6 cups (1.5 L) whole 1 lb (500 g) = 4 cups (1 L) chopped	July to late September
Beets	1 lb (500 g) = 1 bunch = 3 to 4 beets 1 bunch quartered = 2 cups (500 mL) = 2⅓ cups (575 mL) chopped/sliced	July to mid-October
Broccoli	1 lb (500 g) = 1 bunch 1 bunch = 4 cups (1 L) chopped florets; 2 cups (500 mL) sliced peeled stems	July to late October
Brussels sprouts	1 lb (500 g) = 24 sprouts = 4 cups (1 L)	September to November
Cabbage	1 large green cabbage = 4 lb (2 kg) 1 lb (500 g) shredded = 6 cups (1.5 L)	July to November

Carrots	1 lb (500 g) = 4 large carrots
	1 carrot = ¾ cup (175 mL) chopped/sliced =
	    ⅔ cup (150 mL) grated
	1 bunch = 9 small carrots = 12 oz (375 g) tops removed
	1 carrot = ⅓ cup (75 mL) chopped/sliced =
	    ¼ cup (50 mL) grated
		July to late September

Cauliflower	1 large cauliflower = 2¾ lb (1.375 kg) trimmed florets = 12 cups (3 L)	August to late October
Celery	1 bunch = 1½ lb (750 g) 1 stalk = ½ cup (125 mL) sliced = 6 celery sticks	August to September
Corn	1 cob = 8 oz (250 g) = 1 cup (250 mL) kernels	late July to late September
Cucumber	1 English cucumber = 1 lb (500 g) = 12 inches (30 cm) sliced = 4 cups (1 L) chopped = 2½ cups (625 mL) 2 to 8 small field cucumbers = 1 lb (500 g)	year-round June to early September
Eggplant	1 large eggplant = 1 lb (500 g)= 7 cups (1.75 L) sliced or cubed 1 small Asian eggplant = 6 oz (175 g) = 2 cups (500 mL) sliced or cubed	August to late September
Garlic	1 head = about 2 oz (60 g) = 10 cloves 1 clove = 1 tsp (5 mL) minced	August to October
Green onions	1 bunch = 6 onions = 4 oz (125 g) 1 bunch = 1½ cups (375 mL) chopped, white and trimmed green parts	July to September
Leeks	1 bunch = 3 to 4 leeks = 1 lb (500 g) 1 leek = 1 cup (250 mL) sliced, white and pale green parts	August to November

Lettuce, Boston	1 head = 1 lb (500 g) = 11 cups (2.75 L) torn	June to September
Lettuce, iceberg	1 head = 1¼ lb (625 g) = 12 cups (3 L) torn	July to end of September
Lettuce, romaine	1 head = 1½ oz (750 g) = 14 cups (3.5 L) torn	June to end of September
Mushrooms, button	1 lb (500 g) = 30 mushrooms = 6 cups (1.5 L) sliced/chopped	year-round
Onions, cooking	1 lb (500 g) = 3 to 4 onions 1 onion = 1½ cups (375 mL) sliced = 1 cup (250 mL) chopped	August to May
Onions, red	1 lb (500 g) = 2 onions = 2½ cups (625 mL) sliced 1 onion = 2 cups (500 mL) chopped	August to October
Onions, Spanish and other large, sweet varieties	1 lb (500 g) = 1 onion = 3 cups (750 mL) sliced 1 onion = 2 cups (500 mL) chopped	August to October
Parsnips	1 lb (500 g) = 3 to 4 parsnips 1 parsnip = 1 cup (250 mL) chopped = ⅓ cup (75 mL) mashed	September to November
Peas	1 lb (500 g) fresh peas in pod = 1⅓ cups (325 mL) shelled	mid-June to late July
Potatoes	1 lb (500 g) = 3 to 4 potatoes 1 potato = 1 cup (250 mL) sliced = ¾ cup (175 mL) chopped = ½ cup (125 mL) cooked, mashed	late August to late October
Potatoes (new/mini)	1 lb (500 g) = 15 new/mini-potatoes	July to September
Potatoes, sweet	1 lb (500 g) = 2 to 3 sweet potatoes 1 potato = 2½ cups (625 mL) sliced = 2 cups (500 mL) cubed = 1 cup (250 mL) mashed	late summer
Radishes	1 bag = 1 lb (500 g) = 27 radishes = 3½ cups (875 mL) sliced 1 bunch = 12 radishes = 1½ cups (375 mL) sliced	June to September
Rutabaga	1 rutabaga = 2½ lb (1.25 kg) = 5 cups (1.25 L) cubed 1 cup (250 mL) cubed = ½ cup (125 mL) cooked, mashed	October to December

Spinach	1 bag = 10 oz (300 g) = 19 cups (4.75 L), trimmed
	  and lightly packed; 10 cups (2.5 L) packed
	1 bunch = 12 oz (375 g) = 16 cups (4 L), trimmed
	  and lightly packed; 8 cups (2 L) packed
		June to October

Squash, butternut	1 large squash = 3 lb (1.5 kg) = 11 cups (2.75 L) cubed 1 cup (250 mL) cubed = ½ cup (125 mL) mashed	September to November
Sweet peppers	1 lb (500 g) = 2 to 4 peppers 1 pepper = 1½ cups (375 mL) sliced = 1¼ cups (300 mL) chopped	August to September; year-round greenhouse
Tomatoes	1 lb (500 g) = 2 to 3 tomatoes 1 tomato = 1 cup (250 mL) chopped	late July to late September
Zucchini	1 lb (500 g) = 4 zucchini 1 zucchini, halved and sliced = 2 cups (500 mL) 1 zucchini, chopped = 1½ cups (375 mL)	July to late September

Appetizers

1

Baked Brie with Strawberry Mint Topping 18
Stuffed Jalapeño Peppers 19
Crab Cakes 20
Steamed Lemongrass Mussels 21
Sushi Platter 22
Thai Curry Shrimp 24
Grilled Jumbo Shrimp Skewers with Dipping Sauce 25
Grilled Teriyaki Ginger Chicken Satays 26
Honey Garlic Chicken Wings 27
Chicken Liver Pâté with Basil 28
Layered Mexican Dip 29
Hummus 30
Grilled Vegetable Antipasto 31
Peking Hamburger Dumplings 32
Cornmeal "Blini" with Smoked Salmon 33
Party Meatballs with Southwestern Barbecue Sauce 34
Balsamic Mushroom Crostini 35
Smoked Salmon–Stuffed Baguette 36
Picadillo Empanadas 37
Prosciutto Roll-Ups 38
Brie, Pear and Onion Strudel on a Bed of Greens 39
Curried Lamb Phyllo Triangles 40
Quesadillas 41

Baked Brie with Strawberry Mint Topping

A guaranteed crowd-pleaser, a baked round or wedge of creamy Brie cheese is delectable spread with something tart or fruity — everything from strawberries to chutney. Provide plenty of plain water crackers and a spreader so that guests can help themselves.

SUBSTITUTION: For a shortcut, spread Brie with bought or homemade pesto (page 235) or bruschetta topping (page 35). Or top liberally with hot pepper jelly or a prepared sauce such as raspberry chipotle pepper.

1	round (8 oz/250 g) Brie cheese	1

STRAWBERRY MINT TOPPING:

½ cup	chopped strawberries	125 mL
2 tbsp	white wine or vermouth	25 mL
1 tbsp	chopped fresh mint	15 mL

1 STRAWBERRY MINT TOPPING: In bowl, combine strawberries, wine and mint. (MAKE-AHEAD: Cover and refrigerate for up to 8 hours.)

2 Place Brie on baking sheet; spread with topping. Bake in 350°F (180°C) oven for 5 to 10 minutes or until cheese is softened.

TEST KITCHEN TIPS

• You can microwave Brie instead of baking to soften if desired. Place on plate and microwave at Medium-High (70%) for 1 minute or until cheese is slightly softened.

• Brie's downy white rind is perfectly edible. The same applies to Camembert, another famous soft-ripened cheese originally from France. Both are delicious served with fresh fruit, especially ripe pears, for dessert.

Makes 10 to 15 servings.

PER EACH OF 15 SERVINGS, ABOUT:

cal	58	carb	trace
pro	4 g	fibre	trace
total fat	5 g	chol	17 mg
sat. fat	3 g	sodium	105 mg

PERCENTAGE RDI:

calcium	3%	vit. A	3%
iron	1%	vit. C	3%
folate	5%		

TOPPING VARIATIONS

Substitute one of the following for the Strawberry Mint Topping.

Fruit Chutney Topping: Spread ⅓ cup (75 mL) Peach Chutney (page 388) or other chutney over Brie and bake.

Tangy Cranberry Topping: In saucepan, bring 1 cup (250 mL) fresh or frozen cranberries, ¼ cup (50 mL) packed brown sugar and 1 tbsp (15 mL) water to boil. Reduce heat and simmer, stirring occasionally, for 5 minutes. Add 2 tbsp (25 mL) chopped green onions, 2 tsp (10 mL) lime juice, 1 tsp (5 mL) chopped jalapeño pepper and pinch each salt and pepper. Let cool slightly. (MAKE-AHEAD: Cover and refrigerate for up to 4 days.) Spoon over Brie and bake.

Bacon and Sun-Dried Tomato Topping: Stir together ¼ cup (50 mL) crumbled cooked bacon, 2 tbsp (25 mL) chopped drained oil-packed sun-dried tomatoes, 2 tsp (10 mL) of the oil from the tomatoes and 2 tsp (10 mL) chopped fresh parsley. Spoon over Brie and bake.

Hazelnut Pear Topping: Stir together half a ripe pear (or 2 canned pear halves, patted dry), chopped, ¼ cup (50 mL) chopped toasted skinned hazelnuts, 1 tbsp (15 mL) packed brown sugar and 1 tsp (5 mL) hazelnut liqueur or brandy. Spoon over Brie and bake.

Stuffed Jalapeño Peppers

Deep-fried stuffed jalapeño peppers were the inspiration for these irresistible and lightened-up baked peppers. But while you won't get all the fat, you will still get the thrill from the peppers, especially as you nibble your way toward the stem.

10	fresh jalapeño peppers (8 oz/250 g)	10
½ cup	shredded Cheddar cheese	125 mL
¼ cup	light cream cheese, softened	50 mL

¼ cup	salsa	50 mL
¾ cup	fresh bread crumbs	175 mL
2 tbsp	chopped fresh parsley	25 mL
2 tbsp	butter, melted	25 mL

1 Wearing rubber gloves to protect hands, cut jalapeño peppers in half lengthwise. With small knife, scrape out seeds and membranes, leaving stems intact.

2 In bowl, combine Cheddar cheese, cream cheese and salsa; mix in ¼ cup (50 mL) of the bread crumbs. Spoon evenly into each pepper half.

3 In small bowl, toss together remaining bread crumbs, parsley and butter; spoon onto each filling. (MAKE-AHEAD: Cover and refrigerate for up to 1 day.)

4 Bake on baking sheet in 375°F (190°C) oven for 20 minutes or until topping is golden and crisp.

TEST KITCHEN TIPS

• When handling hot peppers, it is always wise to wear rubber gloves.

• Since the hottest parts of the peppers — the membranes and seeds — have been removed, these morsels are not nearly as fiery as you might imagine.

Makes 20 pieces.

PER PIECE, ABOUT:

cal	37	carb	2 g
pro	1 g	fibre	trace
total fat	3 g	chol	9 mg
sat. fat	2 g	sodium	61 mg

PERCENTAGE RDI:

calcium	3%	vit. A	11%
iron	1%	vit. C	32%
folate	2%		

Crab Cakes

Frozen crab is a convenient head start when making crab cakes. Virtually unknown a few years ago, crab cakes now have a stylish reputation and are one of the first appetizers to disappear as trays make the rounds at a party. Chipotles, a Mexican ingredient, are smoked jalapeño peppers packed in adobo sauce. They are available in 7-oz (217 mL) cans in specialty shops and some supermarkets.

TEST KITCHEN TIP: Since you use only 2 chipotle peppers in this recipe, freeze the remainder for batches of chili or for dips when you want a hot, smoky flavour. Dollop individual chipotles, along with enough adobo sauce to moisten, about 1 inch (2.5 cm) apart on bottom edge of 16-inch (40 cm) length of plastic wrap. Roll up, twist ends and twist between peppers so that each is separate, like beads on a necklace; pack into resealable freezer bag and freeze for up to 6 months. Snip off peppers and sauce as needed.

1	pkg (7 oz/200 g) frozen crabmeat, thawed	1
⅓ cup	finely diced sweet red pepper	75 mL
¼ cup	finely diced sweet green pepper	50 mL
¼ cup	chopped green onions	50 mL
1	egg, beaten	1
1¼ cups	dry bread crumbs	300 mL
2 tbsp	vegetable oil	25 mL
CHIPOTLE MAYONNAISE:		
2	chipotle peppers	2
½ cup	light mayonnaise	125 mL
1 tbsp	adobo sauce	15 mL
Dash	Worcestershire sauce	Dash

1 CHIPOTLE MAYONNAISE: Wearing rubber gloves, finely chop chipotle peppers. In small bowl, whisk together chipotles, mayonnaise, adobo sauce and Worcestershire sauce; set aside.

2 Place crabmeat in sieve; pick through to remove any cartilage. Press firmly to remove liquid. Transfer to large bowl. Add red and green peppers, onions, egg, 2 tbsp (25 mL) of the bread crumbs and 3 tbsp (50 mL) of the Chipotle Mayonnaise; stir until well combined.

3 Sprinkle remaining bread crumbs in shallow dish. Form crabmeat mixture by rounded tablespoonfuls (15 mL) into balls; roll in bread crumbs. Place on waxed paper–lined baking sheet; flatten to 2-inch (5 cm) diameter. (MAKE-AHEAD: Cover and refrigerate for up to 1 day.)

4 In nonstick skillet, heat half of the oil over medium-high heat; cook crab cakes, in batches and adding enough of the remaining oil as necessary, for 3 minutes per side or until golden. Serve with remaining Chipotle Mayonnaise.

Makes 16 pieces.

PER PIECE, ABOUT:
cal 73   carb . . . . 4 g
pro . . . . 4 g   fibre . . . . trace
total fat . . . . . 5 g   chol . . . . . . 22 mg
sat. fat . . . . trace   sodium . . 176 mg

PERCENTAGE RDI:
calcium . . . . . . 1%   vit. A 4%
iron . . . . 5%   vit. C 13%
folate 4%

MAYONNAISE VARIATIONS

Curried Mango Chutney Mayonnaise: Substitute 1 tbsp (15 mL) mango chutney and 1 tsp (5 mL) mild curry paste for the chipotles and adobo sauce.

Cajun Mayonnaise: Substitute 1 tbsp (15 mL) grainy mustard and ½ tsp (2 mL) Cajun seasoning for the chipotles and adobo sauce.

Steamed Lemongrass Mussels

Serve mussels hot or cold — redolent with lemongrass, coriander and lime or flavoured the classic French way with wine and herbs — in individual bowls or on a deep help-yourself platter.

2	stalks lemongrass	2
3 lb	mussels	1.5 kg
1 tbsp	vegetable oil	15 mL
2	cloves garlic, minced	2
1	Thai bird chili pepper, sliced (or ¼ tsp/1 mL hot pepper flakes)	1

½ cup	chopped fresh coriander	125 mL
¼ cup	white wine	50 mL
¼ cup	water	50 mL
2 tbsp	fish or soy sauce	25 mL
½ tsp	grated lime rind	2 mL
2 tbsp	lime juice	25 mL

SUBSTITUTION: If serving dish hot, you can substitute chicken stock for wine.

1 Trim tops and ends of lemongrass; remove outer layers. Using back of knife, gently bruise stalks. Cut in half lengthwise; cut crosswise into thin slices. Set aside.

2 Scrub mussels, removing any beards. Discard any that do not close when tapped. Set aside.

3 In Dutch oven or large saucepan, heat oil over medium heat. Add lemongrass, garlic and chili pepper; cook, stirring, for 1 minute or until fragrant. Add half of the coriander, the wine, water, fish sauce, and lime rind and juice; bring to boil.

4 Add mussels; cover and cook, stirring once, for 5 minutes or until mussels open. Discard any that do not open. Serve sprinkled with remaining coriander.

VARIATIONS

Chilled Lemongrass Mussels: Cook as directed; transfer mussels to bowl, reserving cooking liquid. Boil liquid for about 5 minutes or until reduced by half; let cool. Remove mussels from shells and add to reduced liquid. Reserve half of each shell. To serve, fill each shell with a mussel; drizzle with reduced cooking liquid.

Steamed Herbed Mussels in Wine: In Dutch oven or large saucepan, heat 1 tbsp (15 mL) vegetable oil over medium heat; cook 1 onion or 2 shallots, chopped, and 2 cloves garlic, minced, for 5 minutes or until softened. Stir in ½ cup (125 mL) white wine, 2 dashes hot pepper sauce and ¼ tsp (1 mL) each salt and pepper along with prepared mussels. Serve hot or chilled, sprinkled with ½ cup (125 mL) chopped fresh chives, chervil, basil or dill.

Makes 6 servings (60 pieces).

PER SERVING, ABOUT:

cal 89	carb . . . . 4 g
pro . . . . 8 g	fibre . . . . trace
total fat . . . . . 4 g	chol . . . . . . 18 mg
sat. fat . . . . trace	sodium . . 654 mg

PERCENTAGE RDI:

calcium 2%	vit. A 4%
iron 21%	vit. C 10%
folate 14%	

Sushi Platter

Sushi is the pizza and pasta of the new decade; all kinds are now available in restaurants and at takeout counters. Sushi that does not include any raw fish is not difficult to prepare at home and is a lot less expensive and just as delicious. The trick to shaping the sticky seasoned rice or pressing it onto the nori wrapper is having a small bowl of cold water nearby to wet your fingers. Presto — no sticking.

TEST KITCHEN TIP: To toast nori sheets, quickly brush 10 times per side over electric element on high heat or gas element on medium heat.

2 cups	sushi rice, rinsed and drained	500 mL
⅓ cup	rice vinegar	75 mL
2 tbsp	granulated sugar	25 mL
2 tbsp	mirin (Japanese rice wine)	25 mL
2 tsp	salt	10 mL
6	sheets toasted nori	6

FILLING:

1 tbsp	wasabi powder	15 mL
1	pkg (7 oz) frozen crabmeat, thawed and drained	1
6	strips (6 inches x ½ inch/15 x 1 cm) cucumber	6
1	avocado, sliced	1
	Fish roe (optional)	
	Black or toasted sesame seeds (optional)	

1 In large shallow saucepan, bring rice and 2⅓ cups (575 mL) water to boil; cover and boil for 2 minutes. Reduce heat to low; cook for 20 minutes. Remove from heat; let stand, covered, for 15 minutes.

2 Meanwhile, in small saucepan, bring vinegar, sugar, mirin and salt to boil, stirring just until sugar dissolves. Let cool.

3 Spread rice in large shallow dish. Drizzle with vinegar mixture; toss with fork just until combined. Cover with damp tea towel; let cool to room temperature.

4 Place rolling mat on work surface with bamboo slats parallel to edge; place 1 nori sheet, shiny side down, on mat. With wet fingers, press one-sixth of the rice evenly over nori, leaving 1-inch (2.5 cm) border on far side.

5 FILLING: Dab thin line of wasabi over rice about ½ inch (1 cm) from closest edge. Top with one-sixth of the crab, then cucumber strip; arrange some of the avocado slices in row alongside.

Makes 48 pieces.

PER PIECE, ABOUT:

cal 46	carb . . . . 8 g
pro . . . . 2 g	fibre . . . . trace
total fat . . . . . 1 g	chol . . . . 3 mg
sat. fat . . . . trace	sodium . . 126 mg

PERCENTAGE RDI:

calcium 0%	vit. A 2%
iron 2%	vit. C 3%
folate 4%	

6 Holding filling in place with fingers, tightly roll mat over filling. Using mat as guide, continue to roll up firmly, jelly roll–style, squeezing to compress. (MAKE-AHEAD: Wrap in plastic wrap and refrigerate for up to 4 hours.) With sharp wet serrated knife, trim ends; cut roll into 8 slices. Repeat with remaining ingredients. Sprinkle with roe and sesame seeds (if using).

VARIATIONS

California Rolls: Add 3 tbsp (50 mL) black or toasted sesame seeds to rice along with vinegar mixture. Increase cucumber to 10 strips. Using scissors, cut 5 nori sheets in half crosswise to make ten 7- x 4-inch (18 x 10 cm) rectangles. Place rolling mat on work surface with bamboo slats parallel to edge. Cut same-size piece of plastic wrap and place on mat; brush with vegetable oil. With wet fingers, press rounded ½ cup (125 mL) rice on wrap into 7- x 4-inch (18 x 10 cm) rectangle, leaving 1-inch (2.5 cm) border at closest edge. Place nori on rice. Top with filling ingredients. Using wrap and mat as guide, roll up tightly, jelly roll–style, squeezing to compress. Peel off wrap. Repeat with remaining rice, nori and filling ingredients. Cut each roll into thirds. Slice each into 2 diagonal pieces. Top with fish roe (if using). **Makes 60 pieces.**

Sushi Balls or Nigiri: Place heaping 1 tbsp (15 mL) rice onto oiled square of plastic wrap. Wrap around rice; twist to form ball, or thumb shape for nigiri. Unwrap. Top with dab of wasabi mixture and slice of cucumber, smoked salmon, crabmeat or cooked shrimp. Or tie ball with strip of nori, or garnish with fish roe (if using). Repeat with remaining ingredients. **Makes about 50 pieces.**

Simple Sushi: Cut each of 3 nori sheets into 16 equal squares. Dab wasabi mixture in centre of each square. Top with heaping 1 tbsp (15 mL) rice, then slice smoked salmon, crabmeat, cooked shrimp, sliced cucumber, avocado, radish or cherry tomato. **Makes 48 pieces.**

OTHER FILLING Ingredients

🍃 **SHIITAKE MUSHROOMS:** In small saucepan, soak 10 dried shiitake mushrooms in ½ cup (125 mL) warm water for 30 minutes. Add 1 tbsp (15 mL) soy sauce and 1 tsp (5 mL) granulated sugar; simmer for 10 minutes or until no liquid remains. Discard stems; slice caps thinly.

🍃 **EGG OMELETTE:** In small nonstick skillet, heat 1 tsp (5 mL) oil over medium heat. In bowl, whisk 2 eggs; pour into skillet and cook for about 30 seconds, stirring. Cook for about 1 minute or until set. Cut into thin strips.

🍃 2 oz (60 g) smoked salmon, cut in strips.

🍃 Half bunch fresh watercress, coarse stems removed, chopped.

Thai Curry Shrimp

Whether grilled, oven-roasted or tossed in a skillet, shrimp is the number 1 appetizer pick. Three marinades provide plenty of inspiration for any party.

TEST KITCHEN TIPS

• You can broil or roast shrimp in oven, or grill in a grill pan or on the barbecue. To grill, place in single layer in grill basket or thread onto skewers, starting at tail end, through centre of shrimp.

• Thai fish sauce is available in many Asian grocery stores. It is made from fermented fish, so don't let your first whiff put you off. It mellows and blends with other flavours and adds an authenticity to a dish.

1¼ lb	large raw shrimp (about 40)	625 g
THAI MARINADE:		
1 tbsp	ground coriander	15 mL
1 tbsp	chopped fresh coriander, mint or parsley	15 mL
1 tbsp	grated lemon rind	15 mL
1 tbsp	lemon juice	15 mL
1 tbsp	vegetable oil	15 mL
1 tbsp	fish or soy sauce	15 mL
½ tsp	Thai red or green curry paste	2 mL
2	cloves garlic, minced	2

1 Peel and devein shrimp, leaving tails intact; place in bowl.

2 THAI MARINADE: In bowl, stir together ground and fresh coriander, lemon rind and juice, oil, fish sauce, curry paste and garlic. Add shrimp and toss to coat. (MAKE-AHEAD: Cover and refrigerate for up to 1 hour.)

3 Heat large nonstick skillet over medium-high heat. With tongs, add shrimp to pan, discarding any excess marinade; cook, stirring, for about 4 minutes or until pink.

VARIATIONS

Cajun Shrimp: Omit Thai Marinade. In bowl, stir together 2 tbsp (25 mL) lime juice, 1 tbsp (15 mL) vegetable oil, 2 cloves garlic, minced, 2 tsp (10 mL) paprika, 1 tsp (5 mL) each dried oregano and thyme and ¼ tsp (1 mL) each cayenne pepper and salt. Add shrimp and toss to coat.

Lemon Garlic Shrimp: Omit Thai Marinade. In bowl, stir together 1 tbsp (15 mL) olive oil, ½ tsp (2 mL) grated lemon rind, 1 tbsp (15 mL) lemon juice, 2 cloves garlic, minced, 2 tsp (10 mL) dried oregano or basil and ¼ tsp (1 mL) salt. Add shrimp and toss to coat.

Makes about 40 pieces.

PER PIECE, ABOUT:

cal 14	carb ....trace
pro ....2 g	fibre ....trace
total fat ...trace	chol ......16 mg
sat. fat ....trace	sodium ...39 mg

PERCENTAGE RDI:

calcium 0%	vit. A 1%
iron 1%	vit. C 2%
folate 0%	

Grilled Jumbo Shrimp Skewers with Dipping Sauce

Shrimp are reputation-making appetizers. Get ready for rave reviews whether you're entertaining around the barbecue or nibbling, sipping and chatting in the kitchen.

1 lb	jumbo shrimp, peeled and deveined	500 g
¼ cup	olive oil	50 mL
½ tsp	each salt and pepper	2 mL
CORIANDER DIPPING SAUCE:		
1 cup	packed fresh coriander leaves	250 mL

¼ cup	light mayonnaise	50 mL
2 tbsp	light sour cream	25 mL
4 tsp	lime juice	20 mL
1 tbsp	ground almonds	15 mL
1 tbsp	chopped jalapeño pepper	15 mL
1	clove garlic, minced	1

1 CORIANDER DIPPING SAUCE: In food processor, purée coriander leaves, mayonnaise, sour cream, lime juice, almonds and jalapeño pepper; scrape into bowl. Stir in garlic. Set aside in refrigerator until serving. (MAKE-AHEAD: Cover and refrigerate for up to 4 hours.)

2 Toss shrimp with oil, salt and pepper. Holding 2 shrimp curled back to back, thread onto soaked wooden skewers. Or with thicker end of 1 shrimp at top, thread straight through length of body. (MAKE-AHEAD: Cover and refrigerate for up to 4 hours.) Place on greased grill over medium-high heat; close lid and cook, turning once, for about 5 minutes or until opaque. Serve with Coriander Dipping Sauce.

DIPPING SAUCE VARIATIONS

Seafood Sauce: In small bowl, stir together ⅓ cup (75 mL) ketchup, 2 tsp (10 mL) prepared horseradish, 1 tsp (5 mL) lemon or lime juice and ¼ tsp (1 mL) Worcestershire sauce. For added snap, stir in dash hot pepper sauce.

Thai Dipping Sauce: Substitute ½ cup (125 mL) sweet Thai chili sauce for dipping sauce.

VARIATION

Grilled Chicken Skewers with Dipping Sauce: Substitute 4 boneless skinless chicken breasts for shrimp; cut into chunks. Thread onto skewers and grill as for shrimp, turning once and increasing time to about 10 minutes or until no longer pink inside. **Makes 20 pieces.**

Makes 11 to 15 pieces.

PER EACH OF 15 PIECES, ABOUT:

cal	74	carb	1 g
pro	5 g	fibre	trace
total fat	6 g	chol	35 mg
sat. fat	1 g	sodium	100 mg

PERCENTAGE RDI:

calcium	1%	vit. A	2%
iron	4%	vit. C	3%
folate	1%		

THE SCOOP ON Shrimp

This curvaceous crustacean is usually called shrimp in North America, but on the other side of the Atlantic, the general term is prawn.

➦ TO BUY: Generally, the larger the shrimp, the fewer there are per pound (500 g), the more expensive they are and the less work there is to peel and devein. Processors often label their shrimp differently, but here is a general guide to help (all numbers are by the pound/500 g): colossal, 10 or fewer; jumbo, 11 to 15; extra-large, 16 to 20; large, 21 to 30; medium, 31 to 35; small, 36 to 45; miniature or salad, about 100.

➦ TO CLEAN: Using scissors, cut shell of shrimp along arc of back. Gently pull off shell, leaving tail intact if desired. Cut shallow slit along outer arc of shrimp; pull out intestinal vein if present, then rinse shrimp.

Grilled Teriyaki Ginger Chicken Satays

The method of marinating strips of chicken or pork with ginger and soy, threading them onto skewers for grilling and serving them with a peanut sauce has its origins in southeast Asia but can be traced back to India and the Middle East.

VARIATIONS

Grilled Pork Satays: Replace chicken with 1 lb (500 g) boneless pork loin roast; cut across the grain into ¼-inch (5 mm) thick strips. Weave onto skewers and cook, turning once, for 3 to 4 minutes or until browned and just a hint of pink remains inside.

Grilled Beef Satays: Replace chicken with 1 lb (500 g) thick boneless grilling sirloin steak. Cut across the grain into ¼-inch (5 mm) thick strips. Weave onto skewers; cook, turning once, for 4 to 6 minutes or until browned on outside yet still pink inside.

Makes 24 pieces.

PER PIECE, ABOUT:

cal	63	carb	2 g
pro	5 g	fibre	trace
total fat	4 g	chol	11 mg
sat. fat	1 g	sodium	153 mg

PERCENTAGE RDI:

calcium	0%	vit. A	0%
iron	1%	vit. C	2%
folate	2%		

1 lb	boneless skinless chicken breasts	500 g
⅓ cup	smooth peanut butter	75 mL
¼ cup	finely chopped green onions	50 mL

TERIYAKI GINGER MARINADE:

1	slice (½ inch/1 cm thick) gingerroot	1
4	cloves garlic, minced	4
¼ cup	teriyaki sauce	50 mL
3 tbsp	vegetable oil	50 mL
2 tbsp	chopped fresh coriander	25 mL
2 tbsp	rice vinegar	25 mL
2 tsp	grated lemon rind	10 mL
1 tsp	lemon juice	5 mL
¼ tsp	hot pepper sauce	1 mL
1 tbsp	hoisin sauce	15 mL
1 tbsp	sherry	15 mL

1 TERIYAKI GINGER MARINADE: With sharp knife, peel gingerroot; chop finely. In bowl, whisk together ginger, garlic, teriyaki sauce, oil, coriander, vinegar, lemon rind and juice and hot pepper sauce; pour ⅓ cup (75 mL) of the marinade into measuring cup and reserve for peanut sauce. Whisk hoisin sauce and sherry into bowl of marinade.

2 Cut chicken across the grain into ¼-inch (5 mm) thick strips. Add to bowl. Cover and marinate in refrigerator, stirring occasionally, for at least 2 hours or for up to 4 hours.

3 Meanwhile, whisk peanut butter, onions and 3 tbsp (50 mL) warm water into ⅓ cup (75 mL) reserved marinade. (MAKE-AHEAD: Cover peanut sauce and set aside for up to 4 hours.)

4 In shallow dish, soak 24 small wooden skewers in water for at least 30 minutes. Weave chicken strip onto each skewer; brush with marinade.

5 Place on greased grill over medium-high heat or under broiler; cook, turning once, for 4 minutes or until browned and juices run clear. Serve with peanut sauce.

Honey Garlic Chicken Wings

From around the world, chicken wings take on frisky new flavours in an easy three-step cooking method: marinate, bake, then crisp under the broiler.

2½ lb	chicken wings (about 15)	1.25 kg
HONEY GARLIC MARINADE:		
⅓ cup	hoisin sauce	75 mL
¼ cup	soy sauce	50 mL

¼ cup	liquid honey	50 mL
1 tbsp	dry sherry or chicken stock	15 mL
1 tbsp	cider vinegar	15 mL
2	large cloves garlic, minced	2

1 HONEY GARLIC MARINADE: In large bowl, whisk together hoisin sauce, soy sauce, honey, sherry, cider vinegar and garlic.

2 Cut off wing tips at first joint; reserve tips for stock (page 47). Separate wings at remaining joint; trim excess skin. Add wings to marinade; cover and marinate in refrigerator for at least 4 hours, turning occasionally. (MAKE-AHEAD: Marinate in refrigerator for up to 1 day, turning occasionally.)

3 Reserving marinade, arrange wings on rack on foil-lined baking sheet or on greased foil-lined baking sheet. Spoon half of the marinade over wings. Bake in 400°F (200°C) oven for 20 minutes. Turn and brush with remaining marinade; cook for about 20 minutes or until juices run clear when chicken is pierced.

4 Broil for about 1 minute per side or until wings are crisp and browned.

VARIATIONS

Saucy Barbecued Wings: Omit Honey Garlic Marinade. In saucepan, combine 1 cup (250 mL) ketchup, ¼ cup (50 mL) packed brown sugar, ¼ cup (50 mL) water, 1 onion, chopped, 2 cloves garlic, minced, 3 tbsp (50 mL) cider vinegar, 1 tbsp (15 mL) Dijon mustard, 2 tsp (10 mL) Worcestershire sauce and ¼ tsp (1 mL) salt; bring to boil, stirring often. Reduce heat to medium; simmer for 10 minutes. Let cool. In food processor, purée until smooth. Marinate and bake as directed.

Black Bean Chicken Wings: Omit Honey Garlic Marinade. In large bowl, mash ¼ cup (50 mL) Chinese fermented black beans, drained and rinsed. Stir in ⅓ cup (75 mL) hoisin sauce, ¼ cup (50 mL) each soy sauce, liquid honey and ketchup, 2 tbsp (25 mL) each sesame oil, rice vinegar and Dijon mustard, 2 cloves garlic, minced, and ½ tsp (2 mL) chili oil or hot pepper sauce. Marinate and bake as directed.

TEST KITCHEN TIPS

• Place chicken and marinade in resealable bag and freeze for up to 3 weeks. Let thaw in refrigerator and bake as directed.

• Keep a resealable bag in the freezer for handy storage of wing tips and other uncooked chicken bones for making stock (page 47).

Makes about 30 pieces.

PER PIECE, ABOUT:

cal	54	carb	3 g
pro	4 g	fibre	trace
total fat	3 g	chol	12 mg
sat. fat	1 g	sodium	159 mg

PERCENTAGE RDI:

calcium	0%	vit. A	1%
iron	2%	vit. C	0%
folate	0%		

Chicken Liver Pâté with Basil

Pared down in fat and calories but not in taste, this creamy, smooth spread is so fool-proof its title should be "Pâté 101." Equally easy, especially with a food processor, is the Mushroom Pâté, a tasty alternative offering for vegetarians and nonvegetarians alike.

VARIATION

Mushroom Pâté: Omit chicken livers and substitute 8 cups (2 L) mushrooms (1½ lb/750 g). Chop mushrooms coarsely; add to softened onions and garlic. Increase heat to high and cook for about 10 minutes or until liquid is evaporated and mushrooms are beginning to brown. Continue as directed.

⅓ cup	butter, softened	75 mL	3 tbsp	cognac or brandy	50 mL
1	onion, chopped	1	¼ cup	packed fresh basil leaves	50 mL
1	clove garlic, minced	1	¼ cup	light cream cheese	50 mL
12 oz	chicken livers, trimmed	375 g	Pinch	each salt and pepper	Pinch

1 In skillet, melt half of the butter over medium heat; cook onion and garlic, stirring occasionally, for about 5 minutes or until softened.

2 Add chicken livers; cook for about 5 minutes or until browned but still slightly pink inside. Stir in cognac; cook for about 1 minute or until almost evaporated. Let cool.

3 Transfer to food processor. Add basil, cream cheese, remaining butter, salt and pepper; purée until smooth. Spoon into serving bowl. Place plastic wrap directly on surface and refrigerate for at least 1 hour or until chilled and firm. (MAKE-AHEAD: Refrigerate for up to 1 day or overwrap with heavy-duty foil and freeze for up to 2 weeks.)

Makes about 2 cups (500 mL).

PER 1 TBSP (15 mL), ABOUT:

cal 39	carb . . . . 1 g
pro . . . . 2 g	fibre . . . . trace
total fat . . . . . 3 g	chol . . . . . . 53 mg
sat. fat . . . . . . 2 g	sodium . . . 37 mg

PERCENTAGE RDI:

calcium 0%	vit. A 54%
iron 6%	vit. C 5%
folate 25%	

Layered Mexican Dip

Wonderfully scoopable and delicious, this layered appetizer is ideal for a help-yourself occasion. Serve with tortilla chips.

1	can (14 oz/398 mL) refried beans	1
1¼ cups	light sour cream	300 mL
½ tsp	each ground cumin and salt	2 mL
¼ tsp	hot pepper sauce	1 mL
2	avocados	2
⅓ cup	finely chopped onion	75 mL

2 tbsp	lime juice	25 mL
¼ tsp	hot pepper flakes	1 mL
2 cups	shredded old Cheddar cheese	500 mL
2	tomatoes, chopped	2
⅓ cup	sliced green onions	75 mL
½ cup	sliced pitted black olives	125 mL

TEST KITCHEN TIP: If avocados need ripening, place them in a paper bag and let stand at room temperature for 2 to 3 days.

1 In bowl, stir together refried beans, ¼ cup (50 mL) of the sour cream, cumin, ¼ tsp (1 mL) of the salt and hot pepper sauce; spread in 12-inch (30 cm) round serving dish at least 1½ inches (4 cm) deep.

2 Peel and pit avocados. In bowl, mash together avocados, onion, ¼ cup (50 mL) of the remaining sour cream, lime juice, hot pepper flakes and remaining salt; spread over bean layer. Top with remaining sour cream.

3 Starting at outside, garnish with concentric rings of cheese, tomatoes, green onions and olives. (MAKE-AHEAD: Cover and refrigerate for up to 1 day.)

Makes about 24 servings.

PER SERVING, ABOUT:

cal	105	carb	7 g
pro	5 g	fibre	2 g
total fat	7 g	chol	12 mg
sat. fat	3 g	sodium	217 mg

PERCENTAGE RDI:

calcium	10%	vit. A	5%
iron	5%	vit. C	8%
folate	14%		

Hummus

When tahini, the crushed sesame seed equivalent of peanut butter, is added to this Middle Eastern purée of chickpeas, garlic, lemon juice and olive oil, it is rightly called hummus bi tahina. Serve with warmed pita bread, an assortment of raw vegetables or hearts of romaine lettuce.

1	can (19 oz/540 mL) chickpeas, drained and rinsed	1
⅓ cup	tahini	75 mL
3 tbsp	each lemon juice and water	50 mL
1 tbsp	olive oil	15 mL
¾ tsp	ground cumin	4 mL
¼ tsp	salt	1 mL
2	cloves garlic, minced	2

1 In food processor, blend chickpeas, tahini, lemon juice, water, oil, cumin and salt until smooth. Stir in garlic. (MAKE-AHEAD: Cover and refrigerate for up to 3 days.)

TEST KITCHEN TIP: While chickpeas are traditional for hummus, you can make similar dips with canned beans such as white or red kidney beans or black beans.

VARIATIONS

Spicy Hummus: Increase cumin to 1½ tsp (7 mL). Add ½ tsp (2 mL) hot pepper sauce and 2 tbsp (25 mL) chopped jalapeño pepper. **Makes 2 cups (500 mL).**

Herbed Hummus: Omit tahini and cumin. Stir in ¼ cup (50 mL) chopped fresh parsley, 2 green onions, chopped, and 1 tsp (5 mL) dried oregano. **Makes 2 cups (500 mL).**

Creamy Hummus: Omit tahini and cumin. Stir in ¼ cup (50 mL) herbed cream cheese, softened. **Makes 2 cups (500 mL).**

Black Olive Hummus: Stir in ¼ cup (50 mL) chopped oil-cured black olives. **Makes 2 cups (500 mL).**

Sun-Dried Tomato Hummus: Omit tahini, cumin and salt. Substitute sun-dried tomato oil for olive oil and blend in ¼ cup (50 mL) drained oil-packed sun-dried tomatoes. **Makes 2 cups (500 mL).**

Roasted Red Pepper Hummus: Omit tahini and cumin. Blend in ¼ cup (50 mL) chopped roasted red peppers. **Makes 2 cups (500 mL).**

Makes 2 cups (500 mL).

PER 1 TBSP (15 mL), ABOUT:

cal 34	carb . . . . 3 g
pro . . . . 1 g	fibre . . . . 1 g
total fat . . . . . 2 g	chol . . . . 0 mg
sat. fat . . . . trace	sodium . . . 44 mg

PERCENTAGE RDI:

calcium 1%	vit. A 0%
iron 2%	vit. C 2%
folate 4%	

Grilled Vegetable Antipasto

A platter of grilled herb-dressed vegetables has become a modern appetizer classic. Colourful with eggplant, peppers and zucchini, the platter can serve more guests with tasty additions (see tip) from the deli. It is a grand addition to a buffet table or potluck barbecue, especially if there are vegetarian guests.

2	large eggplants (about 3½ lb/1.75 kg)	2
1 tbsp	salt	15 mL
1	each sweet red, yellow and green pepper	1
3	zucchini (about 1½ lb/750 g)	3
2 tbsp	extra-virgin olive oil	25 mL

DRESSING:		
⅓ cup	extra-virgin olive oil	75 mL
¼ cup	chopped fresh oregano (or 1 tsp/5 mL dried)	50 mL
1 tbsp	lemon juice	15 mL
2 tsp	Dijon mustard	10 mL
2	large cloves garlic, minced	2
¼ tsp	each salt and pepper	1 mL

1 Cut eggplants into ½-inch (1 cm) thick slices. In colander, sprinkle eggplant slices with salt; toss to coat and let drain for 30 minutes.

2 Meanwhile, place red, yellow and green peppers on greased grill over medium-high heat or on foil-lined baking sheet under broiler; close lid and cook, turning often, for 15 to 20 minutes or until charred. Let cool slightly. Peel, seed and cut into 1-inch (2.5 cm) thick strips. Set aside.

3 Cut zucchini diagonally into ½-inch (1 cm) thick slices. Rinse eggplant under cold running water; pat dry. Lightly brush zucchini and eggplant with oil. Cook on grill, covered, over medium-high heat or under broiler, turning occasionally, for 10 to 15 minutes or until tender but not charred. Set aside separately.

4 DRESSING: In bowl, whisk together oil, oregano, lemon juice, mustard, garlic, salt and pepper. Toss each vegetable in dressing separately and arrange on large shallow serving platter. (MAKE-AHEAD: Cover and refrigerate for up to 8 hours, spooning any accumulated dressing over vegetables before serving.)

TEST KITCHEN TIPS

• Antipasto means "before the pasta" — in effect, an appetizer served before the meal that should be light enough to allow enjoyment of courses to follow.

• Add variety to your antipasto platter and stretch it to serve many more with thinly sliced salami, prosciutto, mortadella; grilled shrimp, smoked oysters; homemade Giardiniera (page 393), marinated artichokes, capers, mushrooms, hot peppers, olives; bocconcini, provolone, mild feta and goat cheese.

Makes 6 to 8 servings.

PER EACH OF 8 SERVINGS, ABOUT:

cal	188	carb	19 g
pro	3 g	fibre	7 g
total fat	13 g	chol	0 mg
sat. fat	2 g	sodium	98 mg

PERCENTAGE RDI:

calcium	3%	vit. A	12%
iron	9%	vit. C	105%
folate	21%		

Peking Hamburger Dumplings

In northern China, where wheat is a staple, these pot-stickers are served with soup or pickled or fresh vegetables. They make great party food. Kids love them dipped in ketchup!

DIPPING SAUCE: Mix 3 tbsp (50 mL) rice vinegar with 1 tbsp (15 mL) soy sauce. Divide among small saucers. Sprinkle with toasted sesame seeds if desired. Pass chili paste or oil, if desired, to add to sauce.

2 tbsp	vegetable oil	25 mL
DOUGH:		
3 cups	all-purpose flour	750 mL
4 tsp	vegetable oil	20 mL
¼ tsp	salt	1 mL
FILLING:		
2	eggs	2
1 cup	sliced green onions	250 mL
¼ cup	water	50 mL
¼ cup	soy sauce	50 mL
1 tbsp	minced gingerroot	15 mL
1 tbsp	minced fresh hot pepper (or 1½ tsp/7 mL hot pepper flakes)	15 mL
2 tsp	sesame oil	10 mL
½ tsp	each salt and pepper	2 mL
2 lb	extra-lean ground beef	1 kg

1 DOUGH: In bowl, divide flour into 2 mounds. Stirring with fork, pour ½ cup (125 mL) boiling water over 1 of the mounds, mixing well. Add oil and salt to remaining mound. Gradually mix ½ cup (125 mL) cold water into both mounds to form dry, shaggy dough, adding up to 1 tbsp (15 mL) more water if necessary. Turn out onto lightly floured surface; knead for 7 to 10 minutes or until smooth. Wrap in plastic wrap; let rest for 30 minutes. (MAKE-AHEAD: Refrigerate for up to 2 days; let come to room temperature before using.)

2 FILLING: Meanwhile, in large bowl, beat eggs. Stir in onions, water, soy sauce, ginger, hot pepper, sesame oil, salt and pepper. Add beef; mix well. Set aside.

3 On lightly floured surface, roll dough into log; cut into 16 pieces. Flatten each into disc. Keeping remaining discs covered, roll each into 6-inch (15 cm) circle.

4 Place ¼ cup (50 mL) filling in centre of each disc. Gather dough up around filling; pinch at top to seal. Pinch off excess dough. Flatten slightly. Reroll scraps to make 20 dumplings. (MAKE-AHEAD: Cover and refrigerate for up to 1 day or freeze in airtight container for up to 1 month; do not thaw before cooking.)

5 In each of 2 large nonstick skillets, heat half of the oil over medium heat. Add dumplings, pinched side up and without touching. Add enough water to come three-quarters of the way up dumplings. Increase heat to high; cover and cook for 8 minutes or until water evaporates. Reduce heat to medium and cook, uncovered, for about 5 minutes or until bottoms are golden and crusty.

Makes 20 dumplings.

PER DUMPLING (WITH SAUCE), ABOUT:

cal	184	carb	15 g
pro	12 g	fibre	1 g
total fat	8 g	chol	45 mg
sat. fat	2 g	sodium	381 mg

PERCENTAGE RDI:

calcium	1%	vit. A	2%
iron	14%	vit. C	2%
folate	13%		

Cornmeal "Blini" with Smoked Salmon

Restaurateurs Bob Bermann and Barbara Gordon of Boba in Toronto shared the recipe for these tiny salmon-topped pancakes to mark the new millennium.

½ cup	cornmeal	125 mL
¼ cup	all-purpose flour	50 mL
1 tsp	granulated sugar	5 mL
½ tsp	baking soda	2 mL
¼ tsp	salt	1 mL
Pinch	pepper	Pinch
¾ cup	buttermilk	175 mL
1	egg yolk	1

1 tbsp	butter, melted	15 mL
½ cup	shredded Cheddar or Monterey Jack cheese	125 mL
¼ cup	corn kernels	50 mL
GARNISH:		
2 oz	smoked salmon	60 g
½ cup	sour cream	125 mL
	Fresh dill sprigs	

TEST KITCHEN TIP: Top blini stylishly with other smoked seafood: a chevron of trout or mackerel; half a smoked oyster or mussel; or a dab of golden caviar.

1 In bowl, whisk together cornmeal, flour, sugar, baking soda, salt and pepper.

2 In separate bowl, whisk together buttermilk, egg yolk and butter; pour over flour mixture. Sprinkle with cheese and corn. Stir just until flour is incorporated.

3 Heat large nonstick skillet over medium-high heat; brush lightly with oil. Using 1 tbsp (15 mL) batter for each corn cake and brushing skillet with oil as necessary, cook corn cakes for about 1 minute per side or until golden. (MAKE-AHEAD: Cover and refrigerate for up to 4 hours; let come to room temperature before garnishing.)

4 GARNISH: Cut salmon into 2- x ½-inch (5 x 1 cm) strips; twist into rosette shape. Spoon scant 1 tsp (5 mL) sour cream onto centre of each corn cake. Top with salmon rosette and dill sprig.

Makes about 24 pieces.

PER PIECE, ABOUT:

cal 47	carb . . . . 4 g
pro . . . . 2 g	fibre . . . . trace
total fat . . . . . 2 g	chol . . . . . . 16 mg
sat. fat . . . . . . 1 g	sodium . . . 97 mg

PERCENTAGE RDI:

calcium 3%	vit. A 3%
iron 1%	vit. C 0%
folate 2%	

Party Meatballs with Southwestern Barbecue Sauce

If you want to please your guests, don't neglect the humble meatball. While these bite-size nuggets may sound ordinary, serving them with a fabulous sauce elevates them to come-again party fare.

TEST KITCHEN TIPS

• **Lean ground pork, lamb, chicken or turkey is as good as ground beef for meatballs. You can simmer meatballs in prepared sauces with Asian, Indian and Southwestern barbecue flavours.**

• **To keep meatballs warm, serve in a slow-cooker or on a chafing dish. Serve with toothpicks or party skewers.**

• **Make a meal by serving over rice or mashed potatoes.**

2	eggs	2
½ cup	fine dry bread crumbs	125 mL
½ tsp	each salt and pepper	2 mL
2 lb	lean ground beef	1 kg
SOUTHWESTERN BARBECUE SAUCE:		
1 tsp	vegetable oil	5 mL
1	small onion, minced	1
1	clove garlic, minced	1

1 tsp	each chili powder and ground cumin	5 mL
¾ cup	ketchup	175 mL
⅓ cup	water	75 mL
¼ cup	packed brown sugar	50 mL
¼ cup	cider vinegar	50 mL
1 tbsp	each Dijon mustard and Worcestershire sauce	15 mL
Dash	hot pepper sauce	Dash

1 In large bowl, beat eggs; mix in bread crumbs, salt and pepper. Mix in beef. Roll level tablespoonfuls (15 mL) into balls. Bake on foil-lined rimmed baking sheet in 375°F (190°C) oven for about 13 minutes or until no longer pink inside. (MAKE-AHEAD: Freeze in airtight container for up to 3 weeks. Add frozen to sauce, increasing heating time slightly.)

2 SOUTHWESTERN BARBECUE SAUCE: In saucepan, heat oil over medium heat; cook onion, garlic, chili powder and cumin, stirring often, for 5 minutes. Stir in ketchup, water, sugar, vinegar, mustard, Worcestershire sauce and hot pepper sauce; bring to simmer and cook for 5 minutes. (MAKE-AHEAD: Let cool. Freeze in airtight container for up to 3 weeks. Thaw and bring to simmer.) Add meatballs; turn to coat. Simmer, stirring gently, for 5 minutes or until hot.

VARIATIONS

Party Meatballs with Instant Tangy Sauce: Omit Southwestern Barbecue Sauce. In saucepan over medium heat, simmer 1½ cups (375 mL) chili sauce with 1¼ cups (300 mL) grape jelly. Add meatballs and continue as directed.

Party Meatballs with Curry Sauce: Omit Southwestern Barbecue Sauce. In saucepan, heat 1 tsp (5 mL) vegetable oil over medium heat; cook 1 onion, diced, and 1 tbsp (15 mL) mild Indian curry paste, stirring, for 5 minutes or until onion is softened. Add 1 cup (250 mL) each chicken stock and coconut milk or whipping cream; bring to boil. Boil for 5 minutes or until thickened slightly. Stir in ¼ cup (50 mL) chopped fresh coriander. Add meatballs and continue as directed.

Makes about 70 meatballs.

PER MEATBALL (WITH SAUCE), ABOUT:

cal 36	carb . . . . 2 g
pro . . . . 3 g	fibre . . . . trace
total fat . . . . . 2 g	chol . . . . . . 13 mg
sat. fat . . . . . . 1 g	sodium . . . 70 mg

PERCENTAGE RDI:

calcium 1%	vit. A 1%
iron 3%	vit. C 2%
folate 1%	

Balsamic Mushroom Crostini

Tomato bruschetta introduced us to the pleasures of piling intensely seasoned ingredients onto grilled or toasted Italian bread. There are many more choices now, starting with mushrooms and including roasted peppers and ricotta, roasted tomatoes, and the Tuscan-inspired sage and white bean variation here.

1	baguette (French stick)	1
2 tbsp	olive oil	25 mL
2	cloves garlic, minced	2
6 cups	sliced mushrooms (1 lb/500 g)	1.5 L
½ tsp	herbes de Provence	2 mL
¼ tsp	each salt and pepper	1 mL
¼ cup	chopped fresh parsley	50 mL
3 tbsp	balsamic vinegar	50 mL
1 tsp	Dijon mustard	5 mL
¼ cup	shaved Asiago cheese	50 mL

TEST KITCHEN TIP: If you don't have herbes de Provence on hand, just use a generous pinch each dried thyme, rosemary and savory.

1 Cut baguette diagonally into 24 slices. Broil on baking sheet for 30 seconds per side or until golden. Set aside.

2 In large skillet, heat oil over medium-high heat; cook garlic, mushrooms, herbes de Provence, salt and pepper, stirring occasionally, for about 5 minutes or until browned and moisture is evaporated. Remove from heat; stir in parsley, vinegar and mustard. (MAKE-AHEAD: Refrigerate in airtight container for up to 8 hours; let stand at room temperature for 30 minutes before continuing.) Spoon onto prepared toasts. Sprinkle with Asiago.

VARIATION

Warm Garlic Bean Crostini: In nonstick skillet, heat 2 tbsp (25 mL) extra-virgin olive oil over medium-high heat; cook 3 cloves garlic, minced, ½ tsp (2 mL) dried sage, crumbled, and ¼ tsp (1 mL) pepper for 1 minute or until garlic is golden. Meanwhile, drain and rinse 1 can (19 oz/540 mL) white kidney beans; mash one-third. Add mashed and whole beans, 1 tsp (5 mL) grated lemon rind and 1 tbsp (15 mL) lemon juice to skillet; cook for 3 minutes or until hot. Spoon heaping 1 tbsp (15 mL) onto each crostini. Garnish with chopped fresh sage or parsley if desired. **Makes 24 pieces.**

Bruschetta

Chop 4 tomatoes, seeded if desired. Mix with 2 large cloves garlic, minced, ¼ cup (50 mL) chopped fresh basil, 2 tbsp (25 mL) extra-virgin olive oil and generous pinch each salt and pepper. Spoon onto 12 grilled or toasted baguette slices. **Makes 12 pieces.**

Makes 24 pieces.

PER PIECE, ABOUT:

cal	52	carb	7 g
pro	2 g	fibre	1 g
total fat	2 g	chol	1 mg
sat. fat	trace	sodium	108 mg

PERCENTAGE RDI:

calcium	2%	vit. A	1%
iron	4%	vit. C	2%
folate	5%		

Smoked Salmon–Stuffed Baguette

Smoked salmon is hard to resist, and with Canada's supply of farmed and wild salmon, it's now more affordable than ever. Serve thin slices with cream cheese, capers, diced red onion and rye or pumpernickel bread, or enjoy in this stuffed baguette.

TEST KITCHEN TIPS

• Double the cream cheese mixture if you like lots on your sandwiches.

• Both fillings can be used to make tortilla spirals. Top large tortillas with salmon filling ingredients and roll up firmly. Wrap and chill for at least 30 minutes or for up to 1 day. Cut each diagonally into ½-inch (1 cm) thick slices. Use 4 large tortillas.

1	baguette (French stick)	1	1 tsp	wine vinegar	5 mL
SMOKED SALMON FILLING:			4 oz	smoked salmon	125 g
¼ cup	light cream cheese	50 mL	1 tbsp	capers	15 mL
2 tbsp	chopped fresh dill	25 mL	1 tbsp	chopped red onion	15 mL
1 tbsp	grainy mustard	15 mL			

1 Slice baguette in half horizontally; hollow out each half, leaving about ½-inch (1 cm) thick walls.

2 SMOKED SALMON FILLING: In small bowl, stir together cream cheese, dill, mustard and vinegar. Spread cut sides of baguette halves with cheese mixture. Arrange smoked salmon, capers and onion in bottom half; replace top of loaf. Firmly press together. (MAKE-AHEAD: Wrap in plastic wrap and refrigerate for up to 1 day or overwrap with heavy-duty foil and freeze for up to 1 week; thaw in refrigerator for 6 hours.) Using serrated knife, cut into 1-inch (2.5 cm) thick slices.

VARIATION

Artichoke and Gorgonzola–Stuffed Baguette: Omit Smoked Salmon Filling. In bowl, stir together 1 pkg (8 oz/250 g) light cream cheese, softened, 1 jar (6 oz/170 mL) marinated artichoke hearts, drained and chopped, ½ cup (125 mL) Gorgonzola or blue cheese, crumbled, ¼ cup (50 mL) chopped fresh parsley, half sweet red pepper, diced, 1 tsp (5 mL) dried oregano, 1 clove garlic, minced, and pinch pepper. (MAKE-AHEAD: Wrap in plastic wrap and refrigerate for up to 1 day or overwrap with heavy-duty foil and freeze for up to 1 week; thaw in refrigerator for 6 hours.)

Makes 30 pieces.

PER PIECE, ABOUT:

cal	32	carb	4 g
pro	2 g	fibre	trace
total fat	1 g	chol	3 mg
sat. fat	trace	sodium	100 mg

PERCENTAGE RDI:

calcium	1%	vit. A	0%
iron	2%	vit. C	0%
folate	4%		

Picadillo Empanadas

Empanadas are savoury filled pastry crescents popular in Latin America. The delicately sweet and tangy filling has a soupçon of heat from jalapeño pepper.

	Pastry for 9-inch (23 cm) double-crust pie (recipe, page 326)		1	onion, chopped	1
1	egg, beaten	1	½ cup	tomato sauce	125 mL
2 tbsp	poppy seeds	25 mL	⅓ cup	chopped sweet red or green pepper	75 mL
PICADILLO FILLING:			Half	jalapeño pepper, minced	Half
1 tsp	vegetable oil	5 mL	6	green olives, chopped	6
8 oz	lean ground beef	250 g	1 tsp	packed brown sugar	5 mL
			¼ tsp	salt	1 mL

TEST KITCHEN TIP: Try either of the empanada fillings as tasty toppers for baked potatoes.

1 PICADILLO FILLING: In skillet, heat oil over medium-high heat; cook beef and onion for 3 to 5 minutes or until meat is no longer pink. Reduce heat to medium; add tomato sauce, red pepper and jalapeño pepper. Simmer for 2 to 4 minutes or until thickened slightly. Remove from heat; add olives, sugar and salt. Let cool completely. (MAKE-AHEAD: Cover and refrigerate for up to 1 day.)

2 Roll out pastry to about ⅛-inch (3 mm) thickness; cut into 3-inch (8 cm) rounds. Place heaping 1 tsp (5 mL) of the filling on half of each pastry round. Moisten edges with cold water; fold over and seal with fork. Place on ungreased baking sheet. (MAKE-AHEAD: Cover and refrigerate for up to 12 hours.)

3 Brush with egg. Sprinkle with poppy seeds. Bake in 425°F (220°C) oven for 15 to 20 minutes or until golden brown.

VARIATION

Mushroom Empanadas: Omit Picadillo Filling. In large skillet, melt ¼ cup (50 mL) butter over medium heat; cook 2 small onions, chopped, 6 cloves garlic, minced, 1½ tsp (7 mL) each dried thyme and sage, 1 tsp (5 mL) pepper and ½ tsp (2 mL) salt, stirring occasionally, for about 3 minutes or until onion is softened. Increase heat to medium-high; add 3 cups (750 mL) finely chopped portobello mushrooms (about 6 oz/175 g) and 3 cups (750 mL) finely chopped button mushrooms (about 8 oz/250 g). Cook, stirring occasionally, for about 10 minutes or until browned. Stir in ⅔ cup (150 mL) white wine or water, stirring and scraping up brown bits from bottom of pan. Cook for about 5 minutes or until liquid is evaporated. Let cool to room temperature. (MAKE-AHEAD: Cover and refrigerate in airtight container for up to 1 day.)

Makes about 35 empanadas.

PER EMPANADA, ABOUT:

cal	104	carb	8 g
pro	3 g	fibre	1 g
total fat	7 g	chol	24 mg
sat. fat	3 g	sodium	158 mg

PERCENTAGE RDI:

calcium	1%	vit. A	4%
iron	5%	vit. C	3%
folate	5%		

Prosciutto Roll-Ups

Puff pastry—flaky and layered with butter—is the ultimate pastry, and when rolled into hors d'oeuvres, it signals special occasions. Serve these delicious canapés with cocktails.

TEST KITCHEN TIP: Instead of rolling up pastry from both sides to make palmier shape, roll up from 1 side only to make pinwheels.

1	pkg (397 g) frozen puff pastry, thawed	1

PROSCIUTTO PARMESAN FILLING:

2 tbsp	sweet mustard	25 mL
¼ cup	grated Parmesan cheese	50 mL

4 oz	thinly sliced prosciutto (or 6 oz/175 g sliced smoked ham)	125 g
1	egg, beaten	1

1 On lightly floured surface, roll out half of the pastry to 12- x 10-inch (30 x 25 cm) rectangle. Set remaining aside in refrigerator.

2 **PROSCIUTTO PARMESAN FILLING:** Spread pastry with half of the mustard, leaving ½-inch (1 cm) border. Sprinkle with half of the cheese; arrange half of the prosciutto in single layer over cheese. Brush border with water.

3 Starting at short end, roll up jelly roll–style just to centre of rectangle. Roll up other end to meet in centre; turn over. Using serrated knife, trim ends; cut into ½-inch (1 cm) thick slices. Place on parchment paper–lined baking sheets; press lightly.

4 Repeat with remaining ingredients. Cover and refrigerate for 1 hour. (MAKE-AHEAD: Refrigerate for up to 1 day.)

5 Brush egg over roll-ups. Bake in 400°F (200°C) oven for 15 to 18 minutes or until puffed and light golden.

VARIATIONS

Pesto Roll-Ups: Omit Prosciutto Parmesan Filling. Spread ¼ cup (50 mL) pesto (page 235) over pastry.

Smoked Salmon Roll-Ups: Omit Prosciutto Parmesan Filling. In bowl, blend together ½ cup (125 mL) cream cheese, 3 tbsp (50 mL) finely chopped smoked salmon, 1 tbsp (15 mL) chopped fresh dill and pinch pepper; spread over pastry.

Makes about 34 pieces.

PER PIECE, ABOUT:

cal 78	carb . . . . 6 g
pro . . . . 2 g	fibre . . . . trace
total fat . . . . . 5 g	chol . . . . 9 mg
sat. fat . . . . . . 1 g	sodium . . . 87 mg

PERCENTAGE RDI:

calcium 1%	vit. A 0%
iron 3%	vit. C 0%
folate 3%	

Brie, Pear and Onion Strudel on a Bed of Greens

Ripe, juicy pears have a natural affinity to cheese, especially the soft and slightly funky Brie. Puff pastry turns this attractive pairing into a special-occasion appetizer.

1 tbsp	vegetable oil	15 mL
1	onion, sliced	1
1 tsp	granulated sugar	5 mL
¼ cup	chopped walnuts, toasted	50 mL
2 tbsp	chopped dried cranberries	25 mL
Half	pkg (397 g) frozen puff pastry, thawed	Half
2 tsp	Dijon mustard	10 mL
4 oz	Brie cheese, thinly sliced	125 g

1	pear, peeled, cored and thinly sliced	1
1	egg, beaten	1
SALAD:		
6 cups	frisée lettuce	1.5 L
2 cups	torn radicchio lettuce	500 mL
3 tbsp	walnut or extra-virgin olive oil	50 mL
4 tsp	cider vinegar	20 mL
¼ tsp	granulated sugar	1 mL
Pinch	each salt and pepper	Pinch

SUBSTITUTION: Other greens can replace the pale green curly frisée or the assertive red radicchio.

1 In large skillet, heat oil over medium heat; cook onion and sugar, stirring occasionally, for about 20 minutes or until golden and very soft. Stir in walnuts and cranberries. Set aside.

2 On lightly floured surface, roll out puff pastry into 12- x 9-inch (30 x 23 cm) rectangle. Spread mustard along middle third of pastry. Spoon onion mixture over mustard. Top with Brie and pear slices.

3 Starting at corner of 1 long edge of pastry, make diagonal cuts 1 inch (2.5 cm) apart almost to filling. Repeat on other side in opposite direction. Alternating strips from side to side, fold over filling to resemble braid, brushing each strip with egg to secure. Brush top with egg. Transfer to parchment paper–lined baking sheet.

4 Bake in 450°F (230°C) oven for about 25 minutes or until pastry is golden and pears are tender. Let cool slightly. (MAKE-AHEAD: Cover loosely with foil and set aside at room temperature for up to 4 hours; reheat to serve.) Cut into 8 pieces.

5 SALAD: Meanwhile, in bowl, toss together frisée and radicchio lettuce. Whisk together oil, vinegar, sugar, salt and pepper; pour over greens and toss to coat. Divide among 8 plates. Top each with strudel.

Makes 8 servings.

PER SERVING, ABOUT:

cal	314	carb	19 g
pro	7 g	fibre	2 g
total fat	24 g	chol	42 mg
sat. fat	5 g	sodium	196 mg

PERCENTAGE RDI:

calcium	6%	vit. A	12%
iron	9%	vit. C	8%
folate	40%		

Curried Lamb Phyllo Triangles

Myth: Phyllo pastry is hard to work with. Truth: Since availability and supermarket handling have improved, it's rare to find a package with crumbly unwrappable leaves. Always impressive, phyllo permits the cook to freeze trays of savoury appetizers for upcoming parties. Replace lamb with lean ground beef if desired.

TEST KITCHEN TIP: Flaky phyllo cups are handy for preparing party hors d'oeuvres. To make, butter and layer 3 sheets phyllo pastry; cut into 24 squares. Press squares into 24 greased mini muffin or tart tins. Bake in centre of 400°F (200°C) oven for 5 minutes or until golden. Let cool on rack. Repeat to make 48 cups. Fill phyllo cups with cube of Brie cheese, cream cheese or goat cheese; top with smoked salmon or whitefish caviar and dill sprig, or with Peppy Salsa (page 390) or Peach Chutney (page 388). Or fill with Hummus (page 30) and a sliver of black olive or egg salad and a dab of golden caviar or lumpfish caviar.

8	sheets phyllo pastry	8
1/3 cup	butter, melted	75 mL
FILLING:		
1 tsp	vegetable oil	5 mL
8 oz	ground lamb	250 g
1/2 cup	chicken stock	125 mL
1/4 cup	currants	50 mL
1	onion, chopped	1
1	clove garlic, minced	1
1 tbsp	mild curry paste or powder	15 mL
2 tsp	minced gingerroot	10 mL
1 tsp	ground cumin	5 mL
1/4 tsp	each salt and pepper	1 mL
1/2 cup	fresh bread crumbs	125 mL

1 FILLING: In large nonstick skillet, heat oil over medium-high heat; cook lamb, breaking up with wooden spoon, for 8 to 10 minutes or until no longer pink. Drain off fat. Stir in stock, currants, onion, garlic, curry paste, ginger, cumin, salt and pepper. Cover and simmer for 15 minutes or until onions are softened. Remove from heat; stir in bread crumbs. Let cool. (MAKE-AHEAD: Cover and refrigerate for up to 1 day.)

2 Place 1 phyllo sheet on work surface. Cover remaining phyllo with damp tea towel to prevent drying out. Using ruler and sharp knife, cut sheet lengthwise into 5 strips, each about 2½ inches (6 cm) wide.

3 Using pastry brush, lightly brush each strip with butter. Spoon heaping teaspoonful (5 mL) of the filling about ½ inch (1 cm) from end of each strip. Fold 1 corner of phyllo strip over filling so bottom edge of phyllo meets side edge to form triangle. Fold up triangle. Continue folding triangle sideways and upward until end of phyllo strip is reached. Fold end flap over to adhere. Working quickly, form triangles with remaining strips. Repeat with remaining phyllo sheets and filling.

4 Brush lightly with butter. (MAKE-AHEAD: Freeze in airtight containers in layers separated by waxed paper for up to 2 months. Do not thaw before baking.) Place on baking sheets. Bake in 375°F (190°C) oven for 15 to 18 minutes or until golden. Serve hot.

Makes about 40 pieces.

PER PIECE, ABOUT:

cal	50	carb	4 g
pro	2 g	fibre	trace
total fat	3 g	chol	8 mg
sat. fat	1 g	sodium	70 mg

PERCENTAGE RDI:

calcium	0%	vit. A	2%
iron	2%	vit. C	0%
folate	1%		

Quesadillas

Simple but satisfying, quesadillas make for affordable party appetizers, brunch novelties and snacks.

4	large flour tortillas	4
1 cup	shredded cheese (such as Monterey Jack)	250 mL
¼ cup	chopped pickled or fresh jalapeño peppers	50 mL

1 Lay each tortilla on work surface. Sprinkle ¼ cup (50 mL) shredded cheese on half of each; top with one-quarter of the jalapeño peppers. Fold uncovered half over filling. (MAKE-AHEAD: Cover and refrigerate for up to 4 hours.)

2 Bake on greased baking sheet in 400°F (200°C) oven, turning once, for about 8 minutes per side or until golden. Or cook in skillet, grill pan or on greased grill over medium-high heat for about 3 minutes per side or until crisp. Cut each into 8 wedges.

FILLING VARIATIONS

Instead of the cheese and jalapeño filling, try any of these.

Barbecue Chicken: ½ cup (125 mL) barbecue sauce, 1 cup (250 mL) chopped cooked chicken and 1 cup (250 mL) shredded mozzarella cheese.

Bruschetta: 1 cup (250 mL) bruschetta topping (page 35) and ½ cup (125 mL) shredded Asiago cheese.

Mediterranean: ¼ cup (50 mL) prepared pesto or tapenade and 1 cup (250 mL) crumbled goat cheese.

Pear and Brie: Thin slices of pear and Brie cheese.

Prosciutto and Artichoke: 4 slices prosciutto ham, 1 jar (6 oz/170 mL) marinated artichokes, drained and chopped, 1 cup (250 mL) shredded provolone cheese and 2 tbsp (25 mL) grated Parmesan cheese.

Salami: ¼ cup (50 mL) grainy mustard, 12 thin slices salami and 1 cup (250 mL) shredded Swiss cheese.

Spinach and Cheese: 1 pkg (10 oz/300 g) frozen spinach, thawed, squeezed dry and chopped finely, ¼ tsp (1 mL) dried dillweed and ½ cup (125 mL) each shredded mozzarella and crumbled feta cheese.

Jalapeño Corn: 1 cup (250 mL) shredded Monterey Jack cheese, ⅔ cup (150 mL) cooked corn kernels, half sweet red pepper, diced, 2 tsp (10 mL) minced seeded jalapeño pepper, ¾ tsp (4 mL) ground cumin.

TEST KITCHEN TIPS

• Choose coloured or flavoured tortillas for a touch of whimsy. For a party, invite guests to assemble their favourite fillings or get creative with other ingredients.

• A good-quality nonstick or cast-iron grill pan is ideal for cooking quesadillas, imparting attractive grill marks on the tortillas. Using a grill pan is a healthful way to cook meat year-round: fat drips off into the grooves between the ridges of the pan.

Makes 32 pieces.

PER PIECE, ABOUT:

cal	37	carb	4 g
pro	2 g	fibre	trace
total fat	2 g	chol	3 mg
sat. fat	1 g	sodium	71 mg

PERCENTAGE RDI:

calcium	3%	vit. A	1%
iron	2%	vit. C	2%
folate	1%		

Soups

2

Chunky Mushroom Soup 44

Corn Chowder 45

Beet and Vegetable Borscht 46

Soup Stocks 47

Eight No-Cream Creamed Soups 48

Asparagus Miso Soup 49

Gazpacho 50

Vichyssoise 51

Mediterranean Seafood Soup with Rouille 52

Hearty Seafood Chowder 53

Spicy Thai Shrimp and Noodle Soup 54

Black Bean Soup 55

Lentil Soup 56

Pasta e Fagioli 57

Hungarian Goulash Soup 58

Beef and Barley Soup 59

Dutch Meatball Soup 60

Jamaican Beef Pepper Pot 61

Five Turkey Soups 62

Chicken Noodle Soup 63

Chunky Mushroom Soup

Exotic mushrooms provide a stylish flourish to a very satisfying soup. Use crimini, shiitake or oyster mushrooms or a combination. Shiitake mushrooms have tough stems, which should be removed before mushrooms are cooked.

2 tbsp	vegetable oil	25 mL
2	onions, finely chopped	2
2	cloves garlic, minced	2
2	carrots, finely chopped	2
4 cups	sliced exotic mushrooms (about 12 oz/375 g)	1 L
3 cups	sliced button mushrooms (about 8 oz/250 g)	750 mL
½ tsp	dried thyme	2 mL
¼ tsp	each paprika and pepper	1 mL
5 cups	vegetable or chicken stock	1.25 L
1	potato, peeled and cubed	1
2 tbsp	sherry	25 mL

1 In large heavy saucepan, heat oil over medium heat; cook onions, garlic and carrots, stirring occasionally, for 5 minutes or until softened.

2 Stir in exotic and button mushrooms, thyme, paprika and pepper; cook, stirring often, for about 20 minutes or until mushrooms start to turn golden and no liquid remains.

3 Meanwhile, in small saucepan, bring 1½ cups (375 mL) of the vegetable stock to boil. Add potato; cover and cook over medium heat for about 10 minutes or until tender. Pour into blender or food processor; purée until smooth.

4 Stir potato purée and remaining stock into mushroom mixture; bring to boil. Reduce heat and simmer for 5 minutes. Stir in sherry; simmer for 2 minutes.

TEST KITCHEN TIPS

• When buying mushrooms, choose unblemished specimens. Refrigerate small amounts in paper bags (provided in good produce departments) for up to 3 days; if purchased in a large quantity, arrange in single layer on towel-lined tray and cover with damp towel.

• To clean cultivated mushrooms, trim away obvious dirt. Wipe with damp paper towel or mushroom brush. Kitchen lore has discouraged rinsing in water: the already moist mushrooms will absorb even more liquid. But if you need a lot for a cooked dish, try a quick rinse in a salad spinner and immediately spin off rinse water. Never soak mushrooms. Let them dry on towels before using.

Makes 4 servings.

PER SERVING, ABOUT:

cal	183	carb	24 g
pro	4 g	fibre	4 g
total fat	8 g	chol	0 mg
sat. fat	1 g	sodium	816 mg

PERCENTAGE RDI:

calcium	4%	vit. A	92%
iron	17%	vit. C	17%
folate	15%		

Fresh CULTIVATED MUSHROOMS

For supermarket shoppers, there are new choices when buying mushrooms. Best known, cultivated on a large scale and therefore the least expensive is the **white mushroom:** ½ to 3 inches (1 to 8 cm) in diameter, sometimes called the **button mushroom,** but officially known as the *Agaricus bisporus*. When mushrooms are called for in an ingredient list, this is the mushroom to choose. Agaricus mushrooms have a mild taste, but their earthiness still delivers a soupçon of elegance to salads, soups, stews, vegetable side dishes, pastas and dressings.

➤ The common white mushroom has been joined in produce bins by three other cultivated mushrooms, generally referred to as "exotic" mushrooms. The first, called **crimini,** is simply the brown counterpart of the common white mushroom. When grown to saucer size, the crimini becomes a **portobello** mushroom. The portobello, with a meatier, more pronounced woodsy flavour, is a natural for grilling and

Corn Chowder

Corn chowders are as old as Canada and always include some milk or cream. Here, the soup is hearty but light, the kind of soup you can pair up with a sandwich and call supper. Corn chowder reheats like a dream for lunch the next day.

2 tsp	olive oil	10 mL
2	onions, chopped	2
2	potatoes, peeled and diced	2
2	stalks celery, chopped	2
½ cup	diced sweet red pepper	125 mL
¼ tsp	hot pepper flakes	1 mL
2 cups	chicken stock	500 mL

1 cup	milk	250 mL
2	cans (each 10 oz/284 mL) creamed corn	2
½ cup	frozen corn kernels	125 mL
½ tsp	each salt and pepper	2 mL
2 tbsp	chopped fresh coriander, basil, thyme or parsley	25 mL

1 In heavy saucepan, heat oil over medium heat; cook onions, potatoes, celery, red pepper and hot pepper flakes, covered and stirring often, for 5 minutes. Pour in stock and bring to boil; reduce heat and simmer, covered, for 10 minutes or until potato is tender.

2 Add milk, creamed corn, frozen corn, salt and pepper; heat gently until steaming. Serve sprinkled with coriander.

TEST KITCHEN TIP: The surprise about creamed corn is that its creaminess is the result of puréeing, not the addition of dairy cream.

SUBSTITUTION: In the First Nations tradition, the Three Sisters that grow together — corn, squash and beans — simmer together in a soup. Feel free to continue the spirit of the tradition and add lima beans and cubed squash to Corn Chowder.

stuffing. Portobellos cook up dark and, when sliced or chopped, suit robust dishes in which a light colour is not important. Smaller versions are called portobellini.

 Oyster mushrooms come in various shades, but are usually dove grey, which with their flat shape and artistically fringed end does make them look like oysters. Mild in flavour, oyster mushrooms can be used in cooked dishes as you would common white mushrooms, and they are especially suited to Asian dishes and grilling.

 Shiitake mushrooms are the most expensive, the best keepers and the most assertive of the exotics. Stems are tough; remove and use to flavour stocks. Take advantage of the shiitake's flavour in pastas, vegetable side dishes, stir-fries, sauces, soups and wherever you want to up the heartiness of a dish.

 Also available are spindly, tiny-capped white **enoki,** or enokitake, mushrooms, usually grown in clumps and sold packaged in the produce department. They are delightful as a garnish or salad ingredient.

Makes 4 servings.

PER SERVING, ABOUT:

cal 272	carb . . . . 54 g
pro . . . . 10 g	fibre . . . . 4 g
total fat . . . . . 4 g	chol . . . . 2 mg
sat. fat . . . . . . 1 g	sodium 1,169 mg

PERCENTAGE RDI:

calcium 10%	vit. A 10%
iron 11%	vit. C 60%
folate 44%	

Beet and Vegetable Borscht

Gloriously colourful, the vegetables in this soup glow like jewels in a bowl. Caraway seeds add an authentic Eastern European touch to the stock, which can be vegetable, chicken or beef.

TEST KITCHEN TIP: Choose round red-skinned waxier potatoes because they will stay in neat cubes.

SUBSTITUTION: When beets with tops are not available, substitute the same amount of shredded cabbage or Swiss chard for beet greens.

1 tbsp	vegetable oil	15 mL
1	large onion, chopped	1
1	large carrot, chopped	1
2	stalks celery, chopped	2
1	bay leaf	1
Pinch	caraway seeds	Pinch
4	beets (with leaves)	4
2	large red-skinned potatoes	2

4 cups	beef, chicken or vegetable stock	1 L
1	can (19 oz/540 mL) tomatoes, chopped	1
4 tsp	vinegar	20 mL
	Salt and pepper	
¼ cup	light sour cream	50 mL
2 tbsp	chopped fresh dill	25 mL

1 In large heavy saucepan or Dutch oven, heat oil over medium heat; cook onion, carrot, celery, bay leaf and caraway seeds, stirring often, for about 10 minutes or until onion is softened.

2 Meanwhile, trim stalks from beets. Coarsely chop enough of the most tender leaves to make 2 cups (500 mL); set aside. Peel and cube beets. Peel potatoes if desired and cube.

3 Add beets, potatoes and stock to pan; bring to boil. Cover and reduce heat; simmer for about 20 minutes or until vegetables are tender. Add tomatoes; cook for 20 minutes. (MAKE-AHEAD: Let cool; cover and refrigerate for up to 1 day. Reheat before continuing.)

4 Stir in reserved beet greens; cook for about 2 minutes or until tender. Add vinegar; season with salt and pepper to taste. Discard bay leaf. Serve dolloped with sour cream and sprinkled with dill.

Makes 4 to 6 servings.

PER EACH OF 6 SERVINGS, ABOUT:
cal 153   carb ....26 g
pro ....6 g   fibre ....4 g
total fat .....4 g   chol ....1 mg
sat. fat ......1 g   sodium ..754 mg

PERCENTAGE RDI:
calcium .....8%   vit. A 48%
iron ....14%   vit. C 37%
folate 26%

SOUP STOCKS

In Canadian Living *recipes, the word* stock *refers to the strained liquid that results from cooking poultry, meat, fish or vegetables and seasonings in water. Other terms for this flavoured liquid are* broth *and* bouillon.

For homemade stocks, see below. For convenience, you can use good-quality powdered, fresh chilled or canned concentrated stock, increasing the ratio of water to lower sodium content if desired. Stock is also available frozen and may or may not be concentrated. Specialty or bulk stores may sell no- or low-sodium stock bases. If using commercial stocks, avoid adding salt until soup is cooked; at that point, season to taste. Be particularly vigilant when using other cured or canned already salted ingredients (bacon, ham, sausage, clams, tomatoes, beans).

CHICKEN OR TURKEY STOCK

🍃 Pour 16 cups (4 L) cold water into large stockpot. Add 5 lb (2.2 kg) chicken bones, backs and necks, cut into pieces, or 1 turkey carcass, cut into 3 or 4 pieces. Bring to boil; skim off any foam.

🍃 Add 2 each stalks celery, carrots and unpeeled onions, coarsely chopped, 1 bay leaf, 1 tbsp (15 mL) each dried thyme and black peppercorns and 6 stems parsley; reduce heat and simmer for 4 hours.

🍃 Strain through cheesecloth-lined sieve set over bowl; let cool. Refrigerate for about 8 hours or until fat solidifies on surface; remove fat. (MAKE-AHEAD: Refrigerate in airtight container for up to 3 days or freeze for up to 4 months.) **Makes 12 cups (3 L).**

TEST KITCHEN TIP: Too many turkey soups taste flat because the carcass sits too long in the refrigerator. After the meal, remove all meat and package separately. Refrigerate the carcass, then make stock early the next day. The soup can follow a day or two later. The taste difference is dramatic, making turkey soup something to look forward to.

BEEF STOCK

🍃 In roasting pan, combine 4 lb (2 kg) beef bones, 1 lb (500 g) veal bones, 3 tomatoes, coarsely chopped, 2 each stalks celery, carrots and unpeeled onions, coarsely chopped, and 1 clove garlic. Roast in 450°F (230°C) oven for 1 hour or until browned.

🍃 Transfer to large stockpot. Add 16 cups (4 L) cold water. Bring to boil; skim off any foam. Add 1 cup (250 mL) dry red wine, 10 black peppercorns, 1 tsp (5 mL) dried thyme, 4 stems parsley, 2 whole cloves and 1 bay leaf; reduce heat and simmer for 5 hours.

🍃 Strain through cheesecloth-lined sieve set over bowl; let cool. Refrigerate for about 8 hours or until fat solidifies on surface; remove fat. (MAKE-AHEAD: Refrigerate in airtight container for up to 3 days or freeze for up to 4 months.) **Makes 8 cups (2 L).**

FISH STOCK

🍃 Pour 16 cups (4 L) cold water into large stockpot. Add 5 lb (2.2 kg) fish bones, heads and tails from lean, mild fish such as sole or halibut (avoid fatty strong-flavoured fish such as mackerel and salmon). Bring to boil; skim off any foam.

🍃 Add 1 each unpeeled onion and stalk celery, coarsely chopped, 1 leek (white and light green parts only), chopped, 1 bay leaf, 10 black peppercorns, 6 stems parsley, 1 whole clove and ½ cup (125 mL) dry white wine; reduce heat and simmer for 30 minutes.

🍃 Strain through cheesecloth-lined sieve set over bowl; let cool. Refrigerate for about 8 hours or until fat solidifies on surface; remove fat. (MAKE-AHEAD: Refrigerate in airtight container for up to 3 days or freeze for up to 4 months.) **Makes 16 cups (4 L).**

TEST KITCHEN TIPS

• Freeze stock in amounts that you will use in recipes; for example, 2 cups (500 mL).

• These stocks are all unsalted, so you may need to increase the salt in a given recipe for which you use the stock.

Eight No-Cream Creamed Soups

This is soup in its simplest form — vegetables, stock, seasonings and simmering time. Since potatoes provide the creaminess, choose higher-starch oval baking potatoes. An immersion blender is ideal for puréeing the soup right in the pot without having to transfer it to a blender or food processor.

TEST KITCHEN TIPS

• An immersion blender is a very handy kitchen appliance, especially to add an elegant puréed touch to a soup. Be sure to hold it straight with the blender in the bottom of the saucepan before turning it on.

• Dress up bowls of vegetable soup with seasoned croutons, shredded cheese, sour cream or a dab of goat cheese.

VEGETABLES AND SEASONINGS FOR 4 CUPS (1 L) DENSE VEGETABLES			VEGETABLES AND SEASONINGS FOR 4 CUPS (1 L) TENDER VEGETABLES		
1 lb	large parsnips (3 to 5)	500 g	1 lb	frozen peas	500 g
1¼ lb	large beets (2 to 4)	625 g	1 lb	broccoli (1 small bunch)	500 g
1¼ lb	sweet potatoes (2)	625 g	1 lb	cauliflower (1 small head)	500 g
1¼ lb	squash (1 small)	625 g	Season with about 1 tsp (5 mL) dried Italian herb seasoning, crumbled dried basil, crumbled dried mint or herbes de Provence.		
1 lb	carrots (4)	500 g			
Season with about 2 tsp (10 mL) curry paste, ground ginger or ground cumin.					

1 Choose vegetable and seasoning according to chart. Chop vegetable (except peas).

2 In saucepan, heat 2 tsp (10 mL) vegetable oil over medium heat. Add 2 onions, chopped, 2 cloves garlic, minced, 1 potato, peeled and cubed, and your choice of seasoning. Cook, stirring often, for 5 minutes or until onions are softened.

3 Add 4 cups (1 L) prepared vegetables and 4 cups (1 L) chicken, vegetable or beef stock; bring to boil. Reduce heat to medium-low, cover and simmer for 10 minutes for tender vegetables (right column) or 20 minutes for dense vegetables (left column).

4 With immersion blender or in blender, purée until smooth. If desired, thin with more water, stock or milk. Season with salt and pepper to taste. (MAKE-AHEAD: Except for pea soup and broccoli soup, let cool, cover and refrigerate for up to 1 day. Reheat to serve.)

Makes 6 servings.

Asparagus Miso Soup

Soybean paste, or miso, adds protein to a fresh spring vegetarian soup.

3 cups	vegetable stock	750 mL	8 oz	asparagus, cut in 1-inch (2.5 cm) lengths	250 g
3 cups	water	750 mL	1	green onion, chopped	1
¼ cup	white miso	50 mL			
2	carrots, finely diced	2			

1 In large saucepan, bring stock and water to boil. In small bowl, whisk miso with 2 tbsp (25 mL) water until smooth; whisk into pan. Reduce heat to medium-low; simmer for 30 minutes.

2 Add carrots and asparagus; cook for about 5 minutes or until asparagus is tender-crisp. Serve sprinkled with green onion.

ASPARAGUS Appreciation

 The highest quality asparagus is thick and apple green with tight purple-tinged tips. Thinner spears are becoming more common, especially as an imported crop, and are useful for salads and dishes such as risotto.

 To produce white asparagus, a luxury item more popular in Europe than in North America, sandy soil is mounded up around the asparagus plants so that the emerging shoots remain white.

 To prepare asparagus, snap off the tough butt: hold the end of the butt in one hand and grasp the spear about halfway up; bend until the spear snaps. (Keep ends for flavouring soup.)

 Steam-boil upright in tall pot or horizontally in shallow saucepan for about 4 minutes or until tender-crisp. Or roll in olive oil and roast in single layer on baking sheet in 425°F (220°C) oven or grill over medium-high heat for about 8 minutes, turning once.

 After steaming or boiling asparagus for salads, plunge into large bowl of ice water to stop cooking process. Drain on paper towels.

TEST KITCHEN TIPS

• Miso, fermented soybean paste usually combined with a grain such as rye, barley or rice, comes in various shades. Lighter pale yellow miso, called white miso, is more quickly fermented and milder than darker miso. In shades of red to brownish black, this darker, more mature miso is stronger and often saltier. Lighter miso tends to be more expensive. Store all miso in the refrigerator. (See page 68 for Crunchy Iceberg Lettuce Salad with Miso Dressing.)

• Since miso settles to the bottom of the bowl, stir soup before each spoonful.

Makes 4 servings.

PER SERVING, ABOUT:

cal	78	carb	13 g
pro	4 g	fibre	3 g
total fat	2 g	chol	0 mg
sat. fat	trace	sodium	1,135 mg

PERCENTAGE RDI:

calcium	4%	vit. A	94%
iron	9%	vit. C	12%
folate	41%		

MAKE-
AHEAD   BUDGET-   CLASSIC
WISE

Gazpacho

When you think gazpacho, think crisp, cool and refreshing. This summer cross between a salad and a soup is attractive served ice-cold in glasses — maxi martini glasses are stylish.

TEST KITCHEN TIP: To dice cucumber, slice thin strip off side to form flat base. With knife tip at end, cut length-wise into ¼-inch (5 mm) thick slices. Stacking slices, cut into ¼-inch (5 mm) strips; cut crosswise into ¼-inch (5 mm) dice. For tomatoes and green pepper, place flat side down and slice and stack as for cucumber.

3	tomatoes, peeled	3
1	each sweet red and green pepper, halved	1
1	English cucumber, peeled	1
2	cloves garlic, chopped	2
2 tbsp	red wine vinegar	25 mL
1 tbsp	olive oil	15 mL
3½ cups	vegetable cocktail (approx)	875 mL

¼ tsp	hot pepper sauce	1 mL
	Salt and pepper	
GARNISH:		
1 tbsp	olive oil	15 mL
1	clove garlic, minced	1
2	slices day-old bread, crusts removed	2
2	green onions, sliced	2

1 Halve tomatoes; scoop out seeds. Coarsely chop 2 of the tomatoes, red pepper, and half each of the green pepper and cucumber; set remaining vegetables aside.

2 In food processor, or in blender in batches, purée chopped tomatoes, sweet peppers, cucumber, garlic, vinegar and oil until smooth. Transfer to large bowl; stir in vegetable cocktail and hot pepper sauce. Dice remaining cucumber, tomato and green pepper.

3 Refrigerate ¼ cup (50 mL) each cucumber and pepper. Add remaining vegetables to soup; cover and refrigerate for at least 2 hours or until chilled. (MAKE-AHEAD: Refrigerate for up to 12 hours.) Thin with more vegetable cocktail if desired. Season with salt and pepper to taste.

4 GARNISH: Whisk oil with garlic; brush over bread. Cut into ½-inch (1 cm) cubes; bake on baking sheet in 350°F (180°C) oven for 10 to 15 minutes or until croutons are golden, stirring once. Serve gazpacho in chilled bowls; sprinkle with reserved chopped cucumber and green pepper, croutons and green onions.

Makes 8 servings.

PER SERVING, ABOUT:

cal 89	carb .... 13 g
pro .... 2 g	fibre .... 2 g
total fat ..... 4 g	chol .... 0 mg
sat. fat ...... 1 g	sodium .. 421 mg

PERCENTAGE RDI:

calcium 3%	vit. A 25%
iron 8%	vit. C 135%
folate 21%	

VARIATIONS

Herbed Gazpacho: To serve, stir in ¼ cup (50 mL) chopped fresh basil, coriander or dill.

Fire and Ice Gazpacho: For medium heat, increase the hot pepper sauce to ½ tsp (2 mL). For fiery heat, also add 1 tbsp (15 mL) minced hot pepper. If desired, add a splash of plain or peppered vodka just before serving.

Vichyssoise

Although this soup has a fancy French name meaning "in the style of Vichy," its soul is in a peasant leek and potato soup. It is delicious hot but became famous when served cold with a sprinkle of fresh chives by French chef Louis Diat in New York in the early 1900s.

1 tbsp	butter	15 mL
2	leeks (white part only), sliced	2
3 cups	chicken stock	750 mL
2	large potatoes, peeled and cubed	2

1 cup	light cream (10%) or milk	250 mL
¼ tsp	each salt and pepper	1 mL

1 In heavy saucepan, melt butter over low heat; cook leeks, covered and stirring occasionally, for 10 minutes or until softened. Add chicken stock and potatoes; increase heat to medium-high, cover and bring to boil. Reduce heat to medium; simmer for 20 minutes.

2 In blender or food processor, purée in batches until smooth. Blend in cream. Refrigerate for at least 4 hours or until chilled. (MAKE-AHEAD: Cover and refrigerate for up to 1 day.) Season with salt and pepper.

VARIATION

Watercress Vichyssoise: Wash 1 bunch watercress. Pluck off and set aside ½ cup (125 mL) leaves. After simmering soup for 20 minutes, add remaining leaves and stems to saucepan. Cook for about 1 minute or just until wilted. Purée soup and chill. Chop reserved watercress; sprinkle over individual servings.

Makes 4 servings.

PER SERVING, ABOUT:

cal 255	carb . . . . 24 g
pro . . . . 7 g	fibre . . . . 3 g
total fat . . . . 15 g	chol . . . . . . 44 mg
sat. fat . . . . . . 9 g	sodium . . 790 mg

PERCENTAGE RDI:

calcium 8%	vit. A 13%
iron 10%	vit. C 15%
folate 12%	

Mediterranean Seafood Soup with Rouille

Inspired by Marseillaise bouillabaisse, and combining the goodness of the garden with the wonders of the sea, this soup is more chunky main-course stew than starter. The classic topping is rouille, a palate-rousing garlic and saffron mayonnaise.

ROUILLE: In bowl, soak 2 cups (500 mL) cubed French or Italian bread in ¼ cup (50 mL) dry white wine for 5 minutes. In small dish, soak 1 tsp (5 mL) saffron threads in 1 tbsp (15 mL) hot water for 5 minutes. In food processor, purée together bread and saffron mixtures, 3 tbsp (50 mL) light mayonnaise, 2 cloves garlic, minced, and ¼ tsp (1 mL) each salt and hot pepper flakes until very smooth. With machine running, pour in ⅓ cup (75 mL) extra-virgin olive oil in thin steady stream until creamy. Refrigerate.

½ tsp	saffron threads	2 mL
2 tbsp	extra-virgin olive oil	25 mL
1	leek (white and pale green parts only), chopped	1
Half	bulb fennel, thinly sliced	Half
4	cloves garlic, minced	4
½ tsp	dried oregano	2 mL
1	sweet red pepper, chopped	1
1 cup	dry white wine	250 mL
1 tbsp	grated orange rind	15 mL
1 tsp	salt	5 mL

2	cans (each 28 oz/796 mL) tomatoes, drained and chopped	2
3 cups	fish stock	750 mL
3	potatoes, peeled and cubed	3
2 lb	mussels and/or clams	1 kg
1 lb	firm fish fillets (monkfish, cod, halibut, red snapper), cut in chunks	500 g
1 lb	large shrimp, peeled and deveined	500 g
½ cup	chopped fresh parsley	125 mL

1 Soak saffron in ¼ cup (50 mL) hot water; set aside. In large Dutch oven, heat oil over medium heat; cook leek, fennel, garlic and oregano for 5 minutes. Add red pepper, wine, rind and salt; cover and cook for 10 minutes.

2 Add tomatoes, stock and saffron mixture; bring to boil. Reduce heat and simmer, uncovered, for 20 minutes. Meanwhile, in pot of boiling salted water, cook potatoes for 10 minutes or until tender; drain and add to soup.

3 Meanwhile, scrub mussels and remove beards if necessary. Discard any that do not close when tapped. Add mussels and fish to pot, stirring gently; cover and cook for 10 minutes. Add shrimp; cook for 5 minutes or until mussels open, fish is opaque and shrimp are pink.

4 Discard any mussels that do not open. Gently stir in parsley. Ladle soup into warmed bowls. Top each serving with spoonful of rouille.

Makes 6 servings.

PER SERVING, ABOUT:

cal 491	carb . . . . 36 g
pro . . . . 33 g	fibre . . . . 5 g
total fat . . . . 23 g	chol . . . . . 117 mg
sat. fat . . . . . . 3 g	sodium 1,588 mg

PERCENTAGE RDI:

calcium 12%	vit. A 26%
iron 40%	vit. C 113%
folate 33%	

Hearty Seafood Chowder

You have choices: cod, haddock, crab, lobster, clams, shrimp, salmon, mussels, mixed seafood and more! The basics remain the same: a chowder base of onion, potatoes and milk with a last-minute addition of seafood timed so that it cooks through but doesn't flake apart or harden.

2 tbsp	butter	25 mL
1	onion, chopped	1
3 tbsp	all-purpose flour	50 mL
3 cups	fish or chicken stock	750 mL
2	potatoes, peeled and diced	2
1	carrot, diced	1

1	stalk celery, chopped	1
½ tsp	each dried savory and thyme	2 mL
¼ tsp	each salt and pepper	1 mL
1 lb	mixed fish or seafood, cut in chunks	500 g
1 cup	light cream (10%) or milk	250 mL

1 In large heavy saucepan, melt butter over medium heat; cook onion until softened, about 3 minutes. Stir in flour; cook, stirring, for 1 minute. Add stock, potatoes, carrot, celery, savory, thyme, salt and pepper; cover and bring to boil. Reduce heat and simmer until vegetables are tender, about 15 minutes.

2 Add fish; cook for 3 minutes or until opaque. Pour in cream; heat through.

VARIATIONS

Hearty Seafood and Corn Chowder: Add ½ cup (125 mL) corn kernels with seafood.

Hearty Clam Chowder: Omit mixed fish. Add 2 cans (each 5 oz/142 g) clams, drained, along with cream. Use liquid from clams to replace fish or chicken stock.

Hearty Tuna Chowder: Omit mixed fish. Add 2 cans (each 6½ oz/184 g) white tuna, drained, along with cream.

Hearty Fresh Clam Chowder: Omit half of the stock and cream. Omit salt. Add 1½ cups (375 mL) water. Substitute 4 lb (2 kg) fresh littleneck clams, rinsed, for mixed fish; cook for about 10 minutes or until clams open. (Discard any that do not open.)

Hearty Mussel Chowder: Substitute 2 lb (1 kg) fresh mussels (scrub and remove beards; discard any that do not close when tapped) for mixed fish. Cook for about 5 minutes or until mussels open. (Discard any that do not open.)

Makes 4 servings.

PER SERVING, ABOUT:

cal 379	carb . . . . 27 g
pro . . . . 26 g	fibre . . . . 2 g
total fat . . . . 19 g	chol . . . . . 163 mg
sat. fat . . . . . 11 g	sodium . . 837 mg

PERCENTAGE RDI:

calcium 10%	vit. A 63%
iron 16%	vit. C 15%
folate 14%	

Spicy Thai Shrimp and Noodle Soup

This dish is a wonderful example of the way Thai cuisine balances a blend of heat (tiny peppers), sweetness (sugar), saltiness (soy and fish sauces) and sourness (lime juice and leaves).

TEST KITCHEN TIP: Makrut lime is sometimes referred to as kaffir lime, but the knobbly bitter citrus fruit is known as makrut in Thailand. "Kaffir" is pejorative.

2 oz	rice noodles (about 1 cup/250 mL)	60 g
8 cups	chicken stock	2 L
5	makrut lime leaves (optional)	5
1 tbsp	grated gingerroot	15 mL
1	clove garlic, minced	1
3 tbsp	lime or lemon juice	50 mL
2 tbsp	each soy sauce and fish sauce	25 mL
1	Thai or serrano chili pepper, chopped	1

1 tsp	granulated sugar	5 mL
1 lb	large shrimp, peeled and deveined	500 g
1	large carrot, julienned	1
2	green onions, cut in 2-inch (5 cm) pieces	2
¼ cup	chopped fresh coriander	50 mL
¼ cup	chopped fresh mint or Thai basil	50 mL
1	lime, cut in 8 wedges	1

1 In bowl, pour boiling water over noodles to cover; let soak for 15 minutes or until tender. Drain.

2 Meanwhile, in saucepan, bring stock, lime leaves (if using), ginger and garlic to boil; reduce heat and simmer for 15 minutes. Discard lime leaves. Add lime juice, soy and fish sauces, chili pepper and sugar; simmer for 5 minutes. Stir in shrimp, noodles and carrot; simmer for about 3 minutes or just until shrimp are opaque.

3 Divide soup among 8 serving bowls. Sprinkle with green onions, coriander and mint. Garnish with lime wedges.

Makes 8 servings.

PER SERVING, ABOUT:

cal 128	carb . . . . 11 g
pro . . . . 15 g	fibre . . . . 1 g
total fat . . . . . 2 g	chol . . . . . . 65 mg
sat. fat . . . . . . 1 g	sodium 1,461 mg

PERCENTAGE RDI:

calcium 3%	vit. A 33%
iron 12%	vit. C 12%
folate 8%	

Black Bean Soup

MAKE-AHEAD   FREEZABLE   BUDGET-WISE

Whether you choose the long soak method or the quick and convenient canned bean method, this Southwestern-inspired soup will take the chill off a winter's day.

3 cups	black beans	750 mL
1 tbsp	olive oil	15 mL
3	cloves garlic, minced	3
2	onions, chopped	2
2	stalks celery, chopped	2
2 tsp	chili powder	10 mL
2 tsp	chopped jalapeño pepper	10 mL
1½ tsp	dried oregano	7 mL

1 tsp	ground cumin	5 mL
½ tsp	aniseeds	2 mL
6 cups	chicken stock	1.5 L
1	can (14 oz/398 mL) stewed tomatoes	1
¾ tsp	salt	4 mL
¼ tsp	pepper	1 mL
4 tsp	lime juice	20 mL

TEST KITCHEN TIP: Serve with sour cream, coriander and a slice of green pepper. Or serve with Lime Coriander Cream: In bowl, stir together ½ cup (125 mL) sour cream, 2 tbsp (25 mL) finely chopped fresh coriander and 2 tbsp (25 mL) lime juice. Spoon over centre of each bowlful of soup.

1 Rinse beans, discarding any grit. In large heavy saucepan or Dutch oven, cover beans with 3 times their volume of water; bring to boil, cover and cook for 2 minutes. Remove from heat; let soak for 1 hour. Drain.

2 Wipe out pot and heat oil over medium heat; cook garlic, onions and celery, stirring occasionally, for 5 minutes or until onions are softened. Add chili powder, jalapeño pepper, oregano, cumin and aniseeds; cook, stirring occasionally, for 1 minute.

3 Add beans and stock; bring to boil. Reduce heat, cover and simmer for 75 minutes or until beans are very tender. Add tomatoes, salt and pepper; simmer for 10 minutes.

4 In food processor or blender, purée 8 cups (2 L) of the soup in batches. Return to pot; heat through. Stir in lime juice. Taste and adjust seasoning. (MAKE-AHEAD: Let cool; cover and refrigerate for up to 3 days or freeze for up to 2 months. Reheat gently to serve.)

VARIATION

Quick Black Bean Soup: Substitute 3 cans (each 19 oz/540 mL) black beans, drained, for the soaked beans. Reduce stock to 5 cups (1.25 L). To onion mixture, add beans, stock, tomatoes, salt and pepper; simmer for only 30 minutes.

Makes 6 servings.

PER SERVING, ABOUT:

cal	453	carb	71 g
pro	29 g	fibre	17 g
total fat	5 g	chol	0 mg
sat. fat	1 g	sodium	1,270 mg

PERCENTAGE RDI:

calcium	11%	vit. A	8%
iron	50%	vit. C	25%
folate	178%		

Lentil Soup

It is fitting that a delicious soup like this one comes from Agribition, Canada's international agricultural fair in Regina, Saskatchewan, the province where lentils thrive.

TEST KITCHEN TIP: Use green or brown lentils, not smaller red lentils, which break down during cooking.

1 tbsp	vegetable oil	15 mL
2 cups	chopped onions	500 mL
8 cups	chicken or beef stock	2 L
1	can (19 oz/540 mL) tomatoes	1
1 cup	dried lentils, rinsed	250 mL
1 cup	thinly sliced carrots	250 mL
½ tsp	each dried thyme and marjoram	2 mL
	Salt and pepper	
¼ cup	dry sherry	50 mL
1 cup	shredded Cheddar cheese	250 mL

1 In large heavy saucepan or Dutch oven, heat oil over medium heat; cook onions until softened, about 3 minutes.

2 Add stock, tomatoes, lentils, carrots, thyme and marjoram; simmer, covered, for 45 minutes or until lentils and vegetables are tender. Season with salt and pepper to taste. Stir in sherry. (MAKE-AHEAD: Let cool; refrigerate in airtight container for up to 2 days or freeze for up to 2 weeks. Reheat to serve.) Place 1 to 2 tbsp (15 to 25 mL) of the cheese in each soup bowl; ladle soup into bowls.

Makes 10 servings.

PER SERVING, ABOUT:

cal 188	carb .... 19 g
pro .... 13 g	fibre .... 4 g
total fat ..... 7 g	chol ...... 12 mg
sat. fat ...... 3 g	sodium .. 791 mg

PERCENTAGE RDI:

calcium 11%	vit. A 34%
iron 21%	vit. C 13%
folate 52%	

HERB Garnishes

With fresh herbs and a little imagination, it's easy to dress up a simple bowl of soup.

🌿 Instead of the usual sprig of parsley, chop parsley finely and dust it lightly over the soup and wide rim of bowl. Do the same with other fresh herbs such as coriander, dill, chives, basil and chervil.

🌿 Create a design with herbs. Out of the centre of a piece of cardboard, cut a shape, initial or number, depending on the occasion. Hold cutout just above the soup bowl and sprinkle finely chopped parsley or other herb through it to create a pattern on the soup.

Pasta e Fagioli

When you buy a piece of real Parmesan, Parmigiano-Reggiano, it always comes with the name of the cheese printed on the rind to authenticate the purchase. Too tough to grate and eat, the rind stars as a flavouring element in this rustic pasta and bean soup.

1 tbsp	olive oil	15 mL		1	slice prosciutto (¼ inch/5 mm thick)	1
1	onion, chopped	1		1	piece (3 inches/8 cm long) Parmesan rind	1
2	cloves garlic, minced	2				
2	stalks celery, chopped	2		1 cup	tubetti pasta (4 oz/125 g)	250 mL
2	carrots, chopped	2		1	can (19 oz/540 mL) romano beans, drained and rinsed	1
5 cups	chicken stock	1.25 L				
1 cup	water	250 mL		¼ tsp	pepper	1 mL
1	can (28 oz/796 mL) diced tomatoes	1		2 tbsp	grated Parmesan cheese	25 mL

1 In large heavy saucepan or Dutch oven, heat oil over medium heat. Add onion, garlic, celery and carrots; cook, stirring, for about 5 minutes or until onion is tender.

2 Stir in stock, water, tomatoes, prosciutto and Parmesan rind. Bring to boil; reduce heat and simmer for about 30 minutes or until vegetables are tender. (MAKE-AHEAD: Let cool; cover and refrigerate for up to 1 day. Reheat before continuing.)

3 Meanwhile, in large pot of boiling salted water, cook pasta for about 8 minutes or until tender but firm. Drain; add to soup along with beans and pepper. Heat through.

4 Discard Parmesan rind. Serve sprinkled with Parmesan cheese.

Makes 6 servings.

PER SERVING, ABOUT:

cal	268	carb	41 g
pro	15 g	fibre	7 g
total fat	5 g	chol	3 mg
sat. fat	1 g	sodium	1,357 mg

PERCENTAGE RDI:

calcium	12%	vit. A	69%
iron	25%	vit. C	27%
folate	56%		

Hungarian Goulash Soup

Long simmering blends the rich beef, tomato, pepper and mushroom flavours with caraway seeds and paprika. Truly a meal in a bowl, author Rose Murray's goulash soup improves when reheated.

2 tbsp	vegetable oil	25 mL	2	sweet green peppers, diced	2
1½ lb	lean beef, cut in ¾-inch (2 cm) cubes	750 g	¼ cup	water	50 mL
2	onions, sliced	2	1¼ tsp	dried basil	6 mL
3 cups	thickly sliced mushrooms (8 oz/250 g)	750 mL	4	potatoes, peeled and diced	4
2 tbsp	caraway seeds, crushed	25 mL	7 cups	beef stock	1.75 L
1 tbsp	sweet paprika	15 mL	1¼ tsp	dried marjoram	6 mL
½ tsp	salt (approx)	2 mL	¾ tsp	pepper	4 mL
1	can (19 oz/540 mL) tomatoes, chopped	1	4 oz	egg noodles	125 g

1 In large heavy saucepan or Dutch oven, heat oil over medium-high heat; brown meat. Drain off fat. Add onions and mushrooms; reduce heat to medium and cook, stirring occasionally, for 5 to 8 minutes or until onions are softened. Remove from heat; stir in caraway seeds, paprika and salt. Reduce heat to low, cover and cook for 20 minutes, stirring occasionally. Stir in tomatoes, peppers, water and basil; bring to boil. Reduce heat, cover and simmer for 1 hour or until meat is almost tender, adding more water if necessary to prevent sticking.

2 Add potatoes and stock; bring to boil. Reduce heat, cover and simmer for 40 to 45 minutes or until potatoes and meat are tender. Season with more salt to taste. Stir in marjoram and pepper. (MAKE-AHEAD: Let cool for 30 minutes; refrigerate, uncovered, in shallow airtight containers until cold. Cover and refrigerate for up to 2 days. Reheat slowly, stirring often.) Stir in noodles; cook for about 7 minutes or until tender.

Makes 8 servings.

PER SERVING, ABOUT:

cal 292	carb . . . . 33 g
pro . . . . 23 g	fibre . . . . 4 g
total fat . . . . . 8 g	chol . . . . . . 52 mg
sat. fat . . . . . . 2 g	sodium . . 967 mg

PERCENTAGE RDI:

calcium 6%	vit. A 11%
iron 28%	vit. C 58%
folate 15%	

Beef and Barley Soup

Thick and hearty, this soup can simmer all day long in a slow-cooker, or more briefly on top of the stove. Adjust the consistency of the soup to your taste, adding more stock or water if the barley expands and the soup is too thick.

2 tbsp	vegetable oil	25 mL
1 lb	beef stewing cubes	500 g
2 tbsp	all-purpose flour	25 mL
2	onions, chopped	2
3	cloves garlic, minced	3
3 cups	sliced fresh mushrooms (8 oz/250 g)	750 mL
2	carrots, chopped	2
2	stalks celery, chopped	2
1 tsp	dried thyme	5 mL

½ tsp	crumbled dried sage	2 mL
5 cups	beef stock	1.25 L
½ cup	red wine	125 mL
1	can (19 oz/540 mL) tomatoes	1
2 cups	water	500 mL
½ tsp	pepper	2 mL
¼ tsp	salt	1 mL
½ cup	pearl barley	125 mL

1 In large heavy saucepan or Dutch oven, heat oil over medium-high heat. Toss beef with flour; in batches, brown all over, about 5 minutes. Transfer to plate. Drain any fat from pan.

2 Increase heat to high; cook onions, garlic, mushrooms, carrots, celery, thyme and sage, stirring, for about 5 minutes or until liquid is evaporated.

3 Stir stock and wine into pot; cook for 1 minute, stirring and scraping up any brown bits from bottom of pot. Add beef, tomatoes, water, pepper and salt; bring to boil, reduce heat and simmer, covered, for 1½ hours or until beef is tender.

4 Add barley; cover and simmer for 30 minutes or until tender. (MAKE-AHEAD: Let cool for 30 minutes; refrigerate, uncovered, in shallow airtight containers until cold. Cover and refrigerate for up to 2 days. Reheat to serve.)

TEST KITCHEN TIPS

• Barley is a grain that's widely available in bulk and health food stores as well as supermarkets. Grown in more northerly climates, it tends to turn up in Northern European cuisines. Both pot and pearl barley are polished — pearl more so than pot — and can be used interchangeably.

• To make in slow-cooker, after Step 2, transfer to slow-cooker, add remaining ingredients and cook on Low for 6 to 8 hours or until beef is tender.

Makes 6 to 8 servings.

PER EACH OF 8 SERVINGS, ABOUT:

cal 216	carb . . . . 21 g
pro . . . . 17 g	fibre . . . . 3 g
total fat . . . . . 7 g	chol . . . . . . 31 mg
sat. fat . . . . . . 2 g	sodium . . 729 mg

PERCENTAGE RDI:

calcium 5%	vit. A 50%
iron 22%	vit. C 17%
folate 13%	

Dutch Meatball Soup

Here are two versions of a hearty soup from Test Kitchen home economist Susan Van Hezewijk: the first is the long method using beef shank to flavour and enrich the soup; the substitution shows how to get away with canned stock and still produce a deliciously wholesome soup.

SUBSTITUTIONS

• If you don't have time to make stock, substitute 3 cans (each 10 oz/284 mL) beef stock and 10 cups (2.5 L) water.

• Maggi, a traditional seasoning, is sold in grocery stores featuring Dutch products. Instead of Maggi seasoning, you can use 1 tbsp (15 mL) soy sauce plus 1 tsp (5 mL) Worcestershire sauce.

3	leeks (white and light green parts only), chopped	3
1½ cups	each chopped celery and carrots	375 mL
1 lb	lean ground beef	500 g
½ cup	dry bread crumbs	125 mL
2 tbsp	chopped fresh parsley	25 mL
½ tsp	each salt and pepper	2 mL
Pinch	nutmeg	Pinch
1 cup	fine egg noodles	250 mL
1 tbsp	Maggi seasoning	15 mL

STOCK:		
20 cups	cold water	5 L
2½ lb	shank stewing beef bone-in (about 3)	1.25 kg
2	carrots, coarsely chopped	2
2	stalks celery, coarsely chopped	2
1	onion, cut in wedges	1
1 tbsp	salt	15 mL

1 STOCK: In large stockpot or Dutch oven, bring water, beef, carrots, celery and onion to boil. Reduce heat and simmer for 2 hours. Drain, reserving liquid and beef. Cut beef off bone; discard bone and set beef aside. Add salt to stock.

2 Bring stock to simmer. Add leeks, celery and carrots; cook for 30 minutes.

3 Meanwhile, in bowl, mix together ground beef, bread crumbs, 2 tsp (10 mL) of the parsley, salt, pepper and nutmeg; form by tablespoonfuls (15 mL) into balls. Add to soup with reserved beef; simmer for 15 minutes or until meatballs are no longer pink inside. (MAKE-AHEAD: Let cool for 30 minutes; refrigerate, uncovered, in shallow airtight containers until cold. Cover and refrigerate for up to 2 days or freeze for up to 2 weeks. Reheat to continue.)

4 Add noodles; cook for 8 to 10 minutes or until tender but firm. Stir in Maggi seasoning and remaining parsley.

Makes 8 servings.

PER SERVING, ABOUT:

cal 355	carb . . . . 15 g
pro . . . . 33 g	fibre . . . . 3 g
total fat . . . . 17 g	chol . . . . . . 88 mg
sat. fat . . . . . . 7 g	sodium 1,290 mg

PERCENTAGE RDI:

calcium 6%	vit. A 53%
iron 31%	vit. C 7%
folate 15%	

Jamaican Beef Pepper Pot

There are as many variations of this chunky soup as there are kitchens in Jamaica. If you like, doctor this one with hot pepper sauce and let the Caribbean breezes blow.

1 tbsp	vegetable oil	15 mL
2 lb	stewing beef, cubed	1 kg
6	slices bacon, chopped	6
2	onions, chopped	2
4	cloves garlic, minced	4
¼ cup	all-purpose flour	50 mL
6 cups	beef stock	1.5 L
4 cups	water	1 L
¼ cup	tomato paste	50 mL

1 tsp	dried thyme	5 mL
½ tsp	each salt and pepper	2 mL
4	sweet potatoes, peeled and cubed (2 lb/1 kg)	4
1	each sweet red and green pepper, chopped	1
1 tbsp	wine vinegar	15 mL
1 tsp	hot pepper sauce	5 mL

TEST KITCHEN TIP: A stockpot is the ideal pot for making soup. It should have a high side so you can boil without splattering, and it should have a lid and a heavy bottom for even cooking.

1 In large stockpot or Dutch oven, heat oil over high heat; brown beef in batches. Transfer to plate.

2 Add bacon to pot; cook over medium heat for about 5 minutes or until crisp. Drain off fat. Add onions and garlic; cook, stirring occasionally, for 5 minutes or until softened.

3 Sprinkle with flour; cook, stirring, for 1 minute. Add stock and water; bring to boil. Reduce heat to medium-low. Return beef and any juices to pan; add tomato paste, thyme, salt and pepper. Cover and simmer, stirring occasionally, for 1 hour.

4 Add sweet potatoes and red and green peppers; cook, covered, for 30 minutes or until potatoes are tender. (MAKE-AHEAD: Let cool for 30 minutes; refrigerate, uncovered, in shallow airtight containers until cold. Cover and refrigerate for up to 2 days. Reheat to continue.) Stir in vinegar and hot pepper sauce.

VARIATION

Slow-Cooker Jamaican Beef Pepper Pot: Reduce water to 2 cups (500 mL). Brown beef in oil. Cook bacon, onions and garlic as directed. Return beef and any juices to pan. Add stock, 1½ cups (375 mL) of the water, tomato paste, thyme, salt and pepper; bring to boil. Pour into slow-cooker. Add sweet potatoes; cover and cook on Low for 8 to 10 hours or until tender. Increase heat to high. Add peppers. Whisk flour with remaining water; stir into slow-cooker and cook for 15 minutes. Stir in vinegar and hot pepper sauce as directed. **Makes 9 servings.**

Makes 10 servings.

PER SERVING, ABOUT:

cal	301	carb	24 g
pro	25 g	fibre	3 g
total fat	12 g	chol	53 mg
sat. fat	4 g	sodium	716 mg

PERCENTAGE RDI:

calcium	4%	vit. A	118%
iron	21%	vit. C	73%
folate	12%		

Five Turkey Soups

If turkey on December 25 is predictable, then so is turkey soup a few days later. It's a soup that begs for variations depending on what's in your crisper.

	SOFTEN	ADD	SIMMER
Turkey Mushroom Barley Soup	4 cups (1 L) sliced mushrooms; ½ tsp (2 mL) dried thyme	¼ cup (50 mL) barley; 2 tbsp (25 mL) tomato paste; 2 tsp (10 mL) wine vinegar	1 hour or until barley is tender
Turkey Vegetable Soup	1 leek (white part only), sliced; half sweet red pepper, chopped; 1 tsp (5 mL) dried sage	2 potatoes, peeled and cubed; 1 cup (250 mL) cubed peeled rutabaga; ½ cup (125 mL) frozen peas; 1 tbsp (15 mL) lemon juice	25 minutes or until vegetables are tender
Turkey Rice Gumbo Soup	Half sweet green pepper, chopped; 1 tsp (5 mL) Cajun seasoning; ½ tsp (2 mL) dried thyme	1 can (28 oz/796 mL) stewed tomatoes; 1 cup (250 mL) each fresh or frozen cut beans and corn kernels; ¼ cup (50 mL) long-grain rice	25 minutes or until rice is tender
Turkey Chili Soup	2 tbsp (25 mL) chili powder; 1 tsp (5 mL) dried oregano; ½ tsp (2 mL) ground cumin	1 can (28 oz/796 mL) diced tomatoes; 1 can (19 oz/540 mL) red kidney beans, drained and rinsed	15 minutes
Asian Turkey Noodle Soup	2 green onions, chopped; 1 tbsp (15 mL) minced gingerroot (or ¼ tsp/1 mL ground ginger)	2 oz (60 g) wide rice-stick noodles or 1 cup (250 mL) medium egg noodles; 1 cup (250 mL) snow peas, halved; 2 tbsp (25 mL) soy sauce; 2 tsp (10 mL) rice vinegar; ½ tsp (2 mL) sesame oil	6 minutes or until noodles are tender but firm

TEST KITCHEN TIP: If using canned chicken stock, reduce salt to ¼ tsp (1 mL).

1 In large saucepan, heat 1 tbsp (15 mL) vegetable oil over medium heat; cook 1 onion, chopped, 2 each carrots and stalks celery, chopped, and ingredients in first column for about 8 minutes or until softened.

2 Add 6 cups (1.5 L) turkey or chicken stock (see page 47), 1 tsp (5 mL) salt, pinch pepper and ingredients in second column; bring to boil.

3 Reduce heat, cover and simmer for time specified in third column. Add 2 cups (500 mL) chopped cooked turkey; heat through.

Makes 4 to 6 servings.

Chicken Noodle Soup

Chicken legs produce a rich flavoured stock and plenty of meat for this classic soup.

2 cups	each sliced carrots and celery	500 mL
1 cup	chopped onions	250 mL
1 tbsp	salt	15 mL
½ tsp	pepper	2 mL
3 cups	broad egg noodles	750 mL
½ cup	frozen peas	125 mL
2 tbsp	chopped fresh parsley	25 mL

	STOCK:	
5 lb	chicken legs	2.2 kg
16 cups	water	4 L
2	each carrots and stalks celery, coarsely chopped	2
1	onion, coarsely chopped	1
1	bay leaf	1
1 tsp	each salt and dried thyme	5 mL
½ tsp	whole peppercorns	2 mL

1 STOCK: In stockpot, bring chicken and water to boil; skim off foam. Add carrots, celery, onion, bay leaf, salt, thyme and peppercorns; simmer, uncovered, over medium-low heat for 2 hours.

2 Remove chicken; cover and refrigerate. Strain stock through cheesecloth-lined sieve into large bowl, pressing vegetables to extract liquid. Refrigerate for 8 hours or until fat congeals on surface. Lift off and discard fat.

3 In large saucepan or Dutch oven, bring stock to simmer. Add carrots, celery, onions, salt and pepper; cook for 20 to 25 minutes or until tender.

4 Meanwhile, remove chicken meat from bones; chop and add to soup. Add noodles; cook for 10 minutes or until tender. Stir in peas and parsley.

VARIATIONS

Chicken and Wild Rice Soup: Omit noodles. Add ½ cup (125 mL) rinsed wild rice along with vegetables; cover and simmer for 45 to 55 minutes or until rice is tender. Add chicken meat, peas and parsley; heat through. **Makes 8 servings.**

Slow-Cooker Chicken Noodle Soup: Reduce chicken to 3 lb (1.5 kg) and water to 8 cups (2 L); cook stock in slow-cooker on Low for 10 hours. Proceed as directed but reduce soup ingredients by half. **Makes 5 servings.**

Makes 8 servings.

PER SERVING, ABOUT:

cal	467	carb	19 g
pro	56 g	fibre	3 g
total fat	17 g	chol	167 mg
sat. fat	5 g	sodium	1,125 mg

PERCENTAGE RDI:

calcium	6%	vit. A	74%
iron	28%	vit. C	8%
folate	15%		

Salads and
Side Dishes

Fatouche	66
Baby Spinach and Goat Cheese Salad	67
Crunchy Iceberg Lettuce Salad with Miso Dressing	68
Caesar Salad	69
Bread Salad	70
Creamy Coleslaw	71
Keeper Coleslaw	71
Greek Salad	72
Peanut Jicama Salad	73
Roasted Roots Salad	74
Potato Salad	75
Tabbouleh Salad	76
Sushi Rice Salad	77
Penne Salad with Artichokes and Spinach	78
Curried Lentil, Wild Rice and Orzo Salad	79
Red Barn Corn and Bean Salad	80
Salad Dressings and Vinaigrettes	81
Pick-a-Grain Pilaf	83
No-Fail Rice	84
Risotto Milanese	85
Grain and Pasta Side Dishes	86
Baked Beans	87
Simply the Best Scalloped Potatoes	88
Golden Latkes	89
Guides to Boiling and Steaming Vegetables, Roasting Vegetables, Grilling Vegetables	90

Fatouche

This healthful fresh green salad with crisp radishes, pieces of toasted pita and grace notes of fresh mint originated in a Lebanese restaurant in Ottawa.

TEST KITCHEN TIP: Sumac spice, made from the powdered dried berries of the sumac shrub, is a sour element, like lemon, and complements the citrus tang of the dressing. A few shavings of lemon rind can replace it in the dressing.

6	radishes	6
3	tomatoes	3
1	cucumber, peeled and seeded	1
1	sweet green pepper, seeded	1
1	small mild white or Spanish onion	1
1	head romaine lettuce	1
1	whole wheat pita bread	1

1 cup	chopped fresh parsley	250 mL
1 tbsp	chopped fresh mint	15 mL
DRESSING:		
⅓ cup	lemon juice	75 mL
⅓ cup	olive oil	75 mL
2 tsp	ground sumac spice (optional)	10 mL
¾ tsp	salt	4 mL

1 Quarter radishes. Cube tomatoes, cucumber, green pepper and onion. Chop lettuce. In large bowl, combine vegetables. Separate pita bread into 2 layers; broil, turning once, for 2 minutes or until crisp. Break into ½-inch (1 cm) pieces.

2 DRESSING: In small bowl, whisk together lemon juice, oil, ground sumac spice (if using) and salt; pour over vegetables. Add parsley, mint and pita pieces; toss lightly.

Makes 6 to 8 servings.

PER EACH OF 8 SERVINGS, ABOUT:

cal	145	carb	14 g
pro	3 g	fibre	3 g
total fat	10 g	chol	0 mg
sat. fat	1 g	sodium	273 mg

PERCENTAGE RDI:

calcium	5%	vit. A	23%
iron	13%	vit. C	83%
folate	54%		

PREPARING Greens

⌁ Cut out core or stem of lettuce; separate leaves.

⌁ In cold water, gently swish leaves to clean well. For tightly furled heads, such as iceberg, Belgian endive or radicchio, just remove outer leaves and wash head. Place leaves in colander or towel, shaking off excess water.

⌁ Discard any wilted leaves; tear off any discoloured parts. Loosely fill salad spinner half-full of greens; spin, pouring off water occasionally. Blot leaves gently with towel to remove any remaining moisture. Or pat leaves dry by hand between towels.

⌁ Layer greens loosely between dry towels; roll up and place in plastic bag. Refrigerate greens for up to five days.

⌁ Just before serving, tear greens into bite-size pieces. Place in salad bowl. Drizzle with dressing and toss gently just until greens are coated and glistening.

⌁ You need ⅓ cup (75 mL) dressing to dress 8 cups (2 L) greens.

Baby Spinach and Goat Cheese Salad

Rounds of creamy goat cheese coated in crumbs and crisped quickly in a skillet add a pure bistro flourish to salad greens. Much of the goat cheese we find in dairy cases is the soft, unripened, eminently spreadable variety extruded into plastic tubes. This salad is best with firmer unripened goat cheese sold in chubbier logs or partial logs, about 3 inches (8 cm) in diameter.

10 cups	baby spinach	2.5 L
1 cup	thinly sliced mushrooms	250 mL
Half	sweet red pepper, thinly sliced	Half
4	radishes, thinly sliced	4
1	egg	1
1¼ cups	fresh bread crumbs	300 mL
12 oz	goat cheese (3 inches/ 8 cm in diameter)	375 g
2 tbsp	olive oil	25 mL

DRESSING:		
¼ cup	olive oil	50 mL
2 tbsp	sherry or red wine vinegar	25 mL
1 tsp	Dijon mustard	5 mL
1	clove garlic, minced	1
¼ tsp	each salt and pepper	1 mL

TEST KITCHEN TIP: Instead of coating goat cheese in egg and crumbs and frying, you can take a crostini shortcut: simply spread soft goat cheese on 12 thin slices of toasted baguette and add 2 to each salad serving.

1 DRESSING: In bowl, whisk together oil, sherry, mustard, garlic, salt and pepper; set aside. (MAKE-AHEAD: Cover and refrigerate for up to 2 days.)

2 In large bowl, combine spinach, mushrooms, red pepper and radishes.

3 In small bowl, beat egg. Spread bread crumbs in shallow dish. Using waxed dental floss or thread, slice cheese into 6 rounds, each about ¼ inch (5 mm) thick; dip 1 round into egg, then into crumbs, turning to coat all over. Repeat with remaining rounds. (MAKE-AHEAD: Place rounds on baking sheet. Refrigerate for up to 4 hours.)

4 In nonstick skillet, heat oil over medium-high heat; cook cheese rounds for 3 to 5 minutes per side or until slightly melted inside and crisp and golden outside.

5 Drizzle dressing over salad and toss; divide among 6 plates. Top each with cheese round.

Makes 6 servings.

PER SERVING, ABOUT:

cal	342	carb	10 g
pro	15 g	fibre	3 g
total fat	27 g	chol	62 mg
sat. fat	10 g	sodium	450 mg

PERCENTAGE RDI:

calcium	17%	vit. A	96%
iron	31%	vit. C	78%
folate	93%		

Crunchy Iceberg Lettuce Salad with Miso Dressing

Iceberg lettuce may needlessly be out of fashion but not in Japanese restaurants in Canada, where it is happily combined with a slightly sweet but balanced miso dressing. This vinaigrette features miso, fermented soybean paste, which is now available commercially and dresses other greens very tastily.

TEST KITCHEN TIPS

• Sprinkle salad with black sesame seeds if desired.

• White miso is a mellow-tasting variety (see page 49) that is actually a yellow-tan colour. Nori is iridescent black sheets of dried seaweed used to make sushi. Look for both in Asian specialty stores; they are also available in some supermarkets.

2	small tomatoes	2
1	piece (2 inches/5 cm) cucumber	1
2 cups	shredded iceberg lettuce	500 mL
Half	sheet nori, shredded (optional)	Half

MISO DRESSING:		
1 tbsp	white miso	15 mL
1 tbsp	rice vinegar	15 mL
1 tbsp	vegetable oil	15 mL
1½ tsp	granulated sugar	7 mL
1 tsp	water	5 mL
¼ tsp	Dijon mustard	1 mL

1 Core tomatoes; cut into eighths. Cut cucumber in half lengthwise; slice crosswise. In bowl, toss together tomatoes, cucumber, lettuce, and nori (if using).

2 MISO DRESSING: In small bowl, whisk together miso, vinegar, oil, sugar, water and mustard; spoon over salad.

Makes 4 servings.

PER SERVING, ABOUT:

cal 61	carb ....6 g
pro ....1 g	fibre ....1 g
total fat .....4 g	chol ....0 mg
sat. fat ....trace	sodium ..168 mg

PERCENTAGE RDI:

calcium 1%	vit. A 4%
iron 4%	vit. C 18%
folate 12%	

Caesar Salad

Caesar salad has nothing to do with Roman emperors but rather was an inspired creation in 1924 of Italian chef Caesar Cardini, who owned a restaurant in Tijuana, Mexico. This recipe achieves its creaminess with light mayonnaise, instead of chef Cardini's coddled egg.

1	head romaine lettuce	1	2 tsp	Dijon mustard	10 mL
2 cups	croutons (see below)	500 mL	2 tsp	anchovy paste	10 mL
¼ cup	grated Parmesan cheese	50 mL	2	cloves garlic, minced	2
DRESSING:			½ tsp	each salt and pepper	2 mL
¼ cup	vegetable oil	50 mL	½ tsp	Worcestershire sauce	2 mL
2 tbsp	grated Parmesan cheese	25 mL	3 tbsp	light mayonnaise	50 mL
1 tbsp	white wine vinegar	15 mL			

TEST KITCHEN TIP: Sprinkle with 6 slices crisply cooked, crumbled bacon and an extra 2 tbsp (25 mL) grated Parmesan cheese if desired.

1 DRESSING: In bowl, whisk together oil, cheese, vinegar, mustard, anchovy paste, garlic, salt, pepper and Worcestershire sauce. Whisk in mayonnaise until smooth. (MAKE-AHEAD: Cover and refrigerate for up to 1 day.)

2 Tear lettuce into bite-size pieces to make about 20 cups (5 L); place in large bowl. Add dressing, croutons and cheese; toss to combine.

VARIATIONS

Chicken Caesar Salad: Place 4 boneless skinless chicken breasts on greased grill over medium-high heat; close lid and cook, turning once, for about 12 minutes or until no longer pink inside. Slice into thin strips; add to salad.

Shrimp Caesar Salad: In large nonstick skillet, heat 1 tbsp (15 mL) vegetable oil over medium-high heat; cook 2 lb (1 kg) jumbo shrimp, peeled and deveined, for about 5 minutes or until pink, opaque and firm. Add to salad.

Makes 12 servings.

PER SERVING, ABOUT:

cal	124	carb	8 g
pro	4 g	fibre	1 g
total fat	9 g	chol	4 mg
sat. fat	1 g	sodium	298 mg

PERCENTAGE RDI:

calcium	7%	vit. A	15%
iron	8%	vit. C	23%
folate	35%		

MAKE YOUR OWN Croutons

🍂 Use any kind of dense bread, such as sourdough, crusty Mediterranean loaf, multigrain and rye. Day-old bread is preferable. One slice of bread generally yields ¾ cup (175 mL) croutons.

🍂 Cut bread into ½-inch (1 cm) thick slices. Trim off crusts if desired. Brush lightly with olive oil or melted butter. You can flavour the oil or butter with herbs such as rosemary, thyme and oregano, spices such as chili powder, zahtar and black pepper, or finely minced fresh garlic or, for convenience, garlic powder.

🍂 Cut bread into ½-inch (1 cm) cubes. Arrange in single layer on rimmed baking sheet. Bake in 350°F (180°C) oven for about 18 minutes or until golden and crisp, stirring once or twice.

🍂 For no-added-fat croutons, simply cube bread and bake, either with or without seasonings, as above.

🍂 Let croutons cool; store in airtight container for up to 1 week.

Bread Salad

Some of the most inspired recipes are devised from a blend of thrift and good taste. Leftover bread? Toss it with ripe tomatoes (and only ripe ones will do) and vinaigrette. Presto! Panzanella — the bread salad of Italy.

TEST KITCHEN TIPS

• To shred basil, roll leaves tightly, about 10 at a time, into cigar shape. Cut crosswise into shreds (called *chiffonade* in French).

• To make a Caprese sandwich, layer sliced tomatoes, mozzarella and basil between slices of focaccia. Drizzle with olive oil and sprinkle with salt and pepper to taste.

5	tomatoes (about 2 lb/1 kg)	5		3	green onions, sliced	3
5	slices (1 inch/2.5 cm thick) day-old ciabatta bread	5		1	sweet yellow pepper, chopped	1
¼ cup	packed fresh basil leaves	50 mL		**DRESSING:**		
Half	English cucumber (about 6 inches/15 cm), peeled and sliced	Half		3 tbsp	extra-virgin olive oil	50 mL
				1 tbsp	red wine vinegar	15 mL
				¼ tsp	each salt and pepper	1 mL

1 Core and roughly cube tomatoes; place in large bowl. Cut bread into 1-inch (2.5 cm) cubes; toss with tomatoes. Let stand for 10 minutes.

2 Shred basil very thinly; add to bowl along with cucumber, onions and yellow pepper.

3 DRESSING: In separate bowl, whisk together oil, vinegar, salt and pepper; add to salad and toss.

Makes 6 servings.

PER SERVING, ABOUT:

cal	239	carb	35 g
pro	6 g	fibre	4 g
total fat	9 g	chol	0 mg
sat. fat	1 g	sodium	403 mg

PERCENTAGE RDI:

calcium	6%	vit. A	15%
iron	18%	vit. C	112%
folate	39%		

CAPRESE Salad

One of the most popular Italian restaurant salads, Caprese consists of sliced ripe tomatoes, thinly sliced buffalo milk mozzarella and fresh basil sprinkled with extra-virgin olive oil. The success of the salad, to be enjoyed with crusty bread, depends entirely on the quality of ingredients.

Creamy Coleslaw

Because a good cabbage salad is both crunchy and tangy, it's an ideal sidekick for burgers, hotdogs, ribs and any kind of sausage, and it begs to go out to the deck for a barbecue or to the park for a picnic. For a tangier salad, replace mayonnaise with Old-Fashioned Cooked Salad Dressing (page 82).

3 cups	finely shredded cabbage	750 mL	1 tbsp	cider vinegar	15 mL
2	large carrots, grated	2	2 tsp	granulated sugar	10 mL
2	green onions, sliced	2	½ tsp	Dijon mustard	2 mL
DRESSING:			¼ tsp	celery seeds	1 mL
¼ cup	light mayonnaise	50 mL	¼ tsp	each salt and pepper	1 mL
¼ cup	light sour cream	50 mL			

1 **DRESSING:** In large bowl, stir together mayonnaise, sour cream, vinegar, sugar, mustard, celery seeds, salt and pepper.

2 Add cabbage, carrots and green onions to bowl; stir to coat well. (MAKE-AHEAD: **Cover and refrigerate for up to 1 day.**)

TEST KITCHEN TIP: Check the refrigerator crisper when making cabbage salad. For variety, include diced sweet red or green pepper, sliced radishes, shredded zucchini, sliced crisp apples, pears or jicama.

Makes 4 servings.

PER SERVING, ABOUT:

cal	109	carb	14 g
pro	2 g	fibre	2 g
total fat	6 g	chol	2 mg
sat. fat	1 g	sodium	292 mg

PERCENTAGE RDI:

calcium	7%	vit. A	143%
iron	6%	vit. C	52%
folate	19%		

Keeper Coleslaw

This salad is perfect for a party or to keep on hand for busy-time dinners and lunches.

Half	large cabbage, finely shredded (about 12 cups/3 L)	Half	DRESSING:		
1	large carrot, grated	1	¾ cup	vinegar	175 mL
1	onion, finely diced	1	½ cup	granulated sugar	125 mL
			¼ cup	vegetable oil	50 mL
			2 tsp	celery seeds	10 mL
			1½ tsp	salt	7 mL

1 In large bowl, toss together cabbage, carrot and onion.

2 **DRESSING:** In saucepan, heat together vinegar, sugar, oil, celery seeds and salt. Pour over cabbage mixture and toss well. Let cool; cover and refrigerate for 4 hours. (MAKE-AHEAD: **Refrigerate for up to 5 days.**)

Makes 12 servings.

PER SERVING, ABOUT:

cal	94	carb	13 g
pro	1 g	fibre	1 g
total fat	5 g	chol	0 mg
sat. fat	trace	sodium	299 mg

PERCENTAGE RDI:

calcium	3%	vit. A	24%
iron	4%	vit. C	40%
folate	14%		

QUICK   CLASSIC

Greek Salad

Greek salad is one of those summer delights when tomatoes are ripe and juicy and cucumbers come from the garden. Serve as in Greece, as an appetizer, and savour the way feta cheese and olive oil glorify the vegetables. And note, no lettuce.

TEST KITCHEN TIP: Feta cheese varies in saltiness; it's hard to judge unless you can taste a sample before purchasing. The best advice is to first buy small and judiciously, then stick with a brand or provenance — Greece, Canada or Bulgaria, for example — that suits your palate.

3	large ripe tomatoes	3
1	English cucumber (about 12 inches/30 cm long)	1
Half	red onion, chopped	Half
4 oz	feta cheese, crumbled	125 g
½ cup	Kalamata olives	125 mL

DRESSING:		
¼ cup	extra-virgin olive oil	50 mL
2 tbsp	chopped fresh oregano (or 1 tsp/5 mL dried)	25 mL
2 tbsp	lemon juice	25 mL
Pinch	each salt and pepper	Pinch

1 Core and cut tomatoes into 1-inch (2.5 cm) chunks. Peel cucumber; cut into similar-size pieces. Set aside.

2 DRESSING: In large bowl, whisk together oil, oregano, lemon juice, salt and pepper. Add tomatoes, cucumber and onion; toss with dressing.

3 Arrange cheese and olives over salad.

Makes 6 servings.

PER SERVING, ABOUT:

cal 210	carb . . . . 11 g
pro . . . . 5 g	fibre . . . . 3 g
total fat . . . . 18 g	chol . . . . . . 17 mg
sat. fat . . . . . . 5 g	sodium . . 600 mg

PERCENTAGE RDI:

calcium 12%	vit. A 10%
iron 7%	vit. C 40%
folate 16%	

Peanut Jicama Salad

The star ingredient, jicama, provides a crunchy contrast to the creamy dressing, which, by the way, is also excellent with finely shredded cabbage.

1	jicama (about 12 oz/375 g), peeled	1
1	sweet red pepper, chopped	1

DRESSING:

⅓ cup	warm water	75 mL
¼ cup	chopped fresh coriander	50 mL
¼ cup	smooth peanut butter	50 mL
3 tbsp	rice vinegar	50 mL
2 tbsp	teriyaki sauce	25 mL
2	cloves garlic, minced	2
1 tsp	each dry mustard and sesame oil	5 mL
¼ tsp	hot pepper sauce	1 mL

Makes 4 to 6 servings.

1 Cut jicama into scant ¼- x ¼-inch (5 x 5 mm) strips 2 to 3 inches (5 to 8 cm) long to make about 4 cups (1 L); place in salad bowl. Add red pepper. (MAKE-AHEAD: Cover and refrigerate for up to 4 hours.)

2 DRESSING: In small bowl, whisk together warm water, coriander, peanut butter, vinegar, teriyaki sauce, garlic, mustard, sesame oil and hot pepper sauce. Pour over jicama mixture; toss to coat.

PER EACH OF 6 SERVINGS, ABOUT:

cal 106	carb . . . . .10 g
pro . . . . .4 g	fibre . . . . .3 g
total fat . . . . .6 g	chol . . . . . . .0 mg
sat. fat . . . . . .1 g	sodium . . 286 mg

PERCENTAGE RDI:

calcium 2%	vit. A 12%
iron 6%	vit. C 82%
folate 19%	

WHAT IS Jicama?

🌱 Jicama is a common ingredient in Mexican cooking. Pronounced HEE-ka-mah, this tuberous vegetable native to Mexico has a pleasantly crunchy, refreshingly moist flesh that's low in calories. Raw, its slightly sweet, bland taste suits piquant vegetable salads or even tangy fruit salads. Cut into sticks, it's a welcome addition to a platter of crudités. Cooked jicama keeps its crunch and colour and makes a fresh substitute for water chestnuts.

🌱 Choose firm, fresh-looking, thin-skinned jicamas with almost unblemished light tan skins and creamy white flesh. Depending on their freshness, you can store unwrapped jicamas for up to three weeks in the refrigerator or, even better, in a cold room. Once they're cut, you should cover jicamas tightly with plastic wrap and use within a week.

Roasted Roots Salad

Roasting root vegetables caramelizes them, releasing their natural sweetness to balance the roasted garlic dressing.

SUBSTITUTION: You can improvise with the kinds of root vegetables used as long as you respect the amounts and method of preparation. For example, a half rutabaga can replace the carrots, and 4 potatoes the celery root.

Makes 6 servings.

PER SERVING, ABOUT:

cal	247	carb	35 g
pro	4 g	fibre	6 g
total fat	12 g	chol	0 mg
sat. fat	2 g	sodium	441 mg

PERCENTAGE RDI:

calcium	8%	vit. A	273%
iron	13%	vit. C	37%
folate	33%		

1	head garlic	1
4	beets (about 1 lb/500 g), peeled	4
4	carrots (about 1 lb/500 g), peeled	4
2	sweet potatoes (about 1 lb/500 g), peeled	2
1	celery root (about 1 lb/500 g), peeled	1
3 tbsp	olive oil	50 mL
½ tsp	each salt and pepper	2 mL

ROASTED GARLIC DRESSING:

¼ cup	chopped fresh mint (or 1 tsp/5 mL dried)	50 mL
2 tbsp	each olive oil and balsamic vinegar	25 mL
¼ tsp	salt	1 mL

1 Trim tip off garlic head. Cut beets, carrots, sweet potatoes and celery root into 1-inch (2.5 cm) cubes; place in large bowl along with garlic. Add oil, salt and pepper; toss to coat. Spread on large greased or foil-lined rimmed baking sheet; roast in 425°F (220°C) oven, stirring once, for 45 to 55 minutes or until tender and potatoes are golden.

2 **ROASTED GARLIC DRESSING:** Squeeze garlic pulp into large bowl. Add mint, oil, vinegar and salt; mash together. Add vegetables; toss to coat. (MAKE-AHEAD: Cover and refrigerate for up to 4 hours.) Serve hot or warm.

A Variety OF VINEGARS

The English *vinegar* is a direct translation from the French *vin aigre*, "sour wine." Before the invention of the wine bottle cork, that is indeed what happened to a lot of wine because alcohol turned into acetic acid in the presence of air. No longer left to chance, vinegar is now commercially made from white and red wines, sherry and even champagne. Price is a good indication of quality.

There are plenty of vinegars made from other sources: **cider** vinegar from fermented apple cider is delicious and readily available. Check labels to ensure the cider vinegar is indeed made from apples and not just flavoured with the fruit. Mellow **rice** vinegar from a rice base comes in three shades, the most common being the clear and slightly golden vinegar from Japan and China, and Chinese red or black vinegars.

White distilled vinegar, made from grain alcohol, is harsher and better kept for pickles and relishes. Strong brown **malt** vinegar has a role in pickling and as the sprinkle of choice over fish and chips.

Balsamic vinegar, with its range of sweet and sour, is the vinegar in vogue. Unfortunately, real balsamic vinegar, from Modena and Reggio in Italy, is extremely expensive — in the hundreds of dollars for about half a cup (125 mL). It is made from concentrated Trebbiano grape juice or must, which is fermented, acidified and aged for years in ever smaller barrels of different woods. Even among producers, this rare vinegar is treated as a luxury and dispensed with an eye-dropper or enjoyed as a digestif. Most of the balsamic vinegars useful for salads or sauces result from some version of the process, usually with significant aging missing. It is possible to improve an inexpensive balsamic by simmering gently until slightly thickened and a darker, richer colour.

Potato Salad

MAKE-AHEAD   BUDGET-WISE   CLASSIC

Think of potato salad as ready and able to take on all different kinds of dressings and embellishments, from a mustardy French vinaigrette to a classic summer reunion–style creamy dressing, Caesar seasonings, pesto and an over-the-top bacon and blue cheese version.

10	new potatoes (2½ lb/1.25 kg)	10
10	large radishes	10
2	stalks celery	2
6	green onions	6

DRESSING:		
¼ cup	white wine vinegar	50 mL
2 tsp	Dijon mustard	10 mL
1	clove garlic, minced	1
½ tsp	salt	2 mL
¼ tsp	pepper	1 mL
⅓ cup	vegetable oil	75 mL
2 tbsp	chopped fresh parsley	25 mL

TEST KITCHEN TIPS

• **New potatoes of any shape, either white or red, are waxy and very well suited to salads. Later in the year, choose round red potatoes.**

• **Buy potatoes of the same size so that they will cook evenly. Boiling potatoes with skins on helps to keep them intact while cooking.**

1 In saucepan of boiling salted water, cook potatoes for 10 to 15 minutes or just until tender but not mushy. Let cool.

2 Meanwhile, trim and cut radishes in half; with flat sides down, thinly slice and place in large bowl. Finely dice celery; add to bowl. Chop green onions; add to bowl. Peel potatoes; cut into ¾-inch (2 cm) cubes. Add to bowl.

3 DRESSING: In small bowl, whisk together vinegar, mustard, garlic, salt and pepper; gradually whisk in oil until blended. Stir in parsley. Pour over potato mixture; gently toss to coat well. (MAKE-AHEAD: Cover and refrigerate for up to 4 hours.)

VARIATIONS

Classic Potato Salad: Add 3 hard-cooked eggs, chopped, and ½ cup (125 mL) minced sweet or dill pickles. Omit dressing and substitute ¾ cup (175 mL) light mayonnaise, ¼ cup (50 mL) each chopped fresh dill and low-fat yogurt, 1 tbsp (15 mL) each white wine vinegar and Dijon mustard, 1 clove garlic, minced, ¾ tsp (4 mL) salt and ½ tsp (2 mL) pepper.

Blue Cheese and Bacon Potato Salad: Top with 4 slices bacon, cooked and crumbled, and ½ cup (125 mL) crumbled blue cheese. Use grainy mustard instead of Dijon.

Creamy Caesar Potato Salad: Omit dressing and substitute dressing for Caesar Salad (page 69), adding a little more mayonnaise if desired.

Pesto Potato Salad: Add 2 tbsp (25 mL) Pesto (page 235) to dressing.

Makes 4 to 6 servings.

PER EACH OF 6 SERVINGS, ABOUT:

cal	247	carb	32 g
pro	3 g	fibre	3 g
total fat	13 g	chol	0 mg
sat. fat	1 g	sodium	579 mg

PERCENTAGE RDI:

calcium	3%	vit. A	1%
iron	7%	vit. C	48%
folate	16%		

Tabbouleh Salad

Parsley and bulgur are the main ingredients in this healthful Lebanese salad. Also known as burghul, bulgur is made from wheat kernels that have been steamed, dried and crushed. Serve as an appetizer with warmed pita wedges or as a side dish with grilled chicken.

TEST KITCHEN TIPS

• This fresh-tasting salad is best served as soon as it's made because the tomatoes will release water if it stands. To make ahead, add tomatoes just before serving.

• For variety, stir in 1 can (6½ oz/184 g) white tuna, drained and broken into chunks, or 8 oz (250 g) cooked shrimp just before serving.

⅓ cup	bulgur	75 mL
2 cups	finely chopped fresh Italian parsley	500 mL
4	green onions, chopped	4
¼ cup	finely chopped fresh mint	50 mL
4	large tomatoes, diced	4

DRESSING:		
3 tbsp	lemon juice	50 mL
1 tsp	salt	5 mL
¼ tsp	pepper	1 mL
¼ cup	olive oil	50 mL

1 In bowl, pour 2 cups (500 mL) boiling water over bulgur; let stand for 10 minutes or just until softened. Drain well.

2 DRESSING: In large bowl, whisk together lemon juice, salt and pepper; gradually whisk in oil. Add bulgur, parsley, onions, mint and tomatoes; toss gently.

Makes 4 servings.

PER SERVING, ABOUT:

cal	216	carb	22 g
pro	4 g	fibre	5 g
total fat	14 g	chol	0 mg
sat. fat	2 g	sodium	610 mg

PERCENTAGE RDI:

calcium	7%	vit. A	29%
iron	26%	vit. C	113%
folate	48%		

SALAD Oils

~ **VEGETABLE OILS:** When a dressing or vinaigrette calls for a clear oil with a flavour that will not conflict with the seasoning of the salad or dressing, choose Canadian-grown and processed canola oil.

~ **OLIVE OILS:** When the oil itself contributes to the flavour of the dressing or salad ingredients, choose olive oil. The best olive oil comes from freshly gathered ripe olives pressed mechanically without heat. The lowest acid oil, less than one per cent, earns the classification "extra virgin." This oil is more expensive but generally considered worth the extra money for the pleasantly assertive flavour that comes with this quality.

~ Avoid "light" olive oil, which is simply light in colour and flavour; all oils have 14 grams fat per tablespoon (15 mL).

~ Store olive oil in a cool, dark place and use within one year.

~ Olive oil comes from many countries around the Mediterranean, notably Greece, Spain, Italy, France, Turkey, Morocco and Tunisia, and more recently and in much smaller quantities from California, Australia and South Africa.

Sushi Rice Salad

Here's a casual sushi option that delivers all the vinegared rice, mushroom and seafood flavours without the need to master your rolling and shaping skills. Serve as is or with grilled seafood.

3	dried shiitake mushrooms	3
1 cup	hot water	250 mL
1 tbsp	soy sauce	15 mL
1	egg, lightly beaten	1
1 cup	snow peas, cut in half on diagonal	250 mL
1 cup	rinsed drained sliced bamboo shoots	250 mL
4 oz	cooked small shrimp or chopped crab	125 g
1 tbsp	finely chopped pickled ginger	15 mL

1 tbsp	toasted sesame seeds (optional)	15 mL
RICE:		
1 cup	sushi rice	250 mL
1¼ cups	water	300 mL
3 tbsp	rice vinegar	50 mL
1 tbsp	granulated sugar	15 mL
1 tbsp	mirin (Japanese rice wine) or dry sherry	15 mL
1 tsp	salt	5 mL

1 RICE: Rinse rice under cold running water; drain. In shallow saucepan, bring water and rice to boil; reduce heat to low, cover and cook for 25 minutes or until tender. Transfer to large bowl. Add vinegar, sugar, mirin and salt; toss with fork. Let cool completely.

2 Meanwhile, soak mushrooms in hot water for 30 minutes. Drain, reserving ¼ cup (50 mL) of the soaking liquid. Remove and discard stems; slice caps thinly and place in saucepan. Add reserved liquid and soy sauce; boil for about 5 minutes or until liquid is evaporated.

3 In greased nonstick skillet, cook egg over medium heat for about 4 minutes or just until set, turning once. Let cool; cut in half, then into thin strips.

4 In small saucepan of boiling water, cook snow peas for 3 minutes or until tender-crisp. Drain and chill under cold water; drain well.

5 Add mushrooms, egg, snow peas, bamboo shoots, shrimp and pickled ginger to bowl; toss gently. Garnish with sesame seeds (if using).

Makes 4 servings.

PER SERVING, ABOUT:

cal 271	carb . . . . 49 g
pro . . . . 12 g	fibre . . . . 2 g
total fat . . . . . 2 g	chol . . . . . 109 mg
sat. fat . . . . . . 1 g	sodium . . 916 mg

PERCENTAGE RDI:

calcium 3%	vit. A 5%
iron 15%	vit. C 17%
folate 9%	

Penne Salad with Artichokes and Spinach

Use the amounts in this summery pasta salad with Mediterranean ingredients as a model for other pasta salads.

TEST KITCHEN TIP: If not served immediately, pasta absorbs dressing. Save some pasta water to moisten and keep the salad creamy.

SUBSTITUTION: A mix of ¼ cup (50 mL) chopped fresh parsley and ½ to 1 tsp (2 to 5 mL) dried herb such as basil or oregano can stand in for the fresh oregano.

3 cups	penne pasta (10 oz/300 g)	750 mL
2	jars (each 6 oz/170 mL) marinated artichokes	2
2 cups	packed fresh spinach or arugula, shredded	500 mL
Quarter	red onion, thinly sliced	Quarter
1	can (19 oz/540 mL) red kidney beans, drained and rinsed	1

DRESSING:		
¼ cup	chopped fresh oregano or parsley	50 mL
2 tbsp	each wine vinegar and olive oil	25 mL
½ tsp	salt	2 mL
¼ tsp	pepper	1 mL
Dash	hot pepper sauce	Dash

1 In large pot of boiling salted water, cook pasta for 8 to 10 minutes or until tender but firm. Drain and rinse under cold water; drain well and place in large bowl.

2 Drain artichokes, reserving liquid for dressing. Add artichokes, spinach, onion and kidney beans to pasta; toss to combine.

3 DRESSING: Whisk together reserved artichoke liquid, oregano, vinegar, oil, salt, pepper and hot pepper sauce. Pour over salad; toss to coat.

Makes 4 servings.

PER SERVING, ABOUT:

cal 539	carb . . . . 81 g
pro . . . . 19 g	fibre . . . . 14 g
total fat . . . . 17 g	chol . . . . 0 mg
sat. fat . . . . . . 2 g	sodium . . 835 mg

PERCENTAGE RDI:

calcium 8%	vit. A 21%
iron 31%	vit. C 28%
folate 103%	

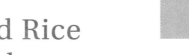

Curried Lentil, Wild Rice and Orzo Salad

Crunchy, attractive and sweetly spiced, this salad is a favourite in The Canadian Living Test Kitchen and, whenever served, garners raves and requests for seconds. Like many grain salads, it's a good keeper and is ideal for summer barbecue parties as well as year-round potlucks and buffets.

½ cup	wild rice	125 mL
⅔ cup	green or brown lentils	150 mL
½ cup	orzo pasta	125 mL
½ cup	currants	125 mL
¼ cup	finely chopped red onion	50 mL
⅓ cup	slivered almonds, toasted	75 mL

DRESSING:		
¼ cup	white wine vinegar	50 mL
1 tsp	ground cumin	5 mL
1 tsp	Dijon mustard	5 mL
½ tsp	each granulated sugar, salt and ground coriander	2 mL
¼ tsp	each turmeric, paprika, nutmeg and ground cardamom	1 mL
Pinch	each cinnamon, ground cloves and cayenne	Pinch
⅓ cup	vegetable oil	75 mL

TEST KITCHEN TIP: Reduce preparation time by substituting up to 1 tbsp (15 mL) mild curry paste for spices.

1 In large pot of boiling salted water, cover and cook wild rice for 35 minutes or until tender. In separate saucepan of boiling salted water, cover and cook lentils for about 25 minutes or until tender. In third saucepan of boiling salted water, cook orzo for about 5 minutes or just until tender.

2 Drain rice, lentils and orzo; transfer to large bowl. Add currants and onion; set aside.

3 DRESSING: In small bowl, whisk together vinegar, cumin, mustard, sugar, salt, coriander, turmeric, paprika, nutmeg, cardamom, cinnamon, cloves and cayenne; whisk in oil. Pour over rice mixture and toss gently.

4 Let salad cool completely; cover and refrigerate for 4 hours. (MAKE-AHEAD: Refrigerate for up to 2 days.) To serve, sprinkle with almonds.

Makes 6 servings.

PER SERVING, ABOUT:

cal	361	carb	45 g
pro	11 g	fibre	5 g
total fat	17 g	chol	0 mg
sat. fat	1 g	sodium	352 mg

PERCENTAGE RDI:

calcium	5%	vit. A	1%
iron	26%	vit. C	3%
folate	60%		

MAKE-AHEAD BUDGET-WISE CLASSIC

Red Barn Corn and Bean Salad

The Canadian Living Test Kitchen originally created this colourful salad for the late broadcaster-author Peter Gzowski's annual literacy fund-raising barbecue for 300 at the Red Barn Theatre in Jacksons Point, Ontario. Your guest list doesn't have to be as long in order to enjoy the salad's crowd-pleasing taste.

TEST KITCHEN TIP: Because fresh basil blackens in the cold of the refrigerator, it is best to add it just before serving.

1	can (19 oz/540 mL) chickpeas, drained and rinsed	1
1	can (19 oz/540 mL) red kidney beans, drained and rinsed	1
1	can (15 oz/425 g) black beans, drained and rinsed	1
1	can (12 oz/341 mL) corn kernels, drained	1
½ cup	chopped red onion	125 mL
1	sweet red pepper, diced	1
½ cup	chopped celery	125 mL
½ cup	chopped fresh basil (or 1 tbsp/15 mL dried)	125 mL
¼ cup	chopped fresh parsley	50 mL
DRESSING:		
½ cup	red wine vinegar	125 mL
⅓ cup	olive oil	75 mL
1 tbsp	Dijon mustard	15 mL
1	clove garlic, minced	1
1½ tsp	salt	7 mL
½ tsp	pepper	2 mL
½ tsp	hot pepper sauce	2 mL

1 In large bowl, combine chickpeas, kidney beans, black beans, corn, onion, red pepper and celery.

2 DRESSING: Whisk together vinegar, oil, mustard, garlic, salt, pepper and hot pepper sauce; pour over bean mixture and toss to coat. (MAKE-AHEAD: Cover and refrigerate for up to 1 day.) Just before serving, add basil and toss. Sprinkle with parsley.

Makes 12 servings.

PER SERVING, ABOUT:

cal	202	carb	28 g
pro	9 g	fibre	7 g
total fat	7 g	chol	0 mg
sat. fat	1 g	sodium	623 mg

PERCENTAGE RDI:

calcium	3%	vit. A	7%
iron	12%	vit. C	38%
folate	44%		

SALAD DRESSINGS AND VINAIGRETTES

There are as many salad dressings as there are cooks. The choices here are among our most popular and versatile. Try a few, and once you have the hang of it, concoct your own special house dressing. Bye-bye, bottled dressings!

EVER-READY HOUSE DRESSING

¾ cup	extra-virgin olive oil	175 mL
⅔ cup	white wine vinegar or cider vinegar	150 mL
2 tbsp	Dijon mustard	25 mL
1 tbsp	dried basil	15 mL
2 tsp	granulated sugar	10 mL
¾ tsp	pepper	4 mL
¼ tsp	salt	1 mL

～ Whisk together oil, vinegar, mustard, basil, sugar, pepper and salt until blended. (MAKE-AHEAD: Cover and refrigerate for up to 1 week.) **Makes 1½ cups (375 mL).** Per 1 tbsp (15 mL): about 63 cal, trace pro, 7 g total fat (1 g sat. fat), 1 g carb, trace fibre, 0 mg chol, 41 mg sodium. % RDI: 1% iron.

RASPBERRY VINAIGRETTE

¼ cup	raspberry juice	50 mL
1 tbsp	white wine vinegar	15 mL
1 tsp	Dijon mustard	5 mL
Pinch	each salt and pepper	Pinch
1 tbsp	vegetable oil	15 mL

～ Whisk together juice, vinegar, mustard, salt and pepper. Whisk in oil. **Makes ⅓ cup (75 mL).** Per 1 tbsp (15 mL): about 29 cal, trace pro, 3 g total fat (trace sat. fat), 2 g carb, 0 g fibre, 0 mg chol, 13 mg sodium.

HONEY DIJON VINAIGRETTE

⅓ cup	vegetable oil	75 mL
⅓ cup	apple juice	75 mL
⅓ cup	liquid honey	75 mL
¼ cup	Dijon mustard	50 mL
¼ cup	white wine vinegar	50 mL
½ tsp	each salt and pepper	2 mL

～ Whisk together oil, apple juice, honey, mustard, vinegar, salt and pepper. (MAKE-AHEAD: Cover and refrigerate for up to 1 week.) **Makes 1½ cups (375 mL).** Per 1 tbsp (15 mL): about 45 cal, trace pro, 3 g total fat (trace sat. fat), 5 g carb, trace fibre, 0 mg chol, 82 mg sodium. % RDI: 1% iron, 2% vit C.

SUN-DRIED TOMATO VINAIGRETTE

2 tbsp	minced oil-packed sun-dried tomatoes	25 mL
2 tbsp	balsamic or red wine vinegar	25 mL
1 tsp	Dijon mustard	5 mL
1	clove garlic, minced	1
Pinch	each salt and pepper	Pinch
⅓ cup	extra-virgin olive oil	75 mL

～ Whisk together tomatoes, vinegar, mustard, garlic, salt and pepper; whisk in oil. **Makes ½ cup (125 mL).** Per 1 tbsp (15 mL): about 87 cal, trace pro, 9 g total fat (1 g sat. fat), 2 g carb, trace fibre, 0 mg chol, 29 mg sodium. % RDI: 1% iron, 2% vit C.

THOUSAND ISLAND DRESSING

¼ cup	light mayonnaise	50 mL
¼ cup	chili sauce	50 mL
1 tbsp	cider vinegar	15 mL
1 tsp	water	5 mL
Pinch	each salt and pepper	Pinch

～ Whisk together mayonnaise, chili sauce, vinegar, water, salt and pepper. **Makes ½ cup (125 mL).** Per 1 tbsp (15 mL): about 32 cal, trace pro, 2 g total fat (trace sat. fat), 3 g carb, 1 g fibre, 0 mg chol, 163 mg sodium. % RDI: 1% iron, 1% vit A, 2% vit C, 2% folate.

TOMATO FRENCH DRESSING

½ cup	ketchup	125 mL
¼ cup	wine vinegar	50 mL
1 tbsp	packed brown sugar	15 mL
1 tbsp	Worcestershire sauce	15 mL
½ tsp	dry mustard	2 mL
½ tsp	salt	2 mL
	Pepper	
¾ cup	vegetable oil	175 mL

～ Whisk together ketchup, vinegar, sugar, Worcestershire sauce, mustard, salt, and pepper to taste; whisk in oil. (MAKE-AHEAD: Cover and refrigerate for up to 2 weeks.) **Makes 1½ cups (375 mL).** Per 1 tbsp (15 mL): about 69 cal, trace pro, 7 g total fat (trace sat. fat), 2 g carb, trace fibre, 0 mg chol, 123 mg sodium. % RDI: 1% iron, 1% vit A, 2% vit C.

BUTTERMILK RANCH DRESSING

1⅓ cups	buttermilk	325 mL
⅔ cup	light mayonnaise	150 mL
4 tsp	cider vinegar	20 mL
1 tsp	Dijon mustard	5 mL
¾ tsp	dried dillweed	4 mL
½ tsp	dried parsley	2 mL
¼ tsp	each salt, pepper and granulated sugar	1 mL
Pinch	garlic powder	Pinch

➤ Whisk together buttermilk, mayonnaise, vinegar, mustard, dillweed, parsley, salt, pepper, sugar and garlic powder. (MAKE-AHEAD: Cover and refrigerate for up to 1 week.) **Makes 2 cups (500 mL).** *Per 1 tbsp (15 mL): about 20 cal, trace pro, 2 g total fat (trace sat. fat), 1 g carb, 0 g fibre, 0 mg chol, 63 mg sodium. % RDI: 1% calcium.*

VARIATIONS

Peppercorn Ranch Dressing: Stir ½ tsp (2 mL) crushed black peppercorns into ½ cup (125 mL) Buttermilk Ranch Dressing.

Creamy Cucumber Dressing: Shred peeled cucumber to make ¼ cup (50 mL). Gently squeeze out excess liquid. Finely chop and add to ½ cup (125 mL) Buttermilk Ranch Dressing.

SUBSTITUTION: If using dressing immediately, replace dried dillweed with 1 tbsp (15 mL) chopped fresh dill, and dried parsley with 2 tsp (10 mL) chopped fresh parsley.

CREAMY GARLIC DRESSING

1	large clove garlic, chopped	1
¼ tsp	salt	1 mL
1 tbsp	mayonnaise	15 mL
1 tbsp	white wine vinegar	15 mL
1½ tsp	Dijon mustard	7 mL
Pinch	pepper	Pinch
⅓ cup	vegetable or extra-virgin olive oil	75 mL

➤ In bowl and using back of spoon or fork, mash garlic with salt to form paste. Whisk in mayonnaise, vinegar, mustard and pepper; whisk in oil. (MAKE-AHEAD: Cover and refrigerate for up to 5 days; whisk to reblend.) **Makes ½ cup (125 mL).** *Per 1 tbsp (15 mL): about 95 cal, trace pro, 11 g total fat (1 g sat. fat), trace carb, trace fibre, 1 mg chol, 93 mg sodium.*

VARIATIONS

Creamy Poppy Seed Dressing: Omit garlic. Add 1 tsp (5 mL) granulated sugar. Substitute lemon juice for vinegar. Stir in 1 green onion, chopped, and 2 tsp (10 mL) poppy seeds after the oil. (With a poppy seed dressing, these make excellent additions to greens: 1 orange, sliced; ½ cup/125 mL sliced red onion; ¼ cup/50 mL toasted slivered almonds.)

Creamy Light Yogurt Dressing: Omit mayonnaise. Reduce oil to 1 tbsp (15 mL). Stir in ½ cup (125 mL) low-fat plain yogurt and 1 tbsp (15 mL) chopped fresh parsley or dill after the oil.

OLD-FASHIONED COOKED SALAD DRESSING

1 cup	granulated sugar	250 mL
2 tbsp	all-purpose flour	25 mL
2 tsp	dry mustard	10 mL
1 tsp	salt	5 mL
1	egg, beaten	1
1 cup	vinegar	250 mL
1 cup	milk	250 mL
1 tbsp	butter	15 mL

➤ In top of double boiler or in heavy saucepan, stir together sugar, flour, mustard and salt; blend in egg, beating well. Stir in vinegar, milk and butter.

➤ Cook over simmering water or over medium-low heat, stirring constantly, for 10 to 15 minutes or until thickened. Let cool, stirring often. Dressing will continue to thicken as it cools. (MAKE-AHEAD: Refrigerate in airtight jar for up to 1 month.) **Makes 2 cups (500 mL).** *Per 1 tbsp (15 mL): about 37 cal, 1 g pro, 1 g total fat (trace sat. fat), 7 g carb, trace fibre, 8 mg chol, 81 mg sodium. % RDI: 1% calcium, 1% iron, 1% vit A.*

Pick-a-Grain Pilaf

The pilaf method of cooking rices starts with lightly frying the rice in a little oil or butter with seasonings such as onion and herbs. Only after that is the liquid added, and the dish is simmered until the rice is tender and liquid absorbed. The technique works with many different grains, and various seasonings.

1 tbsp	vegetable oil	15 mL		2 cups	chicken stock or water	500 mL
1	onion, chopped	1		¼ tsp	salt	1 mL
1	large carrot, diced	1		½ cup	frozen peas (optional)	125 mL
½ tsp	dried oregano	2 mL		1 tbsp	lemon juice	15 mL
1 cup	white rice	250 mL		¼ tsp	pepper	1 mL

1 In heavy saucepan, heat oil over medium-high heat; cook onion, carrot and oregano, stirring occasionally, for 3 minutes or until softened. Add rice; cook, stirring, for 1 minute.

2 Add stock and salt; bring to boil. Reduce heat to low; cover and simmer for 20 minutes. With fork, stir in peas (if using); cover and cook for 5 minutes or until rice is tender and liquid is absorbed. Add lemon juice and pepper; toss with fork.

VARIATIONS

Bulgur Pilaf: Substitute bulgur for rice and dried tarragon for oregano.

Barley Pilaf: Substitute barley for rice and dried savory for oregano; increase cooking time to about 50 minutes.

Quinoa Pilaf: Substitute quinoa, rinsed and drained, for rice and dried herb of choice for oregano. Decrease stock to 1¼ cups (300 mL) and simmer for 15 minutes.

Coconut Thai Rice Pilaf: Substitute rinsed Thai jasmine rice for white rice; omit carrot, peas and oregano. Cook 1 tsp (5 mL) chopped fresh gingerroot along with onion. Omit stock; substitute ¾ cup (175 mL) coconut milk and 1½ cups (375 mL) water.

Couscous Pilaf: Substitute couscous for rice and dried basil for oregano. Decrease stock to 1½ cups (375 mL). Cook onions, carrot and basil as directed. Add stock, salt and peas; bring to boil. Stir in couscous; cover, remove from heat and let stand for 5 minutes. Add lemon juice and pepper; fluff with fork.

TEST KITCHEN TIP: When cooking grains, it's easy to increase the amounts in the recipe and make enough for more than 1 meal. Be sure to transfer cooled freshly cooked grains to airtight container and refrigerate for up to 2 days only.

Makes 4 servings.

PER SERVING, ABOUT:

cal	238	carb	42 g
pro	7 g	fibre	2 g
total fat	5 g	chol	0 mg
sat. fat	1 g	sodium	552 mg

PERCENTAGE RDI:

calcium	3%	vit. A	57%
iron	6%	vit. C	3%
folate	6%		

QUICK   BUDGET-   CLASSIC
         WISE

No-Fail Rice

The Canadian Living Test Kitchen uses this method to cook any long-grain white or brown rice. Use a heavy saucepan with a tight-fitting lid. There are many flavour enhancers you can add to the water with this basic recipe: a bay leaf, a strip of lemon or orange peel, a sprig of parsley or a few slices of gingerroot. Or toss the cooked rice with fresh herbs, a little olive oil or butter, or a squeeze of lemon.

2⅔ cups	water	650 mL
¼ tsp	salt	1 mL
1⅓ cups	basmati, Thai jasmine or other white or brown long-grain rice	325 mL

Makes 4 cups (1 L).

PER 1 CUP (250 mL), ABOUT:

cal 222	carb .... 48 g
pro .... 5 g	fibre .... 1 g
total fat ..... 1 g	chol .... 0 mg
sat. fat .... trace	sodium .. 147 mg

PERCENTAGE RDI:

calcium 2%	vit. A 0%
iron 2%	vit. C 0%
folate 2%	

1 In saucepan, bring water and salt to boil over medium-high heat; stir in rice.

2 Cover and reduce heat to low; simmer for 20 minutes for white rice, 45 minutes for brown rice, or until tender and liquid is absorbed. Fluff with fork.

TEST KITCHEN TIPS

• Rice is grouped according to size and shape. Long-, medium- and short-grain are common, but the terms *patna*, *rose* and *pearl* are still used and designate, in order, the same size differences. The stickiness of rice depends on the proportion of the starches amylose and amylopectin. The stickiest rice contains more amylopectin. Generally, the shorter and rounder the rice, the stickier it is, and the easier it is to shape or pick up with chopsticks.

• Buy rice in quantities you can use within a few weeks. For larger amounts, store in the freezer.

Rice: A VARIETY OF SHAPES AND SIZES

🌾 **ARBORIO**: A fat, short-grain Italian rice with a high percentage of amylopectin starch content, which makes it ideal for creamy risotto, rice puddings and moulded rice desserts. Vialone and Carnaroli are other Italian rice types suited to risotto.

🌾 **BASMATI**: This nutty, fragrant rice, grown in the foothills of the Himalayas, is an aged, long-grain rice. When cooked, basmati expands in length but not width and is very fluffy. Available in white and brown versions. A similarly perfumed long-grain rice, called popcorn or

Texmati, is now grown in America.

🌾 **BROWN**: This name refers to all rice with only the inedible outer husk removed, leaving the bran and germ attached. This least processed rice is the most nutritious and takes the longest to cook. Store in the freezer for up to six months.

🌾 **PARBOILED** (Converted™): This term refers to white long-grain rice that has been soaked, pressure-steamed, then dried. It retains more nutrients than plain white rice and takes slightly longer to cook.

🌾 **SUSHI**: A short- to medium-grain rice that is moist and clumps together when cooked, making it ideal for moulding and rolling into sushi.

🌾 **THAI JASMINE**: A slim long-grain rice with a distinctive jasmine fragrance, popular in Southeast Asian cooking.

🌾 **WHITE**: The term usually refers to long-grain rice. White rice is typically four to five times longer than its width. With its husk, bran and germ removed, long-grain rice cooks up into fluffy, separate grains.

🌾 **WILD**: This long-grain marsh grass, harvested principally in Manitoba, Saskatchewan and Ontario, is not really rice although it is eaten in much the same way. Chewy and nutty, wild rice takes about 45 minutes to cook, twice the time of regular white long-grain rice.

Risotto Milanese

While separate grains of rice are usually what you want with long-grain rice, risotto relies on short-grain rice, such as arborio, and constant stirring to produce a velvety, creamy dish to serve as an appetizer course or side dish. Saffron is essential to call this Milanese, but there are many other flavours, such as wild mushrooms, and sun-dried tomatoes and herbs, that are delightful with risotto.

4 cups	chicken stock	1 L	2	cloves garlic, minced	2
1 cup	water	250 mL	¼ tsp	pepper	1 mL
¼ tsp	saffron threads, crumbled	1 mL	1½ cups	arborio rice	375 mL
			¾ cup	white wine	175 mL
3 tbsp	butter	50 mL	½ cup	grated Parmesan cheese	125 mL
1	onion, chopped	1			

1 In saucepan, bring stock, water and saffron just to simmer over medium heat; reduce heat to low and keep warm.

2 In separate large shallow saucepan, melt butter over medium heat; cook onion, garlic and pepper, stirring, for 3 minutes or until softened. Stir in rice until well coated.

3 Stir in ½ cup (125 mL) of the warm stock; cook, stirring constantly, until all liquid is absorbed. Stir in wine; cook, stirring, until all wine is absorbed. Continue to add stock, ½ cup (125 mL) at a time, stirring after each addition until completely absorbed, for about 20 minutes or until rice is creamy and tender.

4 Stir in cheese and any remaining stock; cook, stirring, for 2 minutes or until risotto is very creamy but still fluid.

VARIATIONS

Squash Risotto: Omit saffron. Add 3 cups (750 mL) diced peeled butternut squash along with onion. Stir in 2 tsp (10 mL) chopped fresh thyme along with Parmesan cheese.

Risotto Primavera: Omit saffron. During final 15 minutes of cooking, stir in 1 lb (500 g) asparagus, trimmed and cut into 1-inch (2.5 cm) pieces, 1 sweet red pepper, chopped, and 1 cup (250 mL) trimmed sugar snap peas or shelled fresh peas. If you have only frozen peas, stir in with Parmesan cheese.

TEST KITCHEN TIPS

• You can stir in sautéed vegetables, mushrooms or seafood during the last addition of liquid and cheese.

• For a weeknight risotto without all the stirring, simply add the stock and wine with the rice; bring to boil. Cover and simmer over low heat for 10 minutes. Stir once; cover and cook for 10 minutes longer or until liquid is almost absorbed and rice is still slightly firm to the bite. Stir in enough of the water along with cheese to make it creamy.

Makes 6 servings.

PER SERVING, ABOUT:

cal	311	carb	43 g
pro	10 g	fibre	1 g
total fat	10 g	chol	22 mg
sat. fat	6 g	sodium	736 mg

PERCENTAGE RDI:

calcium	12%	vit. A	7%
iron	6%	vit. C	2%
folate	4%		

GRAIN AND PASTA SIDE DISHES

Here's a quick reference to solve all your "how much" and "how long" questions for basic grain, pasta and potato side dishes.

WHEAT BERRIES

4 cups	water	1 L
½ tsp	salt	2 mL
1½ cups	soft wheat berries	375 mL

~ In large saucepan, bring water and salt to boil over high heat; add wheat berries. Reduce heat to low; cover and simmer for 45 to 60 minutes or until tender but firm. Drain. Serve hot or cold with chopped fresh herbs and enough vinaigrette to moisten. **Makes 4 to 6 servings.**

KASHA

1 cup	kasha	250 mL
1	egg	1
½ tsp	salt	2 mL
Pinch	pepper	Pinch
1½ cups	boiling water	375 mL
1 tbsp	butter	15 mL

~ In saucepan, combine kasha, egg, salt and pepper; cook over medium-low heat, stirring, for 3 minutes or until dry and kernels separate. Stir in water and butter; cover and cook, without stirring, for 10 to 12 minutes or until water is absorbed. Fluff with fork. **Makes 2 servings.**

BARLEY

2 cups	water or vegetable or chicken stock	500 mL
¼ tsp	salt	1 mL
1 cup	pot or pearl barley	250 mL

~ In saucepan, bring water and salt to boil over high heat; stir in barley. Reduce heat to low; cover and simmer for 40 minutes or until tender and liquid is evaporated. **Makes 4 servings.**

COUSCOUS

1½ cups	water or vegetable or chicken stock	375 mL
Pinch	salt	Pinch
1 cup	couscous	250 mL

~ In saucepan, bring water and salt to boil; stir in couscous. Remove from heat; cover and let stand for 5 minutes. Fluff with fork. **Makes 4 servings.**

POLENTA

4 cups	water	1 L
½ tsp	salt	2 mL
1 cup	cornmeal	250 mL

~ In large saucepan, bring water and salt to boil over high heat; reduce heat to low. Gradually whisk in cornmeal; cook, stirring often with wooden spoon, for 20 to 25 minutes or until thick enough to mound. **Makes 4 servings.**

DRIED PASTA

20 cups	water	5 L
2 tbsp	salt	25 mL
1 lb	dried pasta	500 g

~ In large covered pot, bring water and salt to full rolling boil. Stir in pasta, separating pieces; return to boil. Boil, uncovered and stirring occasionally, for 8 to 10 minutes or until tender but firm. Drain well. **Makes 4 servings.**

FRESH PASTA

16 cups	water	4 L
4 tsp	salt	20 mL
1 lb	fresh pasta	500 g

~ In large covered pot, bring water and salt to full rolling boil. Stir in pasta, separating pieces; return to boil. Boil, uncovered and stirring occasionally, for 1 to 3 minutes or until tender but firm. Drain well. **Makes 4 servings.**

MASHED POTATOES

2 lb	hot boiled peeled potatoes (4 potatoes)	1 kg
1 cup	buttermilk or milk	250 mL
4 tsp	butter	20 mL
½ tsp	each salt and pepper	2 mL

~ In saucepan, mash together potatoes, buttermilk, butter, salt and pepper until smooth. **Makes 4 servings.**

Baked Beans

*Nothing is more Canadian than baked beans. For purists, there's the bacon and
molasses classic, and for adventuresome fans, salsa and maple apple versions.*

3 cups	white pea (navy) beans	750 mL
4 oz	slab bacon or salt pork	125 g
1	can (28 oz/796 mL) tomatoes	1
2 cups	chopped onions	500 mL
¾ cup	ketchup	175 mL

¾ cup	fancy molasses	175 mL
⅓ cup	packed brown sugar	75 mL
1 tbsp	dry mustard	15 mL
½ tsp	salt	2 mL
¼ tsp	pepper	1 mL

TEST KITCHEN TIP: If using
salt pork, omit the salt. If
you opt to make a meatless
version, increase salt to
1 tsp (5 mL).

1 Rinse beans and sort, if necessary, discarding any blemished ones and any
grit.

2 In large Dutch oven or stockpot, cover beans with 3 times their volume of
water. Bring to boil; boil gently for 2 minutes. Remove from heat; cover and let
stand for 1 hour. Drain, discarding liquid.

3 Return soaked beans to pot along with 3 times their volume of fresh water.
Bring to boil; reduce heat and simmer, covered, for 30 to 45 minutes or until tender. Drain, reserving 2 cups (500 mL) cooking liquid.

4 Meanwhile, dice bacon; set aside. In bowl and using potato masher, mash
tomatoes in their juice. In bean pot or 16-cup (4 L) casserole, combine beans,
reserved cooking liquid, bacon, tomatoes, onions, ketchup, molasses, sugar,
mustard, salt and pepper.

5 Bake, covered, in 300°F (150°C) oven for 2½ hours. Uncover and bake for 1 to
1½ hours longer or until sauce is thickened and coats beans well. (MAKE-AHEAD:
Let cool slightly; transfer to shallow airtight container. Finish cooling, uncovered, in refrigerator. Cover and refrigerate for up to 2 days. Reheat over
medium-low heat.)

VARIATIONS

Salsa Baked Beans: Substitute salsa or bottled taco sauce for ketchup. Add 1 tsp
(5 mL) ground cumin and 1 tbsp (15 mL) dried oregano along with crushed tomatoes.
Increase salt to 1 tsp (5 mL) and pepper to ½ tsp (2 mL). Stir in 2 sweet green or red
peppers, chopped, for the last hour of cooking.

Maple Apple Beans: Substitute maple syrup for molasses. Add 3 cups (750 mL) diced
peeled apples and 1 tbsp (15 mL) cider vinegar along with crushed tomatoes.

Makes 6 to 8 servings.

PER EACH OF 8 SERVINGS, ABOUT:

cal 510	carb .... 91 g
pro .... 19 g	fibre .... 16 g
total fat .... 10 g	chol .... 9 mg
sat. fat ...... 3 g	sodium .. 730 mg

PERCENTAGE RDI:

calcium 21%	vit. A 8%
iron 50%	vit. C 27%
folate 118%	

BUDGET-WISE   CLASSIC

Simply the Best
Scalloped Potatoes

This crusty-topped, layered potato dish never goes out of style.

TEST KITCHEN TIPS

• You can use virtually any potato: a starchy long russet baking potato will give you softer, more melting slices; a waxier round boiling potato renders more distinct slices.

• If time is tight, omit the sauce. Instead, mix together 1½ cups (375 mL) whipping cream, 1 cup (250 mL) milk, 1 tsp (5 mL) salt and ½ tsp (2 mL) pepper; pour over potatoes and bake as directed.

6	Yukon Gold potatoes (2 lb/1 kg)	6
1	small onion, sliced	1
SAUCE:		
¼ cup	butter	50 mL
¼ cup	all-purpose flour	50 mL

1 tsp	salt	5 mL
½ tsp	pepper	2 mL
½ tsp	dried thyme or marjoram	2 mL
2½ cups	milk	625 mL

1 SAUCE: In saucepan, melt butter over medium heat. Add flour, salt, pepper and thyme; cook, stirring, for 1 minute. Gradually whisk in milk; cook, whisking constantly, for 5 to 8 minutes or until boiling and thickened. Set aside.

2 Peel and thinly slice potatoes. Arrange one-third in layer in greased 8-inch (2 L) square glass baking dish or casserole; spread half of the onions over top. Repeat layers. Arrange remaining potatoes over top. Pour sauce over top.

3 Cover and bake in 350°F (180°C) oven for 1 hour. Uncover and bake for 30 minutes longer or until lightly browned and potatoes are tender. Let stand for 5 minutes before serving.

Makes 6 servings.

PER SERVING, ABOUT:

cal	256	carb	36 g
pro	6 g	fibre	2 g
total fat	10 g	chol	28 mg
sat. fat	6 g	sodium	518 mg

PERCENTAGE RDI:

calcium	13%	vit. A	12%
iron	6%	vit. C	18%
folate	10%		

BOILED Potatoes

Scrub or peel potatoes; place in large saucepan. Cover with water; add salt (about 1 tsp/2 mL for 2 lb/1 kg potatoes). Cover and bring to boil; boil for about 20 minutes or until fork-tender. Drain and return to pot over low heat for 30 seconds to evaporate excess moisture. For mashed potatoes, see page 86.

OVEN-ROASTED Potatoes

Scrub and cut 2 lb (1 kg) baking potatoes into chunks, fries or wedges. Toss with 2 tbsp (25 mL) olive or vegetable oil, 1 tsp (5 mL) dried rosemary, ½ tsp (2 mL) salt and ¼ tsp (1 mL) pepper. Roast on greased rimmed baking sheet in 425°F (220°C) oven for 45 to 60 minutes or until golden and tender.

Golden Latkes

Crispy, lacy and utterly addictive: that's how to describe latkes, the fried shredded potato rounds so much a part of Hanukkah celebrations. When making latkes, don't try to stint on the oil. Latke experts all say the same thing: just a little soaks in.

10	large potatoes, peeled (about 5 lb/2.2 kg)	10
1	large onion	1
2	eggs	2
½ cup	matzo meal or finely crushed saltine crackers	125 mL

1½ tsp	salt	7 mL
½ tsp	pepper	2 mL
	Vegetable oil for frying	

TEST KITCHEN TIP: Between batches, use a slotted spoon to scoop out shreds of potato that may have escaped into the oil.

1 By hand, or in food processor using shredder blade, grate potatoes and onion.

2 In large bowl, beat together eggs, matzo meal, salt and pepper. Add potato mixture; toss to combine.

3 Pour ¼ inch (5 mm) vegetable oil into each of 2 large skillets over high heat; heat until hot but not smoking. Add ¼ cup (50 mL) potato mixture per latke, leaving 1 inch (2.5 cm) between each; flatten slightly. Fry for 3 minutes or until edges are golden and crisp. Turn; fry for 3 minutes longer or until golden. Drain on paper towel–lined racks. Repeat with remaining potato mixture, adding more oil as necessary. (MAKE-AHEAD: Cover and refrigerate for up to 8 hours. Recrisp on baking sheets in 450°F/230°C oven for about 5 minutes.)

HERBED Rösti

For a typically Swiss crisp potato pancake, boil 4 unpeeled potatoes just until tender. Let cool. (If possible, refrigerate for at least 4 hours or for up to 12 hours.) Peel and shred potatoes coarsely. Toss with 1 tbsp (15 mL) minced fresh parsley, ¼ tsp (1 mL) each salt and dried thyme or basil, and pinch pepper. Melt 1 tbsp (15 mL) butter in small nonstick skillet over medium heat; spread potato mixture evenly over pan, pressing firmly. Cook for 10 minutes or until edges are golden; invert onto large plate. Melt another 1 tbsp (15 mL) butter in skillet; flip rösti into skillet and cook for 10 minutes or until golden on bottom. Cut into wedges. **Makes 6 servings.**

Makes about 10 servings.

PER SERVING, ABOUT:

cal	463	carb	40 g
pro	5 g	fibre	3 g
total fat	32 g	chol	43 mg
sat. fat	3 g	sodium	365 mg

PERCENTAGE RDI:

calcium	2%	vit. A	2%
iron	6%	vit. C	22%
folate	13%		

GUIDE TO BOILING
AND STEAMING VEGETABLES

BOILING: Unless otherwise indicated, place vegetables in enough lightly salted boiling water to cover by 1 inch (2.5 cm); cover and cook for specified time or until tender when pierced with fork.

STEAMING: Place vegetables on rack above boiling water and cover tightly. Vegetables should be at least 1 inch (2.5 cm) above surface of water. This method is most suitable for small quantities of vegetables so that the steam can easily reach each piece to cook evenly.

VEGETABLE	PREPARATION	BOILING	STEAMING
Asparagus	snap off woody ends; peel stems if large	5 minutes per lb (500 g)	7 minutes
Beets	remove stems; keep whole and unpeeled until after cooking	30 minutes (do not prick with fork to check tenderness; if skin wrinkles when pressed, they are done)	40 minutes
Bok choy	trim and chop coarsely, or quarter if small	3 minutes	5 minutes
Broccoli	cut into florets; peel and slice stalks	4 minutes	7 minutes
Brussels sprouts	trim off wilted or coarse outer leaves; cut thin end off stem and score shallow X in bottom	8 minutes	10 minutes
Cabbage	remove coarse outer leaves; quarter and remove core; shred finely or cut into wedges	10 minutes	10 to 12 minutes
Carrots/Parsnips	cut into coins, sticks or chunks	8 to 10 minutes	15 minutes
Cauliflower	cut into florets	4 to 6 minutes	10 minutes
Corn	husk; do not salt water	7 minutes for small cobs; 9 minutes for medium cobs; 11 minutes for large cobs	8 to 12 minutes
Green beans	cut off stem end	3 to 6 minutes	10 minutes

VEGETABLE	PREPARATION	BOILING	STEAMING
Peas	separate pods to shell peas into bowl; for snow peas, pull off vein	2 minutes	8 minutes
Potatoes/ Sweet potatoes	peel if directed; cut into similar-size shapes	20 to 30 minutes	30 to 40 minutes for whole new potatoes
Rutabaga	peel and cube	8 to 10 minutes	15 minutes
Spinach	wash and remove stems and coarse outer leaves	In large pot, cover and cook, with just the water clinging to leaves, over medium heat for 2 minutes or until wilted. Drain and press to remove excess moisture.	
Squash	peel and cut into chunks	10 minutes	12 minutes
White turnips	peel	8 to 10 minutes for cubed; 20 to 30 minutes for whole	15 to 20 minutes

Microwaving

This method is most suitable for small quantities of vegetables or frozen vegetables such as corn or peas. Microwave at High. Below is a list of vegetables best suited to microwaving.

Potatoes: Choose uniform-size, regular-shaped potatoes. Wash and dry; pierce skins several times. Arrange like spokes of wheel with small ends in centre. Microwave for 4 to 6 minutes for 1 potato, 6 to 8 minutes for 2 potatoes, and 8 to 12 minutes for 3 potatoes.

Corn on the cob: Husk corn. Place on microwaveable dish and cover with plastic wrap (for 1 or 2 cobs, wrap individually); cook for 2 minutes per cob. Let stand for 2 minutes before unwrapping.

Squash: Halve; scoop out seeds and fibrous strings. Place, flesh side down, on microwaveable plate or dish. Cover with plastic wrap; microwave for 8 to 12 minutes for large squash such as hubbard, acorn, butternut and turban, and for 6 to 8 minutes for varieties such as delicata and sweet dumpling.

Carrots: Peel and slice carrots. For 2 cups (500 mL) sliced, combine with 2 tbsp (25 mL) water in microwaveable bowl; cover with plastic wrap and microwave at High, stirring once, for about 6 minutes or until fork-tender. Decrease time slightly for frozen carrots as they are already cooked.

Parsnips and rutabaga: Peel and cut into bite-size pieces to make 4 cups (1 L). Place in microwaveable bowl with ¼ cup (50 mL) boiling salted water. Cover with plastic wrap and microwave at High for 4 to 6 minutes or until fork-tender.

GUIDE TO ROASTING VEGETABLES

You can roast a cornucopia of vegetables by following this chart. Amounts for each vegetable will serve about four people. Make a medley of vegetables by combining them from within the same cooking time range.

VEGETABLE	AMOUNT	PREPARATION	ROASTING
Beets	1 lb (500 g)	peeled and quartered	
Carrots	1 lb (500 g)	peeled and cut in 1½-inch (4 cm) lengths	
Celery	1 head	quartered lengthwise, cut into thirds	SEASONING: Toss with 2 tbsp (25 mL) olive or vegetable oil, 1 tsp (5 mL) dried basil, thyme or rosemary (optional) and ¼ tsp (1 mL) each salt and pepper. Roast on greased rimmed baking sheet in 425°F (220°C) oven for specified time.
Eggplant	1 lb (500 g)	cut in 1½-inch (4 cm) chunks	
Fennel	1 bulb	quartered lengthwise	
Parsnips	1 lb (500 g)	cut in 1½-inch (4 cm) lengths	
Red or Spanish onions	1 lb (500 g)	cut lengthwise in wedges	
Rutabaga	1 lb (500 g)	peeled and cut in 1½-inch (4 cm) chunks	Roast for 45 to 60 minutes or until browned and tender.
Sweet peppers	1 lb (500 g)	seeded and cut lengthwise in sixths	
White turnips	1 lb (500 g)	peeled and quartered	
Zucchini	1 lb (500 g)	cut in 1½-inch (4 cm) lengths	
Potatoes	2 lb (1 kg)	cut in 1½-inch (4 cm) chunks	Season as above. Increase salt and pepper to ½ tsp (2 mL) each.
Sweet potatoes	2 lb (1 kg)	cut in 1½-inch (4 cm) chunks	
Leeks	1 bunch	white and pale green part halved lengthwise	Season as above. Roast for 30 to 40 minutes.
Plum tomatoes	1 lb (500 g)	quartered lengthwise	
Portobello mushrooms	1 lb (500 g)	whole cap, stem removed	
Broccoli	1 bunch	florets separated; stalks peeled and cut in 1½-inch (4 cm) chunks	Season as above. Roast for 15 to 25 minutes.
Asparagus	1 lb (500 g)	stalks trimmed	Season as above. Roast for 10 minutes.
Green or wax beans	1 lb (500 g)	trimmed	

Roasted Vegetable Dress-Ups

Add extra flavour to roasted vegetables by tossing them with one of these seasonings before roasting. Each of these mixtures will season 1 lb (500 g) of vegetables. For more, multiply the seasonings accordingly, but use only 1 tbsp (15 mL) more oil per extra pound (500 g).

Moroccan Seasoning: Mix together 2 tbsp (25 mL) chopped fresh parsley, 2 tbsp (25 mL) olive oil, ½ tsp (2 mL) each dried thyme and ground cumin and pinch each cinnamon, salt and pepper.

Greek Seasoning: Mix together 2 tbsp (25 mL) each olive oil and lemon juice, 2 cloves garlic, minced, ½ tsp (2 mL) dried oregano and ¼ tsp (1 mL) each dried mint, salt and pepper.

Parmesan Pepper Seasoning: Mix together 2 tbsp (25 mL) grated Parmesan cheese, 2 tbsp (25 mL) olive oil and ¾ tsp (4 mL) pepper.

GUIDE TO GRILLING VEGETABLES

Vegetables are categorized by grilling time. Brush with a little olive or vegetable oil and sprinkle with salt and pepper and/or your favourite dried herbs. To grill, thread loosely onto skewers or place in grill basket or, if large, directly on greased grill; close lid and cook over medium-high heat, turning once, until lightly browned and tender-crisp.

10-MINUTE VEGETABLES

Asparagus: trimmed

Eggplant: ¼-inch (5 mm) thick slices

Mushrooms: halved or whole mushroom caps

Onions: 1-inch (2.5 cm) wedges or ½-inch (1 cm) thick slices

Sweet peppers: quarters, eighths or 1½-inch (4 cm) chunks

Zucchini and summer squash: 1½-inch (4 cm) chunks or ¼-inch (5 mm) thick slices lengthwise

15-MINUTE VEGETABLES

Carrots: ¼-inch (5 mm) thick slices

Parsnips: halved lengthwise

Potatoes and sweet potatoes: ¼-inch (5 mm) thick slices; for thicker slices, increase grilling time

VEGGIE PACKETS

This method works well for potatoes, sweet potatoes, carrots, beets, peppers and onions. We don't recommend vegetables such as zucchini or mushrooms because they get too watery. For 4 servings, cut 1 lb (500 g) vegetables into 1½-inch (4 cm) pieces. Toss with 1 tbsp (15 mL) olive or vegetable oil and pinch each salt and pepper. Arrange on large square of greased heavy-duty or double-thickness foil. Fold edges to seal; grill, turning once, for 20 to 30 minutes or until tender.

Poultry

4

Chicken Hot Pot with Ginger, Green Onions and Mushrooms   96

Braised Chicken and Bok Choy   97

Sicilian Chicken   98

Quick Chicken in Wine   99

Thai Green Curry Chicken   100

Chicken Adobo   101

Roast Chicken Dijonnaise   102

Spicy Chicken with Couscous Stuffing   103

Roast Turkey with Bacon and Chestnut Stuffing   104

Honey Rosemary Duck   106

Cornish Hens with Tuscan Touches   107

Charmoula Roast Turkey Breast   108

Turkey Breast Stuffed with Fennel and Red Pepper   109

Roasted Chicken Breasts Five Ways   110

Crispy Baked Chicken   111

Breaded Lemon Chicken with Ricotta Leek Stuffing   112

Chicken Phyllo Bundles with Herbed Sabayon   113

Barbecue-Roasted Turkey   114

Buttermilk Basil Chicken Legs   115

Chipotle Mojo Chicken   116

Portuguese Paprika Chicken   117

Grilled Stuffed Chicken Breasts Many Ways   118

Ginger Chicken and Green Onion Kabobs   119

Parmesan Chicken Burgers   120

Chicken and Seafood Paella   121

Old-Fashioned Chicken Pot Pie   122

Chicken Hot Pot with Ginger, Green Onions and Mushrooms

This recipe was inspired by the Singing Chicken Hot Pot dish, a mainstay in Chinese restaurants, where it is brought to the table bubbling hot — hence the fanciful name "Singing Chicken."

6	boneless skinless chicken thighs	6
2 tsp	cornstarch	10 mL
¼ tsp	each salt and pepper	1 mL
1 tbsp	vegetable oil	15 mL
5 cups	halved large mushrooms (12 oz/375 g)	1.25 L
1	onion, sliced	1
4	large cloves garlic, minced	4

1 tbsp	minced gingerroot	15 mL
4	green onions, cut in 2-inch (5 cm) lengths	4
SAUCE:		
¼ cup	chicken stock	50 mL
2 tbsp	soy sauce	25 mL
1 tbsp	oyster sauce	15 mL
1 tbsp	sherry (optional)	15 mL
1 tsp	Dijon mustard	5 mL

1 Trim fat from chicken; cut into bite-size pieces. In bowl, combine cornstarch, salt and pepper; add chicken, stirring to coat. Set aside.

2 SAUCE: In small bowl, whisk together chicken stock, soy sauce, oyster sauce, sherry (if using) and mustard; set aside.

3 In wok, heat oil over high heat; stir-fry chicken for about 6 minutes or until golden brown. Transfer to plate. Drain off all but 1 tbsp (15 mL) fat from pan. Add mushrooms, onion, garlic and ginger; stir-fry for 3 minutes or until mushrooms are golden.

4 Return chicken to pan; mix in sauce. Cover and cook over medium heat for 3 minutes. Add green onions, mixing well; cook over medium-high heat, uncovered, for 1 minute or until sauce is glossy and thickened.

Makes 4 servings.

PER SERVING, ABOUT:

cal 212	carb . . . . 11 g
pro . . . . 22 g	fibre . . . . 2 g
total fat . . . . . 9 g	chol . . . . . . 71 mg
sat. fat . . . . . . 2 g	sodium . . 905 mg

PERCENTAGE RDI:

calcium 4%	vit. A 2%
iron 19%	vit. C 12%
folate 14%	

Braised Chicken and Bok Choy

Chicken simmered in soy sauce and ginger with a whiff of cinnamon is Chinese cooking, comfort-style.

2 tbsp	vegetable oil	25 mL
2 lb	skinless chicken thighs or drumsticks	1 kg
½ cup	chicken stock	125 mL
¼ cup	soy sauce	50 mL
1 tbsp	granulated sugar	15 mL
3	green onions, thinly sliced	3
6	thin slices gingerroot (or ¼ tsp/1 mL ground ginger)	6

¼ tsp	cinnamon	1 mL
Pinch	each ground cloves and pepper	Pinch
6 cups	coarsely chopped bok choy (6 to 8 stalks bok choy), about 1 lb (500 g)	1.5 L
2 tsp	cornstarch	10 mL

SUBSTITUTIONS

• Substitute 4 baby bok choy, quartered lengthwise, for chopped bok choy.

• If bok choy is unavailable, you can use about 4 cups (1 L) chopped broccoli.

1 In shallow Dutch oven, heat oil over medium-high heat; brown chicken, in batches if necessary. Spoon off fat.

2 Add stock, soy sauce, sugar, two-thirds of the onions, the ginger, cinnamon, cloves and pepper; bring to boil. Cover and simmer over medium-low heat for 25 minutes or until juices run clear when chicken is pierced.

3 Increase heat to high and return chicken mixture to boil. Stir in bok choy; cook for 2 minutes. Dissolve cornstarch in 2 tsp (10 mL) water; add to pan and cook, stirring, for 1 minute or until thickened and bok choy is tender-crisp. Serve sprinkled with remaining green onions.

Air CHILLING VERSUS Water CHILLING

Is there a difference? Well, yes and no. Air chilling is a process imported from Europe whereby a scalded defeathered chicken is cooled using blasts of cold air. An air-chilled chicken tends to have a creamier colour, and its skin often has a yellowish tinge, the result of an extra layer being left on during processing. Water chilling, as the name indicates, uses cold water to cool the chicken. As a result, water-chilled chicken tends to be whiter in colour and retain more moisture. The different processing methods have no impact on the nutritional value of the meat nor on the cooking time.

Makes 4 servings.

PER SERVING, ABOUT:

cal	372	carb	10 g
pro	47 g	fibre	2 g
total fat	15 g	chol	188 mg
sat. fat	3 g	sodium	1,364 mg

PERCENTAGE RDI:

calcium	13%	vit. A	33%
iron	30%	vit. C	62%
folate	31%		

Sicilian Chicken

In this dish, chicken breasts, or thighs if you prefer, are nestled in a saucy bed of robust Sicilian ingredients, including tomatoes, capers and a touch of cinnamon.

1 tsp	each dried basil and oregano	5 mL	1	can (19 oz/540 mL) stewed tomatoes	1
¼ tsp	each salt and pepper	1 mL	2 tsp	chopped capers or green olives	10 mL
4	boneless skinless chicken breasts	4	2 tsp	red wine vinegar	10 mL
1 tbsp	olive oil	15 mL	½ tsp	cinnamon	2 mL
1	onion, chopped	1	¼ cup	chopped fresh parsley	50 mL
1	clove garlic, minced	1			

1 In small bowl, combine basil, oregano, salt and pepper; sprinkle half over both sides of chicken. In large nonstick skillet, heat half of the oil over medium-high heat; brown chicken all over, about 4 minutes. Transfer to plate.

2 In skillet, heat remaining oil over medium heat; cook onion, garlic and remaining basil mixture, stirring, for about 5 minutes or until onion is softened. Add tomatoes, breaking up with spoon. Add capers, vinegar and cinnamon.

3 Return chicken to pan; bring to boil. Reduce heat, cover and simmer for about 10 minutes or until chicken is no longer pink inside. Serve sprinkled with parsley.

Makes 4 servings.

PER SERVING, ABOUT:

cal	232	carb	13 g
pro	32 g	fibre	2 g
total fat	6 g	chol	77 mg
sat. fat	1 g	sodium	613 mg

PERCENTAGE RDI:

calcium	7%	vit. A	10%
iron	16%	vit. C	42%
folate	9%		

Quick Chicken in Wine

Coq au vin is simply chicken browned in a skillet with a touch of smoky bacon and wine added to the pan to simmer up and dissolve all the delicious brown bits. Embellish this tasty foundation with mushrooms, onions and garlic, and you have a fine rustic dish, a cooking cousin to chicken cacciatore. Both partner nicely with noodles, rice or crusty bread.

3½ lb	chicken pieces	1.75 kg		½ tsp	pepper	2 mL
2	slices bacon, chopped	2		¼ cup	all-purpose flour	50 mL
6 cups	button mushrooms (1 lb/500 g)	1.5 L		1½ cups	dry white or red wine	375 mL
				1 cup	chicken stock	250 mL
2 cups	pearl onions, peeled	500 mL		1 tbsp	tomato paste	15 mL
3	cloves garlic, minced	3		1	bay leaf	1
3	carrots, cut in bite-size pieces	3		¼ cup	chopped fresh parsley	50 mL
1 tsp	each dried thyme and salt	5 mL				

1 Separate chicken legs at joint. If breasts are large, cut diagonally across each breast to make 2 portions. Remove skin if desired.

2 In Dutch oven, cook bacon over medium heat until crisp; using slotted spoon, transfer to plate. Add chicken to pan; brown on all sides over medium-high heat, in batches if necessary, about 10 minutes. Transfer to plate.

3 Remove all but 1 tbsp (15 mL) fat from pan. Add mushrooms, onions, garlic, carrots, thyme, salt and pepper; cook, stirring often, for 10 minutes or until almost no liquid remains and mushrooms are browned. Stir in flour; cook for 1 minute.

4 Stir in wine, stock, tomato paste and bay leaf; bring to boil. Nestle chicken into vegetable mixture. Sprinkle bacon and any accumulated chicken juices over top. Reduce heat, cover and simmer for 20 minutes. Uncover and simmer for about 20 minutes or until juices run clear when chicken is pierced. Discard bay leaf. Serve sprinkled with parsley.

Makes 6 servings.

PER SERVING, ABOUT:

cal	304	carb	15 g
pro	38 g	fibre	3 g
total fat	9 g	chol	117 mg
sat. fat	2 g	sodium	693 mg

PERCENTAGE RDI:

calcium	5%	vit. A	95%
iron	24%	vit. C	18%
folate	16%		

Thai Green Curry Chicken

Green curry paste adds a refreshing, albeit hot, accent to what is in essence a chicken stew. Serve to aficionados with Thai jasmine or basmati rice. To speed preparation, use commercial green curry paste.

TEST KITCHEN TIP: Vary the recipe by trying it with Thai red curry paste or, if you prefer, mild Indian curry paste.

4	boneless skinless chicken breasts	4
1 tbsp	vegetable oil	15 mL
2 tbsp	finely chopped shallots	25 mL
5	cloves garlic, minced	5
1 tbsp	finely chopped gingerroot	15 mL
3 tbsp	Green Curry Paste (recipe below)	50 mL

1 tbsp	fish sauce	15 mL
4	lime leaves	4
1	can (400 mL) coconut milk	1
1 cup	Thai basil leaves	250 mL
2 tsp	lime juice	10 mL

1 Cut chicken into 1-inch (2.5 cm) pieces; set aside.

2 In large skillet, heat oil over medium heat; cook shallots, garlic and ginger, stirring, for about 2 minutes or until softened. Stir in curry paste, fish sauce, lime leaves and coconut milk until combined.

3 Add chicken to pan; simmer for about 8 minutes or until slightly thickened and chicken is no longer pink inside. Discard lime leaves. Stir in basil leaves and lime juice.

Makes 4 servings.

PER SERVING, ABOUT:

cal	437	carb	8 g
pro	34 g	fibre	1 g
total fat	31 g	chol	79 mg
sat. fat	19 g	sodium	439 mg

PERCENTAGE RDI:

calcium	5%	vit. A	3%
iron	30%	vit. C	7%
folate	13%		

Green CURRY PASTE

You can buy green curry paste ready-made or, for a freshness advantage, prepare your own. In blender, purée together 8 small green chilies, seeded and chopped, ½ cup (125 mL) chopped fresh coriander (roots and stems included), ½ cup (125 mL) chopped shallots, ¼ cup (50 mL) chopped trimmed lemongrass, 5 cloves garlic, chopped, 1 piece (1 inch/2.5 cm) galangal, peeled, 2 tsp (10 mL) each ground coriander and vegetable oil, 1 tsp (5 mL) each ground cumin, turmeric and shrimp paste and ½ tsp (2 mL) each salt and pepper. (MAKE-AHEAD: Freeze in convenient amounts for up to 1 month.) Makes ¾ cup (175 mL).

Chicken Adobo

*From the Philippines comes a tangy simmered chicken dish with an untraditional
but delicious addition of new potatoes. It's very popular with children.*

2 tbsp	vegetable oil	25 mL
8	chicken thighs, skinned	8
3	onions, chopped	3
2	cloves garlic, minced	2
¼ cup	soy sauce	50 mL
¼ cup	vinegar	50 mL

1 tbsp	liquid honey	15 mL
¼ tsp	pepper	1 mL
5	small (unpeeled) new potatoes (1 lb/500 g), cubed	5

1 In shallow Dutch oven, heat oil over medium-high heat; brown chicken in batches. Transfer to plate. Drain off any fat from pan. Add onions and garlic; cook over medium-low heat, stirring often, for 10 minutes or until softened and golden.

2 Add ¼ cup (50 mL) water, soy sauce, vinegar, honey and pepper; bring to boil. Return chicken to pan. Add potatoes; cover and cook over medium-low heat, turning chicken once, for about 40 minutes or until juices run clear when chicken is pierced.

Makes 4 servings.

PER SERVING, ABOUT:

cal	331	carb	31 g
pro	28 g	fibre	3 g
total fat	11 g	chol	95 mg
sat. fat	2 g	sodium	1,126 mg

PERCENTAGE RDI:

calcium	4%	vit. A	2%
iron	16%	vit. C	17%
folate	13%		

Roast Chicken Dijonnaise

Mustard, a Prairie-grown crop, but famous in culinary circles for its preparation in Dijon, France, enhances the most popular roasted fowl. Choose an air-chilled chicken for the crispiest skin and juiciest flesh.

HOW TO Carve
A CHICKEN

🌾 Cut through string holding legs together. If chicken is stuffed, remove stuffing with long spoon and place in warmed serving bowl. If cavity holds aromatics such as herbs, vegetables or lemon, remove and discard, adding any juices to pan drippings.

🌾 Using kitchen shears, cut chicken in half along backbone and breastbone. Cut around natural crease at thigh to make two breast and two leg portions. Cut each breast in half diagonally. Cut through each leg at joint to separate into drumstick and thigh.

1	chicken (3½ to 5 lb/ 1.75 to 2.2 kg)	1
⅓ cup	Dijon mustard	75 mL
2 tsp	soy sauce	10 mL
1 tsp	minced gingerroot	5 mL

1	clove garlic, minced	1
4 tsp	all-purpose flour	20 mL
1 cup	chicken stock	250 mL

1 Remove giblets and neck from chicken. Rinse and pat chicken dry inside and out. Tie legs together with string; tuck wings under back. Place, breast side up, on rack in roasting pan.

2 In small bowl, combine mustard, soy sauce, ginger and garlic; brush all over chicken. Roast in 325°F (160°C) oven, basting occasionally, for 1¾ to 2 hours for smaller chicken, or up to 3 hours for larger, or until juices run clear when chicken is pierced and meat thermometer inserted in thigh registers 185°F (85°C). (Or roast at 375°F/190°C and reduce time by 1 hour.) Transfer to platter and tent with foil; let stand for 20 minutes before carving.

3 Meanwhile, skim fat from pan juices. Sprinkle flour over juices; cook over medium-high heat, stirring, for 1 minute. Pour in chicken stock and any juices from platter; boil, stirring, until thickened. Strain into warmed gravy boat and serve with chicken.

VARIATIONS

Roast Chicken with Lemon and Garlic: Omit mustard mixture. Insert 1 small onion, quartered, 4 cloves garlic, half small lemon, squeezing out juices, and sprig or 2 of thyme, sage, oregano or rosemary, if desired, into chicken cavity. Brush outside of chicken with 1 tbsp (15 mL) olive oil or butter, melted; sprinkle with 1 tsp (5 mL) crumbled dried thyme, sage, oregano or rosemary and ¼ tsp (1 mL) each salt and pepper. After roasting, discard contents of cavity, but tip juices from cavity into pan drippings before adding flour.

Garlic Roast Chicken: Cut off tips from 1 or 2 heads of garlic; add garlic to roasting pan for last hour of cooking Roast Chicken with Lemon and Garlic. Serve broken into buds if desired or squeeze into pan juices and mash when making gravy.

Makes 4 or 5 servings.

PER EACH OF 5 SERVINGS, ABOUT:

cal	361	carb	3 g
pro	33 g	fibre	trace
total fat	23 g	chol	114 mg
sat. fat	6 g	sodium	606 mg

PERCENTAGE RDI:

calcium	3%	vit. A	5%
iron	12%	vit. C	0%
folate	5%		

Spicy Chicken with Couscous Stuffing

An aromatic Moroccan-inspired stuffing infuses the chicken with flavour and adds a delicious element to the menu. Couscous is the star here, but you can easily choose other dressings.

2 tbsp	butter	25 mL	1 cup	couscous	250 mL
4	green onions, chopped	4	¼ cup	currants	50 mL
1	clove garlic, minced	1	¼ cup	chopped almonds	50 mL
1½ tsp	ground cumin	7 mL	3 tbsp	chopped fresh parsley	50 mL
½ tsp	each ground coriander and ginger	2 mL	1	chicken (4 lb/2 kg)	1
Pinch	each cinnamon, salt and pepper	Pinch	¼ tsp	curry powder	1 mL
2½ cups	chicken stock	625 mL	1 tbsp	liquid honey	15 mL
			4 tsp	all-purpose flour	20 mL

1 In saucepan, melt butter over medium heat; cook onions and garlic, stirring often, for 3 minutes or until softened. Stir in ½ tsp (2 mL) of the cumin, ¼ tsp (1 mL) each of the coriander and ginger, the cinnamon, salt and pepper; cook, stirring, for 1 minute.

2 Pour in 1½ cups (375 mL) of the chicken stock; bring to boil. Stir in couscous, currants, almonds and parsley; remove from heat. Cover and let stand for 5 minutes; fluff with fork.

3 Remove giblets and neck from chicken. Rinse and pat chicken dry inside and out. Stuff neck and body cavities with about half of the couscous mixture; place remaining couscous in ovenproof dish. Tie legs together with string; tuck wings under back. Skewer neck cavity closed. Place, breast side up, on rack in roasting pan.

4 Combine remaining cumin, coriander, ginger and the curry powder; sprinkle over chicken. Roast in 325°F (160°C) oven, basting occasionally, for 1½ hours. Brush with honey. Place dish of couscous in oven. Roast for about 30 minutes longer or until juices run clear when chicken is pierced and meat thermometer inserted in thigh registers 185°F (85°C). Transfer to platter and tent with foil; let stand for 20 minutes before carving.

5 Meanwhile, skim fat from pan juices. Sprinkle flour over juices; cook over medium-high heat, stirring, for 1 minute. Pour in remaining chicken stock; boil, stirring, until thickened. Strain into warmed gravy boat and serve with chicken.

HOW TO Stuff A CHICKEN

- Always stuff chicken just before cooking. Rinse neck and body cavities; pat dry.
- Fill neck cavity (wishbone area) first, spooning in stuffing until full but not compacted.
- Pull neck skin to back of chicken and fasten with skewer. Fill body cavity without packing.
- Place any extra stuffing in casserole or heavy-duty foil packet and drizzle with pan drippings; cover or seal and bake alongside chicken for last 30 to 45 minutes.

Makes 5 or 6 servings.

PER EACH OF 6 SERVINGS, ABOUT:

cal	423	carb	35 g
pro	32 g	fibre	3 g
total fat	17 g	chol	92 mg
sat. fat	6 g	sodium	444 mg

PERCENTAGE RDI:

calcium	5%	vit. A	7%
iron	19%	vit. C	5%
folate	14%		

Roast Turkey with Bacon and Chestnut Stuffing

Turkey is the ultimate big roast associated with family holiday gatherings. And while it is familiar, it's not a dish one cooks every week. Considering the attention this centrepiece entrée gets, it's no wonder cooks get the turkey jitters. Take heart. Our stuffing is a tried-and-true Canadian Living Test Kitchen favourite. So is the all-important gravy. Consult the box at right for preparing the perfect roast turkey and set your mind at ease.

SUBSTITUTION: Replace chestnuts with 1 cup (250 mL) of the following: chopped nuts such as pecans or walnuts; dried fruit such as cranberries, apricots or figs; chopped fresh apple; or 1 lb (500 g) sausage, crumbled and cooked.

5	slices bacon, chopped	5	1 tsp	pepper	5 mL
¼ cup	butter	50 mL	½ tsp	salt	2 mL
3	onions, chopped	3	12 cups	cubed day-old Italian or French bread	3 L
3	stalks celery, chopped	3	1	can (425 mL) chestnuts, drained	1
¼ cup	chopped fresh sage (or 2 tbsp/25 mL crumbled dried)	50 mL	¼ cup	chopped fresh parsley	50 mL
1	sweet red pepper, chopped	1	1¼ cups	chicken stock	300 mL

1 In large skillet, cook bacon over medium heat for 5 minutes or until cooked but not crisp. Add butter, onions, celery and sage; cook, stirring occasionally, for 30 minutes or until softened. Add red pepper, pepper and salt; cook for 5 minutes.

2 In large bowl, toss vegetable mixture with bread. Add chestnuts and parsley; drizzle with stock and toss to combine. Let cool.

3 Loosely stuff into cavity of turkey (see Golden Roast Turkey, next page).

Makes 12 cups (3 L) stuffing, enough for 15-lb (6.75 kg) turkey.

PER EACH OF 16 SERVINGS
STUFFING, ABOUT:

cal	165	carb	21 g
pro	4 g	fibre	2 g
total fat	8 g	chol	13 mg
sat. fat	3 g	sodium	357 mg

PERCENTAGE RDI:

calcium	2%	vit. A	9%
iron	9%	vit. C	52%
folate	13%		

STUFFING VARIATIONS

Bacon and Fresh Chestnut Stuffing: Substitute 12 oz (375 g) fresh chestnuts for canned. Cut X in flat side of each. In saucepan of boiling water, cook chestnuts, 4 at a time, for about 2 minutes or until skins can be easily peeled off. Add to stuffing as above.

Italian Bread Stuffing: Substitute 1 tbsp (15 mL) dried rosemary, crumbled, for the sage and 1 cup (250 mL) chopped oil-packed sun-dried tomatoes for the chestnuts.

GOLDEN ROAST Turkey

🌿 **TURKEY:** Count on 1 lb (500 g) uncooked per person. A 15-lb (6.75 kg) turkey will serve 12 to 16 people.

🌿 **PREPARING:** Remove giblets and neck; reserve for stock or gravy. Rinse turkey under cold water; pat dry inside and out. Loosely stuff neck opening with stuffing, if desired; fold skin over stuffing and skewer to back. Lift wings and twist under back. Stuff body cavity if desired. Tuck legs under band of skin or tie together with kitchen string.

🌿 **ROASTING:** Place turkey on rack in roasting pan. Brush with about 2 tbsp (25 mL) butter, melted; sprinkle with salt and pepper. Tent with foil, tucking in sides but leaving ends open. Roast in 325°F (160°C) oven for 3½ hours, basting every 30 minutes. Uncover and roast for about 1 hour longer or until meat thermometer inserted in thickest part of thigh registers 180°F (82°C) for stuffed or unstuffed turkey.

🌿 **CARVING:** Transfer to cutting board; tent with foil and let stand for 30 minutes. With carving knife and fork, cut skin between leg and body; press thigh down, then cut through joint. Cut through joint in leg; slice off dark meat from drumstick. Repeat with other leg. Repeat as for leg to cut off wings. Starting at breastbone, carve breast meat thinly in long sweeping motions.

Wild MUSHROOM GRAVY

🌿 In bowl, pour 1½ cups (375 mL) boiling water over 1 pkg (10 g) dried porcini mushrooms; let soak for 15 minutes. Drain in paper towel–lined sieve, reserving liquid. Chop finely. Set aside.

🌿 Pour pan drippings into large measuring cup; skim off fat, reserving ¼ cup (50 mL) fat. Add mushroom liquid, 1 can (10 oz/284 mL) chicken stock and enough water to pan drippings to make 4 cups (1 L).

🌿 Pour reserved fat back into roasting pan. Stir in ⅓ cup (75 mL) all-purpose flour, ½ tsp (2 mL) dried sage, ¼ tsp (1 mL) each salt and pepper, then reserved mushrooms; cook over medium heat, stirring, for 1 minute. Gradually whisk in stock mixture; bring to boil, stirring and scraping up brown bits from bottom of pan. Reduce heat and simmer, stirring often, for 2 minutes or until thickened. **Makes about 4 cups (1 L).**

TEST KITCHEN TIPS

• Stuff stuffing into neck and body cavities of turkey; wrap excess in foil and add to oven for final hour of roasting. (Or spread in greased 13- x 9-inch/3 L glass baking dish. Cover with foil; bake in 375°F/190°C oven for 30 minutes. Uncover and bake for 30 minutes or until golden and crisp.)

• When respondents on canadianliving.com revealed their turkey tragedies, the 2 most common were: not allowing enough time for a frozen turkey to thaw (5 hours per lb/500 g in the refrigerator or 1 hour per lb/500 g when submerged in cold water refreshed hourly); and failing to remove the bag of giblets neatly hidden in 1 of the 2 turkey cavities. Check both before seasoning or stuffing and you won't get a surprise when you carve.

Honey Rosemary Duck

Canadian Living *associate food editor Andrew Chase perfected this technique of brining, steaming and roasting a whole duck, ridding it of most of its fat to get the crispiest skin and most succulent meat.*

Chinoise Duck: Substitute rice wine or dry sherry for brandy. Omit garlic, rosemary, pepper and lemon. Substitute 1¼ tsp (6 mL) five-spice powder, rubbing ¼ tsp (1 mL) inside duck and 1 tsp (5 mL) outside. Place 4 thin slices gingerroot inside duck, 4 in steaming water and 4 on top of breast when steaming. For glaze, mix 1 tbsp (15 mL) liquid honey with 1½ tsp (7 mL) soy sauce.

1	duck, about 4 lb (2 kg)	1	2 tsp	pepper	10 mL
2 tsp	brandy or vermouth	10 mL	1	lemon	1
⅓ cup	coarse salt (or ¼ cup/ 50 mL fine salt)	75 mL	4	sprigs fresh rosemary	4
4	cloves garlic, smashed	4	1 tbsp	liquid honey	15 mL
2 tbsp	chopped fresh rosemary	25 mL	½ tsp	soy sauce	2 mL

1 Rinse duck well and pat dry thoroughly with paper towels. Rub inside and out with brandy, then salt, distributing evenly. Place in large dish; cover with plastic wrap and refrigerate for at least 1 day or for up to 3 days, turning daily.

2 Rinse salt off duck under cold running water; pat dry with paper towels. Pull off excess fat in cavity; cut off tailbone and excess neck skin. Using metal skewer or toothpick, prick skin all over on angle, especially in fatty areas, being careful not to prick meat under fat.

3 In small bowl, lightly mash together garlic, chopped rosemary and pepper; rub inside cavity. Using vegetable peeler, peel rind off lemon; set aside.

4 Pour water into wok or large pot to come 2 inches (5 cm) up side. Add all but 4 strips of the lemon rind and half of the rosemary sprigs; bring to boil. Place duck, breast side up, in large bamboo steamer. Lay remaining lemon rind and rosemary sprigs on duck. Place steamer on top of wok. Reserving 1½ tsp (7 mL) juice, squeeze remaining lemon juice over duck. Cover and steam over medium-high heat for 70 minutes, adding more boiling water to wok as necessary to maintain level.

5 Remove duck from steamer; carefully pour out excess liquid from body cavity. (MAKE-AHEAD: Let cool slightly; transfer to glass dish and refrigerate until cold. Cover with plastic wrap and refrigerate for up to 1 day.) Discard rosemary and lemon rind.

6 Place duck, breast side down, on rack in roasting pan. In small bowl, mix together honey, soy sauce and reserved lemon juice; lightly brush over bottom skin of duck. Roast in 425°F (220°C) oven for 15 minutes or until golden. Turn duck over; brush with remaining honey mixture. Roast for about 15 minutes longer or until well browned, watching to avoid burning.

Makes 4 servings.

PER SERVING, ABOUT:

cal	372	carb	7 g
pro	41 g	fibre	trace
total fat	19 g	chol	153 mg
sat. fat	7 g	sodium	156 mg

PERCENTAGE RDI:

calcium	3%	vit. A	4%
iron	37%	vit. C	3%
folate	8%		

Cornish Hens with Tuscan Touches

Depending on the time of year and location of your barbecue, you can grill or roast these diminutive hens. For hearty appetites, count on one hen per person, but often a half is sufficient.

⅓ cup	lemon juice	75 mL
¼ cup	extra-virgin olive oil	50 mL
4	cloves garlic, minced	4
1 tbsp	chopped fresh rosemary (or 1 tsp/5 mL dried)	15 mL

2 tsp	fennel seeds, crushed	10 mL
½ tsp	each salt and pepper	2 mL
4	Cornish hens (about 4½ lb/2.25 kg total)	4

TEST KITCHEN TIP: Let a slice of Shallot Peppercorn Butter (page 152) melt over breasts of hens just before serving. You can also leave hens whole and fill cavities with bread or grain stuffing.

1 In large glass bowl, combine lemon juice, oil, garlic, rosemary, fennel seeds, salt and pepper; set aside.

2 Using kitchen shears, cut Cornish hens down each side of backbone; remove backbone. Turn breast side up; press firmly on breastbone to flatten. Tuck wings behind back. Add to bowl; turn to coat all over with marinade. Cover and refrigerate for 4 hours. (MAKE-AHEAD: Refrigerate for up to 1 day.)

3 Place hens, skin side up, on greased grill over medium heat. Close lid and cook for 15 minutes. Using tongs, turn hens over and cook for about 20 minutes or until juices run clear when thigh is pierced, turning if necessary.

4 Transfer hens to cutting board and tent with foil; let stand for 10 minutes. Using chef's knife or kitchen scissors, cut each hen in half vertically down breastbone.

SUBSTITUTION: You can use 4 to 6 whole chicken legs (about 3 lb/1.5 kg) instead of Cornish hens.

VARIATIONS

Micro-Grilled Cornish Hens with Tuscan Touches: Arrange hens with thickest parts to outside of microwaveable bowl containing marinade. Cover with vented plastic wrap and microwave at High, turning and basting twice, for 5 minutes or until juices run slightly pink when leg is pierced. Reserving marinade, place hens on greased grill over medium heat; close lid and cook, turning and basting once with marinade, for 15 minutes or until golden and juices run clear when thigh is pierced.

Oven-Roasted Cornish Hens with Tuscan Touches: Place hens, breast side up, on foil-lined baking sheet. Roast in 425°F (220°C) oven for 45 minutes or until juices run clear when thigh is pierced.

Makes 4 servings.

PER SERVING, ABOUT:

cal	586	carb	2 g
pro	45 g	fibre	trace
total fat	43 g	chol	262 mg
sat. fat	11 g	sodium	274 mg

PERCENTAGE RDI:

calcium	3%	vit. A	7%
iron	15%	vit. C	5%
folate	2%		

Charmoula Roast Turkey Breast

Roasting a lean no-waste turkey breast is the answer to dinner-party and special-occasion menus. Its mild flavour is perfectly complemented by charmoula, a fresh herb-and-spice mixture of Moroccan origin, but you can also opt to use ½ cup (125 mL) Pesto (page 235).

TEST KITCHEN TIP: If you can't find a large single turkey breast, use a double breast of the same weight. Omit cutting step and spread seasoning mixture over both sides of breast.

½ cup	finely chopped fresh coriander	125 mL
⅓ cup	finely chopped fresh parsley	75 mL
2	cloves garlic, minced	2
¼ cup	extra-virgin olive oil	50 mL
2 tbsp	lemon juice	25 mL

1 tsp	each paprika and salt	5 mL
½ tsp	ground cumin	2 mL
¼ tsp	each cayenne pepper and pepper	1 mL
Pinch	cinnamon	Pinch
1	boneless single turkey breast (about 3 lb/1.5 kg)	1

1 In bowl, stir together coriander, parsley, garlic, oil, lemon juice, paprika, salt, cumin, cayenne pepper, pepper and cinnamon.

2 Pat turkey breast dry. With sharp knife held horizontally, cut turkey in half to within 1 inch (2.5 cm) of edge; open like book. Spread half of the seasoning mixture over top. Starting at 1 long edge, roll up; tie around each end and at centre with kitchen string. Rub remaining seasoning mixture all over turkey roll. (MAKE-AHEAD: Wrap and refrigerate for up to 4 hours.)

3 Place on greased rack in roasting pan. Roast in 325°F (160°C) oven for 2 hours or until juices run clear when turkey is pierced and meat thermometer registers 170°F (75°C). Transfer to cutting board and tent with foil; let stand for 20 minutes before slicing thinly.

Makes 8 servings.

PER SERVING, ABOUT:

cal 272	carb . . . . 1 g
pro . . . . 40 g	fibre . . . . trace
total fat . . . . 11 g	chol . . . . . . 92 mg
sat. fat . . . . . . 2 g	sodium . . 374 mg

PERCENTAGE RDI:

calcium 3%	vit. A 4%
iron 16%	vit. C 5%
folate 5%	

Turkey Breast Stuffed with Fennel and Red Pepper

Bulb fennel is not a new vegetable, but its popularity in Canada is. Crunchy when fresh and sliced into a salad, its mild licorice flavour comes to the fore when cooked.

1	boneless double turkey breast (3½ lb/1.75 kg)	1	Half	bulb fennel, chopped (2 cups/500 mL)	Half
1 tbsp	olive oil	15 mL	1 tbsp	chopped fresh thyme (or ½ tsp/2 mL dried)	15 mL
¼ tsp	each salt and pepper	1 mL	½ tsp	salt	2 mL
2 cups	chicken stock	500 mL	¼ tsp	each pepper and dried rosemary	1 mL
2 tbsp	all-purpose flour	25 mL	¼ tsp	fennel seeds, crushed	1 mL
½ cup	dry white wine	125 mL	½ cup	chopped roasted red pepper	125 mL
STUFFING:			½ cup	fresh bread crumbs	125 mL
4 oz	pancetta or bacon, chopped	125 g	2 tbsp	chopped fresh parsley	25 mL
1	onion, chopped	1	2 tbsp	pine nuts, toasted	25 mL
2	cloves garlic, minced	2			

1 STUFFING: In large skillet, cook pancetta over medium-high heat for about 5 minutes or until crisp. Spoon off all but 1 tbsp (15 mL) fat. Reduce heat to medium. Add onion, garlic, fennel, thyme, salt, pepper, rosemary and fennel seeds; cook, stirring often, for about 10 minutes or until vegetables are softened. Stir in red pepper, bread crumbs, parsley and pine nuts. Let cool.

2 Open turkey breast and lay flat on work surface. Fold back filets toward outside of breast. Spread stuffing over breast, leaving 1-inch (2.5 cm) border on all sides. Starting at 1 short end, roll up; tie with kitchen string. Brush with oil; sprinkle with salt and pepper. Place on greased rack in roasting pan; pour in ½ cup (125 mL) of the stock.

3 Roast in 325°F (160°C) oven for about 2½ hours or until no longer pink inside and meat thermometer registers 180°F (82°C), adding more stock to pan if necessary to maintain level. Transfer to cutting board; tent with foil and let stand for 20 minutes.

4 Skim fat from pan juices. Place pan over medium heat; whisk in flour. Whisk in remaining stock and wine; bring to boil. Cook, stirring, for 3 minutes or until thickened; strain. Slice turkey and serve with gravy.

Makes 8 servings.

PER SERVING, ABOUT:

cal	339	carb	7 g
pro	52 g	fibre	1 g
total fat	10 g	chol	114 mg
sat. fat	3 g	sodium	719 mg

PERCENTAGE RDI:

calcium	5%	vit. A	4%
iron	21%	vit. C	28%
folate	11%		

Roasted Chicken Breasts
Five Ways

A variety of seasonings make roasted chicken breasts a reliable and pleasing busy-night supper. Bone-in breasts, legs and thighs are just as convenient to roast as their boneless counterparts. A thrifty choice, they also are considered more succulent.

	LIQUID ADD-INS	FLAVOURINGS
Lemon Mint Chicken Breasts	2 tbsp (25 mL) each lemon juice and olive oil	1 tsp (5 mL) each dried mint and finely grated lemon rind; ½ tsp (2 mL) ground cumin; ¼ tsp (1 mL) each salt, pepper and cinnamon; 1 clove garlic, minced
Cajun Chicken Breasts	¼ cup (50 mL) vegetable oil	2 tsp (10 mL) each dried oregano, paprika and dry mustard; 1 tsp (5 mL) each pepper and dried thyme; ½ tsp (2 mL) salt; ¼ tsp (1 mL) cayenne pepper
Honey Mustard Chicken Breasts	1 tbsp (15 mL) vegetable oil	¼ cup (50 mL) each liquid honey and grainy Dijon mustard; 1 tsp (5 mL) dried thyme; ¼ tsp (1 mL) each salt, pepper and Worcestershire sauce
Ginger Apricot Chicken Breasts	2 tbsp (25 mL) lemon juice	¼ cup (50 mL) apricot preserves; 1 tbsp (15 mL) each minced gingerroot and Dijon mustard; ¼ tsp (1 mL) each salt and pepper
Sticky Hoisin Chicken Breasts	½ cup (125 mL) hoisin sauce	2 tbsp (25 mL) sesame seeds; 1 tbsp (15 mL) soy sauce; 2 tsp (10 mL) sesame oil; 1 tsp (5 mL) grated orange rind

TEST KITCHEN TIPS

• You can brush flavourings under skin of chicken and, if desired, remove skin before eating.

• Roast potatoes or other vegetables at same time for a complete oven meal. See page 92 for inspiration.

1 In bowl, combine Liquid Add-Ins in first column with Flavourings in second column. Brush onto 4 chicken breasts or 4 legs; reserve remaining liquid for glaze. Place chicken, skin side down, on greased foil-lined rimmed baking sheet.

2 Bake in 425°F (220°C) oven, turning and brushing with reserved glaze halfway through, for about 35 minutes or until no longer pink inside.

Makes 4 servings.

Crispy Baked Chicken

The centrepiece for a family-pleasing supper is a platter of crisp oven-baked chicken breasts. You can oven-bake some fries at the same time, jacking up the heat for a few minutes after taking the chicken out.

16	melba toasts	16
2 tbsp	butter, melted	25 mL
2 tbsp	light mayonnaise	25 mL
2 tbsp	Dijon mustard	25 mL

1 tsp	dried thyme	5 mL
¼ tsp	each salt and pepper	1 mL
4	boneless skinless chicken breasts	4

1 In food processor or plastic bag, crush melba toasts until in coarse crumbs; transfer to bowl. Add butter; toss to combine. Set aside.

2 In small bowl, whisk together mayonnaise, mustard, thyme, salt and pepper; spread over chicken. Dip into crumb mixture, turning and pressing to coat.

3 Place chicken on rack on rimmed baking sheet; bake in 425°F (220°C) oven for about 20 minutes or until golden and juices run clear when chicken is pierced.

COATING VARIATIONS

Omit melba toasts and substitute 1 of the following:

🍂 1½ cups (375 mL) coarsely crushed cornflakes.
🍂 ⅓ cup (75 mL) dry bread crumbs mixed with ⅓ cup (75 mL) grated Parmesan cheese; reduce salt in mustard mixture to pinch.
🍂 ½ cup (125 mL) finely chopped pecans or walnuts mixed with ¼ cup (50 mL) dry bread crumbs.
🍂 ½ cup (125 mL) each toasted sesame seeds and dry bread crumbs.

TEST KITCHEN TIP: Substitute 8 chicken drumsticks (about 2 lb/1 kg), skinned if desired; bake for about 35 minutes or until juices run clear when chicken is pierced.

Makes 4 servings.

PER SERVING, ABOUT:

cal	309	carb	17 g
pro	33 g	fibre	1 g
total fat	11 g	chol	93 mg
sat. fat	4 g	sodium	592 mg

PERCENTAGE RDI:

calcium	4%	vit. A	6%
iron	12%	vit. C	2%
folate	4%		

Breaded Lemon Chicken with Ricotta Leek Stuffing

It doesn't take a lot of time to stuff chicken breasts — they're not fiddly. But they still look and taste as though the cook has cared, and that's what entertaining is all about.

TEST KITCHEN TIP: To clean leeks, slit each stalk lengthwise almost to root end. Holding root end up and spreading leaves, flush out grit under cold running water.

SUBSTITUTION: If you can't find leeks, substitute 1 cup (250 mL) chopped onions combined with ½ cup (125 mL) chopped green onions.

4	boneless skinless chicken breasts	4
¼ cup	all-purpose flour	50 mL
1½ tsp	finely grated lemon rind	7 mL
¼ tsp	each salt and pepper	1 mL
1	egg	1
1	egg yolk	1
4 tsp	lemon juice	20 mL
¾ cup	dry bread crumbs	175 mL
2 tbsp	vegetable oil	25 mL

RICOTTA LEEK STUFFING:		
1 tbsp	butter	15 mL
1½ cups	chopped leeks (white part only)	375 mL
1	clove garlic, minced	1
¾ cup	ricotta cheese	175 mL
3 tbsp	grated Parmesan cheese	50 mL
1 tbsp	minced fresh parsley	15 mL
1½ tsp	finely grated lemon rind	7 mL
1 tsp	lemon juice	5 mL
1	egg white	1
¼ tsp	pepper	1 mL

1 RICOTTA LEEK STUFFING: In nonstick skillet, melt butter over medium-low heat; cook leeks and garlic, stirring often, for about 15 minutes or until very soft. Transfer leek mixture to bowl; let cool. Mix in ricotta cheese, Parmesan cheese, parsley, lemon rind and juice, egg white and pepper; set aside.

2 Trim any fat from chicken. With knife held horizontally and starting at thinner side, cut chicken in half almost but not all the way through; open like book.

3 Spread one-quarter of the stuffing evenly over inside of each breast, leaving ½-inch (1 cm) border uncovered. Sprinkle pinch of the flour over bottom border; close breast, pressing around edge to seal. Set aside.

4 In shallow dish, combine remaining flour, lemon rind, salt and pepper. In separate shallow bowl, whisk together egg, egg yolk and lemon juice. Place bread crumbs in another shallow dish. Coat breasts first with flour, then with egg mixture, then with bread crumbs, turning to coat all over. (MAKE-AHEAD: Cover and refrigerate on waxed paper–lined tray for up to 12 hours.)

5 In nonstick skillet, heat half of the oil over medium-high heat; brown chicken, in 2 batches and using remaining oil as needed, about 3 minutes per side. Place on rack on rimmed baking sheet. Bake in 400°F (200°C) oven for 15 to 20 minutes or until springy to the touch and chicken is no longer pink inside.

Makes 4 servings.

PER SERVING, ABOUT:

cal	440	carb	17 g
pro	42 g	fibre	1 g
total fat	22 g	chol	183 mg
sat. fat	8 g	sodium	468 mg

PERCENTAGE RDI:

calcium	19%	vit. A	13%
iron	16%	vit. C	10%
folate	14%		

Chicken Phyllo Bundles with Herbed Sabayon

Chicken breasts are the start for an entertaining main course that can be made ahead and will dazzle guests.

8	boneless skinless chicken breasts	8
2 tbsp	Dijon mustard	25 mL
½ tsp	pepper	2 mL
¼ tsp	salt	1 mL
8	thin slices prosciutto ham	8
16	sheets phyllo pastry	16
¾ cup	butter, melted	175 mL

HERBED SABAYON:

4	egg yolks	4
3 tbsp	chicken stock	50 mL
2 tbsp	dry vermouth	25 mL
⅓ cup	finely chopped fresh parsley	75 mL
2 tbsp	each finely chopped fresh basil and oregano or thyme	25 mL
1 tbsp	lemon juice	15 mL
¼ tsp	each salt and pepper	1 mL

SUBSTITUTION: Instead of the prosciutto, you can use shaved Black Forest ham, roasted sweet red pepper, sautéed mushrooms, shredded Gruyère, Gouda or Jarlsberg cheese, or crumbled feta cheese. Other choices include omitting the mustard and smearing the opened chicken breasts with prepared pesto or sun-dried-tomato pesto or chopped fresh herbs such as basil or sage.

1 With sharp knife held horizontally, cut chicken in half almost but not all the way through; open like book. Brush with mustard; sprinkle with pepper and salt. Lay 1 prosciutto slice on each breast; fold breast over to enclose.

2 Place 1 sheet of phyllo on work surface, keeping remainder covered with damp towel to prevent drying out. Brush with butter; top with second sheet. Centre 1 breast on phyllo about 2 inches (5 cm) from short edge; fold edge over chicken. Fold sides over and roll up. Place, seam side down, on greased rimmed baking sheet; brush with butter. Repeat with remaining phyllo, butter and chicken. (MAKE-AHEAD: **Cover with plastic wrap and refrigerate for up to 8 hours.**) Bake in 350°F (180°C) oven for about 45 minutes or until golden and chicken is no longer pink inside.

3 HERBED SABAYON: In large heatproof bowl or top of double boiler, whisk egg yolks until pale; whisk in stock and vermouth. Place over simmering water; whisk for about 8 minutes or until thickened and frothy. Whisk in parsley, basil, oregano, lemon juice, salt and pepper. Serve with chicken bundles.

Makes 8 servings.

PER SERVING, ABOUT:

cal	500	carb	27 g
pro	37 g	fibre	1 g
total fat	26 g	chol	238 mg
sat. fat	13 g	sodium	794 mg

PERCENTAGE RDI:

calcium	4%	vit. A	23%
iron	21%	vit. C	7%
folate	12%		

Barbecue-Roasted Turkey

As barbecues have become bigger, fancier and more reliable, Canadians have graduated from steaks and burgers into the realm of roasts, whole chickens and turkeys. When turkey is the centrepiece of a festive meal, let it take on a hint of smoky flavour while keeping the kitchen stove freed up for vegetables and dessert.

TEST KITCHEN TIP: A turkey 14 lb (6.25 kg) or smaller is ideal for the barbecue. Collect the pan drippings, skim off the fat and make gravy (page 105).

1	turkey, 14 lb (6.25 kg)	1	2 tbsp	chopped fresh sage, rosemary or thyme (or 2 tsp/10 mL dried)	25 mL
¾ tsp	each salt and pepper	4 mL	1 tbsp	Dijon mustard	15 mL
6	sprigs fresh sage, rosemary or thyme	6			
⅓ cup	each white wine vinegar and vegetable oil	75 mL			

1 Remove neck and giblets from turkey; rinse inside and out, then pat dry. Season inside cavity with salt and pepper. Place sage sprigs in cavity. Skewer neck skin to back. Using kitchen string, tie legs together and wings to body.

2 In bowl, whisk together vinegar, oil, chopped sage and mustard; set aside.

3 Heat 1 burner of 2-burner barbecue or 2 outside burners of 3-burner barbecue to medium. Place foil drip pan under unlit burner. Place turkey on greased grill over unlit burner. Close lid and cook, brushing every 45 minutes with vinegar mixture and adjusting heat to keep temperature between 250° and 300°F (120° and 150°C), for 3½ to 4 hours or until meat thermometer inserted in thigh registers 180°F (82°C).

4 Transfer to cutting board. Tent with foil and let stand for about 20 minutes before carving.

Makes 8 to 10 servings.

PER EACH OF 10 SERVINGS, ABOUT:

cal 754	carb . . . . 1 g
pro . . . . 93 g	fibre . . . . trace
total fat . . . . 40 g	chol . . . . . 271 mg
sat. fat . . . . . 10 g	sodium . . 417 mg

PERCENTAGE RDI:

calcium 8%	vit. A 0%
iron 44%	vit. C 0%
folate 10%	

Buttermilk Basil Chicken Legs

Buttermilk tenderizes chicken and is the vehicle that marries it with fresh herbs. Grilling chicken without the skin ensures a leaner meal and more flavour penetration, and because there is a lot less fat dripping onto the flames, there are fewer flare-ups and less charring.

¾ cup	buttermilk	175 mL
2 tbsp	chopped fresh basil (or 2 tsp/10 mL dried)	25 mL
2 tsp	vegetable oil	10 mL
1 tsp	dry mustard	5 mL
2	cloves garlic, minced	2
¼ tsp	each salt and pepper	1 mL
4	chicken legs, skinned	4

FRESH TOMATO SALSA:		
3	plum tomatoes, chopped	3
2 tbsp	chopped fresh basil (or 2 tsp/10 mL dried)	25 mL
1 tsp	lemon juice	5 mL
1 tsp	olive oil	5 mL
¼ tsp	each salt and pepper	1 mL

TEST KITCHEN TIP: To shorten grilling time to about 25 minutes, separate the chicken legs into drumsticks and thighs. You can also use skinless chicken breasts and grill them, starting meaty side up, for about 25 minutes for bone-in or 12 to 15 minutes for boneless.

1 In glass dish, whisk together buttermilk, basil, oil, mustard, garlic, salt and pepper; add chicken, turning to coat. Cover and marinate in refrigerator for 8 hours, turning occasionally. (MAKE-AHEAD: Refrigerate for up to 1 day.)

2 FRESH TOMATO SALSA: In bowl, stir together tomatoes, basil, lemon juice, oil, salt and pepper. Set aside.

3 Place chicken, meaty side up, on greased grill over medium heat; brush with marinade. Close lid and cook, turning occasionally, for 30 to 40 minutes or until juices run clear when chicken is pierced. Serve topped with salsa.

VARIATION

Buttermilk Rosemary Chicken Legs: In marinade, substitute 1 tbsp (15 mL) chopped fresh rosemary or 1 tsp (5 mL) crushed dried rosemary for the fresh basil and add 1 tsp (5 mL) grated lemon rind. In the salsa, substitute 1 tsp (5 mL) chopped fresh rosemary or ¼ tsp (1 mL) finely crushed dried rosemary for the fresh basil.

Makes 4 servings.

PER SERVING, ABOUT:

cal	213	carb	4 g
pro	25 g	fibre	1 g
total fat	10 g	chol	91 mg
sat. fat	2 g	sodium	372 mg

PERCENTAGE RDI:

calcium	4%	vit. A	3%
iron	11%	vit. C	17%
folate	5%		

MAKE-AHEAD   BUDGET-WISE

Chipotle Mojo Chicken

A daring combination of hot, hot, hot smoked jalapeño (chipotle) peppers and citrus creates a taste-tingling entrée.

TEST KITCHEN TIP: Look for cans of chipotle peppers in adobo sauce in the Mexican ingredients section of your supermarket.

SUBSTITUTION: Try either or both of these marinades with 4 chicken breasts or whole legs, 8 thighs or 4 thick boneless pork loin chops.

¼ cup	olive oil	50 mL
1 tbsp	grated orange rind	15 mL
3 tbsp	orange juice	50 mL
2 tbsp	wine vinegar	25 mL
1	chipotle pepper	1

1	clove garlic, minced	1
1 tbsp	adobo sauce	15 mL
¼ tsp	each salt and chili powder	1 mL
4	chicken legs	4

1 In blender or food processor, purée together oil, orange rind and juice, vinegar, chipotle pepper, garlic, adobo sauce, salt and chili powder until smooth. In glass bowl, pour marinade over chicken legs, turning to coat. Cover and refrigerate for 4 hours. (MAKE-AHEAD: **Refrigerate for up to 12 hours.**)

2 Place chicken, meaty side up, on greased grill over medium heat; baste with marinade. Close lid and cook, turning occasionally, for about 45 minutes or until juices run clear when chicken is pierced.

MICRO-GRILL VARIATION

➥ Arrange chicken with thickest part to outside of microwaveable bowl containing marinade. Cover with vented plastic wrap and microwave at High, turning pieces and basting twice, for 8 minutes or until juices run slightly pink when legs are pierced.

➥ Place chicken on greased grill over medium-high heat; baste with marinade. Close lid and cook for 5 minutes per side or until golden and juices run clear when chicken is pierced.

VARIATION

Mojo Chicken: Omit Chipotle Mojo Chicken marinade. In small saucepan, warm ¼ cup (50 mL) olive oil. In bowl, stir together 4 cloves garlic, minced, 1 jalapeño pepper, seeded and minced, 3 tbsp (50 mL) lime juice, 1 tbsp (15 mL) sherry or wine vinegar, 2 tsp (10 mL) ground cumin and ¼ tsp (1 mL) each salt and pepper. Whisk in warm oil; let cool. Add chicken and marinate as above.

Makes 4 servings.

PER SERVING, ABOUT:

cal	422	carb	4 g
pro	25 g	fibre	trace
total fat	34 g	chol	108 mg
sat. fat	7 g	sodium	314 mg

PERCENTAGE RDI:

calcium	2%	vit. A	13%
iron	9%	vit. C	12%
folate	5%		

MAKE-AHEAD BUDGET-WISE

Portuguese Paprika Chicken

Paprika and tomato paste put a burnish on grilled chicken and make it taste like takeout chicken from Portuguese barbecue restaurants. The Piri Piri Chicken variation is a hotter version thanks to hot pepper.

2 lb	chicken pieces	1 kg

PORTUGUESE PAPRIKA MARINADE:

⅓ cup	dry white wine	75 mL
1 tsp	grated lemon rind	5 mL
3 tbsp	lemon juice	50 mL
2 tbsp	tomato paste	25 mL

1 tbsp	olive oil	15 mL
½ tsp	paprika	2 mL
¼ tsp	salt	1 mL
¼ tsp	hot pepper sauce	1 mL
2	cloves garlic, minced	2

1 PORTUGUESE PAPRIKA MARINADE: In glass bowl, combine wine, lemon rind and juice, tomato paste, oil, paprika, salt, hot pepper sauce and garlic; add chicken, turning to coat. Cover and refrigerate for 4 hours, turning occasionally. (MAKE-AHEAD: **Refrigerate for up to 24 hours.**)

2 Reserving marinade, place chicken, skin side down, on greased grill over medium heat; close lid and cook for 10 minutes. Turn and brush with marinade; cook for 30 to 40 minutes or until juices run clear when chicken is pierced.

VARIATION

Piri Piri Chicken: Omit Portuguese Paprika Marinade. In glass bowl, combine 2 tbsp (25 mL) grated lemon rind, 3 tbsp (50 mL) lemon juice, 10 cloves garlic, minced, 2 tbsp (25 mL) olive oil, 2 tsp (10 mL) hot pepper flakes and ½ tsp (2 mL) salt; add chicken and marinate as above.

Makes 4 servings.

PER SERVING, ABOUT:

cal	425	carb	3 g
pro	41 g	fibre	1 g
total fat	26 g	chol	153 mg
sat. fat	7 g	sodium	281 mg

PERCENTAGE RDI:

calcium	2%	vit. A	11%
iron	12%	vit. C	15%
folate	5%		

QUICK   MAKE-
         AHEAD

Grilled Stuffed Chicken Breasts Many Ways

Chicken is a natural at absorbing different taste accents when it's marinated or glazed or, maybe even better, when it's stuffed. The bonus? A surprise inside each portion.

1	roasted sweet red pepper	1	4 tsp	grainy mustard	20 mL
4	boneless skinless chicken breasts	4	8	fresh basil leaves	8
¼ tsp	each salt and pepper	1 mL	¼ cup	shredded Fontina cheese	50 mL

1 Peel red pepper; cut into quarters, coring and removing seeds.

2 With sharp knife held horizontally and starting at thinner side, cut chicken in half almost but not all the way through; open like book. Sprinkle with pinch of the salt and pepper. Spread 1 side of each with 1 tsp (5 mL) mustard; top with red pepper piece, 2 basil leaves and 1 tbsp (15 mL) Fontina cheese. Fold uncovered side over; secure edge with small skewer or toothpicks. (MAKE-AHEAD: Place on waxed paper–lined rimmed baking sheet. Cover and refrigerate for up to 8 hours.) Sprinkle each with remaining salt and pepper.

3 Place chicken on greased grill over medium-high heat or under broiler; close lid and cook, turning once, for about 12 minutes or until golden brown and chicken is no longer pink inside.

VARIATIONS

Prosciutto-Stuffed Chicken Breasts: Divide equally among 4 split and opened chicken breasts 2 tbsp (25 mL) grainy mustard, 2 cloves garlic, minced, ¼ tsp (1 mL) pepper, 8 basil leaves and 4 thin slices prosciutto. Or omit prosciutto from filling and use to wrap chicken breasts.

Sage and Lemon Chicken Breasts: Divide equally among 4 split and opened chicken breasts 2 tsp (10 mL) Dijon mustard, 1 tsp (5 mL) grated lemon rind, ¼ tsp (1 mL) pepper and 4 fresh sage leaves, chopped.

Cordon Bleu Chicken Breasts: Divide equally among 4 split and opened chicken breasts 2 tsp (10 mL) Dijon mustard, ¼ tsp (1 mL) pepper, 4 thin slices Black Forest ham, folded, and ¼ cup (50 mL) shredded Gruyère or Swiss cheese.

Makes 4 servings.

PER SERVING, ABOUT:

cal	194	carb	2 g
pro	35 g	fibre	trace
total fat	5 g	chol	92 mg
sat. fat	2 g	sodium	340 mg

PERCENTAGE RDI:

calcium	5%	vit. A	10%
iron	6%	vit. C	52%
folate	4%		

Peking Hamburger Dumplings

(PAGE 32)

Baked Brie with Strawberry Mint Topping (top)

(PAGE 18)

Stuffed Jalapeño Peppers (bottom)

(PAGE 19)

Cuban Grilled Pork Sandwich

(PAGE 170)

Simply the Best Scalloped Potatoes

(PAGE 88)

Roasted Roots Salad (top left)

(PAGE 74)

Baby Spinach and Goat Cheese Salad (top right)

(PAGE 67)

Herbed Rösti (bottom left)

(PAGE 89)

Bread Salad (bottom right)

(PAGE 70)

Dutch Meatball Soup (top)

(PAGE 60)

Mediterranean Seafood Soup (bottom)

(PAGE 52)

Roast Chicken with Lemon and Garlic

(PAGE 102)

Salsa Barbecued Beef Brisket

(PAGE 153)

Ginger Chicken and Green Onion Kabobs

To eat well with a minimum of effort, try these tender kabobs. Sparked with fresh ginger, they take only minutes to thread onto skewers and sizzle on the grill or under the broiler.

9	green onions	9
3 tbsp	oyster sauce	50 mL
2 tsp	minced gingerroot	10 mL
1½ tsp	each vegetable oil and water	7 mL

1 lb	boneless skinless chicken breasts	500 g
1	lemon or lime, cut in wedges	1

TEST KITCHEN TIP: Soak bamboo skewers in cold water for 30 minutes before threading to prevent charring on the grill.

1 Finely chop white part and most of green part of 2 of the green onions to make about ¼ cup (50 mL); place in small bowl. Stir in oyster sauce, ginger, oil and water; set aside.

2 Cut remaining green onions into 1-inch (2.5 cm) lengths. Cut chicken into bite-size cubes. Alternately thread onions and chicken onto soaked bamboo skewers. Brush with all of the ginger mixture. (MAKE-AHEAD: Cover and refrigerate for up to 4 hours.)

3 Place on greased grill over medium-high heat or under broiler; close lid and cook, turning once, for about 6 minutes or until chicken is browned and no longer pink inside. Serve with lemon wedges to squeeze over top.

Makes 4 servings.

PER SERVING, ABOUT:

cal	193	carb	5 g
pro	33 g	fibre	1 g
total fat	4 g	chol	84 mg
sat. fat	1 g	sodium	407 mg

PERCENTAGE RDI:

calcium	3%	vit. A	2%
iron	8%	vit. C	15%
folate	10%		

Parmesan Chicken Burgers

You can cook these patties in a lightly greased skillet, on the grill or under the broiler.

TEST KITCHEN TIP: You can top chicken and turkey burgers that contain Parmesan cheese with a fresh bruschetta topping. Here's how: stir together 1 tomato, cored and chopped, 1 clove garlic, minced, 1 tbsp (15 mL) chopped fresh basil, 1 tbsp (15 mL) wine vinegar, 4 tsp (20 mL) olive oil and pinch each salt and pepper. Spoon over patties and sprinkle lightly with additional grated Parmesan cheese.

1 lb	ground chicken	500 g
⅔ cup	dry bread crumbs	150 mL
½ cup	chopped green onions	125 mL
2 tbsp	chopped fresh parsley	25 mL
1 tbsp	grated Parmesan cheese	15 mL
2 tsp	dry mustard	10 mL
1	egg, beaten	1
½ tsp	salt	2 mL
¼ tsp	pepper	1 mL
1 tbsp	vegetable oil	15 mL

1 In large bowl, mix together chicken, bread crumbs, onions, parsley, Parmesan cheese, mustard, egg, salt and pepper. Form into 6 patties. (MAKE-AHEAD: Cover and refrigerate for up to 2 hours or layer between waxed paper in airtight container and freeze for up to 2 weeks.)

2 In nonstick skillet, heat oil over medium heat or heat barbecue grill to medium; cook patties for 5 to 6 minutes per side or until golden brown and no longer pink inside.

VARIATIONS

Basil Parmesan Chicken Burgers: Reduce parsley to 1 tbsp (15 mL) and add up to 1 tbsp (15 mL) chopped fresh basil or Pesto (page 235).

Cajun Chicken Burgers: Omit Parmesan cheese; add 2 tsp (10 mL) Cajun seasoning.

Turkey Burgers: Substitute ground turkey for chicken in any of the variations.

Makes 6 patties.

PER PATTY, ABOUT:
cal 238   carb . . . . 10 g
pro . . . . 16 g   fibre . . . . 1 g
total fat . . . . 14 g   chol . . . . . . 95 mg
sat. fat . . . . . . 4 g   sodium . . 373 mg

PERCENTAGE RDI:
calcium . . . . . 6%   vit. A 5%
iron . . . . 14%   vit. C 7%
folate 7%

Chicken and Seafood Paella

A picnic dish from Valencia, Spain, where it is traditionally cooked over a campfire, paella has turned into a popular party dish in Canada. And it's no wonder, with its combination of seafood, chicken, saffron-scented rice, and spicy sausage for good measure.

8 oz	chorizo sausage	250 g
4	chicken legs	4
1 tbsp	olive oil	15 mL
¼ tsp	saffron threads	1 mL
3 cups	warm chicken stock	750 mL
1	onion, chopped	1
2	cloves garlic, minced	2
1	can (28 oz/796 mL) tomatoes	1

1	small sweet green pepper, diced	1
1½ cups	short-grain rice	375 mL
½ tsp	each salt and pepper	2 mL
½ cup	frozen peas	125 mL
12 oz	large raw shrimp	375 g
12 oz	mussels	375 g
2	green onions, minced	2
8	lemon wedges	8

1 Cut sausage into ½-inch (1 cm) thick slices. Remove skin from chicken; trim off fat. Cut through each chicken leg at joint to separate thigh from drumstick.

2 In large paella pan or deep wide skillet, heat oil over high heat; cook sausage, stirring, for about 2 minutes or until browned. Transfer to platter. Add chicken to pan; cook over medium heat for 7 to 10 minutes per side or until browned. Add to platter.

3 Stir saffron into chicken stock; set aside. Add onion and garlic to pan; cook, stirring, for 4 minutes or until softened. Add stock mixture, tomatoes and green pepper; bring to boil, breaking up tomatoes with spoon and stirring to scrape up any brown bits from bottom of pan. Stir in rice, salt and pepper. Add chicken; simmer gently over low heat, stirring often, for 20 minutes. Gently stir in peas and sausage.

4 Meanwhile, peel and devein shrimp. Scrub mussels under running water. Trim off any beards. Discard any mussels with cracked shells or ones that do not close when tapped. Nestle shrimp and mussels in rice until almost covered; cook over low heat for 7 to 10 minutes or until rice is tender, shrimp are pink and mussels are open. Discard any mussels that do not open. Garnish with onions and lemon wedges.

TEST KITCHEN TIP: Make a fluffier paella with parboiled long-grain rice; cook, covered, adding ½ cup (125 mL) more stock near end of cooking to prevent sticking.

SUBSTITUTION: Varying the dish is easy: use clams instead of mussels, or omit the seafood altogether and double up on the chicken. If you can't find chorizo, use any spicy Mediterranean sausage.

Makes 8 servings.

PER SERVING, ABOUT:

cal	458	carb	40 g
pro	33 g	fibre	2 g
total fat	18 g	chol	131 mg
sat. fat	6 g	sodium	1,093 mg

PERCENTAGE RDI:

calcium	5%	vit. A	10%
iron	25%	vit. C	42%
folate	15%		

Old-Fashioned Chicken Pot Pie

There's nothing old-fashioned about the comfort and joy this dish offers everyone who draws up a chair around your table.

4 cups	chicken stock (approx)	1 L
4 lb	chicken thighs, skinned (about 14)	2 kg
1	bunch small carrots (about 7), peeled	1
4	potatoes, peeled and cut in 1-inch (2.5 cm) cubes	4
2 cups	pearl onions (1 bag/284 g), peeled	500 mL
3 tbsp	butter	50 mL
1	onion, chopped	1
3	stalks celery, chopped	3
2 cups	small mushrooms (8 oz/250 g)	500 mL
⅓ cup	all-purpose flour	75 mL

1 tsp	dried thyme	5 mL
½ tsp	each salt and pepper	2 mL
½ cup	frozen peas	125 mL
¼ cup	whipping cream	50 mL

BISCUIT TOPPING:

2 cups	all-purpose flour	500 mL
2 tbsp	finely chopped fresh parsley	25 mL
4 tsp	baking powder	20 mL
1 tsp	salt	5 mL
½ cup	cold butter	125 mL
¾ cup	milk	175 mL
1	egg yolk	1

1 In stockpot, bring stock to boil. Add chicken thighs; cover and simmer over medium-low heat for 30 minutes or until juices run clear when chicken is pierced. With slotted spoon, transfer chicken to plate; let cool. Remove chicken meat from bones; cut into bite-size chunks and set aside.

2 Meanwhile, cut carrots in half attractively on the diagonal. Add to pot along with potatoes; cook, covered, for 10 minutes. Add pearl onions; simmer for 5 minutes or just until tender. Drain in colander, reserving stock. You should have 4 cups (1 L); add more stock if necessary.

3 In clean stockpot, melt butter over medium-high heat; cook chopped onion, celery and mushrooms, stirring often, for about 8 minutes or until softened. Add flour, thyme, salt and pepper; cook, stirring, for 1 minute. Gradually whisk in reserved stock; bring to boil, stirring. Reduce heat and simmer, stirring often, for 5 minutes or until thick enough to coat back of spoon. Stir in chicken, potato mixture, peas and cream. (MAKE-AHEAD: Let cool for 30 minutes; refrigerate, uncovered, in shallow containers until cold. Cover and refrigerate for up to 1 day. Reheat over low heat.) Spoon into 12-cup (3 L) casserole dish.

Makes 8 servings.

4 BISCUIT TOPPING: In large bowl, combine flour, parsley, baking powder and salt. Using pastry blender or 2 knives, cut in butter until mixture resembles coarse crumbs. With fork, stir in milk until soft slightly sticky dough forms. Knead on floured surface 10 times or until smooth. Pat into 8-inch (20 cm) round about ½ inch (1 cm) thick. Using 2-inch (5 cm) cookie cutter, cut out rounds, pressing scraps together to use all dough. Place on top of pot pie. Mix egg yolk with 1 tbsp (15 mL) water. Brush over biscuits. Place casserole on rimmed baking sheet; bake in 400°F (200°C) oven for 20 minutes or until bubbly and biscuits are golden and no longer doughy underneath.

TOPPING VARIATIONS

Instead of Biscuit Topping, use any of the following:

Pastry: Use enough pastry for a double-crust pie (see Perfect Pastry Every Time, page 326). Roll out and trim to fit top of dish. With cookie cutter, cut steam vents in top. Mix 1 egg yolk with 1 tbsp (15 mL) water; brush over pastry. Roll out trimmed pastry scraps to make decorative cutouts. Position cutouts on pastry. Brush with egg mixture. Bake as directed.

Puff Pastry: Roll out 1 pkg (411 g) puff pastry to fit top of dish. With cookie cutter, cut steam vents; glaze and bake as directed for pastry.

Phyllo Topping: Place 1 of 7 sheets of phyllo pastry on work surface, keeping remaining phyllo covered with damp towel to prevent drying out. Brush lightly with some of ¼ cup (50 mL) butter, melted. Scrunch gently with fingertips to form oval; place over chicken filling. Repeat with remaining phyllo and butter. Bake as directed.

Dumplings: When making sauce (Step 3), increase stock to 5 cups (1.25 L) to provide enough liquid for dumplings. In bowl, combine 2 cups (500 mL) sifted cake-and-pastry flour, 2 tbsp (25 mL) chopped fresh parsley, 4 tsp (20 mL) baking powder and ½ tsp (2 mL) salt. Using pastry blender or fingers, cut in 2 tbsp (25 mL) butter. Using fork, add 1 cup (250 mL) milk and stir until sticky dough forms. Drop by tablespoonfuls (15 mL) into simmering stew, spacing evenly. Cover and boil gently for about 15 minutes without lifting lid or until dumplings are no longer doughy underneath.

Beef

5

Steak and Vegetable Fajitas 126
Beef and Broccoli Stir-Fry 127
Pan-Seared Liver and Onions 128
Old-Fashioned Beef Stew 129
Beef Bourguignonne with Noodles 130
Sauerbraten Beef Stew 131
Herb and Onion Swiss Steak 132
People's Choice Chili 133
Cabbage Rolls 134
Meatloaf Many Ways 136
Easy Roast Beef with Onion Gravy 137
Strip Loin with Exotic Mushrooms and Shallots 138
Devilled Prime Rib with Roasted Garlic Gravy 139
Deluxe Roasted Beef Tenderloin 140
Onion Cranberry Brisket 141
Classic Pot Roast with Vegetables 142
Koftas with Cucumber Yogurt Salad 143
Best Burgers 144
Warm Grilled Flank Steak Salad 145
Party Sirloin 146
Tender T-Bones 147
Red Wine and Oregano Grilled Marinating Steak 148
Korean Beef Short Ribs 149
Mustard Devilled Ribs 150
Ginger Soy Beef Kabobs 151
Rib Eye on the Rotisserie 152
Salsa Barbecued Beef Brisket 153

Steak and Vegetable Fajitas

This recipe has "make it tonight" written all over it: it's quick, uses regular super-market ingredients and features family-pleasing tastes. Even better, it's easy enough for the first one in the door to prep and cook.

TEST KITCHEN TIP: Use this recipe as a guide for making pork or chicken fajitas.

1 tbsp	vegetable oil	15 mL
12 oz	beef stir-fry strips	375 g
1	onion, sliced	1
2	carrots, halved lengthwise and sliced	2
1	sweet red pepper, sliced	1
1	zucchini, halved lengthwise and sliced	1
3	cloves garlic, minced	3

2 tsp	chili powder	10 mL
½ tsp	salt	2 mL
¼ tsp	ground cumin	1 mL
½ cup	salsa	125 mL
2 tbsp	lime juice	25 mL
Dash	hot pepper sauce	Dash
8	large flour tortillas	8

1 In large nonstick skillet, heat oil over medium-high heat; stir-fry beef in batches for 2 to 3 minutes or until browned but still pink inside. Transfer to plate.

2 Add onion and carrots to skillet; cook, stirring occasionally, for 5 minutes or until onion is softened. Add red pepper, zucchini, garlic, chili powder, salt and cumin; cook for 3 minutes or until red pepper is tender-crisp.

3 Add salsa, lime juice and hot pepper sauce. Return beef and any accumulated juices to pan; cook for 1 minute or until hot.

4 Meanwhile, stack tortillas and wrap in foil; bake in 350°F (180°C) oven for 8 to 10 minutes or until warmed. Wrap beef mixture in tortillas.

Makes 4 servings.

PER SERVING, ABOUT:

cal 577	carb . . . . 76 g
pro . . . . 31 g	fibre . . . . 7 g
total fat . . . . 16 g	chol . . . . . . 42 mg
sat. fat . . . . . . 3 g	sodium 1,010 mg

PERCENTAGE RDI:

calcium 9%	vit. A 109%
iron 47%	vit. C 102%
folate 19%	

Beef and Broccoli Stir-Fry

The sauce for this star stir-fry is a vibrant balance of sweet, salty and sour — with a touch of heat. Use this recipe as a model for making chicken and pork stir-fries.

8 oz	top sirloin grilling steak	250 g
1 tsp	cornstarch	5 mL
2 tbsp	vegetable oil	25 mL
1	onion, thinly sliced	1
3	cloves garlic, minced	3
1 tbsp	minced gingerroot	15 mL
4 cups	coarsely chopped broccoli	1 L

SAUCE:		
²⁄₃ cup	chicken stock	150 mL
¼ cup	hoisin sauce	50 mL
2 tbsp	each oyster sauce and soy sauce	25 mL
4 tsp	cornstarch	20 mL
1 tbsp	rice vinegar	15 mL
1 tsp	sesame oil	5 mL
½ tsp	Asian chili paste or hot pepper sauce	2 mL

TEST KITCHEN TIP: Serve with half a package (450 g) precooked Chinese noodles. Separate, rinse in hot water, and toss them in at the end of cooking and heat through. Or serve with rice.

1 SAUCE: In bowl or glass measure, whisk together stock, hoisin, oyster and soy sauces, cornstarch, vinegar, sesame oil and chili paste. Set aside.

2 Cut beef across the grain into thin strips. Toss with cornstarch. In wok or large deep skillet, heat 1 tbsp (15 mL) of the oil over high heat; stir-fry beef for 3 minutes or until browned but still pink inside. Transfer to bowl. Add remaining oil to wok; stir-fry onion, garlic and ginger for 1 minute.

3 Add broccoli and ½ cup (125 mL) water. Cover and steam for about 3 minutes or until broccoli is tender-crisp. Pour in sauce; stir-fry for 1 to 2 minutes or until sauce is thickened. Stir in beef and any accumulated juices; stir-fry for 1 minute.

Makes 2 servings.

PER SERVING, ABOUT:

cal 491	carb . . . . 40 g
pro . . . . 34 g	fibre . . . . 6 g
total fat . . . . 23 g	chol . . . . . . 55 mg
sat. fat . . . . . . 3 g	sodium 2,369 mg

PERCENTAGE RDI:

calcium 13%	vit. A 25%
iron 36%	vit. C 227%
folate 54%	

Pan-Seared Liver and Onions

The combination of liver and onions can't be beat. So why argue? But that doesn't mean you can't dress it up with impressive sage and balsamic highlights, or try the equally tasty apple mustard or mushroom bacon variations.

3 tbsp	vegetable oil	50 mL
6	onions, sliced	6
½ tsp	dried sage	2 mL
½ tsp	each salt and pepper	2 mL
1 lb	calves' or beef liver (½ inch/1 cm thick)	500 g

¼ cup	all-purpose flour	50 mL
½ cup	beef stock	125 mL
2 tbsp	balsamic or red wine vinegar	25 mL
1½ tsp	granulated sugar	7 mL
¼ cup	chopped fresh parsley	50 mL

1 In large heavy skillet, heat 1 tbsp (15 mL) of the oil over medium heat; cook onions, sage and half each of the salt and pepper, stirring often, for 8 minutes or until softened. Reduce heat to medium-low; cook, stirring occasionally, for 20 minutes or until deep golden. Remove and keep warm.

2 Meanwhile, peel away any membrane on liver by loosening with sharp knife and gently pulling away from meat. Trim any tough blood vessels. In shallow dish, combine flour and remaining salt and pepper; set aside.

3 Rinse and dry skillet; heat remaining oil over medium-high heat. Dredge liver with flour mixture to coat, shaking off excess; immediately add to skillet. Sauté liver, in batches if necessary, for 1 to 2 minutes or until underside is browned and blood is just coming to surface. Turn and cook for 1 to 2 minutes longer or until browned, slightly pink inside and still springy to the touch. Remove to heated serving plates.

4 Add stock, vinegar and sugar to skillet; bring to boil, stirring and scraping up any brown bits. Boil, stirring, for 1 to 2 minutes or until reduced to about ⅓ cup (75 mL). Mound onions over liver; top with sauce. Sprinkle with parsley.

Makes 4 servings.

PER SERVING, ABOUT:

cal 354	carb . . . . 29 g
pro . . . . 26 g	fibre . . . . 3 g
total fat . . . . 15 g	chol . . . . . 401 mg
sat. fat . . . . . . 3 g	sodium . . 440 mg

PERCENTAGE RDI:

calcium 4%	vit. A 895%
iron 62%	vit. C 48%
folate 99%	

VARIATIONS

Pan-Seared Liver with Apple and Mustard: Substitute 3 unpeeled apples, sliced, and ¼ cup (50 mL) chopped shallots for onions and sage; cook over medium heat for 10 to 15 minutes or until tender. Substitute ½ cup (125 mL) apple juice, ¼ cup (50 mL) white wine and 2 tbsp (25 mL) Dijon mustard for beef stock, vinegar and sugar.

Pan-Seared Liver with Mushroom and Bacon: Cook 4 slices bacon until crisp, reserving fat to use instead of oil; crumble bacon for garnish. Substitute 4 cups (1 L) sliced mushrooms for sliced onions and sage; sauté for 5 minutes or until tender, adding juices to stock.

Old-Fashioned Beef Stew

In this streamlined version of a time-honoured stew, the browning step has been omitted and, interestingly, there's still plenty of beef flavour.

4	large carrots	4
2	stalks celery	2
Half	small rutabaga	Half
1½ lb	cross rib or blade simmering steak (1½ inches/4 cm thick)	750 g
1 tbsp	vegetable oil	15 mL
3	onions, quartered	3
2	large cloves garlic, minced	2
½ tsp	each dried thyme and marjoram	2 mL

¼ cup	all-purpose flour	50 mL
1 cup	beef stock	250 mL
1 cup	dry red wine or beef stock	250 mL
1	can (19 oz/540 mL) tomatoes	1
3	large potatoes, peeled and cut in chunks	3
1 cup	frozen peas	250 mL
½ tsp	each salt and pepper	2 mL
2 tbsp	chopped fresh parsley	25 mL

1 Peel carrots; cut carrots and celery into 2-inch (5 cm) chunks. To peel rutabaga, place flat side down on cutting board; cut away peel with paring knife, then cut into 2-inch (5 cm) chunks.

2 Trim fat from steak. Slice meat into 1½-inch (4 cm) wide strips; cut crosswise into 1½-inch (4 cm) cubes.

3 In large Dutch oven, heat oil over medium heat; cook onions, stirring occasionally, for about 5 minutes or until lightly coloured. Add garlic, thyme and marjoram; cook, stirring, for 1 minute. Add beef, carrots, celery and rutabaga; sprinkle with flour and cook, stirring, for about 1 minute or until flour is well moistened.

4 Stir in stock, wine and tomatoes, breaking up tomatoes with spoon; bring to boil. Cover and bake in 325°F (160°C) oven for 1½ hours. (MAKE-AHEAD: Let cool slightly; transfer to shallow airtight container. Finish cooling, uncovered, in refrigerator. Cover and refrigerate for up to 2 days or freeze for up to 1 month. Thaw and finish baking, adding about 15 minutes.)

5 Stir in potatoes; cover and bake, stirring once, for 60 to 75 minutes or until meat and potatoes are fork-tender. Stir in peas, salt and pepper; cook until heated through, about 2 minutes. Sprinkle with parsley.

VARIATION

Slow-Cooker Beef Stew:
Prepare vegetables and beef and cook onions, garlic and seasoning in Dutch oven as directed. Transfer beef, vegetables and flour to slow-cooker; stir in stock, wine, tomatoes and potatoes. Cover and cook on Low for 8 to 10 hours or until beef is tender. Stir in peas, salt and pepper; heat through. Sprinkle with parsley.

Makes 8 servings.

PER SERVING, ABOUT:

cal	292	carb	32 g
pro	23 g	fibre	5 g
total fat	8 g	chol	43 mg
sat. fat	2 g	sodium	467 mg

PERCENTAGE RDI:

calcium	8%	vit. A	108%
iron	24%	vit. C	40%
folate	23%		

Beef Bourguignonne with Noodles

Dishes such as Burgundy-style beef with mushrooms and red wine are classics for good reason: they deliver exceptional taste to generation after generation of diners.

TEST KITCHEN TIP: A cross-rib, blade or shoulder pot roast is often an economical cut of beef for stews. Trim and cube at home, reserving any extra to freeze and stew later.

3 lb	beef stewing cubes	1.5 kg
2 tbsp	vegetable oil	25 mL
1	Spanish onion, minced	1
7 cups	halved mushrooms (1½ lb/750 g)	1.75 L
3	cloves garlic, minced	3
½ tsp	dried thyme	2 mL

½ tsp	each salt and pepper	2 mL
¼ cup	all-purpose flour	50 mL
1½ cups	red wine	375 mL
1½ cups	hot beef stock	375 mL
1	bay leaf	1
1½ lb	noodles or other pasta	750 g
1 tbsp	chopped fresh parsley	15 mL

1 Trim fat from beef. In Dutch oven, heat 1 tbsp (15 mL) of the oil over medium-high heat; brown beef in batches, adding remaining oil as necessary. Transfer to plate.

2 Add onion, mushrooms, garlic, thyme, salt and pepper to pan; cook over medium heat, stirring occasionally, for about 8 minutes or until softened and liquid is evaporated.

3 Return beef and any accumulated juices to pan. Sprinkle with flour; cook, stirring, for 1 minute. Add wine, stock and bay leaf; bring to boil. Reduce heat, cover and simmer for 2½ hours. Uncover and cook for 30 minutes or until thickened and meat is tender. Discard bay leaf. (MAKE-AHEAD: Let cool slightly; transfer to shallow airtight container. Finish cooling, uncovered, in refrigerator. Cover and refrigerate for up to 2 days or freeze for up to 1 month.)

4 Meanwhile, in large pot of boiling salted water, cook noodles for 8 to 10 minutes or until tender but firm; drain well. Divide among plates. Spoon bourguignonne over top; sprinkle with parsley.

Makes 6 to 8 servings.

PER EACH OF 8 SERVINGS, ABOUT:

cal 682	carb . . . . 72 g
pro . . . . 52 g	fibre . . . . 8 g
total fat . . . . 20 g	chol . . . . . 163 mg
sat. fat . . . . . . 5 g	sodium . . 799 mg

PERCENTAGE RDI:

calcium 6%	vit. A 2%
iron 65%	vit. C 8%
folate 86%	

VARIATION

Slow-Cooker Beef Bourguignonne: Brown beef as directed; transfer to slow-cooker. In same pan, cook onion, mushrooms and seasonings as directed. Transfer to slow-cooker. Toss with flour. Add wine to pan and bring to boil over high heat; boil, stirring and scraping up any brown bits from bottom of pan, for about 3 minutes. Add to slow-cooker along with stock and bay leaf. Cover and cook on Low for 6 to 8 hours or until beef is tender. Discard bay leaf.

Sauerbraten Beef Stew

MAKE-AHEAD FREEZABLE BUDGET-WISE

Gingersnaps and cider vinegar give a sweet-and-tangy touch to this cold-weather stew of German origin. Mashed potatoes and braised red cabbage or cabbage salad are stellar accompaniments.

2 lb	beef stewing cubes	1 kg
4 tsp	vegetable oil	20 mL
2	onions, chopped	2
2½ cups	beef stock or water	625 mL
½ cup	cider vinegar	125 mL
¼ cup	packed brown sugar	50 mL
2	bay leaves	2

¼ tsp	each salt and pepper	1 mL
Pinch	each ground allspice and cloves	Pinch
4	large carrots, thickly sliced	4
½ cup	crushed gingersnap cookies	125 mL
¼ cup	raisins	50 mL

TEST KITCHEN TIP: Brown meat in batches; adding too much meat to the skillet at one time will cause meat to steam, not brown nicely.

1 Cut stewing cubes into 1-inch (2.5 cm) pieces. In Dutch oven, heat half of the oil over high heat; brown beef in batches, adding remaining oil as needed. Transfer to plate and set aside.

2 Pour off any fat from pan. Reduce heat to medium-low; cook onions, stirring occasionally, for 5 minutes or until softened. Return beef to pan; add stock, vinegar, sugar, bay leaves, salt, pepper, allspice and cloves. Bring to boil; reduce heat, cover and simmer for 1 hour.

3 Add carrots; simmer, covered, for about 20 minutes or until tender. Add gingersnaps and raisins; simmer for 5 minutes or until thickened. Discard bay leaves. (MAKE-AHEAD: Let cool slightly; transfer to shallow airtight container. Finish cooling, uncovered, in refrigerator. Cover and refrigerate for up to 2 days or freeze for up to 1 month.)

VARIATION

Slow-Cooker Sauerbraten Beef Stew: Brown beef and cook onions as directed; transfer to slow-cooker. Pour stock into Dutch oven; cook, stirring and scraping up any brown bits from bottom of pan, for 4 minutes. Pour into slow-cooker along with vinegar, sugar, bay leaves, salt, pepper, allspice and cloves. Cover and cook on Low for 5 hours or until beef is beginning to become tender. Stir in carrots, gingersnaps and raisins; cook on High for 1 to 2 hours or until beef and carrots are tender. Discard bay leaves.

Makes 6 servings.

PER SERVING, ABOUT:

cal	437	carb	35 g
pro	36 g	fibre	3 g
total fat	17 g	chol	84 mg
sat. fat	6 g	sodium	640 mg

PERCENTAGE RDI:

calcium	6%	vit. A	152%
iron	34%	vit. C	5%
folate	11%		

MAKE-AHEAD · FREEZABLE · BUDGET-WISE

Herb and Onion Swiss Steak

There's traditional comfort and robust flavour in this dish of tomato-simmered round steak. You can vary the herb according to what's in your pantry: oregano, basil, or an Italian or Provençal mix.

TEST KITCHEN TIP: Instead of wine, you can use more beef stock plus 2 tsp (10 mL) wine vinegar or cider vinegar.

¼ cup	all-purpose flour	50 mL
¼ tsp	each salt and pepper	1 mL
1 lb	inside round marinating steak	500 g
1 tbsp	vegetable oil	15 mL
2	onions, sliced	2
2	cloves garlic, sliced	2

2	carrots, sliced	2
1½ tsp	dried marjoram	7 mL
¼ cup	tomato paste	50 mL
¾ cup	beef stock (approx)	175 mL
½ cup	dry white wine	125 mL
¼ cup	chopped fresh parsley	50 mL

1 In large heavy plastic bag, shake together flour, salt and pepper. Cut steak into 8 pieces. Place steak, 1 piece at a time, in bag and seal; pound with meat mallet to ¼-inch (5 mm) thickness, working flour mixture into meat. Reserve any remaining flour mixture.

2 In Dutch oven, heat oil over medium-high heat; brown steaks well on both sides, in batches if necessary.

3 Reduce heat to low. Add onions, garlic, carrots, marjoram and any remaining flour mixture. Whisk tomato paste into stock; pour into pan along with wine.

4 Cover and cook over very low heat, turning steaks halfway through and adding up to ¼ cup (50 mL) more stock if necessary to thin sauce, for about 2 hours or until tender. Skim off any fat. (MAKE-AHEAD: Let cool slightly; transfer to shallow airtight container. Finish cooling, uncovered, in refrigerator. Cover and refrigerate for up to 2 days or freeze for up to 1 month.) Serve sprinkled with parsley.

Makes 4 servings.

PER SERVING, ABOUT:

cal 272	carb . . . . 19 g
pro . . . . 29 g	fibre . . . . 3 g
total fat . . . . . 9 g	chol . . . . . . 50 mg
sat. fat . . . . . . 2 g	sodium . . 391 mg

PERCENTAGE RDI:

calcium 5%	vit. A 97%
iron 28%	vit. C 25%
folate 17%	

VARIATIONS

Slow-Cooker Herb and Onion Swiss Steak: In skillet, brown meat as in first 2 steps; transfer to slow-cooker. Whisk tomato paste into stock; pour into skillet along with wine and bring to boil, stirring and scraping up any brown bits. Pour into slow-cooker. Add remaining ingredients. Cover and cook on Low for 6 to 8 hours or until tender.

Pressure Cooker Herb and Onion Swiss Steak: Increase stock to 1¼ cups (300 mL) and wine to ¾ cup (175 mL). Using pressure cooker, follow first 3 steps. Secure lid; bring to High pressure over high heat. Reduce heat to just maintain High pressure; cook for 15 minutes. Let pressure release completely, about 10 minutes.

People's Choice Chili

For years, this mild, smoky chili has been the people's pick at the Heartburn Day chili cook-off in Stratford, Ontario; proceeds go to the Heart and Stroke Foundation. There's no chili powder, but you can add a spoonful with the beef.

7	slices lean bacon	7
1 lb	lean ground beef	500 g
1	onion, chopped	1
1	can (19 oz/540 mL) tomatoes	1
1	can (14 oz/398 mL) kidney beans, drained and rinsed	1
1	can (14 oz/398 mL) pork and beans	1

1	clove garlic, minced	1
⅓ cup	vinegar	75 mL
2 tbsp	packed brown sugar	25 mL
2 tbsp	fancy molasses	25 mL
1 tsp	dry mustard	5 mL
1 tsp	Worcestershire sauce	5 mL
½ tsp	salt	2 mL
¼ tsp	pepper	1 mL
¼ tsp	hot pepper sauce	1 mL

1 In Dutch oven, cook bacon until crisp; drain on paper towels. Crumble; set aside. Drain fat from pan; increase heat to medium-high. Add beef and onion; cook, breaking up meat, for 10 minutes or until no longer pink. Drain off fat.

2 Return bacon to pan. Add tomatoes, kidney beans, pork and beans, garlic, vinegar, sugar, molasses, mustard, Worcestershire sauce, salt, pepper and hot pepper sauce; stir well. Cover and bake in 300°F (150°C) oven for 2 hours. Uncover and bake for 1 hour longer or until thickened. (MAKE-AHEAD: Let cool slightly; transfer to shallow airtight container. Finish cooling, uncovered, in refrigerator. Cover and refrigerate for up to 2 days or freeze for up to 1 month.)

VARIATION

Make-Again Chili: In Dutch oven, heat 2 tsp (10 mL) vegetable oil over medium-high heat; cook 1½ lb (750 g) lean ground beef, pork, chicken or turkey, breaking up, until no longer pink. Drain off fat. Reduce heat to medium; add 1 each large onion, stalk celery and carrot, chopped, 2 cloves garlic, minced, half jalapeño pepper, seeded and minced, 2 tbsp (25 mL) chili powder, 1 tsp (5 mL) each ground cumin and dried oregano, and ¼ tsp (1 mL) each salt and pepper. Cook for 5 minutes, stirring. Stir in 1 can (28 oz/796 mL) tomatoes, chopped, and 1 cup (250 mL) tomato sauce; bring to boil. Reduce heat to low and simmer for 15 minutes. Stir in 1 can (19 oz/540 mL) red kidney beans, drained and rinsed. Simmer for 15 minutes or until thick enough to mound on spoon. Sprinkle with ¼ cup (50 mL) chopped fresh coriander; top with shredded Cheddar cheese. (MAKE-AHEAD: Let cool slightly; transfer to shallow airtight container. Finish cooling, uncovered, in refrigerator. Cover and refrigerate for up to 2 days or freeze for up to 2 weeks.) **Makes 4 to 6 servings.**

Makes 4 servings.

PER SERVING, ABOUT:

cal	578	carb	59 g
pro	38 g	fibre	14 g
total fat	22 g	chol	75 mg
sat. fat	8 g	sodium	1,436 mg

PERCENTAGE RDI:

calcium	14%	vit. A	10%
iron	46%	vit. C	28%
folate	41%		

Cabbage Rolls

This is a very fine recipe for cabbage rolls, baked and enjoyed countless times since it was first published as a cooking lesson. Cabbage rolls are quintessential comfort food to the initiated, and a mellow surprise for those not yet having had the good fortune to enjoy them.

TEST KITCHEN TIP: To soften leaves, you can also microwave cabbage: Core and place 1 cabbage in 12-cup (3 L) casserole with 2 tbsp (25 mL) water; cover and microwave at High for 12 to 14 minutes or until leaves are softened.

2	heads cabbage (each 2 lb/1 kg)	2
1¼ cups	chicken stock	300 mL
½ cup	parboiled rice	125 mL
8	slices bacon, finely chopped	8
2 tbsp	butter	25 mL
3	onions, chopped	3
2	cloves garlic, minced	2
½ cup	finely chopped sweet red pepper	125 mL
1½ tsp	dried marjoram	7 mL
½ tsp	dried thyme	2 mL
1½ lb	lean ground beef	750 g
½ cup	chopped fresh parsley	125 mL
¾ tsp	salt	4 mL
½ tsp	pepper	2 mL
1	egg, beaten	1
1	can (28 oz/796 mL) sauerkraut, rinsed and squeezed dry	1
3 tbsp	packed brown sugar	50 mL
1	can (48 oz/1.36 L) tomato juice	1

1 Using sharp knife, remove core from cabbages. In large pot of boiling salted water, blanch cabbages, 1 at a time, for 5 to 8 minutes or until leaves are softened. Remove and chill in cold water. Remove a few outer leaves and set aside.

2 Working from core end, carefully remove 12 leaves from each cabbage, returning cabbage to boiling water for 2 to 3 minutes when leaves become difficult to remove. Drain on towels. Pare off coarse veins; set leaves aside.

3 Meanwhile, in saucepan, bring stock to boil; add rice. Reduce heat, cover and simmer for 15 to 20 minutes or until tender and stock is absorbed. Transfer to large bowl.

4 Meanwhile, in skillet, cook bacon over medium heat for about 5 minutes or until crisp; drain off fat. Add butter to skillet; cook onions, garlic, red pepper, marjoram and thyme for 5 minutes or until onions are softened. Add to rice along with beef, parsley, salt, pepper and egg; mix well. Spoon about ¼ cup (50 mL) onto each leaf just above stem end. Fold end over filling, then sides; roll up.

Makes 24 rolls, or 8 servings.

PER SERVING, ABOUT:

cal	392	carb	36 g
pro	24 g	fibre	7 g
total fat	18 g	chol	84 mg
sat. fat	7 g	sodium	1,721 mg

PERCENTAGE RDI:

calcium	11%	vit. A	18%
iron	37%	vit. C	112%
folate	40%		

5 Line 24-cup (6 L) roasting pan or Dutch oven with one-third of the sauerkraut; sprinkle with one-third of the sugar. Top with half of the cabbage rolls, seam side down; cover with one-third of the sauerkraut and one-third of the sugar. Repeat with remaining rolls, sauerkraut and sugar.

6 Pour tomato juice over rolls. Top with a few of the reserved outer leaves to prevent scorching. Cover and bake in 350°F (180°C) oven for 1½ hours. Uncover and bake for 30 minutes longer or until rolls are tender. Discard top leaves. (MAKE-AHEAD: Let cool slightly; transfer to shallow airtight container. Finish cooling, uncovered, in refrigerator. Cover and refrigerate for up to 1 day or freeze for up to 1 month. Thaw and reheat, covered, in 350°F /180°C oven for 1 hour or until bubbling and heated through.)

Which GROUND BEEF?

Ground beef is one of the least expensive and most versatile sources of high-quality protein. Regulations require that ground beef be labelled as either:

Extra-lean: a maximum fat content of 10%
Lean: a maximum fat content of 17%
Medium: a maximum fat content of 23%
Regular: a maximum fat content of 30%

EXTRA-LEAN/LEAN: Use in such recipes as cabbage rolls and meat loaf, in which the ground beef is not precooked and drained of fat before being added to other ingredients.

MEDIUM: Use in such recipes as hamburgers and meatballs, in which the ground beef is not cooked before other ingredients are added but in which the fat can be drained during cooking.

REGULAR: Use in such recipes as spaghetti sauce and tacos, in which the ground beef is cooked and fat is drained off before beef is combined with other ingredients.

Meatloaf Many Ways

Canadian Living *is proud of its reputation for delicious meat loaf recipes, none better than this master recipe with variations featuring tastes from around the world.*

	VEGETABLES	FLAVOURINGS	TOPPERS
Bistro Meat Loaf	10 cloves garlic, sliced; 1 tsp (5 mL) dried thyme; pinch salt	2 tbsp (25 mL) red wine vinegar	2 plum tomatoes, sliced
Lasagna Meat Loaf	1 sweet green pepper, chopped; 1 tsp (5 mL) dried basil	½ cup (125 mL) tomato sauce	⅓ cup (75 mL) tomato sauce; then ½ cup (125 mL) shredded Monterey Jack cheese
Chili Meat Loaf	1 sweet green pepper, chopped; 1 tbsp (15 mL) chili powder	1 cup (250 mL) drained red kidney beans; ½ cup (125 mL) salsa	½ cup (125 mL) shredded Cheddar cheese
Shepherd's Pie Meat Loaf	2 carrots, chopped	½ cup (125 mL) each peas and chili sauce	1½ cups (375 mL) mashed potatoes
Stroganoff Meat Loaf	2 cups (500 mL) sliced mushrooms; ½ tsp (2 mL) dried thyme	½ cup (125 mL) light sour cream; 1 tbsp (15 mL) Worcestershire sauce	1 tbsp (15 mL) Dijon mustard; then sprinkle of dried thyme

TEST KITCHEN TIPS

• For Speedy Mini Meat Loaves, shape beef mixture into 12 balls and place in muffin cups; add Toppers and bake in 400°F (200°C) oven for 20 to 25 minutes or until no longer pink inside.

• A meat loaf pan set is available with holes in the bottom of the inner one to let the fat drain off.

1 In large bowl and using fork, beat 1 egg; blend in ½ cup (125 mL) dry bread crumbs, ½ tsp (2 mL) salt and ¼ tsp (1 mL) pepper.

2 In large skillet, heat 2 tsp (10 mL) vegetable oil over medium-high heat. Add Vegetables in first column and 1 onion, chopped; cook for 3 minutes. Let cool slightly; add to bowl.

3 Add Flavourings in second column. Mix to combine. Mix in 1½ lb (750 g) lean ground beef. Pack into 8- x 4-inch (1.5 L) loaf pan.

4 Spread with Toppers in in third column. Place on rimmed baking sheet; bake in 350°F (180°C) oven for 60 to 75 minutes or until meat thermometer registers 170°F (77°C). Let stand for 5 minutes; drain off fat.

Makes 6 servings.

Easy Roast Beef with Onion Gravy

For oven roasts (but not the most tender cuts, which are labelled "premium oven roasts"), a quick sear in a high-heat oven followed by low and slow roasting creates a juicy, tender and very lean roast. Be sure not to cook oven roasts beyond the medium-rare stage or you'll risk having tough, dry meat.

1	eye of round or inside round oven roast (3 lb/1.5 kg)	1
1 tsp	vegetable oil	5 mL
1 tsp	Worcestershire sauce	5 mL
½ tsp	pepper	2 mL

GRAVY:		
1 tbsp	butter	15 mL
1 cup	finely chopped onion	250 mL
¼ cup	all-purpose flour	50 mL
3 cups	beef stock or water	750 mL
1 tbsp	red wine vinegar	15 mL
¼ tsp	each salt and pepper	1 mL

1 Brush roast with oil and Worcestershire sauce; sprinkle with pepper. Place on rack in small roasting pan; pour 1½ cups (375 mL) water into pan. Roast in 500°F (260°C) oven for 30 minutes.

2 Reduce heat to 275°F (140°C). Roast for 1 to 1¼ hours or until meat thermometer registers 140°F (60°C) for rare or 150°F (65°C) for medium-rare. Transfer to cutting board; tent with foil and let stand for 15 minutes.

3 GRAVY: Meanwhile, add butter to liquid remaining in roasting pan. Add onion and cook over medium heat, stirring occasionally, for 5 to 8 minutes or until very soft. Stir in flour; cook, stirring, for 1 minute. Add beef stock and vinegar; bring to boil, stirring and scraping up any brown bits from bottom of pan. Reduce heat and simmer for 5 minutes or until thickened. Strain if desired; season with salt and pepper. Slice roast thinly and serve with gravy.

EASY HORSERADISH
Cream Sauce

This sauce is a natural with roast beef. Place 3 tbsp (50 mL) prepared horseradish in fine sieve; press out moisture. Combine with ½ cup (125 mL) light sour cream and 1 tsp (5 mL) Dijon mustard. **Makes about ⅔ cup (150 mL).**

Makes 8 servings.

PER SERVING, ABOUT:

cal	288	carb	5 g
pro	40 g	fibre	trace
total fat	11 g	chol	87 mg
sat. fat	4 g	sodium	427 mg

PERCENTAGE RDI:

calcium	2%	vit. A	1%
iron	27%	vit. C	2%
folate	8%		

Strip Loin with Exotic Mushrooms and Shallots

Amazingly tender and succulent — words to make your mouth water in anticipation of this elegant mushroom-sauced roast created by author Bonnie Stern.

1	strip loin premium oven roast (5 lb/2.2 kg), 2½ inches (6 cm) thick, trimmed	1
1 tbsp	chopped fresh rosemary	15 mL
1 tbsp	pepper	15 mL
1 tbsp	Worcestershire sauce	15 mL
1 tbsp	Dijon mustard	15 mL
2	cloves garlic, minced	2
1 tbsp	olive oil	15 mL
1 tsp	salt	5 mL

SAUCE:		
1 lb	shallots, peeled and cut in quarters	500 g
2 tbsp	balsamic vinegar	25 mL
2 cups	dry red wine	500 mL
2 tbsp	butter	25 mL
1 lb	fresh exotic mushrooms, sliced ½ inch (1 cm) thick	500 g
⅓ cup	oyster sauce	75 mL
2 tbsp	coarsely chopped fresh parsley	25 mL

1 Pat roast very dry. In small bowl, combine rosemary, pepper, Worcestershire sauce, mustard and garlic; rub into roast. Marinate at room temperature for 30 minutes. (MAKE-AHEAD: Marinate in refrigerator for up to 24 hours.)

2 In large skillet, heat oil over medium-high heat. Sprinkle salt over roast; brown well all over, about 10 minutes. Transfer to parchment paper–lined rimmed baking sheet. Roast in 375°F (190°C) oven for 45 minutes or until meat thermometer inserted in thickest part registers 130°F (55°C) for very rare, or until desired doneness. Transfer to cutting board; tent with foil and let stand for about 10 minutes before carving into ½-inch (1 cm) thick slices.

3 SAUCE: Meanwhile, discard all but about 2 tbsp (25 mL) fat from skillet. Add shallots and vinegar; cook over medium-high heat, stirring often, for about 5 minutes or until no liquid remains and shallots begin to brown. Add wine; cook, stirring and scraping up any brown bits from bottom of pan, until reduced to about ½ cup (125 mL) and shallots are tender, about 15 minutes.

4 Meanwhile, in another large skillet, heat butter over medium heat; cook exotic mushrooms, stirring occasionally, for about 10 minutes or until mushrooms are wilted and browned. Add to shallot mixture. Add oyster sauce; cook for 5 minutes. Stir in parsley. Serve over beef.

Makes 8 to 10 servings.

Devilled Prime Rib with Roasted Garlic Gravy

Plenty of mustard and a generous dollop of horseradish put the devil into this handsome roast. The garlic heads roast up sweet and soft to give a mellow note to the gravy.

1	prime rib premium oven roast (about 5 lb/2.2 kg)	1
1	onion, finely chopped	1
2	cloves garlic, minced	2
⅓ cup	each Dijon and grainy mustard	75 mL
2 tbsp	horseradish	25 mL
1 tbsp	lemon juice	15 mL

2 tsp	dried thyme	10 mL
¾ tsp	each salt and pepper	4 mL
2	heads garlic	2
GRAVY:		
2 tbsp	all-purpose flour	25 mL
1 cup	beef stock	250 mL
⅓ cup	red wine	75 mL

1 Place roast, bone side down, on greased rack in roasting pan. Mix together onion, minced garlic, Dijon and grainy mustards, horseradish, lemon juice, thyme, salt and pepper; spread over top and sides of roast. (MAKE-AHEAD: Refrigerate for up to 12 hours.)

2 Roast in 325°F (160°C) oven for 1 hour. Trim off and discard tips from garlic heads; wrap in foil and place beside roast. Roast for 1 hour or until garlic is softened and meat thermometer registers 140°F (60°C) for rare, or for 1½ hours or until meat thermometer registers 150°F (65°C) for medium-rare, or until desired doneness. Transfer to cutting board. Tent with foil; let stand for 15 minutes.

3 GRAVY: Meanwhile, skim fat from juices in pan. Place pan over medium-high heat; sprinkle flour over juices. Cook, stirring, for 1 minute. Unwrap garlic heads; holding base of each with paper towel, squeeze pulp into pan. Pour in stock and wine; bring to boil, stirring and scraping up any brown bits from bottom of pan. Reduce heat and simmer for 2 minutes or until thickened. Strain into warmed gravy boat, pressing pulp through strainer.

4 Slice beef thinly; serve with gravy.

VARIATION

Herbed Prime Rib Roast: Instead of mustard coating (Step 1, above): Cut 1 large firm clove garlic into slivers. Cut slits all over roast; insert garlic slivers into slits. Blend together 2 tbsp (25 mL) olive oil, 1 tbsp (15 mL) each dried oregano and basil, 1 tsp (5 mL) dried mint and pepper; spread evenly over roast. Roast as directed.

Makes 6 to 8 servings.

PER EACH OF 8 SERVINGS, ABOUT:

cal	363	carb	7 g
pro	41 g	fibre	1 g
total fat	18 g	chol	92 mg
sat. fat	7 g	sodium	683 mg

PERCENTAGE RDI:

calcium	6%	vit. A	0%
iron	29%	vit. C	5%
folate	8%		

QUICK MAKE-AHEAD

Deluxe Roasted Beef Tenderloin

The ne plus ultra of roast beef, beef tenderloin is the roast to serve when you want to impress — and take entertaining a little easy. All you need is a simple rub and a shockingly short amount of time in the oven for fork-tender beef. Ask your butcher for the even-size centre part of the tenderloin. Serve hot or cold.

TEST KITCHEN TIPS

• The meat should be quite pink inside for best texture and flavour. Do not cook for longer than indicated.

• Top sirloin is a less expensive alternative. It is not as tender and shrinks more, so you may want to buy more. Pieces 1½ to 2 inches (4 to 5 cm) thick work best.

½ cup	Worcestershire sauce	125 mL
2 tbsp	packed brown sugar	25 mL
2 tbsp	Scotch whisky	25 mL
1 tsp	pepper	5 mL
2	cloves garlic, minced	2

1	piece (1 inch/2.5 cm) gingerroot, thinly sliced	1
1	beef tenderloin premium oven roast (4 lb/2 kg)	1
2 tbsp	coarse salt	25 mL

1 In bowl, whisk together Worcestershire sauce, sugar, whisky, pepper, garlic and ginger until sugar is dissolved. Place tenderloin in long glass baking dish; pour marinade over top, turning beef to coat. Cover and marinate in refrigerator for 24 hours, turning and basting occasionally.

2 Remove tenderloin from marinade, shaking off excess. Place on foil-lined rimmed baking sheet. Rub all over with salt. Roast in 500°F (260°C) oven for 10 minutes. Turn over and roast for 10 to 15 minutes longer or until meat thermometer inserted in centre registers 140°F (60°C) for rare or 150°F (65°C) for medium-rare. (MAKE-AHEAD: Let cool; wrap in foil and refrigerate for up to 2 days.)

Makes 16 servings.

PER SERVING, ABOUT:

cal 160	carb . . . . 2 g
pro . . . . 22 g	fibre . . . . trace
total fat . . . . . 7 g	chol . . . . . . 52 mg
sat. fat . . . . . . 2 g	sodium . . 969 mg

PERCENTAGE RDI:

calcium 1%	vit. A 0%
iron 21%	vit. C 0%
folate 3%	

Onion Cranberry Brisket

Supremely tasty, this braised brisket remains popular year after year with associate food editor Daphna Rabinovitch's family. It's a dream holiday item, all the more attractive because it must be made ahead, giving the cook plenty of time to chill and defat the gravy.

1½	cans (each 398 mL) jellied cranberry sauce	1½
1½	envelopes (each 38.5 g) onion soup mix	1½
3	cloves garlic, minced	3

¼ cup	water	50 mL
¼ tsp	cayenne pepper	1 mL
1	single brisket pot roast (about 4 lb/2 kg)	1

1 In roasting pan just large enough to hold brisket, whisk together cranberry sauce, onion soup mix, garlic, water and cayenne pepper.

2 Add beef brisket to pan; spoon cranberry mixture over top. Cover with plastic wrap; refrigerate for 12 hours or for up to 24 hours.

3 Cover pan with foil or lid; cook in 325°F (160°C) oven, basting every 30 minutes, for about 4 hours or until brisket is fall-apart tender. (MAKE-AHEAD: Let cool for 30 minutes; cover and refrigerate for at least 12 hours or for up to 24 hours.)

4 Skim fat from surface. Slice brisket thinly across the grain. Arrange slices in pan juices. Cover and heat in 325°F (160°C) oven for 1 hour or until hot.

Makes 10 servings.

PER SERVING, ABOUT:

cal 361	carb . . . . 31 g
pro . . . . 28 g	fibre . . . . 1 g
total fat . . . . 13 g	chol . . . . . . 72 mg
sat. fat . . . . . . 5 g	sodium . . 490 mg

PERCENTAGE RDI:

calcium 2%	vit. A 0%
iron 21%	vit. C 5%
folate 3%	

Classic Pot Roast with Vegetables

Unlike fast food, slow food such as this pot roast is much more than fuel. This roast supplies plenty of nutrients, a kitchen full of fragrant anticipation, and plenty of comfort when everyone sits down to enjoy tender slices with vegetables and gravy.

SUBSTITUTION: Substitute apple juice or additional beef stock for the wine in recipe; add 1 tbsp (15 mL) cider vinegar.

1	boneless cross rib or blade pot roast (4 lb/2 kg)	1	1	bay leaf	1
⅓ cup	all-purpose flour	75 mL	1 cup	beef stock	250 mL
2 tbsp	vegetable oil	25 mL	½ cup	red or white wine	125 mL
1½ cups	chopped onions	375 mL	1 tbsp	tomato paste	15 mL
¾ cup	each chopped carrots and celery	175 mL	3	leeks	3
2	cloves garlic, minced	2	6	carrots, sliced thickly	6
1 tsp	dried thyme	5 mL	6	potatoes, quartered	6
¾ tsp	pepper	4 mL	½ tsp	salt	2 mL
½ tsp	dried basil or tarragon	2 mL	¼ cup	finely chopped fresh parsley	50 mL

1 Pat meat dry; coat with flour. Shake off excess and reserve. In Dutch oven, heat oil over medium-high heat; brown beef all over, turning with wooden spoons, about 7 minutes. Transfer to plate and set aside.

2 Drain off fat in pan; reduce heat to medium. Add chopped onions, carrots, celery, garlic, thyme, pepper, basil and bay leaf. Cook, stirring often, for 5 minutes. Sprinkle with reserved flour; cook, stirring, for 1 minute. Add stock, wine and tomato paste; bring to simmer. Return beef to pan; cover and cook over low heat or in 325°F (160°C) oven, turning once, for 1¾ hours.

3 Meanwhile, trim coarse green part from leeks. Slit and rinse thoroughly under running water. Cut into 2-inch (5 cm) lengths. Add leeks, carrots, potatoes and salt to pan; cover and cook, turning roast every 30 minutes, for 60 to 70 minutes or until vegetables are tender. Transfer roast to cutting board; transfer vegetables to serving platter. Cover and keep warm.

4 Discard bay leaf. Skim off fat. Pour cooking liquid into blender or food processor; purée until smooth. Slice roast; add to platter. Sprinkle vegetables with parsley. Pass gravy in sauce boat.

Makes 6 to 8 servings.

PER EACH OF 8 SERVINGS, ABOUT:

cal	482	carb	38 g
pro	40 g	fibre	5 g
total fat	19 g	chol	87 mg
sat. fat	6 g	sodium	376 mg

PERCENTAGE RDI:

calcium	7%	vit. A	164%
iron	35%	vit. C	27%
folate	26%		

Koftas with Cucumber Yogurt Salad

Ground meat assumes many shapes and forms, none more pleasing than this Middle Eastern take on grilled burgers. Serve with warmed pita breads to wrap the koftas and salad.

1	small onion, grated	1
2	cloves garlic, minced	2
2 tbsp	pine nuts or finely chopped almonds	25 mL
1 tbsp	chopped fresh oregano (or 1 tsp/5 mL dried)	15 mL
1 tbsp	lemon juice	15 mL

1 tsp	each ground cumin and cinnamon	5 mL
¼ tsp	each salt and pepper	1 mL
1 lb	lean ground beef	500 g
	Cucumber Yogurt Salad (recipe follows)	

TEST KITCHEN TIP: To broil koftas, place skewers on greased rack on foil-lined baking sheet. Broil for 6 to 8 minutes, turning once.

1 In bowl, mix together onion, garlic, pine nuts, oregano, lemon juice, cumin, cinnamon, salt and pepper. Mix in beef. Divide into 8 portions; mould each around 8-inch (20 cm) soaked wooden skewer, pressing to form 6-inch (15 cm) sausage-shaped oval. (MAKE-AHEAD: Cover and refrigerate for up to 4 hours.)

2 Place on greased grill over medium-high heat; close lid and cook, turning once, for about 4 minutes or until no longer pink inside. Serve with Cucumber Yogurt Salad.

Cucumber Yogurt Salad

1	cucumber (1 lb/500 g)	1
1 cup	Balkan-style plain yogurt	250 mL

1	clove garlic, minced	1
1 tbsp	chopped fresh mint	15 mL
Pinch	salt	Pinch

1 Peel and halve cucumber lengthwise; seed and cut into ¼-inch (5 mm) thick slices. In bowl, mix together yogurt, garlic, mint and salt; stir in cucumber. **Makes 2 cups (500 mL).**

Makes 4 servings.

PER SERVING (WITH SALAD), ABOUT:

cal 339	carb . . . . 15 g
pro . . . . 25 g	fibre . . . . 2 g
total fat . . . . 20 g	chol . . . . . . 85 mg
sat. fat . . . . . . 9 g	sodium . . 268 mg

PERCENTAGE RDI:

calcium 18%	vit. A 6%
iron 26%	vit. C 20%
folate 16%	

MAKE-AHEAD   FREEZABLE   BUDGET-WISE

Best Burgers

Take your hamburger from basic to brilliant five different ways, either on the barbecue or in a grill pan or skillet. To be safe, always cook burgers until no longer pink inside; check with the tip of a pointed knife.

	ADD-INS	TOPPERS
Fajita Burgers	1 sweet red pepper, diced; 2 cloves garlic, minced; 1 tbsp (15 mL) lemon juice; 1 tsp (5 mL) chili powder	salsa; 1 avocado, sliced
French Onion Burgers	1 onion, grated; 1 tbsp (15 mL) each wine vinegar and Worcestershire sauce	Swiss cheese slice added to each for last minute of cooking; grilled thick slices Spanish onion
Hot Asian Burgers	1 tbsp (15 mL) each soy sauce and rice or wine vinegar; 1½ tsp (7 mL) ground ginger; 2 cloves garlic, minced; 1 tsp (5 mL) hot pepper sauce	2 green onions, chopped
Cheddar Burgers	1 cup (250 mL) shredded Cheddar cheese; 1 green apple, grated	Dijonnaise sauce; alfalfa sprouts
Mediterranean Burgers	2 tbsp (25 mL) each pesto and chopped black olives	sliced tomatoes

TEST KITCHEN TIPS

• For juicy burgers, shape patties gently. Overmixing and too much pressing make tough, dry hamburgers. Dip hands in water when shaping patties to prevent sticking, and keep patting to a minimum.

• Turn burgers only once. Don't press or flatten with spatula during grilling because this forces out juices.

1 In bowl and using fork, beat 1 egg; mix in ¼ cup (50 mL) dry bread crumbs, ½ tsp (2 mL) salt, ¼ tsp (1 mL) pepper and Add-Ins in first column. Mix in 1 lb (500 g) medium ground beef.

2 Shape into four ½-inch (1 cm) thick patties. (MAKE-AHEAD: Layer patties between waxed paper in airtight container and refrigerate for up to 4 hours or freeze for up to 2 weeks.) Place on greased grill over medium-high heat; close lid and cook, turning once, for about 10 minutes or until no longer pink inside.

3 Add Toppers in second column. Place each dressed patty in bun.

SUBSTITUTION: You can use lean ground beef if you like. However, medium is a great deal for grilled burgers as they remain moist and juicy in spite of the fat that's released on the barbecue.

Makes 4 servings.

Warm Grilled Flank Steak Salad

When tossing greens with a warm dressing, choose sturdy varieties such as romaine, spinach, curly endive, fancy frisée and napa cabbage; soft greens such as Boston, leaf and baby leaf mixes wilt quickly. For colour, include some torn radicchio with the greens.

1 lb	flank marinating steak	500 g	Half	sweet red pepper, thinly sliced	Half
¼ cup	balsamic or sherry or wine vinegar	50 mL	½ cup	thinly sliced Spanish or Vidalia onion	125 mL
2	cloves garlic, minced	2	2 tbsp	finely chopped fresh basil (or 2 tsp/10 mL dried)	25 mL
¼ tsp	pepper	1 mL			
8 oz	asparagus, cut in 1-inch (2.5 cm) pieces	250 g	2 tbsp	extra-virgin olive oil	25 mL
9 cups	torn mixed salad greens	2.25 L	½ tsp	salt	2 mL

1 Place steak in shallow glass dish. Whisk together vinegar, garlic and pepper; pour over steak and turn to coat. Cover and let stand at room temperature for 30 minutes. (MAKE-AHEAD: **Refrigerate for up to 8 hours.**)

2 In large pot of boiling salted water, blanch asparagus for 2 minutes or until tender-crisp. Drain. Chill under cold water; drain again. Pat dry. In large bowl, gently toss together asparagus, salad greens, red pepper and onion; set aside.

3 Reserving marinade, transfer steak to greased grill over medium-high heat; close lid and cook, turning once, for 6 minutes per side for medium-rare or until desired doneness. Transfer to cutting board and tent with foil; let stand for 5 minutes before slicing thinly across the grain.

4 Meanwhile, in small saucepan, bring reserved marinade to boil; reduce heat and simmer, stirring often, for 5 minutes. Whisk in basil, oil and salt; pour over salad and toss to coat. Divide salad among serving plates. Top with steak and any juices.

Makes 4 servings.

PER SERVING, ABOUT:

cal	309	carb	13 g
pro	29 g	fibre	4 g
total fat	16 g	chol	44 mg
sat. fat	5 g	sodium	515 mg

PERCENTAGE RDI:

calcium	10%	vit. A	56%
iron	31%	vit. C	93%
folate	128%		

Party Sirloin

Sirloin steak is a delight to serve. One thick and generous piece grilled to rare or medium-rare, sliced and fanned invites guests to help themselves to as much as they want. There are occasions when one steak per person is the right choice, but when you have the opportunity, try the sirloin steak route.

TEST KITCHEN TIP: For more marinades, see page 148, and for rubs, page 173. A knob of flavoured butter may seem like too much of a good thing, but let yourself succumb occasionally with one selected from page 152.

2 lb	top sirloin grilling steak or sirloin tip marinating steak (1½ inches/4 cm thick)	1 kg

MARINADE:

⅓ cup	rice or cider vinegar	75 mL
¼ cup	soy sauce	50 mL
3 tbsp	vegetable oil	50 mL
2 tbsp	chopped fresh coriander	25 mL
1 tbsp	sesame oil	15 mL
1 tbsp	sherry	15 mL
3	green onions, finely chopped	3
2	cloves garlic, minced	2
½ tsp	chili paste or hot pepper sauce	2 mL

1 MARINADE: In shallow glass dish, whisk together vinegar, soy sauce, vegetable oil, coriander, sesame oil, sherry, onions, garlic and chili paste.

2 Add steak to dish, turning to coat evenly. Cover and marinate in refrigerator for at least 4 hours or for up to 8 hours, turning steak occasionally.

3 Discarding marinade, place steak on greased grill over medium-high heat; close lid and cook, turning once, for 20 minutes for rare or until desired doneness.

4 Transfer to cutting board; tent with foil and let stand for 5 minutes before slicing thinly.

VARIATION

Beer-Marinated Party Sirloin: Give beef subtly different flavours just by changing the marinade. Use ½ cup (125 mL) beer, ¼ cup (50 mL) beef stock, 3 tbsp (50 mL) each vegetable oil and cider vinegar, 2 tbsp (25 mL) balsamic vinegar (optional), 1 tbsp (15 mL) packed brown sugar, 1 small onion, thinly sliced, and ½ tsp (2 mL) dried thyme.

Makes 8 servings.

PER SERVING, ABOUT:

cal 155	carb . . . . 1 g
pro . . . . 21 g	fibre . . . . trace
total fat . . . . . 7 g	chol . . . . . . 51 mg
sat. fat . . . . . . 2 g	sodium . . 211 mg

PERCENTAGE RDI:

calcium 1%	vit. A 0%
iron 16%	vit. C 0%
folate 4%	

Tender T-Bones

Tenderloin may be more expensive, but no steak has more style or taste than a nice thick T-bone. Serve with a dab of flavoured butter (page 152), over a pool of Tangy Barbecue Sauce (below) or with Dijon mustard.

4	T-bone grilling steaks (each about 6 oz/175 g)	4
2 tbsp	olive oil	25 mL

¼ tsp	each salt and pepper	1 mL
1 cup	Tangy Barbecue Sauce (recipe follows), optional	250 mL

1 Brush steaks with oil; sprinkle with salt and pepper. Place on greased grill over high heat; close lid and cook for 5 minutes per side for medium-rare or until desired doneness.

2 Brush steaks lightly with Tangy Barbecue Sauce just before removing from grill or serve alongside (if using).

Tangy Barbecue Sauce

1 cup	beef stock	250 mL
1 cup	chili sauce	250 mL
⅔ cup	water	150 mL
½ cup	fancy molasses	125 mL
2 tbsp	wine vinegar	25 mL
4 tsp	Dijon mustard	20 mL

2 tsp	chili powder	10 mL
2 tsp	Worcestershire sauce	10 mL
1 tsp	celery seeds, crushed	5 mL
1 tsp	ground cumin	5 mL
½ tsp	each salt and pepper	2 mL

1 In large saucepan, combine stock, chili sauce, water, molasses, vinegar, mustard, chili powder, Worcestershire sauce, celery seeds, cumin, salt and pepper; bring to boil. Reduce heat and simmer for about 20 minutes or until reduced to about 2 cups (500 mL). (MAKE-AHEAD: Refrigerate in airtight container for up to 2 weeks.) **Makes 2 cups (500 mL).**

TEST KITCHEN TIPS

• Grilling steaks come from the loin and rib areas and include rib, rib eye, T-bone, strip loin, top sirloin and tenderloin. All of these steaks can be cooked the same way, and in many recipes, notably grilled recipes, they are interchangeable.

• For the Tangy Barbecue Sauce, use your own home-made Chili Sauce (page 389) or purchase a bottle of this traditional sweet-and-sour tomato relish at any super-market.

Makes 4 servings.

PER SERVING (WITH ¼ CUP/ 50 ML SAUCE), ABOUT:

cal	448	carb	47 g
pro	28 g	fibre	4 g
total fat	17 g	chol	56 mg
sat. fat	5 g	sodium	1,715 mg

PERCENTAGE RDI:

calcium	12%	vit. A	8%
iron	42%	vit. C	20%
folate	14%		

Red Wine and Oregano Grilled Marinating Steak

A thick lean marinating steak has virtually no waste. Serve it all at once, or enjoy half for one meal, then slice and toss the rest in a supper salad the next day.

TEST KITCHEN TIP:

Marinating steaks include sirloin tip, eye of round, inside round, outside round and flank steak. They are usually very tasty and very lean, and because they come from the most exercised hip and shoulder areas, they are chewier than more tender grilling steaks. Marinating helps tenderize the meat but cannot penetrate sufficiently to tenderize fibres throughout. But, in combination with cooking no more than rare or medium-rare and slicing across the grain, these steaks are thrifty options for year-round barbecuing.

3 lb	inside round marinating steak, (1½ inches/4 cm thick)	1.5 kg
3 tbsp	red wine vinegar	50 mL
3 tbsp	olive oil	50 mL

2	cloves garlic, minced	2
2 tbsp	each chopped fresh oregano and mint (or 2 tsp/10 mL dried)	25 mL
¼ tsp	pepper	1 mL

1 Place steak in shallow glass dish. Whisk together vinegar, oil, garlic, oregano, mint and pepper; pour over steak, turning to coat. Cover and marinate in refrigerator for 8 hours. (MAKE-AHEAD: Marinate for up to 24 hours.)

2 Reserving marinade, place steak on greased grill over medium-high heat; close lid and cook, turning once and basting occasionally with marinade, for 15 minutes. Turn and grill without basting for 15 minutes or until rare. Transfer steak to cutting board; tent with foil and let stand for about 10 minutes before slicing thinly across the grain.

Makes 8 servings.

PER SERVING, ABOUT:

cal 232	carb . . . . 1 g
pro . . . . 34 g	fibre . . . . trace
total fat . . . . . 9 g	chol . . . . . . 73 mg
sat. fat . . . . . . 2 g	sodium . . . 58 mg

PERCENTAGE RDI:

calcium 1%	vit. A 0%
iron 24%	vit. C 0%
folate 6%	

TENDERIZING Marinades

Marinades usually contain an acidic ingredient such as vinegar, which helps tenderize meat as it flavours. Try these as an alternative to the marinade in the recipe.

- In small bowl, stir together ingredients for desired marinade (right).
- We calculate that ⅓ cup (75 mL) marinade works for 4 servings (1 lb/ 500 g) boneless or 1½ lb (750 g) bone-in meat or poultry, but you can marinate slightly more.
- Marinate in refrigerator for at least 4 hours or for up to 12 hours.

- **MOROCCAN MARINADE:** Use 3 tbsp (50 mL) olive oil, 2 tbsp (25 mL) each granulated sugar and lemon juice, 2 cloves garlic, minced, 2 tbsp (25 mL) each ground cumin and paprika, ½ tsp (2 mL) each salt and pepper, and ¼ tsp (1 mL) cinnamon. **Makes about ⅓ cup (75 mL).**

- **FIVE-SPICE MARINADE:** Use ¼ cup (50 mL) orange juice, 2 tbsp (25 mL) soy sauce, half small onion, minced, 1 tbsp (15 mL) minced gingerroot, 1 tsp (5 mL) Chinese five-spice powder, 1 tsp (5 mL) sesame oil and ¼ tsp (1 mL) cayenne pepper. **Makes about ⅓ cup (75 mL).**

Korean Beef Short Ribs

Short ribs, now labelled "beef simmering short ribs," need a spunky marinade and long, slow cooking. That's what they get with a Korean blend of ginger, soy, garlic and sake and an hour wrapped in foil tenderizing over low flames.

3 lb	lean beef simmering short ribs, trimmed	1.5 kg		1 cup	Korean Marinade (recipe follows)	250 mL

1 Place beef ribs in large shallow glass dish; pour Korean Marinade over top, turning to coat. Cover and marinate in refrigerator for 4 hours, turning occasionally. (MAKE-AHEAD: Refrigerate ribs for up to 48 hours.)

2 Reserving marinade, divide ribs between 2 large pieces of heavy-duty foil; drizzle marinade evenly over ribs. Loosely wrap foil over ribs and seal package tightly. Place packages on grill over medium-low heat; close lid and cook for about 1 hour or until meat is tender.

3 Reserving marinade, unwrap ribs and place directly on greased grill over medium-high heat; cook ribs, turning and basting frequently with marinade, for 10 to 15 minutes or until crisp.

SUBSTITUTION: You can use meaty beef rib bones instead of short ribs. Marinate as per recipe. Omit wrapping in foil. To cook, place ribs, curved side down, on greased grill over medium heat; close lid and cook, turning and brushing with marinade every 5 minutes, for about 25 minutes or until glazed and crusty.

Korean Marinade

1	small apple, sliced	1		2 cups	soy sauce	500 mL
1	small onion, thinly sliced	1		1 cup	granulated sugar	250 mL
1	piece (1 inch/2.5 cm) gingerroot, thinly sliced	1		½ cup	sake or dry sherry	125 mL
5	cloves garlic, thinly sliced	5		½ cup	mirin (Japanese rice wine)	125 mL
15	black peppercorns	15				

1 In saucepan, combine sliced apple, onion, ginger, garlic, peppercorns, soy sauce, granulated sugar, sake and mirin; bring to boil.

2 Reduce heat and simmer for about 40 minutes or until marinade is reduced by half.

3 Cover and refrigerate for 12 hours. Strain through fine sieve. (MAKE-AHEAD: Refrigerate in airtight container for up to 2 weeks.) **Makes 2 cups (500 mL).**

SUBSTITUTION: If you don't have mirin, you can increase the sake to ¾ cup (175 mL) and add ¼ cup (50 mL) corn syrup.

Makes 4 servings.

PER SERVING, ABOUT:

cal	655	carb	36 g
pro	39 g	fibre	1 g
total fat	38 g	chol	105 mg
sat. fat	16 g	sodium	4,213 mg

PERCENTAGE RDI:

calcium	5%	vit. A	0%
iron	33%	vit. C	3%
folate	10%		

Mustard Devilled Ribs

Meaty rib bones — you may have to ask your butcher for any left over from preparing boneless rib roasts — may look like the makings for a caveman's feast, but they are so crusty and delicious.

½ cup	Dijon mustard	125 mL	2	cloves garlic, minced	2
½ cup	grainy mustard	125 mL	¼ tsp	dried thyme	1 mL
1 tbsp	Worcestershire sauce	15 mL	¼ tsp	hot pepper sauce	1 mL
1 tbsp	vegetable oil	15 mL	4 lb	meaty beef rib bones	2 kg
1 tbsp	prepared horseradish	15 mL	¼ cup	minced fresh parsley	50 mL

1 In small bowl, whisk together Dijon and grainy mustards, Worcestershire sauce, oil, horseradish, garlic, thyme and hot pepper sauce.

2 Arrange ribs in large shallow glass dish; brush all over with mustard mixture. Cover and refrigerate for at least 3 hours, turning and brushing ribs occasionally. (MAKE-AHEAD: Refrigerate for up to 12 hours, turning and brushing occasionally.)

3 Reserving any marinade and using tongs, place ribs on greased grill over medium heat; close lid and cook, turning every 5 minutes and brushing with marinade, for 25 minutes. Grill, without brushing, for 10 minutes longer or until crusty and brown. Serve sprinkled with parsley.

VARIATION

Barbecued Beef Ribs: Substitute 1½ cups (375 mL) Tangy Barbecue Sauce (page 147) for the mustard sauce.

Makes 8 servings.

PER SERVING, ABOUT:

cal 309	carb . . . . 2 g
pro . . . . 13 g	fibre . . . . trace
total fat . . . . 28 g	chol . . . . . . 46 mg
sat. fat . . . . . 11 g	sodium . . 466 mg

PERCENTAGE RDI:

calcium 5%	vit. A 1%
iron 11%	vit. C 3%
folate 3%	

Ginger Soy Beef Kabobs

Ginger, soy and sesame seeds make one of the many choice marinades to flavour kabobs, which, by the way, are an excellent make-ahead for a barbecue.

1 lb	top sirloin grilling steak or sirloin tip marinating steak (1 inch/2.5 cm thick)	500 g	2 tbsp	minced gingerroot	25 mL
2 tsp	sesame seeds	10 mL	2 tbsp	soy sauce	25 mL
GINGER SOY MARINADE:			2 tsp	rice or cider vinegar	10 mL
4	green onions, thinly sliced	4	2 tsp	vegetable oil	10 mL
3	cloves garlic, minced	3	½ tsp	granulated sugar	2 mL
			Dash	hot pepper sauce	Dash

1 Trim fat from steak; cut into 1-inch (2.5 cm) cubes.

2 GINGER SOY MARINADE: In glass bowl, combine onions, garlic, ginger, soy sauce, vinegar, oil, sugar and hot pepper sauce; add beef, stirring to coat. Cover and marinate in refrigerator for at least 1 hour. (MAKE-AHEAD: Refrigerate for up to 12 hours.)

3 Thread beef onto metal or soaked wooden skewers. Place on greased grill over medium-high heat; close lid and cook, turning 3 times, for 10 minutes or until browned but still pink inside.

4 Meanwhile, in dry skillet, heat sesame seeds over medium heat, stirring often, until golden and fragrant, about 6 minutes. Sprinkle over kabobs.

VARIATIONS

Mild Jerked Kabobs: Omit sesame seeds. For marinade, substitute 1 tbsp (15 mL) vegetable oil, 1 tbsp (15 mL) soy sauce, 2 tsp (10 mL) vinegar, ¼ tsp (1 mL) ground ginger, ¼ tsp (1 mL) pepper, ¼ tsp (1 mL) mild curry paste and pinch each allspice and cayenne.

Classic Greek Kabobs: Omit sesame seeds. For marinade, substitute 2 tbsp (25 mL) lemon juice, 1 tbsp (15 mL) olive oil, ½ tsp (2 mL) dried oregano, ½ tsp (2 mL) grated lemon rind, ¼ tsp (1 mL) dried mint and pinch pepper.

Provençal Beef Kabobs: Omit sesame seeds. For marinade, substitute 2 tbsp (25 mL) olive oil, 4 tsp (20 mL) red or white wine vinegar, 1 tsp (5 mL) each dried thyme and either oregano or rosemary, and 1 clove garlic, minced.

Makes 4 servings.

PER SERVING, ABOUT:

cal	154	carb	3 g
pro	19 g	fibre	trace
total fat	7 g	chol	45 mg
sat. fat	2 g	sodium	425 mg

PERCENTAGE RDI:

calcium	2%	vit. A	0%
iron	17%	vit. C	3%
folate	6%		

Rib Eye on the Rotisserie

Barbecuing a roast, whether you do it on a rotisserie or over indirect heat, is surprisingly effortless and a nice change from steaks for barbecue parties.

TEST KITCHEN TIP: If you don't have a rotisserie on your barbecue, cook the roast using the indirect heat method: Heat 1 of the burners of a 2-burner barbecue or 2 outside burners of a 3-burner barbecue to medium-low. Place drip pan under unlit burner; pour in water to depth of 1 inch (2.5 cm). Place roast on greased grill over unlit burner; close lid and cook for 2½ to 3 hours, giving roast one-quarter turn every 30 minutes.

½ cup	Dijon mustard	125 mL
½ cup	beef stock	125 mL
2 tbsp	vegetable oil	25 mL
1 tbsp	crushed peppercorns	15 mL
1 tbsp	light soy sauce	15 mL

1 tbsp	red wine vinegar or balsamic vinegar	15 mL
1	rib eye premium oven roast (boneless), 8 lb (3.5 kg)	1

1 In bowl, whisk together mustard, beef stock, oil, peppercorns, soy sauce and vinegar.

2 Insert rotisserie rod lengthwise through centre of roast, making sure to balance roast for even turning. Secure firmly with clamps. Position on barbecue over drip pan.

3 Brush all over with one-quarter of the mustard mixture. Close lid and cook over medium-low heat, brushing 3 times with remaining mustard mixture, for about 2½ hours or until meat thermometer registers 140°F (60°C) for rare or 150°F (65°C) for medium-rare.

4 Transfer roast to cutting board; tent with foil and let stand for 15 minutes before slicing.

Makes 20 servings.

PER SERVING, ABOUT:

cal	250	carb	1 g
pro	34 g	fibre	trace
total fat	11 g	chol	74 mg
sat. fat	4 g	sodium	203 mg

PERCENTAGE RDI:

calcium	2%	vit. A	0%
iron	19%	vit. C	0%
folate	4%		

FLAVOURED Butters FOR GRILLED BEEF

Flavoured butters are an inspired addition to any barbecued meat, poultry and fish. Place a round on each portion of hot food to serve, or melt and brush on food while grilling.
~ In small bowl, stir ½ cup (125 mL) butter, softened, with ingredients for desired flavour (right) until smooth. Spoon onto plastic wrap; shape into log and wrap tightly. Refrigerate until firm; slice into ½-inch (1 cm) thick rounds to serve. (MAKE-AHEAD: Refrigerate for up to 2 weeks.) Makes about ½ cup (125 mL).

~ HORSERADISH BUTTER: Use 1 tbsp (15 mL) horseradish and pinch pepper.
~ SHALLOT PEPPERCORN BUTTER: In small saucepan, melt 1 tsp (5 mL) butter; cook 1 shallot, minced, until softened. Let cool completely. Use shallot, 2 tbsp (25 mL) pink peppercorns, crushed, and 1 tbsp (15 mL) dry red wine.
~ ANCHOVY BUTTER: Use 4 anchovy fillets, drained and mashed (or 2 tsp/ 10 mL anchovy paste), ¼ cup (50 mL) minced green onions, 1 clove garlic, minced, and 1 tsp (5 mL) grated lemon rind.

Salsa Barbecued Beef Brisket

Ever since barbecues went fancy and started performing more and more like ovens, the range of dishes you can cook over the flames has blossomed. Here's one, for example: brisket, usually a cold-weather braised dish, is transformed into a summer weekend treat. Serve with corn muffins, crusty buns or warmed flour tortillas.

1	jar (650 mL) salsa	1
⅔ cup	packed brown sugar	150 mL
¼ cup	Worcestershire sauce	50 mL

1 tsp	pepper	5 mL
1	single brisket pot roast (4 lb/2 kg)	1

1 In saucepan, bring salsa, sugar, Worcestershire sauce and pepper to boil. Reduce heat and cook, stirring occasionally, for 5 minutes. Let cool. Transfer half to bowl; cover and set aside in refrigerator.

2 Place brisket in shallow roasting pan just large enough to hold brisket. Pour remaining salsa mixture over meat and turn to coat. Cover and refrigerate for 4 hours, turning occasionally. (MAKE-AHEAD: Refrigerate for 24 hours, turning occasionally.)

3 Heat 1 burner of 2-burner barbecue or 2 outside burners of 3-burner barbecue to medium. Reserving marinade and using tongs, transfer brisket to greased grill over unlit burner. Close lid and cook for 1 hour, adjusting burner heat if necessary to keep temperature between 250° and 300°F (120° and 150°C) and using oven thermometer if necessary. Turn and brush generously with some of the marinade. Cook, turning and basting twice, for 2½ to 3 hours or until knife inserted in centre comes out easily.

4 Transfer brisket to cutting board and tent with foil; let stand for 10 minutes before slicing thinly across the grain.

5 Meanwhile, heat reserved salsa mixture. Serve with brisket.

Makes 10 servings.

PER SERVING, ABOUT:

cal	289	carb	16 g
pro	29 g	fibre	1 g
total fat	12 g	chol	70 mg
sat. fat	4 g	sodium	289 mg

PERCENTAGE RDI:

calcium	4%	vit. A	4%
iron	25%	vit. C	20%
folate	6%		

Pork and Lamb

6

Pork and Three-Pepper Teriyaki Stir-Fry   156

Lemon Olive Pork Chops   157

Five Speedy Pork Chop Suppers   158

Caraway Pork Goulash   159

Lemon Oregano Pork Stew   160

Pepper Orange Pork Stew   161

Mussel Sausage Simmer   162

Triple Pork Tenderloin with Mushroom Stuffing   163

Orange Fennel Rack of Pork   164

Jerk Roast Pork   165

Glazed Pork Tenderloin with Chinese Noodles   166

Chutney-Glazed Ham with Mango Salsa   167

Barbecued Pork Loin with Rosemary   168

Pulled Pork on a Bun   169

Cuban Grilled Pork Sandwich   170

Honey Garlic Ribs   171

Slow and Easy Real Barbecued Ribs   172

Maple-Glazed Peameal Bacon Dinner   174

Choucroute Garnie   175

Deep-Dish Tourtière   176

Lamb Shanks with Beans   177

Lamb Moussaka   178

Roast Leg of Lamb   180

Rosemary-Crusted Rack of Lamb   181

Butterflied Leg of Lamb   182

Herbed Lamb Chops   183

Pork and Three-Pepper Teriyaki Stir-Fry

Serve this colourful and quick stir-fry over rice or noodles. Chinese presteamed noodles take just minutes to break apart and warm in hot water and are particularly well suited to this dish.

4	boneless pork loin chops (about 1 lb/500 g)	4
Pinch	each salt and pepper	Pinch
2 tbsp	vegetable oil	25 mL
1	onion, thinly sliced	1
1	each sweet red, yellow and green pepper, thinly sliced	1
¼ cup	chicken stock or water	50 mL
¼ cup	teriyaki sauce	50 mL
1 tbsp	wine vinegar or cider vinegar	15 mL
1 tsp	cornstarch	5 mL
1 tsp	water	5 mL
1 tsp	toasted sesame seeds (optional)	5 mL

1 Cut pork crosswise into thin strips; sprinkle with salt and pepper. In large skillet or wok, heat oil over high heat; brown pork, in batches if necessary. Transfer to plate.

2 Add onion and red, yellow and green peppers to pan; stir-fry over medium-high heat for 3 minutes. Return pork and any accumulated juices to pan. Add stock, teriyaki sauce and vinegar; bring to boil. Whisk cornstarch with water; whisk into sauce and cook, stirring, until glossy and pork mixture is coated. Serve sprinkled with sesame seeds (if using).

Makes 4 servings.

PER SERVING, ABOUT:

cal 321	carb . . . . 12 g
pro . . . . 26 g	fibre . . . . 2 g
total fat . . . . 19 g	chol . . . . . . 76 mg
sat. fat . . . . . . 5 g	sodium . . 810 mg

PERCENTAGE RDI:

calcium 4%	vit. A 19%
iron 12%	vit. C 193%
folate 12%	

Lemon Olive Pork Chops

Pork chops are a healthy and speedy supper solution. Just make sure the fat is trimmed and that you nick the edges at 1-inch (2.5 cm) intervals so that the chops remain flat.

2 tbsp	all-purpose flour	25 mL
¼ tsp	pepper	1 mL
4	boneless pork loin chops (1 lb/500 g)	4
1 tbsp	olive oil	15 mL
3	cloves garlic, minced	3

1⅓ cups	chicken stock	325 mL
⅓ cup	sliced green olives	75 mL
2 tbsp	capers, rinsed	25 mL
1 tsp	grated lemon rind	5 mL
1 tbsp	lemon juice	15 mL
1 tbsp	chopped fresh parsley	15 mL

SUBSTITUTION: You can always replace boneless chops with bone-in chops. This dish is also delicious with veal chops and with ground pork patties. Cook patties until well done.

1 In sturdy plastic bag, shake together flour and pepper. Shake chops, 1 at a time, in flour mixture to coat.

2 In skillet, heat oil over medium-high heat; brown chops, 2 to 3 minutes per side. Transfer to plate.

3 Add garlic to pan; cook, stirring, for 1 minute. Add chicken stock, olives, capers and lemon rind and juice; bring to boil. Return pork to pan. Cover and simmer over medium heat, turning once, for 3 to 4 minutes or until glazed and just a hint of pink remains inside. Serve sprinkled with parsley.

Makes 4 servings.

PER SERVING, ABOUT:

cal	284	carb	5 g
pro	26 g	fibre	1 g
total fat	17 g	chol	76 mg
sat. fat	5 g	sodium	694 mg

PERCENTAGE RDI:

calcium	4%	vit. A	1%
iron	11%	vit. C	7%
folate	6%		

Five Speedy Pork Chop Suppers

Our master method encourages you to try skillet pork chops many ways.

	WHISK TOGETHER, ADD TO SKILLET AND BOIL FOR 3 MINUTES	ADD TO SKILLET, COVER AND COOK OVER MEDIUM HEAT FOR 3 TO 5 MINUTES OR UNTIL TENDER	RETURN PORK AND ACCUMULATED JUICES TO SKILLET ALONG WITH
Barbecue Chops	¾ cup (175 mL) water; ½ cup (125 mL) barbecue sauce; 1 clove garlic, minced; 1 tsp (5 mL) chili powder	2 zucchini, sliced	1 cup (250 mL) shredded Monterey Jack cheese
Orange Broccoli Chops	1½ cups (375 mL) orange juice; 1 tbsp (15 mL) cornstarch; 1 tsp (5 mL) dried thyme; ½ tsp (2 mL) granulated sugar; ¼ tsp (1 mL) salt	2 cups (500 mL) broccoli florets	¼ cup (50 mL) toasted sliced almonds
Asian Chops	1 cup (250 mL) water; ¼ cup (50 mL) soy sauce; 2 tbsp (25 mL) ketchup; 1 tbsp (15 mL) each cornstarch and honey	1 sweet red pepper, sliced; 1 can (227 mL) sliced water chestnuts, drained	1½ cups (375 mL) snow peas, trimmed and halved; cook, covered, for 4 minutes or until tender-crisp
Curried Chops	1 can (400 mL) light coconut milk; 1 tbsp (15 mL) mild curry paste	2 cups (500 mL) baby carrots	½ cup (125 mL) frozen peas; cook for 2 minutes or until hot. Add 2 tbsp (25 mL) chopped fresh coriander
Apple Chops	1 cup (250 mL) apple juice; 2 tbsp (25 mL) cider vinegar; ½ tsp (2 mL) granulated sugar; ¼ tsp (1 mL) salt	2 red apples, cut in thin wedges	1 tbsp (15 mL) chopped fresh parsley

SUBSTITUTION: Bone-in chops are cheaper than boneless and can easily replace them in any of these skillet suppers.

1 Season 4 trimmed boneless pork loin chops (1 lb / 500 g total) with ¼ tsp (1 mL) each salt and pepper. In skillet, heat 2 tsp (10 mL) vegetable oil over medium-high heat; cook chops for 3 to 4 minutes per side or until browned and just a hint of pink remains inside. Transfer to plate and keep warm.

2 Add 2 onions, chopped, to pan; cook over medium heat, stirring occasionally, for 5 minutes or until softened. Follow instructions in columns 1, 2 and 3.

Makes 4 servings.

Caraway Pork Goulash

Buttered noodles or new potatoes and a dollop of sour cream, light if you wish, round out this hearty stew. Good fresh Hungarian paprika is essential for success; it's worth searching out at delis or specialty shops.

3 lb	lean boneless pork shoulder butt	1.5 kg
2 tbsp	butter	25 mL
2 tbsp	vegetable oil	25 mL
5 cups	sliced onions	1.25 L
1	clove garlic, minced	1
2 tbsp	sweet Hungarian paprika	25 mL
1 tbsp	caraway seeds	15 mL
2 tsp	crushed dried marjoram	10 mL
1½ tsp	salt	7 mL
¾ cup	dry red wine	175 mL
¼ cup	lemon juice	50 mL
¼ cup	water	50 mL
2 tbsp	tomato paste	25 mL
½ cup	finely chopped fresh parsley	125 mL

TEST KITCHEN TIP: For a thicker goulash, uncover during the last 30 minutes of cooking.

SUBSTITUTION: For pork stew, it's convenient to buy already cubed pork shoulder.

1 Cut pork into 1-inch (2.5 cm) cubes. In Dutch oven or large heavy saucepan, heat half of the butter and oil over medium-high heat; brown pork in batches, adding remaining butter and oil as necessary. Transfer to plate.

2 Add onions and garlic to pan; cook over medium heat, stirring occasionally, for 5 to 8 minutes or until softened. Blend in paprika, caraway seeds, marjoram and salt; cook, stirring, for 3 minutes.

3 Return pork and any accumulated juices to pan. Stir in wine, lemon juice, water and tomato paste; cover and simmer, stirring occasionally, for about 1½ hours or until meat is tender. (MAKE-AHEAD: Let cool slightly; transfer to shallow airtight container. Finish cooling, uncovered, in refrigerator. Cover and refrigerate for up to 2 days or freeze for up to 1 month. Thaw and reheat.) Serve sprinkled with parsley.

Makes 6 to 8 servings.

PER EACH OF 8 SERVINGS, ABOUT:

cal 364	carb . . . . 12 g
pro . . . . 35 g	fibre . . . . 2 g
total fat . . . . 19 g	chol . . . . . 122 mg
sat. fat . . . . . . 6 g	sodium . . 599 mg

PERCENTAGE RDI:

calcium 6%	vit. A 17%
iron 24%	vit. C 22%
folate 12%	

Lemon Oregano Pork Stew

The no-fuss make-ahead factor is what gives stew its appeal, not only for busy week-nights but also for come-on-over dinners. Pork shoulder butt has the necessary marbling and connective tissue to tenderize during slow, moist simmering.

TEST KITCHEN TIP: To peel pearl onions as quickly as possible, cover them with boiling water and let stand for 2 minutes before draining and peeling.

3 lb	boneless pork shoulder butt	1.5 kg
¼ cup	all-purpose flour	50 mL
½ tsp	salt	2 mL
¼ tsp	pepper	1 mL
3 tbsp	olive oil	50 mL
1	onion, chopped	1
7	carrots, cut in chunks	7

4	cloves garlic, minced	4
1 tbsp	grated lemon rind	15 mL
1 tbsp	dried oregano	15 mL
2½ cups	chicken stock	625 mL
4 cups	pearl onions (2 bags/ each 284 g), peeled	1 L
¼ cup	chopped fresh parsley	50 mL
2 tbsp	lemon juice	25 mL

1 Trim fat from pork; cut into 1½-inch (4 cm) cubes. In bowl or plastic bag, toss together pork, flour and pinch each of the salt and pepper to coat. In Dutch oven or large heavy saucepan, heat 1 tbsp (15 mL) of the oil over medium-high heat; brown pork in batches, adding more oil as necessary. Transfer to plate.

2 Add any remaining oil to pan. Cook chopped onion, carrots, garlic, lemon rind, oregano and remaining salt and pepper over medium heat, stirring occasionally, for 5 minutes. Add chicken stock; bring to boil, stirring and scraping up any brown bits from bottom of pan. Return pork and any accumulated juices to pan. Cover and simmer over medium-low heat for 45 minutes.

3 Stir in pearl onions; cook for 45 minutes or until pork is tender. (MAKE-AHEAD: Let cool slightly; transfer to shallow airtight container. Finish cooling, uncovered, in refrigerator. Cover and refrigerate for up to 2 days. Reheat over medium-low heat.) Stir in parsley and lemon juice.

Makes 8 servings.

PER SERVING, ABOUT:

cal 377	carb . . . . 16 g
pro . . . . 37 g	fibre . . . . 3 g
total fat . . . . 18 g	chol . . . . . 114 mg
sat. fat . . . . . . 5 g	sodium . . 561 mg

PERCENTAGE RDI:

calcium 6%	vit. A 161%
iron 23%	vit. C 17%
folate 15%	

Pepper Orange Pork Stew

The contrast between rich braised pork and bright tangy citrus gives this stew broad appeal. While it simmers, cook rice and steam a complementary green vegetable. Broccoli is always a good choice.

2 lb	lean boneless pork shoulder butt	1 kg	2	sweet red peppers, cut in strips	2
3 tbsp	olive oil	50 mL	4 oz	prosciutto or ham, coarsely chopped	125 g
½ tsp	salt	2 mL	10	cloves garlic, thinly sliced	10
¼ tsp	pepper	1 mL	1 tsp	each paprika and dried thyme	5 mL
2	onions, thickly sliced	2	¼ tsp	hot pepper flakes	1 mL
1 cup	chicken stock	250 mL	1	orange	1
2 tbsp	tomato paste	25 mL			

1 Trim off any fat from pork; cut into 1½-inch (4 cm) cubes. In Dutch oven or large heavy saucepan, heat 1 tbsp (15 mL) of the oil over medium-high heat; brown pork in batches, adding more oil as necessary. Sprinkle with salt and pepper. Transfer to plate.

2 Drain off fat in pan. Add onions; cook over medium heat, stirring occasionally, for 5 minutes. Add stock and tomato paste; bring to boil, stirring and scraping up any brown bits from bottom of pan. Return pork to pan; stir in red peppers, prosciutto, garlic, paprika, thyme and hot pepper flakes.

3 Grate rind from orange; add to stew. Peel orange; chop coarsely and stir into stew. Cover and simmer over low heat, stirring occasionally, for 1 to 1½ hours or until pork is tender. (MAKE-AHEAD: Let cool slightly; transfer to shallow airtight container. Finish cooling, uncovered, in refrigerator. Cover and refrigerate for up to 2 days or freeze for up to 1 month. Thaw in refrigerator and bring to room temperature. Reheat over medium-low heat.)

Makes 4 servings.

PER SERVING, ABOUT:

cal	500	carb	19 g
pro	53 g	fibre	4 g
total fat	23 g	chol	167 mg
sat. fat	7 g	sodium	1,025 mg

PERCENTAGE RDI:

calcium	9%	vit. A	29%
iron	31%	vit. C	213%
folate	15%		

Mussel Sausage Simmer

This exuberantly seasoned dish gets its inspiration from Portuguese cataplana — a lusty blend of sausage, pork chunks and clams. It is a heady antidote to midwinter blues or a glorious welcome back after brisk forays into Canadian cold weather.

SUBSTITUTION: Choose other well-seasoned sausages such as Portuguese chouriço or Spanish chorizo.

1 tbsp	olive oil	15 mL
2½ lb	mild Portuguese or Italian sausage, cut in chunks	1.25 kg
2	red onions, chopped	2
4	cloves garlic, minced	4
1 tbsp	paprika	15 mL
¼ tsp	hot pepper flakes	1 mL
1 cup	tomato juice	250 mL
¾ cup	dry red wine	175 mL
2½ lb	mussels	1.25 kg
¼ cup	sliced green onions	50 mL

1 In Dutch oven or large heavy saucepan, heat oil over medium-high heat; brown sausage in batches. Transfer to plate.

2 Drain off fat in pan. Add red onions, garlic, paprika and hot pepper flakes to pan; cook, stirring occasionally, for 5 minutes or until softened. Pour in tomato juice and wine; bring to boil. Return sausage to pan; reduce heat, cover and simmer for 45 minutes.

3 Meanwhile, scrub mussels under running water; trim off any beards. Discard any with cracked shells and any that do not close when tapped. Add mussels to pan; cook, covered, for 12 minutes or until mussels open. Discard any that do not open. Serve sprinkled with green onions.

Makes 8 servings.

PER SERVING, ABOUT:

cal	374	carb	15 g
pro	27 g	fibre	2 g
total fat	23 g	chol	71 mg
sat. fat	7 g	sodium	1,118 mg

PERCENTAGE RDI:

calcium	6%	vit. A	9%
iron	28%	vit. C	20%
folate	17%		

Triple Pork Tenderloin with Mushroom Stuffing

Tenderloin, the incredibly tender, lean, moist cut of pork with no waste, lends itself perfectly to a flavourful stuffing and is as delectable hot as it is cold. Layer three tenderloins together and you have an impressive dish more than ample for a party.

3	pork tenderloins (each 12 oz/375 g)	3	¾ cup	finely chopped onions or shallots	175 mL
¼ cup	Dijon mustard	50 mL	1	apple (unpeeled), diced	1
1	apple (unpeeled), thinly sliced	1	1	carrot, finely chopped	1
¼ tsp	each salt and pepper	1 mL	2 cups	coarse fresh bread crumbs	500 mL
6	sprigs fresh thyme	6	⅓ cup	chopped fresh parsley	75 mL
STUFFING:			1 tbsp	chopped fresh thyme (or ½ tsp/2 mL dried)	15 mL
2 tbsp	each butter and vegetable oil	25 mL	¼ tsp	crumbled dried sage	1 mL
4 cups	finely diced mushrooms (14 oz/400 g)	1 L	¼ tsp	each salt and pepper	1 mL

1 STUFFING: In large skillet, heat butter with oil over medium-high heat; cook mushrooms and onions, stirring occasionally, for about 8 minutes or until liquid is evaporated. Add apple and carrot; cook for 1 minute. Remove from heat. Add bread crumbs, parsley, thyme, sage, salt and pepper; combine well. Set aside.

2 Cut each tenderloin lengthwise halfway through; open like book. Place between plastic wrap or waxed paper; using meat pounder or rolling pin, pound to generous ¼-inch (5 mm) thickness.

3 Cut about 7 pieces of kitchen string into 15-inch (38 cm) lengths; arrange crosswise about 1½ inches (4 cm) apart in lightly greased roasting pan. Place 1 piece of meat on strings. Press half of the stuffing over meat to cover surface. Top with second piece of meat, placing wide end over thin end of first piece; tuck thin ends under and press firmly in place. Top with remaining stuffing and meat.

4 Tie strings around roast, trimming any excess. Spread mustard all over roast. Arrange apple slices in lengthwise row on top; sprinkle with salt and pepper. Arrange thyme sprigs over top. Place in 400°F (200°C) oven; reduce heat to 350°F (180°C). Roast for 1¼ to 1¾ hours or until meat thermometer inserted in centre registers 160°F (70°C). Transfer to cutting board; tent with foil and let stand for 10 minutes. (MAKE-AHEAD: Let cool; cover and refrigerate for up to 24 hours.) Slice roast and arrange on platter.

TEST KITCHEN TIP: When serving hot, accompany tenderloin roast with pan-seared onions and apples: Cut 3 uncored apples crosswise into scant ½-inch (1 cm) thick slices, discarding ends. Repeat with 1 red onion. In large skillet, heat 1 tbsp (15 mL) vegetable oil over medium-high heat; sear apples and onion for 1 to 2 minutes per side or until light golden, adding more oil as needed. Season with salt and pepper to taste. Arrange around roast.

Makes 8 to 10 servings.

PER EACH OF 10 SERVINGS, ABOUT:

cal	234	carb	12 g
pro	26 g	fibre	2 g
total fat	9 g	chol	64 mg
sat. fat	3 g	sodium	319 mg

PERCENTAGE RDI:

calcium	3%	vit. A	22%
iron	17%	vit. C	8%
folate	10%		

Orange Fennel Rack of Pork

It's no secret that pork and fruit go together. In this stylish rib-end rack of pork, both are complemented by licorice accents of fennel.

TEST KITCHEN TIP: In order to cut between the rib bones and serve 1 chop-size portion per person, ensure that the butcher has removed the chine, or backbone, which runs the length of the roast.

1	loin rack of pork, rib end (4 lb/2 kg)	1
3	cloves garlic, slivered	3
2 tbsp	minced gingerroot	25 mL
4 tsp	fennel seeds, crushed	20 mL
½ tsp	salt	2 mL
¼ tsp	pepper	1 mL

GLAZE:		
½ cup	thawed orange juice concentrate	125 mL
½ cup	water	125 mL
¼ cup	orange marmalade	50 mL
2 tsp	grated orange rind	10 mL
2 tsp	cornstarch	10 mL

1 Make tiny slits all over pork; insert garlic slivers. Combine ginger, fennel seeds, salt and pepper; rub over pork. Wrap ends of ribs in foil to prevent charring. Roast, rib end up, on rack in shallow roasting pan in 325°F (160°C) oven for 30 minutes.

2 GLAZE: Meanwhile, in small saucepan, cook orange juice concentrate, water, marmalade, orange rind and cornstarch over medium-high heat, whisking constantly, for 3 to 5 minutes or until boiling and thickened. Remove ½ cup (125 mL) for basting; set aside remainder in saucepan.

3 Brush pork lightly with some of the basting glaze. Roast, basting with glaze every 20 minutes, for 2 to 2¼ hours or until meat thermometer inserted in centre registers 160° to 170°F (70° to 75°C). Transfer to cutting board; tent with foil and let stand for 15 minutes before slicing.

4 Rewarm reserved glaze over low heat; spoon over meat.

VARIATION

Red Pepper–Glazed Pork Loin: Omit garlic and glaze and substitute the following: Combine 1 tbsp (15 mL) dried sage, ¾ tsp (4 mL) salt and 3 cloves garlic, minced; rub over pork and roast for 1½ hours. Brush roast with ¼ cup (50 mL) red pepper jelly, melted; roast for 30 minutes. Brush again with ¼ cup (50 mL) melted jelly and continue roasting to doneness as above.

Makes 8 servings.

PER SERVING, ABOUT:

cal	296	carb	16 g
pro	29 g	fibre	1 g
total fat	12 g	chol	78 mg
sat. fat	4 g	sodium	181 mg

PERCENTAGE RDI:

calcium	5%	vit. A	1%
iron	11%	vit. C	35%
folate	10%		

Jerk Roast Pork

Live a little and take your taste buds on a fantasy holiday to Jamaica, home of reggae, Blue Mountain coffee and jerk. The roast, with its characteristic Island pepperiness and touch of allspice, is big enough that you can include your friends in the fun.

1	loin rack of pork, rib end (4 lb/2 kg)	1

JERK MARINADE:

4	green onions, chopped	4
3	cloves garlic	3
1	Scotch bonnet pepper or hot pepper, halved	1
1	onion, chopped	1
¼ cup	orange juice	50 mL

3 tbsp	soy sauce	50 mL
1 tbsp	vegetable oil	15 mL
2 tsp	ground allspice	10 mL
2 tsp	vinegar	10 mL
½ tsp	dried thyme	2 mL
½ tsp	each salt and pepper	2 mL
¼ tsp	each curry powder and cinnamon	1 mL

1 JERK MARINADE: In food processor, purée together green onions, garlic, Scotch bonnet pepper, onion, orange juice, soy sauce, oil, allspice, vinegar, thyme, salt, pepper, curry powder and cinnamon. (MAKE-AHEAD: Refrigerate in airtight container for up to 4 days.)

2 In bowl, pour marinade over pork; cover and marinate in refrigerator for at least 2 hours or for up to 12 hours, turning occasionally.

3 Roast on rack in roasting pan in 325°F (160°C) oven for 1¾ to 2 hours or until meat thermometer inserted in centre registers 160°F (70°C). Transfer to cutting board; tent with foil and let stand for 10 minutes before slicing.

TEST KITCHEN TIPS

• In Jamaica, moist pork shoulder butt roasts are more typical jerk cuts. However, loin roasts are easier to carve, especially if the roasts have had the backbone removed.

• Scotch bonnet peppers are fiery-hot peppers shaped like little bonnets, hence the name. They add not only heat but taste to foods. Be wary when handling these peppers; wear disposable rubber gloves and do not touch any part of your body.

SUBSTITUTION: Instead of Scotch bonnet peppers, use jalapeños, hot banana peppers or hot green chilies.

Makes 8 servings.

PER SERVING, ABOUT:

cal 260	carb . . . . 3 g
pro . . . . 29 g	fibre . . . . 1 g
total fat . . . . 14 g	chol . . . . . . 78 mg
sat. fat . . . . . . 5 g	sodium . . 461 mg

PERCENTAGE RDI:

calcium 4%	vit. A 2%
iron 12%	vit. C 10%
folate 5%	

Glazed Pork Tenderloin with Chinese Noodles

Chefs use a trick that's handy for home cooks: they sear meat to get a good colour, then finish cooking it in the oven, or sometimes even under the broiler, as in this recipe. This technique works perfectly with tenderloins.

SUBSTITUTION: If you can't find precooked Chinese noodles, cook 12 oz (375 g) spaghetti in a large pot of boiling salted water for about 8 minutes or until tender but firm.

2	pork tenderloins (1½ lb/750 g total)	2
1 tbsp	vegetable oil	15 mL
½ cup	hoisin sauce	125 mL
2 tbsp	minced gingerroot	25 mL
2 tbsp	each soy sauce and red wine vinegar	25 mL
1 tbsp	liquid honey	15 mL

2	cloves garlic, minced	2
1½ tsp	toasted sesame seeds	7 mL
2	pkg (each 450 g) precooked Chinese noodles	2
1	onion, thinly sliced	1
1	each sweet green and red pepper, thinly sliced	1
1 tbsp	lemon juice	15 mL

1 Trim any fat from pork. Tuck thin ends under and tie each tenderloin with kitchen string. In skillet, heat oil over high heat; sear pork all over, about 5 minutes. Place on rack on rimmed foil-lined baking sheet.

2 In bowl, whisk together hoisin sauce, ginger, soy sauce, vinegar, honey and garlic; set ½ cup (125 mL) aside. Brush pork with half of the remaining sauce. Broil 6 inches (15 cm) from heat, turning halfway through and brushing with remaining sauce, for 10 to 12 minutes or until just a hint of pink remains inside and juices run clear when pork is pierced.

3 Transfer to cutting board. Sprinkle with sesame seeds. Tent with foil and let stand for 5 minutes before slicing thinly on the diagonal.

4 Meanwhile, loosen noodles under cold water. In bowl, cover noodles with boiling water; let stand for 4 minutes. Drain.

5 Meanwhile, in large skillet, cook onion and green and red peppers over medium-high heat for 5 minutes. Add lemon juice and reserved sauce; cook for 1 minute. Add noodles and toss. Serve with pork.

Makes 6 servings.

PER SERVING, ABOUT:

cal 638	carb . . . . 92 g
pro . . . . 44 g	fibre . . . . 5 g
total fat . . . . 10 g	chol . . . . . 158 mg
sat. fat . . . . . . 2 g	sodium . . 760 mg

PERCENTAGE RDI:

calcium 4%	vit. A 10%
iron 26%	vit. C 82%
folate 95%	

Chutney-Glazed Ham with Mango Salsa

MAKE-AHEAD   CLASSIC

From the kitchen of Canada's foremost proponent of healthy eating, Anne Lindsay, comes this ham accented with chutney and ginger and served with a tropical salsa.

1	fully cooked bone-in smoked ham, 12 to 15 lb (5.5 to 6.75 kg)	1
3 cups	orange juice, heated	750 mL
	Mango Salsa (recipe follows)	
GLAZE:		
½ cup	packed brown sugar	125 mL
½ cup	strained mango chutney	125 mL

2 tbsp	Dijon mustard	25 mL
1 tbsp	chopped gingerroot	15 mL
1 tbsp	wine vinegar	15 mL
¼ tsp	five-spice powder (optional)	1 mL
Dash	hot pepper sauce	Dash

TEST KITCHEN TIPS

• For a smaller crowd, use a 7- to 10-lb (3.15 to 4.5 kg) ham; cook for about 2 hours.

• For salsa, be sure to dice sweet red pepper, cucumber and coriander finely. You can use mint instead of coriander if you like.

1 GLAZE: In small bowl, combine sugar, chutney, mustard, ginger, vinegar, five-spice powder (if using) and hot pepper sauce; set aside. (MAKE-AHEAD: Cover and refrigerate for up to 1 day.)

2 Remove skin and all but ¼-inch (5 mm) thick layer of fat from ham. Diagonally score fat side of ham to form diamond pattern; place, fat side up, in roasting pan. Pour warm orange juice over ham. Bake in 325°F (160°C) oven, basting occasionally and adding water to pan if liquid evaporates, for 1 hour.

3 Brush one-third of the glaze over ham. Bake, brushing with more glaze every 20 minutes, for 2 hours or until meat thermometer inserted in centre registers 140°F (60°C). Transfer to cutting board; tent with foil and let stand for 10 minutes before carving. Serve with Mango Salsa.

Mango Salsa

2	mangoes, peeled and cut in ½-inch (1 cm) cubes	2
1	jalapeño pepper, minced	1
½ cup	each diced sweet red pepper and cucumber	125 mL

¼ cup	minced red onion	50 mL
2 tbsp	chopped fresh coriander	25 mL
2 tbsp	lemon or lime juice	25 mL
¼ tsp	ground cumin	1 mL

Makes 16 to 20 servings.

1 In bowl, gently stir together mangoes, jalapeño pepper, red pepper, cucumber, onion, coriander, lemon juice and cumin. (MAKE-AHEAD: Cover and refrigerate for up to 6 hours.) **Makes 3½ cups (875 mL).**

PER 4-OZ (125 G) SERVING (WITH SALSA), ABOUT:

cal	223	carb	11 g
pro	29 g	fibre	trace
total fat	6 g	chol	62 mg
sat. fat	2 g	sodium	1,639 mg

PERCENTAGE RDI:

calcium	2%	vit. A	1%
iron	9%	vit. C	13%
folate	5%		

Barbecued Pork Loin with Rosemary

Roast-size cuts of pork, beef and lamb, and whole poultry add up to a lot less fussing when you're entertaining. They deliver all the smoky magic and outdoor atmosphere of steaks, chicken parts and chops but require a lot less tending. Rosemary and prosciutto add a dress-up touch.

SUBSTITUTION: You can use 2 large pork tenderloins instead of the single loin, butterflying each just once and arranging thin ends over thick ends for an even roll.

1	boneless centre-cut single loin pork roast (2 lb/1 kg)	1
2 tbsp	olive oil	25 mL
2	cloves garlic, minced	2
1 tbsp	Dijon mustard	15 mL

2 tsp	chopped fresh rosemary (or ½ tsp/2 mL dried)	10 mL
½ tsp	pepper	2 mL
4 oz	thinly sliced smoked ham or prosciutto	125 g

1 Slice pork lengthwise down centre almost but not all the way through; open like book. Repeat slicing for each half; open out.

2 In small bowl, whisk together oil, garlic, mustard, rosemary and pepper; brush half over cut side of pork. Cover with prosciutto. Roll up and tie at both ends and centre with wet kitchen string. Brush remaining oil mixture all over roast.

3 Place roast on greased grill over high heat; brown all over. Turn off 1 burner of 2-burner barbecue or centre burner of 3-burner barbecue and place roast over unlit burner; reduce heat on other side burner or outer burners to medium. Close lid and cook for 1¾ to 2 hours or until meat thermometer inserted in centre registers 160°F (70°C). Transfer to cutting board; tent with foil and let stand for 10 minutes before slicing.

Makes 8 servings.

PER SERVING, ABOUT:

cal 196	carb . . . . 1 g
pro . . . . 25 g	fibre . . . . trace
total fat . . . . 10 g	chol . . . . . . 68 mg
sat. fat . . . . . . 3 g	sodium . . 257 mg

PERCENTAGE RDI:

calcium 2%	vit. A 0%
iron 7%	vit. C 2%
folate 1%	

Pulled Pork on a Bun

If your idea of heaven is a juicy barbecue sandwich with lots of tangy sauce and a mound of tender shredded pork (and you thought you had to seek it out at some barbecue shack in Texas), you'll want to try this slow-barbecued pork shoulder on kaisers.

2 tbsp	each paprika and packed brown sugar	25 mL	1	boneless pork shoulder butt roast (about 3 lb/1.5 kg)		1
1 tbsp	each chili powder, ground cumin and dried thyme	15 mL		Tangy Barbecue Sauce (recipe, page 147)		
1 tsp	each salt and pepper	5 mL	8	crusty kaiser rolls, halved		8

1 In small bowl, combine paprika, brown sugar, chili powder, cumin, thyme, salt and pepper. Untie roast if necessary. Rub spice mixture over pork; transfer to glass bowl or resealable plastic bag. Cover and refrigerate for 4 hours. (MAKE-AHEAD: Refrigerate for up to 24 hours.)

2 Heat 1 burner of 2-burner barbecue or 2 outside burners of 3-burner barbecue to medium. Place pork, fat side up, on greased grill over unlit burner; close lid and cook, adjusting heat if necessary to keep temperature between 250° and 300°F (120° and 150°C), for 3 to 3¼ hours or until meat thermometer inserted in centre registers 160°F (70°C). Transfer to cutting board. Tent with foil and let stand for 20 minutes. Using 2 forks or hands, pull pork into shreds and place in bowl.

3 Meanwhile, in saucepan, heat barbecue sauce. Pour 1½ cups (375 mL) of the sauce over pork, tossing to coat. Pile onto rolls. Drizzle with remaining sauce.

SUBSTITUTION: Instead of Tangy Barbecue Sauce, you can make this quick sauce based on convenient ready-made barbecue sauce: Simmer together 1 bottle (455 mL) hickory barbecue sauce, ¼ cup (50 mL) packed brown sugar, ¼ cup (50 mL) cider vinegar and ½ tsp (2 mL) hot pepper sauce for 5 minutes.

Makes 8 servings.

PER SERVING, ABOUT:

cal	507	carb	62 g
pro	35 g	fibre	7 g
total fat	13 g	chol	78 mg
sat. fat	4 g	sodium	1,477 mg

PERCENTAGE RDI:

calcium	16%	vit. A	19%
iron	49%	vit. C	13%
folate	35%		

Cuban Grilled Pork Sandwich

*This is an extravaganza of a sandwich, with layers of fresh roast pork, cheese, ham
and pickle. Ideally, the sandwich is grilled in a hot press, but you can approximate the
effect by heating the foil-wrapped loaf in a 350°F (180°C) oven or on a grill over
medium-high heat for about 20 minutes or until the cheese begins to melt and ooze.*

2 tbsp	vegetable oil	25 mL		1	oblong loaf of bread (450 g)	1
1 tbsp	chili powder	15 mL		¼ cup	light mayonnaise	50 mL
1	clove garlic, minced	1		2 tsp	Dijon mustard	10 mL
¼ tsp	pepper	1 mL		6 oz	sliced Black Forest ham	175 g
Pinch	salt	Pinch		6	slices dill pickle	6
1	pork tenderloin (12 oz/375 g)	1		4 oz	sliced Swiss cheese	125 g

1 In glass bowl, whisk together oil, chili powder, garlic, pepper and salt; add
pork, turning to coat. (MAKE-AHEAD: Cover and refrigerate for up to 24 hours.)

2 Place pork on greased grill over medium-high heat; close lid and cook, turning once, for 16 to 20 minutes or until just a hint of pink remains inside and
juices run clear when pork is pierced. Transfer to cutting board; tent with foil
and let cool. Slice thinly on the diagonal.

3 Cut bread in half horizontally. Combine mayonnaise with mustard; spread
on cut sides of loaf. Layer sliced pork, ham and dill pickle, then cheese, on
bottom half. Sandwich with top half of loaf. (MAKE-AHEAD: Wrap in foil and
refrigerate for up to 6 hours. If desired, heat foil-wrapped loaf before serving.)
Cut into eighths to serve.

Makes 8 servings.

PER SERVING, ABOUT:

cal	349	carb	34 g
pro	24 g	fibre	1 g
total fat	13 g	chol	46 mg
sat. fat	4 g	sodium	822 mg

PERCENTAGE RDI:

calcium	14%	vit. A	7%
iron	16%	vit. C	2%
folate	19%		

Honey Garlic Ribs

Pork ribs are so versatile, adapting here to four different flavours. You can also marinate precooked ribs with 1 cup (250 mL) Tangy Barbecue Sauce (page 147).

3 lb	pork side or back ribs	1.5 kg	2 tbsp	plum sauce	25 mL
HONEY GARLIC MARINADE:			2 tbsp	liquid honey	25 mL
¼ cup	teriyaki sauce	50 mL	1 tbsp	rice vinegar	15 mL
¼ cup	hoisin sauce	50 mL	2	cloves garlic, minced	2
2 tbsp	sherry	25 mL			

1 Cut ribs into 2- or 3-rib portions. Place in large pot; cover with cold water. Bring to boil; skim off froth. Reduce heat, cover and simmer for 40 minutes or until tender. Drain; arrange in single layer in large shallow glass dish. Set aside.

2 HONEY GARLIC MARINADE: Combine teriyaki sauce, hoisin sauce, sherry, plum sauce, honey, vinegar and garlic. Pour over ribs, turning to coat. Cover and marinate in refrigerator for 4 hours, turning occasionally. (MAKE-AHEAD: Refrigerate for up to 24 hours.) Set aside ⅓ cup (75 mL) of the marinade.

3 Reserving marinade in glass dish, place ribs on greased grill over medium-high heat; cook, brushing often with remaining marinade and turning once, for 10 to 15 minutes or until browned. Add 2 tbsp (25 mL) water to reserved ⅓ cup (75 mL) marinade and bring to boil; boil for 3 minutes. To serve, brush reserved boiled marinade over ribs.

MARINADE VARIATIONS

Thai Ribs: Omit Honey Garlic Marinade. Combine ⅓ cup (75 mL) hoisin sauce, ¼ cup (50 mL) each soy sauce and lime juice, 2 tbsp (25 mL) each minced gingerroot, chopped fresh coriander and sherry, 2 cloves garlic, minced, 1 tsp (5 mL) sesame oil and ½ tsp (2 mL) each granulated sugar and chili paste. Use as marinade and brush all remaining marinade on ribs during grilling.

Korean Ribs: Omit Honey Garlic Marinade. Combine ⅓ cup (75 mL) soy sauce, ¼ cup (50 mL) chopped green onions, 2 tbsp (25 mL) sherry, 2 tsp (10 mL) vegetable oil, 1 tsp (5 mL) sesame oil, ¼ tsp (1 mL) hot pepper flakes and 1 clove garlic, minced. Use as marinade and brush all remaining marinade on ribs during grilling. To serve, sprinkle ribs with sesame seeds.

Black Bean Ribs: Omit Honey Garlic Marinade. Combine ⅓ cup (75 mL) black bean sauce, 2 tbsp (25 mL) rice vinegar, 4 tsp (20 mL) each liquid honey and ketchup, 2 tsp (10 mL) chopped gingerroot, 2 tsp (10 mL) sesame oil, 2 cloves garlic, minced, and pinch pepper. Use as marinade and brush all remaining marinade on ribs during grilling.

Makes 4 servings.

PER SERVING, ABOUT:

cal	633	carb	23 g
pro	48 g	fibre	1 g
total fat	37 g	chol	180 mg
sat. fat	14 g	sodium	1,113 mg

PERCENTAGE RDI:

calcium	8%	vit. A	1%
iron	26%	vit. C	2%
folate	6%		

Slow and Easy
Real Barbecued Ribs

While Canadians call a grill a barbecue, and talk about barbecuing food instead of grilling, authentic barbecuing involves slow cooking for a long time, preferably with a whisper of natural smoke from time to time. We've duplicated this process on a modern gas barbecue, omitting another Canadian tradition when cooking ribs: boiling them before glazing on the grill.

5 lb	pork back ribs (3 racks)	2.2 kg
RUB:		
¼ cup	packed brown sugar	50 mL
2 tbsp	each paprika and chili powder	25 mL
1 tbsp	each ground cumin and salt	15 mL
1 tsp	each pepper and cayenne pepper	5 mL
½ tsp	ground cloves	2 mL
SAUCE:		
2 tbsp	vegetable oil	25 mL
1	onion, chopped	1
4	cloves garlic, minced	4
1 tbsp	each paprika and chili powder	15 mL
1 tsp	each salt and pepper	5 mL
1	can (19 oz/540 mL) tomatoes	1
1	can (5½ oz/156 mL) tomato paste	1
⅔ cup	vinegar	150 mL
⅓ cup	packed brown sugar	75 mL
2 tbsp	Dijon mustard	25 mL
½ cup	fancy molasses	125 mL

1 Trim any visible fat from ribs. If necessary, remove membrane from underside. Place ribs in large shallow glass dish.

2 RUB: In small dish, stir together sugar, paprika, chili powder, cumin, salt, pepper, cayenne and cloves; rub all over ribs. Cover and refrigerate for 4 hours. (MAKE-AHEAD: Refrigerate for up to 24 hours.)

3 SAUCE: Meanwhile, in large saucepan, heat oil over medium heat; cook onion and garlic, stirring occasionally, for 5 minutes or until softened. Add paprika, chili powder, salt and pepper; cook for 2 minutes. Add tomatoes, tomato paste, vinegar, sugar and mustard; bring to boil. Reduce heat and simmer, stirring occasionally, for about 1 hour or until thickened and reduced by one-third. Let cool slightly. Pour into blender; purée until smooth. Stir in molasses. Set aside 1 cup (250 mL) for dipping.

Makes 6 to 8 servings.

PER EACH OF 8 SERVINGS, ABOUT:

cal 642	carb . . . . 43 g
pro . . . . 31 g	fibre . . . . 3 g
total fat . . . . 40 g	chol . . . . . 137 mg
sat. fat . . . . . 13 g	sodium 1,489 mg

PERCENTAGE RDI:

calcium 15%	vit. A 36%
iron 42%	vit. C 35%
folate 5%	

4 Heat 1 burner of 2-burner barbecue or 2 outside burners of 3-burner barbecue to medium. Place ribs on greased grill over unlit burner. Close lid and cook for 50 minutes, keeping temperature between 250° and 300°F (120° and 150°C) and using oven thermometer if necessary. Turn and cook for 50 minutes or until tender and bones are visible at ends.

5 Brush ribs generously with some of the sauce. Cook, turning once and basting often, for 20 minutes or until crisp on both sides. Cut into 2- or 3-rib pieces. Serve with reserved sauce.

SPICE RUBS FOR Pork

~ In bowl, stir together ingredients for desired spice mix (right). These mixes are good for beef, lamb and poultry, too. **Makes about ⅓ cup (75 mL).**

~ For every 4 servings (1 lb/500 g boneless, 1½ lb/750 g bone-in pork), rub with 2 tbsp (25 mL) spice mix. Cover and refrigerate for at least 4 hours or for up to 12 hours.

~ Store dry spice mixes in airtight containers for up to 6 months.

~ **MEDITERRANEAN SPICE MIX:** Use 3 tbsp (50 mL) dried rosemary, 2 tbsp (25 mL) ground cumin, 2 tbsp (25 mL) ground coriander, 1 tbsp (15 mL) dried oregano, 2 tsp (10 mL) cinnamon and ½ tsp (2 mL) salt.

~ **CHILI SPICE MIX:** Use 3 tbsp (50 mL) chili powder, 2 tbsp (25 mL) paprika, 2 tbsp (25 mL) packed brown sugar, 1 tbsp (15 mL) ground cumin, 1 tsp (5 mL) garlic powder and ½ tsp (2 mL) each salt and pepper.

~ **CAJUN SPICE MIX:** Use 3 tbsp (50 mL) dried thyme, 2 tbsp (25 mL) each paprika and packed brown sugar, 1 tbsp (15 mL) each ground cumin, dry mustard and hot pepper flakes, and 1 tsp (5 mL) salt.

~ **MIDDLE EASTERN SPICE MIX:** Use 3 tbsp (50 mL) paprika, 2 tbsp (25 mL) each ground coriander and cumin, 1 tsp (5 mL) each ground ginger and cinnamon, ½ tsp (2 mL) each salt and ground allspice, and ¼ tsp (1 mL) each cayenne pepper and ground cloves.

Maple-Glazed
Peameal Bacon Dinner

*Nothing is quicker or easier than grilling thick slices of peameal bacon and using the
barbecue to cook sweet potatoes and hobo packs of apples to serve alongside.*

4	sweet potatoes (unpeeled), about 2 lb (1 kg)	4	⅓ cup	maple syrup	75 mL
1½ lb	peameal bacon (unsliced)	750 g	2 tsp	Dijon mustard	10 mL
2	apples (unpeeled)	2	Pinch	ground cloves	Pinch

1 Scrub and prick potatoes. Place on greased grill over medium heat; close lid
and cook, turning occasionally, for 25 minutes.

2 Meanwhile, cut bacon into ¾-inch (2 cm) thick slices. Core apples; cut into
eighths. In small bowl, combine maple syrup, mustard and cloves. Place apples
on large buttered square of foil; drizzle with 2 tbsp (25 mL) of the maple syrup
mixture. Seal packet and set aside.

3 Add bacon to grill; close lid and cook for 10 minutes. Turn and brush with
some of the maple syrup mixture. Add apple packet to grill; close lid and cook
for about 10 minutes or until apples and potatoes are tender. Slash each potato
just enough to drizzle in 1 tsp (5 mL) maple syrup mixture.

VARIATION

Peameal Bacon Roast: Place 2½-lb (1.25 kg) peameal bacon or back bacon roast on
rack in small foil-lined roasting pan. In bowl, stir together ¼ cup (50 mL) maple
syrup, 2 tbsp (25 mL) Dijon mustard and ¼ tsp (1 mL) dried thyme; brush over roast,
reserving any leftover to brush on halfway through roasting time. Roast in 425°F (220°C)
oven for about 70 minutes or until meat thermometer inserted in centre registers
130°F (55°C). Transfer to cutting board; tent with foil and let stand for 10 minutes
before slicing. **Makes 8 servings.**

Makes 4 servings.

PER SERVING, ABOUT:

cal	609	carb	84 g
pro	39 g	fibre	8 g
total fat	13 g	chol	84 mg
sat. fat	4 g	sodium	2,294 mg

PERCENTAGE RDI:

calcium	9%	vit. A	495%
iron	19%	vit. C	98%
folate	26%		

Choucroute Garnie

There has to be a little smoky bacon to season this robust sauerkraut dish simmered with apples, juniper berries and onion. As for the sausages, to be authentic they should come from an Alsatian charcuterie, but realistically, choose ones from delis or butchers specializing in food from Northern and Eastern Europe.

3	large onions, sliced	3
3	Golden Delicious apples, cored and sliced	3
4	cloves garlic, minced	4
6 cups	sauerkraut, rinsed and drained	1.5 L
8 oz	chunk slab bacon	250 g
1 tbsp	cracked peppercorns	15 mL
20	juniper berries	20
1 tsp	caraway seeds	5 mL

1 cup	dry white wine or chicken stock	250 mL
1 tbsp	vegetable oil	15 mL
1	boneless pork loin (about 2 lb/1 kg)	1
4	fresh bratwurst sausages	4
4	knackwurst sausages or wieners	4
16	small new potatoes (unpeeled), boiled	16

TEST KITCHEN TIP: For the best flavour, choose fresh sauerkraut sold by weight in delicatessens. It has a truer, more subtle flavour than canned or even jarred varieties; in fact, it will be a revelation to people who think sauerkraut is too strong and coarse.

1 In Dutch oven, combine half each of the onions, apples and garlic. Cover with half of the sauerkraut; add bacon. Sprinkle with peppercorns, juniper berries and caraway seeds. Add remaining onions, apples and garlic; cover with remaining sauerkraut. Pour in wine. Cover and cook in 300°F (150°C) oven for 2½ hours.

2 In large skillet, heat oil over medium-high heat; brown pork loin. Nestle into sauerkraut; cook, covered, for 1 hour.

3 In same skillet, brown bratwurst; add to sauerkraut mixture along with knackwurst. Cook, covered, for 1 hour or until sausages are cooked through and tender. Transfer pork loin and bacon to cutting board; cut into slices. Heap sauerkraut onto large platter; surround with sausages, sliced pork and bacon, and potatoes.

Makes 8 servings.

PER SERVING, ABOUT:

cal	644	carb	38 g
pro	43 g	fibre	8 g
total fat	36 g	chol	134 mg
sat. fat	12 g	sodium	2,048 mg

PERCENTAGE RDI:

calcium	11%	vit. A	1%
iron	38%	vit. C	62%
folate	26%		

Deep-Dish Tourtière

Tourtière is always served with a sweet-and-sour pickle, green tomato relish or a fruity Chili Sauce (page 389) to temper the richness of pastry plus pork. While tourtière is traditionally made as a double-crust pie, this top-crust-only version is practical for buffets, especially potluck suppers.

TEST KITCHEN TIP: If pie shape is integral to your enjoyment of this Quebec holiday-time special dish, use the seasoned pork mixture to mound generously in 1 deep 10-inch (25 cm) double-crust pie, or more thinly in two 9-inch (23 cm) double-crust pies. For the latter, you will need to double the amount of pastry.

2	potatoes (1 lb/500 g)	2
2 lb	lean ground pork, chicken or turkey	1 kg
1 tbsp	vegetable oil	15 mL
2	large onions, chopped	2
6	cloves garlic, minced	6
1	stalk celery, chopped	1
6 cups	sliced mushrooms (about 1 lb/500 g)	1.5 L
1½ tsp	dried thyme	7 mL
¾ tsp	each salt and dried savory	4 mL
½ tsp	pepper	2 mL
¼ tsp	each ground cloves and cinnamon	1 mL
2 cups	chicken stock	500 mL
¼ cup	chopped fresh parsley	50 mL
	Pastry for 1 double-crust pie (see Perfect Pastry Every Time, page 326)	
1	egg, beaten	1

1 Peel and quarter potatoes. In saucepan of boiling salted water, cover and cook potatoes for about 15 minutes or until tender. Drain and return to pan; dry potatoes over low heat for 30 seconds. Mash until smooth.

2 In Dutch oven or large deep skillet, cook pork over medium-high heat in batches, stirring and scraping up any brown bits from bottom of pan, for about 5 minutes or until no longer pink. Strain through large sieve set over bowl. Skim off any fat from juices; reserve juices and pork.

3 Add oil to pan; heat over medium heat. Add onions, garlic, celery, mushrooms, thyme, salt, savory, pepper, cloves and cinnamon; cook, stirring often, for about 10 minutes or until softened and liquid is evaporated. Add reserved meat and juices, chicken stock and potatoes; cook for about 5 minutes or until thickened. Stir in parsley. Scrape into 13- x 9-inch (3 L) glass baking dish; refrigerate until cooled.

4 On lightly floured surface, roll out pastry slightly larger than top of baking dish. Place over filling, letting pastry rise loosely over rim. Tuck under any pastry beyond rim; press to inner rim. (MAKE-AHEAD: Cover and refrigerate for up to 1 day. Or wrap in heavy-duty foil and freeze for up to 2 weeks; thaw in refrigerator for 48 hours or until no longer icy in middle.) Brush pastry with egg. Cut steam hole in centre. Bake in lower third of 425°F (220°C) oven for about 45 minutes or until golden brown and filling is piping hot. Let stand on rack for 5 minutes before serving.

Makes 8 servings.

PER SERVING, ABOUT:

cal	667	carb	48 g
pro	30 g	fibre	3 g
total fat	39 g	chol	153 mg
sat. fat	17 g	sodium	959 mg

PERCENTAGE RDI:

calcium	5%	vit. A	14%
iron	31%	vit. C	15%
folate	35%		

Lamb Shanks with Beans

This classic French braised dish demonstrates beautifully how budget cuts taste so good thanks to browning that creates a deep flavour, then slow, moist cooking that tenderizes these tougher cuts.

1 tbsp	vegetable oil	15 mL
6	lamb shanks (about 4 lb/2 kg)	6
4	large onions, sliced vertically	4
4	cloves garlic, minced	4
1	can (28 oz/796 mL) tomatoes	1
2 cups	water	500 mL
1 cup	dry red wine or beef stock	250 mL
2 tsp	crushed dried rosemary	10 mL
1 tsp	salt	5 mL
¾ tsp	dried thyme	4 mL
½ tsp	pepper	2 mL
2	bay leaves	2
2 cups	cubed carrots	500 mL
1 cup	each cubed peeled parsnip and rutabaga	250 mL
¼ cup	minced fresh parsley	50 mL

BRAISED BEANS:

2 tsp	vegetable oil	10 mL
2	onions, chopped	2
2	cloves garlic, minced	2
4 cups	cooked white beans	1 L
½ cup	chicken stock	125 mL
¼ tsp	each salt and pepper	1 mL

TEST KITCHEN TIP: For cooked white beans, either open 2 cans (each 19 oz/540 mL) white beans, rinse and drain or cook 2 cups (500 mL) dry white beans according to method on page 87.

1 In large Dutch oven, heat oil over medium-high heat; brown shanks in batches. Transfer to plate.

2 Drain fat from pan. Add onions and garlic; cook over medium heat, stirring occasionally, for 8 minutes or until tender.

3 Return shanks to pan. Add tomatoes, breaking up with spoon, water, wine, rosemary, salt, thyme, pepper and bay leaves; bring to boil. Reduce heat, cover and simmer for 1 hour.

4 Add carrots, parsnip and rutabaga; simmer, covered, for 40 minutes or until tender.

5 **BRAISED BEANS:** Meanwhile, in heavy saucepan, heat oil over medium-low heat; cook onions and garlic, stirring occasionally, for 4 to 6 minutes or until softened. Add beans, stock, salt and pepper; bring to boil. Reduce heat and simmer for 15 to 20 minutes or until almost no liquid remains.

6 Meanwhile, using slotted spoon, transfer meat and vegetables to platter; discard bay leaves. Cover and keep warm. Skim fat from pan juices; boil for 10 minutes to thicken slightly. Transfer beans to platter; spoon juices over meat, vegetables and beans. Sprinkle with parsley.

Makes 6 servings.

PER SERVING, ABOUT:

cal	525	carb	59 g
pro	44 g	fibre	13 g
total fat	13 g	chol	95 mg
sat. fat	4 g	sodium	853 mg

PERCENTAGE RDI:

calcium	21%	vit. A	101%
iron	63%	vit. C	50%
folate	68%		

Lamb Moussaka

This excellent Greek layered casserole is ideal for potlucks, buffets and casual entertaining. Even people who normally turn up their noses at eggplant love it in this make-ahead dish.

SUBSTITUTION: You can also make Beef Moussaka, substituting lean ground beef for lamb.

2	eggplants (2½ lb/1.25 kg total)	2
1 tbsp	salt	15 mL
2 tbsp	olive oil	25 mL
½ cup	fresh bread crumbs	125 mL
¼ cup	grated Parmesan cheese	50 mL

MEAT SAUCE:

2 lb	lean ground lamb	1 kg
2	onions, chopped	2
4	cloves garlic, minced	4
1 tbsp	dried oregano	15 mL
1 tsp	cinnamon	5 mL
¼ tsp	pepper	1 mL
1 cup	red wine	250 mL
1	can (19 oz/540 mL) tomatoes	1
1	can (5½ oz/156 mL) tomato paste	1
½ cup	chopped fresh parsley	125 mL

CHEESE SAUCE:

¼ cup	butter	50 mL
¼ cup	all-purpose flour	50 mL
2 cups	milk	500 mL
½ tsp	salt	2 mL
¼ tsp	each nutmeg and pepper	1 mL
1 cup	crumbled feta cheese	250 mL
4	eggs, beaten	4
2 cups	pressed dry cottage cheese	500 mL

1 Cut eggplants into ¼-inch (5 mm) thick slices; layer in colander, sprinkling each layer with salt. Let stand for 30 minutes.

2 MEAT SAUCE: Meanwhile, in large skillet, cook lamb over high heat, breaking up with spoon, for 5 minutes or until no longer pink. Spoon off any fat. Add onions, garlic, oregano, cinnamon and pepper; cook over medium-high heat, stirring often, for 5 minutes or until onions are softened.

3 Add wine, tomatoes and tomato paste, breaking up tomatoes with spoon; bring to boil. Reduce heat and simmer vigorously for 10 minutes or until mixture does not fill in when spoon is drawn through pan. Stir in parsley. Set aside.

4 Rinse eggplants; drain well and pat dry. In batches, brush eggplants with oil and broil on baking sheet, turning once, for 8 to 12 minutes or until golden and translucent. Set aside.

Makes 8 servings.

PER SERVING, ABOUT:

cal 593	carb .... 29 g
pro .... 41 g	fibre .... 6 g
total fat .... 35 g	chol ..... 223 mg
sat. fat ..... 16 g	sodium .. 712 mg

PERCENTAGE RDI:

calcium 27%	vit. A 28%
iron 32%	vit. C 37%
folate 36%	

5 CHEESE SAUCE: In saucepan, melt butter over medium heat; whisk in flour and cook, whisking, for 2 minutes, without browning. Gradually whisk in milk until boiling and thickened enough to coat back of spoon. Stir in salt, nutmeg and pepper. Let stand for 10 minutes, stirring occasionally.

6 Rinse feta under cold water; drain well. In large bowl, whisk together feta, eggs and cottage cheese; whisk in cheese sauce.

7 Spread half of the meat sauce in greased 13- x 9-inch (3 L) glass baking dish. Spoon ½ cup (125 mL) of the cheese sauce on top, spreading evenly. Layer with half of the eggplant, overlapping if necessary. Repeat layers once. Pour remaining cheese sauce over top. (MAKE-AHEAD: Let cool slightly. Finish cooling, uncovered, in refrigerator. Cover with plastic wrap and refrigerate for up to 1 day or overwrap with heavy-duty foil and freeze for up to 3 weeks. Thaw in refrigerator for 48 hours before continuing.)

8 Combine bread crumbs with Parmesan cheese; sprinkle over moussaka. Bake in 350°F (180°C) oven for 70 minutes or until browned and bubbly. Let stand for 15 minutes; cut into squares.

MAKE-
AHEAD

Roast Leg of Lamb

For festive occasions, nothing impresses as much as a whole leg of lamb, here with three pleasing taste variations.

TEST KITCHEN TIPS

• The size of a leg of lamb ranges from 3½ to 6 lb (1.75 to 2.7 kg), depending on the way it is butchered and its country of origin. Canadian lamb is often larger than imported. A short-cut leg has the sirloin removed; a whole leg includes the sirloin.

• To carve leg of lamb, place lamb on cutting board with meatier portion facing up. Grip shank end firmly with towel. Cutting down to bone, cut ¼-inch (5 mm) thick slices. With knife parallel to bone, cut slices from along bone. Turn lamb so that remaining meaty portion faces up. Carve as for first side.

1	leg of lamb (3½ lb/1.75 kg), trimmed	1
1	onion, chopped	1
1½ cups	chicken stock (approx)	375 mL
2 tbsp	cornstarch	25 mL
¼ tsp	each salt and pepper	1 mL

MEDITERRANEAN:

1 cup	red wine	250 mL
1	onion, chopped	1
1 tsp	each dried mint, tarragon and thyme	5 mL
¼ tsp	salt	1 mL

OR CARIBBEAN:

2 tbsp	vegetable oil	25 mL
1 tbsp	grated gingerroot	15 mL
1 tsp	ground cumin	5 mL
¾ tsp	salt	4 mL
½ tsp	each pepper, ground coriander and turmeric	2 mL
¼ tsp	cayenne pepper	1 mL

OR ITALIAN:

10	cloves garlic	10
2 tbsp	olive oil	25 mL
½ tsp	each salt and pepper	2 mL
½ cup	grated Romano cheese	125 mL

1 MEDITERRANEAN: In large shallow glass dish, mix together wine, onion, mint, tarragon and thyme. Add lamb, turning to coat. Cover and refrigerate for 8 hours, turning and brushing often with marinade. (MAKE-AHEAD: Refrigerate for up to 24 hours.) Brush off onion; sprinkle with salt. Strain marinade into saucepan; boil for 5 minutes.

2 CARIBBEAN: In small bowl, stir together oil, ginger, cumin, salt, pepper, coriander, turmeric and cayenne pepper; brush evenly over lamb.

3 ITALIAN: Make 10 tiny slits all over lamb; insert garlic clove completely into each slit. Brush lamb with oil; sprinkle with salt and pepper. Press cheese all over lamb to adhere.

4 Place lamb on greased rack in roasting pan; roast in 350°F (180°C) oven for about 1¾ hours or until meat thermometer inserted in centre registers 150°F (65°C) for medium-rare, or to desired doneness. Transfer to platter and tent with foil; let stand for 15 minutes before carving.

5 Skim fat from pan juices. Add onion to pan; cook for 5 minutes. (For Mediterranean version, add enough stock to boiled marinade to make 1½ cups/375 mL.) Pour in stock; bring to boil, stirring and scraping up brown bits from bottom of pan. Mix cornstarch with 2 tbsp (25 mL) water; stir into pan. Add salt and pepper. Cook, stirring, until thickened. Strain if desired. Serve with lamb.

Makes 6 servings.

PER SERVING, ABOUT:

cal	289	carb	5 g
pro	37 g	fibre	trace
total fat	11 g	chol	129 mg
sat. fat	5 g	sodium	446 mg

PERCENTAGE RDI:

calcium	2%	vit. A	0%
iron	24%	vit. C	2%
folate	2%		

Rosemary-Crusted Rack of Lamb

The technique of searing the lamb racks before roasting ensures that this small cut of meat will be beautifully brown and crusty outside yet still pink and tender inside. Couscous Timbales (recipe below) are an attractive accompaniment.

½ cup	fresh bread crumbs	125 mL		¼ tsp	each salt and pepper	1 mL
¼ cup	toasted chopped pecans	50 mL		¼ cup	Dijon mustard	50 mL
2 tbsp	chopped fresh rosemary	25 mL		2	racks of lamb (18 bones total), 1½ lb (750 g) total	2
2 tbsp	grated Parmesan cheese	25 mL				
2	cloves garlic, minced	2		2 tbsp	olive oil	25 mL

1 In small bowl, combine bread crumbs, pecans, rosemary, Parmesan cheese, garlic, salt and pepper. Spread mustard evenly over lamb racks. Coat racks with bread crumb mixture.

2 In large ovenproof skillet, heat oil over medium-high heat. Add racks, fat side down; cook for 2 minutes or until golden. Transfer to 425°F (220°C) oven; roast for about 15 minutes or until meat thermometer inserted in centre registers 140°F (60°C) for rare or until desired doneness.

3 Transfer lamb to cutting board; tent with foil and let stand for 10 minutes before carving.

couscous Timbales

In small saucepan, heat 1 tbsp (15 mL) olive oil over medium heat; cook 1 small onion, finely chopped, 1 carrot, finely chopped, half sweet red pepper, diced, and ¼ tsp (1 mL) each dried thyme, salt and pepper for 5 minutes or until softened. Pour in 1½ cups (375 mL) vegetable or chicken stock; bring to boil. Add 1 cup (250 mL) couscous; cover and remove from heat. Let stand for 5 minutes; fluff. Pack into six 6-oz (175 mL) greased ramekins or timbale moulds; to serve, invert onto plates. **Makes 6 servings.**

Makes 6 servings.

PER SERVING, ABOUT:

cal	178	carb	4 g
pro	12 g	fibre	trace
total fat	13 g	chol	37 mg
sat. fat	3 g	sodium	306 mg

PERCENTAGE RDI:

calcium	5%	vit. A	1%
iron	9%	vit. C	2%
folate	2%		

Butterflied Leg of Lamb

Caraway is a novel spice to connect to lamb, but well worth trying with this easy-to-carve company lamb.

¼ cup	chopped fresh parsley	50 mL
1 tsp	grated lemon rind	5 mL
¼ cup	lemon juice	50 mL
3 tbsp	olive oil	50 mL
4	cloves garlic, minced	4
1 tbsp	chopped fresh marjoram (or 1 tsp/5 mL dried)	15 mL

2 tsp	caraway seeds, crushed	10 mL
¼ tsp	each salt and pepper	1 mL
1	butterflied leg of lamb (about 3 lb/1.5 kg)	1
2	slices bacon, chopped	2

1 In large shallow glass dish, combine parsley, lemon rind and juice, oil, garlic, marjoram, caraway seeds, salt and pepper; set aside.

2 Trim fat from lamb. Cut slits all over; insert bacon piece into each. Add to marinade, turning to coat. Cover and refrigerate for 8 hours, turning occasionally. (MAKE-AHEAD: **Refrigerate for up to 24 hours.**)

3 Place lamb on greased grill over medium-high heat; close lid and cook, turning once, for 20 to 30 minutes or until meat thermometer inserted in centre registers 140°F (60°C) for rare or until desired doneness.

4 Transfer lamb to cutting board; tent with foil and let stand for 10 minutes. Slice thinly across the grain.

Makes 8 to 10 servings.

PER EACH OF 10 SERVINGS, ABOUT:

cal 215	carb . . . . 1 g
pro . . . . 29 g	fibre . . . . trace
total fat . . . . 10 g	chol . . . . . 107 mg
sat. fat . . . . . . 4 g	sodium . . 109 mg

PERCENTAGE RDI:

calcium 1%	vit. A 0%
iron 18%	vit. C 3%
folate 0%	

Herbed Lamb Chops

Harvest your garden or visit your local market for herbs to dress up these succulent lamb chops.

¼ cup	red wine vinegar	50 mL
2 tbsp	each chopped fresh rosemary and thyme or marjoram	25 mL
2	cloves garlic, minced	2

1 tbsp	olive oil	15 mL
½ tsp	pepper	2 mL
¼ tsp	salt	1 mL
8	lamb loin chops (1½ lb/750 g total)	8

SUBSTITUTION: Using the same marinade ingredients, you can substitute 1 lb (500 g) top sirloin grilling steak, 4 pork loin chops or 4 boneless skinless chicken breasts for the lamb chops.

1 In large glass bowl, whisk together vinegar, rosemary, thyme, garlic, oil, pepper and salt; add lamb chops, turning to coat. Let stand for 5 minutes. (MAKE-AHEAD: **Cover and refrigerate for up to 4 hours.**)

2 Reserving any marinade, place chops on greased grill over medium-high heat; close lid and cook, turning halfway through and brushing once with marinade, for about 14 minutes for medium-rare or until desired doneness.

Makes 4 servings.

PER SERVING, ABOUT:

cal 157	carb . . . . 2 g
pro . . . . 18 g	fibre . . . . trace
total fat . . . . . 8 g	chol . . . . . . 68 mg
sat. fat . . . . . . 3 g	sodium . . 179 mg

PERCENTAGE RDI:

calcium 3%	vit. A 0%
iron 16%	vit. C 2%
folate 0%	

Fish and Seafood

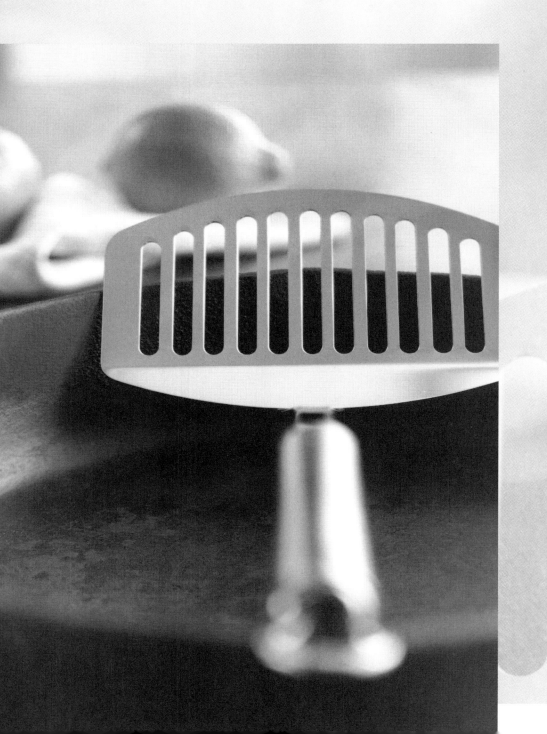

7

Coconut Curry Fish 186

Halibut Braised in Tomato Sauce 187

Spiced Shrimp and Rice Pilaf 188

Red Curry Mussels 189

Poached Salmon with Beurre Blanc 190

Boiled Lobster 191

Crusty Salmon Cakes 192

Batter-Fried Fish 193

Cod au Gratin 194

Roasted Arctic Char with Shrimp 195

Herbed Seafood Casserole 196

Glazed Sea Bass with Red Curry Sauce 197

Oven-Baked Fish and Chips 198

Slow-Grilled Salmon with Garlic and Basil 199

Cumin and Lime Fish Kabobs 200

Grilled Halibut with Tomato Salsa 201

Apple Mustard–Glazed Trout Fillets 202

Grilled Salmon Fillets 203

Cedar-Planked Salmon 204

Fresh Tuna Salade Niçoise 205

Coconut Curry Fish

The coconut milk, the curry powder and especially the whole allspice mark this dish as Jamaican in origin. It's at its most delicious served with the classic Jamaican side dish rice and peas (see below).

SUBSTITUTION: You can use other kinds of fish steaks or fillets. Tilapia, red snapper, halibut and haddock are good choices.

1 tbsp	vegetable oil	15 mL
2	onions, chopped	2
3	cloves garlic, minced	3
2 tsp	curry powder	10 mL
½ tsp	each salt and pepper	2 mL
1	can (400 mL) coconut milk	1

1 cup	diced tomatoes	250 mL
½ cup	chicken or fish stock	125 mL
10	whole allspice	10
2 lb	kingfish or grouper steaks	1 kg
½ tsp	lime juice	2 mL
2	green onions, sliced	2

1 In shallow Dutch oven, heat oil over medium heat; cook onions and garlic, stirring occasionally, for 5 minutes or until softened. Add curry powder, salt and pepper; stir for 1 minute.

2 Add coconut milk, tomatoes, stock and allspice; bring to boil. Reduce heat and simmer for about 25 minutes or until reduced by about half.

3 Add fish; cover and cook for 10 minutes or until fish flakes easily when tested with fork. Discard allspice. Stir in lime juice. Serve sprinkled with green onions.

Makes 6 servings.

PER SERVING, ABOUT:

cal	294	carb	8 g
pro	28 g	fibre	1 g
total fat	17 g	chol	48 mg
sat. fat	13 g	sodium	338 mg

PERCENTAGE RDI:

calcium	6%	vit. A	9%
iron	28%	vit. C	15%
folate	14%		

RICE AND PEAS

2 tsp	vegetable oil	10 mL
4	green onions, sliced	4
2	cloves garlic, minced	2
2¼ cups	chicken stock	550 mL
1 cup	coconut milk	250 mL
1	Scotch bonnet pepper (or pinch cayenne pepper)	1
½ tsp	dried thyme	2 mL
¼ tsp	salt	1 mL

8	whole allspice	8
1½ cups	parboiled rice	375 mL
1 cup	drained rinsed red kidney beans	250 mL

In saucepan, heat oil over medium heat; cook onions and garlic for 1 minute. Add stock, coconut milk, pepper, thyme, salt and allspice; bring to boil. Add rice; return to boil. Cover and cook over medium-low heat for 15 minutes. Stir in beans; cook for 10 minutes or until rice is tender. Discard pepper and allspice. **Makes 6 servings.**

Halibut Braised in Tomato Sauce

One reason why fish can be the ideal solution for quick weeknight meals is the speed at which it cooks. It's also versatile, as this version with a quick tomato sauce shows. Serve with rice, short pasta or crusty bread and a salad.

1 tbsp	olive oil	15 mL
1	onion, chopped	1
2	cloves garlic, minced	2
½ cup	diced sweet red pepper	125 mL
1 tsp	dried basil or oregano	5 mL

½ tsp	each salt and pepper	2 mL
Pinch	hot pepper flakes	Pinch
1	can (28 oz/796 mL) tomatoes	1
1 lb	halibut, cod, haddock or red snapper fillets	500 g
¼ cup	minced fresh parsley	50 mL

1 In large deep skillet, heat oil over medium heat; cook onion, garlic, diced red pepper, basil, salt, pepper and hot pepper flakes for about 5 minutes or until softened.

2 Add tomatoes; with potato masher or back of spoon, break into bits. Bring to boil; reduce heat and simmer, stirring often, for about 15 minutes or until thick enough to mound on spoon. (MAKE-AHEAD: Let sauce cool. Refrigerate in airtight container for up to 3 days or freeze for up to 2 weeks. Thaw and reheat gently before continuing.)

3 If necessary, cut fish fillets into serving-size portions. Nestle in sauce, spooning some of the sauce over top. Cover and simmer over low heat for about 8 minutes or until fish flakes easily when tested with fork. Sprinkle with parsley.

VARIATION

Shrimp Braised in Tomato Sauce with Feta: Substitute 12 oz (375 g) deveined peeled raw shrimp for the fish. Use dried oregano instead of basil. Cook for about 3 minutes or until shrimp start to turn pink. Stir in 4 oz (125 g) feta cheese, broken into chunks. Remove from heat, cover and let stand for about 2 minutes or until shrimp are pink and cheese starts to melt. Sprinkle with parsley, and black olives if desired. **Makes 4 servings.**

Makes 4 servings.

PER SERVING, ABOUT:

cal 213	carb . . . . 13 g
pro . . . . 26 g	fibre . . . . 3 g
total fat . . . . . 7 g	chol . . . . . . 36 mg
sat. fat . . . . . . 1 g	sodium . . 678 mg

PERCENTAGE RDI:

calcium 11%	vit. A 23%
iron 19%	vit. C 73%
folate 15%	

Spiced Shrimp and Rice Pilaf

The combination of rice, spices and shrimp might price this dish into fare for company, but it's also quick for weeknights. Serve with Cucumber Raita, Tomato and Mint Salad (recipes below), basmati rice and, when there's time, crispy pappadams.

TEST KITCHEN TIP: To prepare pappadams, shallow-fry in vegetable oil in skillet over medium-high to high heat. Drain on paper towel–lined plate.

1 lb	large raw shrimp	500 g
1 tbsp	each vegetable oil and butter	15 mL
1	onion, chopped	1
3	cloves garlic, minced	3
2 tsp	mild curry paste	10 mL
1 tsp	grated gingerroot	5 mL

4	each whole cardamom pods and cloves, bruised	4
½ tsp	salt	2 mL
1	small stick cinnamon	1
Half	sweet red pepper, diced	Half
1½ cups	long-grain rice	375 mL
¼ cup	fresh coriander leaves	50 mL

Makes 4 servings.

PER SERVING, ABOUT:

cal . . . . 426 carb . . . . 60 g
pro . . . . 23 g fibre . . . . 2 g
total fat . . . . 10 g chol . . . . . 137 mg
sat. fat . . . . . . 3 g sodium . . 453 mg

PERCENTAGE RDI:

calcium . . . . . 5% vit. A 13%
iron . . . . 16% vit. C 47%
folate 8%

1 Peel and devein shrimp; rinse and pat dry. In wide heavy saucepan, heat oil over medium-high heat; cook shrimp for about 3 minutes or just until pink. Transfer to plate and set aside.

2 Add butter to pan; reduce heat to medium. Cook onion, garlic, curry paste, ginger, cardamom, cloves, salt and cinnamon stick, stirring occasionally, for about 5 minutes or until onion is softened. Stir in red pepper, rice and 3 cups (750 mL) water; bring to boil. Cover and reduce heat to low; cook for about 20 minutes or until water is absorbed and rice is tender.

3 Sprinkle shrimp over rice; using fork, gently toss together, at the same time picking out whole spices if desired. Remove from heat. Cover and let shrimp reheat. Transfer to serving bowl; garnish with coriander.

CUCUMBER Raita

Thinly slice 1 piece (6 inches/15 cm) English cucumber and 4 small radishes. Add to colander; toss with 1 tsp (5 cm) salt. Let stand for 30 minutes. Press out moisture; toss with 1 cup (250 mL) thick yogurt, 1 tbsp (15 mL) lemon juice, 1 small clove garlic, minced, and pinch grated gingerroot. **Makes 1½ cups (375 mL).**

TOMATO AND MINT Salad

Core and cut 2 tomatoes into thin wedges; place in shallow bowl along with 2 green onions, thinly sliced, and ¼ cup (50 mL) chopped fresh mint. In separate bowl, stir together 1 tbsp (15 mL) lemon juice, 1 tsp (5 mL) granulated sugar, ¼ tsp (1 mL) salt and pinch cayenne pepper until sugar is dissolved. Drizzle over tomato mixture; toss to serve. **Makes 2 cups (500 mL).**

Red Curry Mussels

Ever since mussels made it big in the '80s, they have been a popular eatery item across Canada. From a fine Halifax seafood restaurant, McKelvie's, here is a version of mussels with a Thai twist. Serve as a main course for four or as eight appetizer servings.

4 lb	mussels	2 kg
2 tbsp	butter	25 mL
1 tbsp	grated gingerroot	15 mL
3	cloves garlic, minced	3
1	small tomato, peeled and diced	1

1 tbsp	mild Thai red curry paste	15 mL
1	can (400 mL) coconut milk	1
2 tbsp	each finely chopped fresh coriander and chives	25 mL

1 Scrub mussels and remove beards, if necessary. Discard any that do not close when tapped. Set aside.

2 In Dutch oven or large saucepan, melt butter over medium heat; cook ginger, garlic and tomato for 4 minutes, stirring. Add curry paste; cook, mashing into tomato mixture, for 1 minute.

3 Pour in coconut milk; bring to boil, whisking. Add mussels; cover and cook, stirring occasionally, for about 7 minutes or until mussels open. Discard any that do not open.

4 Ladle mussels and coconut broth into 4 shallow soup bowls. Sprinkle with coriander and chives.

TEST KITCHEN TIP: Freshly harvested cultivated mussels hardly need more preparation than a rinse under cold water, thanks to efficient machinery that declumps, debeards and scrubs them. But judge for yourself and scrub and snip off beards if necessary. Discard any mussels that do not close when tapped.

SUBSTITUTION: You can replace the Thai red curry paste with green curry paste, or with mild Indian curry paste.

Makes 4 servings.

PER SERVING, ABOUT:

cal	380	carb	10 g
pro	18 g	fibre	1 g
total fat	31 g	chol	53 mg
sat. fat	22 g	sodium	317 mg

PERCENTAGE RDI:

calcium	5%	vit. A	16%
iron	56%	vit. C	25%
folate	30%		

Poached Salmon with Beurre Blanc

For salmon, king of fishes, here is a classic and classy French technique: poaching fillets in wine, then serving them with some of the reduced liquid, enriched with butter and cream.

TEST KITCHEN TIP: Serve with saffron rice. Here's how to turn plain rice into this fancier version: Stir together 1 tbsp (15 mL) milk or water, ¼ tsp (1 mL) saffron threads and pinch granulated sugar. Stir into boiling water when adding rice.

6 cups	water	1.5 L
1 cup	dry white wine	250 mL
1	onion, sliced	1
2	stalks celery, sliced	2
6	sprigs fresh parsley	6
2	bay leaves	2
Half	lemon, sliced	Half
1½ tsp	dried tarragon	7 mL
1 tsp	black peppercorns	5 mL
½ tsp	each dried thyme and salt	2 mL

6	salmon fillets, each about 6 oz (175 g)	6
⅓ cup	white wine vinegar	75 mL
2 tbsp	finely chopped shallots	25 mL
Pinch	white or black pepper	Pinch
½ cup	cold butter, cut in small cubes	125 mL
1 tbsp	whipping cream	15 mL
1 tbsp	chopped fresh chives and/or parsley	15 mL

1 In shallow Dutch oven or skillet large enough to hold fish in single layer, combine water, wine, onion, celery, parsley, bay leaves, lemon, tarragon, peppercorns, thyme and salt; bring to boil. Simmer over medium heat for 20 minutes. (MAKE-AHEAD: Cover and set aside for up to 6 hours; return to simmer.)

2 Add salmon to liquid. Cover and cook at bare simmer for 7 to 9 minutes or until fish flakes easily when tested with fork. With slotted spatula, transfer fish to platter and keep warm. Strain liquid, reserving 1 cup (250 mL).

3 In saucepan, combine reserved liquid, vinegar, shallots and pepper; bring to boil. Boil over high heat for 5 to 6 minutes or until reduced to ¼ cup (50 mL). Reduce heat to low. Whisk in butter, 1 cube at a time, until thickened; whisk in cream. Serve over salmon. Garnish with chives.

Makes 6 servings.

PER SERVING, ABOUT:

cal 423	carb . . . . 1 g
pro . . . . 30 g	fibre . . . . trace
total fat . . . . 33 g	chol . . . . . 128 mg
sat. fat . . . . . 13 g	sodium . . 240 mg

PERCENTAGE RDI:

calcium 3%	vit. A 17%
iron 4%	vit. C 8%
folate 21%	

Boiled Lobster

What would a trip to Atlantic Canada be without at least one lobster experience, whether it's a bib-on boiled lobster by the wharf, a lobster roll or a full-fledged cold lobster and potato salad supper? And don't leave the coast without a box of the crustaceans to take home for a lobster party.

4	live lobsters (each 1½ lb/750 g)	4

½ cup	butter, melted, or Lemon Chive Dipping Sauce (recipe below)	125 mL

1 Fill large deep pot with enough salted water (1 tbsp/15 mL salt per 4 cups/1 L water) to completely cover lobsters; bring to full rolling boil over high heat. Grasp back of each lobster; plunge headfirst into water. Cover and return to boil.

2 Start cooking time when water boils; reduce to bubbly simmer. Cook each lobster for 10 minutes for first pound (500 g) and 1 minute for each additional 4 oz (125 g) or until lobster is bright red and small leg comes away easily when twisted and pulled. Immediately remove from water.

3 Remove meat from lobster, discarding shells and setting meat aside or dipping into melted butter to eat as you proceed. First, twist off claws at joint at body; separate into claw and arm sections. Break off smaller part of claw and remove meat with lobster pick or nut pick. Using lobster cracker or nutcracker, crack larger part of claw at widest part; lift out meat. Crack arm; pick out meat.

4 Separate tail piece from body by twisting apart. Bend tail backward and break off flippers; pick out meat from each flipper.

5 Using kitchen shears or steak knife, cut through shell along underside of tail to expose meat. With fingers or fork, pry meat from shell. Remove and discard intestinal vein (if any).

6 Holding legs and inner section of body, pull off back shell. Remove and eat red coral (if any) and green tomalley (liver). Insert thumbs in inner section of body and pry apart to separate in half lengthwise; extract any meaty tidbits. Break off legs; press out juice and meat.

Lemon Chive Dipping Sauce

In bowl, combine ½ cup (125 mL) plain yogurt, ¼ cup (50 mL) light mayonnaise, 4 tsp (20 mL) chopped fresh chives or green onion, 1 tbsp (15 mL) lemon juice, 1 tsp (5 mL) mustard and pinch cayenne pepper. (MAKE-AHEAD: Cover and refrigerate for up to 8 hours.) **Makes ¾ cup (175 mL).**

TEST KITCHEN TIPS

• For even cooking, buy lobsters of similar weight.

• If you don't have lobster crackers, use kitchen shears to cut along edge of claws. If you don't have any picks, use small forks to remove meat.

Makes 4 servings.

PER SERVING (WITH SAUCE), ABOUT:

cal 241	carb . . . . 6 g
pro . . . . 38 g	fibre . . . . trace
total fat . . . . . 6 g	chol . . . . . 129 mg
sat. fat . . . . . . 1 g	sodium . . 801 mg

PERCENTAGE RDI:

calcium 14%	vit. A 6%
iron 5%	vit. C 3%
folate 9%	

Crusty Salmon Cakes

What's interesting about something as old-fashioned as salmon cakes is just how enthusiastically they are greeted by an upcoming generation of young cooks and eaters.

2	large potatoes (1 lb/500 g)	2
3	green onions, chopped	3
¼ cup	chopped fresh coriander or parsley	50 mL
1 tbsp	Dijon mustard	15 mL
½ tsp	salt	2 mL
¼ tsp	grated lemon rind	1 mL
¼ tsp	pepper	1 mL
¼ tsp	hot pepper sauce	1 mL
1	egg, beaten	1
2	cans (each 7½ oz/213 g) salmon, drained and coarsely flaked	2
2 tbsp	vegetable oil	25 mL
4	lemon wedges	4

TEST KITCHEN TIPS

• Mash canned salmon bones into the fish for a calcium boost of more than 30 per cent.

• To serve with tartar sauce, stir together ¼ cup (50 mL) finely chopped dill pickle, 3 tbsp (50 mL) light mayonnaise and 1 tbsp (15 mL) each light sour cream and chopped fresh dill. For a sweeter tartar sauce, substitute chopped bread-and-butter pickles for the dill pickle and fresh dill.

SUBSTITUTION: Leftover cooked fish can be used instead of the canned salmon. You will need 2 cups (500 mL) flaked fish.

1 Peel and cut potatoes in half crosswise. In 6-cup (1.5 L) microwaveable dish, microwave potatoes with 1 cup (250 mL) water at High, covered, for 10 minutes or until tender. (Or cook in saucepan of boiling salted water, covered, for 15 to 20 minutes or until tender.) Drain.

2 In large bowl, mash potatoes until smooth; stir in onions, coriander, mustard, salt, lemon rind, pepper and hot pepper sauce. Blend in egg. Fold in salmon. Let cool for 5 minutes. Using hands, shape into eight ¾-inch (2 cm) thick patties. (MAKE-AHEAD: Cover and refrigerate for up to 4 hours.)

3 In large nonstick skillet, heat half of the oil over medium heat; cook 4 of the patties for about 5 minutes per side or until golden. Repeat with remaining oil and patties. Serve with lemon wedges.

Makes 4 servings.

PER SERVING, ABOUT:

cal 280	carb . . . . 18 g
pro . . . . 21 g	fibre . . . . 2 g
total fat . . . . 14 g	chol . . . . . . 78 mg
sat. fat . . . . . . 2 g	sodium . . 709 mg

PERCENTAGE RDI:

calcium 23%	vit. A 5%
iron 11%	vit. C 17%
folate 12%	

Batter-Fried Fish

Fish and chips are wonderful just as they emerge crisp and golden from the fryer, so avoid the soggy fish from takeouts and opt for crisp, delicious fillets done at home. Pair them with oven fries (page 198).

	Vegetable oil for deep-frying	
1 lb	haddock or cod fillets	500 g
¼ tsp	salt	1 mL

BATTER:		
¾ cup	all-purpose flour	175 mL
1½ tsp	baking powder	7 mL
½ tsp	salt	2 mL
1	egg	1
⅔ cup	milk	150 mL

1 Fill deep fryer half full with oil; heat to 375°F (190°C).

2 Cut fillets into serving-size pieces; sprinkle with salt. (If fillets are more than ½ inch/1 cm thick, cut 3 or 4 slits in sides so they will cook evenly.)

3 BATTER: In bowl, mix together flour, baking powder and salt. In small bowl, beat egg; stir in milk. Add milk mixture to dry ingredients and beat just until smooth.

4 Dip fish into batter and fry in hot oil, turning once, until golden brown, about 7 minutes. Remove with slotted spoon; drain on paper towels before serving.

VARIATION

Pan-Fried Fish: For 2-lb (1 kg) fish fillets or small fish such as smelts, beat together 2 eggs, ¼ cup (50 mL) milk and ½ tsp (2 mL) salt. Place about ½ cup (125 mL) all-purpose flour in shallow bowl. Spread 1 cup (250 mL) fine dry bread crumbs or cornmeal in separate bowl. Dip fish first into flour, shaking off excess, then into egg mixture, allowing liquid to drip off. Dip into crumbs, pressing to coat. In large skillet, heat 1 tbsp (15 mL) each vegetable oil and butter over medium-high heat; pan-fry fish in batches for about 2 minutes per side or until golden and crunchy outside and flaky inside, heating more oil and butter as needed between batches. Sprinkle with salt and pepper and serve with lemon wedges. **Makes 4 servings.**

Makes 4 servings.

PER SERVING, ABOUT:

cal 307	carb . . . . 17 g
pro . . . . 26 g	fibre . . . . 1 g
total fat . . . . 14 g	chol . . . . . 112 mg
sat. fat . . . . . . 2 g	sodium . . 568 mg

PERCENTAGE RDI:

calcium 11%	vit. A 5%
iron 16%	vit. C 0%
folate 15%	

Cod au Gratin

While cod is the traditional fish blanketed and baked under a Cheddar cheese sauce, nowadays you can enjoy the dish with other fresh fillets.

1 lb	cod fillets	500 g
1½ cups	hot milk	375 mL
¼ cup	butter	50 mL
¼ cup	all-purpose flour	50 mL

½ tsp	salt	2 mL
Pinch	each white pepper and dry mustard	Pinch
1 cup	shredded Cheddar cheese	250 mL

1 Cut fish into large pieces and place in single layer in greased baking dish.

2 Pour milk over fish and bake in 350°F (180°C) oven for 12 to 15 minutes or just until fish flakes easily when tested with fork. Pour off milk and reserve. (Flake fish with fork in dish if desired.)

3 In heavy saucepan, melt butter over medium heat; stir in flour, salt, pepper and mustard. Gradually stir in reserved milk; cook, whisking, for about 8 minutes or until smooth and thickened.

4 Pour sauce over fish; top with cheese. Place dish in shallow pan of water; bake for 20 minutes or until bubbling and heated through.

Makes 4 servings.

PER SERVING, ABOUT:

cal 382	carb .... 11 g
pro .... 31 g	fibre .... trace
total fat .... 23 g	chol ..... 116 mg
sat. fat ..... 14 g	sodium .. 686 mg

PERCENTAGE RDI:

calcium 31%	vit. A 25%
iron 7%	vit. C 2%
folate 12%	

FISH "En Papillote"

For an elegant way to serve fish — be it salmon, halibut, trout, pickerel or cod — cut one 8-inch (20 cm) square of heavy-duty foil per serving. Or cut heart-shaped pieces of parchment paper large enough to generously accommodate fish. On centre of each, place 4- to 6-oz (125 to 175 g) fish fillet. Drizzle with 1 tsp (5 mL) dry vermouth or white wine. Sprinkle with thinly sliced green onion or chives and fresh dill or tarragon, a fine dice of sweet red pepper, and salt and pepper. Seal foil tightly around fish. For heart-shaped parchment pieces, start at dip in top of heart and make ¾-inch (2 cm) folds around edge of paper. Bake on baking sheet in 450°F (230°C) oven for 10 minutes per inch (2.5 cm) of thickness. Transfer to plate; cut into packet. Serve with lemon wedges.

Roasted Arctic Char
with Shrimp

When author Bonnie Stern travelled to Iqaluit in the Arctic, she came back with this memorable way to serve that region's prize fish. Ask your fishmonger to debone the fish from the inside, leaving the skin and flesh of the char intact so that you can cut the fish crosswise to serve.

⅓ cup	butter	75 mL
1	onion, chopped	1
2	stalks celery, chopped	2
4 cups	fresh bread crumbs	1 L
2 tbsp	chopped fresh parsley	25 mL
2 tbsp	chopped fresh dill	25 mL
2	green onions, chopped	2

1 tsp	salt	5 mL
½ tsp	pepper	2 mL
1 lb	frozen cooked baby shrimp, thawed	500 g
1	boned arctic char or salmon, about 5 lb (2.2 kg)	1
¼ tsp	each salt and pepper	1 mL

1 In skillet, melt butter over medium heat; cook onion and celery, stirring occasionally, for 5 to 8 minutes or until softened. Remove from heat. Stir in bread crumbs, parsley, dill, green onions, salt and pepper. Stir in shrimp.

2 Pat fish cavity dry; sprinkle cavity with salt and pepper. Fill cavity with stuffing; sew or skewer closed. Bake on greased rimmed baking sheet in 425°F (220°C) oven for 45 to 55 minutes or until flesh is opaque and flakes easily when tested with fork.

TEST KITCHEN TIP: You can use a bone-in char or salmon. To serve, run knife along backbone to cut through skin; pull off skin, then ease knife along between the flesh and bones on top side. Ease off top fillet. Cut into portions to serve with some of the stuffing from inside the fish. Turn fish over and repeat with fillet on other side and remaining stuffing inside.

Makes 8 servings.

PER SERVING, ABOUT:

cal	301	carb	13 g
pro	27 g	fibre	1 g
total fat	15 g	chol	107 mg
sat. fat	5 g	sodium	393 mg

PERCENTAGE RDI:

calcium	5%	vit. A	11%
iron	14%	vit. C	5%
folate	12%		

Herbed Seafood Casserole

A rice crust holds a delectable blend of scallops, shrimp and crab in a cream sauce.

TEST KITCHEN TIPS

• If making this dish ahead to freeze, be sure to allow enough time for thawing: a 13- x 9-inch (3 L) casserole usually takes about 48 hours to thaw in the refrigerator.

• Before serving, garnish with chopped fresh parsley.

1 cup	long-grain rice	250 mL
1	egg, beaten	1
⅓ cup	chopped fresh parsley	75 mL
⅓ cup	butter	75 mL
1	onion, chopped	1
3	cloves garlic, minced	3
1	large carrot, finely chopped	1
1½ cups	chopped fennel or celery	375 mL
1 tbsp	chopped fresh dill	15 mL
1 tsp	each salt and pepper	5 mL

1 lb	scallops	500 g
1 lb	large raw shrimp	500 g
1	pkg (7 oz/200 g) frozen crabmeat, thawed	1
¼ cup	all-purpose flour	50 mL
1½ cups	milk	375 mL
1	pkg (8 oz/250 g) cream cheese, cubed	1
¼ tsp	dried thyme	1 mL
TOPPING:		
1½ cups	fresh bread crumbs	375 mL
2 tbsp	butter, melted	25 mL

1 In saucepan, add rice to 2 cups (500 mL) boiling salted water; return to boil. Reduce heat to low, cover and simmer for 15 to 20 minutes or until tender and water is absorbed. Let cool. Stir in egg and 2 tbsp (25 mL) of the parsley.

2 Meanwhile, in skillet, melt 1 tbsp (15 mL) of the butter over medium heat; cook onion, garlic, carrot and fennel, stirring often, for 5 minutes. Stir in ½ tsp (2 mL) of the dill and ¼ tsp (1 mL) each of the salt and pepper; transfer to large bowl.

3 In clean skillet, bring 2 cups (500 mL) water to simmer; poach scallops just until opaque, 1 to 3 minutes. Using slotted spoon, add to bowl. Poach shrimp for 3 minutes or just until firm and pink. Drain, reserving 1 cup (250 mL) liquid. Peel and devein shrimp; add to bowl. Press liquid from crabmeat; chop into bite-size chunks and add to bowl.

4 In same skillet, melt remaining butter over medium heat; cook flour, whisking, for 2 minutes, without browning. Whisk in poaching liquid and milk; cook, stirring, for 5 minutes. Add cheese, thyme and remaining dill, salt and pepper, whisking until cheese is melted. Add to bowl along with remaining parsley.

5 Line greased 13- x 9-inch (3 L) glass baking dish with rice; spoon seafood mixture over top. (MAKE-AHEAD: Let cool slightly; finish cooling, uncovered, in refrigerator. Cover and refrigerate for up to 2 days or overwrap with heavy-duty foil and freeze for up to 2 weeks. Thaw in refrigerator for 48 hours.)

6 TOPPING: Mix bread crumbs with butter; sprinkle over casserole. Bake in 325°F (160°C) oven for 40 to 50 minutes or until bubbly and golden.

Makes 8 servings.

PER SERVING, ABOUT:

cal	489	carb	34 g
pro	31 g	fibre	2 g
total fat	25 g	chol	190 mg
sat. fat	15 g	sodium	962 mg

PERCENTAGE RDI:

calcium	14%	vit. A	60%
iron	21%	vit. C	10%
folate	20%		

Glazed Sea Bass with Red Curry Sauce

From Calgary author Cinda Chavich comes this Thai-inspired fish her gourmet club has enjoyed atop Thai jasmine rice and accompanied by braised baby bok choy.

8	Chilean sea bass or halibut fillets (skin on), each about 4 oz (125 g)	8
¼ cup	cornstarch	50 mL
3 tbsp	peanut or vegetable oil	50 mL
1 tsp	sesame oil	5 mL
	Red Curry Sauce (recipe below)	

GLAZE:		
¾ cup	chicken stock	175 mL
⅓ cup	each liquid honey and soy sauce	75 mL
3 tbsp	lime juice	50 mL
¼ tsp	Asian chili paste	1 mL
1	clove garlic, minced	1

1 GLAZE: In saucepan, combine stock, honey, soy sauce, lime juice, Asian chili paste and garlic over medium heat; simmer for about 20 minutes or until reduced to ½ cup (125 mL). (MAKE-AHEAD: Refrigerate for up to 1 day.)

2 In shallow dish, dip fish into cornstarch, turning to coat; shake off excess. In large nonstick skillet, heat peanut and sesame oils over high heat; reduce heat to medium and cook fish, skin side up, for 4 minutes or until crisp on bottom. Transfer to foil-lined rimmed baking sheet, cooked side up.

3 Spoon 1 tbsp (15 mL) of the glaze over each fillet. Bake in 400°F (200°C) oven for about 8 minutes or until fish flakes easily when tested with fork. Drizzle with Red Curry Sauce.

Red Curry Sauce

1 cup	coconut milk	250 mL
1 cup	chicken stock	250 mL
2 tbsp	lime juice	25 mL
2 tbsp	Thai red curry paste	25 mL

1 tsp	packed brown sugar	5 mL
1 tsp	fish sauce	5 mL
2 tbsp	chopped fresh coriander	25 mL

1 In saucepan, bring coconut milk, stock, lime juice, curry paste, brown sugar and fish sauce to boil; reduce heat and simmer, stirring occasionally, for about 30 minutes or until reduced to 1 cup (250 mL). Stir in coriander just before drizzling over fish. **Makes 1 cup (250 mL).**

Makes 8 servings.

PER SERVING (WITH SAUCE), ABOUT:

cal	321	carb	18 g
pro	26 g	fibre	trace
total fat	16 g	chol	37 mg
sat. fat	7 g	sodium	982 mg

PERCENTAGE RDI:

calcium	6%	vit. A	6%
iron	18%	vit. C	2%
folate	10%		

Oven-Baked Fish and Chips

Fish with crunchy edges and moist steaming flakes — fries, too! Very high heat is the key to both. To be Canadian, sprinkle with vinegar.

3	large baking potatoes	3
2 tbsp	vegetable oil	25 mL
¾ tsp	each salt and pepper	4 mL
3 cups	cornflakes	750 mL
¼ cup	all-purpose flour	50 mL
1 tsp	dried Italian herb seasoning	5 mL

1 tsp	grated lemon rind	5 mL
1	egg	1
1 tbsp	milk	15 mL
4	halibut, haddock or cod fillets (1 lb/500 g total)	4

1   Scrub potatoes; cut each into 8 wedges. Toss with oil and ¼ tsp (1 mL) each of the salt and pepper; place on large rimmed baking sheet. Bake in 450°F (230°C) oven for 20 minutes. Turn and bake for 10 minutes longer or until crisp and golden outside and tender inside; move to edges of baking sheet.

2   Meanwhile, pour cornflakes into plastic bag. Using rolling pin, crush to make coarse crumbs; transfer to plate. On separate plate, stir together flour, herb seasoning, lemon rind and remaining salt and pepper.

3   In shallow dish, whisk egg with milk. Dip each fillet into flour mixture, shaking off excess. Dip into egg mixture, then into crumbs, pressing lightly to coat. Place in centre of baking sheet. Return to oven for about 8 minutes or until fish is crispy and flakes easily when tested with fork.

Makes 4 servings.

PER SERVING, ABOUT:

cal 418	carb . . . . 52 g
pro . . . . 29 g	fibre . . . . 4 g
total fat . . . . 10 g	chol . . . . . . 61 mg
sat. fat . . . . . . 1 g	sodium . . 636 mg

PERCENTAGE RDI:

calcium 7%	vit. A 6%
iron 39%	vit. C 30%
folate 18%	

Slow-Grilled Salmon with Garlic and Basil

Slicing the salmon through to the skin into portion-size fillets makes serving easy. It also gives the garlic basil brush-on more coverage and therefore more taste.

4	large cloves garlic, chopped	4
¼ tsp	salt	1 mL
¼ cup	minced fresh basil	50 mL
3 tbsp	olive oil	50 mL
2 tbsp	finely chopped fresh parsley	25 mL
1 tbsp	minced dry-packed sun-dried tomatoes	15 mL
1	boned whole side salmon (skin on), about 3 lb (1.5 kg)	1

1 On cutting board and using fork, mash garlic with salt. In small bowl, combine garlic mixture, basil, oil, parsley and sun-dried tomatoes. Place salmon, skin side down, on board. Slicing through flesh but not skin, cut whole side of salmon into portions about 2 inches (5 cm) wide. Brush top and between portions with garlic mixture. Cover and refrigerate for 30 minutes. (MAKE-AHEAD: Refrigerate for up to 12 hours.)

2 Place salmon, skin side down, on greased grill over medium-low heat; close lid and cook for about 30 minutes or until fish flakes easily when tested with fork.

Makes 4 servings.

PER SERVING, ABOUT:

cal 553	carb . . . . 2 g
pro . . . . 47 g	fibre . . . . trace
total fat . . . . 36 g	chol . . . . . 133 mg
sat. fat . . . . . . 7 g	sodium . . 294 mg

PERCENTAGE RDI:

calcium 4%	vit. A 4%
iron 7%	vit. C 17%
folate 35%	

Cumin and Lime Fish Kabobs

Choose a fish that holds together on the grill: monkfish, salmon, halibut and sword-fish are good ones. Or mix chunks of fish with scallops and jumbo shrimp.

1½ lb	salmon, halibut, swordfish or monkfish fillets	750 g
1	lime, cut in 8 wedges	1
MARINADE:		
1 tsp	grated lime rind	5 mL
¼ cup	lime juice	50 mL

¼ cup	vegetable oil	50 mL
4 tsp	Worcestershire sauce	20 mL
1	small onion, minced	1
2	cloves garlic, minced	2
1½ tsp	ground cumin	7 mL
¼ tsp	pepper	1 mL

1 MARINADE: In large glass bowl, whisk together lime rind and juice, oil, Worcestershire sauce, onion, garlic, cumin and pepper; set aside.

2 Cut fish into 1½-inch (4 cm) chunks to make 24 pieces; add to marinade, tossing to coat. Cover and refrigerate for 30 minutes.

3 Remove fish from marinade, reserving marinade. On each of 4 skewers, thread 2 pieces of fish, 1 lime wedge, 2 pieces of fish, 1 lime wedge, then 2 pieces of fish.

4 Place on greased grill over medium heat; baste with marinade. Close lid and cook, turning twice, for 10 to 12 minutes or until fish flakes easily when tested with fork.

Makes 4 servings.

PER SERVING, ABOUT:

cal 393	carb . . . . 5 g
pro . . . . 30 g	fibre . . . . trace
total fat . . . . 28 g	chol . . . . . . 84 mg
sat. fat . . . . . . 4 g	sodium . . 133 mg

PERCENTAGE RDI:

calcium 3%	vit. A 2%
iron 6%	vit. C 18%
folate 22%	

Grilled Halibut with Tomato Salsa

No longer does a piece of fish need a rich sauce to win approval at the table. A simple toss of tomatoes with herbs — call it salsa or a fresh relish — is enough to dress it up. It's healthful, too.

2 tbsp	lime juice	25 mL
1 tbsp	olive oil	15 mL
¼ tsp	each salt and pepper	1 mL
1	halibut steak (1½ lb/750 g total)	1

TOMATO SALSA:

2	plum tomatoes, diced	2
¼ cup	chopped fresh coriander or basil	50 mL
1 tbsp	minced jalapeño pepper	15 mL
1	green onion, finely chopped	1
1 tbsp	lime juice or wine vinegar	15 mL
1 tbsp	olive oil	15 mL
¼ tsp	each salt and pepper	1 mL

Makes 4 servings.

1 In glass bowl, whisk together lime juice, oil, salt and pepper. Add fish, turning to coat. Cover and refrigerate for up to 30 minutes.

2 TOMATO SALSA: Meanwhile, in bowl, stir together tomatoes, coriander, jalapeño pepper, onion, lime juice, oil, salt and pepper.

3 Place fish on greased grill over medium-high heat; close lid and cook, turning once, for about 10 minutes per inch (2.5 cm) of thickness or until fish is opaque and flakes easily when tested with fork. Serve with salsa.

PER SERVING, ABOUT:

cal	247	carb	3 g
pro	36 g	fibre	1 g
total fat	10 g	chol	54 mg
sat. fat	1 g	sodium	336 mg

PERCENTAGE RDI:

calcium	8%	vit. A	12%
iron	13%	vit. C	23%
folate	12%		

FLAVOURED BUTTERS FOR Fish

For variety, replace the salsa in the recipe above with one of these flavoured butter toppings. Place a round on each serving hot from the grill or melt and brush on the fish while grilling. Try them with any grilled, baked or poached fish.

➤ In small bowl, stir ½ cup (125 mL) butter, softened, with ingredients for desired flavouring (below) until smooth. Spoon onto plastic wrap; shape into log and wrap tightly. Refrigerate until firm. Slice into ½-inch (1 cm) thick rounds to serve. (MAKE-AHEAD: Refrigerate for up to 2 weeks.) Makes about ½ cup (125 mL).

➤ **HERB BUTTER:** Use ¼ cup (50 mL) minced fresh parsley, 2 tbsp (25 mL) minced green onion or chives, 1 tbsp (15 mL) minced fresh basil, dill, tarragon or chervil and pinch pepper.

➤ **CAPER MUSTARD BUTTER:** Use 2 tbsp (25 mL) each drained capers and Dijon mustard, ½ tsp (2 mL) grated lemon rind and 1 tsp (5 mL) lemon juice.

➤ **LIME AND CHILI BUTTER:** Use 2 tbsp (25 mL) minced fresh coriander, 1 tsp (5 mL) grated lime rind, 2 tbsp (25 mL) lime juice and 1 tsp (5 mL) chili powder.

Apple Mustard–Glazed Trout Fillets

Choose two trout fillets that weigh 12 to 16 oz (375 to 500 g) each, enough to serve four, or choose four smaller ones.

4	rainbow trout fillets, each 6 to 8 oz (175 to 250 g)	4

APPLE MUSTARD GLAZE:

2 tbsp	frozen apple juice concentrate, thawed	25 mL
1 tbsp	Dijon mustard	15 mL

1 tsp	cider vinegar	5 mL
½ tsp	paprika	2 mL
¼ tsp	pepper	1 mL
Pinch	salt	Pinch

1 Pat trout fillets dry. Arrange, skin side down, on plate; set aside.

2 **APPLE MUSTARD GLAZE:** In bowl, combine apple juice concentrate, mustard, vinegar, paprika, pepper and salt. Brush onto fillets.

3 Place fillets, skin side down, on greased grill over medium heat; drizzle with any remaining glaze. Close lid and cook for 12 to 14 minutes or until fish flakes easily when tested with fork.

VARIATION

Grilled Trout Fillets with Tandoori Marinade: Omit Apple Mustard Glaze. For about 1½ lb (750 g) fish fillets, stir together ½ cup (125 mL) plain yogurt, 1 tbsp (15 mL) each minced fresh coriander and lemon juice, 1 large clove garlic, minced, 2 tsp (10 mL) minced gingerroot, 1 tsp (5 mL) ground cumin, ¾ tsp (4 mL) paprika, ½ tsp (2 mL) turmeric and pinch each salt and pepper. Marinate fish in refrigerator for up to 45 minutes. **Makes 4 servings.**

Makes 4 servings.

PER SERVING, ABOUT:

cal 287	carb . . . . 4 g
pro . . . . 47 g	fibre . . . . trace
total fat . . . . . 8 g	chol . . . . . 129 mg
sat. fat . . . . . . 2 g	sodium . . 113 mg

PERCENTAGE RDI:

calcium 15%	vit. A 6%
iron 33%	vit. C 25%
folate 8%	

Grilled Salmon Fillets

Grilling is one of the most flavourful ways to cook salmon fillets. Three different marinades give plenty of options.

1	salmon fillet (skin on), 1 lb (500 g)	1

LEMON DILL MARINADE:

¼ cup	olive oil	50 mL
2 tbsp	chopped fresh dill (or 2 tsp/10 mL dried dillweed)	25 mL
1 tsp	grated lemon rind	5 mL
2 tbsp	lemon juice	25 mL
¼ tsp	each salt and pepper	1 mL

1 On cutting board, slice salmon into 4 pieces. If necessary, remove any bones with tweezers. Measure thickest portion of fillet to determine cooking time.

2 LEMON DILL MARINADE: In bowl, whisk together olive oil, dill, lemon rind and juice, salt and pepper; pour into shallow glass dish. Add salmon and turn to coat evenly. Cover and marinate in refrigerator for up to 30 minutes, turning occasionally.

3 Reserving marinade, place salmon, skin side down, on greased grill over medium-high heat; brush with marinade. Close lid and cook, turning once, for 10 minutes per inch (2.5 cm) of thickness or just until opaque and fish flakes easily when tested with fork.

VARIATIONS

Grilled Salmon Fillets with Teriyaki Marinade: Omit Lemon Dill Marinade. Substitute ¼ cup (50 mL) soy sauce, 4 tsp (20 mL) white wine vinegar, 2 tsp (10 mL) granulated sugar, 2 tsp (10 mL) vegetable oil and 1 clove garlic, minced.

Grilled Salmon Fillets with Lime Cumin Marinade: Omit Lemon Dill Marinade. Substitute ¼ cup (50 mL) olive oil, 1 tsp (5 mL) grated lime rind, 2 tbsp (25 mL) lime juice, 1 tbsp (15 mL) Worcestershire sauce, 1½ tsp (7 mL) ground cumin, 2 cloves garlic, minced, and ¼ tsp (1 mL) each salt and pepper.

Grilled Salmon Fillets with Quick Curry Marinade: Omit Lemon Dill Marinade. Substitute ¼ cup (50 mL) vegetable oil, 2 tbsp (25 mL) lemon juice, 2 tsp (10 mL) mild Indian or Thai red curry paste and ¼ tsp (1 mL) each salt and pepper.

TEST KITCHEN TIPS

• Always check salmon fillets for bones before marinating; rub your fingers along the flesh surface and if you encounter bones, pull out with tweezers.

• To turn fillets over halfway through cooking, place 1 metal spatula under fillet and another on top.

• Note that the marinades are for flavour, not tenderness. Marinating fish for more than 45 minutes in the refrigerator may allow the acids in the marinade to "cook" the outside of the fish, which means that when the fish is grilled, the outside will be dry and woolly.

Makes 4 servings.

PER SERVING, ABOUT:

cal	304	carb	1 g
pro	20 g	fibre	trace
total fat	24 g	chol	56 mg
sat. fat	4 g	sodium	199 mg

PERCENTAGE RDI:

calcium	1%	vit. A	1%
iron	3%	vit. C	10%
folate	14%		

Cedar-Planked Salmon

As the salmon grills or bakes on the piece of soaked cedar, the wood infuses the fish with a delightfully smoky flavour. Grill asparagus alongside for an easy but very special menu.

TEST KITCHEN TIP: You can opt to roast the salmon planks in a 425°F (220°C) oven for about 12 minutes or until fish flakes easily when tested with fork.

6	salmon fillets, each about 6 oz (175 g)	6
2 tbsp	olive oil	25 mL
½ tsp	grated lemon rind	2 mL
2 tbsp	lemon juice	25 mL
1 tbsp	chopped chives or green onions	15 mL
2 tsp	Dijon mustard	10 mL
Pinch	each salt and pepper	Pinch

DILL SAUCE:		
½ cup	light sour cream	125 mL
2 tbsp	finely chopped cucumber	25 mL
1 tbsp	chopped fresh dill (or ½ tsp/2 mL dried dillweed)	15 mL
2 tsp	minced chives or green onion	10 mL
Pinch	each salt and pepper	Pinch

1 Soak two 7- x 12-inch (18 x 30 cm) untreated cedar planks in water for at least 30 minutes or for up to 24 hours. Place 3 salmon fillets on top of each plank.

2 In small bowl, whisk together oil, lemon rind and juice, chives, mustard, salt and pepper; brush half over salmon. Place planks on grill over medium-high heat; close lid and cook, turning fish once and brushing with remaining lemon mixture, for 10 minutes. Cook for about 10 minutes longer or until fish flakes easily when tested with fork.

3 DILL SAUCE: Meanwhile, combine sour cream, cucumber, dill, chives, salt and pepper. Serve with salmon.

Makes 6 servings.

PER SERVING, ABOUT:

cal 337   carb ....4 g
pro ....31 g   fibre ....trace
total fat ....21 g chol ......85 mg
sat. fat ......4 g sodium ..121 mg

PERCENTAGE RDI:

calcium .....6%   vit. A 3%
iron ....4%   vit. C 12%
folate 21%

Quarterdeck PLANKED SALMON

At the Quarterdeck Grill near Liverpool, Nova Scotia, a side of salmon is laced to a cedar plank and smoke-cooked over an outdoor fire. For your home barbecue, skip the plank and brush salmon skin with vegetable oil. Place one 4-lb (2 kg) salmon fillet, skin side down, on greased grill over medium heat. Brush with a blend of ¼ cup (50 mL) each butter and rum and pinch each salt and pepper. Reduce heat to low; close lid and cook, brushing on rum mixture, for about 20 minutes or until fish flakes easily when tested with fork. **Makes 12 servings.**

Fresh Tuna Salade Niçoise

This composed salad is a classic from the city of Nice in the south of France. Instead of the usual canned tuna, this salad has a glamorous upgrade: grilled fresh tuna.

5	new red potatoes (unpeeled), 1½ lb (750 g)	5
1 lb	green beans, trimmed	500 g
5	plum tomatoes	5
Half	small red onion	Half
4	hard-cooked eggs	4
1	tuna fillet (1½ lb/750 g)	1
2 tbsp	extra-virgin olive oil	25 mL
Pinch	each salt and pepper	Pinch
⅓ cup	niçoise olives	75 mL

DRESSING:		
¼ cup	red wine vinegar	50 mL
1 tbsp	Dijon mustard	15 mL
1	clove garlic, minced	1
2 tsp	anchovy paste	10 mL
¼ tsp	each salt and pepper	1 mL
½ cup	extra-virgin olive oil	125 mL

1 DRESSING: In bowl, whisk together vinegar, mustard, garlic, anchovy paste, salt and pepper; gradually whisk in oil until blended. Set aside.

2 In saucepan of boiling salted water, cook potatoes, covered, for 20 to 25 minutes or just until tender. Remove with slotted spoon; let cool slightly. Cut into quarters.

3 In same pan, cook green beans for 5 to 7 minutes or until tender-crisp. Drain and cool in cold water. Drain well.

4 Cut each tomato into 6 wedges. Slice red onion thinly. Peel eggs; cut eggs into quarters.

5 Brush both sides of tuna with oil; sprinkle with salt and pepper. Place on greased grill over medium-high heat; close lid and cook, turning once, for 6 to 8 minutes or until firm and opaque outside with a pink and translucent rare band inside. Cut into ¼-inch (5 mm) thick slices.

6 On large platter, attractively arrange potatoes, green beans, tomatoes, onion, eggs, olives and tuna; drizzle with dressing.

CLASSIC

SUBSTITUTIONS

• Instead of grilling and slicing fresh tuna, you can use 3 cans (each 6 oz/ 170 g) white tuna, drained and broken into chunks.

• You can substitute any oil-cured black olives for the niçoise olives.

Makes 6 servings.

PER SERVING, ABOUT:

cal	570	carb	30 g
pro	36 g	fibre	5 g
total fat	35 g	chol	189 mg
sat. fat	6 g	sodium	947 mg

PERCENTAGE RDI:

calcium	8%	vit. A	81%
iron	29%	vit. C	50%
folate	26%		

Eggs, Cheese and Vegetarian

Foolproof Frittatas	208
Rolled Cheese Omelette	209
Eggs Benedict	210
Southwestern Poached Eggs	211
Quiche Lorraine	212
French Toast Sandwiches	213
Smoked Salmon Strata	214
Layered Chorizo Bake	215
Breakfast Strudels	216
Puffy Dutch Pancake with Bananas and Strawberries	217
Cheese Soufflé	218
Portobello Asparagus Strudels	219
Mediterranean Vegetable Pie	220
Two-Cheese Tomato Tart	221
Mushroom Lentil Burgers	222
Barbecued Tofu Sandwiches with Aïoli	223
Vegetarian Moussaka	224
Black Bean Chili with Avocado Salsa	226
Perogies	227

Foolproof Frittatas

Like its rolled French cousin, the omelette, this hearty flat Italian frittata is a godsend for a quick supper, lunch or even brunch. Tuck leftovers into pita pockets with lettuce, tomatoes, cucumber and mayo or sour cream for a satisfying lunch.

	SOFTEN	ADD	SPRINKLE
Pasta Primavera Frittata	1 onion, sliced; 1 carrot, thinly sliced; 2 cloves garlic, minced; ½ tsp (2 mL) dried Italian herb seasoning	1 cup (250 mL) cooked short pasta (about ¾ cup/ 175 mL uncooked); 1½ cups (375 mL) frozen broccoli florets, thawed and patted dry; dash hot pepper sauce	⅓ cup (75 mL) grated Parmesan cheese
Zucchini, Sweet Red Pepper and Feta Frittata	1 onion, sliced; 1 zucchini, thinly sliced; 2 cloves garlic, minced	1 sweet red pepper, thinly sliced; 4 tsp (20 mL) chopped fresh dill (or 1 tsp/ 5 mL dried dillweed)	¾ cup (175 mL) crumbled feta cheese; 9 Kalamata olives, pitted and quartered
Frittata Lorraine	½ cup (125 mL) diced ham; 1 onion, chopped	¾ cup (175 mL) shredded Swiss cheese	2 green onions, minced
Smoked Turkey and Mushroom Frittata	1 onion, chopped; 2 cups (500 mL) sliced mushrooms; ½ tsp (2 mL) dried sage	8 oz (250 g) smoked turkey or ham, cut in ½-inch (1 cm) cubes; 2 plum tomatoes, diced	¾ cup (175 mL) shredded Gouda cheese (smoked or plain)
Smoked Salmon and Leek Frittata	2 leeks (white and light green parts only) or 1 onion, thinly sliced	1 potato, peeled, cooked and diced; 4 oz (125 g) smoked salmon, coarsely chopped; 1 tbsp (15 mL) chopped fresh parsley	2 oz (60 g) cream cheese, diced

TEST KITCHEN TIPS

• To ovenproof a nonstick skillet with nonmetal handle, wrap handle in 2 layers of foil.

• These frittatas are delicious straight from the oven or at room temperature. They keep well in the refrigerator for up to 2 days and can be reheated.

1 In 9- or 10-inch (23 or 25 cm) ovenproof nonstick or cast-iron skillet, heat 1 tbsp (15 mL) vegetable oil over medium heat. Add ingredients listed in first column; cook, stirring often, for 5 to 8 minutes or until softened.

2 In large bowl, whisk together 8 eggs, ¼ cup (50 mL) milk, ½ tsp (2 mL) salt and ¼ tsp (1 mL) pepper; add ingredients listed in second column. Pour into skillet, stirring to combine. Reduce heat to medium-low.

3 Sprinkle with ingredients listed in third column; cook for about 10 minutes or until bottom and side are firm yet top is still slightly runny. Broil for 3 to 5 minutes or until golden brown and set. Slice into wedges.

Makes 4 servings.

Rolled Cheese Omelette

Omelettes are scrambled eggs with attitude: they look and sound fancier. Mastering omelette making is a cooking benchmark worth achieving. A nonstick or seasoned omelette pan reserved only for omelettes is a great help in folding and rolling the tender egg mixture around a delectable filling — of which there are so many.

2	eggs	2
1 tbsp	water	15 mL
Pinch	each salt and pepper	Pinch
2 tsp	butter	10 mL

	FILLING:	
¼ cup	shredded Cheddar cheese	50 mL

1 In bowl, combine eggs, water, salt and pepper. With fork, stir briskly just until blended but not frothy. In 8-inch (20 cm) nonstick skillet, melt butter over medium-high heat until foaming, tilting pan to coat bottom and side.

2 When foam starts to subside and butter just begins to darken, pour egg mixture into middle of pan. Immediately shake pan back and forth while using underside of fork to stir eggs in circular motion for 10 seconds.

3 Cook, shaking pan occasionally and using spatula to push cooked egg to centre and allow uncooked eggs to flow underneath (tipping pan if necessary), for about 1 minute longer or until set but still creamy and bottom is light golden.

4 Tilt handle up and shake pan to slide omelette up opposite side of pan.

5 FILLING: Spoon cheese across centre of omelette. With spatula, lift third of omelette closest to handle over filling. Tilting pan, lift and roll filled part of omelette over remaining uncovered third of omelette. Slide out, seam side down, onto warmed plate.

VARIATIONS

Asparagus and Ham Omelette: Omit cheese filling. Use 3 stalks cooked asparagus and 1 slice Black Forest ham. **Makes 1 serving.**

Mushroom Duxelles Omelette for Two: Double eggs, water, salt, pepper and butter. Omit cheese filling. Before cooking eggs, melt 1 tbsp (15 mL) butter in skillet over medium-high heat; cook 1 shallot or small onion, finely chopped, 1 clove garlic, minced, 1½ cups (375 mL) finely chopped mushrooms and pinch each salt and pepper for about 8 minutes or until liquid is evaporated. Stir in 1 tbsp (15 mL) chopped fresh parsley, and 1 tbsp (15 mL) light cream (10%) if desired. Fill omelettes as above. **Makes 2 servings.**

Makes 1 serving.

PER SERVING, ABOUT:

cal	331	carb	2 g
pro	20 g	fibre	0 g
total fat	27 g	chol	479 mg
sat. fat	14 g	sodium	380 mg

PERCENTAGE RDI:

calcium	23%	vit. A	35%
iron	11%	vit. C	0%
folate	18%		

Eggs Benedict

Here's the stellar brunch dish, with variations for smoked salmon on top and a choice of ultra-rich hollandaise or a creamy chive sauce.

4	English muffins, halved and toasted	4
8	thin slices ham (about 10 oz/300 g)	8
8	eggs, poached (see page 211)	8
HOLLANDAISE SAUCE:		
4	egg yolks	4
¼ cup	water	50 mL

¼ tsp	pepper	1 mL
¼ cup	butter, softened	50 mL
2 tsp	lemon juice	10 mL
	Tomato wedges (optional)	
	Fresh chives, chopped (optional)	

1 HOLLANDAISE SAUCE: In small heavy saucepan, whisk together egg yolks, water and pepper; cook, whisking, over medium-low heat for about 5 minutes or until pale and thick enough to coat back of spoon. Remove from heat. Whisk in butter and lemon juice.

2 Top each muffin half with 1 ham slice and 1 poached egg; spoon 2 tbsp (25 mL) of the sauce over top. Garnish with tomato wedges and chives (if using).

VARIATIONS

Eggs Benedict with Herbed Cream Sauce: Omit Hollandaise Sauce. In small heavy saucepan, melt 1 tbsp (15 mL) butter over medium-low heat. Add 1 tbsp (15 mL) all-purpose flour; cook, stirring, for 2 minutes. Increase heat to medium. Whisk in 1 cup (250 mL) warm milk; cook, stirring constantly, for 8 to 10 minutes or until thickened. Whisk in 2 tbsp (25 mL) light cream cheese until blended, then ¼ tsp (1 mL) each salt and pepper and pinch cayenne pepper. Stir in 1 tbsp (15 mL) chopped fresh chives or green onions.

Salmon Eggs Benedict: Substitute 8 slices smoked salmon for the ham.

Peameal Bacon Eggs Benedict: Substitute 8 slices peameal bacon (4 oz/125 g), cooked, for the ham.

Eggs Florentine: Omit English muffins. Substitute 1 pkg (10 oz/284 g) fresh spinach, cooked, squeezed to remove liquid, dabbed with butter and seasoned. Top eggs with Herbed Cream Sauce as above. Sprinkle with grated Parmesan cheese; broil just until cheese is lightly browned.

Makes 8 servings.

PER SERVING, ABOUT:

cal	291	carb	16 g
pro	16 g	fibre	1 g
total fat	18 g	chol	361 mg
sat. fat	7 g	sodium	731 mg

PERCENTAGE RDI:

calcium	8%	vit. A	20%
iron	16%	vit. C	0%
folate	22%		

Southwestern Poached Eggs

QUICK BUDGET-WISE

A chunky, mildly piquant tomato chili pairs off with eggs for a quick brunch or supper dish. Serve with crusty rolls or warmed pitas to scoop up the delicious mess as the yolks break into the sauce.

1 tsp	vegetable oil	5 mL
1	small onion, chopped	1
2	cloves garlic, minced	2
1	sweet yellow or green pepper, chopped	1
1 tbsp	chili powder	15 mL
1 tsp	dried oregano	5 mL
1	can (19 oz/540 mL) tomatoes	1

1 cup	cooked black beans	250 mL
¾ cup	water	175 mL
2 tbsp	tomato paste	25 mL
2 tsp	packed brown sugar	10 mL
1½ tsp	Worcestershire sauce	7 mL
4	eggs	4
1 tbsp	chopped fresh coriander	15 mL

SUBSTITUTION: Opt for red kidney beans or chickpeas if you don't have black beans in your pantry.

1 In nonstick skillet, heat oil over medium heat; cook onion, garlic, yellow pepper, chili powder and oregano, stirring occasionally, for 5 minutes or until softened.

2 Stir in tomatoes, breaking up with spoon; stir in beans, water, tomato paste, brown sugar and Worcestershire sauce. Bring to boil; reduce heat and simmer for 10 minutes.

3 With spatula, shape 4 nests in mixture; crack 1 egg into each. Cook for about 8 minutes or until whites are almost set. Cover and cook for about 2 minutes longer or until whites are just set but yolks are still runny. Sprinkle with coriander.

Makes 2 to 4 servings.

PER EACH OF 4 SERVINGS, ABOUT:

cal	209	carb	26 g
pro	13 g	fibre	6 g
total fat	7 g	chol	214 mg
sat. fat	2 g	sodium	336 mg

PERCENTAGE RDI:

calcium	9%	vit. A	32%
iron	24%	vit. C	105%
folate	45%		

How to Cook AN EGG PERFECTLY

➤ **POACHED:** Pour enough water into shallow saucepan to come 2 inches (5 cm) up side; bring to boil. Reduce heat to simmer. Break each egg into small dish; gently slip into water. Cook for 3 to 5 minutes or until desired doneness. Remove with slotted spoon and drain well.

➤ **HARD-COOKED:** Arrange eggs in single layer in large deep saucepan; pour in enough cold water to come at least 1 inch (2.5 cm) above eggs. Cover and bring to boil over high heat. Immediately remove from heat; let stand for 20 minutes. Drain and run cold water over eggs for 2 minutes. Peel off shells.

➤ **SOFT-COOKED:** Cook in same way as for hard-cooked eggs, but let stand in cooking water for 4 to 5 minutes or until desired doneness.

Microwave SCRAMBLED EGGS FOR ONE OR TWO

➤ In microwaveable bowl, whisk 2 eggs with 2 tbsp (25 mL) milk or water. Microwave, uncovered, at High, whisking every 30 seconds, for 1 to 2 minutes or until set but still moist and creamy.

➤ Serve in split pita breads with salsa or chili sauce, or on a toasted English muffin layered with slices of ham and cheese.

Quiche Lorraine

Quiche may be as old as the hills — that's the 1970s in culinary parlance — but don't let culinary fashion mongering keep you away from this versatile and satisfying dish. There's a basic formula — single crust, four eggs and 1¼ cups (300 mL) milk — that you can vary several enticing ways.

TEST KITCHEN TIP: Update a slice of quiche by serving it on a bed of dressed salad greens. Mesclun mix is ideal.

	Pastry for 9-inch (23 cm) single-crust pie (see page 326)		1	green onion, finely chopped	1
1 tbsp	Dijon mustard	15 mL	4	eggs	4
¾ cup	shredded Swiss cheese	175 mL	1¼ cups	milk	300 mL
4 oz	bacon (about 5 slices), cooked and crumbled	125 g	¼ tsp	each salt and pepper	1 mL

1 On lightly floured surface, roll out pastry to fit 9-inch (23 cm) quiche dish or pie plate. Place in plate, trimming to leave 1 inch (2.5 cm) extending over rim. Fold back inside rim; flute edge if using pie plate. Prick all over with fork. Line with foil; fill with pie weights or dried beans. Bake in bottom third of 400°F (200°C) oven for about 15 minutes or until rim is light golden. Remove foil and weights; let cool on rack.

2 Brush shell with mustard; sprinkle with ½ cup (125 mL) of the cheese, bacon and onion. In bowl, whisk together eggs, milk, salt and pepper; pour into shell. Sprinkle with remaining cheese. Bake in 375°F (190°C) oven for about 35 minutes or until knife inserted in centre comes out clean. Let cool on rack for 10 minutes. Cut into wedges.

VARIATIONS

Smoked Salmon Asparagus Quiche: Omit bacon and onion. Use shredded Jarlsberg or Swiss cheese. Sprinkle shell with 1 cup (250 mL) chopped cooked asparagus, 4 oz (125 g) smoked salmon or Black Forest ham, cut in thin strips, ½ cup (125 mL) of the cheese and 1 tbsp (15 mL) chopped fresh dill. Pour egg mixture over top. Sprinkle with remaining cheese. Bake as directed.

Caramelized Onion Artichoke Quiche: Omit bacon and onion. Use shredded Jarlsberg or Swiss cheese. In skillet, melt 2 tbsp (25 mL) butter over medium-low heat; cook 2 large onions, thinly sliced, for about 30 minutes or until golden. In bowl, stir onions with 1 jar (6 oz/170 mL) marinated artichoke hearts, drained and chopped, and ½ cup (125 mL) chopped roasted sweet red peppers. Sprinkle shell with ½ cup (125 mL) of the cheese. Spoon in onion mixture. Pour egg mixture over top. Sprinkle with remaining cheese. Bake as directed.

Makes 4 to 6 servings.

PER EACH OF 6 SERVINGS, ABOUT:

cal	408	carb	26 g
pro	15 g	fibre	1 g
total fat	27 g	chol	208 mg
sat. fat	13 g	sodium	573 mg

PERCENTAGE RDI:

calcium	21%	vit. A	20%
iron	14%	vit. C	2%
folate	22%		

French Toast Sandwiches

Simple French toast is stale but good bread (the kind that actually dries out in a day or two) dipped in egg and milk and fried. Preferable is the sandwich version: two slices held together with a filling that adds oomph, variety and substance, changing the dish from leftover thrift into a house classic.

3	eggs	3	8	slices bread (each about ¾ inch/2 cm thick)	8
⅔ cup	milk	150 mL	1 tbsp	Dijon mustard	15 mL
1 tsp	dried basil	5 mL	4	slices Fontina, Swiss or old Cheddar cheese (4 oz/125 g)	4
¼ tsp	pepper	1 mL			
Pinch	salt	Pinch			

1 In large shallow dish, whisk together eggs, milk, basil, pepper and salt; set aside. Spread 4 of the bread slices with mustard; top each with cheese slice and sandwich with remaining bread slice. Dip into egg mixture, turning to soak well.

2 Place on greased rimmed baking sheet; gradually pour any remaining egg mixture over top. (MAKE-AHEAD: Cover and refrigerate for up to 12 hours.) Bake in 375°F (190°C) oven, turning once, for about 25 minutes or until golden. (Or, in nonstick skillet, melt 2 tsp/10 mL butter over medium heat; cook sandwiches in batches, turning once, for about 6 minutes or until browned.)

SWEET FILLING VARIATIONS

Omit basil, pepper, Dijon mustard and cheese; add ¼ tsp (1 mL) cinnamon to egg mixture and choose 1 of these sandwich fillings:

Fruity Cream Cheese: Spread bread slices with ¼ cup (50 mL) spreadable cream cheese and ⅓ cup (75 mL) raspberry jam.

Peanut Butter and Banana: Spread bread slices with ¼ cup (50 mL) peanut butter and top with 2 bananas, sliced.

Sweet Pineapple: Lay 1 ring canned pineapple on each bread slice; sprinkle evenly with ¼ cup (50 mL) packed brown sugar.

Basic FRENCH TOAST

For every 2 thick slices of bread, whisk together 1 egg and ⅓ cup (75 mL) milk. Dip each slice into egg mixture, turning to soak well. In greased nonstick skillet, cook slices over medium heat in batches for about 3 minutes per side or until crisp and golden brown. Serve with maple syrup, ketchup or salsa. **Makes 1 serving.**

Makes 4 servings.

PER SERVING, ABOUT:

cal	402	carb	43 g
pro	20 g	fibre	2 g
total fat	17 g	chol	198 mg
sat. fat	8 g	sodium	773 mg

PERCENTAGE RDI:

calcium	29%	vit. A	18%
iron	23%	vit. C	0%
folate	34%		

Smoked Salmon Strata

Brunch is made easy when it features a strata, a fancy version of layered French toast baked in a shallow casserole. With a filling such as smoked salmon and herbed cream cheese, a strata is definitely company fare.

VARIATION

Asparagus Ham Strata:
Substitute 12 oz (375 g) shaved Black Forest ham for the salmon. Snap off and discard ends from 1 lb (500 g) asparagus; chop into bite-size chunks. In large pot of boiling water, blanch asparagus for 2 minutes. Chill under cold water; drain and pat dry. Spread bread with cheese. Sprinkle asparagus evenly over half of the bread slices. Top with ham before sandwiching with remaining bread slices.

⅓ cup	herbed cream cheese, softened	75 mL
12	slices egg bread (challah)	12
2	green onions, minced	2
12	slices smoked salmon (about 5 oz/150 g)	12
4	eggs	4

2 cups	milk	500 mL
2 tsp	Dijon mustard	10 mL
¼ tsp	each dried dillweed and pepper	1 mL
Pinch	salt	Pinch
½ cup	shredded Swiss cheese	125 mL
	Chopped green onions	

1 Spread cream cheese evenly over each bread slice; sprinkle half of the slices with minced onions, then top with smoked salmon slices. Sandwich with remaining bread slices, cheese side down; cut in half diagonally.

2 Arrange 3 sandwich halves, cut side down and overlapping slightly, along centre of greased 13- x 9-inch (3 L) glass baking dish. Arrange remaining halves, cut side down, in circle around centre layer, overlapping and curving slightly to fit.

3 In bowl, whisk together eggs, milk, mustard, dill, pepper and salt; pour evenly over sandwich halves, then sprinkle with cheese. Cover with plastic wrap and refrigerate for 4 hours. (MAKE-AHEAD: Refrigerate for up to 12 hours.)

4 Bake in 350°F (180°C) oven for about 35 minutes or until light golden and set. Let stand on rack for 10 minutes. Garnish with chopped onions.

Makes 8 servings.

PER SERVING, ABOUT:

cal	324	carb	34 g
pro	17 g	fibre	1 g
total fat	13 g	chol	164 mg
sat. fat	6 g	sodium	584 mg

PERCENTAGE RDI:

calcium	20%	vit. A	13%
iron	19%	vit. C	2%
folate	20%		

BREADS FOR Stratas

✎ Stratas are an ideal use for leftover bread. Stale bread lends structure to the strata and doesn't turn extremely soggy when the egg mixture is poured over it. Feel free to substitute another kind for what's called for in the recipe.

✎ Day-old bread should be slightly dry, not soft. If soft or moist, here's how to make it stale quickly: Lay slices on rimless baking sheets; bake in 200°F (100°C) oven, turning once, for about 20 minutes. Let cool.

Layered Chorizo Bake

This Mexican-inspired breakfast and brunch bake is an irresistible combination of a crusty top layer and creamy smooth corn-studded pudding and paprika-spiced sausage. Jalapeño peppers add a tingle of heat, too; cut back if you prefer.

8 oz	chorizo sausage, thinly sliced	250 g
6 oz	cream cheese, softened	175 g
½ cup	cornmeal	125 mL
3 tbsp	granulated sugar	50 mL
4	eggs	4
1	can (12 oz/341 mL) corn kernels, drained (or 1½ cups/375 mL fresh or frozen)	1

1½ cups	shredded old Cheddar cheese (about 6 oz/175 g)	375 mL
6	green onions, sliced	6
Half	jalapeño pepper, seeded and minced	Half
1 tsp	dried oregano	5 mL
½ tsp	each salt and pepper	2 mL

1 In skillet, cook sausage over medium heat, stirring often, for about 5 minutes or until crisp and lightly browned.

2 Meanwhile, in bowl, beat together cream cheese, cornmeal and sugar until smooth. Beat in eggs, 1 at a time, beating until smooth after each addition. Stir in corn, 1 cup (250 mL) of the Cheddar cheese, onions, jalapeño pepper, oregano, salt and pepper.

3 Pour half of the egg mixture into greased 8-inch (2 L) square glass baking dish or casserole; cover with three-quarters of the sausage. Pour remaining egg mixture evenly over top; sprinkle with remaining sausage and cheese.

4 Bake in 375°F (190°C) oven for about 30 minutes or until light golden and set. Let cool for 5 minutes.

TEST KITCHEN TIP: Chorizo (or, in Portuguese, *chouriço*), is pork sausage seasoned with sweet or hot paprika or red-pepper pulp. It is soft and suitable for grilling or frying and used in many dishes. Air-cured, the sausage dries and becomes very sliceable to use in soups, add to pizza or to eat as is. Hot or mild Italian sausage, or other well-seasoned fresh sausage, can be substituted for the chorizo; you can also use kielbasa sausage instead, but omit the cooking in skillet.

Makes 4 to 6 servings.

PER EACH OF 6 SERVINGS, ABOUT:

cal	546	carb	28 g
pro	25 g	fibre	2 g
total fat	38 g	chol	237 mg
sat. fat	19 g	sodium	1,099 mg

PERCENTAGE RDI:

calcium	24%	vit. A	30%
iron	16%	vit. C	10%
folate	25%		

Breakfast Strudels

Creamy seasoned scrambled eggs rolled in crisp phyllo pastry and popped into the oven are an inspired idea for weekend breakfasts, especially when there's company.

2 tbsp	butter	25 mL		1 cup	diced smoked ham	250 mL
2 tbsp	all-purpose flour	25 mL		2 tbsp	minced fresh parsley	25 mL
1 cup	milk	250 mL		2 tsp	minced fresh chives or green onion tops	10 mL
½ cup	shredded old Cheddar cheese	125 mL		½ tsp	dried thyme	2 mL
¼ tsp	salt (approx)	1 mL		8	sheets phyllo pastry	8
¼ tsp	pepper	1 mL		¼ cup	butter, melted	50 mL
6	eggs, lightly beaten	6		3 tbsp	grated Parmesan cheese	50 mL

1 In heavy saucepan, melt butter over medium heat; stir in flour. Gradually whisk in milk; cook, stirring constantly, for about 5 minutes or until smooth and thickened. Add Cheddar cheese, ¼ tsp (1 mL) salt and half of the pepper; stir until cheese is melted. Set aside.

2 In large nonstick skillet over medium-high heat, stir together eggs, ham, parsley, chives, thyme, remaining pepper and pinch more salt; cook, stirring almost constantly, for about 3 minutes or until eggs are scrambled and just cooked but still moist. Stir into cheese sauce. Let cool.

3 Place 1 sheet of the phyllo on work surface, keeping remainder covered with damp tea towel to prevent drying out. Brush sheet lightly with some of the butter. Fold in half lengthwise; brush lightly with some of the butter. Spoon about ⅓ cup (75 mL) of the egg mixture along 1 narrow end of phyllo, leaving 1-inch (2.5 cm) border; sprinkle about 1 tsp (5 mL) of the Parmesan cheese over egg mixture. Fold sides over to enclose filling; roll up.

4 Brush top with butter. Place, seam side down, on greased rimmed baking sheet. Repeat with remaining ingredients to make 7 more strudels. (MAKE-AHEAD: Wrap in plastic wrap and refrigerate for up to 48 hours, or overwrap with heavy-duty foil and freeze in airtight container for up to 1 month. Unwrap but do not thaw before baking.)

5 Bake in 375°F (190°C) oven for 13 to 16 minutes, or for 35 to 40 minutes if frozen, or until golden. Let stand for 5 to 10 minutes before serving.

Makes 8 servings.

PER SERVING, ABOUT:

cal 289	carb . . . . 17 g
pro . . . . 14 g	fibre . . . . 1 g
total fat . . . . 18 g	chol . . . . . 204 mg
sat. fat . . . . . . 9 g	sodium . . 651 mg

PERCENTAGE RDI:

calcium 13%	vit. A 20%
iron 13%	vit. C 2%
folate 11%	

Puffy Dutch Pancake with Bananas and Strawberries

This dramatically large crusty puff is rather like an overgrown Yorkshire pudding, elbowing its way up and out of the skillet and forming a deep cup in the centre. There, you can nestle a lovely surprise: a sauce starring fresh bananas and strawberries.

1 tbsp	butter, melted	15 mL		**TOPPING:**		
4	eggs	4		1 cup	orange juice	250 mL
1 cup	all-purpose flour	250 mL		¼ cup	packed brown sugar	50 mL
1 cup	milk	250 mL		4	bananas, sliced	4
¾ tsp	salt	4 mL		2 tsp	cornstarch	10 mL
2 tbsp	icing sugar	25 mL		1 tbsp	water	15 mL
				1½ cups	sliced strawberries	375 mL
				4 tsp	rum (optional)	20 mL

1 Brush butter over bottom and side of 12-inch (30 cm) ovenproof nonstick or cast-iron skillet; heat in centre of 450°F (230°C) oven for 5 minutes.

2 Meanwhile, in large bowl, whisk together eggs, flour, milk and salt until smooth. Pour into pan; return to oven and bake for 15 minutes. Reduce heat to 350°F (180°C); bake for about 10 minutes or until puffed and browned. With metal spatula, loosen from skillet and slide onto platter.

3 TOPPING: Meanwhile, in separate skillet, bring orange juice and sugar to boil over medium-high heat, stirring; boil for 1 minute. Reduce heat to medium; add bananas and cook for 1 minute.

4 Dissolve cornstarch in water; add to pan and cook, stirring, for 1 minute or until thickened. Stir in strawberries, and rum (if using). Spoon into centre of puff; sprinkle with icing sugar.

Makes 6 servings.

PER SERVING, ABOUT:

cal	308	carb	55 g
pro	9 g	fibre	3 g
total fat	7 g	chol	151 mg
sat. fat	3 g	sodium	373 mg

PERCENTAGE RDI:

calcium	8%	vit. A	11%
iron	14%	vit. C	62%
folate	26%		

Cheese Soufflé

Soufflés have a reputation for being temperamental, even difficult for the home cook. Nothing could be further from the truth now that electric mixers beat egg whites speedily and ovens heat reliably. This master recipe with variations should be enough for soufflés to beat their unwarranted rap and for everyone to ooh and aah at their billowing height.

3 tbsp	butter	50 mL	½ tsp	salt	2 mL
3 tbsp	all-purpose flour	50 mL	Pinch	pepper	Pinch
1 cup	milk	250 mL	4	eggs, separated	4
1½ cups	shredded Cheddar, Swiss or Gouda cheese	375 mL	¼ tsp	cream of tartar	1 mL

1 In heavy saucepan, melt butter over medium heat; add flour and cook, whisking, for 30 seconds. Stir in milk; cook, whisking constantly, for 3 to 5 minutes or until boiling and thickened. Remove from heat; stir in cheese, salt and pepper. Whisk in egg yolks, 1 at a time, whisking thoroughly after each addition.

2 In large bowl, beat egg whites with cream of tartar until stiff peaks form. Whisk one-third into egg yolk mixture; fold in remaining whites.

3 Scrape into greased 6- x 3-inch or 7- x 3-inch (1 L or 1.5 L) soufflé dish. Place on baking sheet and bake in 375°F (190°C) oven for about 35 minutes or until puffed and golden and top is firm to the touch.

VARIATIONS

Cheese and Broccoli or Asparagus Soufflé: After whisking in egg yolks, stir in 1½ cups (375 mL) finely chopped cooked broccoli florets or asparagus.

Italian Soufflé: Substitute 1 cup (250 mL) shredded mozzarella cheese and ½ cup (125 mL) grated Parmesan cheese for Cheddar cheese. Add 1 tbsp (15 mL) each chopped fresh basil and oregano.

Mexican Soufflé: Substitute Monterey Jack cheese for Cheddar cheese. After whisking in egg yolks, stir in ½ cup (125 mL) cooked corn kernels, ½ cup (125 mL) chopped sweet red peppers and 2 tbsp (25 mL) chopped jalapeño pepper.

Spinach and Feta Soufflé: Substitute ½ cup (125 mL) crumbled feta cheese for shredded Cheddar cheese. After whisking in egg yolks, stir in 1 cup (250 mL) chopped cooked spinach, squeezed dry, and 2 tbsp (25 mL) chopped fresh dill.

Makes 2 to 4 servings.

PER EACH OF 4 SERVINGS, ABOUT:

cal	373	carb	9 g
pro	20 g	fibre	trace
total fat	29 g	chol	287 mg
sat. fat	17 g	sodium	731 mg

PERCENTAGE RDI:

calcium	37%	vit. A	33%
iron	9%	vit. C	0%
folate	15%		

Portobello Asparagus Strudels

When an impressive main course or appetizer is in order, this lusty bundle of meaty mushrooms, fresh asparagus, roasted pepper and zesty Asiago cheese rolled in easy-to-handle phyllo pastry meets the criteria.

6	portobello mushrooms (about 1½ lb/750 g), stemmed	6	8	sheets phyllo pastry	8
2 tbsp	olive oil	25 mL	¼ cup	butter, melted	50 mL
2 tbsp	balsamic vinegar	25 mL	¼ cup	fresh bread crumbs	50 mL
2 tsp	dried thyme	10 mL	2 cups	shredded Asiago cheese	500 mL
¼ tsp	each salt and pepper	1 mL	2	jars (each 313 mL) roasted sweet red peppers, drained	2
3 tbsp	Dijon mustard	50 mL			
1 tbsp	water	15 mL	1 lb	asparagus, trimmed	500 g

1 Slice mushroom caps. In large skillet, heat oil over medium-high heat; cook mushrooms, stirring often, for about 10 minutes or until liquid is evaporated. Stir in vinegar, thyme, salt and pepper; cook for 2 minutes.

2 In small bowl, blend mustard with water; set aside. Place 1 sheet of the phyllo on work surface with 1 long edge closest, keeping remainder covered with damp tea towel to prevent drying out. Brush sheet lightly with some of the butter. Top with second sheet; brush lightly with some of the mustard mixture. About 4 inches (10 cm) to the right of left-hand edge, top with third sheet to extend pastry slightly; brush lightly with some of the butter. Align fourth sheet over third; brush with some of the mustard mixture.

3 Sprinkle phyllo stack with half of the bread crumbs in 3-inch (8 cm) wide strip, about 1 inch (2.5 cm) from closest edge and leaving 2-inch (5 cm) border at each side edge. Sprinkle with ½ cup (125 mL) of the cheese. Arrange half of the mushrooms over cheese. Top with half each of the red peppers and asparagus; sprinkle with ½ cup (125 mL) of the cheese.

4 Along closest edge, fold 1-inch (2.5 cm) border over filling; fold side edges over to enclose filling and roll up. Place, seam side down, on greased baking sheet; brush with some of the butter. Repeat with remaining ingredients. (MAKE-AHEAD: Cover and refrigerate for up to 2 hours; bake for 10 minutes longer.) Bake in 425°F (220°C) oven for about 25 minutes or until golden. Let stand for 5 minutes before serving. Slice each strudel diagonally into thirds.

Makes 6 servings.

PER SERVING, ABOUT:

cal	412	carb	32 g
pro	15 g	fibre	5 g
total fat	27 g	chol	52 mg
sat. fat	13 g	sodium	773 mg

PERCENTAGE RDI:

calcium	29%	vit. A	40%
iron	32%	vit. C	133%
folate	45%		

Mediterranean Vegetable Pie

This pie's olive oil pastry forms a sturdy base that folds up in attractive ragged edges to enclose a medley of roasted vegetables, garlic, cheese and oregano.

SUBSTITUTION: Instead of roasting your own peppers, you can use 1 jar (313 mL) roasted sweet red peppers, drained.

TEST KITCHEN TIP: Roast vegetables in top and bottom thirds of oven, rotating and switching pans halfway through for even cooking.

1¾ cups	all-purpose flour	425 mL
1 tsp	each salt and baking powder	5 mL
⅓ cup	each olive oil and milk	75 mL
2	eggs	2
FILLING:		
2	each zucchini and onions	2
1	eggplant	1
¼ cup	olive oil	50 mL

1 tsp	salt	5 mL
1	head garlic	1
3	roasted sweet red peppers, peeled, seeded and sliced	3
1 cup	shredded Fontina or mozzarella cheese	250 mL
¼ cup	chopped fresh oregano (or 2 tsp/10 mL dried)	50 mL
½ tsp	pepper	2 mL

1 In large bowl, whisk together flour, salt and baking powder. In separate bowl, whisk together oil, milk and 1 of the eggs; add to dry ingredients. Using fingers or mixer with dough hook, blend until smooth and liquid is absorbed. Turn out onto lightly floured surface; knead for about 2 minutes or until velvety smooth. Form into ball. Transfer to bowl; cover and refrigerate for 30 minutes. (MAKE-AHEAD: Wrap in plastic wrap and refrigerate for up to 5 days.)

2 FILLING: Cut zucchini, onions and eggplant crosswise into ½-inch (1 cm) thick slices; brush with all but 1 tbsp (15 mL) of the oil. Place in single layer on 2 large baking sheets. Sprinkle with ½ tsp (2 mL) of the salt. Without peeling, separate garlic cloves; in bowl, toss with remaining oil. Add garlic to pans, reserving oil in bowl.

3 Roast in 425°F (220°C) oven for about 40 minutes or until vegetables are tender. Let cool. Squeeze garlic from skins into reserved oil in bowl; mash with fork. (MAKE-AHEAD: Refrigerate vegetables in airtight container and cover and refrigerate garlic for up to 12 hours.)

4 On floured surface, roll out pastry into 18-inch (45 cm) circle; transfer to large parchment paper–lined baking sheet. Spread garlic mixture into 9-inch (23 cm) circle in centre of pastry. Top with one-third of the vegetable mixture, then one-third of the red peppers; sprinkle with one-third of the cheese, oregano, pepper and remaining salt. Repeat layers twice. Fold pastry border over filling to form attractive irregular edge, leaving 2-inch (5 cm) opening on top. Lightly beat remaining egg; brush over pastry to seal folds.

5 Bake in lower third of 375°F (190°C) oven for about 30 minutes or until pastry is golden. Let cool on pan on rack for 5 minutes before cutting into wedges.

Makes 6 servings.

PER SERVING, ABOUT:

cal	488	carb	45 g
pro	13 g	fibre	5 g
total fat	29 g	chol	94 mg
sat. fat	7 g	sodium	993 mg

PERCENTAGE RDI:

calcium	17%	vit. A	33%
iron	20%	vit. C	173%
folate	36%		

Two-Cheese Tomato Tart

Celebrate summer with a tomato-topped tart underpinned with creamy Fontina and stretchy mozzarella.

3	sheets phyllo pastry	3
¼ cup	butter, melted	50 mL
⅓ cup	Dijon mustard	75 mL
3 oz	mozzarella cheese, thinly sliced	90 g
3 oz	Fontina cheese, thinly sliced	90 g

2	tomatoes, thinly sliced	2
1	large clove garlic, minced	1
2 tbsp	chopped fresh oregano (or 1 tsp/5 mL dried)	25 mL
2 tbsp	olive oil	25 mL
¼ tsp	each salt and pepper	1 mL

TEST KITCHEN TIP: You can also serve this tart as an appetizer to serve 8.

1 Cut each sheet of phyllo in half crosswise. Lay 1 half on work surface, keeping remainder covered with damp tea towel to prevent drying out. Brush sheet lightly with some of the butter. Place second sheet on top, making sure edges are not perfectly aligned; brush with 1 tbsp (15 mL) of the mustard. Roughly layer remaining sheets, alternating butter and mustard and ending with layer of mustard. Gently lift into 14¾- x 4½-inch (37.5 x 11.5 cm) rectangular tart pan with removable bottom; press gently. Spread remaining mustard on top; fold phyllo edges under to create ruffled effect.

2 Cover with layer of mozzarella and Fontina cheeses; arrange tomato slices on top, overlapping in long rows. Sprinkle with garlic, oregano, oil, salt and pepper. Place tart pan on rimmed baking sheet. Bake in 375°F (190°C) oven for 35 to 40 minutes or until phyllo is golden.

Makes 4 servings.

PER SERVING, ABOUT:

cal	400	carb	15 g
pro	13 g	fibre	1 g
total fat	33 g	chol	75 mg
sat. fat	16 g	sodium	881 mg

PERCENTAGE RDI:

calcium	26%	vit. A	30%
iron	11%	vit. C	15%
folate	5%		

Mushroom Lentil Burgers

Ready-made vegetarian patties available in supermarkets inspired these terrific, inexpensive and superior-tasting burgers. Pop them into toasted poppy seed buns with lettuce, juicy slices of tomato and cucumber.

1 tsp	vegetable oil	5 mL	3 tbsp	grated Parmesan cheese	50 mL
1	onion, finely chopped	1	2 tbsp	chopped pine nuts or pecans	25 mL
1 cup	finely chopped mushrooms	250 mL	¼ tsp	pepper	1 mL
½ tsp	dried thyme	2 mL	4	lettuce leaves	4
1	can (19 oz/540 mL) lentils, drained and rinsed	1	4	poppy seed hamburger buns	4
½ cup	quick-cooking rolled oats (not instant)	125 mL			

Makes 4 servings.

PER SERVING, ABOUT:

cal	400	carb	61 g
pro	20 g	fibre	8 g
total fat	9 g	chol	4 mg
sat. fat	2 g	sodium	663 mg

PERCENTAGE RDI:

calcium	17%	vit. A	3%
iron	48%	vit. C	8%
folate	115%		

1 In large nonstick skillet, heat oil over medium heat; cook onion, stirring occasionally, for about 4 minutes or until softened. Add mushrooms and thyme; cook, stirring, for about 4 minutes or just until starting to brown. Let cool slightly.

2 In bowl, coarsely mash lentils; stir in mushroom mixture, oats, cheese, pine nuts and pepper. Shape into four ¾-inch (2 cm) thick patties. (MAKE-AHEAD: Place on large waxed paper–lined plate; cover and refrigerate for up to 8 hours.)

3 In same skillet or on greased grill over medium heat, cook patties for 3 to 4 minutes per side or until golden brown. Sandwich with lettuce in buns.

Bean Burgers WITH CORIANDER CREAM

This is the easiest vegetarian burger ever. No one will believe it has only three ingredients.

➤ Drain and rinse 1 can (19 oz/ 540 mL) red kidney, black or romano beans. Place in large bowl; mash with fork until smooth but still with some small lumps. Stir in ½ cup (125 mL) dry bread crumbs and ⅓ cup (75 mL) salsa. With wet hands, shape into four ½-inch (1 cm) thick patties. (MAKE-AHEAD: Place on large waxed paper–lined plate; cover and refrigerate for up to 8 hours.) In large nonstick skillet, heat 2 tsp (10 mL) vegetable oil over medium-high heat; cook patties, turning once, for about 10 minutes or until crusty on outside and piping hot inside. Or cook on grill as above. Sandwich in whole wheat buns along with lettuce leaves and ⅓ cup (75 mL) light sour cream mixed with 2 tbsp (25 mL) minced fresh coriander.

Barbecued Tofu Sandwiches with Aïoli

This enthusiastically seasoned sandwich, made with two different kinds of tofu, could confound a person who says he doesn't like tofu. The "patty" is extra-firm tofu, ideal for grilling, and the garlicky sauce is whizzed up with soft silken tofu, not mayonnaise. This recipe is suitable for vegans.

1	pkg (350 g) extra-firm tofu	1
3 tbsp	olive oil	50 mL
2 tbsp	chopped fresh basil	25 mL
1 tbsp	wine vinegar	15 mL
1	clove garlic, minced	1
Pinch	each salt and pepper	Pinch
2	sweet yellow peppers	2

4	soft rolls	4
1	large tomato, sliced	1
4	large basil leaves	4
TOFU AÏOLI:		
1 cup	silken tofu	250 mL
1 tbsp	lemon juice	15 mL
Pinch	each salt and pepper	Pinch
1	clove garlic, minced	1

1 Drain extra-firm tofu; cut horizontally into 4 slices. In shallow dish, whisk together oil, basil, vinegar, garlic, salt and pepper; add tofu, turning to coat. Set aside. (MAKE-AHEAD: Cover and refrigerate for up to 24 hours, turning occasionally.)

2 Cut yellow peppers in half; core, seed and flatten. Place on greased grill over medium-high heat; close lid and cook, turning often, for 15 to 20 minutes or until softened and charred. Let cool; peel off and discard skin.

3 Reserving marinade, place tofu on greased grill over medium-high heat; close lid and cook for 5 minutes. Brush with half of the reserved marinade; turn and cook for about 5 minutes or until crisp and grill-marked.

4 TOFU AÏOLI: In food processor, combine silken tofu, lemon juice, salt and pepper; pulse until smooth. Stir in garlic. (MAKE-AHEAD: Refrigerate in airtight container for up to 3 days.)

5 Meanwhile, cut rolls in half horizontally; brush cut sides with remaining marinade. Place, cut side down, on grill; toast for about 2 minutes or until golden.

6 Spread bottom half of each roll with 2 tbsp (25 mL) of the aïoli; top with tofu slice, yellow pepper half, tomato slices and basil leaf. Top with aïoli; sandwich with tops of rolls.

Makes 4 servings.

PER SERVING, ABOUT:

cal	402	carb	42 g
pro	17 g	fibre	4 g
total fat	20 g	chol	0 mg
sat. fat	4 g	sodium	321 mg

PERCENTAGE RDI:

calcium	17%	vit. A	16%
iron	28%	vit. C	163%
folate	36%		

Vegetarian Moussaka

If time management is a goal in your kitchen, this recipe is for you! There are enough components — broiled eggplant, chunky tomato sauce, feta cheese and ricotta custard topping — to make two casseroles. Enjoy one right away, freeze the second.

TEST KITCHEN TIP: To make only 1 moussaka, divide ingredients in half, decreasing tomatoes and tomato paste to half can each and cinnamon to rounded ¼ tsp (1 mL). You can use the remaining tomatoes and paste for pasta or soup.

4	eggplants (about 3½ lb/1.75 kg)	4
1 tbsp	salt	15 mL
¼ cup	olive oil	50 mL
2 cups	crumbled feta cheese	500 mL
CUSTARD:		
¼ cup	butter	50 mL
¼ cup	all-purpose flour	50 mL
1½ cups	milk	375 mL
1 tsp	salt	5 mL
¼ tsp	each nutmeg and pepper	1 mL
4	eggs	4
2 cups	ricotta or cottage cheese	500 mL

TOMATO SAUCE:		
2 tbsp	olive oil	25 mL
3	onions, chopped	3
2	zucchini, diced	2
1	sweet red pepper, diced	1
4	cloves garlic, minced	4
2 tsp	dried oregano	10 mL
¾ tsp	cinnamon	4 mL
¼ tsp	pepper	1 mL
1	can (19 oz/540 mL) tomatoes, drained and chopped	1
1	can (5½ oz/156 mL) tomato paste	1

1 Cut eggplants crosswise into ½-inch (1 cm) thick slices; layer in colander, sprinkling each layer with salt. Let stand for 30 minutes. Rinse thoroughly and drain; pat dry.

2 In batches, brush eggplants with oil and broil on baking sheet, turning once, for 8 to 12 minutes or until lightly browned. Set aside.

3 CUSTARD: Meanwhile, in heavy saucepan, melt butter over medium heat; whisk in flour and cook, whisking, for 2 minutes, without browning. Gradually whisk in milk until smooth; cook, whisking often, for 2 to 4 minutes or until boiling and thickened. Stir in salt, nutmeg and pepper. Transfer to large bowl; let cool slightly. Whisk in eggs and ricotta cheese; place plastic wrap directly on surface and set aside.

4 TOMATO SAUCE: In large skillet, heat oil over medium heat; cook onions, zucchini, red pepper and garlic, stirring occasionally, for about 5 minutes or until softened. Stir in oregano, cinnamon and pepper; cook, stirring, for 1 minute. Add tomatoes and tomato paste; bring to boil. Reduce heat and simmer for about 10 minutes or until zucchini is tender.

Makes 8 servings.

PER SERVING, ABOUT:

cal	 512	carb .... 34 g
pro	.... 20 g	fibre .... 8 g
total fat	.... 35 g	chol ..... 185 mg
sat. fat	..... 16 g	sodium .. 894 mg

PERCENTAGE RDI:

calcium	.... 37%	vit. A 39%
iron	.... 22%	vit. C 75%
folate	...... 35%	

5 In each of two 8-inch (2 L) square glass baking dishes, spread one-quarter of the tomato sauce; top with one-quarter of the eggplant and sprinkle with ½ cup (125 mL) of the feta cheese. Top with remaining tomato sauce, then remaining eggplant. Spread custard evenly over top; sprinkle with remaining feta cheese. (MAKE-AHEAD: Refrigerate until cool; cover and refrigerate for up to 1 day or overwrap with heavy-duty foil and freeze for up to 2 months. Thaw completely in refrigerator before baking.)

6 Bake in 350°F (180°C) oven for 1 hour or until top is browned and set. Let stand for 15 minutes; cut into squares.

GRAINS Glossary

BARLEY: Barley is available as pearl or pot barley, both of which have had the bran removed and have been polished and steamed. Both take about 40 minutes to cook.

BUCKWHEAT: Actually not a grain at all but in the same family as rhubarb and sorrel, buckwheat is available as a flour or as seeds or groats. Buckwheat flour is popular for pancakes and yeast-raised blini. Buckwheat groats, called kasha, come in three different grades (fine, medium and coarse) and can be toasted in a dry skillet before steaming to enhance flavour.

BULGUR: A staple in Middle Eastern cooking, bulgur (also known as burghul) is wheat kernels that have been steamed, dried and crushed. Bulgur comes in coarse, medium and fine varieties, has a tender, chewy texture and is usually soaked, not cooked, before eating. Use in salads, pilafs and as a side dish.

COUSCOUS: Made from semolina, this ground hard durum wheat has long been a staple in North African cuisine, where it is steamed and rolled to expand in size. Couscous is widely available in instant precooked form and needs only a five-minute soak in hot liquid. Couscous is a fine accompaniment to almost any stew. Like rice, pasta and potatoes, it is an excellent salad ingredient.

MILLET: Rich in protein, millet cooks quickly and, because of its mildness, is the perfect culinary foil for any stew. It adds a seedy crunch to quick breads. Store in the refrigerator or freezer.

OATS: Known most commonly in their ground "oatmeal" form and their steamed and rolled flake form, oats are the basis of porridge and are combined with wheat flour in baking breads, cookies and muffins. For baking, use old-fashioned or large-flake oats or quick-cooking oats; avoid instant oats.

PEARL COUSCOUS: Often called Israeli or Middle Eastern couscous, this is a small round wheat flour pasta. Cook and enjoy as such.

QUINOA: An ancient grain, quinoa is considered a supergrain because of its high nutritional status (it contains all eight essential amino acids, making it a complete protein). Ivory in colour and somewhat bland, quinoa cooks like rice but in half the time. Store quinoa in the refrigerator or freezer since it turns rancid quickly. Always rinse very well before using.

WHEAT BERRIES: Noted for their chewy texture, wheat berries are unprocessed whole soft or hard wheat kernels. Soft wheat berries take less time to cook than hard and are a more golden colour. Use like rice in salads.

Black Bean Chili with Avocado Salsa

It's this kind of sassy chili with freshly dressed avocado topping that has dispelled forever the myth that vegetarian food is bland and unappealing. Guess what? Vegetarians and nonvegetarians alike will enjoy this chili.

VARIATION

Slow-Cooker Black Bean Chili with Avocado Salsa:
Reduce chili powder to 1 tbsp (15 mL). Cook vegetables as directed in Step 1; place in 18- to 24-cup (4.5 to 6 L) slow-cooker. Add ¼ cup (50 mL) tomato paste and all remaining ingredients except Avocado Salsa. Cover and cook on Low for 6 hours. Prepare and serve Avocado Salsa as directed.

1 tbsp	vegetable oil	15 mL
2	onions, chopped	2
2	cloves garlic, minced	2
2	carrots, chopped	2
1	jalapeño pepper, seeded and minced	1
2 tbsp	chili powder	25 mL
1 tsp	each ground cumin and dried oregano	5 mL
¼ tsp	salt	1 mL
2	cans (each 28 oz/796 mL) stewed tomatoes	2

2	cans (each 19 oz/540 mL) black beans, drained and rinsed	2
2	sweet red peppers, chopped	2

AVOCADO SALSA:

2	avocados, peeled, pitted and diced	2
2 tbsp	minced red onion	25 mL
2 tbsp	chopped fresh coriander	25 mL
2 tbsp	lime juice	25 mL
Pinch	each salt and pepper	Pinch

1 In large saucepan, heat oil over medium heat; cook onions, garlic, carrots, jalapeño pepper, chili powder, cumin, oregano and salt, stirring occasionally, for about 5 minutes or until onions are softened.

2 Add tomatoes, black beans and red peppers; cover and simmer for about 40 minutes or until carrots are tender.

3 AVOCADO SALSA: In bowl, stir together avocados, onion, coriander, lime juice, salt and pepper; spoon onto each serving.

Makes 8 servings.

PER SERVING, ABOUT:

cal	311	carb	48 g
pro	12 g	fibre	11 g
total fat	11 g	chol	0 mg
sat. fat	2 g	sodium	873 mg

PERCENTAGE RDI:

calcium	11%	vit. A	78%
iron	34%	vit. C	145%
folate	86%		

COOKED DRIED Beans

Canned beans are convenient, but when you have time, it's more economical to precook the beans yourself. To replace the contents of each 19-oz (540 mL) can (about 2 cups/500 mL), combine 1 cup (250 mL) dried black beans and 3 cups (750 mL) water in large saucepan; bring to boil. Boil for 2 minutes; remove from heat. Cover and let stand for 1 hour. Drain. Add 6 cups (1.5 L) water; bring to boil. Reduce heat, cover and simmer for about 1 hour or until tender. Drain. Rehydrate and cook chickpeas and other dried beans in the same way, adjusting cooking time as necessary.

Perogies

Plump filled dumplings served with onions and sour cream are a delicious gift brought from Eastern Europe to Canadian tables.

2 tbsp	butter	25 mL
1	onion, sliced	1
	Sour cream	
DOUGH:		
3 cups	all-purpose flour	750 mL
1½ tsp	salt	7 mL
1	egg	1
¾ cup	water (approx)	175 mL
4 tsp	vegetable oil	20 mL

POTATO FILLING:		
1 tbsp	butter	15 mL
⅓ cup	finely chopped onion	75 mL
1 cup	cold mashed potatoes	250 mL
¾ cup	shredded Cheddar cheese	175 mL
½ tsp	salt	2 mL
¼ tsp	pepper	1 mL

1 DOUGH: In bowl, whisk flour with salt. In separate bowl, beat together egg, water and oil; stir into flour mixture to make soft, not sticky, dough that holds together in ball. If necessary, add more water, 1 tbsp (15 mL) at a time, being careful not to make dough sticky. Turn out onto lightly floured surface; knead about 10 times or just until smooth. Halve dough; cover with plastic wrap or damp tea towel. Let rest for 20 minutes.

2 POTATO FILLING: Meanwhile, in skillet, heat butter over medium heat; cook onion for 3 to 5 minutes or until tender. Transfer to bowl; stir in potatoes, cheese, salt and pepper.

3 Working with half of the dough at a time and keeping remainder covered to prevent drying out, roll out on lightly floured surface to about 1/16-inch (1.5 mm) thickness; with 3-inch (8 cm) round cookie cutter, cut out rounds. Place 1 tsp (5 mL) of the filling on centre of each round; with water, lightly moisten edge of 1 half of round. Fold each round in half; pinch edges together to seal and crimp attractively. Place on tea towel–lined rimmed baking sheets; cover with damp tea towel to prevent drying out. (MAKE-AHEAD: Refrigerate for up to 8 hours, or freeze on baking sheets, then pack in freezer bags and freeze for up to 1 month. Do not thaw before cooking.)

4 In large pot of boiling salted water, cook perogies in batches, stirring gently to prevent them from sticking together or to bottom of pot, for 1½ to 2 minutes or until they float to top. With slotted spoon, transfer to colander to drain.

5 Meanwhile, in large heavy skillet, melt butter over medium heat; cook onion for about 5 minutes or until golden. Add perogies; toss to coat and warm through. Serve with sour cream.

FILLING VARIATIONS

Mushroom: In large skillet, melt 2 tbsp (25 mL) butter over medium heat; cook 3 cups (750 mL) chopped mushrooms and ⅓ cup (75 mL) finely chopped onion, stirring often, for 7 to 9 minutes or until liquid is evaporated. Remove from heat; stir in 1 egg yolk, 1 tbsp (15 mL) chopped fresh dill and ¼ tsp (1 mL) each salt and pepper.

Cottage Cheese: Stir together 1 cup (250 mL) pressed cottage cheese, 1 egg, beaten, 1 tbsp (15 mL) chopped green onion or fresh dill, ½ tsp (2 mL) salt and ¼ tsp (1 mL) pepper.

Makes about 36 perogies.

PER PEROGY, ABOUT:

cal	66	carb	9 g
pro	2 g	fibre	trace
total fat	2 g	chol	11 mg
sat. fat	1 g	sodium	171 mg

PERCENTAGE RDI:

calcium	2%	vit. A	2%
iron	4%	vit. C	0%
folate	6%		

Pasta and Pizza

9

A Fine Tomato Pasta Sauce 230

Pasta Puttanesca 231

Big-Batch Beef Ragu 232

Penne with Garlicky Rapini 233

Macaroni and Cheese Five Ways 234

Chicken Pesto Pasta 235

Spaghetti Carbonara 236

Fettuccine Alfredo — The Classic 237

Pastitsio 238

Creamy Shrimp Bake 240

Spicy Sausage and Rigatoni Bake 241

Luscious Mushroom Lasagna 242

Old Favourite Lasagna 244

Potato Gnocchi 245

Singapore Noodles 246

Pad Thai 247

Pizza Dough 248

Grilled Pepper and Sausage Pizza 249

Mushroom Pizza 250

Pesto and Roasted Eggplant Pizza 251

QUICK   FREEZABLE   BUDGET-
WISE

A Fine Tomato Pasta Sauce

There may be plenty of ready-made pasta sauces, but you can create your own fresh-tasting tomato sauce or use it as a starting point for your own signature sauces, adding mushrooms, fennel and sausage, vegetables, clams or creamy cheese. Each batch is plenty to coat 1 lb (500 g) pasta, cooked.

1 tsp	olive oil	5 mL
2	cloves garlic, minced	2
1	onion, chopped	1
Half	carrot, grated	Half
1 tsp	dried basil	5 mL
½ tsp	dried oregano	2 mL

¼ tsp	each salt and pepper	1 mL
1	can (28 oz/796 mL) tomatoes	1
1 tbsp	tomato paste	15 mL
½ tsp	granulated sugar	2 mL
2 tbsp	chopped fresh parsley	25 mL

1 In large saucepan, heat oil over medium heat; cook garlic, onion, carrot, basil, oregano, salt and pepper, stirring often, for 5 minutes or until onion is softened.

2 Add tomatoes, breaking up with spoon. Stir in tomato paste and sugar; bring to boil. Reduce heat to medium; simmer for about 20 minutes or until thickened. (MAKE-AHEAD: Let cool. Refrigerate in airtight container for up to 2 days or freeze for up to 1 month. Reheat to serve.) Stir in parsley.

VARIATIONS

Mushroom Pasta Sauce: In skillet, heat 2 tsp (10 mL) butter with 1 tsp (5 mL) olive oil over medium heat; cook 2 cups (500 mL) sliced mushrooms (shiitake, oyster, portobello, button) for 5 to 7 minutes or until golden. Add to Tomato Pasta Sauce along with ½ tsp (2 mL) granulated sugar; simmer for 10 minutes. **Makes 3½ cups (875 mL).**

Ratatouille Pasta Sauce: In skillet, heat 1 tbsp (15 mL) olive oil over medium heat; cook 1 cup (250 mL) cubed peeled eggplant, stirring often, for 5 minutes. Add half sweet green pepper, chopped, and 1 small zucchini, chopped; cook for 5 minutes. Add to Tomato Pasta Sauce along with ½ tsp (2 mL) granulated sugar; simmer for 10 minutes. Stir in 2 tbsp (25 mL) each chopped fresh parsley and basil. **Makes 4 cups (1 L).**

Sausage Fennel Pasta Sauce: In skillet, heat 2 tsp (10 mL) olive oil over medium-high heat. Remove casings from 8 oz (250 g) mild or hot Italian sausage; add to pan and cook, breaking up, for 4 minutes. Add ½ tsp (2 mL) crushed fennel seeds; cook for 1 minute. Drain off fat. Add to Tomato Pasta Sauce; simmer for 10 minutes. **Makes 4 cups (1 L).**

Quick Clam Pasta Sauce: Omit salt. Add generous pinch hot pepper flakes to onion mixture. Drain 1 can (5 oz/142 g) baby clams; add juice along with canned tomatoes. Increase tomato paste to 3 tbsp (50 mL). Stir reserved clams into cooked thickened sauce; heat through. Stir in parsley. **Makes 3½ cups (875 mL).**

Makes 3 cups (750 mL).

Pasta Puttanesca

Anyone who indulges in robust flavours will enjoy this quick sauce, allegedly named for the ladies of the night whose work did not allow for much kitchen time. You can keep all the makings in your cupboard for a very tasty short-notice supper.

2 tbsp	olive oil	25 mL
4	cloves garlic, minced	4
½ tsp	dried oregano	2 mL
¼ tsp	hot pepper flakes	1 mL
4	anchovy fillets, chopped	4
1	can (28 oz/796 mL) tomatoes	1

½ cup	oil-cured olives, pitted and halved	125 mL
2 tbsp	drained rinsed capers	25 mL
¼ cup	chopped fresh Italian parsley	50 mL
12 oz	spaghetti	375 g

TEST KITCHEN TIP: To create curls and shavings from hard cheeses such as Parmesan (Parmigiano-Reggiano), Grana Padano, Pecorino Romano or Asiago, scrape vegetable peeler or cheese plane firmly against chunk of cold cheese, easing up as the curl forms.

1 In large skillet, heat oil over medium heat; cook garlic, oregano, hot pepper flakes and anchovies, stirring occasionally, for about 3 minutes or just until garlic starts to colour.

2 Add tomatoes, breaking up with spoon. Add olives and capers; bring to boil. Reduce heat and simmer for about 10 minutes or until thickened to consistency of salsa. (MAKE-AHEAD: Let cool. Refrigerate in airtight container for up to 2 days or freeze for up to 1 month. Reheat to serve.) Stir in parsley.

3 Meanwhile, in large pot of boiling salted water, cook pasta for 8 to 10 minutes or until tender but firm; drain and return to pot. Add sauce; toss to coat.

VARIATIONS

Arrabbiata Pasta: Omit anchovies, olives, capers and parsley. Increase hot pepper flakes to ½ tsp (2 mL). Add 1 cup (250 mL) fresh basil leaves, chopped, and ¼ tsp (1 mL) each salt and pepper. Toss with 5 cups (1.25 L) penne, cooked, instead of spaghetti.

Artichoke Pasta: Omit anchovies. Add ¼ cup (50 mL) slivered dry-packed sun-dried tomatoes and 1 jar (6 oz/170 mL) marinated artichoke hearts, drained and quartered. Reduce olives to ¼ cup (50 mL). Toss with 5 cups (1.25 L) penne, cooked, instead of spaghetti.

Makes 4 servings.

PER SERVING, ABOUT:

cal 488	carb . . . . 75 g
pro . . . . .14 g	fibre . . . . 7 g
total fat . . . .15 g	chol . . . . 3 mg
sat. fat . . . . . .2 g	sodium 1,327 mg

PERCENTAGE RDI:

calcium 9%	vit. A 14%
iron 28%	vit. C 37%
folate 61%	

Big-Batch Beef Ragu

Fill the kitchen with the heady aroma of simmering ragu, a satisfying chunky meat sauce. For a faster, smoother sauce, purée the tomatoes before adding them to the pan and reduce cooking time to a little more than two-and-a-half hours.

TEST KITCHEN TIP: For a vegetarian ragu, omit beef and add the following along with carrots: 3 cups (750 mL) quartered mushrooms, 3 zucchini (1 lb/500 g total), chopped, 1 each sweet red and green pepper, chopped, and ¼ tsp (1 mL) granulated sugar; cook over medium-high heat for 20 minutes or just until mushrooms are golden. Add wine or vegetable stock. Add 1 can (19 oz/540 mL) chickpeas or kidney beans, drained and rinsed, or 2 cups (500 mL) cubed firm tofu if desired. **Makes 10 cups (2.5 L).**

1 tbsp	olive oil (approx)	15 mL
2 lb	beef stewing cubes	1 kg
2	onions, chopped	2
5	cloves garlic, minced	5
2	each carrots and stalks celery, chopped	2
2 tsp	dried basil	10 mL
1½ tsp	each dried thyme and oregano	7 mL
½ cup	red wine or beef stock	125 mL
3	cans (each 28 oz/796 mL) tomatoes	3
½ tsp	each salt and pepper	2 mL

1 In Dutch oven or large heavy saucepan, heat 1 tsp (5 mL) of the oil over medium-high heat; brown beef in batches, adding enough of the remaining oil as necessary. Transfer to plate.

2 Add more oil to pan if necessary; cook onions and garlic over medium heat, stirring occasionally, for 5 minutes or until softened. Add carrots, celery, basil, thyme and oregano; cook for 5 minutes. Add wine; cook, stirring and scraping up any brown bits from bottom of pan, for about 2 minutes or until liquid is almost evaporated.

3 Add tomatoes, salt and pepper; bring to boil, breaking up tomatoes with spoon. Reduce heat to low. Return beef and any accumulated juices to pan; cook, stirring often, for about 3½ hours or until thickened and only small amount of liquid remains on surface.

VARIATIONS

Big-Batch Cacciatore Sauce: Omit beef; substitute 12 chicken thighs (about 4 lb/2 kg), skinned, boned and cut into 1½-inch (4 cm) pieces. After browning, cover and refrigerate. Add 3 cups (750 mL) sliced mushrooms along with carrots. Substitute 1½ tsp (7 mL) dried rosemary for basil; substitute marjoram for oregano. Cook for about 10 minutes or until mushrooms begin to brown. Return chicken to pan after simmering for 3 hours; cook for 30 minutes or until chicken is tender. **Makes 10 cups (2.5 L).**

Big-Batch Sausage and Pepper Sauce: Omit beef; substitute 2 lb (1 kg) Italian sausage. Remove casings; cut into ½-inch (1 cm) pieces. Brown pieces in batches, keeping pieces whole, about 8 minutes. Drain off all but 2 tsp (10 mL) fat. Substitute 2 each sweet green and red peppers, chopped, for carrots and celery. Omit thyme, oregano and salt. Add 1 tsp (5 mL) fennel seeds. Simmer for 4 hours. **Makes 9 cups (2.25 L).**

Makes 10 cups (2.5 L).

PER 1 CUP (250 mL), ABOUT:

cal	235	carb	15 g
pro	22 g	fibre	3 g
total fat	10 g	chol	50 mg
sat. fat	3 g	sodium	579 mg

PERCENTAGE RDI:

calcium	8%	vit. A	51%
iron	26%	vit. C	42%
folate	11%		

Penne with Garlicky Rapini

By cooking the rapini separately instead of with the pasta, you can better control the pungent rapini's tenderness and maintain its vibrant green colour. If heat is your thing, increase the hot pepper flakes.

1	bunch rapini (about 1 lb/500 g)	1
3 tbsp	extra-virgin olive oil	50 mL
6	cloves garlic, minced	6

¼ tsp	hot pepper flakes	1 mL
½ tsp	salt	2 mL
4 cups	penne rigate pasta (12 oz/375 g)	1 L

SUBSTITUTION: Use broccoli or broccolini instead of the rapini. They are all part of the same family.

1 Trim off 1 inch (2.5 cm) from base of rapini stalks. In large skillet, bring 4 cups (1 L) water to boil. Add rapini; cover and cook for about 6 minutes or until stalks are tender. Drain and chill under cold water; drain again and pat dry. Chop coarsely; set aside.

2 In same skillet, heat oil over medium heat; cook garlic and hot pepper flakes for 2 minutes or until garlic begins to brown. Add rapini and salt; cook for about 4 minutes or until hot.

3 Meanwhile, in large pot of boiling salted water, cook pasta for 8 to 10 minutes or until tender but firm. Drain and return to pot, reserving ½ cup (125 mL) cooking water. Add rapini mixture to pasta; toss to coat. If desired, add enough of the reserved cooking water to moisten.

PASTA Perfecto

❧ Pasta must be cooked in lots of water in a large pot. A small pot or too little water crowds the pasta, causing it to cook unevenly and become gluey. For each pound (500 g) dry pasta, boil vigorously in 20 cups (5 L) water with 2 tbsp (25 mL) salt. For 12 oz (375 g) pasta, reduce water to 16 cups (4 L) and salt to 4 tsp (20 mL).

❧ To check if pasta is cooked properly, remove a piece from the pot and let it cool slightly before tasting. It is ready if it is tender but still holds its shape and is al dente, or slightly firm, to the bite.

❧ Reserving up to 1 cup (250 mL) of the cooking water in case you need to moisten your dish before serving, pour cooked pasta into colander to drain, shaking colander slightly.

❧ Do not rinse under cold water unless you are using it in a salad or in baked dishes such as lasagna.

Makes 4 servings.

PER SERVING, ABOUT:

cal 448	carb . . . . 70 g
pro . . . . 15 g	fibre . . . . 6 g
total fat . . . . 12 g	chol . . . . 0 mg
sat. fat . . . . . . 2 g	sodium . . 531 mg

PERCENTAGE RDI:

calcium 25%	vit. A 32%
iron 26%	vit. C 57%
folate 57%	

Macaroni and Cheese Five Ways

Canadians and macaroni and cheese — it's a love affair. Whether we bake the elbows in a creamy sauce or toss everything in a pot for a quick supper, these versions are better than anything you can buy in a box — and not much more work, either.

	CHEESE	ADD-INS	TOPPINGS
Spinach Ricotta Macaroni and Cheese	1 tub (500 mL) ricotta cheese; ½ cup (125 mL) grated Romano cheese	1 pkg (10 oz/300 g) frozen chopped spinach, thawed and squeezed dry; 1 jar (313 mL) roasted red peppers, drained and chopped	¼ cup (50 mL) each dry bread crumbs and grated Romano cheese
Bacon Macaroni and Cheese	2¾ cups (675 mL) shredded old Cheddar cheese	2 green onions, chopped; 4 slices bacon, cooked and crumbled	½ cup (125 mL) shredded old Cheddar cheese
Broccoli Macaroni and Cheese	2¾ cups (675 mL) shredded Jarlsberg cheese	2 cups (500 mL) frozen chopped broccoli or 1 cup (250 mL) frozen peas	½ cup (125 mL) shredded Jarlsberg cheese
Fiesta Macaroni and Cheese	2¾ cups (675 mL) shredded Monterey Jack cheese	½ cup (125 mL) mild salsa; ½ cup (125 mL) frozen corn kernels; dash hot pepper sauce	1 cup (250 mL) crushed tortilla chips
Tomato Macaroni and Cheese	2¾ cups (675 mL) shredded Fontina or Gruyère cheese	2 green onions, chopped	2 plum tomatoes, thinly sliced; ¼ cup (50 mL) grated Parmesan cheese

1 In large pot of boiling salted water, cook 2 cups (500 mL) macaroni for about 8 minutes or until tender but firm. Drain and return to pot.

2 Meanwhile, in saucepan, melt 2 tbsp (25 mL) butter over medium heat; cook 1 onion, chopped, for about 5 minutes or until softened. Add ⅓ cup (75 mL) all-purpose flour; cook, stirring, for 1 minute. Gradually whisk in 3 cups (750 mL) milk; cook, whisking, for about 8 minutes or until sauce is thickened.

3 Add 2 tsp (10 mL) Dijon mustard, ¾ tsp (4 mL) salt and ½ tsp (2 mL) pepper. Stir in Cheese in first column just until melted. Pour over macaroni.

4 Stir Add-Ins in second column into macaroni mixture until combined.

5 Spread in 8-inch (2 L) square glass baking dish. Add Toppings in third column. Bake, uncovered, in 350°F (180°C) oven for about 30 minutes or until bubbly.

Makes 4 to 6 servings.

Chicken Pesto Pasta

This recipe is inspired by a favourite pasta salad from Hannah's Kitchen in Toronto, where it is served as a cold salad to a loyal lunch crowd.

12	dry-packed sun-dried tomatoes	12
3	boneless skinless chicken breasts	3
1 tbsp	olive oil	15 mL

5 cups	rotini pasta (1 lb/500 g)	1.25 L
¾ cup	Pesto (recipe follows)	175 mL
¼ tsp	each salt and pepper	1 mL
2 tbsp	toasted pine nuts	25 mL

TEST KITCHEN TIP: Top pasta with crumbled goat cheese if desired.

1   In bowl, cover tomatoes with boiling water; let stand for 5 minutes or until softened. Drain and cut into thin strips; set aside. Cut chicken crosswise into ¼-inch (5 mm) thick strips.

2   In skillet, heat oil over medium-high heat; cook chicken, stirring often, for 5 minutes or until no longer pink inside. Set aside.

3   Meanwhile, in large pot of boiling salted water, cook pasta for 8 to 10 minutes or until tender but firm; drain and return to pot, reserving ½ cup (125 mL) of the cooking liquid. Add softened sun-dried tomatoes, chicken, pesto, salt and pepper; toss to coat, adding a little of the cooking water to moisten if desired. Heat through. Garnish with pine nuts.

Pesto

2 cups	packed fresh basil leaves	500 mL
½ cup	grated Parmesan cheese	125 mL
¼ cup	pine nuts	50 mL

¼ tsp	each salt and pepper	1 mL
⅓ cup	extra-virgin olive oil	75 mL
3	cloves garlic, minced	3

1   In food processor, finely chop together basil, Parmesan cheese, pine nuts, salt and pepper. With motor running, add oil in thin steady stream. Stir in garlic. (MAKE-AHEAD: Refrigerate in airtight container for up to 3 days or freeze for up to 6 months.) **Makes ¾ cup (175 mL).**

Makes 6 servings.

PER SERVING, ABOUT:

cal 597	carb . . . . 62 g
pro . . . . 34 g	fibre . . . . 6 g
total fat . . . . 25 g	chol . . . . . . 50 mg
sat. fat . . . . . . 5 g	sodium . . 672 mg

PERCENTAGE RDI:

calcium 15%	vit. A 2%
iron 23%	vit. C 5%
folate 57%	

Spaghetti Carbonara

Serve up comfort food to your family with this quick, pantry-friendly dish. Be sure to use flat-leaf Italian parsley for best flavour.

2 tbsp	butter or olive oil	25 mL
1	onion, chopped	1
2	cloves garlic, minced	2
4 oz	pancetta or bacon, diced	125 g
3	eggs	3

1 tsp	salt	5 mL
12 oz	spaghetti	375 g
½ cup	grated Parmesan cheese	125 mL
2 tbsp	chopped fresh Italian parsley	25 mL

1 In small skillet, melt butter over medium heat; cook onion and garlic, stirring occasionally, for 3 minutes or until softened. Add pancetta; cook, stirring occasionally, for about 6 minutes. In small bowl, lightly beat eggs with salt; set aside.

2 Meanwhile, in large pot of boiling salted water, cook spaghetti for 8 to 10 minutes or until tender but firm. Drain and return to pot over medium heat.

3 Immediately stir in Parmesan, parsley and pancetta mixture. Stir in eggs; cook, stirring, for about 30 seconds or until eggs are lightly cooked and pasta is coated.

Makes 4 servings.

PER SERVING, ABOUT:

cal	537	carb	68 g
pro	27 g	fibre	4 g
total fat	17 g	chol	200 mg
sat. fat	8 g	sodium	1,510 mg

PERCENTAGE RDI:

calcium	20%	vit. A	16%
iron	21%	vit. C	5%
folate	63%		

THE BEST CHEESES for Pasta

Cheeses with distinctive taste and/or creaminess are the best matches for pasta.

↳ **PARMESAN:** Parmigiano-Reggiano is the authentic cow's milk cheese from the area around Parma, Italy. Although it is more expensive than its imitators, a little of its magnificent full taste goes a long way. A wedge keeps in the refrigerator for weeks, at the ready to grate over pasta. Grana Padano is a less expensive cheese in the same hard grating family.

↳ **PECORINO ROMANO:** Grate this pungent sheep's milk cheese over pasta to boost flavour and to make a crusty top on baked pasta dishes. Use as you would Parmigiano-Reggiano.

↳ **ASIAGO:** This sharp hard cow's milk cheese is wonderful shaved or

Fettuccine Alfredo — The Classic

The mild, smooth sauce cloaking tender strands of fettuccine makes this dish a favourite with kids and adults alike. There are lighter variations, but when you think of Alfredo as a special and very occasional treat, you should enjoy it in traditional style.

12 oz	fettuccine	375 g
1 cup	whipping cream	250 mL
¼ cup	butter	50 mL
1 cup	grated Parmesan cheese	250 mL

½ tsp	salt	2 mL
¼ tsp	pepper	1 mL
Pinch	nutmeg	Pinch
	Finely chopped fresh parsley	

1 In large pot of boiling salted water, cook pasta for 8 to 10 minutes or until tender but firm; drain well and return to pot.

2 Meanwhile, in saucepan, bring cream and butter just to boil. Reduce heat and stir in Parmesan, salt, pepper and nutmeg; add to pasta and toss to coat. Serve sprinkled with parsley.

VARIATION

Pasta Primavera: Just before tossing pasta, add 1 lb (500 g) tender-crisp cooked vegetables such as asparagus, sugar snap or shelled peas, green beans, broccoli, sweet red pepper or halved cherry tomatoes. Top finished dish with shredded fresh basil or chervil.

TEST KITCHEN TIP: Vary your repertoire with seafood and smoked salmon versions of the classic. Just before tossing pasta, add 1 lb (500 g) cooked, peeled, deveined shrimp or other seafood; top finished dish with sprinkle of chopped fresh tarragon. Or add 4 oz (125 g) smoked salmon, cut in strips, and 1 tbsp (15 mL) chopped fresh dill; top finished dish with sprinkle of chopped fresh dill and finely grated lemon rind.

grated over pasta. Use as you would Parmigiano-Reggiano.

 MOZZARELLA: This ivory-colour unripened cheese gives creaminess and stretch to dishes, especially baked pastas, in which other stronger ingredients make up for its mildness.

 PROVOLONE: A stretchy cheese that starts out mild with a bit of an edge but becomes tangy and robust as it ages, provolone blends well with other cheeses and gives depth to their flavour.

 RICOTTA: This soft, moist, slightly granular unripened cheese has a milky taste and comes in varying degrees of milk fat. It is often used in stuffed or baked pasta. It is sold in tubs. Choose smooth ricotta for sauces.

 Even nontraditional cheeses — Old Cheddar, Gruyère, Emmenthal, Gorgonzola, feta and goat cheese — all add enough distinctly robust taste.

Makes 4 servings.

PER SERVING, ABOUT:

cal	726	carb	66 g
pro	22 g	fibre	4 g
total fat	41 g	chol	127 mg
sat. fat	25 g	sodium	1,114 mg

PERCENTAGE RDI:

calcium	37%	vit. A	34%
iron	16%	vit. C	0%
folate	55%		

Pastitsio

This hearty Greek casserole, with its layers of creamy pasta custard and savoury meat sauce, can be prepared a day ahead, making it perfect for buffet suppers.

1 tbsp	vegetable oil	15 mL
1	large onion, finely chopped	1
2	cloves garlic, minced	2
1½ lb	lean ground beef	750 g
1 tsp	each dried oregano and basil	5 mL
¾ tsp	cinnamon	4 mL
½ tsp	each salt, pepper, granulated sugar and dried thyme	2 mL
½ cup	dry white wine or chicken stock	125 mL
⅓ cup	tomato paste	75 mL
1	can (19 oz/540 mL) tomatoes	1
¼ cup	minced fresh parsley	50 mL

PASTA CUSTARD LAYERS:		
2½ cups	medium pasta shells	625 mL
⅓ cup	butter	75 mL
⅓ cup	all-purpose flour	75 mL
3½ cups	milk	875 mL
½ tsp	salt	2 mL
¼ tsp	nutmeg	1 mL
Pinch	pepper	Pinch
2	eggs	2
1 cup	creamed cottage cheese	250 mL
1 cup	shredded mozzarella or Swiss cheese	250 mL
¼ cup	grated Parmesan cheese	50 mL

1 In Dutch oven or large heavy saucepan, heat oil over medium heat; cook onion and garlic, stirring occasionally, for about 5 minutes or until softened. Add beef; cook over high heat, stirring to break up, for about 3 minutes or until no longer pink. Stir in oregano, basil, cinnamon, salt, pepper, sugar and thyme; cook for 3 minutes.

2 Add wine, tomato paste and tomatoes, mashing tomatoes; bring to boil. Reduce heat and simmer, uncovered, for 15 minutes. Add parsley; set aside.

3 PASTA CUSTARD LAYERS: Meanwhile, in large pot of boiling salted water, cook pasta until tender but firm, about 8 minutes. Drain and transfer to large bowl. Toss with 1 tbsp (15 mL) of the butter. Set aside.

4 In large heavy saucepan, melt remaining butter over medium heat; stir in flour and cook, stirring, without browning, for 1 minute. Gradually whisk in milk until smooth; cook for about 5 minutes or until thickened. Stir in salt, nutmeg and pepper.

Makes 6 servings.

PER SERVING, ABOUT:

cal	773	carb	50 g
pro	46 g	fibre	4 g
total fat	43 g	chol	200 mg
sat. fat	21 g	sodium	1,225 mg

PERCENTAGE RDI:

calcium	40%	vit. A	38%
iron	38%	vit. C	30%
folate	43%		

5 In large bowl, whisk eggs; whisk in about ½ cup (125 mL) of the hot cream sauce. Return mixture to saucepan; cook for 2 minutes, stirring. Remove from heat; blend in cottage cheese and mozzarella. Stir into pasta.

6 Spread one-half of the pasta mixture in 13- x 9-inch (3 L) glass baking dish. Spread meat filling over top. Spread remaining pasta mixture evenly over meat. Sprinkle with Parmesan. (MAKE-AHEAD: Let cool in refrigerator; cover and refrigerate for up to 1 day. Or overwrap with heavy-duty foil and freeze for up to 2 weeks; thaw in refrigerator for 48 hours. Add about 20 minutes to baking time.) Bake in 375°F (190°C) oven for 1 hour or until bubbly and top is lightly browned. Let stand for 10 minutes.

MATCHING Pasta Types TO RECIPES

Different pasta shapes match some sauces better than others. As a rule of thumb, you can interchange each of these pasta types within each group.

➤ **Spaghetti, vermicelli, spaghettini, linguine or fettuccine:** serve these long strand pastas with smooth sauces that will cling to them.

➤ **Fusilli, rotini, radiatori, orecchiette, conchiglie, farfalle or rigatone:** serve these short shaped pastas with chunky sauces that will nestle in the grooves of the pasta; they are also great baked.

➤ **Penne, ziti or macaroni:** these tubular pastas are suitable for most sauces.

➤ **Stellini, alphabet, orzo or tubetti:** these tiny shapes are perfect for soups and stews.

Creamy Shrimp Bake

Shrimp says company fare more enthusiastically than almost any other ingredient. Here it fancies up a béchamel-based (cream sauce) pasta dish that has the extra bonus of broccoli florets.

TEST KITCHEN TIPS

• You can buy shrimp already peeled, deveined, cooked and frozen, or you can prepare and cook your own. Starting at underside, pull off shells from 12 oz (375 g) shrimp. With sharp knife, make shallow cut lengthwise along back to locate dark vein just below surface. Pull out vein; pull off tail. Rinse shrimp. Cook in simmering water for about 3 minutes or until pink and firm. Drain and plunge into cold water just long enough to stop cooking. Drain.

• If desired, increase shrimp content by starting with 1 lb (500 g); decrease broccoli to 1 cup (250 mL) or omit.

2 tbsp	butter	25 mL		5 cups	medium pasta shells (12 oz/375 g)	1.25 L
¼ cup	all-purpose flour	50 mL		2 cups	small broccoli florets	500 mL
¾ tsp	dried tarragon	4 mL		**TOPPING:**		
½ cup	white wine or chicken stock	125 mL		1 cup	fresh bread crumbs	250 mL
3 cups	milk	750 mL		¼ cup	grated Parmesan cheese	50 mL
1	pkg (4 oz/125 g) cream cheese	1		¼ cup	chopped fresh parsley	50 mL
¾ tsp	salt	4 mL		1 tsp	grated lemon rind	5 mL
½ tsp	pepper	2 mL		1	clove garlic, minced	1
8 oz	cooked peeled shrimp	250 g		2 tbsp	butter, melted	25 mL

1 In large saucepan, melt butter over medium heat; whisk in flour and tarragon and cook, whisking, for 1 minute. Gradually whisk in wine until smooth. Whisk in milk; bring to boil. Reduce heat to medium; cook, stirring, for 10 minutes or until smooth and thickened. Remove from heat. Whisk in cream cheese, salt and pepper until melted. Add shrimp.

2 Meanwhile, in large pot of boiling salted water, cook pasta for 6 minutes. Add broccoli; cook for 2 minutes or until pasta is tender but firm. Drain and return to pot. Add sauce; toss to coat. Pour into 11- x 7-inch (2 L) glass baking dish, pressing pasta to submerge. (MAKE-AHEAD: Let cool in refrigerator; cover and refrigerate for up to 1 day. Or overwrap with heavy-duty foil and freeze for up to 2 weeks; thaw in refrigerator for 48 hours. Bake, covered, in 400°F/200°C oven for 30 minutes before uncovering and continuing.)

3 TOPPING: In small bowl, combine bread crumbs, cheese, parsley, lemon rind and garlic; drizzle with butter and stir to combine. Sprinkle over pasta mixture. Bake in 425°F (220°C) oven for 15 minutes or until topping is golden and crusty and shrimp mixture is bubbling.

Makes 4 to 6 servings.

PER EACH OF 6 SERVINGS, ABOUT:

cal	518	carb	58 g
pro	24 g	fibre	3 g
total fat	20 g	chol	130 mg
sat. fat	12 g	sodium	881 mg

PERCENTAGE RDI:

calcium	25%	vit. A	29%
iron	26%	vit. C	25%
folate	51%		

Spicy Sausage and Rigatoni Bake

When lasagna is too much work, you can still enjoy all its robust flavours in this zesty cold-weather warm-up.

1 tbsp	olive oil	15 mL
2	onions, sliced	2
1	sweet red pepper, chopped	1
3	cloves garlic, minced	3
½ tsp	fennel seeds, crushed	2 mL
1 lb	hot Italian sausage	500 g
2	jars (each 700 mL) tomato-basil pasta sauce	2

1 tbsp	wine vinegar	15 mL
5 cups	rigatoni pasta (12 oz/375 g)	1.25 L
2 cups	shredded mozzarella cheese	500 mL
¼ cup	grated Parmesan cheese	50 mL
2 tbsp	chopped fresh parsley	25 mL

1 In Dutch oven or large heavy skillet, heat oil over medium-high heat; cook onions, stirring occasionally, for 5 minutes. Add red pepper, garlic and fennel seeds; reduce heat to medium and cook for 10 minutes or until onions are very soft and golden. Transfer to bowl.

2 Cut sausage into 1-inch (2.5 cm) chunks; add to pan and brown well on all sides, about 8 minutes. Drain off fat. Stir in pasta sauce and vinegar. Return vegetable mixture to pan; reduce heat to medium-low and simmer for 15 minutes.

3 Meanwhile, in large pot of boiling salted water, cook pasta for about 8 minutes or until tender but firm. Drain, reserving 1 cup (250 mL) of the cooking water. Return pasta to pot; add sauce and reserved cooking water.

4 Combine mozzarella and Parmesan cheeses; set 1 cup (250 mL) aside. Stir remaining cheese into pasta mixture. Pour into 13- x 9-inch (3 L) glass baking dish, pressing pasta to submerge. Sprinkle with reserved cheese and parsley. (MAKE-AHEAD: Let cool in refrigerator; cover and refrigerate for up to 1 day. Or overwrap with heavy-duty foil and freeze for up to 2 weeks; thaw in refrigerator for 48 hours. Bake, covered, in 400°F/200°C oven for 30 to 45 minutes; uncover and continue.) Bake in 400°F (200°C) oven for 15 minutes or until golden.

Makes 8 servings.

VARIATION

Meatball and Rigatoni Bake: Instead of sausage, make meatballs: In bowl, mix together 1 egg, ⅓ cup (75 mL) finely chopped onion, ¼ cup (50 mL) dry bread crumbs, 2 cloves garlic, minced, 3 tbsp (50 mL) grated Parmesan cheese, 1 tsp (5 mL) dried oregano, ¾ tsp (4 mL) salt and ½ tsp (2 mL) pepper. Mix in 1 lb (500 g) lean ground turkey, chicken, pork or beef. Shape heaping tablespoonfuls (15 mL) into balls.

PER SERVING, ABOUT:

cal	582	carb	66 g
pro	25 g	fibre	6 g
total fat	25 g	chol	53 mg
sat. fat	9 g	sodium	1,606 mg

PERCENTAGE RDI:

calcium	26%	vit. A	36%
iron	22%	vit. C	77%
folate	44%		

MAKE-AHEAD   FREEZABLE

Luscious Mushroom Lasagna

A creamy béchamel sauce binds a rich blend of woodsy wild and cultivated mushrooms in a special-occasion lasagna.

10 oz	lasagna noodles (about 16)	300 g		⅔ cup	dry white wine	150 mL
2 tbsp	finely chopped fresh Italian parsley	25 mL		2 tbsp	finely chopped fresh thyme	25 mL
MUSHROOMS:				**SAUCE:**		
½ oz	dried porcini mushrooms	15 g		¼ cup	butter	50 mL
2 tbsp	butter	25 mL		½ cup	all-purpose flour	125 mL
2	onions, chopped	2		4½ cups	milk	1.125 L
4	cloves garlic, minced	4		¾ tsp	salt	4 mL
½ tsp	each salt and pepper	2 mL		¼ tsp	pepper	1 mL
16 cups	sliced button mushrooms (2½ lb/1.25 kg)	4 L		Pinch	nutmeg	Pinch
8 cups	sliced stemmed shiitake mushrooms (1½ lb/750 g)	2 L		2½ cups	shredded Gruyère cheese	625 mL
				¾ cup	grated Parmesan cheese	175 mL

1 MUSHROOMS: In small bowl, cover dried porcini mushrooms with 1 cup (250 mL) warm water; let stand for 10 minutes. Drain, reserving soaking liquid. Finely chop mushrooms. Strain liquid. Set aside.

2 In large Dutch oven, melt butter over medium heat; cook onions, garlic, salt and pepper, stirring occasionally, for about 5 minutes or until softened. Add half of the button and all of the shiitake mushrooms; increase heat to high and cook for 5 minutes. Stir in remaining button mushrooms; cook, stirring often, for about 10 minutes or until no liquid remains. Stir in wine, reserved porcini mushrooms and soaking liquid; cook for 5 to 10 minutes or until no liquid remains. Remove from heat; stir in thyme. (You should have about 6 cups/1.5 L mushroom mixture.)

3 SAUCE: In large saucepan, melt butter over medium heat; whisk in flour and cook, whisking, for 1 minute. Whisking constantly, add milk, ½ cup (125 mL) at a time. Stir in salt, pepper and nutmeg. Cook, stirring, for about 15 minutes or until bubbly and thickened. Whisk in 2 cups (500 mL) of the Gruyère cheese and ½ cup (125 mL) of the Parmesan; simmer until melted. (You should have about 5½ cups/1.375 L.)

Makes 8 servings.

PER SERVING, ABOUT:

cal	609	carb	62 g
pro	30 g	fibre	6 g
total fat	27 g	chol	80 mg
sat. fat	16 g	sodium	946 mg

PERCENTAGE RDI:

calcium	63%	vit. A	28%
iron	34%	vit. C	15%
folate	55%		

4 In large pot of boiling salted water, cook noodles for 8 minutes or until tender but firm. Transfer to cold water. Drain and arrange in single layer between damp tea towels.

5 Spread 1 cup (250 mL) of the sauce in 13- x 9-inch (3 L) glass baking dish. Top with 4 noodles in single layer and overlapping slightly. Top with 2 cups (500 mL) of the mushroom mixture. Repeat layers twice. Top with 1 cup (250 mL) of the sauce, remaining noodles, then remaining sauce. (MAKE-AHEAD: Let cool in refrigerator; cover and refrigerate for up to 1 day. Or overwrap with heavy-duty foil and freeze for up to 2 weeks; thaw in refrigerator for 48 hours. Add about 20 minutes to covered baking time.)

6 Cover with foil and place on rimmed baking sheet; bake in 375°F (190°C) oven for 30 minutes. Sprinkle with remaining cheeses; bake, uncovered, for 30 minutes or until bubbly and golden. Let stand for 10 minutes before serving. Sprinkle with parsley.

How Much PASTA TO COOK

~ For main-course servings, count on 12 oz to 1 lb (375 to 500 g) for 4 servings.

~ In all our recipes, short pasta such as fusilli is measured in cups (mL) wherever possible; spaghetti and other long-strand pastas are measured by weight. If you don't have a kitchen scale, wrap a tape measure around a bundle of pasta to measure the circumference:

~ About 2½ inches (6 cm) = 3 oz (90 g) = 1 serving

~ About 4½ inches (11 cm) = 8 oz (250 g) = 2 to 3 servings

~ About 5¼ inches (13 cm) = 12 oz (375 g) = 3 to 4 servings

~ About 5¾ inches (14 cm) = 1 lb (500 g) = 4 servings

Old Favourite Lasagna

A really good lasagna is the start of a party. With this recipe, let the fun begin for everyone in the family, from little folks to big.

8 oz	lasagna noodles (about 12)	250 g
1	pkg (300 g) frozen chopped spinach, thawed and squeezed dry	1
2 cups	shredded mozzarella cheese	500 mL
¼ cup	grated Parmesan cheese	50 mL

MEAT FILLING:

8 oz	Italian sausage	250 g
8 oz	ground beef	250 g
1	each onion, carrot and stalk celery, chopped	1
4	cloves garlic, minced	4
1½ tsp	each dried oregano and basil	7 mL

¼ tsp	pepper	1 mL
Pinch	hot pepper flakes	Pinch
1	can (28 oz/796 mL) tomatoes, chopped	1
1	can (14 oz/398 mL) tomato sauce	1

CHEESE FILLING:

2	eggs	2
¼ tsp	each pepper and nutmeg	1 mL
2 cups	cottage cheese	500 mL
1 cup	shredded mozzarella cheese	250 mL
½ cup	grated Parmesan cheese	125 mL

1 MEAT FILLING: Remove sausage from casings. In Dutch oven, cook sausage and beef over medium-high heat, breaking up with spoon, for 5 minutes or until no longer pink; transfer to plate. Spoon off all but 1 tbsp (15 mL) fat. Add onion, carrot, celery, garlic, oregano, basil, pepper and hot pepper flakes to pan; cook, stirring often, for 3 to 5 minutes. Add tomatoes, tomato sauce and meat; bring to boil. Reduce heat and simmer, stirring often, for 25 minutes or until thickened.

2 CHEESE FILLING: Meanwhile, in bowl, beat together eggs, pepper and nutmeg. Blend in cottage, mozzarella and Parmesan cheeses. Set aside.

3 In large pot of boiling salted water, cook noodles for 6 to 8 minutes or until almost tender. Transfer to cold water. Drain and arrange in single layer between damp tea towels. Spread 1 cup (250 mL) of the meat filling in 13- x 9-inch (3 L) glass baking dish. Top with one-third of the noodles; spread with one-third of the remaining meat filling, then half of the cheese filling and half of the spinach. Starting with noodles, repeat layers once.

4 Top with remaining noodles; spread with remaining meat filling. Sprinkle with mozzarella and Parmesan cheeses. Cover loosely with foil; bake in 375°F (190°C) oven for 20 minutes. Uncover and bake for 20 to 25 minutes or until bubbly and heated through. Let stand for 10 minutes before serving.

Makes 8 servings.

PER SERVING, ABOUT:

cal 533	carb . . . . 37 g
pro . . . . 38 g	fibre . . . . 4 g
total fat . . . . 26 g	chol . . . . . 131 mg
sat. fat . . . . . 13 g	sodium 1,370 mg

PERCENTAGE RDI:

calcium 47%	vit. A 69%
iron 25%	vit. C 28%
folate 43%	

Potato Gnocchi

You don't have to have an Italian grandmother, or nònna, *to make these featherlight potato dumplings. Their fragrant fresh sage and butter sauce is typical of Tuscany, where simple flavours are allowed to sing.*

6	Yukon Gold potatoes (unpeeled), 2½ lb (1.25 kg)	6
1	egg yolk	1
1 tbsp	salt	15 mL
2⅓ cups	all-purpose flour	575 mL

SAGE AND BUTTER SAUCE:		
10	fresh sage leaves	10
½ cup	butter	125 mL
¼ tsp	pepper	1 mL
¼ cup	grated Parmesan cheese	50 mL

TEST KITCHEN TIP: To give the butter sauce a nutty flavour, heat the butter until light golden.

1 In large saucepan of boiling water, cook potatoes, covered, for about 30 minutes or until tender. Drain and let cool for about 10 minutes or until easy to handle. Peel and place in large bowl. Refrigerate until cold, about 30 minutes.

2 Through medium disc of food mill or ricer, press potatoes into bowl to make 8 cups (2 L) unpacked. Mix in egg yolk and 1 tsp (5 mL) of the salt. With wooden spoon, stir in 2 cups (500 mL) of the flour. Turn out onto unfloured work surface. Knead to form soft, slightly sticky, spongy dough. Divide into 8 pieces.

3 Roll each piece into 20-inch (50 cm) rope about ¾ inch (2 cm) thick. Cut each rope into ½-inch (1 cm) lengths. On work surface, toss with ¼ cup (50 mL) more flour.

4 Dip fork into remaining flour. Hold fork with tines facing down; with fingertips of other hand, lightly roll each piece down tines of fork to create ridges. Dust baking sheet with remaining flour. Place gnocchi on sheet. (MAKE-AHEAD: Freeze for about 2 hours or until firm. Using metal spatula, transfer to freezer bags and freeze for up to 2 weeks.)

5 Bring large pot of water to boil; add remaining salt. Cook half of the gnocchi, stirring gently, for about 3 minutes or until tender and gnocchi float to top. With slotted spoon, transfer to warmed bowl. Repeat with remaining gnocchi.

6 SAGE AND BUTTER SAUCE: Meanwhile, chop 4 of the sage leaves. In large skillet, heat butter over medium heat; cook chopped and whole sage leaves and pepper for 1 minute or until fragrant. Pour sauce over gnocchi; toss to coat. Sprinkle with Parmesan.

SAUCE VARIATION

Mushroom Butter Sauce: Add 2 cups (500 mL) sliced oyster or sliced stemmed shiitake mushrooms to butter. Cook for about 5 minutes or until softened.

Makes 4 to 6 servings.

PER EACH OF 6 SERVINGS, ABOUT:

cal 467	carb . . . . 66 g
pro . . . . 10 g	fibre . . . . 4 g
total fat . . . . 18 g	chol . . . . . . 81 mg
sat. fat . . . . . 11 g	sodium . . 952 mg

PERCENTAGE RDI:

calcium 8%	vit. A 17%
iron 19%	vit. C 32%
folate 32%	

Singapore Noodles

Curry paste adds a distinctive taste to this noodle dish, which features the fresh crunch of bean sprouts and peanuts.

8 oz	boneless pork loin chops (about 2)	250 g
1	pkg (350 g) steamed chow mein noodles (or 8 oz/250 g uncooked thin rice noodles)	1
2 tbsp	vegetable oil	25 mL
8 oz	small raw shrimp, peeled and deveined	250 g
Half	jalapeño pepper, seeded and sliced	Half
1 tbsp	mild curry paste	15 mL
4	cloves garlic, minced	4
1 tbsp	minced gingerroot	15 mL
1	sweet red pepper, thinly sliced	1
1	large carrot, julienned	1
1½ cups	chicken stock	375 mL
2 tbsp	rice vinegar	25 mL
2 tbsp	soy sauce	25 mL
1 tbsp	granulated sugar	15 mL
3	green onions, sliced	3
1 cup	bean sprouts	250 mL
¼ cup	each finely chopped peanuts and fresh coriander	50 mL

1 Cut pork into very thin strips about 2 inches (5 cm) long; set aside. In bowl, pour boiling water over noodles; let stand for 1 minute. Drain and set aside.

2 In wok or large skillet, heat oil over medium-high heat. Add pork; stir-fry for about 2 minutes or until just a hint of pink remains inside. Transfer to plate. Add shrimp to wok; stir-fry just until pink and firm. Add to pork.

3 Add jalapeño pepper, curry paste, garlic and ginger to wok; stir-fry for 30 seconds. Add red pepper and carrot; stir-fry for about 3 minutes or until carrot is tender-crisp.

4 In small bowl, stir together chicken stock, rice vinegar, soy sauce and sugar. Add to wok along with noodles; cook, stirring, for 5 minutes or until most of the liquid is absorbed but noodles are still coated with sauce. Add green onions, bean sprouts and reserved pork mixture; cook for about 2 minutes or until hot. Serve sprinkled with peanuts and coriander.

Makes 4 to 6 servings.

PER EACH OF 6 SERVINGS, ABOUT:

cal	356	carb	42 g
pro	20 g	fibre	3 g
total fat	12 g	chol	65 mg
sat. fat	2 g	sodium	668 mg

PERCENTAGE RDI:

calcium	4%	vit. A	48%
iron	14%	vit. C	65%
folate	15%		

Lamb Moussaka

(PAGE 178)

Pasta Puttanesca (top)
(PAGE 231)

Cedar-Planked Salmon (bottom)
(PAGE 204)

Orange Fennel Rack of Pork

(PAGE 164)

Quick Orange Buns

(PAGE 262)

Country Seed Bread with Raspberry and Red Currant Jelly

(PAGES 269 and 385)

Classic Angel Food Cake

(PAGE 310)

Bumbleberry Cobbler on the Barbecue (top left)
(PAGE 281)

Mandarin Sorbet (top right)
(PAGE 294)

Brutti ma Buoni (bottom left)
(PAGE 356)

Chocolate Caramel Macadamia Tart (bottom right)
(PAGE 346)

Strawberry Rhubarb Galette
(PAGE 333)

Pad Thai

Once exotic but now popular, Pad Thai is one of those dishes that has caught the imagination of restaurant-goers and home cooks alike. The ingredient list looks long, but all items are available in most supermarkets and none of the steps is complicated.

1	pkg (227 g) wide rice stick noodles	1
½ cup	chicken stock	125 mL
¼ cup	granulated sugar	50 mL
¼ cup	fish sauce	50 mL
3 tbsp	lime juice	50 mL
2 tbsp	ketchup	25 mL
¼ tsp	hot pepper flakes	1 mL
4 oz	boneless pork loin	125 g
6 oz	extra-firm tofu	175 g
1	sweet red pepper	1

¼ cup	vegetable oil	50 mL
1	egg, beaten	1
8 oz	large raw shrimp, peeled and deveined	250 g
3	cloves garlic, minced	3
2 cups	bean sprouts	500 mL
½ cup	fresh coriander leaves, coarsely chopped	125 mL
6	green onions, thinly sliced diagonally	6
¼ cup	unsalted peanuts, chopped	50 mL

TEST KITCHEN TIPS

• Buy clear amber-colour fish sauce, which can be shrimp or anchovy flavoured; refrigerate after opening.

• Soaking times for rice noodles are important because the noodles absorb liquid as long as they are in it and can become too soft and swollen.

SUBSTITUTION: You can use chicken instead of pork.

1 In large bowl, soak noodles in warm water for 15 minutes; drain and set aside. Meanwhile, in small bowl, whisk together chicken stock, sugar, fish sauce, lime juice, ketchup and hot pepper flakes; set sauce aside.

2 Cut pork across the grain into ¼-inch (5 mm) thick strips. Set aside. Cut tofu into ½-inch (1 cm) cubes. Core, seed and dice red pepper.

3 In wok or large skillet, heat 1 tsp (5 mL) of the oil over medium heat; cook egg, stirring occasionally, for 3 minutes or until scrambled and set. Transfer to plate. Wipe out wok; add 1 tbsp (15 mL) of the oil. Increase heat to medium-high; stir-fry shrimp, garlic and pork for about 3 minutes or until shrimp are bright pink. Add to egg.

4 Heat remaining oil in pan. Stir in tofu and red pepper; cook, stirring occasionally, for 2 minutes or until tofu begins to brown. Gently stir in noodles until beginning to wilt, about 1 minute. Pour in sauce; stir-fry for 3 minutes or until noodles are tender.

5 Return egg mixture to pan. Add bean sprouts, coriander and half of the green onions; stir-fry for 2 to 3 minutes or until heated through. Serve garnished with peanuts and remaining green onions.

Makes 4 servings.

PER SERVING, ABOUT:

cal	631	carb	74 g
pro	29 g	fibre	5 g
total fat	25 g	chol	135 mg
sat. fat	3 g	sodium	1,737 mg

PERCENTAGE RDI:

calcium	13%	vit. A	18%
iron	26%	vit. C	102%
folate	39%		

PIZZA DOUGH

You have choices — buying fresh or frozen dough or prebaked crusts at the supermarket or making your own at a fraction of the cost. The first two recipes make 1 lb (500 g) dough, enough for a 12-inch (30 cm) pizza to share or for two 8-inch (20 cm) personal-size pizzas; the bread machine version doubles the yield.

FOOD PROCESSOR PIZZA DOUGH

2 cups	all-purpose flour	500 mL
1½ tsp	quick-rising (instant) dry yeast	7 mL
¾ tsp	salt	4 mL
¾ cup	hot water (120°F/50°C)	175 mL
2 tsp	olive oil	10 mL

In food processor, pulse together flour, yeast and salt. With motor running, pour in hot water and oil; whirl for about 1 minute or until ball forms. With floured hands, shape into smooth ball. Place in greased bowl, turning to grease all over. Cover with plastic wrap; let rise in warm draft-free place for about 1 hour or until doubled in bulk. (MAKE-AHEAD: Or refrigerate unrisen dough to rise for 24 hours. Or freeze in plastic bag for up to 1 month; let thaw and rise in refrigerator overnight.)

Turn out dough onto lightly floured surface; divide in half and shape into discs. Roll out each disc into 8-inch (20 cm) circle, letting dough rest, covered, if too elastic to roll. Place side by side on large baking sheet. Let rest for 15 minutes. Press all over to form slightly raised rim. Or form all the dough into one 12-inch (30 cm) pizza base on pizza pan. **Makes one 12-inch (30 cm) pizza base or two 8-inch (20 cm) personal pizza bases.**

HANDMADE PIZZA DOUGH

2 cups	all-purpose flour	500 mL
1½ tsp	quick-rising (instant) dry yeast	7 mL
¾ tsp	salt	4 mL
¾ cup	hot water (120°F/50°C)	175 mL
2 tsp	olive oil	10 mL

In bowl, combine flour, yeast and salt. With wooden spoon, gradually stir in water and oil until dough forms, using hands if necessary.

Turn out onto lightly floured surface; knead for 8 minutes or until smooth and elastic. Continue with rising and rolling out as for Food Processor Pizza Dough. **Makes one 12-inch (30 cm) pizza base or two 8-inch (20 cm) personal pizza bases.**

BREAD MACHINE PIZZA DOUGH

1½ cups	water	375 mL
4 tsp	olive oil	20 mL
1¼ tsp	salt	6 mL
4 cups	all-purpose flour	1 L
2½ tsp	quick-rising (instant) dry yeast	12 mL

Into pan of 2-lb (1 kg) bread machine, place (in order) water, oil, salt, flour and yeast. (Do not let yeast touch liquid.) Choose dough setting. Shape into 4 discs. Roll out as for Food Processor Pizza Dough. (Or divide dough in half. Form each half into one 12-inch/30 cm pizza base.) **Makes two 12-inch (30 cm) pizza bases or four 8-inch (20 cm) personal pizza bases.**

VARIATIONS

Whole Wheat or Multigrain Pizza Dough: Replace ½ cup (125 mL) of the all-purpose flour with whole wheat or multigrain flour (preferably bread flour).

Herbed Pizza Dough: Flavour the dough by adding ½ tsp (2 mL) dried oregano to the dry ingredients.

TEST KITCHEN TIP: For thin-crust pizza, bake shaped dough without letting it rise. For thicker crust, let shaped dough rise for up to 45 minutes.

Grilled Pepper and Sausage Pizza

Put down the phone — homemade pizza is a snap. Instead of waiting for the door-bell to ring, you can inhale the aromas as the pizza bubbles and crisps in your oven.

1	each sweet red and green pepper	1
1	red onion	1
2 tbsp	olive oil	25 mL
1	small clove garlic, minced	1
1 tsp	minced jalapeño pepper (or ¼ tsp/1 mL hot pepper sauce)	5 mL

8 oz	hot or mild Italian sausage	250 g
1	unbaked 12-inch (30 cm) pizza base (see Pizza Dough, page 248)	1
½ cup	pizza or pasta sauce	125 mL
2 cups	shredded mozzarella cheese	500 mL
2 tbsp	chopped fresh parsley	25 mL

1 Core, seed and cut red and green peppers into quarters. Cut onion into ½-inch (1 cm) thick slices. Whisk together oil, garlic and jalapeño pepper; brush over vegetables.

2 Place peppers on greased grill over medium-high heat; close lid and cook for 5 minutes. Add onion and sausage; cook, covered and turning occasionally, for about 15 minutes or until vegetables are tender and sausage is no longer pink inside. Let cool.

3 Cut peppers into thin slices. Separate onion into rings. Cut sausage on diagonal into ¼-inch (5 mm) thick slices. Spread pizza base with sauce; sprinkle with onion, then mozzarella cheese, sweet peppers and sausage.

4 Bake in bottom third of 500°F (260°C) oven for 10 minutes or until cheese is bubbly and crust is golden and slightly puffed. Sprinkle with parsley.

TEST KITCHEN TIP: To bake the pizza on the barbecue, lightly brush top of pizza base with oil. Place, oiled side down, on grill over medium-high heat; close lid and cook for 4 minutes. Invert onto greased pizza pan. Top as directed. Place on grill over medium heat; close lid and cook for 15 minutes, rotating pan occasionally.

Makes 8 slices.

PER SLICE, ABOUT:

cal 338	carb . . . . 33 g
pro . . . . 15 g	fibre . . . . 2 g
total fat . . . . 16 g	chol . . . . . . 37 mg
sat. fat . . . . . . 6 g	sodium . . 608 mg

PERCENTAGE RDI:

calcium 17%	vit. A 17%
iron 15%	vit. C 93%
folate 25%	

FETA AND TOMATO Pizza

There's no cooking required to make this Greek-style topping. Brush unbaked 12-inch (30 cm) pizza base with 2 tbsp (25 mL) olive oil. Sprinkle with 1 tsp (5 mL) dried oregano, then 2 cups (500 mL) shredded mozzarella cheese. Top with 3 tomatoes, thinly sliced, half sweet green pepper, thinly sliced, and ⅓ cup (75 mL) sliced pitted oil-cured or Kalamata olives. Sprinkle with 1 cup (250 mL) crumbled feta cheese. Bake in bottom third of 500°F (260°C) oven for about 10 minutes or until golden and slightly puffed. **Makes 8 slices.**

Mushroom Pizza

Exotic mushrooms — shiitake, oyster, crimini and even portobello — boost the woodsy flavour of regular button mushrooms.

1 tbsp	olive oil	15 mL
3	cloves garlic, minced	3
8 cups	sliced stemmed fresh exotic mushrooms (1½ lb/750 g)	2 L
3 cups	sliced button mushrooms	750 mL
1	unbaked 12-inch (30 cm) pizza base (see Pizza Dough, page 248)	1

½ cup	pasta sauce	125 mL
1 cup	shredded mozzarella cheese	250 mL
2 oz	feta cheese (or ¼ cup/50 mL grated Parmesan cheese)	60 g
2 tbsp	chopped fresh basil	25 mL

Makes 8 slices.

PER SLICE, ABOUT:

cal .... 236 carb .... 30 g
pro .... 9 g fibre .... 3 g
total fat ..... 9 g chol ...... 19 mg
sat. fat ...... 4 g sodium .. 435 mg

PERCENTAGE RDI:

calcium .... 12% vit. A 7%
iron .... 17% vit. C 35%
folate 25%

1 In large skillet, heat oil over medium-high heat; cook garlic and exotic and button mushrooms, stirring occasionally, for about 15 minutes or until tender and liquid is evaporated.

2 Spread pizza base with sauce; sprinkle with mushrooms, then mozzarella cheese. Crumble feta cheese over top.

3 Bake in bottom third of 500°F (260°C) oven for 10 minutes or until crust is golden and slightly puffed and cheese is bubbly. Sprinkle with basil.

AT-HOME Pizzeria

Making your own pizza is easy; you can top it with just about anything you like. Use these guidelines — and your imagination and taste buds — to create a delicious variety of home-made pizzas. If you're sharing the pizza, but not the tastes, divide the pie visually into portions and top according to individual likes.

For a 12-inch (30 cm) round, enough for 2 adult dinner servings, you need about 2 cups (500 mL) shredded cheese, ½ to ¾ cup (125 to 175 mL) tomato pizza or pasta sauce and about 2 cups (500 mL) total toppings.

For maximum distribution of flavours and ease of serving, the pizza should be layered as follows: Spread base with sauce; sprinkle with half of the cheese, all of the toppings, then the rest of the cheese (this keeps the toppings from drying out).

Bake topped pizzas on bottom rack of 500°F (260°C) oven for about 12 minutes, slightly more if crust is thick, slightly less if crust is thin and toppings are few.

Pesto and Roasted
Eggplant Pizza

*Eggplant may not be your first choice for a pizza topping, but that will change when
you taste how delicious this versatile vegetable is with pesto and Fontina.*

1	eggplant (about 12 oz/375 g)	1
3 tbsp	olive oil	50 mL
¼ tsp	each salt and pepper	1 mL
⅔ cup	Pesto (recipe, page 235)	150 mL

1	unbaked 12-inch (30 cm) pizza base (see Pizza Dough, page 248)	1
1½ cups	shredded Fontina or mozzarella cheese	375 mL
½ cup	diced plum tomatoes	125 mL

1 Cut eggplant into ½-inch (1 cm) thick slices; brush with half of the oil. Arrange
in single layer on baking sheet; sprinkle with salt and pepper. Roast in 425°F
(220°C) oven, turning halfway through, for about 30 minutes or until dark and
tender.

2 Spread ½ cup (125 mL) of the pesto over pizza base; sprinkle with Fontina
cheese. Arrange eggplant over top, then tomatoes. Combine remaining oil and
pesto; drizzle over tomatoes.

3 Bake in bottom third of 500°F (260°C) oven for 10 minutes or until cheese is
bubbly and crust is golden and slightly puffed.

VARIATION

Grilled Vegetable Pizza: Instead of just eggplant, cover pizza base with roasted or
leftover grilled eggplant, sweet peppers, onions and zucchini. You can also wrap whole
heads of garlic in foil and cook on ledge over grill for about 30 minutes or until tender
enough to squeeze out onto crust.

Makes 8 slices.

PER SLICE, ABOUT:

cal 376	carb . . . . 28 g
pro . . . . 12 g	fibre . . . . 3 g
total fat . . . . 24 g	chol . . . . . . 28 mg
sat. fat . . . . . . 7 g	sodium . . 633 mg

PERCENTAGE RDI:

calcium 17%	vit. A 9%
iron 13%	vit. C 32%
folate 23%	

Quick Breads
and Yeast Breads

10

Easy-Mix Muffins   254

Morning Sunshine Bars   255

Honey Bran Muffins   256

Lemon Poppy Seed Loaf   257

Blueberry Orange Almond Loaf   258

Banana Chocolate Chip Loaf   259

Soda Bread   260

Tea Biscuits   261

Quick Orange Buns   262

Classic Pancakes   263

Waffles with Apple Cranberry Sauce   264

The Versatile Crêpe   265

Basic Bread: By Hand and Machine   266

Buttermilk Loaf   268

Country Seed Bread   269

Caraway Rye Bread   270

Ciabatta   271

Lavash   272

Nova Scotia Oatmeal Rolls   273

Cinnamon Buns   274

Hot Cross Buns   275

Pecan Kugelhopf   276

Challah   277

Easy-Mix Muffins

Muffin mania may have subsided, replaced by bagel ballyhoo, but muffins are still the multichangeable easy-bakes that satisfy as breakfast staples and quick snacks.

	DRY ADD-INS	LIQUID ADD-INS	SPECIAL ADD-INS
Raspberry Lemon Muffins	1 cup (250 mL) quick-cooking rolled oats; 1 tbsp (15 mL) grated lemon rind	1¼ cups (300 mL) buttermilk	¾ cup (175 mL) frozen raspberries
Chocolaty Banana Muffins	½ cup (125 mL) all-purpose flour	1 cup (250 mL) buttermilk; 1 cup (250 mL) mashed bananas (2 large)	¾ cup (175 mL) chocolate chips
Apple Spice Muffins	½ cup (125 mL) wheat bran; 1 tsp (5 mL) each ground cinnamon, nutmeg and allspice	1 cup (250 mL) sweetened applesauce; ½ cup (125 mL) milk	1½ cups (375 mL) diced peeled apples
Zucchini Pecan Raisin Muffins	½ cup (125 mL) oat bran or wheat bran; 1½ cups (375 mL) shredded zucchini; 1 tsp (5 mL) each ground cinnamon and ginger	1¼ cups (300 mL) buttermilk	½ cup (125 mL) chopped pecans; ½ cup (125 mL) raisins
Piña Colada Muffins	½ cup (125 mL) all-purpose flour; ½ cup (125 mL) shredded sweetened coconut; ½ tsp (2 mL) ground nutmeg	½ cup (125 mL) milk; ½ cup (125 mL) pineapple juice; 1 tbsp (15 mL) grated lemon rind	¾ cup (175 mL) drained canned crushed pineapple

MUFFIN DRESS-UPS

Sprinkle one of the following over batter just before muffins go into the oven.

Raspberry Lemon Muffins: quick-cooking rolled oats

Chocolaty Banana Muffins: chocolate chips

Apple Spice Muffins: cinnamon sugar

Piña Colada Muffins: shredded coconut

1 In large bowl, whisk together 2 cups (500 mL) all-purpose flour, 1 cup (250 mL) packed brown sugar, 1½ tsp (7 mL) baking powder, 1 tsp (5 mL) baking soda and ½ tsp (2 mL) salt. Add Dry Add-Ins in first column.

2 In separate bowl, whisk together 2 eggs, ⅓ cup (75 mL) vegetable oil and 1 tsp (5 mL) vanilla. Add Liquid Add-Ins in second column. Pour over dry ingredients.

3 Sprinkle with Special Add-Ins in third column. Stir just until dry ingredients are moistened. Spoon into 12 greased or paper-lined muffin cups. Bake in centre of 375°F (190°C) oven for 20 to 25 minutes or until tops are firm to the touch. Let cool in pan on rack for 5 minutes. Transfer to racks; let cool completely. (MAKE-AHEAD: Store in airtight container for up to 2 days or wrap individually in plastic wrap and freeze in airtight container for up to 2 weeks.)

Makes 12 muffins.

Morning Sunshine Bars

Bountifully sized and packed with good things — dates, pecans, bananas and carrots — bars like these are good candidates to take away for a cottage or country weekend.

1½ cups	each all-purpose and whole wheat flours	375 mL
2 tsp	baking powder	10 mL
2 tsp	cinnamon	10 mL
1 tsp	baking soda	5 mL
½ tsp	ground ginger	2 mL
¼ tsp	salt	1 mL
2	eggs	2
1 cup	packed brown sugar	250 mL
1 cup	mashed very ripe bananas (2 large)	250 mL
⅔ cup	plain yogurt	150 mL
⅓ cup	vegetable oil	75 mL
2 cups	grated carrots (about 4)	500 mL
1 cup	chopped dates or raisins	250 mL
½ cup	chopped toasted pecans	125 mL
16	pecan halves	16

TEST KITCHEN TIP: Pop a frozen muffin (see variation) into a lunch box to thaw in time for a morning break or for lunch.

1 In large bowl, whisk together all-purpose and whole wheat flours, baking powder, cinnamon, baking soda, ginger and salt.

2 In separate bowl, whisk together eggs, sugar, bananas, yogurt and oil; pour over dry ingredients. Sprinkle with carrots, dates and chopped pecans; mix just until dry ingredients are moistened.

3 Spread batter in greased waxed paper–lined 13- x 9-inch (3.5 L) metal cake pan. Position pecan halves in grid to have 1 per bar. Bake in centre of 375°F (190°C) oven for about 30 minutes or until firm to the touch and tester inserted in centre comes out clean. Let cool completely in pan on rack. Cut into bars. (MAKE-AHEAD: Store in airtight container for up to 2 days or wrap individually in plastic wrap and freeze in airtight container for up to 2 weeks.)

VARIATION

Morning Sunshine Muffins: Reduce pecan halves to 12. Spoon batter into large greased or paper-lined muffin cups until heaping but not overflowing; press pecan half into top of each. Bake as directed. Let cool in pan on rack for 5 minutes. Transfer to rack; let cool completely. (MAKE-AHEAD: Store at room temperature or freeze as for bars.) **Makes 12 muffins.**

Makes 16 bars.

PER BAR, ABOUT:

cal	276	carb	46 g
pro	5 g	fibre	4 g
total fat	9 g	chol	28 mg
sat. fat	1 g	sodium	173 mg

PERCENTAGE RDI:

calcium	6%	vit. A	47%
iron	13%	vit. C	3%
folate	12%		

MAKE-AHEAD FREEZABLE CLASSIC

Honey Bran Muffins

Choose a dark honey, such as buckwheat, for these lighter-than-usual bran muffins.

SUBSTITUTION: Any dried (not candied) fruit — such as chopped dates, apricots or figs — or mix of dried fruit is delicious in these muffins instead of raisins.

2	eggs	2
1⅓ cups	buttermilk	325 mL
⅓ cup	vegetable oil	75 mL
¼ cup	liquid honey	50 mL
2 tsp	vanilla	10 mL
1½ cups	100% Bran or All-Bran cereal	375 mL

1¾ cups	all-purpose flour	425 mL
½ cup	packed brown sugar	125 mL
1½ tsp	baking soda	7 mL
½ tsp	cinnamon	2 mL
½ tsp	salt	2 mL
1½ cups	raisins	375 mL

Makes 12 muffins.

PER MUFFIN, ABOUT:

cal	281	carb	53 g
pro	5 g	fibre	4 g
total fat	8 g	chol	37 mg
sat. fat	1 g	sodium	357 mg

PERCENTAGE RDI:

calcium	6%	vit. A	2%
iron	19%	vit. C	2%
folate	13%		

1 In bowl, whisk together eggs, buttermilk, oil, honey and vanilla; stir in cereal. Let stand for 5 minutes.

2 Meanwhile, in large bowl, whisk together flour, sugar, baking soda, cinnamon and salt. Pour bran mixture over dry ingredients; sprinkle with raisins. Stir just until moistened. Spoon into greased or paper-lined muffin cups, filling to top.

3 Bake in centre of 375°F (190°C) oven for about 25 minutes or until golden and tops are firm to the touch. Let cool in pan on rack for 5 minutes. Transfer to rack; let cool completely. (MAKE-AHEAD: Store in airtight container for up to 2 days or wrap individually in plastic wrap and freeze in airtight container for up to 2 weeks.)

MUFFIN Know-How

🍃 Because canola oil has a very mild taste, it is ideal for muffin baking. Also noteworthy: of all oils, it has the least amount of saturated fat. When vegetable oil is called for in muffin recipes, you can substitute canola oil.

🍃 If brown sugar is lumpy when combining with dry ingredients, pass through a sieve or crumble with fingertips.

🍃 Grease muffin cups with butter or oil using a pastry brush or spray with vegetable oil or line with paper liners, available in the baking section of the supermarket.

🍃 When the batter does not fill all the muffin cups in a pan, pour about 1 inch (2.5 cm) water into empty cups to prevent them from burning.

🍃 Let baked muffins cool in pan for about five minutes. This allows the still-hot and delicate structure to firm up before being transferred to racks.

🍃 Run a blunt knife around edge of muffins to loosen before lifting out of pan. Serve immediately or remove to racks and let cool.

🍃 Muffins can be stored in freezer for up to two weeks. To freeze, let cool completely before wrapping individually in plastic wrap and enclosing in airtight freezer bag or freezer container.

🍃 To warm a muffin straight from the freezer, microwave at High for about 20 seconds.

Lemon Poppy Seed Loaf

The tangy lemon syrup seeps seductively into this pretty loaf. It's perfect for a bake sale or to share with colleagues at work.

½ cup	butter, softened	125 mL
1 cup	granulated sugar	250 mL
2	eggs	2
1½ cups	all-purpose flour	375 mL
3 tbsp	poppy seeds	50 mL
1 tbsp	grated lemon rind	15 mL
1 tsp	baking powder	5 mL

¼ tsp	salt	1 mL
½ cup	milk	125 mL
LEMON SYRUP:		
⅓ cup	granulated sugar	75 mL
1 tsp	grated lemon rind	5 mL
⅓ cup	lemon juice	75 mL

TEST KITCHEN TIP: To ensure easy removal of loaf from pan, line bottom of pan with waxed or parchment paper cut to fit.

1 In large bowl, beat butter with sugar until fluffy; beat in eggs, 1 at a time, beating well after each addition. In separate bowl, whisk together flour, poppy seeds, lemon rind, baking powder and salt; stir into butter mixture alternately with milk, making 3 additions of dry ingredients and 2 of milk.

2 Spread batter in greased 8- x 4-inch (1.5 L) loaf pan. Bake in centre of 325°F (160°C) oven for about 1 hour or until tester inserted in centre comes out clean. Place pan on rack.

3 **LEMON SYRUP:** In microwaveable measure or in saucepan on stove, warm sugar, lemon rind and lemon juice until sugar dissolves. With skewer, pierce hot loaf in 12 places right to bottom; gradually pour lemon syrup over loaf, allowing time for syrup to seep into holes. Let cool in pan on rack for 30 minutes; turn out onto rack and let cool completely. Wrap in plastic wrap and let stand for 1 day before slicing. (MAKE-AHEAD: Store for up to 3 days or overwrap with heavy-duty foil and freeze in airtight container for up to 1 month.)

Makes 1 loaf, 12 slices.

PER SLICE, ABOUT:

cal	242	carb	36 g
pro	4 g	fibre	1 g
total fat	10 g	chol	57 mg
sat. fat	5 g	sodium	164 mg

PERCENTAGE RDI:

calcium	6%	vit. A	9%
iron	7%	vit. C	5%
folate	10%		

Blueberry Orange Almond Loaf

This loaf has it all — fruit, nuts and a sparkling top.

SUBSTITUTION: You can
replace the dried blueberries
with other dried fruit such
as golden raisins, cranberries
or cherries.

¾ cup	butter, softened	175 mL
¾ cup	granulated sugar	175 mL
2	eggs	2
2 tbsp	finely grated orange rind	25 mL
½ tsp	almond extract	2 mL
3 cups	all-purpose flour	750 mL
1 tsp	baking powder	5 mL
1 tsp	baking soda	5 mL

½ tsp	salt	2 mL
1 cup	milk	250 mL
1 cup	dried blueberries	250 mL
½ cup	sliced almonds, toasted	125 mL

TOPPING:

2 tbsp	sliced almonds	25 mL
1 tbsp	granulated sugar	15 mL

1 In large bowl, beat butter with sugar until light and fluffy. Beat in eggs, 1 at a time, beating well after each addition. Beat in orange rind and almond extract.

2 In separate bowl, whisk together flour, baking powder, baking soda and salt; stir into butter mixture alternately with milk, making 3 additions of dry ingredients and 2 of milk. Stir in blueberries and almonds. Spread batter in greased and parchment paper–lined 9- x 5-inch (2 L) loaf pan.

3 TOPPING: Sprinkle evenly with almonds and sugar.

4 Bake in centre of 350°F (180°C) oven for about 1 hour or until cake tester inserted in centre comes out clean. Let cool in pan on rack for 15 minutes. Turn out onto rack; let cool completely. (MAKE-AHEAD: Wrap in plastic wrap and store at room temperature for up to 3 days or overwrap with heavy-duty foil and freeze in airtight container for up to 2 weeks.)

Makes 1 loaf, 16 slices.

PER SLICE, ABOUT:

cal 261	carb . . . . 35 g
pro . . . . 5 g	fibre . . . . 2 g
total fat . . . . 12 g	chol . . . . . . 51 mg
sat. fat . . . . . . 6 g	sodium . . 266 mg

PERCENTAGE RDI:

calcium 7%	vit. A 10%
iron 9%	vit. C 2%
folate 14%	

Banana Chocolate Chip Loaf

The affordability and availability of bananas usually ensure a few brown speckled ones waiting in the fruit bowl to be mashed and baked into a loaf.

2 cups	all-purpose flour	500 mL
¼ cup	granulated sugar	50 mL
2 tsp	baking powder	10 mL
1 tsp	baking soda	5 mL
Pinch	salt	Pinch
1 cup	chocolate chips	250 mL

2 cups	mashed ripe bananas (about 4 large)	500 mL
½ cup	butter, melted	125 mL
¼ cup	milk	50 mL
2	eggs	2

SUBSTITUTION: When an oversupply of ripe bananas begins to perfume your kitchen, freeze without peeling (or peel and mash in convenient amounts) to thaw and use for banana bread or muffins.

1 In large bowl, whisk together flour, sugar, baking powder, baking soda and salt; add chocolate chips. In separate bowl, whisk together bananas, butter, milk and eggs; pour over flour mixture and stir just until blended.

2 Spread batter in greased 9- x 5-inch (2 L) loaf pan. Bake in centre of 350°F (180°C) oven for 50 to 60 minutes or until cake tester inserted in centre comes out clean. Let cool in pan on rack for 15 minutes. Turn out onto rack; let cool completely. (MAKE-AHEAD: Wrap in plastic wrap and store at room temperature for up to 2 days or overwrap with heavy-duty foil and freeze in airtight container for up to 1 month.)

VARIATIONS

Mini Banana Chocolate Chip Loaves: Spoon batter into 4 greased 5¾- x 3¼-inch (625 mL) loaf pans. Bake for about 40 minutes. **Makes 4 mini loaves.**

Banana Chocolate Chip Muffins: Spoon batter into greased or paper-lined muffin cups, filling three-quarters full. Bake for 25 minutes or until golden brown and tops are firm to the touch. **Makes 12 muffins.**

Makes 1 loaf, 16 slices.

PER SLICE, ABOUT:

cal	208	carb	29 g
pro	3 g	fibre	2 g
total fat	10 g	chol	43 mg
sat. fat	6 g	sodium	176 mg

PERCENTAGE RDI:

calcium	3%	vit. A	7%
iron	9%	vit. C	5%
folate	11%		

QUICK   BUDGET-   CLASSIC
          WISE

Soda Bread

Bread in less than half an hour, and moist and memorable bread at that.

3 cups	all-purpose flour	750 mL		½ tsp	salt	2 mL
1 cup	whole wheat flour	250 mL		1¾ cups	buttermilk	425 mL
1 cup	raisins, dried currants or chopped dried fruit (optional)	250 mL		3 tbsp	vegetable oil	50 mL
				1	egg	1
3 tbsp	granulated sugar	50 mL		**TOPPING:**		
1 tbsp	baking powder	15 mL		1 tbsp	whole wheat flour	15 mL
1 tsp	baking soda	5 mL				

1 In large bowl, whisk together all-purpose and whole wheat flours, raisins (if using), sugar, baking powder, baking soda and salt. In separate bowl, whisk together buttermilk, oil and egg; pour over dry ingredients and stir just until moistened and ragged.

2 Turn out dough onto lightly floured surface. With lightly floured hands, knead gently 10 times or just until dough holds together. Place on greased baking sheet; flatten into 9-inch (23 cm) circle 3 inches (8 cm) thick. With serrated knife, score top into sixths.

3 TOPPING: Dust with flour.

4 Bake in centre of 350°F (180°C) oven for 45 to 50 minutes or until cake tester inserted in centre comes out clean. Let cool on pan on rack for 5 minutes. Cut into wedges or slices.

VARIATION

Fruity Soda Bread: Omit whole wheat flour and increase all-purpose flour to 4 cups (1 L). Add ⅓ cup (75 mL) each raisins, dried currants, mixed candied fruit and chopped dried figs. Add 1½ tsp (7 mL) grated orange rind to buttermilk mixture. Omit dusting with flour. While bread is cooling, mix ½ cup (125 mL) icing sugar with 1 tbsp (15 mL) orange juice; spread over warm bread.

Makes 1 loaf, 20 wedges.

PER WEDGE, ABOUT:

cal	128	carb	22 g
pro	4 g	fibre	1 g
total fat	3 g	chol	11 mg
sat. fat	trace	sodium	181 mg

PERCENTAGE RDI:

calcium	4%	vit. A	1%
iron	8%	vit. C	0%
folate	11%		

Tea Biscuits

Call them scones if you like and dress them up or down with dried fruit or cheese.

2¼ cups	all-purpose flour	550 mL		½ cup	cold butter, cubed	125 mL
2 tbsp	granulated sugar	25 mL		1 cup	milk	250 mL
1 tbsp	baking powder	15 mL		1	egg, lightly beaten	1
½ tsp	salt	2 mL				

1 In large bowl, whisk together flour, sugar, baking powder and salt. Using pastry blender or 2 knives, cut in butter until mixture resembles coarse crumbs. Pour milk over top and stir with fork to form soft, slightly sticky ragged dough.

2 Turn out dough onto lightly floured surface. With lightly floured hands, knead gently 10 times. Gently pat out into ½-inch (1 cm) thick round. Using 2-inch (5 cm) floured cutter, cut out rounds. Place on ungreased baking sheet. Gather up scraps and repat dough; cut out more rounds, pressing remaining scraps into final biscuit.

3 Brush tops of biscuits with egg. Bake in centre of 425°F (220°C) oven for 12 to 15 minutes or until golden. Let cool on pan on racks. (MAKE-AHEAD: Wrap individually in plastic wrap and freeze in airtight container for up to 2 weeks; thaw and reheat in 350°F/180°C oven for 10 minutes.)

VARIATIONS

Dried Fruit and Lemon Tea Biscuits: Add ½ cup (125 mL) raisins, dried currants, dried blueberries, dried cranberries, chopped dried cherries (not candied), apricots or prunes. Add 2 tsp (10 mL) grated lemon or orange rind to dry mixture.

Oat Tea Biscuits with Raisins: Substitute ½ cup (125 mL) rolled oats (not instant) for ½ cup (125 mL) of the flour. Add ½ cup (125 mL) raisins or currants and 1 tsp (5 mL) cinnamon to dry mixture.

Cheese Tea Biscuits: Omit sugar. Add ¼ tsp (1 mL) cayenne pepper to flour mixture. Add 1 cup (250 mL) shredded old Cheddar cheese after butter has been cut in.

Buttermilk Tea Biscuits: Decrease baking powder to 2½ tsp (12 mL). Add ½ tsp (2 mL) baking soda to dry mixture. Substitute buttermilk for milk. (In all the milk-based biscuits above, you can substitute buttermilk.)

TEST KITCHEN TIPS

• Treat tea biscuit dough gently, avoiding overmixing and keeping the kneading process to the bare minimum —just enough to bring the dough together. If you want to eliminate the rerolling, pat out dough into rectangle and cut into squares.

• For real old-fashioned strawberry shortcake, make tea biscuits about 2½ inches (6 cm) wide. While still warm, split each biscuit, place bottom half on dessert plate and cover generously with slightly sweetened sliced strawberries. Centre remaining biscuit half over berries, and garnish with a lavish dollop of whipped cream and a whole berry.

Makes about 12 tea biscuits.

PER BISCUIT, ABOUT:	
cal 179	carb . . . . 21 g
pro . . . . 4 g	fibre . . . . 1 g
total fat . . . . . 9 g	chol . . . . . . 40 mg
sat. fat . . . . . . 5 g	sodium . . 254 mg

PERCENTAGE RDI:	
calcium 6%	vit. A 9%
iron 8%	vit. C 0%
folate 13%	

Quick Orange Buns

Biscuit dough scented with orange, then buttered, rolled, sliced and baked in a tube pan, elevates this quick bread to new heights. This recipe made Cheryl Neely of Ottawa the winner in the bread category of our millennium heritage recipe contest.

3 cups	all-purpose flour	750 mL	¾ cup	orange juice	175 mL
3 tbsp	granulated sugar	50 mL	3 tbsp	butter, softened	50 mL
4 tsp	baking powder	20 mL	**ORANGE SUGAR:**		
1½ tsp	salt	7 mL	¾ cup	granulated sugar	175 mL
⅓ cup	shortening	75 mL	4 tsp	grated orange rind	20 mL
2	eggs	2			

Makes 8 buns.

PER BUN, ABOUT:

cal	405	carb	63 g
pro	7 g	fibre	2 g
total fat	14 g	chol	65 mg
sat. fat	5 g	sodium	621 mg

PERCENTAGE RDI:

calcium	7%	vit. A	7%
iron	16%	vit. C	17%
folate	27%		

1 In large bowl, whisk together flour, sugar, baking powder and salt. With pastry blender or 2 knives, cut in shortening until in fine crumbs. Beat eggs with orange juice; drizzle over crumbs, tossing with fork to moisten.

2 Turn out dough onto lightly floured surface; knead gently for 30 seconds. Roll or pat into 8-inch (20 cm) square; spread with butter.

3 ORANGE SUGAR: Combine sugar with orange rind; sprinkle over dough. Roll up jelly roll–style; cut into 8 slices. Place, side by side and cut side down, in greased 9- or 10-inch (3 or 4 L) tube pan. Bake in centre of 425°F (220°C) oven for 35 minutes or until golden. (MAKE-AHEAD: Store in airtight container at room temperature for up to 1 day.)

Bannock

In Canada's North, bannock has long been a staple scone-type bread, made over an open fire using ingredients at hand. In the absence of dairy products, lard or shortening replaced the butter, and water often had to stand in for milk. Today, bannock is more often baked in an oven, but it is still as welcome.

⟋ In bowl, mix together 3 cups (750 mL) all-purpose flour, 2 tbsp (25 mL) baking powder, 1 tbsp (15 mL) granulated sugar and 1 tsp (5 mL) salt. Cut in ½ cup (125 mL) lard until in fine crumbs. Gradually add enough of 1 cup (250 mL) water (or milk for richer dough) to make soft dough. Press into ball; flatten into 1-inch (2.5 cm) thick circle. Bake on baking sheet in centre of 425°F (220°C) oven for about 25 minutes or until lightly browned. Cut into wedges and serve warm with butter.

Classic Pancakes

From the original Canadian Living Cookbook, *here's the recipe you need when there's a request for pancakes, whether it's a weekend morning or a weekday supper. Serve hot with butter and maple or fruit syrup.*

1	egg	1
1½ cups	milk	375 mL
2 tbsp	butter, melted, or vegetable oil	25 mL

1½ cups	all-purpose flour	375 mL
1 tbsp	baking powder	15 mL
1 tbsp	granulated sugar	15 mL
½ tsp	salt	2 mL

TEST KITCHEN TIP: Freeze any leftover pancakes, separated by waxed paper, in freezer bags. Pop into the toaster to reheat for quick breakfasts and snacks.

1 In large bowl, beat together egg, milk and butter. In separate bowl, whisk together flour, baking powder, sugar and salt; pour over egg mixture and stir until almost smooth.

2 Heat skillet or griddle over medium heat; brush with oil or unsalted fat (optional for nonstick pans). Pour about ¼ cup (50 mL) batter for each pancake into skillet; cook for 1½ to 2 minutes or until underside is brown and bubbles break on top but do not fill in. Turn and cook for 30 to 60 seconds longer or until underside is golden brown. Repeat with remaining batter, brushing skillet with more oil as necessary.

VARIATIONS

Buttermilk Pancakes: Increase eggs to 2. Use 2 cups (500 mL) buttermilk instead of 1½ cups (375 mL) milk. Use 1 tsp (5 mL) each baking powder and baking soda instead of 1 tbsp (15 mL) baking powder. If batter is too thick, add a little water.

Blueberry Pancakes: To either Classic or Buttermilk pancake batter, stir in 1 cup (250 mL) fresh wild blueberries, mixing with as few strokes as possible.

Buckwheat Honey Pancakes: Use ¾ cup (175 mL) buckwheat flour and ¾ cup (175 mL) all-purpose flour instead of 1½ cups (375 mL) all-purpose flour. Substitute liquid honey (buckwheat, if available) for sugar.

Makes 12 pancakes.

PER PANCAKE, ABOUT:

cal	101	carb	15 g
pro	3 g	fibre	trace
total fat	3 g	chol	25 mg
sat. fat	2 g	sodium	200 mg

PERCENTAGE RDI:

calcium	6%	vit. A	4%
iron	5%	vit. C	0%
folate	9%		

FREEZABLE BUDGET-
WISE

Waffles with Apple Cranberry Sauce

Waffles are simply pancakes putting on the ritz. But why not? Drizzle with pure Canadian maple syrup, top with fruit or spoon on the Apple Cranberry Sauce or Cherry Berry Sauce (recipe follows). You can also use the batter for pancakes.

2 cups	all-purpose flour	500 mL
¼ cup	granulated sugar	50 mL
2 tsp	baking powder	10 mL
½ tsp	baking soda	2 mL
½ tsp	cinnamon	2 mL
¼ tsp	salt	1 mL
2	eggs	2
2 cups	buttermilk	500 mL
¼ cup	butter, melted	50 mL
2 tbsp	vegetable oil	25 mL

APPLE CRANBERRY SAUCE:		
1 tbsp	butter	15 mL
2 tbsp	packed brown sugar	25 mL
4	apples, peeled and sliced	4
1 cup	apple juice	250 mL
½ cup	dried cranberries or raisins	125 mL
1 tbsp	cornstarch	15 mL

1 APPLE CRANBERRY SAUCE: In skillet, melt butter over medium heat; stir in brown sugar. Add apples; cook, stirring, for 10 minutes. Add apple juice and cranberries; bring to boil. Dissolve cornstarch in 1 tbsp (15 mL) water; add to skillet and cook, stirring, for 1 minute or until thickened. Set aside and keep warm.

2 In large bowl, whisk together flour, sugar, baking powder, baking soda, cinnamon and salt. In small bowl, whisk together eggs, buttermilk and butter; pour over flour mixture and stir just until combined.

3 Heat waffle iron. For each waffle, brush lightly with some of the oil; pour in ½ cup (125 mL) batter, spreading to edges. Close lid and cook for 4 to 5 minutes or until crisp, golden and steam stops. Serve with warm sauce.

Makes 6 servings.

VARIATION

Waffles with Cherry Berry Sauce: Omit Apple Cranberry Sauce. In saucepan, combine 1½ cups (375 mL) frozen sour cherries (thawed), 1 cup (250 mL) each frozen strawberries and raspberries (thawed), ¼ cup (50 mL) frozen blueberries (thawed), ¼ cup (50 mL) granulated sugar, ¼ cup (50 mL) water and 2 tbsp (25 mL) cornstarch; bring to boil over medium-high heat, stirring gently. Cook for about 1 minute or until thickened. Stir in 1 tsp (5 mL) vanilla. Serve warm.

The Versatile Crêpe

Thin French pancakes, the well-known crêpes, are custom-made to fill with savouries or sweets. Keep a batch handy in the freezer so you can spread them thinly with raspberry jam, fold them over a scoop of ice cream, drizzle them with chocolate sauce — and call them dessert.

1 cup	all-purpose flour	250 mL
¼ tsp	salt	1 mL
3	eggs	3
1¼ cups	milk	300 mL
3 tbsp	butter, melted (approx)	50 mL

STRAWBERRIES ROMANOFF FILLING:		
3 cups	sliced strawberries	750 mL
2 tbsp	orange juice concentrate or orange liqueur	25 mL
2 tsp	granulated sugar	10 mL
½ cup	whipping cream	125 mL
1 tbsp	icing sugar	15 mL

1 In bowl, whisk flour with salt. In small bowl, whisk together eggs, milk and 2 tbsp (25 mL) of the butter; whisk into flour mixture until smooth. Cover and refrigerate for 1 hour. Strain into another bowl.

2 Heat 8-inch (20 cm) crêpe pan or skillet over medium heat. Brush lightly with some of the remaining butter. Pour scant ¼ cup (50 mL) batter into centre of pan, swirling pan to coat; cook for about 1 minute or until bottom is golden. Turn and cook for 30 seconds. Transfer to plate. Repeat with remaining batter and butter. (MAKE-AHEAD: Stack crêpes between waxed paper, wrap and refrigerate for up to 3 days or freeze in airtight container for up to 1 month.)

3 STRAWBERRIES ROMANOFF FILLING: In bowl, stir together strawberries, orange juice concentrate and sugar; let stand for 10 minutes. In separate bowl, whip cream. Spoon strawberry mixture down centre of each crêpe; top with some of the whipped cream. Roll up and sprinkle with icing sugar.

SAVOURY FILLING VARIATION

Ham, Brie and Asparagus Filling: In large saucepan of boiling water, cook 36 asparagus spears; drain on towels. Slice 8 oz (250 g) Brie cheese into 12 slices. Arrange 1 slice shaved Black Forest ham (6 oz/175 g total) in centre of each crêpe; place 3 cooked asparagus spears on each. Top with Brie slice; roll up. Place in greased 13- x 9-inch (3 L) glass baking dish. Brush with 2 tbsp (25 mL) butter, melted. Cover and bake in 350°F (180°C) oven for 12 to 15 minutes or until heated through. Sprinkle with 2 tbsp (25 mL) chopped fresh chives. **Makes 6 servings, 2 crêpes each.**

Makes 6 servings, 2 crêpes each.

PER SERVING, ABOUT:

cal 296	carb . . . . 29 g
pro . . . . 8 g	fibre . . . . 2 g
total fat . . . . 17 g	chol . . . . . 152 mg
sat. fat . . . . . . 9 g	sodium . . 220 mg

PERCENTAGE RDI:

calcium 9%	vit. A 21%
iron 11%	vit. C 87%
folate 26%	

Basic Bread: By Hand and Machine

Afraid of yeast? Here's the recipe that will start your success as a bread baker. It's reassuring to know that modern yeast is very reliable as long as you store it in the refrigerator and respect the best-before date. And to ensure that your bread will rise, our recipes start off by proofing the yeast — that is, letting it work itself into a froth in a small amount of sweetened water. No froth, no rise; get fresh yeast and start again.

1 tsp	granulated sugar	5 mL		2 tbsp	butter	25 mL
1 cup	warm water	250 mL		1 tsp	salt	5 mL
1	pkg active dry yeast (or 1 tbsp/15 mL)	1		5 cups	all-purpose flour (approx)	1.25 L
1 cup	milk	250 mL		1	egg yolk	1
2 tbsp	granulated sugar	25 mL		1 tbsp	water	15 mL

1 In large bowl, dissolve 1 tsp (5 mL) sugar in warm water. Sprinkle in yeast; let stand for 10 minutes or until frothy. Meanwhile, in saucepan, heat together milk, 2 tbsp (25 mL) sugar, butter and salt over low heat just until butter is melted; let cool to lukewarm. Stir into yeast mixture.

2 With electric mixer, gradually beat in 3 cups (750 mL) of the flour until smooth, about 3 minutes. With wooden spoon, gradually stir in enough of the remaining flour to make stiff dough. Turn out onto lightly floured surface; knead for 10 minutes or until smooth and elastic, adding more flour as necessary.

3 Place in greased bowl, turning to grease all over. Cover with plastic wrap; let rise in warm draft-free place for 1 to 1½ hours or until doubled in bulk.

4 Punch down dough; turn out onto lightly floured surface. Knead into ball. Cover with tea towel; let rest for 10 minutes.

5 Divide dough in half; knead each portion into smooth ball. Gently pull into 11- x 8-inch (28 x 20 cm) rectangle. Starting at narrow end, roll up into cylinder; pinch along bottom to smooth and seal. Fit into 2 greased 8- x 4-inch (1.5 L) loaf pans. Cover and let rise for about 1 hour or until doubled in bulk.

6 Whisk egg yolk with water; brush over loaves. Bake in centre of 400°F (200°C) oven for about 30 minutes or until loaves are golden brown and sound hollow when tapped on bottom. Remove from pans; let cool on racks. (MAKE-AHEAD: Wrap in plastic wrap, overwrap with heavy-duty foil and freeze for up to 1 month.)

Makes 2 loaves, 12 slices each.

PER SLICE, ABOUT:

cal 116	carb ....22 g
pro ....3 g	fibre ....1 g
total fat .....2 g	chol ......13 mg
sat. fat ......1 g	sodium ..112 mg

PERCENTAGE RDI:

calcium 2%	vit. A 2%
iron 8%	vit. C 0%
folate 18%	

BREAD MACHINE BASIC BREAD

Into pan of 1½- to 2-lb (750 g to 1 kg) bread machine, place (in order) ½ cup (125 mL) each water and milk, 1 tbsp (15 mL) each granulated sugar and cubed butter, ½ tsp (2 mL) salt, 3 cups (750 mL) all-purpose flour and 1¼ tsp (6 mL) quick-rising (instant) dry yeast. (Do not let yeast touch liquids.) Choose basic or regular/light setting. (Note: If you like, you can simply make the dough in the machine and bake as per hand-kneaded dough, previous page.) Remove baked loaf from pan; let cool on rack. **Makes 1 loaf, 12 slices.**

BREAD MACHINE Success

🍃 Bread machine dough is much lighter in texture than handmade dough. Let it rest between rolling because it will be more elastic than handmade dough.

🍃 Bread machines give best results with quick-rising dry yeast. It is specially formulated to be added to dry ingredients and to dissolve and activate immediately.

🍃 Bread machine yeast is a particularly active strain of yeast with increased levels of ascorbic acid (vitamin C). It was developed specifically for use in bread machines. Use the same measurement as for quick-rising dry yeast. Store yeast in the refrigerator and always check the expiry date before using.

🍃 Have all the ingredients at room temperature for best results.

HOW TO Adapt a Recipe
FOR THE BREAD MACHINE

🍃 It may take a number of attempts to get the formula for your favourite recipe just right for your bread machine. Write down the quantities that work for you.

🍃 Using the manufacturer's manual as a guide, determine the amount of flour (number of cups) that you can use in your bread machine. You must not exceed this amount or you might damage the machine.

🍃 For each 1 cup (250 mL) flour used, you will need approximately ⅓ cup (75 mL) liquid, at least 1 tsp (5 mL) sugar, honey or other sweetener, ¼ tsp (1 mL) salt and ½ tsp (2 mL) bread machine or quick-rising (instant) dry yeast. Do not leave out the sweetener or the salt; both are needed for successful yeast dough.

🍃 If fat is called for in the recipe, use at least 1 tsp (5 mL) room temperature solid fat or vegetable oil per 1 cup (250 mL) flour.

🍃 Remove the bread pan from the machine before adding any ingredients. Add ingredients to the pan in the order suggested. Yeast must remain dry until the machine starts to mix ingredients.

🍃 Be present when the machine starts to knead the ingredients. Open the lid and look at the dough ball during the first knead: if it is too firm and dry, or if the bread machine seems to be straining, add liquid, a few drops at a time, until machine stops straining; if it is too sticky, add enough flour, a spoonful at a time, to make it smooth.

Buttermilk Loaf

These glossy loaves combine a fine, even texture, mild dairy tang and a warm butter-scotch colour. Make one, freeze one and enjoy how beautifully they slice for sandwiches. Or add cheese to one or both of the loaves as suggested in the variation.

Pinch	granulated sugar	Pinch	2 tbsp	liquid honey	25 mL
⅓ cup	warm water	75 mL	1	egg, beaten	1
2½ tsp	active dry yeast	12 mL	6 cups	all-purpose flour (approx)	1.5 L
2 cups	buttermilk	500 mL	1½ tsp	salt	7 mL
⅓ cup	butter, melted	75 mL	1 tbsp	milk	15 mL

1 In large bowl, dissolve sugar in warm water. Sprinkle in yeast; let stand for 10 minutes or until frothy. Stir in buttermilk, butter, honey and egg. With electric mixer, gradually beat in 3 cups (750 mL) of the flour and salt until smooth. With wooden spoon, gradually stir in 2¾ cups (675 mL) of the remaining flour to form slightly moist dough.

2 Turn out dough onto lightly floured surface; knead for about 8 minutes or until smooth and elastic, adding as much of the remaining flour as necessary. Place in greased bowl, turning to grease all over. Cover with plastic wrap; let rise in warm draft-free place for 1 to 1½ hours or until doubled in bulk.

3 Punch down dough; turn out onto lightly floured surface. Divide in half; knead each into ball. Cover with tea towel; let rest for 5 minutes. Press each into 12- x 9-inch (30 x 23 cm) rectangle. Starting at narrow end, roll up into cylinder; pinch along bottom to smooth and seal. Fit into 2 greased 9- x 5-inch (2 L) loaf pans. Cover and let rise for 1 to 1½ hours or until ½ inch (1 cm) above rim of pan and dough does not spring back when lightly pressed.

4 Brush top of each loaf with milk. With sharp knife, cut slash about ¾ inch (2 cm) deep along length of top. Bake in centre of 350°F (180°C) oven for 45 to 55 minutes or until golden brown and loaves sound hollow when tapped on bottom. Remove from pans; let cool on racks.

Makes 2 loaves, 12 slices each.

PER SLICE, ABOUT:

cal	154	carb	26 g
pro	4 g	fibre	1 g
total fat	3 g	chol	17 mg
sat. fat	2 g	sodium	195 mg

PERCENTAGE RDI:

calcium	3%	vit. A	3%
iron	10%	vit. C	0%
folate	20%		

VARIATION

Buttermilk Cheddar Loaf: For each loaf, cut 5 oz (150 g) old Cheddar cheese into ½-inch (1 cm) cubes and freeze until firm. Sprinkle cheese on dough rectangle before rolling up into cylinder. Serve loaf warm.

Country Seed Bread

This nutty-flavoured loaf has an attractive slash along the top. For a higher, lighter loaf, use whole wheat or whole grain flour especially formulated for bread, now available in most supermarkets.

2 cups	all-purpose flour (approx)	500 mL		2 tsp	quick-rising (instant) dry yeast	10 mL
1 cup	whole wheat flour	250 mL		1¼ cups	very warm water	300 mL
¼ cup	flax seeds	50 mL		2 tbsp	liquid honey	25 mL
2 tbsp	sesame seeds	25 mL		2 tbsp	vegetable oil	25 mL
1 tbsp	poppy seeds	15 mL		1½ tsp	salt	7 mL

TEST KITCHEN TIP: For a nuttier flavour, toast seeds on baking sheet in 350°F (180°C) oven for 4 minutes; let cool.

1   In large bowl, whisk together all-purpose and whole wheat flours, flax seeds, sesame seeds, poppy seeds and yeast. In small bowl, stir together water, honey, oil and salt; stir into flour mixture to form sticky dough.

2   Turn out dough onto lightly floured surface; knead for about 8 minutes or until dough springs back when pressed in centre and surface is still slightly sticky, adding up to ¼ cup (50 mL) more all-purpose flour as necessary. Place in greased bowl, turning to grease all over. Cover with plastic wrap; let rise in warm draft-free place for about 1¼ hours or until doubled in bulk.

3   Punch down dough; turn out onto lightly floured surface. Gently pull into 11- x 8-inch (28 x 20 cm) rectangle. Starting at narrow end, roll up into cylinder; pinch along bottom to smooth and seal. Fit into greased 8- x 4-inch (1.5 L) loaf pan. Cover and let rise for 1 hour or until doubled in bulk and ¾ inch (2 cm) above rim of pan.

4   Brush top of loaf with water. With sharp knife, cut slash about 1 inch (2.5 cm) deep along length of top. Bake in centre of 400°F (200°C) oven for 15 minutes. Reduce heat to 350°F (180°C); bake for 30 to 35 minutes or until brown and loaf sounds hollow when tapped on bottom. Remove from pan; let cool on rack.

BREAD MACHINE VARIATION

Country Seed Bread: Into pan of 1½- to 2-lb (750 g to 1 kg) bread machine, place (in order) water, honey, oil, salt, all-purpose and whole wheat flours, flax seeds, sesame seeds, poppy seeds and yeast. (Do not let yeast touch liquids.) Choose whole wheat setting. If machine differentiates between fresh and powdered milk, choose powdered milk setting. (Note: If you like, you can simply make the dough in the machine and bake as per hand-kneaded dough above.) Remove baked loaf from pan; let cool on rack.

Makes 1 loaf, 12 slices.

PER SLICE, ABOUT:

cal	172	carb	28 g
pro	5 g	fibre	3 g
total fat	5 g	chol	0 mg
sat. fat	trace	sodium	292 mg

PERCENTAGE RDI:

calcium	3%	vit. A	0%
iron	13%	vit. C	0%
folate	19%		

Caraway Rye Bread

With a gentle rye flavour that's spiced with caraway, this lovely loaf bakes up into a burnished dome.

1 tsp	packed brown sugar	5 mL		½ tsp	salt	2 mL
1 cup	warm water	250 mL		4 cups	all-purpose flour (approx)	1 L
4 tsp	active dry yeast	20 mL		2 cups	rye flour	500 mL
1 cup	warm milk	250 mL		2 tbsp	cocoa powder, sifted	25 mL
¼ cup	fancy molasses	50 mL		2 tbsp	caraway seeds, crushed	25 mL
¼ cup	butter, softened	50 mL		1	egg, lightly beaten	1
1 tbsp	cider vinegar	15 mL				

1 In large bowl, dissolve sugar in warm water. Sprinkle in yeast; let stand for 10 minutes or until frothy. Whisk in milk, molasses, butter, vinegar and salt. Gradually beat in 2½ cups (625 mL) of the all-purpose flour, rye flour, cocoa and caraway seeds until smooth. With wooden spoon, gradually stir in 1 cup (250 mL) of the remaining flour to make soft but not sticky dough.

2 Turn out dough onto lightly floured surface; knead for 8 to 10 minutes or until smooth and elastic, adding enough of the remaining flour as necessary. Place in greased bowl, turning to grease all over. Cover with plastic wrap; let rise in warm draft-free place for about 1 hour or until doubled in bulk.

3 Punch down dough; divide in half. Form each into oval; fit into 2 greased 8- x 4-inch (1.5 L) loaf pans. Cover and let rise for about 1 hour or until doubled in bulk. Brush with egg.

4 Bake in centre of 350°F (180°C) oven for 35 to 45 minutes or until golden brown and loaves sound hollow when tapped on bottom. Remove from pans; let cool on racks.

Makes 2 loaves, 12 slices each.

PER SLICE, ABOUT:

cal	146	carb	26 g
pro	4 g	fibre	2 g
total fat	3 g	chol	15 mg
sat. fat	1 g	sodium	78 mg

PERCENTAGE RDI:

calcium	3%	vit. A	3%
iron	11%	vit. C	0%
folate	18%		

FLOUR Facts

All-purpose flour is a mixture of 80 per cent hard wheat and 20 per cent soft wheat. Because Canadian wheat has such a high protein content, we can use all-purpose flour for our loaves and still get fabulous results.

Specialty bread flours are also available at supermarkets and at bulk and health food stores. They have a higher gluten content than all-purpose flour, so you may want to increase the liquid and shorten your kneading time slightly.

Whole wheat flour is milled from the entire wheat kernel, including the bran and germ. It has a richer flavour and higher nutritional value than all-purpose flour.

Store all flours in airtight containers; store whole grain flour in the refrigerator or freezer to prevent it from going rancid.

Ciabatta

The new darling of the flatbreads, ciabatta, or slipper bread, features a crusty floured surface. Ciabatta is great company for soups, stews and other dinner entrées.

SPONGE:

¼ tsp	active dry yeast	1 mL
⅔ cup	warm water	150 mL
1¼ cups	all-purpose flour	300 mL

DOUGH:

Pinch	granulated sugar	Pinch
½ cup	warm water	125 mL

½ tsp	active dry yeast	2 mL
¼ cup	milk	50 mL
1 tbsp	olive oil	15 mL
2 cups	all-purpose flour	500 mL
1½ tsp	salt	7 mL

1 SPONGE: In bowl, stir yeast into warm water until dissolved; stir in flour until smooth. Cover with plastic wrap and refrigerate for at least 12 hours or for up to 24 hours.

2 DOUGH: In bowl of electric mixer, dissolve sugar in warm water. Sprinkle in yeast; let stand for 10 minutes or until frothy. Using dough hook on low speed, stir in sponge, milk and oil until combined. Add flour and salt; mix on low speed for 8 minutes, scraping down bowl halfway through.

3 Turn out dough onto well-floured surface; knead lightly into ball. Place in greased bowl, turning to grease all over. Cover with plastic wrap; let rise in warm draft-free place for about 1½ hours or until doubled in bulk and bubbles appear on surface.

4 Scrape dough out of bowl onto lightly floured surface; divide in half. With floured hands, gently form each into cylinder, pinching seam firmly to seal. Pull each out to 9- x 4-inch (23 x 10 cm) rectangle. Place each, seam side up, on well-floured tea towel. Cover with damp tea towel; let rise for about 1½ hours or until not quite doubled in bulk and bubbles appear on surface.

5 Gently flip rectangles over onto 2 floured rimless baking sheets. Spray with water. Bake on bottom and middle racks of 425°F (220°C) oven for 10 minutes. Switch baking sheets; spray with water. Bake for 12 to 15 minutes longer or until golden brown and bread sounds hollow when tapped on bottom. Remove from pans; let cool on racks.

Makes 2 loaves, 4 servings each.

PER SERVING, ABOUT:

cal	205	carb	39 g
pro	6 g	fibre	2 g
total fat	2 g	chol	1 mg
sat. fat	trace	sodium	436 mg

PERCENTAGE RDI:

calcium	2%	vit. A	0%
iron	15%	vit. C	0%
folate	29%		

Lavash

Cracker thin and cracker crisp, lavash is delicious with soups, dips and cheeses. Try a variety of seeds or herbs for a change of pace.

5½ cups	all-purpose flour (approx)	1.375 L
1¼ cups	warm water	300 mL
3	eggs	3
2 tsp	each salt and granulated sugar	10 mL

2 tsp	active dry yeast	10 mL
3 tbsp	each sesame and poppy seeds	50 mL
2 tbsp	fennel seeds or aniseeds	25 mL

1 Set aside ½ cup (125 mL) of the flour for rolling. In large bowl, whisk together water, eggs, salt, sugar and yeast. With wooden spoon, stir in 4 cups (1 L) of the flour, 1 cup (250 mL) at a time; beat until smooth. Stir in enough of the remaining flour to make soft sticky dough.

2 Turn out dough onto lightly floured surface. Knead a few times until dough holds together. Place in greased bowl, turning to grease all over. Cover with plastic wrap; let rise in warm draft-free place for about 1 hour or until doubled in bulk.

3 In small bowl, combine sesame seeds, poppy seeds and fennel seeds; set aside.

4 Punch down dough; cut into quarters. Using reserved flour, dust work surface; place 1 piece on surface. Cover and refrigerate remaining dough. Keeping surface floured, roll out to 15- x 11-inch (38 x 28 cm) rectangle, letting dough rest occasionally to prevent springing back. Place on greased baking sheet; gently stretch back to rectangle. Brush with water; prick all over with fork. Sprinkle with one-quarter of the seeds; press lightly.

5 Bake in centre of 400°F (200°C) oven, turning pan halfway through, for 15 to 20 minutes or until golden and crisp. Let cool on pan on rack. Repeat with remaining dough and seeds. Break cooled breads into random shapes. (MAKE-AHEAD: Store in airtight container for up to 5 days.)

Makes 4 cracker breads, about 80 pieces.

Nova Scotia Oatmeal Rolls

Breadbaskets in this Atlantic province often boast thick slices of moist nutty-flavoured oatmeal bread. The dough makes a dozen rolls or two delicious loaves of bread.

½ cup	packed brown sugar	125 mL
½ cup	warm water	125 mL
2	pkg active dry yeast (or 2 tbsp/25 mL)	2
1¼ cups	boiling water	300 mL
1 cup	quick-cooking rolled oats	250 mL
⅓ cup	butter, softened	75 mL

1½ tsp	salt	7 mL
2	eggs, lightly beaten	2
4½ cups	all-purpose flour (approx)	1.125 L
1 cup	whole wheat flour	250 mL
TOPPING:		
1	egg, lightly beaten	1
¼ cup	quick-cooking rolled oats	50 mL

1 In small bowl, dissolve 1 tsp (5 mL) of the sugar in warm water. Sprinkle in yeast; let stand for 10 minutes or until frothy. Meanwhile, in large bowl, stir together remaining sugar, boiling water, rolled oats, butter and salt, stirring until sugar is dissolved and butter is melted. Let cool to lukewarm. Stir in yeast mixture and eggs. With electric mixer, beat in 2 cups (500 mL) of the all-purpose flour and whole wheat flour. With wooden spoon, stir in enough of the remaining all-purpose flour to make soft dough.

2 Turn out dough onto lightly floured surface; knead for 8 to 10 minutes or until smooth and elastic, adding enough of the remaining flour as necessary. Place in greased bowl, turning to grease all over. Cover with plastic wrap; let rise in warm draft-free place for about 1 hour or until doubled in bulk.

3 Punch down dough; turn out onto lightly floured surface. Divide into 12 portions. Shape each into ball, stretching and pinching dough underneath to make tops smooth. Place 2 inches (5 cm) apart on greased baking sheets. Cover and let rise for 30 to 45 minutes or until doubled in bulk.

4 TOPPING: Brush rolls with egg; sprinkle with rolled oats. Bake in centre of 375°F (190°C) oven for 30 minutes or until rolls sound hollow when tapped on bottom. Remove from pans; let cool on racks.

TEST KITCHEN TIP: Regular and quick-cooking rolled oats are made from oat groats (kernels) that have been steamed and rolled. They are generally interchangeable, but not with instant oats for which the groats have been precooked and dried before rolling. When mixed with liquid, instant oats become very soft — just what you want for cereal but a gooey disaster for the likes of breads and muffins.

Makes 12 rolls.

PER ROLL, ABOUT:

cal	339	carb	58 g
pro	10 g	fibre	4 g
total fat	8 g	chol	67 mg
sat. fat	4 g	sodium	361 mg

PERCENTAGE RDI:

calcium	3%	vit. A	7%
iron	23%	vit. C	0%
folate	41%		

Cinnamon Buns

The bread part is really just an excuse for cinnamon, butter and brown sugar.

¼ cup	granulated sugar	50 mL
½ cup	warm water	125 mL
1	pkg active dry yeast (or 1 tbsp/15 mL)	1
½ cup	milk	125 mL
¼ cup	butter	50 mL
1 tsp	salt	5 mL
2	eggs, beaten	2
4 cups	all-purpose flour (approx)	1 L

FILLING:		
1 cup	butter	250 mL
1½ cups	packed brown sugar	375 mL
1 cup	coarsely chopped pecans	250 mL
1 tbsp	cinnamon	15 mL

1 In large bowl, dissolve 1 tsp (5 mL) of the sugar in warm water. Sprinkle in yeast; let stand for 10 minutes or until frothy. Meanwhile, in saucepan, heat together remaining sugar, milk, butter and salt until butter is melted; let cool to lukewarm. Add eggs and milk mixture to yeast mixture; stir to combine. With electric mixer, gradually beat in 1½ cups (375 mL) of the flour; beat for 2 minutes or until smooth. With wooden spoon, gradually stir in enough of remaining flour to make soft, slightly sticky dough that comes away from side of bowl.

2 Turn out onto lightly floured surface; knead for 7 to 10 minutes or until smooth and elastic, adding enough of the remaining flour as necessary. Place in greased bowl, turning to grease all over. Cover and let rise in warm draft-free place for 1 to 1½ hours (or in refrigerator for 8 hours) or until doubled in bulk and impression remains when fingertips are pressed into dough.

3 FILLING: In saucepan over medium heat, melt ¾ cup (175 mL) of the butter with ¾ cup (175 mL) of the sugar, whisking. Pour into greased 13- x 9-inch (3 L) glass baking dish. Sprinkle with half of the pecans; set aside. Melt remaining butter; set aside. Combine remaining sugar, pecans and cinnamon; set aside.

4 Punch down dough. Turn out onto lightly floured surface; roll out into 18- x 14-inch (45 x 35 cm) rectangle. Brush with all but 2 tbsp (25 mL) of the melted butter, leaving ½-inch (1 cm) border uncovered; sprinkle with sugar mixture. Starting at long side, tightly roll up, pinching seam to seal. Brush with remaining butter. With serrated knife, cut into 15 pieces; place, cut sides down, in pan. Cover and let rise for 1 hour or until doubled in bulk.

5 Bake in centre of 375°F (190°C) oven for 25 to 30 minutes or until golden and tops sound hollow when tapped. Let stand in dish for 3 minutes. Invert onto flat serving platter, scraping off remaining filling in dish to drizzle over buns.

Makes 15 buns.

PER BUN, ABOUT:

cal	420	carb	52 g
pro	6 g	fibre	2 g
total fat	22 g	chol	71 mg
sat. fat	10 g	sodium	330 mg

PERCENTAGE RDI:

calcium	5%	vit. A	16%
iron	17%	vit. C	0%
folate	25%		

Hot Cross Buns

One a penny, two a penny, hot cross buns. Save a penny and make currant-studded hot cross buns that will fill your kitchen with a heavenly spicy fragrance and thrill the whole household.

½ cup	granulated sugar	125 mL
¼ cup	warm water	50 mL
1	pkg active dry yeast (or 1 tbsp/15 mL)	1
3½ cups	all-purpose flour	875 mL
2 tbsp	cinnamon	25 mL
1 tsp	nutmeg	5 mL
½ tsp	salt	2 mL
¼ tsp	ground cloves	1 mL
¾ cup	warm milk	175 mL
¼ cup	butter, melted	50 mL

1	egg	1
1	egg yolk	1
½ cup	dried currants	125 mL
¼ cup	chopped mixed candied peel	50 mL
GLAZE:		
2 tbsp	each granulated sugar and water	25 mL
ICING:		
½ cup	icing sugar	125 mL
2 tsp	water	10 mL

1 In small bowl, dissolve 1 tbsp (15 mL) of the sugar in warm water. Sprinkle in yeast; let stand for 10 minutes or until frothy. Meanwhile, in large bowl, whisk together remaining sugar, flour, cinnamon, nutmeg, salt and cloves; make well in centre. Whisk together milk, butter, egg and egg yolk; pour into well. Pour in yeast mixture. With wooden spoon, stir until soft dough forms.

2 Turn out dough onto lightly floured surface; knead for 8 minutes or until smooth and elastic. Place in greased bowl, turning to grease all over. Cover with plastic wrap; let rise in warm draft-free place for about 1 hour or until doubled in bulk.

3 Punch down dough; turn out onto lightly floured surface. Knead in currants and peel. Shape into 12-inch (30 cm) log; with serrated knife, cut into 9 pieces. Shape each into ball, stretching and pinching dough underneath to make tops smooth. Place 2 inches (5 cm) apart on greased baking sheet. Cover and let rise for about 35 minutes or until doubled in bulk. Bake in centre of 400°F (200°C) oven for about 15 minutes or until golden brown.

4 GLAZE: In saucepan, stir sugar with water over medium heat until dissolved; brush over buns. Let cool on pan.

5 ICING: Stir icing sugar with water. Using piping bag fitted with round tip, pipe cross on top of each cooled bun. Or drizzle on with small spoon.

BREAD MACHINE VARIATION

Hot Cross Loaf: Reduce flour to 3¼ cups (800 mL). Into pan of bread machine, place (in order) water, milk, butter, sugar, egg, egg yolk, salt, flour, cinnamon, nutmeg, cloves and yeast. (Do not let yeast touch liquid.) Choose sweet dough setting; after first kneading, add currants and peel. Remove baked loaf from pan; let cool on rack. **Makes 1 loaf, 12 slices.**

TEST KITCHEN TIP: To make 18 buns by hand, increase the yeast to 4 tsp (20 mL) and double the other ingredients.

Makes 9 buns.

PER BUN, ABOUT:

cal	370	carb 69 g
pro	8 g	fibre 3 g
total fat	7 g	chol 64 mg
sat. fat	4 g	sodium 205 mg

PERCENTAGE RDI:

calcium	6%	vit. A 8%
iron	22%	vit. C 2%
folate	36%	

MAKE-AHEAD

Pecan Kugelhopf

Made like a cake, and just as rich, this tall, proud confection needs but one rise. Traditionally baked in a special fluted mould, kugelhopf can also be made in a tube pan.

SUBSTITUTION: Replace dried cranberries with currants or golden raisins.

1 cup	chopped toasted pecans	250 mL
½ cup	granulated sugar	125 mL
¼ cup	warm water	50 mL
1	pkg active dry yeast (or 1 tbsp/15 mL)	1
1½ cups	dried cranberries	375 mL
¾ cup	butter, softened	175 mL

4	eggs	4
¾ cup	milk	175 mL
1 tbsp	grated lemon rind	15 mL
1 tsp	salt	5 mL
4 cups	all-purpose flour (approx)	1 L
1 tbsp	icing sugar	15 mL

1 Generously butter large kugelhopf pan or 10-inch (4 L) tube pan. Sprinkle with ¼ cup (50 mL) of the pecans. Set aside.

2 In small bowl, dissolve 1 tsp (5 mL) of the sugar in warm water. Sprinkle in yeast; let stand for 10 minutes or until frothy. Meanwhile, in small saucepan, bring cranberries and ⅓ cup (75 mL) water to boil; reduce heat to medium-low, cover and simmer for 3 minutes. Drain if necessary; let cool.

3 In large bowl, beat butter with remaining sugar until light and fluffy. Beat in eggs, 1 at a time, until blended. With electric mixer on low speed, beat in yeast mixture, milk, lemon rind and salt. Beat in 2 cups (500 mL) of the flour; beat at medium speed for 5 minutes. With wooden spoon, stir in cranberries, remaining pecans and enough of the remaining flour, ½ cup (125 mL) at a time, to make slightly stiff sticky dough. Turn into prepared pan. Cover with greased waxed paper; let rise in warm draft-free place for about 1½ hours or until about ½ inch (1 cm) from top of pan. Remove paper.

4 Bake in centre of 375°F (190°C) oven for 45 to 50 minutes or until cake tester inserted in centre comes out clean. Invert onto rack; let cool. (MAKE-AHEAD: Wrap in plastic wrap and store at room temperature for up to 2 days.) Dust with icing sugar.

Makes 1 large loaf, 16 slices.

PER SLICE, ABOUT:

cal 321	carb .... 41 g
pro .... 6 g	fibre .... 2 g
total fat .... 15 g	chol ...... 78 mg
sat. fat ...... 6 g	sodium .. 254 mg

PERCENTAGE RDI:

calcium 3%	vit. A 11%
iron 12%	vit. C 5%
folate 25%	

Challah

The "ch" in this traditional Jewish egg bread is pronounced more like a gutteral "h." Here are two ways to form challah: braided and — especially for Jewish New Year, Rosh Hashanah — a glorious crown.

2 tsp	granulated sugar	10 mL
½ cup	warm water	125 mL
1	pkg active dry yeast (or 1 tbsp/15 mL)	1
3½ cups	all-purpose flour (approx)	875 mL
1 tsp	salt	5 mL
¼ cup	liquid honey	50 mL

2	eggs, lightly beaten	2
2	egg yolks	2
¼ cup	butter, melted, or vegetable oil	50 mL
¾ cup	golden raisins	175 mL
TOPPING:		
1	egg yolk	1
1 tbsp	sesame seeds	15 mL

1 In small bowl, dissolve sugar in warm water. Sprinkle in yeast; let stand for 10 minutes or until frothy. In large bowl, stir 3 cups (750 mL) of the flour with salt. With wooden spoon, stir in yeast mixture, honey, eggs, egg yolks and butter until ragged dough forms. Turn out onto lightly floured surface; knead for 10 minutes or until smooth and elastic, adding enough of the remaining flour as necessary. Place in greased bowl, turning to grease all over. Cover with plastic wrap; let rise in warm draft-free place for about 1 hour or until doubled in bulk and indentation remains when dough is poked with 2 fingers. Punch down dough; knead in raisins. Let rest for 5 minutes.

2 TO MAKE CROWN: Roll dough into 30-inch (76 cm) long rope. Holding 1 end in place, wind remaining rope around end to form fairly tight spiral that is slightly higher in centre. Transfer to lightly greased baking sheet.

3 TO MAKE BRAID: Divide dough into quarters; roll each into 18-inch (45 cm) long rope. Place ropes side by side on greased baking sheet; pinch together at 1 end. Starting at pinched end, move second rope from left over rope on its right. Move far right rope over 2 ropes on left. Move far left rope over 2 ropes on right. Repeat until braid is complete; tuck ends under braid.

4 Cover crown loaf or braid loaf loosely with plastic wrap. Let rise in warm draft-free place for about 1 hour or until doubled in bulk.

5 TOPPING: Lightly beat egg yolk with 1 tsp (5 mL) water; brush over loaf. Sprinkle with sesame seeds. Bake in centre of 350°F (180°C) oven for 35 to 45 minutes or until golden brown and loaf sounds hollow when tapped on bottom. Remove from pan; let cool on rack.

BREAD MACHINE VARIATION

Challah (for dough only): Replace active dry yeast with 2½ tsp (12 mL) quick-rising (instant) dry yeast. Into pan of bread machine, place (in order) water, honey, sugar, butter, eggs, egg yolks, salt, flour and yeast. (Do not let yeast touch liquid.) Choose dough setting. When complete, remove from pan. Knead in raisins if desired. Let rest for 5 minutes. Shape and bake as directed.

TEST KITCHEN TIP: Challah, fresh or day-old, makes the finest French toast and bread puddings.

Makes 1 loaf, 16 servings.

PER SERVING, ABOUT:

cal	190	carb	32 g
pro	5 g	fibre	2 g
total fat	5 g	chol	76 mg
sat. fat	2 g	sodium	184 mg

PERCENTAGE RDI:

calcium	2%	vit. A	6%
iron	11%	vit. C	0%
folate	22%		

Desserts

11

Five Dessert Crisps 280

Bumbleberry Cobbler 281

Lemon Sponge Pudding 282

Very Special Bread Pudding with Orange Crème Anglaise 283

Vanilla Soufflé with Passion Fruit Sauce 284

Icky Sticky Baked Date Pudding 285

Plum Pudding 286

Port Lemon Crème Caramel 288

Crème Brûlée 289

Panna Cotta with Raspberry Strawberry Sauce 290

Tiramisu 291

Very Berry Trifle 292

Fresh Fruit Pavlova 293

Ice and Easy Sorbets 294

Strawberry Ice Cream 295

Frozen Lemon Meringue Torte 296

Rhubarb and Strawberry Compote 297

Caramel-Baked Pear Sundaes 298

Roasted Pears in Port 299

Chocolate Fondue 299

Five Dessert Crisps

Five fruit combos, from strawberries with rhubarb to pears with cranberries, bring you pleasing crunchy-topped fruit desserts from spring right through to fall harvest.

	FRUIT	ADD-INS	TOPPING TOUCHES
Strawberry Rhubarb Crisp	4 cups (1 L) sliced fresh or thawed frozen rhubarb; 2 cups (500 mL) halved fresh strawberries	⅓ cup (75 mL) packed brown sugar; 2 tbsp (25 mL) all-purpose flour	¼ cup (50 mL) all-purpose flour; 1 tsp (5 mL) grated orange rind
Almond Cherry Crisp	4 cups (1 L) drained thawed pitted sour cherries or pitted fresh sweet black cherries; 2 cups (500 mL) diced peeled apples	⅓ cup (75 mL) granulated sugar; 3 tbsp (50 mL) all-purpose flour for sour cherries or 2 tbsp (25 mL) for sweet; 2 tsp (10 mL) lemon juice	¾ cup (175 mL) chopped blanched almonds; ¼ cup (50 mL) all-purpose flour; 1 tsp (5 mL) grated lemon rind
Peach Berry Crisp	5 cups (1.25 L) sliced peeled peaches or nectarines; 1 cup (250 mL) fresh raspberries or blueberries	⅓ cup (75 mL) packed brown sugar; 2 tbsp (25 mL) all-purpose flour	¼ cup (50 mL) all-purpose flour; ½ tsp (2 mL) ground ginger
Spiced Plum Apple Crisp	4 cups (1 L) sliced pitted plums; 2 cups (500 mL) sliced peeled apples	⅓ cup (75 mL) packed brown sugar; 2 tbsp (25 mL) all-purpose flour; 1 tsp (5 mL) cinnamon; ½ tsp (2 mL) ground nutmeg	¾ cup (175 mL) quick-cooking rolled oats (not instant); 2 tbsp (25 mL) packed brown sugar
Pear Cranberry Crisp	4 cups (1 L) sliced peeled pears; 2 cups (500 mL) fresh or frozen cranberries	¼ cup (50 mL) liquid honey; 2 tbsp (25 mL) all-purpose flour	¾ cup (175 mL) quick-cooking rolled oats (not instant); ½ cup (125 mL) chopped pecans; 2 tbsp (25 mL) packed brown sugar

TEST KITCHEN TIP: Fruit crisps have a natural affinity for cream, whether it's ice cream, sour cream, pouring cream or whipped cream. You can cut back on the fat with frozen vanilla yogurt, sour cream or thick yogurt.

1 In large bowl, gently toss Fruit in first column with Add-Ins in second column. Arrange evenly in greased 8-inch (2 L) square glass baking dish.

2 In separate bowl, combine ¾ cup (175 mL) all-purpose flour, ⅔ cup (150 mL) packed brown sugar and Topping Touches in third column. Drizzle with ⅓ cup (75 mL) butter, melted; stir until crumbly. Sprinkle over fruit mixture.

3 Bake in centre of 350°F (180°C) oven for 45 to 60 minutes or until bubbly, topping is golden and fruit is tender.

Makes 6 servings.

Bumbleberry Cobbler

There never has been a bumbleberry bush — nor will there ever be one. Bumbleberry denotes a fragrant combination of berries, fruit and rhubarb.

2 cups	each raspberries and blueberries	500 mL
1½ cups	chopped rhubarb	375 mL
1½ cups	sliced peaches or nectarines	375 mL
½ cup	granulated sugar	125 mL
2 tbsp	cornstarch	25 mL

BISCUIT TOPPING:		
1½ cups	all-purpose flour	375 mL
¼ cup	granulated sugar	50 mL
1 tsp	baking powder	5 mL
½ tsp	baking soda	2 mL
Pinch	salt	Pinch
¼ cup	cold butter	50 mL
⅔ cup	buttermilk	150 mL
½ tsp	vanilla	2 mL

1 In bowl, toss together raspberries, blueberries, rhubarb, peaches, sugar and cornstarch; spoon into greased 8-inch (2 L) square glass baking dish. Set aside.

2 BISCUIT TOPPING: In large bowl, whisk together flour, sugar, baking powder, baking soda and salt. Using pastry blender or 2 knives, cut in butter until crumbly. Stir buttermilk with vanilla; drizzle over flour mixture and stir with fork just until soft sticky dough forms. Gather dough into ball. Turn out onto floured work surface and pat into 8-inch (20 cm) square. Cut into 6 pieces and place on top of fruit. Or drop by spoonfuls over fruit.

3 Bake in centre of 375°F (190°C) oven for about 45 minutes or until filling is bubbly and topping is light golden and no longer doughy underneath when lifted with spoon. Let cool for 20 minutes before serving.

VARIATION

Bumbleberry Cobbler on the Barbecue: Line bottom of 8-inch (2 L) square foil pan with double thickness of foil. Place second foil pan inside and line with double thickness of foil, leaving 1-inch (2.5 cm) overhang; grease pan. Spoon in fruit mixture; top with biscuit topping. Pull up overhang of foil to prevent juices from running over. Place on grill over medium-low heat; close lid and cook for about 45 minutes or until filling is bubbly and topping is light golden and no longer doughy underneath when lifted with spoon.

Makes 6 servings.

PER SERVING, ABOUT:

cal	375	carb	71 g
pro	5 g	fibre	5 g
total fat	9 g	chol	23 mg
sat. fat	5 g	sodium	237 mg

PERCENTAGE RDI:

calcium	12%	vit. A	11%
iron	13%	vit. C	25%
folate	20%		

Lemon Sponge Pudding

Such an old favourite but still a real crowd-pleaser, this tangy-sweet pudding goes into the oven as one batter and comes out with a light sponge cake layer on top and creamy lemon sauce on the bottom.

1 cup	granulated sugar	250 mL	3 tbsp	butter, melted	50 mL
3 tbsp	all-purpose flour	50 mL	3	eggs, separated	3
¼ tsp	salt	1 mL	1 tbsp	finely grated lemon rind	15 mL
1 cup	milk	250 mL	⅓ cup	lemon juice	75 mL

1 In large bowl, whisk together ¾ cup (175 mL) of the sugar, flour and salt; whisk in milk, butter and egg yolks. Whisk in lemon rind and juice.

2 In separate bowl, beat egg whites until soft peaks form; beat in remaining sugar, 1 tbsp (15 mL) at a time, until stiff peaks form. Stir about one-quarter into lemon mixture; fold in remaining egg whites.

3 Scrape into 8-inch (2 L) square glass baking dish. Place in larger shallow pan. Pour enough boiling water into pan to come halfway up sides of dish. Bake in centre of 350°F (180°C) oven for 30 to 40 minutes or until top is lightly browned and set. Remove from heat. Let cool on rack for about 30 minutes. Serve warm or cool.

Makes 6 servings.

PER SERVING, ABOUT:

cal 255	carb . . . . 40 g
pro . . . . 5 g	fibre . . . . trace
total fat . . . . . 9 g	chol . . . . . 126 mg
sat. fat . . . . . . 5 g	sodium . . 207 mg

PERCENTAGE RDI:

calcium 6%	vit. A 12%
iron 4%	vit. C 10%
folate 7%	

Very Special Bread Pudding with Orange Crème Anglaise

This cranberry-studded pudding is a sophisticated take on a down-home dish that's guaranteed to delight both old-fashioned and modern palates. The creamy crème anglaise (pouring custard sauce) is spiked with liqueur.

16	slices egg bread, challah or home-style bread (about 1 loaf, or 1 lb/500 g)	16
1½ cups	cranberries, fresh or frozen	375 mL
1 tbsp	grated orange rind	15 mL
6	eggs	6
3 cups	milk	750 mL
1 cup	whipping cream	250 mL
¾ cup	granulated sugar	175 mL
1 tsp	vanilla	5 mL

ORANGE CRÈME ANGLAISE:

1 cup	whipping cream	250 mL
1	strip (1 inch/2.5 cm wide) orange rind	1
3	egg yolks	3
¼ cup	granulated sugar	50 mL
¼ cup	orange-flavoured liqueur or thawed frozen orange juice concentrate (optional)	50 mL

1 Trim off bread crusts; cut bread into 1-inch (2.5 cm) cubes. Arrange half in greased 12-inch (2.5 L) oval baking dish; scatter two-thirds each of the cranberries and orange rind over top. Cover with remaining bread cubes; top with remaining cranberries and orange rind.

2 In large bowl, whisk together eggs, milk, cream, all but 1 tbsp (15 mL) of the sugar and vanilla; pour over bread mixture. Let stand for 15 minutes. Using baster, drizzle liquid over bread mixture several times. (MAKE-AHEAD: Cover with plastic wrap and refrigerate for up to 24 hours.) Sprinkle with remaining sugar.

3 Bake in centre of 375°F (190°C) oven for 45 to 60 minutes or until puffed and golden and knife inserted in centre comes out clean.

4 ORANGE CRÈME ANGLAISE: Meanwhile, in small saucepan, heat cream with orange rind over medium heat just until steaming. Remove from heat; discard orange rind. In small bowl, whisk egg yolks with sugar until pale; gradually whisk in cream. Return to saucepan and cook, stirring constantly and being careful not to boil, for 3 to 5 minutes or until thick enough to coat back of wooden spoon. Strain into pitcher. Stir in liqueur (if using). (MAKE-AHEAD: Place plastic wrap directly on surface and refrigerate for up to 2 days; reheat over low heat or serve cold.) Serve with pudding.

TEST KITCHEN TIPS

• You can use a 13- x 9-inch (3 L) glass baking dish instead of the 12-inch (2.5 L) oval baking dish, but the pudding will not puff as high.

• The orange liqueur and strip of orange rind in the crème anglaise suit the bread pudding particularly well. For other desserts, you can omit both and replace with 2 tsp (10 mL) vanilla or ¼ cup (50 mL) rum, brandy, eau de vie or other liqueur stirred in at the end.

Makes 8 servings.

PER SERVING, ABOUT:

cal	555	carb	56 g
pro	14 g	fibre	2 g
total fat	31 g	chol	350 mg
sat. fat	17 g	sodium	340 mg

PERCENTAGE RDI:

calcium	20%	vit. A	36%
iron	16%	vit. C	5%
folate	22%		

MAKE-
AHEAD

Vanilla Soufflé with Passion Fruit Sauce

Guests wait for the soufflé — not the other way around. There are other sauce choices: raspberry (page 316), strawberry (page 312) and chocolate (page 312).

TEST KITCHEN TIP: To make with fragrant flecks of real vanilla, slit 4-inch (10 cm) piece of vanilla bean lengthwise. Scrape out seeds. Add seeds to saucepan along with milk and bury pod in granulated sugar to flavour sugar for another dessert. Omit liquid vanilla extract.

2 tbsp	butter	25 mL
2 tbsp	all-purpose flour	25 mL
⅔ cup	milk	150 mL
⅔ cup	granulated sugar	150 mL
1 tbsp	vanilla	15 mL
4	eggs, separated	4

¼ tsp	cream of tartar	1 mL
	Icing sugar	
PASSION FRUIT SAUCE:		
3	passion fruits	3
¼ cup	granulated sugar	50 mL

1 PASSION FRUIT SAUCE: Cut passion fruits in half; scoop out pulp and press through fine-mesh sieve into bowl to collect juice and remove seeds. Stir in sugar until dissolved. Set aside. (MAKE-AHEAD: Cover and refrigerate for up to 4 hours.)

2 In saucepan, melt butter over medium heat; whisk in flour and cook, whisking, for 1 minute. Gradually whisk in milk until smooth. Cook, whisking, for 2 minutes or until thickened. Remove from heat. Whisk in half of the sugar and the vanilla. Whisk in egg yolks, 1 at a time. Return to medium heat and cook, whisking, for about 2 minutes or until thickened. Remove from heat.

3 In separate bowl, beat egg whites with cream of tartar until soft peaks form. Gradually beat in remaining sugar, 2 tbsp (25 mL) at a time, until stiff peaks form. Fold one-quarter of the egg whites into yolk mixture; gently fold in remaining egg whites.

4 Divide among six ¾-cup (175 mL) greased ramekins. Place on baking sheet and bake in centre of 375°F (190°C) oven for about 16 minutes or until puffed and almost firm to the touch. Sieve icing sugar over soufflés. Serve immediately with Passion Fruit Sauce.

Makes 6 servings.

PER SERVING, ABOUT:

cal	234	carb	36 g
pro	6 g	fibre	2 g
total fat	8 g	chol	155 mg
sat. fat	4 g	sodium	98 mg

PERCENTAGE RDI:

calcium	5%	vit. A	12%
iron	6%	vit. C	5%
folate	7%		

Icky Sticky Baked Date Pudding

It's interesting how simple homemade desserts often make a lasting impression on guests, sometimes more than fancy time-consuming confections. That's true of this warm date cake with butterscotch sauce, a much talked about dessert from the early 1990s. You won't be disappointed — it's a real bowl-licker.

1¾ cups	chopped dates	425 mL	2	eggs	2
1 cup	water	250 mL	1 tsp	vanilla	5 mL
1 tsp	grated orange rind	5 mL	1¼ cups	all-purpose flour	300 mL
1 tsp	baking soda	5 mL	2 tsp	baking powder	10 mL
½ cup	butter, softened	125 mL	½ tsp	salt	2 mL
⅓ cup	packed brown sugar	75 mL		Toffee Sauce (recipe follows)	

1 In small saucepan, bring dates, water and orange rind to boil; boil for 3 minutes. Remove from heat; stir in baking soda. Set aside.

2 In large bowl, beat butter with brown sugar until fluffy. Beat in eggs, 1 at a time; beat in vanilla. In small bowl, whisk together flour, baking powder and salt; sprinkle half over batter and fold in gently. Fold in date mixture, then remaining flour mixture.

3 Pour into greased 9-inch (2.5 L) square metal cake pan. Bake in centre of 350°F (180°C) oven for 30 to 40 minutes or until cake tester inserted in centre comes out clean. Transfer to rack; let cool slightly. (MAKE-AHEAD: Wrap in plastic wrap and store at room temperature for up to 24 hours or overwrap with heavy-duty foil and freeze for up to 2 weeks. To reheat, wrap pan in foil and heat in 325°F/160°C oven for 10 to 15 minutes or until steaming.) To serve, cut into squares. Pass Toffee Sauce to drizzle over top.

Toffee Sauce

Makes 8 servings.

⅔ cup	packed brown sugar	150 mL	¼ cup	butter	50 mL
⅓ cup	whipping cream	75 mL	1 tsp	vanilla	5 mL

1 In saucepan, bring sugar, cream and butter to boil, stirring until smooth. Reduce heat and simmer for 3 minutes. Stir in vanilla. (MAKE-AHEAD: Cover and set aside for up to 5 hours; reheat to serve.) Spoon over pudding. **Makes 1¼ cups (300 mL), or 8 servings.**

PER SERVING (WITH TOFFEE SAUCE), ABOUT:

cal	486	carb	71 g
pro	5 g	fibre	4 g
total fat	22 g	chol	113 mg
sat. fat	13 g	sodium	560 mg

PERCENTAGE RDI:

calcium	8%	vit. A	22%
iron	15%	vit. C	0%
folate	13%		

Plum Pudding

Rich and chock-full of fruit, nuts and liquor, a plum pudding can be made months ahead of serving time. In fact, the chefs at Jasper Park Lodge in Jasper, Alberta, make theirs a year ahead to age. Serve with Orange Hard Sauce (recipe follows), Orange Crème Anglaise (page 283) or a double making of Toffee Sauce (page 285).

TEST KITCHEN TIP: To reheat, unwrap and return to mould; cover with paper circle and lid and steam in boiling water for 1 hour or until hot. Or place, flat side down, on microwaveable plate; cover with glass bowl and heat in microwave at High for 5 to 7 minutes or until warmed through.

½ cup	butter, softened	125 mL
¾ cup	packed brown sugar	175 mL
2	eggs	2
1 tbsp	grated orange rind	15 mL
1 cup	all-purpose flour	250 mL
1 cup	fine stale (not dry) bread crumbs	250 mL
1 tsp	baking soda	5 mL
½ tsp	each salt, cinnamon and nutmeg	2 mL
¼ tsp	each ground cloves and ginger	1 mL
1 cup	chopped candied mixed peel	250 mL
1 cup	seeded lexia raisins	250 mL
¾ cup	halved candied cherries	175 mL
½ cup	golden raisins	125 mL
½ cup	slivered almonds	125 mL
⅓ cup	rum, brandy or orange juice	75 mL
¼ cup	rum or brandy (for flaming)	50 mL
	Orange Hard Sauce (recipe follows), optional	

1 Grease 8-cup (2 L) pudding ring mould or 6-cup (1.5 L) pudding bowl; line bottom with circle of greased waxed paper, pressing into any patterns on mould. Set aside.

2 In large bowl, beat butter with sugar until fluffy. Beat in eggs, 1 at a time; add orange rind. In separate bowl, whisk together flour, bread crumbs, baking soda, salt, cinnamon, nutmeg, cloves and ginger; stir in candied peel, seeded raisins, cherries, golden raisins and almonds. With wooden spoon, stir half of the dry ingredients into butter mixture; stir in ⅓ cup (75 mL) rum, then remaining dry ingredients. Scrape into pudding mould or bowl, packing and smoothing top.

3 Place circle of greased waxed paper directly on surface. Cover with lid. Or, for bowl, make 1-inch (2.5 cm) pleat across middle of large piece of foil and fit over top, pressing down sides. Trim edge, leaving 3-inch (8 cm) overhang; press down side. Tie string securely around mould about 1 inch (2.5 cm) from rim; fold foil overhang up over string.

Makes 10 to 12 servings.

PER EACH OF 12 SERVINGS
(WITHOUT ORANGE HARD SAUCE),
ABOUT:

cal 369	carb . . . . 62 g
pro . . . . 4 g	fibre . . . . 3 g
total fat . . . . 12 g	chol . . . . . . 56 mg
sat. fat . . . . . . 5 g	sodium . . 328 mg

PERCENTAGE RDI:

calcium 5%	vit. A 9%
iron 13%	vit. C 5%
folate 9%	

4 Place on rack in deep Dutch oven or stockpot; pour enough boiling water into pan to come two-thirds of the way up side of mould. Cover and bring to boil. Reduce heat to medium-low and simmer, adding boiling water as needed to maintain level, for 1½ to 2 hours for ring mould, 2½ to 3 hours for pudding bowl, or until cake tester inserted in centre comes out clean.

5 Lift out of water onto rack; let stand for 10 minutes. Remove lid and paper and unmould onto plate. (MAKE-AHEAD: Let cool completely. Wrap in plastic wrap and refrigerate for up to 4 weeks. Or overwrap with heavy-duty foil and freeze for up to 3 months; thaw and reheat as per tip.)

6 In saucepan over medium-low heat, warm ¼ cup (50 mL) rum just until heated through but not boiling. Remove from heat. Using long match, ignite rum; pour over pudding. Serve with Orange Hard Sauce (if using).

Orange Hard Sauce

½ cup	butter, softened	125 mL	2 tbsp	orange juice	25 mL
1½ cups	sifted icing sugar	375 mL	1 tsp	lemon juice	5 mL
3 tbsp	grated orange rind	50 mL			

1 In bowl, beat butter with sugar; beat in orange rind, orange juice and lemon juice until smooth and fluffy. Using piece of plastic wrap or waxed paper, roll into log. Or pipe into rosettes onto waxed paper–lined plate. Refrigerate until firm. (MAKE-AHEAD: Refrigerate in airtight container for up to 5 days.) Cut log into 1-inch (2.5 cm) thick slices. Place slice on each serving of warm pudding. **Makes 1½ cups (375 mL).**

Port Lemon Crème Caramel

What starts out as a simple idea takes on a whole new world of flavour! Here, crème caramel, that perennial dinner-party favourite of silky baked custard drenched in caramel, gets prettied up with lemon and port or Madeira.

TEST KITCHEN TIP: If some of the caramel sticks to the custard cups when unmoulding, set cups in pan, with enough boiling water to come halfway up sides, for a few minutes to melt caramel. Spoon caramel over custards.

1¼ cups	granulated sugar	300 mL	6	egg yolks	6
2 cups	milk	500 mL	3	eggs	3
1 cup	whipping cream	250 mL	¼ cup	port or Madeira wine	50 mL
	Strips of rind from 1 lemon				

1 In small heavy saucepan over medium-high heat, stir ½ cup (125 mL) of the sugar with ¼ cup (50 mL) water until dissolved. Reduce heat to medium; cook, without stirring but brushing down side of pan with brush dipped in cold water, for 10 to 12 minutes or until amber. Remove from heat. Immediately divide among eight 6-oz (175 mL) custard cups, swirling to coat bottom and ½ inch (1 cm) up side. Set aside.

2 In saucepan, bring milk, cream and lemon rind just to boil; remove from heat. In bowl, beat together egg yolks, eggs, port and remaining sugar. Slowly strain milk mixture through fine sieve into bowl, gently stirring to blend. Pour into prepared cups.

3 Place cups in large roasting pan; pour enough boiling water into pan to come halfway up sides of cups. Bake in centre of 350°F (180°C) oven for 40 minutes or until knife inserted in centres comes out clean. Remove from water. Let cool to room temperature. (MAKE-AHEAD: Cover and refrigerate for up to 2 days.) Run knife around edge of each; invert onto dessert plates, scraping out any caramel adhering to cup.

VARIATIONS

Classic Vanilla Crème Caramel: Omit lemon rind. Substitute 1 tsp (5 mL) vanilla for port.

Orange Caramel Custard: Substitute orange rind for lemon rind. Substitute 2 tbsp (25 mL) orange liqueur or orange juice concentrate for port.

Makes 8 servings.

PER SERVING, ABOUT:

cal	324	carb	35 g
pro	7 g	fibre	0 g
total fat	17 g	chol	289 mg
sat. fat	9 g	sodium	71 mg

PERCENTAGE RDI:

calcium	11%	vit. A	24%
iron	6%	vit. C	0%
folate	11%		

Crème Brûlée

Very stylish and very rich, crème brûlée is best enjoyed in small quantities.

3 cups	whipping cream	750 mL
8	egg yolks	8
⅓ cup	granulated sugar	75 mL

1½ tsp	vanilla	7 mL
½ cup	packed brown sugar, sifted	125 mL

1 In saucepan, heat cream over medium-high heat until steaming. In bowl, whisk egg yolks with granulated sugar; gradually whisk in cream. Whisk in vanilla. Skim off foam. Divide among eight 6-oz (175 mL) ramekins or custard cups. Place in 2 large shallow pans; pour enough boiling water into pans to come halfway up sides of ramekins.

2 Bake in centre of 350°F (180°C) oven for 30 to 35 minutes or until edges are set but centres still jiggle and knife inserted in centres comes out creamy. Remove from water; let cool on racks. Cover and refrigerate for about 2 hours or until chilled and set. (MAKE-AHEAD: Refrigerate for up to 2 days.)

3 Place cups on rimmed baking sheet; sprinkle brown sugar evenly over custards. Broil 6 inches (15 cm) from heat for 2 to 6 minutes or until sugar bubbles and darkens, removing each when ready. Chill, uncovered, for at least 30 minutes before serving or for up to 3 hours.

VARIATIONS

Pumpkin Crème Brûlée: Along with egg yolks and sugar, whisk in ¾ cup (175 mL) pumpkin purée, ½ tsp (2 mL) cinnamon and ¼ tsp (1 mL) each ground cloves, nutmeg and ginger.

White Chocolate Crème Brûlée: Finely chop 5 oz (150 g) white chocolate and place in bowl; pour steaming cream over top, whisking until smooth. Continue with recipe. Top with brown sugar and caramelize as directed, or melt 3 oz (90 g) bittersweet or semisweet chocolate and spread over chilled custards; melt 1 oz (30 g) white chocolate and drizzle over tops before serving.

Bittersweet Chocolate Crème Brûlée: Finely chop 5 oz (150 g) bittersweet chocolate and place in bowl; pour steaming cream over top, whisking until smooth. Continue with recipe. Top with brown sugar and caramelize as directed, or melt 3 oz (90 g) white chocolate and spread over chilled custards; melt 1 oz (30 g) bittersweet chocolate and drizzle over tops before serving.

Raspberry Crème Brûlée: Divide 1 cup (250 mL) fresh raspberries among custard cups before filling. Substitute ¼ cup (50 mL) raspberry liqueur for vanilla. Decorate caramelized crème brûlées with 2 cups (500 mL) fresh raspberries.

TEST KITCHEN TIPS

• When broiling the crèmes brûlées, watch constantly, because caramel turns from amber to black very quickly.

• While broiling the topping does work, you can follow the lead of pastry chefs who actually use a blowtorch to "brûler" the tops of their creamy custards. Compact versions of the worker's torch are for sale in many kitchenware shops.

Makes 8 servings.

PER SERVING, ABOUT:

cal	437	carb	24 g
pro	5 g	fibre	trace
total fat	36 g	chol	335 mg
sat. fat	21 g	sodium	44 mg

PERCENTAGE RDI:

calcium	9%	vit. A	39%
iron	6%	vit. C	0%
folate	10%		

Panna Cotta with Raspberry Strawberry Sauce

Panna cotta means "cooked cream" in Italian, and that's the basis of this dessert set with gelatin, not eggs, as in its crème caramel and brûlée incarnations.

TEST KITCHEN TIP: Serve panna cotta simply with golden pineapple and kiwifruit, sliced strawberries or mangoes in the spring; raspberries, sweet cherries and blueberries early in the summer; peaches and nectarines later in August; and poached plums in the fall.

1 cup	milk	250 mL
1	pkg (7 g) unflavoured gelatin	1
2 tsp	vanilla	10 mL
1 cup	whipping cream	250 mL
⅓ cup	granulated sugar	75 mL

RASPBERRY STRAWBERRY SAUCE:		
1	pkg (300 g) frozen unsweetened raspberries, thawed	1
½ cup	sliced strawberries	125 mL
2 tbsp	granulated sugar	25 mL

1 Pour milk into small saucepan. Sprinkle with gelatin; let stand for 5 minutes. Warm over very low heat, stirring, until gelatin dissolves; remove from heat. Stir in vanilla.

2 In separate saucepan, stir cream with sugar over medium heat until sugar is dissolved and small bubbles form around edge. Remove from heat; stir in gelatin mixture. Pour into 4 greased ½-cup (125 mL) moulds. Refrigerate for about 4 hours or until set. (MAKE-AHEAD: Cover and refrigerate for up to 2 days.)

3 RASPBERRY STRAWBERRY SAUCE: Press raspberries through sieve set over bowl; add strawberries and sugar, stirring. Unmould custards onto plates. Spoon sauce over and around each.

VARIATION

Orange Panna Cotta with Orange Caramel Sauce: Substitute 1 tsp (5 mL) finely grated orange rind for the vanilla, and ½ cup (125 mL) orange juice for ½ cup (125 mL) of the milk. Omit Raspberry Strawberry Sauce and substitute Orange Caramel Sauce (recipe follows).

Orange Caramel Sauce: In small heavy saucepan, heat ¾ cup (175 mL) orange juice until steaming; keep warm. In separate small heavy saucepan, stir ½ cup (125 mL) granulated sugar with ¼ cup (50 mL) water over medium heat until dissolved. Increase heat to medium-high; boil, without stirring, until very pale caramel colour. Gradually pour in orange juice, stirring constantly; boil vigorously for about 5 minutes or until syrupy and reduced to scant ⅔ cup (150 mL). Let cool. (MAKE-AHEAD: Cover and refrigerate for up to 2 days; let come to room temperature before continuing.) Peel 2 oranges; pare outer membranes. Holding over bowl to catch juice, cut out sections between membranes. Gently stir sections into sauce; stir in some of the juice if desired. **Makes about 1 cup (250 mL).**

Makes 4 servings.

PER SERVING, ABOUT:

cal 346	carb .... 33 g
pro .... 5 g	fibre .... trace
total fat .... 22 g	chol ...... 81 mg
sat. fat ..... 14 g	sodium ... 56 mg

PERCENTAGE RDI:

calcium 12%	vit. A 23%
iron 4%	vit. C 43%
folate 10%	

Tiramisu

It's frightening the way some dishes become fads and then are discarded. Passé! Bye-bye! Prime example: tiramisu, that espresso-scented, creamy cheesecake-trifle hybrid, first elevated to most favoured dessert status, then dumped into the sweets backwater. Tiramisu does not deserve this. Make it and prove that good taste can overrule fickle culinary fashion.

6	egg yolks	6
½ cup	granulated sugar	125 mL
¾ cup	strong brewed coffee	175 mL
⅔ cup	brandy	150 mL
1 lb	mascarpone cheese	500 g
2 cups	whipping cream	500 mL

48	soft ladyfingers, 2¾ inches (7 cm) long (6 oz/175 g)	48
¼ cup	cocoa powder	50 mL
1 oz	bittersweet chocolate, grated	30 g

1 In heatproof bowl, beat egg yolks with sugar for 5 minutes or until pale and thickened. Beat in ¼ cup (50 mL) each of the coffee and brandy. Set bowl over saucepan of simmering water; beat at low speed for 7 minutes or until thickened and foamy. Let cool.

2 In bowl, stir mascarpone until smooth. Stir in one-third of the egg mixture; fold in remaining egg mixture. In separate bowl, whip cream. Stir one-third into cheese mixture; fold in remaining whipped cream.

3 Combine remaining coffee and brandy. Arrange half of the ladyfingers in 13- x 9-inch (3 L) glass baking dish or similar-size shallow serving dish; brush with half of the coffee mixture. Spread with half of the cream mixture. Sift half of the cocoa over top. Repeat layers. Cover and refrigerate for 12 hours. Garnish with chocolate. (MAKE-AHEAD: Overwrap with heavy-duty foil and freeze for up to 2 weeks; thaw in refrigerator for 24 hours before serving.)

TEST KITCHEN TIP: Mascarpone is rich, double- or triple-cream cheese made from cow's milk; it is both imported from Italy and made in Canada. While it's the soul of tiramisu, a small dollop paired with fruit, berries or fresh figs makes a sophisticated little dessert. Or drizzle with honey or Raspberry Strawberry Sauce (page 290).

Makes 12 servings.

PER SERVING, ABOUT:

cal	451	carb	21 g
pro	6 g	fibre	1 g
total fat	37 g	chol	269 mg
sat. fat	22 g	sodium	40 mg

PERCENTAGE RDI:

calcium	7%	vit. A	22%
iron	12%	vit. C	0%
folate	8%		

MAKE-AHEAD   CLASSIC

Very Berry Trifle

What makes this trifle special is the abundance of berries and the real custard made light and fluffy with whipped cream.

TEST KITCHEN TIP: You can use unsweetened individually quick-frozen (IQF) berries in the trifle. IQF berries are not packaged with syrup or sauce, so they won't add excess moisture. If using frozen berries for the garnish, let stand in refrigerator until just thawed.

SUBSTITUTION: Instead of pound cake, you can use store-bought soft ladyfingers, or white or chocolate cake as long as it's the same weight.

1 lb	pound cake	500 g
½ cup	raspberry jam	125 mL
1½ cups	whipping cream	375 mL
¼ cup	sherry	50 mL
2 cups	each blueberries and raspberries	500 mL
1 cup	strawberries, hulled	250 mL

CUSTARD:		
5	egg yolks	5
2½ cups	milk	625 mL
½ cup	granulated sugar	125 mL
⅓ cup	cornstarch	75 mL
2 tsp	vanilla	10 mL
GARNISH:		
1 cup	each blueberries, raspberries and strawberries, hulled	250 mL

1 CUSTARD: In bowl, whisk together egg yolks, ½ cup (125 mL) of the milk, sugar and cornstarch. In saucepan, heat remaining milk over medium heat until bubbles form around edge; gradually whisk into yolk mixture. Return to pan and cook, stirring, for 5 minutes or until thickened. Strain into bowl; stir in vanilla. Place plastic wrap directly on surface. Refrigerate for about 4 hours or until chilled.

2 Cut cake into 1-inch (2.5 cm) thick slices. Spread 1 side of each with jam. Cut into 1-inch (2.5 cm) cubes. Set aside. In bowl, whip ½ cup (125 mL) of the cream; fold into custard.

3 Arrange one-third of the cake in bottom of 12-cup (3 L) glass bowl. Sprinkle with one-third of the sherry; top with one-third each of the berries, then one-third of the custard. Repeat layers twice. Cover and refrigerate for 12 hours. (MAKE-AHEAD: Refrigerate for up to 2 days.) Whip remaining cream; spread over top.

4 GARNISH: Just before serving, top decoratively with blueberries, raspberries and strawberries.

Makes 12 servings.

PER SERVING, ABOUT:

cal 422	carb . . . . 54 g
pro . . . . 6 g	fibre . . . . 4 g
total fat . . . . 21 g	chol . . . . . 156 mg
sat. fat . . . . . 10 g	sodium . . 199 mg

PERCENTAGE RDI:

calcium 12%	vit. A 20%
iron 9%	vit. C 45%
folate 20%	

Fresh Fruit Pavlova

Gossamer and soft inside, crisp and the palest gold outside, billowy Pavlova is a dream dessert for any special dinner. Fill its nestlike centre with cream, rich or lightened up, and garnish with a tumble of seasonal berries, nectarines, peaches or kiwifruit, or tropical mangoes and golden pineapple.

1 cup	granulated sugar	250 mL
4	egg whites	4
¼ tsp	cream of tartar	1 mL
1 tbsp	cornstarch	15 mL
2 tsp	vinegar	10 mL
1 tsp	vanilla	5 mL

TOPPING:		
1 cup	whipping cream	250 mL
2 tsp	granulated sugar	10 mL
3 cups	sliced fruit	750 mL

1 Line baking sheet with parchment paper or greased and floured foil. Using 9-inch (23 cm) round cake pan as guide, mark circle on paper or foil (if using paper, turn over).

2 In food processor, whirl sugar for 30 seconds or until crystals are finer and smaller. In bowl, beat egg whites with cream of tartar until soft peaks form. Beat in sugar, 2 tbsp (25 mL) at a time, until stiff glossy peaks form. Beat in cornstarch, vinegar and vanilla.

3 Spoon egg white mixture onto prepared circle. With back of spoon, form into nest shape with hollow about 5 inches (12 cm) wide and side about 1 inch (2.5 cm) higher than hollow. Bake in centre of 275°F (140°C) oven for 1¼ to 1½ hours or until crisp and light golden but still soft inside. Let cool on sheet on rack. Slide long metal spatula under meringue to loosen from paper; slide onto flat serving plate.

4 TOPPING: In bowl, whip cream with sugar; spoon into meringue nest, leaving raised side bare. Arrange fruit on top of cream. To serve, cut with serrated knife.

VARIATIONS

Hazelnut Pavlova: Spread ⅔ cup (150 mL) coarsely chopped hazelnuts on baking sheet; toast in 350°F (180°C) oven for 5 to 8 minutes or until golden and fragrant. Let cool. Toss with cornstarch; fold into egg whites.

Lightened-Up Pavlova Topping: In cheesecloth-lined sieve set over bowl, drain ⅔ cup (150 mL) plain yogurt in refrigerator for at least 2 hours or until reduced to ⅓ cup (75 mL). Reduce whipping cream to ⅔ cup (150 mL); increase sugar to 1 tbsp (15 mL). Fold yogurt into whipped cream. Increase fruit to 4 cups (1 L).

Makes 8 to 10 servings.

PER EACH OF 10 SERVINGS, ABOUT:

cal	191	carb	28 g
pro	2 g	fibre	1 g
total fat	9 g	chol	31 mg
sat. fat	5 g	sodium	31 mg

PERCENTAGE RDI:

calcium	2%	vit. A	12%
iron	1%	vit. C	18%
folate	2%		

MAKE-AHEAD   BUDGET-WISE

Ice and Easy Sorbets

Get your licks in with these six summer soothers, surprisingly easy to make without any fancy equipment. Note that for all intents and purposes, sorbet is sherbet. For our photograph, we removed membranes from six mandarin halves and froze them. To serve, we filled each with a scoop of Mandarin Sorbet (see variation below).

	PREPARE	PURÉE WITH
Very Strawberry	4 cups (1 L) strawberries, hulled	2 tbsp (25 mL) lemon juice
Really Raspberry	4 cups (1 L) raspberries	1 tbsp (15 mL) each corn syrup and lemon juice; strain through sieve
Peachy Keen	6 peaches or nectarines, peeled and sliced to make 4 cups (1 L)	2 tbsp (25 mL) lemon juice
Fuzzy Raspberry	1 cup (250 mL) raspberries; 5 peaches or nectarines, peeled and sliced to make 3 cups (750 mL)	1 tbsp (15 mL) lemon juice; strain through sieve
Cantaberry	2 cups (500 mL) strawberries, hulled; 1 small cantaloupe, peeled and cubed to make 3 cups (750 mL)	2 tbsp (25 mL) lemon juice

TEST KITCHEN TIPS

• When making sorbets, you can substitute frozen fruit for fresh; thaw slightly before puréeing.

• These desserts can be stored in the freezer for up to 2 days; after that, purée them again in the food processor to enjoy an extra day or 2 of fresh flavour.

• For easy individual party servings, scoop and freeze the finished ices on a foil-lined baking sheet.

1 SIMPLE SYRUP: In saucepan, bring ⅔ cup (150 mL) each granulated sugar and water to boil, stirring to dissolve sugar. Let cool completely.

2 Wash and prepare fruit in first column. Purée with ingredients in second column to make fresh fruit purée. Mix with Simple Syrup.

3 Spoon into shallow metal cake pan; freeze for about 4 hours or until firm. Break into chunks; purée in food processor. Pack into airtight container and refreeze for 4 hours or until firm or for up to 2 days. (Or freeze in ice-cream machine according to manufacturer's instructions.)

Makes 6 to 8 servings.

VARIATION

Mandarin Sorbet: Wash and dry 6 mandarins. Grate rind from 3 of the mandarins. Cut all in half and juice to make 1½ cups (375 mL), keeping ungrated skins intact. Remove membranes from juiced ungrated skins. In saucepan, bring 1½ cups (375 mL) granulated sugar, 1 cup (250 mL) water and reserved rind to boil; boil, stirring, for 5 minutes. Stir in mandarin juice and ½ cup (125 mL) lemon juice. Strain through sieve into shallow pan. Freeze as directed in Step 3. **Makes 6 servings.**

Strawberry Ice Cream

Homemade custard is the basis of this strawberry ice cream, but in no way does its creaminess take away from the essence of summer's finest berry. This recipe proves that you can make first-class ice cream with or without an ice-cream machine.

3 cups	strawberries, sliced	750 mL
¼ cup	granulated sugar	50 mL
CUSTARD:		
3	egg yolks	3
⅓ cup	granulated sugar	75 mL

1 cup	light cream (10%)	250 mL
½ cup	whipping cream	125 mL
1½ tsp	vanilla	7 mL

TEST KITCHEN TIPS

• Homemade ice cream is best made in a small batch and eaten within 3 days.

• You can add a tablespoon (15 mL) of liqueur to the purée; kirsch to the berries; orange liqueur to the peaches; cassis to the plums.

1 CUSTARD: In bowl, whisk egg yolks with sugar for 2 minutes or until pale and thickened; set aside. In heavy saucepan, heat light cream over medium heat just until bubbles form around edge; gradually whisk into yolk mixture. Return to clean pan; cook over low heat, stirring constantly, for about 12 minutes or until thick enough to coat back of wooden spoon.

2 Immediately strain through fine sieve into large bowl. Stir in whipping cream and vanilla. Place plastic wrap directly on surface; refrigerate for at least 2 hours or for up to 24 hours.

3 In bowl, combine strawberries with sugar; let stand for about 20 minutes or until juicy. In food processor or blender, purée strawberries to make about 2 cups (500 mL). Fold into chilled custard.

4 Spoon into shallow metal cake pan; freeze for about 3 hours or until almost firm. Break into chunks; purée in food processor. Pack into airtight container and freeze for 1 hour or until firm. (MAKE-AHEAD: Freeze for up to 3 days.) Transfer to refrigerator 30 minutes before serving. (Or freeze in ice-cream machine according to manufacturer's instructions.)

VARIATIONS

Raspberry Ice Cream: Substitute 4 cups (1 L) raspberries for strawberries; purée and press through sieve before combining with sugar. Omit standing time and puréeing.

Peach Ice Cream: Substitute 6 large ripe peaches (1½ lb/750 g), peeled and sliced, for the strawberries.

Red Plum Ice Cream: Omit strawberries and sugar. In saucepan, combine 3 cups (750 mL) sliced (unpeeled) red plums (about 5), ¼ cup (50 mL) water and 2 tbsp (25 mL) granulated sugar; simmer over low heat for 20 minutes or until tender. Purée, then chill; fold into custard.

Makes 3 cups (750 mL), 6 servings.

PER SERVING, ABOUT:

cal 270	carb . . . . 28 g
pro . . . . 3 g	fibre . . . . 1 g
total fat . . . . 17 g	chol . . . . . 160 mg
sat. fat . . . . . 10 g	sodium . . . 29 mg

PERCENTAGE RDI:

calcium 7%	vit. A 17%
iron 6%	vit. C 52%
folate 10%	

Frozen Lemon Meringue Torte

Garnish this luscious make-ahead dessert created by Bonnie Stern with fresh or sugared violets, violas and/or mint leaves (see Making Candied Flowers, this page).

1¼ cups	granulated sugar	300 mL		**MERINGUES:**		
⅓ cup	butter	75 mL		1½ cups	granulated sugar	375 mL
1 tbsp	grated lemon rind	15 mL		2 tbsp	cornstarch	25 mL
1 cup	lemon juice	250 mL		2 tsp	grated lemon rind	10 mL
6	eggs	6		6	egg whites	6
1½ cups	whipping cream	375 mL		1 tsp	vanilla	5 mL

1 Trace four 8-inch (20 cm) circles onto 2 sheets of parchment paper; turn papers over and place on baking sheets.

2 MERINGUES: Combine ¾ cup (175 mL) of the sugar, cornstarch and lemon rind; set aside. In bowl, beat egg whites until soft peaks form; beat in remaining sugar, 2 tbsp (25 mL) at a time, until stiff peaks form. Add vanilla; fold in reserved sugar mixture. Spoon meringue onto circles, smoothing tops. Bake in centre of 300°F (150°C) oven for 1 hour or until dry and light golden. Let cool. (MAKE-AHEAD: Store in cool, dry place for up to 3 days.)

3 In saucepan, heat sugar, butter, lemon rind and lemon juice over medium-high heat, stirring, until sugar dissolves. In bowl, beat eggs; whisk in lemon mixture. Return to pan and cook, stirring, just until bubbly and thickened; simmer for 1 minute. Pour into bowl. Place plastic wrap directly on surface; chill in refrigerator to room temperature. (MAKE-AHEAD: Refrigerate for up to 24 hours.) In bowl, whip cream; fold into lemon mixture.

4 Crumble least attractive meringue for garnish; set aside. Fit 1 meringue into 9-inch (2.5 L) springform pan. Pour one-third of the lemon mixture over top. Repeat layers twice. Sprinkle crumbled meringue over top. Freeze for at least 8 hours or until solid. (MAKE-AHEAD: Remove from pan, wrap in foil and freeze for up to 1 week.) Let soften in refrigerator for 45 minutes before serving.

Makes 12 servings.

MAKING Candied Flowers

Use egg white or this simple syrup to candy edible flowers (unsprayed).

SYRUP: In small saucepan, bring ½ cup (125 mL) water and ⅓ cup (75 mL) granulated sugar to boil; boil for 1 minute. Let cool.

Lightly beat 1 egg white. With small paintbrush, brush egg white or syrup onto clean, dry flowers or petals. Sprinkle with granulated sugar to coat lightly. Place on waxed paper–lined baking sheet; set aside at room temperature for at least 24 hours or until completely dry.

Rhubarb and Strawberry Compote

This gentle cooking method lets tender chunks of rhubarb keep their shape. The compote is delicious without the strawberries, sensational with, and easy to turn into a fool or frozen yogurt.

1 cup	granulated sugar	250 mL
¼ cup	water	50 mL
6 cups	chopped rhubarb (12 large stalks)	1.5 L

1	strip (4 inches/10 cm) orange rind	1
1 cup	sliced strawberries	250 mL

1 In top of double boiler over direct heat, bring sugar and water to boil. Place over gently boiling water in bottom of double boiler. Stir in rhubarb and orange rind; cover and cook, without stirring, for 15 to 20 minutes or until tender.

2 Turn off heat; let cool in pan over hot water. Chill. To serve, remove orange rind; gently stir in strawberries.

Makes 4 cups (1 L), 4 servings.

PER SERVING, ABOUT:

cal	242	carb	61 g
pro	2 g	fibre	4 g
total fat	1 g	chol	0 mg
sat. fat	trace	sodium	9 mg

PERCENTAGE RDI:

calcium	14%	vit. A	2%
iron	4%	vit. C	52%
folate	6%		

RHUBARB AND STRAWBERRY FOOL

1½ cups	Rhubarb and Strawberry Compote (see above)	375 mL
1 cup	whipping cream	250 mL

≈ In food processor, purée Rhubarb and Strawberry Compote until smooth; transfer to serving bowl.

≈ Whip cream; spoon over compote and fold together, leaving streaks. (MAKE-AHEAD: Cover and refrigerate for up to 4 hours.) **Makes 8 servings.** *Per serving: 143 cal, 1 g pro, 11 g total fat (6 g sat. fat), 12 g carb, 1 g fibre, 38 mg chol, 12 mg sodium. % RDI: 4% calcium, 1% iron, 12% vit A, 10% vit C, 2% folate.*

RHUBARB AND STRAWBERRY FROZEN YOGURT

2 cups	Rhubarb and Strawberry Compote (see above)	500 mL
½ cup	plain yogurt	125 mL
3 tbsp	superfine sugar	50 mL
2 tbsp	orange juice	25 mL

≈ In food processor, purée Rhubarb and Strawberry Compote until smooth; blend in yogurt, sugar and juice.

≈ Freeze in ice-cream machine according to manufacturer's instructions. Or freeze in shallow metal pan for 3 to 4 hours or until almost firm. Break into chunks; purée in food processor, in batches if necessary. Pack into airtight container; freeze for 1 hour or until firm. (MAKE-AHEAD: Freeze for up to 2 days.) **Makes 4 cups (1 L).** *Per ½ cup (125 mL): 91 cal, 1 g pro, 1 g total fat (trace sat. fat), 21 g carb, 1 g fibre, 1 mg chol, 12 mg sodium. % RDI: 6% calcium, 1% iron, 1% vit A, 15% vit C, 3% folate.*

VARIATION

Summer Berry Fools: Fools got their name because they are so foolishly simple and quick to make — with strawberries or raspberries, fresh in season, frozen (thawed) when not. Mash or purée 2 cups (500 mL) fruit to make 1 cup (250 mL) crushed. In large bowl, whip 1½ cups (375 mL) whipping cream, 2 tbsp (25 mL) granulated sugar and dash of vanilla or your favourite liqueur; pour crushed fruit over top and fold in, leaving streaks. Garnish with whole berries. **Makes 6 to 8 servings.**

Caramel-Baked Pear Sundaes

The best pears to choose for this luscious fruit dessert are Bartletts, with the shapely Bosc a pretty good alternative. Buy pears a few days before using; let ripen at room temperature to a firm, juicy stage for this recipe.

1⅓ cups	pear or apple juice	325 mL
2 tbsp	lemon juice	25 mL
1 cup	granulated sugar	250 mL
½ cup	water	125 mL

4	large pears	4
¼ cup	sliced almonds, toasted	50 mL
2 cups	frozen vanilla yogurt or ice cream	500 mL

1 In small saucepan, warm pear juice with lemon juice; keep warm.

2 In deep 16-cup (4 L) heavy saucepan, stir sugar with water over medium heat on burner that is same size as pan; cook, stirring, for about 4 minutes or until dissolved. Increase heat to medium-high; bring to full rolling boil, about 1 minute. Boil, without stirring but brushing down sides of pan with pastry brush dipped in water, for about 6 minutes or until pale caramel colour, watching carefully and turning pan if caramel colours in some spots before others. Remove from heat.

3 Holding an arm's length away and averting face to avoid spatters, add pear juice mixture; stir with long-handled spoon until blended and bubbles subside. Boil for 10 minutes or until thickened and dark amber. Transfer to shallow 10-cup (2.5 L) baking or gratin dish.

4 Peel, halve and core pears. Place, cut side down, in caramel mixture; spoon sauce over top. Bake in centre of 400°F (200°C) oven, basting every 10 minutes and turning over for last 10 minutes, for 35 minutes or until tender. Let cool. Store at room temperature for up to 2 hours. Sprinkle with almonds; serve with frozen yogurt.

Makes 4 servings.

PER SERVING, ABOUT:

cal	509	carb	106 g
pro	6 g	fibre	3 g
total fat	9 g	chol	10 mg
sat. fat	4 g	sodium	64 mg

PERCENTAGE RDI:

calcium	16%	vit. A	3%
iron	7%	vit. C	52%
folate	6%		

BANANAS IN Caramel Sauce

In large skillet, heat ½ cup (125 mL) granulated sugar with ¼ cup (50 mL) water over medium heat, stirring until sugar is dissolved. Increase heat to medium-high, cover and bring to full rolling boil; boil, without stirring but brushing down sides of pan with pastry brush dipped in water, for about 4 minutes or until amber. Holding at arm's length and averting face to avoid spatters, add ½ cup (125 mL) orange juice and 2 tbsp (25 mL) rum. Cook, stirring, for about 5 minutes or until smooth. Cut 4 bananas into 1-inch (2.5 cm) slices; add to sauce and heat through. Serve over ice cream. **Makes 4 servings.**

Roasted Pears in Port

This Italian-inspired dessert is utterly simple and, like many fruit desserts, a real crowd-pleaser. Serve with ice cream if desired.

6	firm ripe Bartlett pears (about 3 lb/1.5 kg)	6	1 cup	ruby port	250 mL
2 tbsp	butter, melted	25 mL	2 tbsp	coarsely broken cinnamon sticks	25 mL
3 tbsp	granulated sugar	50 mL			

1 Trim bottoms of pears so that they stand upright. Using small melon baller or spoon and working from bottom of each pear, remove core. Place pears upright in 11- x 7-inch (2 L) glass baking dish. Brush with butter; sprinkle with sugar. Pour port into dish; sprinkle with cinnamon.

2 Cover dish with foil and bake in centre of 325°F (160°C) oven for 45 minutes; baste. Bake, uncovered and basting 3 or 4 times, for 45 to 75 minutes longer or until tender and skins begin to wrinkle. Transfer to serving dish.

3 Spoon juice from dish into small saucepan; cook over high heat, stirring often, until reduced to about ½ cup (125 mL). Pour over pears. Serve warm or at room temperature.

Makes 6 servings.

PER SERVING, ABOUT:

cal	165	carb	32 g
pro	1 g	fibre	5 g
total fat	5 g	chol	10 mg
sat. fat	2 g	sodium	41 mg

PERCENTAGE RDI:

calcium	2%	vit. A	4%
iron	4%	vit. C	8%
folate	3%		

Chocolate Fondue

Fondue is the most leisurely of desserts. Gather guests around a pot of what is essentially ganache — the filling for truffles — and invite them to dip and devour chunks of fruit (bananas, strawberries, mangoes, pineapples and pears outshine most others) and cake (Banana Chocolate Chip Loaf, page 259, is ideal).

6 oz	bittersweet chocolate, chopped	175 g	¾ cup	whipping cream	175 mL
4 oz	milk chocolate, chopped	125 g	2 tbsp	amaretto, brandy or rum	25 mL

1 Place bittersweet and milk chocolates in fondue pot. In saucepan, heat whipping cream until boiling.

2 Pour whipping cream over chocolate, whisking until melted. Whisk in amaretto. Set over warmer.

Makes 2 cups (500 mL).

PER ¼ CUP (50 mL), ABOUT:

cal	268	carb	17 g
pro	4 g	fibre	4 g
total fat	24 g	chol	32 mg
sat. fat	15 g	sodium	23 mg

PERCENTAGE RDI:

calcium	5%	vit. A	8%
iron	11%	vit. C	0%
folate	1%		

Cakes

12

Chocolate Layer Cake 302

Chocolate Blackout Cake 303

White Butter Cake 304

Lemon-Glazed Pound Cake 305

Orange and Sour Cherry Buttermilk Cake 306

Canada's Best Carrot Cake with Cream Cheese Icing 308

Rich Brandied Fruitcake 309

Classic Angel Food Cake 310

Coconut Chiffon Cake 311

Banana Split Roll 312

Strawberry Shortcake 313

Mocha Marjolaine 314

Raspberry Cookies and Cream Torte 316

Orange Pecan Meringue Cake 317

Cinnamon Toast Coffee Cake 318

Rhubarb Upside-Down Cake 319

Blueberry Cheese Coffee Cake 320

Raspberry Chocolate Chip Bundt Cake 321

Very Gingery Ginger Cake 322

Basic but Beautiful Cheesecake 323

Chocolate Layer Cake

What's a birthday without a cake? And what's a cake without chocolate? Here's the best ever, with a creamy icing to match.

1 cup	butter, softened	250 mL
1½ cups	granulated sugar	375 mL
2	eggs	2
1 tsp	vanilla	5 mL
2 cups	all-purpose flour	500 mL
½ cup	cocoa powder	125 mL
1 tsp	each baking powder and baking soda	5 mL
¼ tsp	salt	1 mL
1½ cups	buttermilk	375 mL

CHOCOLATE ICING:		
1½ cups	unsalted butter, softened	375 mL
½ cup	whipping cream	125 mL
1 tbsp	vanilla	15 mL
3 cups	icing sugar	750 mL
6 oz	unsweetened chocolate, chopped, melted and cooled	175 g

1 Grease two 8-inch (2 L) springform pans or grease two 8-inch (1.2 L) round metal cake pans and line bottoms with parchment or waxed paper. Set aside.

2 In large bowl, beat butter with sugar until light and fluffy. Beat in eggs, 1 at a time; beat in vanilla. In separate bowl, sift together flour, cocoa, baking powder, baking soda and salt. With wooden spoon, stir into butter mixture alternately with buttermilk, making 3 additions of dry ingredients and 2 of buttermilk. Spoon into prepared pans, smoothing tops.

3 Bake in centre of 350°F (180°C) oven for 30 to 35 minutes or until cake tester inserted in centre comes out clean. Let cool on racks for 20 minutes. Remove from pans; let cool completely on racks. (MAKE-AHEAD: Wrap layers separately in plastic wrap and refrigerate for up to 1 day or overwrap with heavy-duty foil and freeze for up to 2 weeks.) Cut each cake horizontally into 2 layers.

4 CHOCOLATE ICING: In bowl, beat butter until fluffy; gradually beat in cream. Beat in vanilla. Beat in icing sugar, 1 cup (250 mL) at a time. Beat in melted chocolate until fluffy and smooth.

5 Place 1 layer, cut side up, on cake plate. Slide strips of waxed paper between cake and plate. Spread cut side with about ¾ cup (175 mL) of the icing; cover with remaining half, cut side down. Spread top with another ¾ cup (175 mL) of the icing. Repeat with remaining layers, spreading remaining icing over side and top. Remove paper strips. (MAKE-AHEAD: Cover loosely and refrigerate for up to 2 days. Let come to room temperature before serving.)

Makes 12 servings.

PER SERVING, ABOUT:

cal	753	carb	75 g
pro	7 g	fibre	4 g
total fat	51 g	chol	153 mg
sat. fat	31 g	sodium	376 mg

PERCENTAGE RDI:

calcium	8%	vit. A	41%
iron	18%	vit. C	0%
folate	14%		

Chocolate Blackout Cake

Dark, chocolaty cake crumbs covering three layers of dark, moist cake and smooth, rich filling earn this superb cake the name "blackout."

2 cups	granulated sugar	500 mL		2 tsp	baking soda	10 mL
2 cups	water	500 mL		½ tsp	salt	2 mL
4 oz	unsweetened chocolate, chopped	125 g		**ICING:**		
⅓ cup	butter	75 mL		1½ cups	granulated sugar	375 mL
1 tsp	vanilla	5 mL		1⅓ cups	whipping cream	325 mL
2	eggs, lightly beaten	2		6 oz	unsweetened chocolate, chopped	175 g
2 cups	all-purpose flour	500 mL		⅔ cup	butter, softened	150 mL
2 tsp	baking powder	10 mL		1 tsp	vanilla	5 mL

1 Grease two 8-inch (1.2 L) round metal cake pans; set aside.

2 In saucepan, bring sugar and water to boil, stirring until sugar dissolves. Place chocolate and butter in large bowl; whisk in sugar mixture until melted and smooth. Stir in vanilla. Let cool slightly. Beat in eggs.

3 In separate bowl, whisk together flour, baking powder, baking soda and salt; add to chocolate mixture all at once. Using electric mixer, beat until smooth. Divide between prepared pans. Bake in centre of 350°F (180°C) oven for about 35 minutes or until tops spring back when lightly touched. Let cool in pans on racks for 30 minutes. Remove from pans; let cool completely on racks. (MAKE-AHEAD: Wrap well with plastic wrap and store at room temperature for up to 1 day or overwrap with heavy-duty foil and freeze for up to 2 weeks.)

4 ICING: In saucepan, heat sugar with cream just until boiling. Remove from heat; whisk in chocolate, butter and vanilla until melted and smooth. Transfer to bowl; refrigerate for 2 hours or until cold. Using electric mixer, beat for about 5 minutes or until thick and glossy.

5 Slice each cake in half horizontally; set 1 layer aside. Place 1 layer on cake plate. Slide strips of waxed paper between cake and plate. Spread top with heaping cupful (250 mL) of the icing; level icing. Top with another cake layer and icing; level icing. Top with third layer of cake; spread top and sides with remaining icing. Refrigerate for 10 minutes.

6 Crumble remaining cake layer into crumbs; sprinkle over top and press small handfuls onto side of cake, pressing lightly to adhere. Remove paper strips. (MAKE-AHEAD: Cover loosely and refrigerate for up to 2 days.) Serve at room temperature.

Makes 12 servings.

PER SERVING, ABOUT:

cal	659	carb	82 g
pro	6 g	fibre	4 g
total fat	39 g	chol	111 mg
sat. fat	23 g	sodium	515 mg

PERCENTAGE RDI:

calcium	6%	vit. A	25%
iron	18%	vit. C	0%
folate	13%		

White Butter Cake

Chocolate cake is indisputably popular, but this vanilla-scented cake has its share of enthusiastic fans. Bake as directed for a sheet cake and decorate for anniversaries, birthdays, showers, retirement parties — whatever the cake occasion. The sheet format cuts easily for a crowd, but if you like, bake it in round cake pans for a layer cake.

4	eggs	4		2 tbsp	baking powder	25 mL
1⅓ cups	milk	325 mL		1 tbsp	grated orange rind	15 mL
1 tbsp	vanilla	15 mL		1 tsp	salt	5 mL
4 cups	sifted cake-and-pastry flour	1 L		1 cup	butter, softened	250 mL
2 cups	granulated sugar	500 mL			Butter Icing (recipe follows)	

1 Grease 13- x 9-inch (3.5 L) metal cake pan; line bottom with parchment or waxed paper. Set aside.

2 In bowl, whisk together eggs, ⅓ cup (75 mL) of the milk and vanilla; set aside. In separate large bowl, whisk together flour, sugar, baking powder, orange rind and salt. Beat in butter and remaining milk at medium speed for 2 minutes or until fluffy. Beat in egg mixture in 3 additions, beating well and scraping down side of bowl after each. Scrape into prepared pan, smoothing top.

3 Bake in centre of 350°F (180°C) oven for 40 to 45 minutes or until golden, top springs back when lightly touched and cake tester inserted in centre comes out clean. Let cool in pan on rack for 20 minutes.

4 Run knife around edge of cake; invert onto baking sheet and peel off paper. Reinvert cake onto rack; let cool completely on rack. (MAKE-AHEAD: Wrap in plastic wrap and store for up to 1 day or overwrap with heavy-duty foil and freeze for up to 2 weeks.) Ice top and sides of cake with Butter Icing.

Makes 16 to 20 servings.

Butter Icing

½ cup	butter, softened	125 mL		⅓ cup	whipping cream	75 mL
2½ cups	icing sugar	625 mL		1 tsp	vanilla	5 mL

1 In bowl, beat butter until light. Gradually beat in sugar and cream, making 3 additions of sugar and 2 of cream. Stir in vanilla. (MAKE-AHEAD: Cover and refrigerate for up to 3 days; beat again before using.) **Makes about 2 cups (500 mL).**

Lemon-Glazed Pound Cake

Pound cake, with its dense crumb and rich flavour, is the exact opposite of fluffy cake-mix cakes. Here it's presented with a lemon glaze — very nice indeed to slice and serve with tea. But you can gussy up this classic with a tumble of fresh berries.

1½ cups	light sour cream	375 mL
1 tsp	baking soda	5 mL
⅔ cup	butter, softened	150 mL
2⅔ cups	granulated sugar	650 mL
5	eggs	5
1½ tsp	vanilla	7 mL
4½ cups	sifted cake-and-pastry flour	1.125 L

1 tbsp	grated lemon rind	15 mL
¼ tsp	salt	1 mL
GLAZE:		
¾ cup	icing sugar	175 mL
2 tsp	grated lemon rind	10 mL
2 tbsp	lemon juice	25 mL

1 Grease 10-inch (4 L) tube pan; set aside.

2 In small bowl, stir sour cream with baking soda; set aside. In large bowl, beat butter until fluffy; gradually beat in sugar until well combined. Beat in eggs, 1 at a time, scraping down bowl and beating well after each addition. Stir in vanilla. In separate bowl, whisk together flour, lemon rind and salt; stir into batter alternately with sour cream mixture, making 3 additions of dry ingredients and 2 of sour cream mixture. Scrape into pan.

3 Bake in centre of 325°F (160°C) oven for 1½ hours or until light golden and cake tester inserted in centre comes out clean. Let cool in pan on rack for 30 minutes. Turn out onto rack; let cool completely. (MAKE-AHEAD: Wrap in plastic wrap and store at room temperature for up to 1 day or overwrap with heavy-duty foil and freeze for up to 2 weeks. Let come to room temperature.) Transfer to cake plate.

4 GLAZE: In small bowl, whisk together icing sugar and lemon rind and juice; pour over cake, spreading evenly over top and letting excess drip down side.

Makes 16 servings.

PER SERVING, ABOUT:

cal	376	carb	65 g
pro	6 g	fibre	1 g
total fat	11 g	chol	91 mg
sat. fat	6 g	sodium	228 mg

PERCENTAGE RDI:

calcium	5%	vit. A	11%
iron	16%	vit. C	3%
folate	18%		

Orange and Sour Cherry Buttermilk Cake

Enhance your reputation as resident pastry chef with this slightly dense, moist, but not too sweet cake. It boasts a tangy cherry layer and a stunning icing sugar–dusted crunchy almond topping. The topping is surprisingly easy to make and apply.

½ cup	butter, softened	125 mL
1½ cups	granulated sugar	375 mL
2	eggs	2
1 tbsp	finely grated orange rind	15 mL
2 tbsp	orange juice	25 mL
¼ tsp	almond extract	1 mL
2 cups	all-purpose flour	500 mL
1 tsp	baking powder	5 mL
½ tsp	baking soda	2 mL
¼ tsp	salt	1 mL
½ cup	ground almonds	125 mL
1 cup	buttermilk	250 mL

SOUR CHERRY FILLING:		
¾ cup	cherry juice or cranberry juice	175 mL
½ cup	tightly packed dried sour cherries	125 mL
2 tbsp	granulated sugar	25 mL
1½ tsp	cornstarch	7 mL
1½ tsp	water	7 mL
SUGARED ALMOND TOPPING:		
2 tbsp	granulated sugar	25 mL
1	egg white	1
1½ cups	sliced almonds	375 mL
⅓ cup	apricot jam	75 mL
1 tsp	water	5 mL
1 tbsp	icing sugar	15 mL

1 **SOUR CHERRY FILLING:** In small saucepan, bring cherry juice, dried cherries and sugar to boil. Reduce heat to medium-low; simmer for 20 minutes or until cherries are softened and plumped. Reserving juice, strain cherries in sieve, pressing gently to extract excess juice. Place cherries in bowl.

2 Return juice to saucepan; bring to boil. Whisk cornstarch with water; add to juice and cook, whisking constantly, until thickened. Pour over cherries, stirring to combine. Let cool completely. (MAKE-AHEAD: Refrigerate in airtight container for up to 4 days.)

3 Grease and flour 10-inch (3 L) springform pan; set aside.

Makes 12 servings.

PER SERVING, ABOUT:

cal 436	carb . . . . 63 g
pro . . . . 8 g	fibre . . . . 2 g
total fat . . . . 18 g	chol . . . . . . 57 mg
sat. fat . . . . . . 6 g	sodium . . 239 mg

PERCENTAGE RDI:

calcium 9%	vit. A 10%
iron 13%	vit. C 12%
folate 17%	

4 In large bowl, beat butter with sugar until light and fluffy. Add eggs, 1 at a time, beating well after each addition. Add orange rind, orange juice and almond extract; beat for about 2 minutes or until light and fluffy. In separate bowl, whisk together flour, baking powder, baking soda and salt; stir in ground almonds. On low speed, beat dry ingredients alternately with buttermilk into butter mixture, making 3 additions of dry ingredients and 2 of buttermilk.

5 Spread half of the batter in prepared pan. Spoon cherry filling evenly over top, leaving 1-inch (2.5 cm) border uncovered around edge. Top with remaining batter. Bake in centre of 350°F (180°C) oven for 55 to 60 minutes or until cake is golden, firm to the touch and pulls away from pan. Let cool in pan on rack. Remove side of pan.

6 SUGARED ALMOND TOPPING: In bowl, whisk sugar with egg white just until combined. Add almonds; toss to coat. Spread in single layer on parchment paper–lined baking sheet. Bake in 325°F (160°C) oven, tossing often, for 20 to 30 minutes or until golden and dry. Let cool completely.

7 In small saucepan, bring jam and water to simmer; spread in thin layer over top and side of cake. Cover top with generous 1 cup (250 mL) sugared almonds. Crush remaining sugared almonds; press evenly onto side of cake. Sift icing sugar over top. (MAKE-AHEAD: Store in airtight container for up to 1 day.)

GETTING READY TO Bake a Cake

~ Adjust oven rack to centre of oven. Ensure that there is plenty of room for air to circulate around cake pan.

~ Use the pan called for in the recipe. If you don't have the exact pan, it is better to choose a very slightly larger pan than a smaller one, as batter will overflow and burn on the bottom of your oven. Shorten baking time to allow for shallower batter in larger pan.

~ Prepare pan before making batter. In most instances, all you need to do is use a pastry brush to grease the cake pan thoroughly with shortening or unsalted butter, or coat with non-stick cooking spray. To ensure that cakes or layers release cleanly from pans, you can also add parchment paper or waxed paper cut to fit bottom of pans. Occasionally, a band of parchment paper around the inside of the pan is called for, notably for cakes in springform pans when a smooth side is important, or when fruit in contact with metal will discolour and take on a metallic taste.

~ Let eggs, butter and liquid come to room temperature before making batter. Room-temperature eggs will give you more volume and will be capable of holding air, so butter will beat up lighter and creamier. To warm cold eggs, immerse in a bowl of warm-to-the-touch water.

MAKE-AHEAD   FREEZABLE   CLASSIC

Canada's Best Carrot Cake with Cream Cheese Icing

Birthdays, weddings, reunions — this moist cake is welcome at all special occasions.

2 cups	all-purpose flour	500 mL
2 tsp	baking powder	10 mL
2 tsp	cinnamon	10 mL
1 tsp	baking soda	5 mL
¾ tsp	salt	4 mL
½ tsp	nutmeg	2 mL
¾ cup	each granulated and packed brown sugar	175 mL
3	eggs	3
¾ cup	vegetable oil	175 mL

1 tsp	vanilla	5 mL
2 cups	grated carrots	500 mL
1 cup	drained canned crushed pineapple	250 mL
½ cup	chopped pecans	125 mL
ICING:		
1	pkg (8 oz/250 g) cream cheese, softened	1
¼ cup	butter, softened	50 mL
½ tsp	vanilla	2 mL
1 cup	icing sugar	250 mL

Makes 18 servings.

PER SERVING, ABOUT:

cal	338	carb	38 g
pro	4 g	fibre	1 g
total fat	20 g	chol	58 mg
sat. fat	6 g	sodium	278 mg

PERCENTAGE RDI:

calcium	4%	vit. A	38%
iron	9%	vit. C	2%
folate	10%		

1 Grease and flour 13- x 9-inch (3.5 L) metal cake pan; set aside.

2 In large bowl, whisk together flour, baking powder, cinnamon, baking soda, salt and nutmeg. In separate bowl, beat together granulated and brown sugars, eggs, oil and vanilla until smooth; pour over flour mixture and stir just until moistened. Stir in carrots, pineapple and pecans. Spread in prepared pan.

3 Bake in centre of 350°F (180°C) oven for 40 minutes or until cake tester inserted in centre comes out clean. Let cool in pan on rack. (MAKE-AHEAD: Cover with plastic wrap and store at room temperature for up to 2 days or overwrap with heavy-duty foil and freeze for up to 2 weeks; let thaw before continuing.)

4 ICING: In bowl, beat cream cheese with butter until smooth. Beat in vanilla. Beat in icing sugar, one-third at a time, until smooth. Spread over top of cake. (MAKE-AHEAD: Cover loosely and refrigerate for up to 1 day.)

When IS THE CAKE DONE?

🍂 Set timer for 5 minutes less than the time specified in recipe; check cake then for the following signs. If the cake is not done, return it to the oven to finish baking.

🍂 A fully baked cake will spring back when lightly touched in the centre. The cake also draws away slightly from the side of the pan, and a cake tester (a toothpick or skewer works well) inserted in the centre comes out clean. Also trust your sense of smell: the fresh aroma of butter and sugar wafting out of the oven can be the signal to check the cake.

🍂 When cakes emerge from the oven, their structure is set, but the set is still fragile. Let cakes stand in pans on rack for time specified in each recipe, usually 15 to 20 minutes. Run knife around edge of cake, then place rack over pan and invert cake onto rack to cool completely.

Rich Brandied Fruitcake

High-quality candied fruit makes this traditional cake easy and quick to prepare. However, when it comes to raisins, only flat, seeded ones, often called muscat or lexia, deliver the authentic rich, winy flavour.

4 cups	candied mixed peel	1 L
3 cups	seeded raisins (lexia)	750 mL
1 cup	dark seedless raisins (Thompson)	250 mL
1 cup	currants	250 mL
1 cup	halved candied cherries	250 mL
1 cup	brandy or rum	250 mL
½ cup	diced candied pineapple	125 mL
1 cup	butter, softened	250 mL
1¼ cups	packed brown sugar	300 mL

3	eggs	3
2 tsp	vanilla	10 mL
2 cups	all-purpose flour	500 mL
1½ tsp	baking powder	7 mL
1 tsp	each cinnamon and nutmeg	5 mL
½ tsp	each salt and ground cloves	2 mL
1 cup	each chopped pecans and blanched slivered almonds	250 mL

1 Line two 9- x 5-inch (2 L) and one 5¾- x 3¼-inch (625 mL) loaf pans with parchment paper. Set aside.

2 In large glass bowl, stir together candied peel, seeded and dark raisins, currants, cherries, brandy and pineapple; cover with plastic wrap. Let stand for 12 hours or microwave at High for 3 minutes or until steaming; stir and let cool.

3 In large bowl, beat butter with sugar until fluffy; beat in eggs, 1 at a time. Beat in vanilla. In separate bowl, whisk together flour, baking powder, cinnamon, nutmeg, salt and cloves; stir into batter, one-third at a time. Scrape fruit mixture over batter; sprinkle with pecans and almonds. Stir just enough to coat fruit and nuts evenly. Spoon into prepared pans, packing with back of spoon; tap pans lightly on counter to release air bubbles.

4 Bake in centre of 300°F (150°C) oven for about 1¼ hours for small loaf and 2 hours for large loaves or until cake tester inserted in centre comes out clean. Let cool in pans on racks for 30 minutes. Remove from pans; let cool completely on racks. Remove paper. Wrap in plastic wrap, then heavy-duty foil; store in cool place for up to 2 months.

TEST KITCHEN TIPS

• Choose shiny pans; line with white parchment paper.

• Before heating oven, place shallow roasting pan on lowest rack; fill half-full with hot water.

• Place foil loosely over cakes after about 1 hour of baking.

• To prevent cakes from drying out over a long span of time, wrap with cheesecloth and brush with brandy before wrapping in plastic wrap and heavy-duty foil. Every few weeks, unwrap cakes and brush cheesecloth again with brandy.

Makes 2 large cakes, 36 slices each, and 1 small cake, 24 slices.

PER SLICE LARGE CAKE, ABOUT:

cal	132	carb	24 g
pro	1 g	fibre	1 g
total fat	4 g	chol	14 mg
sat. fat	2 g	sodium	56 mg

PERCENTAGE RDI:

calcium	2%	vit. A	3%
iron	4%	vit. C	3%
folate	2%		

Classic Angel Food Cake

Store-bought angel food cakes tend to be extremely sweet. So why bother? With an electric mixer, it really isn't hard to whip up one of these impressively ethereal cakes. Flavour it any way you want — with almond and vanilla, with chocolate, with lemon-lime — or celebrate with a cascade of berries and cream.

1¼ cups	sifted cake-and-pastry flour	300 mL		1 tsp	cream of tartar	5 mL
1½ cups	granulated sugar	375 mL		½ tsp	salt	2 mL
1½ cups	egg whites (about 11)	375 mL		2 tsp	vanilla	10 mL
1 tbsp	lemon juice	15 mL		½ tsp	almond extract	2 mL

1 Into bowl, sift flour with ¾ cup (175 mL) of the sugar; sift again into separate bowl. Set aside.

2 In large bowl, beat egg whites until foamy. Add lemon juice, cream of tartar and salt; beat until soft peaks form. Beat in remaining sugar, 2 tbsp (25 mL) at a time, until stiff glossy peaks form. Sift flour mixture over top, one-quarter at a time, gently folding in each addition until blended. Fold in vanilla and almond extract. Pour into ungreased 10-inch (4 L) tube pan. Run spatula through batter to eliminate any large air bubbles; smooth top.

3 Bake in centre of 350°F (180°C) oven for 40 to 45 minutes or until cake springs back when lightly touched. Turn pan upside down and let hang on legs attached to pan, or on bottle, until completely cooled. Remove from pan. (MAKE-AHEAD: Wrap in plastic wrap and store in airtight container for up to 2 days or freeze for up to 1 month.)

VARIATIONS

Lemon-Lime Angel Food Cake: Fold in 1 tbsp (15 mL) each grated lemon and lime rind along with vanilla. Omit almond extract.

Chocolate Angel Food Cake: Replace ¼ cup (50 mL) of the flour with cocoa powder.

Chocolate Espresso Angel Food Cake: Omit almond extract. Stir 4 tsp (20 mL) instant espresso granules or instant coffee granules with vanilla before folding into batter. Fold in 3 oz (90 g) bittersweet chocolate, grated.

Celebration Angel Food Cake: Replace almond extract with 1 tbsp (15 mL) grated orange rind. Whip 2 cups (500 mL) whipping cream; fold in ¼ cup (50 mL) orange liqueur and 2 tbsp (25 mL) icing sugar. Spread over top and side of cake. Fill centre and cover top with 4 cups (1 L) fresh fruit such as berries or sliced mangoes, letting some tumble down side.

Makes 12 servings.

PER SERVING, ABOUT:

cal 153	carb . . . . 34 g
pro . . . . 4 g	fibre . . . . trace
total fat . . . trace	chol . . . . 0 mg
sat. fat . . . . trace	sodium . . 146 mg

PERCENTAGE RDI:

calcium 0%	vit. A 0%
iron 5%	vit. C 0%
folate 6%	

Coconut Chiffon Cake

Surprisingly easy to make — and to make well — this all-occasion cake has an elegant and stylish simplicity. With coconut nicely distributed throughout the cake and crowning the top, this is a truly fancy dessert.

2 cups	sifted cake-and-pastry flour	500 mL
1⅓ cups	granulated sugar	325 mL
2 tsp	baking powder	10 mL
¼ tsp	salt	1 mL
¼ cup	water	50 mL
¼ cup	vegetable oil	50 mL
6	eggs, separated	6
½ tsp	coconut extract	2 mL

1 cup	shredded sweetened coconut	250 mL
¼ tsp	cream of tartar	1 mL
GARNISH:		
⅔ cup	flaked or shredded sweetened coconut	150 mL
1 cup	icing sugar, sifted	250 mL
4 tsp	milk	20 mL
½ tsp	vanilla	2 mL

1 Grease 10-inch (3 L) springform pan; line bottom and side with parchment paper. Set aside.

2 Into bowl, sift together flour, ⅔ cup (150 mL) of the sugar, baking powder and salt. Combine water with oil; pour into dry ingredients and stir to combine. Add egg yolks and coconut extract; beat at low speed just until smooth and thickened, scraping down side of bowl once. Stir in coconut. Set aside.

3 Stir remaining granulated sugar with cream of tartar. In separate bowl, beat egg whites until frothy; beat in sugar mixture in slow steady stream, about 1 minute. Beat until soft peaks form. Fold one-quarter into yolk mixture; fold in remaining whites until no streaks remain. Pour into prepared pan, filling right to top. Bake in centre of 350°F (180°C) oven for about 50 minutes or until top springs back when lightly touched. Let cool in pan on rack. (MAKE-AHEAD: Wrap in plastic wrap and store in airtight container at room temperature for up to 2 days or freeze for up to 2 weeks; let thaw before continuing.)

4 GARNISH: Spread half of the coconut on baking sheet; toast in 300°F (150°C) oven for 10 to 12 minutes or until golden. Let cool. Combine with remaining coconut and set aside.

5 In small bowl, whisk together icing sugar, milk and vanilla until smooth; spread over top of cake, letting some drip down side. Sprinkle coconut over icing.

CAKE-AND-PASTRY Flour

Cake-and-pastry flour is 100 per cent soft wheat flour with low protein content and very fine granulation. It is best for light cakes and pastries, in which a tender, fine texture is desired. It can be used for all baking except yeast breads. Although results will not be identical, all-purpose flour can be substituted for cake-and-pastry flour by using 2 tbsp (25 mL) less per cup (250 mL).

Makes 16 servings.

PER SERVING, ABOUT:

cal	241	carb	38 g
pro	4 g	fibre	1 g
total fat	8 g	chol	81 mg
sat. fat	4 g	sodium	116 mg

PERCENTAGE RDI:

calcium	3%	vit. A	4%
iron	9%	vit. C	0%
folate	10%		

Banana Split Roll

Enjoy all the flavours of an old-fashioned soda-fountain favourite in this fanciful cake.

CHOCOLATE Sauce

In small saucepan, bring 1 cup (250 mL) whipping cream and 2 tbsp (25 mL) corn syrup to boil. Add 6 oz (175 g) bittersweet chocolate, chopped; whisk until smooth. Let stand for 15 minutes or until thickened. (MAKE-AHEAD: Cover with plastic wrap and refrigerate for up to 5 days. Reheat before using.)

⅓ cup	butter, softened	75 mL
¾ cup	granulated sugar	175 mL
3	egg yolks	3
⅔ cup	mashed bananas (about 2)	150 mL
½ cup	buttermilk	125 mL
1 cup	all-purpose flour	250 mL
¾ tsp	each baking powder and baking soda	4 mL
½ tsp	salt	2 mL
6	egg whites	6

FILLING:

1 cup	whipping cream	250 mL
2 tbsp	icing sugar	25 mL
1 tsp	vanilla	5 mL

GARNISH:

¾ cup	Strawberry Sauce (recipe follows)	175 mL
24	banana slices	24
12	pineapple slices	12
¾ cup	Chocolate Sauce (recipe, this page)	175 mL

1 Line 17- x 11-inch (45 x 29 cm) rimmed baking sheet with parchment paper; set aside.

2 In large bowl, beat butter with sugar until light and fluffy; beat in egg yolks, 1 at a time, beating well after each addition. Stir in bananas and buttermilk. In separate bowl, whisk together flour, baking powder, baking soda and salt; add to batter and stir just until combined. In separate bowl and using clean beaters, beat egg whites until soft peaks form. Stir one-quarter into banana mixture; fold in remaining egg whites. Spread in prepared pan, smoothing top.

3 Bake in centre of 350°F (180°C) oven for about 20 minutes or until golden. Loosen edges with knife; let cool in pan on rack for 5 minutes. Invert onto tea towel; peel off paper. Starting at long edge, roll up cake in towel; let cool on rack.

4 FILLING: In bowl, whip cream; beat in sugar and vanilla. Unroll cake. Spread with cream mixture. Using towel as support, roll up cake without towel. (MAKE-AHEAD: Cover and refrigerate for up to 8 hours.)

5 GARNISH: Pool Strawberry Sauce on each plate. Top with 3 thin slices or 1 thick slice cake. Garnish with fruit slices. Drizzle with Chocolate Sauce.

Strawberry Sauce

Purée together 2 cups (500 mL) strawberries, ⅓ cup (75 mL) granulated sugar and ¼ cup (50 mL) water or orange juice. Press through fine sieve to remove seeds, adding up to 2 tbsp (25 mL) more liquid if desired. **Makes 1⅓ cups (325 mL).**

Makes 12 servings.

PER SERVING, ABOUT:

cal 345	carb . . . . 44 g
pro . . . . 5 g	fibre . . . . 1 g
total fat . . . . 18 g	chol . . . . . 100 mg
sat. fat . . . . . 10 g	sodium . . 289 mg

PERCENTAGE RDI:

calcium 5%	vit. A 16%
iron 9%	vit. C 23%
folate 13%	

Strawberry Shortcake

While biscuits, also known as scones, are the traditional base for homemade short-cake, the trend is to layer the strawberries and cream with cake. The combination is lighter and allows you to make the cake up to one day ahead — a liberty you cannot take with biscuits.

¼ cup	milk	50 mL
2 tbsp	butter	25 mL
1 tsp	grated orange rind	5 mL
¾ cup	sifted cake-and-pastry flour	175 mL
1 tsp	baking powder	5 mL
¼ tsp	salt	1 mL
5	eggs	5
¾ cup	granulated sugar	175 mL

FILLING:

1½ cups	whipping cream	375 mL
2 tbsp	granulated sugar	25 mL
1 tsp	vanilla	5 mL
4 cups	sliced strawberries	1 L

GARNISH:

1 tsp	icing sugar	5 mL
5	whole strawberries	5

1 Line 15- x 10-inch (40 x 25 cm) rimmed baking sheet with parchment paper; set aside.

2 In saucepan, heat milk with butter over medium heat until melted; stir in orange rind and keep warm. In bowl, whisk together flour, baking powder and salt; set aside. Separate 3 of the eggs, reserving yolks. In another bowl, beat egg whites until foamy. Beat in ¼ cup (50 mL) of the sugar, 1 tbsp (15 mL) at a time, until soft peaks form.

3 In separate large bowl, beat together egg yolks, remaining eggs and sugar for about 5 minutes or until pale and thick enough that batter leaves ribbons on surface for 3 seconds when beaters are lifted. Fold in egg white mixture. Sift dry ingredients over top; fold in until combined. Make well in centre; pour in milk mixture and fold in. Spread in prepared pan.

4 Bake in centre of 350°F (180°C) oven for about 12 minutes or until golden and top springs back when lightly touched. Let cool in pan on rack. (MAKE-AHEAD: Cover with plastic wrap and store for up to 1 day.)

5 FILLING: In bowl, whip cream with sugar and vanilla. Cut cake crosswise into 3 equal layers. Transfer one layer to serving plate. Spread with half of the whipped cream, then half of the strawberries. Top with second cake layer, spread with remaining cream, then berries. Top with last cake layer. Cover and refrigerate for 1 hour.

6 GARNISH: To serve, dust with icing sugar. Garnish with whole berries.

TEST KITCHEN TIPS

• In June and July, shortcake overflows with strawberries. As the summer heats up, raspberries join their red berry buddies. In August, sliced peaches or nectarines can take their place. Blueberries are a colourful addition to peaches or berries; add them whenever you can.

• Sprinkling the fruit lightly with sugar and letting it macerate for about 30 minutes makes a delicious juice to drench the cake and leave guests besotted.

Makes 12 servings.

PER SERVING, ABOUT:

cal 247	carb .... 25 g
pro .... 4 g	fibre .... 1 g
total fat .... 15 g	chol ..... 133 mg
sat. fat ...... 8 g	sodium .. 129 mg

PERCENTAGE RDI:

calcium 5%	vit. A 18%
iron 7%	vit. C 53%
folate 12%	

Mocha Marjolaine

Invite company to enjoy this rich coffee-and-chocolate meringue dessert, a French pastry-shop specialty.

1½ cups	toasted hazelnuts	375 mL		8 oz	semisweet chocolate	250 g
1 cup	granulated sugar	250 mL		3 cups	whipping cream	750 mL
2 cups	toasted sliced almonds	500 mL		1 tbsp	instant coffee granules	15 mL
2 tbsp	cornstarch	25 mL		1 tbsp	granulated sugar	15 mL
7	egg whites	7		1 tbsp	hot water	15 mL
½ tsp	cream of tartar	2 mL			Whole hazelnuts (optional)	

1 Line 17- x 11-inch (45 x 29 cm) rimmed baking sheet with parchment paper. Draw three 16- x 3-inch (40 x 8 cm) rectangles on paper; turn paper over. Set aside.

2 In food processor, finely grind hazelnuts with ⅓ cup (75 mL) of the sugar; transfer to bowl. Set aside 1 cup (250 mL) of the almonds for garnish. In food processor, finely grind remaining almonds with ⅓ cup (75 mL) of the remaining sugar; stir into hazelnuts along with cornstarch.

3 In large bowl, beat egg whites with cream of tartar until soft peaks form; gradually beat in remaining sugar, 2 tbsp (25 mL) at a time, until stiff peaks form. Fold in nut mixture in 3 additions; spread evenly over rectangles. Bake in centre of 275°F (140°C) oven for 1½ hours or until golden. Let meringues cool in pan on rack.

4 Meanwhile, chop 6 oz (175 g) of the chocolate; place in bowl. In saucepan, bring ½ cup (125 mL) of the cream to boil; pour over chocolate, stirring until melted to form ganache (icing). Refrigerate for 30 minutes or until spreadable.

5 Meanwhile, chop remaining chocolate; melt in bowl set over saucepan of hot (not boiling) water. Let cool. In separate bowl, whip 2 cups (500 mL) of the remaining cream; fold 2 tbsp (25 mL) into cooled chocolate. Fold back into whipped cream.

6 Dissolve coffee granules and sugar in hot water; let cool slightly. In another bowl, whip remaining cream with coffee mixture. Set aside.

7 Gently remove meringues from paper; trim with sharp knife if necessary to make uniform size. Place 1 of the meringues on serving platter; spread with one-third of the chilled ganache. Spread ¼-inch (5 mm) thick layer of chocolate whipped cream over ganache.

Makes 10 servings.

PER SERVING, ABOUT:

cal	712	carb	47 g
pro	12 g	fibre	4 g
total fat	57 g	chol	92 mg
sat. fat	22 g	sodium	69 mg

PERCENTAGE RDI:

calcium	14%	vit. A	27%
iron	16%	vit. C	2%
folate	13%		

8 Spread second meringue with half of the remaining ganache; place on top of first meringue. Spread coffee whipped cream over top. Spread remaining ganache over third meringue; place on top of coffee whipped cream. Spread enough of the remaining chocolate whipped cream to cover sides and top, leaving ends bare.

9 Use remaining chocolate whipped cream to pipe rosettes on top. Garnish top with whole hazelnuts (if using) and sides with reserved almonds. Freeze for at least 4 hours or until solid. (MAKE-AHEAD: Wrap in heavy-duty foil and freeze for up to 2 days.) Serve frozen.

BEATING Egg Whites

➤ Use scrupulously clean metal or glass bowl and clean beaters. A tall, narrow bowl that maximizes the beating action is preferable to a wide, shallow one.

➤ Bring eggs to room temperature in bowl of warm water if necessary; cold eggs do not beat up to as high a volume.

➤ Separate eggs carefully, not allowing the least speck of yolk into the whites. If this happens, use a piece of eggshell to lift out yolk cleanly. To be on the safe side (and in baking, this is the side you want to be on), separate yolks and whites into two separate bowls. Check each white, then transfer to bowl in which you intend to make meringue. This way, a bit of yolk in the last egg white won't ruin the rest, which, when making an angel food cake or dacquoise, can be close to a dozen.

➤ Beat at low speed until foamy; add cream of tartar, if required in the recipe, at this stage to stabilize egg whites.

➤ Increase speed to high and beat until whites mound and form soft peaks that droop when the beaters are lifted.

➤ At this soft peak stage, begin gradually adding sugar, about 2 tbsp (25 mL) at a time, until whites form glossy peaks that stand straight up when beaters are lifted. Sugar helps stabilize and stiffen whites.

Raspberry Cookies and Cream Torte

The cream and raspberry layers of this dessert — lavish enough for entertaining — are separated by thin waferlike cookies, crisp when the torte is assembled but softened enough to be cut into neat wedges after it stands for a few hours in the refrigerator. Serve with extra raspberries if desired.

RASPBERRY Sauce

In food processor or blender, purée 3 pkg (each 300 g) frozen unsweetened raspberries, thawed; press through sieve into bowl to remove seeds. Whisk in ¾ cup (175 mL) instant dissolving (fruit/berry) sugar, and 1 tbsp (15 mL) raspberry liqueur if desired. **Makes about 2½ cups (625 mL).** For smaller amounts, divide into thirds.

2 cups	whipping cream	500 mL	1 cup	all-purpose flour	250 mL
⅓ cup	icing sugar	75 mL	¾ cup	unsalted butter, melted	175 mL
	Raspberry Sauce (recipe this page)		2 tbsp	water	25 mL
	Icing sugar (optional)		1 tbsp	vanilla	15 mL

WAFERS:

6	egg whites	6
1½ cups	granulated sugar	375 mL

1 Line 2 large rimmed baking sheets with parchment paper. Draw two 8-inch (20 cm) circles on each; turn paper over. Set aside.

2 WAFERS: In large bowl, lightly whisk egg whites; gradually whisk in sugar, flour, butter, water and vanilla just until blended. Drop ⅓ cup (75 mL) batter onto each circle; gently spread to cover circle.

3 Bake, 1 sheet at a time, in upper half of 400°F (200°C) oven for 8 to 10 minutes or until edges are just beginning to brown; let cool on baking sheet on rack for 2 minutes. Transfer to flat surface; let cool completely. Repeat with remaining batter to make 9 wafers. (MAKE-AHEAD: Layer between waxed paper and store in airtight container for up to 2 days.)

4 In bowl, whip cream with icing sugar. Place 1 wafer on cake plate; spread with ½ cup (125 mL) of the whipped cream. Drizzle with ¼ cup (50 mL) of the Raspberry Sauce. Repeat layering with 7 of the remaining wafers, cream and sauce. Top with remaining wafer. Cover and refrigerate for 1½ to 2 hours or until wafers have softened just enough to cut into wedges. Dust with icing sugar (if using).

Makes 8 servings.

PER SERVING, ABOUT:

cal 647	carb . . . . 72 g
pro . . . . 6 g	fibre . . . . trace
total fat . . . . 39 g	chol . . . . . 123 mg
sat. fat . . . . . 24 g	sodium . . . 65 mg

PERCENTAGE RDI:

calcium 6%	vit. A 40%
iron 8%	vit. C 25%
folate 16%	

Orange Pecan Meringue Cake

A cake of nut meringues layered with flavoured whipped cream is called a dacquoise in French. Whether chocolate, orange or fruit, dacquoises are impressive and, since they must be made ahead in order for the filling to soften the meringues, are a boon for the baker.

2¼ cups	toasted pecans	550 mL
1½ cups	granulated sugar	375 mL
2 tbsp	cornstarch	25 mL
9	egg whites	9
1 tsp	vanilla	5 mL

ORANGE CREAM:

2 cups	whipping cream	500 mL
¾ cup	sifted icing sugar	175 mL

2 tbsp	orange-flavoured liqueur or orange juice	25 mL
1 tbsp	grated orange rind	15 mL

GARNISH:

	Orange or kumquat slices
	Mint or orange leaves

1 Line 2 large rimmed baking sheets with parchment paper. Using 8-inch (1.2 L) round metal cake pan as guide, draw 2 circles on each paper; turn paper over.

2 In food processor, chop 1½ cups (375 mL) of the pecans with ½ cup (125 mL) of the sugar and cornstarch until finely ground; set aside.

3 In bowl, beat egg whites until soft peaks form; beat in remaining sugar, 2 tbsp (25 mL) at a time, until stiff glossy peaks form. Beat in vanilla. Sprinkle with half of the nut mixture and fold in; fold in remaining nut mixture. Spread over circles.

4 Bake in top and bottom thirds of 275°F (140°C) oven for 60 to 75 minutes or until tops are firm to the touch, switching and rotating baking sheets halfway through. Using sharp knife and same round cake pan as guide, trim meringues into even circles while still hot. Slide long metal spatula under meringues to loosen; carefully transfer to rack and let cool completely. (MAKE-AHEAD: Layer between waxed paper and store in airtight container for up to 1 week.)

5 ORANGE CREAM: In bowl, whip cream with sugar and liqueur; stir in orange rind. Centre 1 meringue on serving plate. Slide strips of waxed paper between meringue and plate. Using two-thirds of the orange cream, stack remaining meringues, spreading orange cream between layers. Spread remaining cream over top and side. Chop remaining pecans; press into side of cake. Refrigerate for 1 hour. (MAKE-AHEAD: Refrigerate for up to 8 hours.) Remove paper strips. Garnish with orange slices and mint. To serve, slice with serrated knife.

TO TOAST Nuts

Spread nuts on baking sheet and toast in 350°F (180°C) oven for 6 to 10 minutes or until fragrant and golden, stirring once. For smaller nuts — such as pine nuts or sliced, chopped or slivered nuts — bake for 4 to 8 minutes, again stirring to prevent burning and to bake evenly.

Makes 10 servings.

PER SERVING, ABOUT:

cal 511	carb .... 47 g
pro .... 6 g	fibre .... 2 g
total fat .... 35 g	chol ...... 61 mg
sat. fat ..... 12 g	sodium ... 67 mg

PERCENTAGE RDI:

calcium 4%	vit. A 18%
iron 4%	vit. C 3%
folate 6%	

Cinnamon Toast Coffee Cake

This fine, moist cake with tunnels of cinnamon, butter and brown sugar comes together thanks to an unusual but easy method.

TEST KITCHEN TIP: To add a glaze to the coffee cake, whisk together ¾ cup (175 mL) icing sugar, 2 tbsp (25 mL) water, 1½ tsp (7 mL) espresso powder or instant coffee granules and ¼ tsp (1 mL) cinnamon; drizzle over cooled coffee cake.

4	egg yolks	4
⅔ cup	sour cream	150 mL
1 tsp	vanilla	5 mL
2 cups	sifted cake-and-pastry flour	500 mL
1 cup	granulated sugar	250 mL
½ tsp	each baking soda and baking powder	2 mL

Pinch	salt	Pinch
¾ cup	butter, softened	175 mL
CINNAMON FILLING:		
⅓ cup	packed brown sugar	75 mL
3 tbsp	butter, softened	50 mL
2 tbsp	cinnamon	25 mL
1 tbsp	cake-and-pastry flour	15 mL

1 Grease 10-inch (3 L) Bundt pan; set aside.

2 FILLING: In small bowl and using wooden spoon, beat together brown sugar, butter, cinnamon and flour; set aside.

3 In separate small bowl, whisk together egg yolks, 1 tbsp (15 mL) of the sour cream and vanilla. In large bowl, whisk together flour, sugar, baking soda, baking powder and salt; beat in butter and remaining sour cream on low speed until ingredients begin to clump. Increase speed to high; beat for 1½ minutes. Add egg mixture in 3 additions, beating well and scraping down side of bowl between each.

4 Scrape 1 cup (250 mL) of the batter into prepared pan; smooth surface. Using back of spoon, make ditch in middle of batter in pan. Fold ¾ cup (175 mL) of the remaining batter into cinnamon filling until streaky. Drop spoonfuls of streaky batter into ditch. Top with remaining batter, smoothing evenly to touch inside edge of pan.

5 Bake in centre of 350°F (180°C) oven for 40 minutes or until cake tester inserted in centre comes out clean. Let cool in pan on rack for 15 minutes. Remove from pan; let cool completely on rack. (MAKE-AHEAD: Store in airtight container for up to 3 days or wrap in plastic wrap, overwrap with heavy-duty foil and freeze for up to 2 weeks.)

Makes 10 to 12 servings.

PER EACH OF 12 SERVINGS, ABOUT:

cal 325	carb . . . . 39 g
pro . . . . 3 g	fibre . . . . 1 g
total fat . . . . 18 g	chol . . . . . 117 mg
sat. fat . . . . . 11 g	sodium . . 217 mg

PERCENTAGE RDI:

calcium 5%	vit. A 18%
iron 14%	vit. C 0%
folate 13%	

Rhubarb Upside-Down Cake

For maximum visual impact, choose the pinkest, most tender rhubarb stalks. Forced rhubarb, available from January until the garden variety pushes up from the soil in April, is often pinker.

3 tbsp	butter, melted	50 mL		2	eggs	2
⅔ cup	granulated sugar	150 mL		1 tsp	vanilla	5 mL
1 lb	trimmed rhubarb (about 10 stalks)	500 g		1½ cups	all-purpose flour	375 mL
				1½ tsp	baking powder	7 mL
1½ tsp	grated orange rind	7 mL		1 tsp	baking soda	5 mL
CAKE:				1 tsp	grated orange rind	5 mL
½ cup	butter, softened	125 mL		¼ tsp	salt	1 mL
¾ cup	granulated sugar	175 mL		1 cup	plain yogurt	250 mL

1 Grease side of 9-inch (2.5 L) springform pan; pour in butter and sprinkle with sugar. Cut rhubarb into 2-inch (5 cm) pieces. Arrange in tight rows in bottom of pan, starting with middle 3 rows and trimming to fit. Chop remaining pieces coarsely; sprinkle on top along with orange rind. Set aside.

2 CAKE: In large bowl, beat butter with sugar until fluffy; beat in eggs, 1 at a time. Beat in vanilla. In separate bowl, whisk together flour, baking powder, baking soda, orange rind and salt; stir half into butter mixture. Stir in yogurt, then remaining flour mixture. Spread over rhubarb without disturbing rows, mounding higher at edge. Wrap foil around bottom of pan and set on baking sheet. Bake in centre of 350°F (180°C) oven for about 1 hour or until top springs back when lightly touched. Let cool in pan on rack for 15 minutes. Invert onto cake plate. Serve warm.

TENDER Rhubarb

To force rhubarb to grow out of season, farmers transplant rhubarb roots in the fall from fields into hothouse sheds. After a period of freezing cold, the space is warmed and the roots sprout into stalks. Unlike such greenhouse crops as tomatoes, peppers, cucumbers and lettuce, rhubarb is forced in the dark to keep the shoots pink and toothsomely tender.

Makes 8 to 10 servings.

PER EACH OF 10 SERVINGS, ABOUT:

cal	332	carb	47 g
pro	5 g	fibre	1 g
total fat	15 g	chol	79 mg
sat. fat	9 g	sodium	372 mg

PERCENTAGE RDI:

calcium	10%	vit. A	14%
iron	8%	vit. C	5%
folate	13%		

Blueberry Cheese Coffee Cake

This sumptuous cake combines the best of creamy cheesecake and moist coffee cake.

TEST KITCHEN TIP: If you don't have the exact size of pan called for, substitute a slightly larger pan. As a general rule, use a pan that is ½ to 1 inch (1 to 2.5 cm) larger — never one that is smaller. Reduce baking time slightly.

⅓ cup	butter, softened	75 mL
⅔ cup	granulated sugar	150 mL
2	eggs	2
2 tsp	vanilla	10 mL
1½ cups	all-purpose flour	375 mL
1 tsp	baking powder	5 mL
½ tsp	baking soda	2 mL
¼ tsp	salt	1 mL
½ cup	sour cream	125 mL
1½ cups	fresh or frozen wild blueberries	375 mL

CRUMB TOPPING:

1 cup	all-purpose flour	250 mL
¼ cup	packed brown sugar	50 mL
¼ cup	granulated sugar	50 mL
½ tsp	cinnamon	2 mL
⅓ cup	butter, melted	75 mL

CREAM CHEESE FILLING:

1	pkg (8 oz/250 g) cream cheese, softened	1
¼ cup	granulated sugar	50 mL
1	egg	1
1 tsp	finely grated lemon rind	5 mL

1 Grease 9-inch (2.5 L) springform pan; set aside.

2 CRUMB TOPPING: In small bowl, combine flour, brown and granulated sugars and cinnamon. Drizzle with butter; toss until thoroughly moistened. Set aside.

3 CHEESE FILLING: In bowl, beat cream cheese with sugar until light and fluffy, scraping down side of bowl occasionally. Beat in egg and lemon rind just until smooth; set aside.

4 In large bowl, beat butter with sugar until well combined. Beat in eggs, 1 at a time, beating well after each addition. Beat in vanilla. In separate bowl, whisk together flour, baking powder, baking soda and salt; stir into butter mixture alternately with sour cream, making 3 additions of dry ingredients and 2 of sour cream. Spread in prepared pan, mounding slightly. Sprinkle 1 cup (250 mL) of the blueberries over top. Gently spread cream cheese filling over blueberries; sprinkle with remaining blueberries. Sprinkle evenly with crumb topping.

5 Bake in centre of 350°F (180°C) oven for about 1¼ hours or until edge is set and just beginning to come away from pan. Let cool in pan on rack for 30 minutes. Serve warm or at room temperature.

Makes 12 servings.

PER SERVING, ABOUT:

cal 394	carb . . . . 48 g
pro . . . . 6 g	fibre . . . . 1 g
total fat . . . . 20 g	chol . . . . . 108 mg
sat. fat . . . . . 12 g	sodium . . 307 mg

PERCENTAGE RDI:

calcium 5%	vit. A 22%
iron 12%	vit. C 3%
folate 17%	

VARIATION

Raspberry Cheese Coffee Cake: Substitute raspberries for blueberries. If desired, bake in 10-inch (3 L) Bundt pan for about 1 hour.

Raspberry Chocolate Chip Bundt Cake

Frozen raspberries make this handsome cake a reality year-round. Of course, you can use fresh raspberries or, for a change of flavour, fresh wild blueberries.

2	pkg (each 300 g) frozen unsweetened raspberries	2
3 tbsp	icing sugar	50 mL
¾ cup	butter, softened	175 mL
1 cup	granulated sugar	250 mL
3	eggs	3
2 tsp	vanilla	10 mL

2¼ cups	all-purpose flour	550 mL
2 tsp	baking powder	10 mL
1½ tsp	baking soda	7 mL
½ tsp	salt	2 mL
1½ cups	sour cream	375 mL
1½ cups	chocolate chips	375 mL
¼ cup	light cream (10%)	50 mL

TEST KITCHEN TIP: When freezing cakes ahead, always let thaw before icing or glazing.

1 Grease 10-inch (3 L) Bundt pan; set aside.

2 Measure out 1 cup (250 mL) of the raspberries; thaw in sieve, reserving juice. Thaw remaining berries; purée in food processor, adding reserved juice. Press through sieve into bowl to remove seeds; add icing sugar. Set sauce aside.

3 In bowl, beat butter with sugar until light and fluffy; beat in eggs, 1 at a time. Beat in vanilla. In separate bowl, whisk together flour, baking powder, baking soda and salt; stir half into butter mixture. Stir in sour cream; stir in remaining flour mixture. Stir in 1 cup (250 mL) of the chocolate chips. Spread half into prepared pan; sprinkle with reserved drained berries. Spread remaining batter over top.

4 Bake in centre of 350°F (180°C) oven for 40 minutes or until top springs back when lightly touched. Let cool in pan on rack for 10 minutes. Remove from pan; let cool completely on rack. (MAKE-AHEAD: Wrap in plastic wrap and store in airtight container at room temperature for up to 1 day or freeze for up to 2 weeks; let thaw before continuing.) Transfer to cake plate.

5 Slide strips of waxed paper between cake and plate. Melt remaining chocolate chips with cream; pour over cake, drizzling down side. Serve with reserved raspberry sauce.

Makes 12 servings.

PER SERVING, ABOUT:

cal	447	carb	55 g
pro	6 g	fibre	2 g
total fat	24 g	chol	99 mg
sat. fat	14 g	sodium	435 mg

PERCENTAGE RDI:

calcium	8%	vit. A	18%
iron	15%	vit. C	17%
folate	20%		

MAKE-AHEAD   FREEZABLE

Very Gingery Ginger Cake

Ginger is a flavour so associated with cookies that sometimes it is forgotten for cake. In this recipe, you get to enjoy ginger to the max, with ground, fresh and crystallized ginger all packing a punch in the batter.

TEST KITCHEN TIP: Serve with lightly whipped cream or Lower-Fat Topping (page 336).

3 cups	all-purpose flour	750 mL
1 tbsp	cinnamon	15 mL
2 tsp	baking soda	10 mL
1½ tsp	ground cloves	7 mL
1 tsp	ground ginger	5 mL
¾ tsp	salt	4 mL
1½ cups	granulated sugar	375 mL

1 cup	each vegetable oil and fancy molasses	250 mL
2	eggs	2
½ cup	water	125 mL
2 tbsp	minced gingerroot	25 mL
½ cup	chopped crystallized ginger	125 mL
1 tbsp	icing sugar	15 mL

1 Grease and flour 10-inch (3 L) Bundt pan; set aside.

2 In bowl, whisk together flour, cinnamon, baking soda, cloves, ground ginger and salt. In large bowl, whisk together sugar, oil, molasses, eggs, water and gingerroot; stir in flour mixture, one-third at a time. Stir in crystallized ginger. Pour into prepared pan.

3 Bake in centre of 350°F (180°C) oven for about 1 hour or until cake tester inserted in centre comes out clean. Let cool in pan on rack for 30 minutes. Remove from pan; let cool completely on rack. (MAKE-AHEAD: Cover with plastic wrap and store at room temperature for up to 1 day or overwrap with heavy-duty foil and freeze for up to 2 weeks.) Dust with icing sugar.

Makes 12 servings.

PER SERVING, ABOUT:

cal 492	carb . . . . 77 g
pro . . . . 4 g	fibre . . . . 1 g
total fat . . . . 19 g	chol . . . . . . 36 mg
sat. fat . . . . . . 2 g	sodium . . 366 mg

PERCENTAGE RDI:

calcium 9%	vit. A 2%
iron 34%	vit. C 7%
folate 17%	

Basic but Beautiful Cheesecake

Basic doesn't sound impressive enough for this taste- and texture-perfect cheesecake. Dress it up with fruit and/or sauces, or try the variation to widen your repertoire.

2	pkg (each 8 oz/250 g) cream cheese	2
¾ cup	granulated sugar	175 mL
3	eggs	3
1 tbsp	lemon juice	15 mL
2 tsp	vanilla	10 mL

Pinch	salt	Pinch
3 cups	sour cream	750 mL
CRUST:		
1 cup	graham cracker crumbs	250 mL
¼ cup	granulated sugar	50 mL
2 tbsp	butter, melted	25 mL

1 CRUST: In bowl, stir together crumbs, sugar and butter until well moistened; press onto bottom of lightly greased 8- or 8½-inch (2 or 2.25 L) springform pan. Centre pan on large square of foil; press up to side of pan. Bake in centre of 325°F (160°C) oven for 8 to 10 minutes or until set. Let cool.

2 Meanwhile, in large bowl, beat cream cheese until softened. Gradually beat in sugar; beat for 3 minutes or until smooth and light, scraping down bowl twice. Using low speed, beat in eggs, 1 at a time, beating well after each addition and scraping down bowl often. Blend in lemon juice, vanilla and salt, then sour cream. Pour over crust.

3 Set springform pan in larger pan; pour enough hot water into larger pan to come 1 inch (2.5 cm) up side of springform pan. Bake in centre of 325°F (160°C) oven for 1¼ hours or until shine disappears and edge is set yet centre still jiggles slightly. Turn off oven. Quickly run knife around edge of cake. Let cool in oven for 1 hour. Remove from water and transfer to rack; remove foil and let cool completely. (MAKE-AHEAD: Cover and refrigerate for up to 2 days or overwrap with heavy-duty foil and freeze for up to 2 weeks.)

VARIATION

Mocha Marble Cheesecake: CRUST: Substitute chocolate wafer crumbs for graham cracker crumbs. Omit sugar. CAKE: After preparing batter, dissolve 2 tsp (10 mL) instant coffee granules in 1 tbsp (15 mL) hot water. Divide batter in half. Whisk 8 oz (250 g) semisweet chocolate, melted and cooled, into one half; whisk coffee into chocolate mixture. By cupfuls (250 mL), alternately pour chocolate batter and plain batter over crust. Swirl handle of spoon through both batches, without disturbing crust, to create marbled effect. Bake as directed.

TEST KITCHEN TIP: Top slices of cheesecake with fresh berries or with Cherry Berry Sauce (see Waffles with Cherry Berry Sauce, page 264), Caramel Sauce (see Bananas in Caramel Sauce, page 298) or Raspberry Sauce (page 316).

Makes 10 to 12 servings.

PER EACH OF 12 SERVINGS, ABOUT:

cal	372	carb	27 g
pro	7 g	fibre	trace
total fat	27 g	chol	127 mg
sat. fat	16 g	sodium	238 mg

PERCENTAGE RDI:

calcium	9%	vit. A	29%
iron	8%	vit. C	0%
folate	7%		

Pies, Tarts
and Pastry

13

Pastry Principles   326

Best-Ever Apple Pie   328

Dutch Apple Pie   329

Tarte Tatin   330

Saskatoon Berry Pie   331

Guidelines for Double-Crust Fruit Pies   332

Strawberry Rhubarb Galette   333

Pear Pandowdy   334

Plum Almond Tart   335

Fresh Blueberry Tart   336

Fresh Strawberry Pie   337

Lemon Meringue Pie   338

Creamy Pumpkin Pie   339

Coconut Cream Pie   340

Gooey Butter Tarts   342

Pecan Pie   343

Cherry Chocolate Baklava   344

Frozen Peanut Butter Pie   345

Chocolate Caramel Macadamia Tart   346

White Chocolate Lemon Tart   347

Phyllo Fruit Cups with Orange White Chocolate Cream   348

PASTRY PRINCIPLES

Here's a selection of pastry recipes in amounts to suit your pie-making needs. The pastries can also be made with all cold butter if desired.

PERFECT PASTRY EVERY TIME

6 cups	sifted cake-and-pastry flour (or 5¼ cups/1.3 L all-purpose flour)	1.5 L
1½ tsp	salt	7 mL
2⅓ cups	lard or shortening (1 lb/454 g)	575 mL
1	egg	1
1 tbsp	vinegar	15 mL
	Ice water	

꙼ In large bowl, combine flour with salt. Using pastry blender or 2 knives, cut in lard until mixture resembles fine crumbs with a few larger pieces.

꙼ In liquid measure and using fork, beat egg with vinegar until blended. Add enough ice water to make 1 cup (250 mL).

꙼ Stirring briskly with fork, gradually add just enough of the egg mixture, 1 tbsp (15 mL) at a time, to flour mixture to make dough hold together. Divide into 6 portions and press each into disc. Wrap in plastic wrap and refrigerate for at least 30 minutes or until chilled. (MAKE-AHEAD: Refrigerate for up to 3 days or freeze for up to 3 months. Let cold pastry stand for 15 minutes at room temperature before rolling out.) **Makes enough for 6 single-crust or 3 double-crust 9-inch (23 cm) pies.**

PERFECT PROCESSOR PASTRY

3 cups	all-purpose flour	750 mL
1 tsp	salt	5 mL
½ cup	cold butter, cubed	125 mL
½ cup	cold lard or shortening, cubed	125 mL
1	egg	1
2 tsp	vinegar or lemon juice	10 mL
	Ice water	

꙼ In food processor fitted with metal blade, blend flour with salt. Using on/off motion, cut in butter and lard until mixture resembles fine crumbs with a few larger pieces.

꙼ In liquid measure, beat egg until foamy; add vinegar and enough ice water to make ⅔ cup (150 mL). With motor running, add egg mixture all at once; process just until dough starts to clump together. Do not let it form ball. Remove and press together into 2 discs. Wrap in plastic wrap and refrigerate for at least 30 minutes or until chilled. (MAKE-AHEAD: Refrigerate for up to 3 days or freeze for up to 3 months. Let cold pastry stand for 15 minutes at room temperature before rolling out.) **Makes enough for 2 single-crust or 1 double-crust 9- or 10-inch (23 or 25 cm) pies.**

BAKED SINGLE-CRUST PIE SHELL

1½ cups	all-purpose flour	375 mL
¼ tsp	salt	1 mL
¼ cup	each cold butter and shortening, cubed	50 mL
1	egg yolk	1
1 tsp	lemon juice	5 mL
	Ice water	

꙼ In bowl, mix flour with salt. Using pastry blender or 2 knives, cut in butter and shortening until mixture resembles fine crumbs with a few larger pieces. In liquid measure, beat egg yolk with lemon juice; mix in enough ice water to make ⅓ cup (75 mL). Drizzle over dry ingredients, stirring briskly with fork until ragged dough forms. Press into disc. Wrap in plastic wrap and refrigerate for at least 30 minutes or until chilled. (MAKE-AHEAD: Refrigerate for up to 3 days.)

꙼ On lightly floured surface, roll out pastry to ⅛-inch (3 mm) thickness; fit into 9-inch (23 cm) pie plate. Trim edge to ¾-inch (2 cm) overhang; fold overhang under and flute edge. Line pie shell with foil; fill with pie weights or dried beans. Bake in bottom third of 400°F (200°C) oven for 15 minutes. Remove weights and foil. Prick shell all over; bake for 10 minutes longer or until evenly golden. Let cool on rack.

Pastry Ingredients and Techniques

In pastry making, the purpose of cutting fat into flour is to produce both tenderness and flakiness. The fat can be lard, shortening, butter, hard margarine or a combination of these.

➤ Shortening and lard are easiest to work with and produce a good "short" (tender) texture. They can be interchanged in most recipes. Lard is animal fat and adds an old-fashioned flavour; shortening is usually made from vegetable oils (hardened by hydrogenation) and adds little flavour.

➤ Butter is used when a buttery flavour is desired; it has a higher moisture content than shortening and lard, and must be kept cold and handled quickly. Using a little shortening along with butter makes the pastry easier to work with.

➤ Regular hard margarine (not soft) can be substituted for butter in most recipes, but the pastry will not be as short and it won't have the same flavour. Butter is animal fat (made from cream); margarine is made from vegetable oils. Recipes using salted butter or margarine will, of course, call for less salt than those using shortening or lard.

Pastry Handling Made Easy

➤ After forming dough, press into disc(s) and wrap in plastic wrap. Chill for at least 30 minutes.

➤ On lightly floured surface or pastry cloth, roll out pastry with a well-floured or stockinette-covered rolling pin. Roll from the centre and lift pin at edge to maintain even thickness. Turn pin clockwise 45 degrees; repeat rolling out and turning rolling pin to desired thickness.

➤ Loosely roll dough around rolling pin; pick up and centre over pie plate. Unroll onto pie plate. Trim edge: for single-crust pie, trim to ¾ inch (2 cm) from rim, fold under and flute; for bottom shell of double-crust pie, trim to edge of pie plate. Moisten pastry on rim with water.

➤ For double-crust pie shells, roll out dough discs separately into same-size circles. Using rolling pin, drape over filling without stretching. Trim, leaving ¾-inch (2 cm) overhang. Gently lift bottom pastry rim and fold overhang under rim; press together to seal. Tilt sealed pastry rim up from pie plate at 45-degree angle.

➤ With hand on outside of tilted pastry rim and using thumb and bent index finger, gently twist rim to form scalloped edge. With small decorative cutter or tip of sharp knife, cut steam vents in centre.

Best-Ever Apple Pie

The apple of choice for apple pie is the Northern Spy. Just "Spies" to their fans, these apples may never win a beauty contest. But what they lack in looks, they more than make up for in taste: spicy and tart without being sour. Best of all, the slices hold together, making the filling as handsome as the glazed, flaky crust.

TEST KITCHEN TIP: The best fruit pies are freshly baked, but you can make fruit pies up to 8 hours before serving. Store at room temperature.

EASY-ROLL PASTRY:

¾ cup	shortening	175 mL
3 tbsp	butter, softened	50 mL
2¼ cups	all-purpose flour	550 mL
¾ tsp	salt	4 mL
½ cup	ice water	125 mL

FILLING:

8 cups	thinly sliced peeled tart apples (2¼ lb/1.125 kg)	2 L
2 tbsp	lemon juice	25 mL
½ cup	granulated sugar	125 mL
3 tbsp	all-purpose flour	50 mL
½ tsp	cinnamon	2 mL

GLAZE:

1	egg yolk	1
2 tsp	granulated sugar	10 mL

1 EASY-ROLL PASTRY: In bowl, beat shortening with butter until smooth; stir in flour and salt until ragged. Pour in water; stir until loose dough forms. Gather into 2 balls. On floured surface, gently press each into ¾-inch (2 cm) thick disc. Wrap in plastic wrap and refrigerate for at least 1 hour or until chilled.

2 On lightly floured surface, roll out 1 of the discs into 13-inch (33 cm) circle. Fit into 9-inch (23 cm) pie plate; trim, leaving ¾-inch (2 cm) overhang.

3 FILLING: In large bowl, toss apples with lemon juice. Stir together sugar, flour and cinnamon; sprinkle over apples and toss until coated. Scrape into pie shell.

4 Roll out remaining pastry to same-size circle. Brush pastry on rim with water; fit pastry over filling. Trim, leaving ¾-inch (2 cm) overhang; fold overhang under pastry rim; seal and flute edge.

Makes 6 to 8 servings.

5 GLAZE: Whisk egg yolk with 1 tbsp (15 mL) water; brush over pastry. Sprinkle with sugar. Cut steam vents in centre. Bake in bottom third of 425°F (220°C) oven for 15 minutes. Reduce heat to 350°F (180°C); bake for 40 minutes longer or until golden, filling is bubbly and apples are soft. Let cool on rack.

PER EACH OF 8 SERVINGS, ABOUT:

cal 445	carb . . . . 59 g
pro . . . . 4 g	fibre . . . . 4 g
total fat . . . . 22 g	chol . . . . . . 38 mg
sat. fat . . . . . . 7 g	sodium . . 238 mg

PERCENTAGE RDI:

calcium 2%	vit. A 5%
iron 11%	vit. C 8%
folate 19%	

VARIATION

Cranberry Apple Filling: Substitute 2 cups (500 mL) fresh or frozen cranberries for 2 cups (500 mL) of the apples. Omit lemon juice. Increase flour to ¼ cup (50 mL). Reduce cinnamon to ¼ tsp (1 mL). Add ¼ tsp (1 mL) nutmeg.

Dutch Apple Pie

The ideal time to eat this southwestern Ontario specialty is just as the last of the oven warmth has left the filling. Be warned, though: this is not one of those store-bought stiff pies in which no juice escapes the razor-sharp wedges. Anticipate some juices as you cut and serve the pie.

	Pastry for deep 10-inch (25 cm) single-crust pie		¾ cup	packed brown sugar	175 mL
			2 tbsp	all-purpose flour	25 mL
5	large Northern Spy apples (about 2 lb/1 kg)	5	3 tbsp	cold butter	50 mL
¼ cup	whipping cream	50 mL	½ tsp	cinnamon	2 mL

1 On lightly floured surface, roll out pastry and fit into deep 10-inch (25 cm) pie plate; trim pastry ¾ inch (2 cm) from edge. Fold under and flute edge. Set aside.

2 Peel and core apples; cut each into 6 wedges. Arrange snugly in single layer in pie shell; drizzle with half of the cream. In small bowl, combine sugar with flour; cut in butter until mixture is crumbly. Sprinkle over apples; dust with cinnamon. Drizzle with remaining cream.

3 Bake in bottom third of 450°F (230°C) oven for 15 minutes. Reduce heat to 350°F (180°C); bake for 30 to 35 minutes longer or until apples are tender, shielding edges of pastry with foil if browning too much. Let cool on rack.

VARIATION

Dutch Pear Pie: Substitute firm, just-ripe Bartlett or Bosc pears for the apples. Increase flour to ⅓ cup (75 mL), sprinkling 2 tbsp (25 mL) over pears and adding remainder to brown sugar.

APPLES FOR Pies

Northern Spy is the preferred apple but, unfortunately, it's not available across the country or even for the entire fall and winter apple season. Others to try include Golden Delicious, Jonagold, Crispin and Idared; they all hold their shape when baked, but because they are sweeter than Northern Spy apples, the pie may need a touch more lemon juice and bits of butter dotted over the apple slices before putting on the top crust. Avoid Granny Smith, Empire, Cortland and any of the McIntosh family because they tend to become mushy when baked. Red Delicious, forever hard, is dry and tasteless in a pie.

Makes 6 to 8 servings.

PER EACH OF 8 SERVINGS, ABOUT:

cal	481	carb	61 g
pro	5 g	fibre	4 g
total fat	25 g	chol	70 mg
sat. fat	13 g	sodium	339 mg

PERCENTAGE RDI:

calcium	4%	vit. A	15%
iron	14%	vit. C	5%
folate	18%		

Tarte Tatin

This show-off French pie is an irresistible trio of buttery crust, gorgeous chunks of apple and caramel drizzle. Mind you, you have to be a little fearless the first time you flip over a hot pastry-topped skilletful of apples onto a plate. It's a kind of coming of age for pie lovers. But practice makes perfect, and a long, thick pair of oven mitts will prevent burns.

TEST KITCHEN TIP: Use oven mitts when working with caramelized sugar; it gets extremely hot.

SUBSTITUTION: You can substitute 10 Golden Delicious apples for the Northern Spies; cut each half into thirds.

1 cup	all-purpose flour	250 mL
1 tbsp	granulated sugar	15 mL
¼ tsp	salt	1 mL
½ cup	cold unsalted butter, cubed	125 mL
1 tsp	vinegar	5 mL
	Ice water	

FILLING:		
8	large Northern Spy apples (about 4 lb/2 kg)	8
2 tbsp	lemon juice	25 mL
¼ cup	unsalted butter	50 mL
¾ cup	granulated sugar	175 mL

1 In large bowl, combine flour, sugar and salt. Using pastry blender or 2 knives, cut in butter until mixture resembles coarse crumbs with a few larger pieces. Stir vinegar with enough ice water to make ¼ cup (50 mL). Drizzle over flour mixture, tossing with fork until dough holds together when pressed and adding a little more water if necessary. Press into ball; flatten into disc. Wrap in plastic wrap and refrigerate for at least 30 minutes or for up to 3 days.

2 FILLING: Meanwhile, peel, quarter and core apples; cut each quarter in half lengthwise. In bowl, toss apples with lemon juice.

3 In 8-inch (20 cm) cast-iron skillet, melt butter over medium-high heat. Add sugar; cook, stirring, for 3 to 5 minutes or until starting to bubble. Remove from heat. Drain apples; arrange, flat side down, in concentric circles in syrup in skillet. Layer remaining apples over top to cover first layer evenly.

4 Cook over medium heat, basting with syrup that bubbles up, for about 15 minutes or until apples begin to soften and syrup starts to thicken. Cover and cook for 5 minutes or until apples in top layer are just tender. Remove from heat; let cool for 5 minutes.

5 Meanwhile, on lightly floured surface, roll out pastry into 10-inch (25 cm) circle; cut 4 small steam vents at centre. Fit over apples and trim pastry extending over rim of pan; press pastry edge down between apples and pan.

6 Bake in bottom third of 425°F (220°C) oven for about 25 minutes or until pastry is golden brown. Let stand for 4 minutes. Invert heatproof serving plate over pastry. Wearing oven mitts, grasp plate and pan; turn over to unmould tart onto plate. With tongs, quickly arrange apples stuck in pan over top. Serve warm.

Makes 6 to 8 servings.

PER EACH OF 8 SERVINGS, ABOUT:

cal	373	carb	57 g
pro	2 g	fibre	4 g
total fat	17 g	chol	44 mg
sat. fat	10 g	sodium	69 mg

PERCENTAGE RDI:

calcium	1%	vit. A	16%
iron	5%	vit. C	8%
folate	7%		

Saskatoon Berry Pie

Strawberries and rhubarb mingle with Prairie saskatoons in this pie from the Station Arts Centre in Rosthern, Saskatchewan.

	Pastry for 9-inch (23 cm) double-crust pie	
1 tsp	milk or cream	5 mL
1 tsp	granulated sugar	5 mL

FILLING:		
3½ cups	saskatoon berries	875 mL
1 cup	quartered strawberries	250 mL
1 cup	chopped rhubarb	250 mL
¾ cup	granulated sugar	175 mL
¼ cup	cornstarch	50 mL
2 tbsp	lemon juice	25 mL

1 FILLING: In small saucepan, combine ½ cup (125 mL) of the saskatoon berries and ¼ cup (50 mL) each of the strawberries and rhubarb; cook over medium heat, stirring occasionally, for 5 minutes or until tender. (Or microwave in covered bowl at High for 2 minutes.) Transfer to food processor; purée until smooth. In bowl, stir together purée, remaining saskatoons, strawberries and rhubarb, sugar, cornstarch and lemon juice.

2 On lightly floured surface, roll out half of the pastry and fit into 9-inch (23 cm) pie plate. Trim pastry; brush pastry rim with water. Spoon in filling. Roll out remaining pastry and fit over top; trim ¾ inch (2 cm) from edge; tuck pastry under and flute edge. Brush pastry with milk; sprinkle with sugar. Cut steam vents in top.

3 Bake in bottom third of 425°F (220°C) oven for 15 minutes. Reduce heat to 350°F (180°C); bake for about 30 minutes longer or until golden and filling is bubbly. Let cool on rack.

Makes 6 to 8 servings.

PER EACH OF 8 SERVINGS, ABOUT:

cal	503	carb	67 g
pro	6 g	fibre	4 g
total fat	24 g	chol	65 mg
sat. fat	12 g	sodium	388 mg

PERCENTAGE RDI:

calcium	3%	vit. A	12%
iron	15%	vit. C	25%
folate	25%		

GUIDELINES FOR
DOUBLE-CRUST FRUIT PIES

TYPE OF PIE	PREPARED FRUIT	GRANULATED SUGAR	THICKENER	FLAVOURINGS
Blueberry	5 cups (1.25 L)	¾ cup (175 mL)	¼ cup (50 mL) all-purpose flour	½ tsp (2 mL) each grated lemon rind and cinnamon
Peach	5 cups (1.25 L), peeled and sliced	¾ cup (175 mL)	¼ cup (50 mL) all-purpose flour	2 tbsp (25 mL) diced crystallized ginger
Plum	5 cups (1.25 L), quartered	1 cup (250 mL)	¼ cup (50 mL) all-purpose flour	½ tsp (2 mL) cinnamon
Raspberry	4 cups (1 L)	1 cup (250 mL)	3 tbsp (50 mL) all-purpose flour	none needed
Bumbleberry	2 cups (500 mL) chopped peeled apples and 1 cup (250 mL) each raspberries, blackberries and diced rhubarb	¾ cup (175 mL)	4 tsp (20 mL) each all-purpose flour and cornstarch	¼ tsp (1 mL) nutmeg and ½ tsp (2 mL) cinnamon
Tart Cherry	6 cups (1.5 L), pitted*	1½ cups (375 mL)	⅓ cup (75 mL) cornstarch	1 tbsp (15 mL) lemon juice and 1 tsp (5 mL) vanilla

Assembling Pies

🍃 Line 9-inch (23 cm) pie plate with pastry.

🍃 In bowl, combine prepared fruit, sugar, thickener, 1 tbsp (15 mL) lemon juice and flavourings (see chart).

🍃 Spoon into pastry shell; dot filling with 1 tbsp (15 mL) butter.

🍃 Moisten edge of bottom crust. Cover with top crust. Trim and flute edge. Brush top with milk or cream; sprinkle lightly with granulated sugar. Cut steam vents.

🍃 Bake in bottom third of 425°F (220°C) oven for 15 minutes. Reduce heat to 350°F (180°C); bake for 35 to 45 minutes longer or until fruit is tender, filling is thickened and pastry is golden.

Glazing Pies

A pie with a beautiful gloss and golden colour is especially appealing. There are several ways to get a professional-looking glaze.

🍃 Whisk 1 egg yolk with 1½ tsp (7 mL) cream for a deep gold colour. Milk or water can replace the cream, but the glaze will be less golden. Or use a whole beaten egg (the white adds particular gloss), cream or milk. Just before baking, brush the pastry top with choice of glaze.

🍃 For fruit pies, especially cherry and apple, and for wintertime pies, such as raisin, sprinkle granulated sugar over the glaze to make the pie glitter.

Freezing Pies

🍃 You can freeze well-wrapped unbaked fruit pies for up to 4 months with the following changes: increase the amount of flour in each pie by 1 tbsp (15 mL) and don't cut steam vents until just before baking.

🍃 Bake still-frozen pies in 450°F (230°C) oven for 15 minutes. Reduce heat to 375°F (190°C); bake for up to 60 minutes longer or until filling is thickened and pastry is golden.

* To use frozen tart cherries from pail, thaw 8 cups (2 L) to yield 6 cups (1.5 L). Drain, reserving ⅓ cup (75 mL) juice. If cherries are presweetened, decrease sugar to ¾ cup (175 mL).

Strawberry Rhubarb Galette

*Although pie making is an honoured skill in Canada, pastry makers here happily
learn new tricks from other countries, such as this free-form no-plate pie from France.
It's novel, easy to assemble and absolutely impressive.*

2½ cups	all-purpose flour	625 mL		⅓ cup	all-purpose flour	75 mL
2 tbsp	granulated sugar	25 mL		⅓ cup	crushed amaretti cookies or vanilla wafers	75 mL
¼ tsp	salt	1 mL				
¾ cup	cold butter, cubed	175 mL		**TOPPING:**		
¾ cup	ice water	175 mL		1	egg yolk	1
STRAWBERRY RHUBARB FILLING:				1 tbsp	water	15 mL
5 cups	chopped (1 inch/2.5 cm) rhubarb	1.25 L		2 tsp	granulated sugar	10 mL
2 cups	quartered strawberries	500 mL		2 tbsp	apple jelly, melted	25 mL
¾ cup	granulated sugar	175 mL				

1 In bowl, whisk together flour, sugar and salt. Using pastry blender or 2 knives, cut in butter until in large crumbs. Add water all at once; mix with fork just until dough comes together. With hands, shape into disc. Wrap in plastic wrap and refrigerate for 30 minutes or until chilled.

2 STRAWBERRY RHUBARB FILLING: In large bowl, toss together rhubarb, strawberries, sugar and flour. Set aside.

3 On floured parchment paper and using floured rolling pin, roll out pastry into 17-inch (43 cm) circle, leaving edge ragged. Transfer paper and pastry to rimless baking sheet or pizza pan. Sprinkle with crushed cookies, leaving 4-inch (10 cm) border uncovered. Spoon filling over cookies. Fold up pastry border over filling, making evenly spaced pleats or rustic folds.

4 TOPPING: Beat egg yolk with water; brush over pastry. Sprinkle with sugar.

5 Bake in bottom third of 425°F (220°C) oven for 10 minutes. Reduce heat to 375°F (190°C) and bake for 50 to 60 minutes longer or until bubbly and crust is golden. Let cool on rack for 30 minutes. Brush filling with apple jelly.

VARIATION

Plum Galette: Omit Strawberry Rhubarb Filling: In bowl, toss together 7 cups (1.75 L) halved (or quartered if large) plums (about 8 whole), ¾ cup (175 mL) granulated sugar, ¼ cup (50 mL) all-purpose flour, 2 tsp (10 mL) finely grated orange rind and ¼ tsp (1 mL) cinnamon. Assemble and bake as directed. Brush baked filling with jelly as directed.

Makes 8 servings.

PER SERVING, ABOUT:

cal	468	carb	69 g
pro	6 g	fibre	4 g
total fat	20 g	chol	74 mg
sat. fat	11 g	sodium	257 mg

PERCENTAGE RDI:

calcium	8%	vit. A	18%
iron	16%	vit. C	32%
folate	26%		

Pear Pandowdy

A pandowdy is a juicy fruit pudding-pie with a crusty covering. Breaking up the pastry top partway through baking and pushing it down into the fruit is known as "dowdying."

8 cups	chopped peeled pears (about 8 large)	2 L
⅓ cup	liquid honey	75 mL
2 tbsp	lemon juice	25 mL
2 tsp	cornstarch	10 mL
2 tsp	grated lemon rind	10 mL
½ tsp	nutmeg	2 mL

TOPPING:		
¾ cup	all-purpose flour	175 mL
1 tbsp	granulated sugar	15 mL
½ tsp	grated lemon rind	2 mL
Pinch	salt	Pinch
⅓ cup	cold butter, cubed	75 mL
2 tbsp	lemon juice	25 mL
GLAZE:		
2 tsp	milk	10 mL
1 tsp	granulated sugar	5 mL

1 In bowl, toss together pears, honey, lemon juice, cornstarch, lemon rind and nutmeg; transfer to 8-inch (2 L) square glass baking dish. Set aside.

2 TOPPING: In bowl, stir together flour, sugar, lemon rind and salt. With pastry blender or 2 knives, cut in butter until crumbly. In small bowl, combine 2 tbsp (25 mL) cold water with lemon juice; drizzle over flour mixture, stirring with fork to form dough. Transfer to lightly floured surface; roll out slightly larger than baking dish. Place over fruit, tucking pastry down inside edges of dish.

3 GLAZE: Brush pastry with milk; sprinkle with sugar. Cut cross in centre. Bake in bottom third of 400°F (200°C) oven for 50 minutes or until filling is tender and bubbly and topping is golden.

4 Using sharp knife, cut pastry topping into 2-inch (5 cm) squares, pressing sides of squares down into fruit. Bake for about 10 minutes longer or until golden. Let cool slightly and serve warm. Or let cool to room temperature before serving.

Makes 6 to 8 servings.

PER EACH OF 8 SERVINGS, ABOUT:

cal	264	carb	49 g
pro	2 g	fibre	4 g
total fat	9 g	chol	21 mg
sat. fat	5 g	sodium	80 mg

PERCENTAGE RDI:

calcium	2%	vit. A	8%
iron	7%	vit. C	13%
folate	9%		

Plum Almond Tart

Glazed plum wedges peek out from under a frangipane, or almond, filling.

PAT-IN SWEET PASTRY:		
1½ cups	all-purpose flour	375 mL
2 tbsp	granulated sugar	25 mL
4 tsp	cornstarch	20 mL
¾ cup	cold butter, cubed	175 mL
PLUM FRANGIPANE FILLING:		
⅔ cup	ground almonds	150 mL
¼ cup	granulated sugar	50 mL

2 tbsp	butter, softened	25 mL
1	egg	1
¼ tsp	almond extract	1 mL
2 tbsp	all-purpose flour	25 mL
5	plums (1 lb/500 g)	5
3 tbsp	apricot jam, melted and strained	50 mL

1 PAT-IN SWEET PASTRY: In large bowl, stir together flour, sugar and cornstarch. Using pastry blender, 2 knives or fingers, work in butter until mixture clumps together. With floured hands, press evenly into 9-inch (23 cm) round tart pan with removable bottom. Cover and refrigerate for at least 1 hour or until chilled. With fork, prick pastry shell all over; bake in bottom third of 350°F (180°C) oven for about 15 minutes or just until starting to turn golden. Let cool completely on rack.

2 PLUM FRANGIPANE FILLING: Meanwhile, in bowl, beat together almonds, sugar and butter; beat in egg and almond extract. Stir in flour. Spread in cooled tart shell. Cut plums into thin wedges; nestle, cut side down, in concentric circles in filling. Bake in bottom third of 375°F (190°C) oven for about 30 minutes or until firm to the touch and tester inserted in centre comes out clean. Let cool on rack for 15 minutes.

3 Remove side of pan; brush apricot jam over filling and crust. (MAKE-AHEAD: Cover and set aside at room temperature for up to 3 hours.)

VARIATION

Puckery Lemon Tart: Omit Plum Frangipane Filling. Increase baking time for crust to about 25 minutes. In heatproof bowl, whisk together 2 eggs, 3 egg yolks and 1 cup (250 mL) granulated sugar. Place over (not touching) simmering water in saucepan; cook, whisking often, for about 10 minutes or until thickened and pale. Whisk in ½ cup (125 mL) butter, cubed, 1 piece at a time, melting each piece completely before adding next. Add 2 tbsp (25 mL) grated lemon rind and ½ cup (125 mL) lemon juice; cook, whisking constantly, for about 4 minutes or until thickened to consistency of pudding and no longer frothy. Pour into baked crust, smoothing top. Refrigerate for at least 1 hour or until set. (MAKE-AHEAD: Refrigerate for up to 4 hours.)

Makes 6 to 8 servings.

PER EACH OF 8 SERVINGS, ABOUT:

cal 416	carb . . . . 43 g
pro . . . . 6 g	fibre . . . . 2 g
total fat . . . . 26 g	chol . . . . . . 81 mg
sat. fat . . . . . 13 g	sodium . . 218 mg

PERCENTAGE RDI:

calcium 3%	vit. A 21%
iron 11%	vit. C 7%
folate 17%	

Fresh Blueberry Tart

A sweet pat-in crust and a filling of fresh and cooked blueberries make this blueberry pie unusual — and unusually delicious. Serve it with whipped cream or Lower-Fat Topping (see below).

1¼ cups	all-purpose flour	300 mL
3 tbsp	icing sugar	50 mL
Pinch	salt	Pinch
⅔ cup	cold butter, cubed	150 mL
FILLING:		
⅔ cup	granulated sugar	150 mL
3 tbsp	cornstarch	50 mL

Pinch	salt	Pinch
5 cups	blueberries	1.25 L
½ tsp	finely grated lemon rind	2 mL
2 tbsp	lemon juice	25 mL
1 tbsp	butter	15 mL

1 In bowl, stir together flour, sugar and salt. Using pastry blender or 2 knives, cut in butter until crumbly. Press into small handfuls until dough holds together. Press into bottom and up side of 10-inch (25 cm) tart pan with removable bottom. Using fork, prick pastry all over. Bake in bottom third of 350°F (180°C) oven for about 20 minutes or until light golden. Let cool on rack.

2 FILLING: Meanwhile, in saucepan, stir together sugar, cornstarch and salt. Whisk in ⅓ cup (75 mL) cold water, 2 cups (500 mL) of the blueberries and lemon rind; bring to simmer over medium heat. Reduce heat and simmer gently, stirring often, for about 10 minutes or until glossy and thickened. Remove from heat. Stir in lemon juice and butter. Let cool slightly.

3 Gently stir remaining berries into saucepan. Spoon into prepared crust, smoothing top. Refrigerate for about 30 minutes or until set. (MAKE-AHEAD: Refrigerate for up to 8 hours.)

Makes 8 servings.

PER SERVING, ABOUT:

cal 356	carb .... 50 g
pro .... 3 g	fibre .... 3 g
total fat ....17 g	chol ...... 45 mg
sat. fat .....10 g	sodium ..178 mg

PERCENTAGE RDI:

calcium 1%	vit. A 16%
iron 7%	vit. C 20%
folate 12%	

LOWER-FAT Topping

Instead of topping desserts with rich whipped cream, lower the fat with a mixture of thickened yogurt and cream. Spoon 1 cup (250 mL) plain yogurt into coffee filter–lined sieve set over bowl. Let drain in refrigerator for 4 hours or until yogurt measures ¾ cup (175 mL). Sweeten as desired and serve as topping. Or enrich with whipped cream: whip ½ cup (125 mL) whipping cream; stir one-quarter into yogurt, then fold in remaining cream. **Makes enough to top 8 wedges of pie, cake or crisps, or 8 servings of fruit.**

Fresh Strawberry Pie

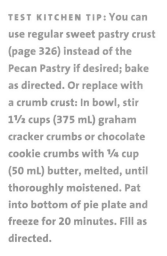

When Canadians think of strawberry pie, they think of a fresh-tasting one like this. Local berries offer the finest flavour and colour for any fresh or baked berry dessert.

8 cups	strawberries, hulled	2 L
1 cup	granulated sugar	250 mL
¼ cup	cornstarch	50 mL
½ cup	water	125 mL
1 tbsp	butter	15 mL
PECAN PASTRY:		
1 cup	all-purpose flour	250 mL
¼ cup	packed brown sugar	50 mL

½ tsp	salt	2 mL
½ cup	cold butter, cubed	125 mL
½ cup	ground pecans	125 mL
2 tbsp	cold water	25 mL
1	egg yolk	1
GARNISH:		
1 cup	whipping cream	250 mL
2 tbsp	icing sugar	25 mL

1 PECAN PASTRY: In bowl, combine flour, sugar and salt. Using pastry blender or 2 knives, cut in butter until mixture resembles coarse crumbs. Stir in pecans. Beat water with egg yolk; using fork, stir into flour mixture until crumbly and moist. Press into 10-inch (25 cm) pie plate; flute edges. Cover and refrigerate for 30 minutes. (MAKE-AHEAD: Refrigerate for up to 1 day.)

2 Using fork, prick pastry all over. Line with foil; fill with dried beans or pie weights. Bake in bottom third of 375°F (190°C) oven for 10 minutes. Remove weights and foil; bake for 10 to 12 minutes longer or until golden. Let cool completely on rack.

3 In food processor or blender, purée 4 cups (1 L) of the strawberries until smooth. In saucepan, combine sugar with cornstarch; blend in water. Add puréed berries; bring to boil over medium-high heat, stirring constantly. Reduce heat to low; cook, stirring constantly, for 1 to 2 minutes or until translucent and slightly thickened. Remove from heat; stir in butter. Press mixture through sieve into bowl; let cool until lukewarm.

4 Arrange remaining whole berries, tips up, in pastry shell; pour in filling. Refrigerate for at least 2 hours or until set. (MAKE-AHEAD: Refrigerate for up to 6 hours.)

5 GARNISH: Just before serving, whip cream with icing sugar; spread or pipe around edge of pie.

TEST KITCHEN TIP: You can use regular sweet pastry crust (page 326) instead of the Pecan Pastry if desired; bake as directed. Or replace with a crumb crust: In bowl, stir 1½ cups (375 mL) graham cracker crumbs or chocolate cookie crumbs with ¼ cup (50 mL) butter, melted, until thoroughly moistened. Pat into bottom of pie plate and freeze for 20 minutes. Fill as directed.

Makes 8 to 10 servings.

PER EACH OF 10 SERVINGS, ABOUT:

cal	400	carb	48 g
pro	3 g	fibre	2 g
total fat	23 g	chol	81 mg
sat. fat	12 g	sodium	234 mg

PERCENTAGE RDI:

calcium	4%	vit. A	20%
iron	9%	vit. C	97%
folate	15%		

Lemon Meringue Pie

So seemingly simple, lemon meringue pie does challenge the baker. The cornstarch that thickens the filling can break down and turn watery if the heat is too high or the filling is stirred too vigorously. Follow our steps for success. Plan on enjoying the finished pie the same day, before the meringue begins to bead.

TEST KITCHEN TIP: Lining the pastry with foil and weighing it down (called "baking blind") prevents it from bubbling and, especially, from shrinking. Pie weights, pellet-shaped or round, are available in kitchenware shops. If you don't have pie weights, any kind of dried bean can be used, and reused for years. Just don't try cooking them up in a recipe afterward.

1	unbaked 9-inch (23 cm) single-crust pie shell	1

FILLING:

1¼ cups	granulated sugar	300 mL
6 tbsp	cornstarch	100 mL
½ tsp	salt	2 mL
2 cups	water	500 mL
4	egg yolks, beaten	4
1 tbsp	grated lemon rind	15 mL
½ cup	lemon juice	125 mL
3 tbsp	butter	50 mL

MERINGUE:

5	egg whites, at room temperature	5
¼ tsp	cream of tartar	1 mL
⅓ cup	instant dissolving (fruit/berry) sugar	75 mL

1 Line pie shell with foil; fill with pie weights or dried beans. Bake in bottom third of 400°F (200°C) oven for 15 minutes. Remove weights and foil. Prick shell all over; bake for 10 minutes longer or until evenly golden. Let cool on rack.

2 **FILLING:** Meanwhile, in heavy saucepan, mix together sugar, cornstarch and salt; stir in water. Bring to boil over medium-high heat, stirring constantly. Reduce heat to medium-low; simmer for 3 minutes, stirring constantly. Remove from heat. Whisk one-quarter into egg yolks; whisk back into pan. Cook over medium heat, stirring, for 2 minutes. Remove from heat. Stir in lemon rind, lemon juice and butter. Set aside.

3 **MERINGUE:** In bowl, beat egg whites with cream of tartar until soft peaks form. Beat in sugar, 1 tbsp (15 mL) at a time, until stiff glossy peaks form. Pour filling into cooled crust, smoothing top. Starting at edge and using spatula, spread meringue around outside of hot filling, sealing to crust, to prevent shrinkage. Spread over remaining filling, making attractive peaks with back of spoon or mounding and smoothing meringue to peak in centre. Bake in centre of 400°F (200°C) oven for 5 to 6 minutes or until golden. Let cool on rack for about 5 hours or until set.

Makes 6 to 8 servings.

PER EACH OF 8 SERVINGS, ABOUT:

cal 432	carb . . . . 62 g
pro . . . . 6 g	fibre . . . . 1 g
total fat . . . . 18 g	chol . . . . . 153 mg
sat. fat . . . . . . 9 g	sodium . . 407 mg

PERCENTAGE RDI:

calcium 2%	vit. A 14%
iron 9%	vit. C 10%
folate 16%	

Creamy Pumpkin Pie

Yes, this pie is old-fashioned, but no other dessert is so connected to the memories of romping in golden fall leaves, country drives and our beloved Thanksgiving.

1½ cups	all-purpose flour	375 mL
2 tsp	finely grated orange rind	10 mL
½ tsp	salt	2 mL
¼ cup	each cold butter and shortening, cubed	50 mL
1	egg yolk	1
1 tsp	vinegar	5 mL
	Ice water	

FILLING:

1	can (14 oz/398 mL) pumpkin purée	1
1 cup	packed brown sugar	250 mL
1	pkg (4 oz/125 g) cream cheese, softened	1
½ cup	whipping cream	125 mL
2	eggs	2
1 tbsp	all-purpose flour	15 mL
1 tsp	each cinnamon and vanilla	5 mL
½ tsp	each ground ginger, nutmeg and salt	2 mL

TOPPING:

½ cup	whipping cream	125 mL

TEST KITCHEN TIP: To decorate the pie, cut out miniature pastry pumpkins and arrange on top. Gather pastry scraps together and roll out. Using small pumpkin-shaped cookie cutter, cut out 11 shapes. Transfer to baking sheet; bake in bottom third of 375°F (190°C) oven for about 12 minutes or until golden. Transfer to rack; let cool.

1 In large bowl, combine flour, orange rind and salt. Using pastry blender or 2 knives, cut in butter and shortening until mixture resembles coarse crumbs. In measuring cup, whisk egg yolk with vinegar; pour in enough ice water to make ⅓ cup (75 mL). Drizzle over flour mixture, tossing with fork until dough holds together and adding a little more ice water if necessary. Form into ball; press into disc. Wrap in plastic wrap; refrigerate for 1 hour.

2 On floured surface, roll out pastry to ⅛-inch (3 mm) thickness; fit into 9-inch (23 cm) pie plate. Trim edge to ¾-inch (2 cm) overhang, reserving scraps; fold edge under and flute. Prick shell all over. Refrigerate for 30 minutes.

3 Line pastry shell with foil; fill evenly with pie weights or dried beans. Bake in bottom third of 375°F (190°C) oven for 15 minutes; remove weights and foil. Bake for 10 to 12 minutes longer or until pastry just starts to turn golden.

4 **FILLING:** Meanwhile, in food processor, purée together pumpkin purée, sugar, cream cheese, whipping cream, eggs, flour, cinnamon, vanilla, ginger, nutmeg and salt. Pour into pie shell; bake in bottom third of 350°F (180°C) oven for 1 hour or until set around edge and slightly jiggly in centre. Let cool on rack. (MAKE-AHEAD: Cover and refrigerate for up to 8 hours.)

5 **TOPPING:** In bowl, whip cream. Pipe or spoon into 8 rosettes around edge. Top each with pastry pumpkin (see tip); stand 3 pumpkins in centre.

Makes 6 to 8 servings.

PER EACH OF 8 SERVINGS, ABOUT:

cal	496	carb	51 g
pro	7 g	fibre	2 g
total fat	30 g	chol	152 mg
sat. fat	16 g	sodium	431 mg

PERCENTAGE RDI:

calcium	8%	vit. A	128%
iron	21%	vit. C	5%
folate	19%		

Coconut Cream Pie

Here's the secret to this cream pie's divine coconut flavour: cream of coconut syrup, which highlights the shredded coconut and coconut liqueur or rum in the filling. It seems that what's good for a piña colada is even better for a pie.

TEST KITCHEN TIP: Whisking some of the hot coconut milk mixture into the egg yolks to warm them is called "tempering." This step ensures that the yolks blend smoothly into the custard and don't scramble and lump.

1½ cups	all-purpose flour	375 mL
2 tbsp	granulated sugar	25 mL
¼ tsp	salt	1 mL
⅔ cup	cold butter, cubed	150 mL
⅓ cup	whipping cream	75 mL
FILLING:		
2½ cups	milk	625 mL
½ cup	granulated sugar	125 mL
⅓ cup	cornstarch	75 mL
¼ tsp	salt	1 mL
¼ cup	cream of coconut syrup (such as Coco López or piña colada mix)	50 mL

4	egg yolks, beaten	4
1 cup	shredded sweetened coconut	250 mL
¼ cup	coconut liqueur or rum	50 mL
2 tbsp	butter	25 mL
1 tsp	vanilla	5 mL
1 cup	whipping cream	250 mL
GARNISH:		
1 cup	whipping cream	250 mL
2 tbsp	toasted shredded sweetened coconut	25 mL

1 In large bowl, combine flour, sugar and salt. With pastry blender or 2 knives, cut in butter until mixture starts to clump together. Pour in ¼ cup (50 mL) of the cream, tossing with fork until dough holds together; add remaining cream to dry spots. Gather dough; press into disc. Wrap in plastic wrap and refrigerate for 30 minutes or until chilled. (MAKE-AHEAD: Refrigerate for up to 3 days. Or freeze for up to 2 weeks; let thawed dough stand at room temperature for 15 minutes.)

2 On lightly floured surface, roll out dough and fit into 10-inch (25 cm) pie plate, leaving ¾-inch (2 cm) overhang. Turn overhang under; flute edge. Prick all over with fork. Line with foil; fill evenly with pie weights or dried beans. Bake in bottom third of 425°F (220°C) oven for 15 minutes. Remove weights and foil. Bake for 5 to 7 minutes longer or until golden. Let cool on rack. (MAKE-AHEAD: Store at room temperature for up to 2 days.)

Makes 12 servings.

PER SERVING, ABOUT:

cal 493	carb . . . . 39 g
pro . . . . 6 g	fibre . . . . 1 g
total fat . . . . 35 g	chol . . . . . 170 mg
sat. fat . . . . . 22 g	sodium . . 288 mg

PERCENTAGE RDI:

calcium 10%	vit. A 34%
iron 8%	vit. C 2%
folate 13%	

3 FILLING: In heavy saucepan, whisk together ½ cup (125 mL) of the milk, the sugar, cornstarch and salt; stir in remaining milk and cream of coconut syrup. Bring to boil over medium heat, stirring constantly; cook, stirring, for about 7 minutes or until thickened. Remove from heat.

4 Stir 1 cup (250 mL) of the hot mixture into egg yolks; pour back into pan and cook for 3 to 4 minutes or until thickened. Remove from heat. Stir in coconut, liqueur, butter and vanilla. Pour into stainless-steel or glass bowl; let stand in larger bowl of ice water just until cooled, about 10 minutes. In separate bowl, whip cream; fold into coconut base. Pour into baked pie crust. Place plastic wrap directly on surface of filling; refrigerate for 3 to 4 hours or until chilled.

5 GARNISH: In bowl, whip cream; using pastry bag, pipe decoratively around edge of pie. Sprinkle coconut over entire surface.

BITTERSWEET CHOCOLATE CREAM PIE

For a sensational chocolate pie, make and bake the pastry for the Coconut Cream Pie (page 340, steps 1 and 2). Fill and garnish with the following

CHOCOLATE CREAM FILLING:

3 cups	milk	750 mL
½ cup	granulated sugar	125 mL
⅓ cup	cornstarch	75 mL
½ tsp	salt	2 mL
4 oz	bittersweet chocolate, chopped	125 g
3	egg yolks	3
2 tbsp	butter	25 mL
2 tsp	vanilla	10 mL

GARNISH:

¾ cup	whipping cream	175 mL
1 oz	bittersweet chocolate	30 g

❧ CHOCOLATE CREAM FILLING: In heavy saucepan, heat milk until bubbles form around edge. In bowl, combine sugar, cornstarch and salt. Gradually add milk, whisking until smooth. Return to saucepan. Add chocolate; cook over medium heat, whisking constantly, for 4 to 7 minutes or until boiling and thickened. Remove from heat.

❧ Whisk about one-quarter of the hot mixture into egg yolks; whisk back into saucepan. Reduce heat to low; simmer for about 1 minute or until no taste of raw starch remains.

Remove from heat; stir in butter and vanilla. Pour into bowl and place plastic wrap directly on surface; refrigerate until cold and almost set. Spread filling over baked pie shell.

❧ GARNISH: In bowl, whip cream; spread or pipe over filling. With vegetable peeler, shave chocolate decoratively over cream. Cover loosely and refrigerate for 2 hours or until filling is set. (MAKE-AHEAD: Refrigerate for up to 1 day.) **Makes 6 to 8 servings.**

Gooey Butter Tarts

Although they're the icon of Canadian cooking, butter tarts are barely 100 years old and probably originated with the popularization of corn syrup. The jury's out about the best of these supersweet tarts: some demand that the filling be gooey, others that it be firm. There are bakers who add nuts, others who prefer currants, and still others who update them according to popular tastes, such as with chunks of chocolate.

VARIATIONS

Drizzled Gooey Butter Tarts:
Drizzle cooled tarts with
2 oz (60 g) semisweet or
white chocolate, melted.

Not-So-Gooey Butter Tarts:
Increase brown sugar to
¾ cup (175 mL); decrease
corn syrup to ¼ cup (50 mL).

Chocolate Butter Tarts:
Reduce all-purpose flour in
pastry to 1¼ cups (300 mL)
and sift into bowl along with
½ cup (125 mL) unsweetened
cocoa powder. Continue
with recipe. To filling, add
¼ cup (50 mL) chopped
bittersweet chocolate
instead of currants, raisins,
pecans or coconut.

1½ cups	all-purpose flour	375 mL
¼ tsp	salt	1 mL
¼ cup	cold butter, cubed	50 mL
¼ cup	shortening, cubed	50 mL
1	egg yolk	1
1 tsp	vinegar	5 mL
	Ice water	

	FILLING:	
½ cup	packed brown sugar	125 mL
½ cup	corn syrup	125 mL
1	egg	1
2 tbsp	butter, softened	25 mL
1 tsp	each vanilla and vinegar	5 mL
Pinch	salt	Pinch
¼ cup	currants, raisins, chopped pecans or shredded coconut	50 mL

1 In large bowl, combine flour with salt. With pastry blender or 2 knives, cut in butter and shortening until in fine crumbs. In 1-cup (250 mL) liquid measure, whisk egg yolk with vinegar; add enough ice water to make ⅓ cup (75 mL). Gradually sprinkle over flour mixture, stirring briskly with fork until pastry holds together. Gather dough; press into disc. Wrap in plastic wrap and refrigerate for at least 1 hour or until chilled.

2 FILLING: In bowl, vigorously whisk together brown sugar, corn syrup, egg, butter, vanilla, vinegar and salt. Set aside.

3 On lightly floured surface, roll out pastry to ⅛-inch (3 mm) thickness. Using 4-inch (10 cm) round cookie cutter (or clean empty 28 oz/796 mL can), cut out 12 circles, rerolling scraps if necessary. Fit into 2¾- x 1¼-inch (7 x 3 cm) muffin cups. Divide currants among pastry shells. Spoon in filling until three-quarters full.

4 Bake in bottom third of 450°F (230°C) oven for about 12 minutes or until filling is puffed and bubbly and pastry is golden. Let stand on rack for 1 minute. To prevent sticking, immediately run metal spatula around tarts to loosen; carefully slide spatula under tarts and transfer to rack to let cool.

Makes 12 tarts.

PER TART, ABOUT:

cal	237	carb	34 g
pro	3 g	fibre	1 g
total fat	11 g	chol	52 mg
sat. fat	5 g	sodium	132 mg

PERCENTAGE RDI:

calcium	2%	vit. A	7%
iron	7%	vit. C	0%
folate	9%		

Pecan Pie

If rich food were a sin, you would need to do penance for a slice of this popular pie.

1	unbaked 9-inch (23 cm) single-crust pie shell	1
FILLING:		
3	eggs	3
¾ cup	packed brown sugar	175 mL
¾ cup	corn syrup	175 mL

2 tbsp	butter, melted	25 mL
1 tsp	vanilla	5 mL
1½ cups	pecan halves	375 mL
GLAZE:		
2 tbsp	corn syrup, warmed	25 mL

TEST KITCHEN TIP: Pecan halves tend to be of higher quality than chopped pecans. In this recipe, you could also use walnut halves, but only if they are fresh California walnuts.

1 FILLING: In bowl, stir together eggs, brown sugar, corn syrup, butter and vanilla; stir in pecans. Pour into pie shell. Bake in bottom third of 375°F (190°C) oven for 40 to 45 minutes or until pastry is golden and filling is just firm to the touch, shielding edge with foil if browning too quickly.

2 GLAZE: Brush filling with corn syrup; let cool. Cut with serrated knife.

VARIATION

Chocolate Pecan Pie: There are two ways to embellish a pecan pie with chocolate. Add 1 cup (250 mL) coarsely chopped bittersweet (not unsweetened) chocolate to the corn syrup mixture along with the pecans. Or omit corn syrup glaze; melt 2 oz (60 g) chopped bittersweet (not unsweetened) chocolate over hot (not boiling) water. Let cool slightly; scrape into small piping bag with fine tip. Or scrape into sturdy plastic bag with resealable top; gently press out air and close top of plastic bag, then carefully snip off a small corner from bottom of plastic bag. Pressing bag gently, zigzag chocolate over surface of cooled pie in a random fashion.

Makes 6 to 8 servings.

PER EACH OF 8 SERVINGS, ABOUT:

cal 553	carb . . . . 68 g
pro . . . . 7 g	fibre . . . . 2 g
total fat . . . . 30 g	chol . . . . . 121 mg
sat. fat . . . . . . 9 g	sodium . . 294 mg

PERCENTAGE RDI:

calcium 4%	vit. A 12%
iron 15%	vit. C 0%
folate 18%	

MAKE-AHEAD   CLASSIC

Cherry Chocolate Baklava

Chocolate and dried cherries add a sophisticated twist to a classic sweet.

TEST KITCHEN TIP: To prevent phyllo from cracking, let thaw completely in refrigerator for 24 hours before unwrapping and unrolling sheets.

VARIATION

Classic Walnut Baklava:

Omit cherries and chocolate. Substitute 3¼ cups (800 mL) toasted chopped walnuts for pecans. Increase sugar to ⅓ cup (75 mL). Add ¼ tsp (1 mL) ground cloves. Prepare syrup as directed.

1 cup	dried cherries or raisins	250 mL
1 cup	water	250 mL
2¼ cups	toasted chopped pecans	550 mL
2 tbsp	granulated sugar	25 mL
1 tsp	cinnamon	5 mL
6 oz	bittersweet chocolate, chopped	175 g
⅔ cup	butter, melted	150 mL
12	sheets phyllo pastry	12

SYRUP:		
1 cup	granulated sugar	250 mL
½ cup	liquid honey	125 mL
⅓ cup	water	75 mL
1	strip (2 inches/5 cm) lemon rind	1
1 tbsp	lemon juice	15 mL
2	cloves	2

1 In bowl, soak cherries in water for 5 minutes. Drain and pat dry; chop coarsely.

2 Meanwhile, in food processor, grind pecans, sugar and cinnamon until in coarse crumbs; transfer to bowl. Stir in cherries and chocolate; set aside.

3 Lightly brush 13- x 9-inch (3.5 L) metal cake pan with some of the butter; set aside. Cut phyllo in half into 14- x 8-inch (35 x 20 cm) sheets. Place 1 sheet on work surface, keeping remainder covered with plastic wrap and damp towel to prevent drying out. Brush lightly with some of the butter. Layer with 5 more sheets, brushing each with butter. Place stack in pan; sprinkle with 1 cup (250 mL) of the pecan mixture. Stack 4 more sheets, brushing each with butter; place on pecan mixture. Sprinkle with 1 cup (250 mL) more of the pecan mixture.

4 Stack 4 more sheets, brushing each with butter; place on pecan mixture. Sprinkle with 1 cup (250 mL) more pecan mixture. Stack 4 more sheets, brushing each with butter; place on pecan mixture. Sprinkle with remaining pecan mixture. Stack remaining sheets, brushing each with butter. Place on top.

5 Using tip of knife and without cutting all the way through to filling, cut phyllo diagonally from 1 corner to opposite corner; make parallel cuts, 1½ inches (4 cm) apart, to edge. Repeat in opposite direction to form diamonds. Bake in centre of 350°F (180°C) oven for 40 to 45 minutes or until golden brown and crisp.

6 SYRUP: In small saucepan, whisk together sugar, honey, water, lemon rind and juice, and cloves. Bring to boil over medium-high heat; cook, stirring, for 1 minute. Discard rind and cloves. Pour over hot baklava. Let cool on rack. Cut into diamond shapes. (MAKE-AHEAD: Cover with plastic wrap and store at room temperature for up to 1 day.)

Makes 24 servings.

PER SERVING, ABOUT:

cal	271	carb	30 g
pro	3 g	fibre	2 g
total fat	17 g	chol	14 mg
sat. fat	6 g	sodium	113 mg

PERCENTAGE RDI:

calcium	2%	vit. A	6%
iron	9%	vit. C	5%
folate	4%		

Frozen Peanut Butter Pie

Nostalgic for peanut butter and hungry for chocolate? Here they are together in a no-bake pie that lives up to your fondest memories.

1 cup	chocolate wafer crumbs	250 mL
¼ cup	butter, melted	50 mL
FILLING:		
⅔ cup	sour cream	150 mL
3 tbsp	icing sugar	50 mL
2 tbsp	whipping cream	25 mL
⅔ cup	smooth peanut butter	150 mL

TOPPING:		
2 oz	semisweet chocolate, coarsely chopped	60 g
¼ cup	whipping cream	50 mL
¼ cup	chopped peanuts	50 mL

1 In bowl, stir wafer crumbs with butter until thoroughly moistened; pat onto bottom only of 9-inch (23 cm) pie plate. Freeze for 20 minutes.

2 FILLING: In bowl, whisk together sour cream, sugar and whipping cream; whisk in peanut butter until smooth. Spread evenly over crust; freeze for 1 hour.

3 TOPPING: Meanwhile, in small saucepan, melt chocolate with cream over medium-low heat, stirring until smooth. Let cool for 15 minutes.

4 Spread chocolate mixture evenly over filling. Sprinkle peanuts around edge of pie. Freeze for about 1 hour or until completely set. (MAKE-AHEAD: Wrap in foil and freeze for up to 1 week.) Let stand at room temperature for 10 minutes before serving.

Makes 12 servings.

PER SERVING, ABOUT:

cal	249	carb	15 g
pro	6 g	fibre	1 g
total fat	20 g	chol	25 mg
sat. fat	8 g	sodium	181 mg

PERCENTAGE RDI:

calcium	3%	vit. A	8%
iron	6%	vit. C	0%
folate	8%		

Chocolate Caramel Macadamia Tart

There's no halfway with this layered caramel and silky chocolate ganache tart. While it takes a little more time to prepare than some desserts, none of the steps is difficult, and the end result is pure pleasure.

TEST KITCHEN TIP: For a shortcut, omit caramelizing the nuts for the topping. Instead, sprinkle whipped cream rosettes with toasted macadamias, chopped if you like.

2 cups	chocolate wafer crumbs	500 mL
⅓ cup	butter, melted	75 mL
CARAMEL FILLING:		
¾ cup	granulated sugar	175 mL
3 tbsp	water	50 mL
2 tbsp	corn syrup	25 mL
⅓ cup	butter, cut in pieces	75 mL
⅔ cup	chopped macadamia nuts	150 mL
¼ cup	whipping cream	50 mL

GANACHE:		
⅔ cup	whipping cream	150 mL
6 oz	bittersweet chocolate, chopped	175 g
2 tbsp	butter	25 mL
TOPPING:		
½ cup	macadamia nuts	125 mL
½ cup	granulated sugar	125 mL
2 tbsp	water	25 mL
¾ cup	whipping cream	175 mL

1 In bowl, stir wafer crumbs with butter. Press onto bottom and up side of 9-inch (23 cm) round or square tart pan with removable bottom. Bake in centre of 350°F (180°C) oven for 10 minutes or until set. Let cool completely on rack.

2 CARAMEL FILLING: In heavy saucepan, bring sugar, water and corn syrup to boil; boil, without stirring, but brushing down side of pan with wet pastry brush, for about 8 minutes or until caramel colour. Remove from heat; whisk in butter, then nuts and cream. Pour into prepared crust. Refrigerate for about 1 hour or until set.

3 GANACHE: In saucepan, heat cream just until boiling; pour over chocolate and butter in bowl, whisking until melted and smooth. Let cool slightly. Pour over caramel filling. Refrigerate for at least 8 hours or until set. (MAKE-AHEAD: Refrigerate for up to 2 days.)

4 TOPPING: Arrange nuts closely together on foil-lined baking sheet. In saucepan, bring sugar and water to boil; boil, without stirring, but brushing down side of pan with wet pastry brush, for 5 to 7 minutes or until caramel colour. Pour over nuts; let cool completely (MAKE-AHEAD: Store, uncovered, for up to 1 day.) Break into pieces; finely chop in food processor.

5 Remove side of tart pan; slide tart onto serving platter, removing bottom. In bowl, whip cream; spoon into pastry bag fitted with rosette tip. Pipe border of rosettes around edge of tart. Sprinkle with nut topping.

Makes 12 servings.

PER SERVING, ABOUT:

cal	551	carb	44 g
pro	5 g	fibre	3 g
total fat	44 g	chol	76 mg
sat. fat	22 g	sodium	251 mg

PERCENTAGE RDI:

calcium	5%	vit. A	23%
iron	14%	vit. C	0%
folate	3%		

White Chocolate Lemon Tart

White chocolate is rather too sweet for some palates, but when cut with a tart fruit such as lemon, orange or cranberry, it's nothing short of ethereal.

2	eggs	2	**PASTRY:**			
2	egg yolks	2	1½ cups	all-purpose flour	375 mL
⅔ cup	granulated sugar	150 mL	4 tsp	cornstarch	20 mL
2 tsp	grated lemon rind	10 mL	1 tbsp	icing sugar	15 mL
½ cup	lemon juice	125 mL	¾ cup	cold butter, cubed	175 mL
3 oz	white chocolate, chopped	90 g	1 tbsp	vinegar	15 mL
⅔ cup	whipping cream	150 mL	2 oz	semisweet chocolate, chopped	60 g

1 In heatproof bowl or top of double boiler over hot (not boiling) water, whisk together eggs, egg yolks, sugar and lemon rind and juice; cook, whisking frequently, for 10 minutes or until translucent and thickened to consistency of pudding. Remove lemon curd from heat; add white chocolate, stirring until melted. Pour into clean bowl; place plastic wrap directly on surface and refrigerate for 1 hour or until chilled. (MAKE-AHEAD: Refrigerate for up to 3 days.)

2 PASTRY: In large bowl, stir together flour, cornstarch and icing sugar. With pastry blender or 2 knives, cut in butter until mixture resembles fine crumbs with a few larger pieces. With fork, lightly stir in vinegar until mixture is moistened; let stand for 20 minutes. With floured hands, squeeze together small handfuls of dough just until mixture holds together. Press evenly into ¼-inch (5 mm) thick layer on bottom and up side of 9-inch (23 cm) tart pan with removable bottom. Cover and refrigerate for at least 1 hour or until chilled. (MAKE-AHEAD: Refrigerate for up to 3 days.)

3 Prick bottom of pastry shell all over with fork; bake in centre of 350°F (180°C) oven for 35 to 40 minutes or until golden. Let cool on rack.

4 In bowl over saucepan of hot (not boiling) water, melt semisweet chocolate, stirring occasionally. Using pastry brush, coat inside of pastry shell with chocolate. Let cool.

5 In bowl, whip cream. Fold half into lemon curd; fold in remaining whipped cream just until combined. Pour into shell, swirling top. Refrigerate for 1 hour or until set. (MAKE-AHEAD: Cover and refrigerate for up to 24 hours.)

TEST KITCHEN TIP: The white chocolate lemon filling is lovely spooned over fresh berries, especially wild blueberries. Top with a sprig of mint.

Makes 8 servings.

PER SERVING, ABOUT:

cal	505	carb	49 g
pro	6 g	fibre	1 g
total fat	33 g	chol	181 mg
sat. fat	19 g	sodium	214 mg

PERCENTAGE RDI:

calcium	6%	vit. A	29%
iron	11%	vit. C	10%
folate	17%		

MAKE-AHEAD · CLASSIC

Phyllo Fruit Cups with Orange White Chocolate Cream

These crisp phyllo cups are so versatile. Fill them with this orange-accented white chocolate cream, or spoon in vanilla ice cream, then add a tumble of your favourite berries and Raspberry Sauce (page 316) or Bananas in Caramel Sauce (page 298). You can even get creative with coffee ice cream, toasted almonds and a drizzle of Chocolate Sauce (page 312).

¼ cup	granulated sugar	50 mL
¼ cup	water	50 mL
ORANGE WHITE CHOCOLATE CREAM:		
1	egg	1
1	egg yolk	1
¼ cup	granulated sugar	50 mL
1 tsp	grated lemon rind	5 mL
3 tbsp	lemon juice	50 mL
1 tsp	grated orange rind	5 mL
2 tbsp	orange juice	25 mL
2 oz	white chocolate, chopped	60 g
⅓ cup	whipping cream	75 mL

PHYLLO CUPS:		
4	sheets phyllo pastry	4
3 tbsp	butter, melted	50 mL
3 tbsp	granulated sugar	50 mL
3 oz	bittersweet chocolate, melted	90 g
TOPPING:		
⅓ cup	apricot jam	75 mL
1 tbsp	water	15 mL
2	kiwifruit, peeled and thinly sliced	2
1 cup	sliced strawberries	250 mL

1 In saucepan, bring sugar and water to boil over medium heat; boil for 2 minutes. Let sugar syrup cool. (MAKE-AHEAD: Cover and refrigerate for up to 3 days.)

2 ORANGE WHITE CHOCOLATE CREAM: In heatproof bowl or top of double boiler over simmering water, whisk together egg, egg yolk, sugar, lemon rind and juice, and orange rind and juice; cook, whisking frequently, for 10 minutes or until translucent and thickened to consistency of pudding. Remove from heat; whisk in white chocolate until melted. Place plastic wrap directly on surface; refrigerate for about 1 hour or until chilled. In bowl, whip cream; fold into orange mixture. Refrigerate for 1 hour. (MAKE-AHEAD: Refrigerate for up to 24 hours.)

3 PHYLLO CUPS: Meanwhile, place 1 sheet of phyllo on work surface, keeping remainder covered with damp towel to prevent drying out. Cut in half lengthwise; cut into thirds crosswise to make 6 squares. Lightly brush 1 of the squares with some of the butter. Top with another square, turning slightly so edges do

Makes 8 servings.

PER SERVING, ABOUT:

cal	337	carb	44 g
pro	4 g	fibre	3 g
total fat	18 g	chol	79 mg
sat. fat	10 g	sodium	132 mg

PERCENTAGE RDI:

calcium	5%	vit. A	11%
iron	11%	vit. C	48%
folate	11%		

348

not align; brush with butter. Repeat with third square. Brush lightly with sugar syrup. Gently fit into greased muffin cup, pressing against side and bottom. Repeat with remaining squares, staggering placement in cups so they are not beside one another. Repeat with remaining phyllo.

4 Bake in centre of 400°F (200°C) oven for 8 minutes or until golden and crisp. Sprinkle sugar over edges. Let cool in pan on rack for 5 minutes. Remove from pan; let cool completely on rack. Brush inside of each with bittersweet chocolate; let stand for 15 minutes or until set. (MAKE-AHEAD: Cover lightly and store at room temperature for up to 8 hours.) Divide Orange White Chocolate Cream among chocolate-lined cups.

5 TOPPING: In saucepan, bring jam and water to boil; immediately strain and let cool. Arrange kiwifruit and strawberry slices over filling. Brush apricot glaze over fruit; let set before serving.

PHYLLO CUP Fillings

Phyllo cups invite you to fill them with all kinds of fruits and sauces. Here are a few ideas.

↶ Scoop vanilla ice cream, frozen yogurt or a fruity sorbet (page 294) into cups. Top with a lavish spoonful of a complementary fruit such as raspberries, blueberries, blackberries, sliced strawberries, pineapple or mango chunks, fresh orange sections or other fragrant seasonal fruit.

Or top ice cream with raspberries or strawberries and drizzle with Raspberry Sauce (page 316).

↶ Dip into your preserves cupboard and top the ice cream or frozen yogurt with a dollop of Wild Blueberry Preserve (page 378), or half a pear (with some juice) from Five-Spice Pears (page 386).

↶ Briefly sautéed fruit is another not-to-be missed filling for phyllo cups. As you might expect, luscious sautéed fruit pairs well with anything creamy, such as whipped cream. See Bananas in Caramel Sauce (page 298), or enjoy Apple Cranberry Sauce (page 264), Cherry Berry Sauce (page 264) or Rhubarb and Strawberry Compote (page 297) with strawberries over ice cream-filled cups or nestled under a dollop of whipped cream. Hold back on some of the juices if necessary.

↶ And don't forget chocolate. Drizzle Chocolate Sauce (page 312) over coffee or caramel ice cream, or over raspberry or mango sorbet (page 294).

Cookies, Bars and Squares

14

Oatmeal Cookies 352

Best-Ever Chocolate Chip Cookies 353

Hermits Galore 354

Amaretti 355

Brutti ma Buoni 356

Spicy Ginger Crinkle Cookies 357

Almond Biscotti 358

Peanut Butter Cookies 359

Pecan Snowballs 360

Glazed Almond Spritz Rosettes 361

Shortbread Cookies 362

Icebox Cookies 363

Speculaas 364

Sugar Cookies 365

Rugalahs 366

Glazed Apricot Blondies 367

Oodles of Brownies 368

Panforte 369

Florentine Bars 370

Simply Lovely Lemon Squares 371

Nanaimo Bars 372

Date Squares 373

Granola Bars 374

Chocolate Truffles 375

Oatmeal Cookies

Whoever said that the best cookies are homemade spoke the truth. To get you into the cookie-making mode, here are six versions of the ever-popular oatmeal cookie. Be sure to use large-flake or old-fashioned rolled oats.

	FLAVOURINGS	ADD-INS
Classic Oatmeal Cookies	1 tbsp (15 mL) vanilla; 1 tsp (5 mL) cinnamon	1 cup (250 mL) raisins
Chocolate Orange Pecan Oatmeal Cookies	1 tsp (5 mL) grated orange rind	¾ cup (175 mL) chocolate chips; ½ cup (125 mL) chopped pecans
Butterscotch Crisp Oatmeal Cookies	1 tbsp (15 mL) vanilla	1 cup (250 mL) rice crisp cereal; ½ cup (125 mL) each quick-cooking rolled oats and butterscotch chips
Health Nut Oatmeal Cookies	1 tsp (5 mL) vanilla; ¾ tsp (4 mL) nutmeg	½ cup (125 mL) chopped hazelnuts; ½ cup (125 mL) wheat germ; ¼ cup (50 mL) sunflower seeds; 2 tbsp (25 mL) flaxseeds
Trail Mix Oatmeal Cookies	Dash almond extract	⅓ cup (75 mL) each slivered almonds, raisins and shredded coconut
Hermit Oatmeal Cookies	1 tsp (5 mL) cinnamon; ½ tsp (2 mL) nutmeg; ¼ tsp (1 mL) ground cloves	⅓ cup (75 mL) each raisins, chopped dried apricots and chopped walnuts

VARIATION

Oatmeal Date Sandwich Cookies: In saucepan over medium heat, bring 2 cups (500 mL) chopped pitted dates, 1 tbsp (15 mL) grated orange rind, ⅔ cup (150 mL) orange juice and ⅓ cup (75 mL) water to boil, stirring often. Reduce heat to low; cover and simmer, stirring often, for 45 minutes. Uncover and cook, stirring, for 5 minutes or until thickened and fairly smooth. Let cool. Sandwich between 2 cookies.

1 In large bowl, beat ⅔ cup (150 mL) softened butter with 1 cup (250 mL) packed brown sugar until fluffy. Beat in 1 egg and Flavourings in first column.

2 In separate bowl, mix together 1½ cups (375 mL) rolled oats (not instant), 1 cup (250 mL) all-purpose flour, ½ tsp (2 mL) each baking powder and baking soda and ¼ tsp (1 mL) salt; stir into butter mixture along with Add-Ins in second column until blended.

3 Drop by heaping tablespoonfuls (15 mL), about 2 inches (5 cm) apart, onto parchment paper–lined or greased rimless baking sheets.

4 Bake in 375°F (190°C) oven for 10 minutes or until golden. Let cool on pans on racks for about 2 minutes. Transfer to racks; let cool completely. (MAKE-AHEAD: Layer between waxed paper in airtight container and store at room temperature for up to 5 days or freeze for up to 2 weeks.)

Makes about 36 cookies.

Best-Ever Chocolate Chip Cookies

Canadian Living *has published many chocolate chip cookie recipes, but founding food editor Carol Ferguson's recipe, with a punchy hit of vanilla, is the standout.*

½ cup	butter	125 mL
½ cup	shortening	125 mL
1 cup	granulated sugar	250 mL
½ cup	packed brown sugar	125 mL
2	eggs	2
1 tbsp	vanilla	15 mL

2 cups	all-purpose flour	500 mL
1 tsp	baking soda	5 mL
½ tsp	salt	2 mL
2 cups	semisweet chocolate chips	500 mL
1 cup	chopped walnuts or pecans	250 mL

TEST KITCHEN TIP: To make a giant chocolate chip cookie "greeting card," press dough onto parchment paper–lined 12-inch (30 cm) pizza pan. Bake in centre of 375°F (190°C) oven for 25 minutes or until golden. Let cool on rack. Pipe greeting on top with melted chocolate.

1 In bowl, beat butter with shortening; gradually beat in granulated and brown sugars until smooth. Beat in eggs and vanilla. In separate bowl, whisk together flour, baking soda and salt; stir into butter mixture. Stir in chocolate chips and walnuts. Refrigerate for 30 minutes.

2 Drop by rounded tablespoonfuls (15 mL), about 2 inches (5 cm) apart, onto parchment paper–lined or greased rimless baking sheets. With fork, flatten to ½ inch (1 cm) thickness. Bake in 375°F (190°C) oven for 8 to 9 minutes or until edges are golden and centres are still slightly underbaked. Let cool on pans on racks for 5 minutes. Transfer to racks; let cool completely. (MAKE-AHEAD: Layer between waxed paper in airtight container and store at room temperature for up to 5 days or freeze for up to 2 weeks.)

VARIATIONS

Chewy Chocolate Chip Cookies: Omit shortening; increase butter to 1 cup (250 mL) and flour to 2¾ cups (675 mL). Bake in 350°F (180°C) oven for 8 to 12 minutes.

Reverse Chocolate Chip Cookies: Substitute cocoa powder for ⅓ cup (75 mL) of the flour, sifting with flour before adding to batter; use white chocolate chips instead of dark chocolate chips. Bake as directed.

Chocolate Chip Ice-Cream Sandwiches: Drop dough by ¼ cupfuls (50 mL) onto parchment paper–lined baking sheets. Flatten slightly with fork. Bake in 375°F (190°C) oven for 15 minutes or until golden. Let cool on pans on racks for 3 minutes. Transfer to racks and let cool completely. Spread about ½ cup (125 mL) slightly softened ice cream on bottom of each of 4 cookies; top each with second cookie and roll in mini candy-coated chocolates. Wrap individually in plastic wrap and freeze in airtight container for at least 4 hours or until firm.

Makes about 48 cookies.

PER COOKIE, ABOUT:

cal 132	carb . . . . .15 g
pro . . . . .1 g	fibre . . . . .1 g
total fat . . . . .8 g	chol . . . . . .14 mg
sat. fat . . . . . .3 g	sodium . . .72 mg

PERCENTAGE RDI:

calcium 1%	vit. A 2%
iron 4%	vit. C 0%
folate 4%	

Hermits Galore

Hermits are a moist, mildly spicy cookie usually pumped up with raisins and nuts. For fun, we've named new taste combinations after famous real or fictional hermits.

½ cup	butter, softened	125 mL
½ cup	shortening	125 mL
1 cup	packed brown sugar	250 mL
⅓ cup	granulated sugar	75 mL
2	eggs	2
1 tsp	vanilla	5 mL
2½ cups	all-purpose flour	625 mL
1 tsp	each baking powder and cinnamon	5 mL
¾ tsp	each nutmeg, ground allspice and ground cloves	4 mL
½ tsp	each baking soda and salt	2 mL
1½ cups	raisins	375 mL
1 cup	chopped pitted dates	250 mL
1 cup	chopped pecans, toasted	250 mL

1 In large bowl, beat together butter, shortening and brown and granulated sugars until light and fluffy; beat in eggs, 1 at a time. Beat in vanilla.

2 In separate bowl, stir together flour, baking powder, cinnamon, nutmeg, allspice, cloves, baking soda and salt; stir into butter mixture in 2 additions. Stir in raisins, dates and pecans.

3 Drop by tablespoonfuls (15 mL), about 2 inches (5 cm) apart, onto parchment paper–lined or greased rimless baking sheets. Bake in 350°F (180°C) oven for about 15 minutes or until golden. Let cool on pans on racks for 5 minutes. Transfer to racks; let cool completely. (MAKE-AHEAD: Layer between waxed paper in airtight container and store at room temperature for up to 5 days or freeze for up to 2 weeks.)

Makes about 80 cookies.

PER COOKIE, ABOUT:

cal	 76	carb . . . . 11 g
pro	. . . . 1 g	fibre . . . . 1 g
total fat	. . . . . 4 g	chol . . . . 8 mg
sat. fat	. . . . . . 1 g	sodium . . . 40 mg

PERCENTAGE RDI:

calcium 1%	vit. A 1%
iron 3%	vit. C 0%
folate 2%	

VARIATIONS

Mountain Man Hermits: Omit raisins, dates and pecans; substitute 3½ cups (875 mL) trail mix.

Robinson Crusoe Hermits: Omit raisins, dates and pecans; substitute 1¼ cups (300 mL) shredded coconut, 1 cup (250 mL) chopped toasted macadamia or Brazil nuts, ¾ cup (175 mL) chopped dried pineapple and ½ cup (125 mL) chopped dried papaya.

Morning Grumps Hermits: Omit dates and pecans; substitute 1¼ cups (300 mL) rice crisp cereal and ¾ cup (175 mL) roasted peanuts.

Greta Garbo Hermits: Omit cloves; substitute ½ tsp (2 mL) ground cardamom. Omit raisins, dates and pecans; substitute 2 cups (500 mL) candied fruit, 1½ cups (375 mL) chopped toasted almonds and 2 tsp (10 mL) each grated orange and lemon rind.

Amaretti

With a hefty splash of almond extract and a full measure of chopped almonds, this is the cookie for almond lovers to enjoy with espresso to finish a meal. This recipe is from the family of Test Kitchen home economist and "Canadian Living Cooks" cohost Emily Richards.

2 cups	unblanched almonds	500 mL
2	egg whites	2
1 cup	granulated sugar	250 mL

2 tbsp	all-purpose flour	25 mL
1 tbsp	almond extract	15 mL
1 tsp	baking powder	5 mL

1 In food processor, chop almonds until in small pieces with some powdery granules. Set aside.

2 In large bowl, beat egg whites until soft peaks form; beat in sugar, 2 tbsp (25 mL) at a time, until ribbons fall from lifted beaters. Stir in almonds, flour, almond extract and baking powder.

3 Drop by level tablespoonfuls (15 mL), about 2 inches (5 cm) apart, onto parchment paper–lined or greased rimless baking sheets. With fingertips, shape each into neat circle.

4 Bake in centre of 350°F (180°C) oven for about 20 minutes or until light brown and tops are crisp. Let cool on pans on racks for 2 minutes. Transfer to racks; let cool completely. (MAKE-AHEAD: Store in airtight container for up to 2 weeks.)

TEST KITCHEN TIPS

• Batter is sticky; dust hands with icing sugar before shaping each dough circle.

• For these delicate cookies, dark baking sheets are not recommended as they cause overbrowning.

Nut KNOW-HOW

To ensure freshness, buy nuts from a store with a high turnover. If possible, sample before buying.

In cookies, most nuts taste better if they're toasted. To toast whole nuts, spread single layer on rimmed baking sheet; toast in 350°F (180°C) oven (or toaster oven for small amounts) for 8 to 10 minutes or until fragrant and darkened slightly. Watch carefully: nuts brown quickly once they're hot. Chopped nuts need less time.

To toast nuts in the microwave, spread on microwaveable plate; microwave at High for 5 to 10 minutes or until fragrant, stirring about every 2 minutes. Reduce time for chopped nuts.

To remove skins from hazelnuts, rub hot toasted hazelnuts in clean tea towel until most or all of the skins are removed. If you like the colour and taste that the toasted skin adds to cookies, rub lightly to retain some of the skins.

Store nuts in airtight container in freezer (for up to several months) to ensure freshness.

Makes about 48 cookies.

PER COOKIE, ABOUT:

cal	53	carb	6 g
pro	1 g	fibre	trace
total fat	3 g	chol	0 mg
sat. fat	trace	sodium	8 mg

PERCENTAGE RDI:

calcium	2%	vit. A	0%
iron	1%	vit. C	0%
folate	2%		

Brutti ma Buoni

"Ugly but good" is the translation of the name for these crunchy-on-the-outside and chewy-on-the-inside Italian cookies. You can make them with coarsely chopped toasted almonds, hazelnuts or walnuts, but they are even more addictive when chunks of chocolate are added.

TEST KITCHEN TIP: Use a nougat milk chocolate bar such as Toblerone.

4	egg whites	4
1 cup	granulated sugar	250 mL
3 tbsp	all-purpose flour	50 mL
1 tsp	vanilla	5 mL

2 cups	coarsely chopped nougat milk chocolate bar	500 mL
2 tbsp	icing sugar	25 mL

1 In large heatproof bowl over saucepan of gently simmering water, cook egg whites with granulated sugar, whisking occasionally, for about 10 minutes or until opaque. Remove from heat; beat for about 7 minutes or until cooled, thickened and glossy. Fold in flour and vanilla; fold in chocolate.

2 Drop by heaping tablespoonfuls (15 mL), about 2 inches (5 cm) apart, onto parchment paper–lined or greased foil-lined rimless baking sheets. Bake, 1 sheet at a time, in centre of 350°F (180°C) oven for 25 to 30 minutes or until light brown. Let cool on racks. Sprinkle with icing sugar. (MAKE-AHEAD: **Store in airtight container for up to 3 days.**)

VARIATION

Ginger Brutti ma Buoni: Substitute 1 tsp (5 mL) ground ginger for vanilla and 1 cup (250 mL) chopped crystallized ginger for chopped chocolate bar.

Makes about 24 cookies.

PER COOKIE, ABOUT:

cal 110	carb ....22 g
pro ....1 g	fibre ....trace
total fat .....2 g	chol ....1 mg
sat. fat ......1 g	sodium ...44 mg

PERCENTAGE RDI:

calcium 2%	vit. A 0%
iron 1%	vit. C 0%
folate 1%	

Spicy Ginger Crinkle Cookies

Crunchy little spice cookies are made for dunking in milk or tea.

¾ cup	shortening	175 mL
1 cup	packed brown sugar	250 mL
1	egg	1
¼ cup	fancy molasses	50 mL
1 tsp	vanilla	5 mL
2 cups	all-purpose flour	500 mL

2 tsp	each baking soda and ground ginger	10 mL
1 tsp	cinnamon	5 mL
½ tsp	ground allspice or cloves	2 mL
½ tsp	salt	2 mL
¼ cup	granulated sugar	50 mL

TEST KITCHEN TIP: Boost the ginger by adding 2 tbsp (25 mL) chopped crystallized ginger.

1 In large bowl, beat shortening with brown sugar until fluffy. Beat in egg, molasses and vanilla until smooth. In separate bowl, whisk together flour, baking soda, ginger, cinnamon, allspice and salt; stir into molasses mixture in 2 additions.

2 Scoop dough by level tablespoonfuls (15 mL) and roll into balls. Roll in granulated sugar to coat and place, about 2 inches (5 cm) apart, on parchment paper–lined or greased rimless baking sheets.

3 Bake in 350°F (180°C) oven for about 12 minutes or until flattened, tops are cracked and bottoms are browned. Let cool on pans on racks. (MAKE-AHEAD: Layer between waxed paper in airtight container and store at room temperature for up to 5 days or freeze for up to 2 weeks.)

Makes about 46 cookies.

PER COOKIE, ABOUT:

cal	78	carb	11 g
pro	1 g	fibre	trace
total fat	3 g	chol	5 mg
sat. fat	1 g	sodium	79 mg

PERCENTAGE RDI:

calcium	1%	vit. A	0%
iron	4%	vit. C	0%
folate	3%		

COOKIE BAKING Basics

⌁ Baking sheets with no rims or with slightly slanted lips allow heat to circulate around the baking cookies. Rimmed sheets are less suitable, but if they are all you have, you can just turn them over and use the rimless underside.

⌁ Heavy, shiny bright sheets are best: they don't warp and they bake cookies evenly and prevent them from browning too quickly.

⌁ For most drop, sliced or shaped cookies, line baking sheets with parchment paper. Cookies lift off parchment effortlessly; wipe paper after use and reuse until it becomes brittle. Or brush baking sheets lightly with shortening or unsalted butter.

⌁ The ideal way to bake cookies is one sheet at a time on the centre rack of the oven. In the name of speed, you can bake two sheets at a time, in top and bottom thirds of oven, switching and rotating pans halfway through baking time.

Almond Biscotti

The darlings of the latte and cappuccino crowd, biscotti can feature almost any nut or dried fruit, even a double dose of chocolate.

TEST KITCHEN TIPS

• For long biscotti, cut cookie logs on diagonal.

• If you have only 1 or 2 baking sheets, let them cool between batches. Hot baking sheets will melt cookie dough, resulting in changes to the texture and shape of cookies.

½ cup	butter, softened	125 mL
1 cup	granulated sugar	250 mL
3	eggs	3
1 tsp	each vanilla and almond extract	5 mL
2¾ cups	all-purpose flour	675 mL
1½ tsp	baking powder	7 mL
¼ tsp	salt	1 mL
1 cup	unblanched almonds	250 mL
1 tbsp	icing sugar	15 mL

1 In bowl, beat butter with sugar until fluffy; beat in eggs, 1 at a time, then vanilla and almond extract. In separate bowl, whisk together flour, baking powder and salt; add to butter mixture all at once, stirring just until combined. Stir in almonds.

2 Divide dough in half; with floured hands, shape each half into log about 12 inches (30 cm) long. Place, about 4 inches (10 cm) apart, on parchment paper–lined or greased rimless baking sheet; flatten each until about 3 inches (8 cm) wide, leaving top slightly rounded.

3 Bake in centre of 325°F (160°C) oven for about 30 minutes or until firm and tops are just turning golden. Let cool on pan on rack for 10 minutes. Transfer to cutting board; with serrated knife, cut into ½-inch (1 cm) thick slices. Stand slices upright on 2 rimless baking sheets. Return to oven; bake for 30 to 40 minutes or until dry and crisp. Let cool on pans on racks. (MAKE-AHEAD: Layer between waxed paper in airtight container and store at room temperature for up to 1 week or freeze for up to 2 weeks.) Dust with icing sugar just before serving.

VARIATIONS

Cherry Almond Biscotti: Decrease almonds to ½ cup (125 mL); add ¾ cup (175 mL) dried cherries, cranberries or blueberries.

Double Chocolate Biscotti: Omit almond extract. Decrease flour to 2 cups (500 mL); add ⅔ cup (150 mL) cocoa powder, sifted, and ½ tsp (2 mL) baking soda. Stir in ½ cup (125 mL) mini chocolate chips along with almonds.

Other Nut Biscotti: Substitute whole hazelnuts, pecan or walnut halves, or shelled pistachios for almonds; replace almond extract with additional vanilla.

Makes about 40 cookies.

PER COOKIE, ABOUT:

cal 98	carb ....13 g
pro ....2 g	fibre ....1 g
total fat .....5 g	chol ......22 mg
sat. fat ......2 g	sodium ...53 mg

PERCENTAGE RDI:

calcium 2%	vit. A 3%
iron 4%	vit. C 0%
folate 6%	

Peanut Butter Cookies

Test Kitchen manager Heather Howe arms her kids with forks and gets them to help flatten the balls of dough. You can add crunch by mixing in 1 cup (250 mL) chopped peanuts before forming the dough into balls.

1 cup	butter, softened	250 mL
¾ cup	packed brown sugar	175 mL
¾ cup	granulated sugar	175 mL
1 cup	peanut butter	250 mL
2	eggs	2

1 tsp	vanilla	5 mL
2½ cups	all-purpose flour	625 mL
1 tsp	each baking soda and baking powder	5 mL
¼ tsp	salt	1 mL

1 In large bowl, beat butter until light and fluffy; beat in brown and granulated sugars. Beat in peanut butter and eggs, 1 at a time; beat in vanilla until smooth.

2 In separate bowl, whisk together flour, baking soda, baking powder and salt; add all at once to butter mixture and stir until blended.

3 Scoop dough by rounded tablespoonfuls (15 mL) and roll into balls; place, 2 inches (5 cm) apart, on parchment paper–lined or greased rimless baking sheets. With fork dipped in flour or granulated sugar, press each to make criss-cross pattern and flatten to ½-inch (1 cm) thickness.

4 Bake in 350°F (180°C) oven for 10 to 12 minutes or until firm and edges and bottoms are golden. Transfer to racks; let cool. (MAKE-AHEAD: Layer between waxed paper in airtight container and store at room temperature for up to 5 days or freeze for up to 2 weeks.)

VARIATION

Chocolate Peanut Butter Thumbprints: Instead of flattening balls of dough with a fork, press each with your thumb to create indent. Bake as directed; while each cookie is still hot, use handle of wooden spoon to indent again if necessary to reform, then fill with chocolate candy.

Makes about 44 cookies.

PER COOKIE, ABOUT:

cal	128	carb	14 g
pro	3 g	fibre	1 g
total fat	7 g	chol	21 mg
sat. fat	3 g	sodium	119 mg

PERCENTAGE RDI:

calcium	1%	vit. A	4%
iron	4%	vit. C	0%
folate	6%		

Pecan Snowballs

The irresistible icing-sugar coating melts in your mouth as it introduces the toasted pecan cookie.

1 cup	butter, softened	250 mL
1¼ cups	icing sugar	300 mL
1½ tsp	vanilla	7 mL
2 cups	all-purpose flour	500 mL

2 cups	toasted pecans, finely chopped	500 mL
½ tsp	salt	2 mL

1 In large bowl, beat butter with 1 cup (250 mL) of the sugar until smooth; beat in vanilla. Stir in flour, pecans and salt; mix with hands and press together firmly. Wrap in plastic wrap; refrigerate for 30 minutes.

2 Scoop by scant tablespoonfuls (15 mL) and roll into balls; place, 1 inch (2.5 cm) apart, on ungreased rimless baking sheets. Bake in 325°F (160°C) oven for 18 to 20 minutes or until light golden. Transfer to racks; let cool for 5 minutes.

3 Meanwhile, sift remaining sugar into shallow bowl. Roll balls in icing sugar; return to racks and let cool completely. Roll again in icing sugar. (MAKE-AHEAD: Layer between waxed paper in airtight container and store at room temperature for up to 1 week or freeze for up to 2 months.)

VARIATION

Almond Snowballs or Crescents: Substitute finely chopped blanched almonds for pecans. Add ¼ tsp (1 mL) almond extract along with vanilla. For Almond Snowballs, form into balls. For Almond Crescents, scoop by scant tablespoonfuls (15 mL) and shape into 2½-inch (6 cm) long logs, then bend into crescents; place, about 2 inches (5 cm) apart, on baking sheets.

Makes about 42 cookies.

PER COOKIE, ABOUT:

cal 110	carb ....9 g
pro ....1 g	fibre ....1 g
total fat .....8 g	chol ......12 mg
sat. fat ......3 g	sodium ...72 mg

PERCENTAGE RDI:

calcium 0%	vit. A 4%
iron 3%	vit. C 0%
folate 4%	

Glazed Almond Spritz Rosettes

Pretty, delicate and festive only begin to describe these delicious little almond bites. The glaze gives a lovely shimmer, and the silver dragées add a celebratory touch, whether you're serving these cookies for a wedding, shower or Christmas gathering.

1 cup	butter, softened	250 mL
⅔ cup	icing sugar	150 mL
1	egg yolk	1
1½ tsp	vanilla	7 mL
¼ tsp	almond extract	1 mL
Pinch	salt	Pinch
2 cups	all-purpose flour	500 mL
½ cup	ground almonds	125 mL

GLAZE:

1 cup	icing sugar (approx)	250 mL
¼ cup	whipping cream (approx)	50 mL
¼ tsp	almond extract	1 mL
	Silver dragées or candied cherries	

TEST KITCHEN TIPS

• With a cookie press, you can press out any festive shape.

• If desired, leave unglazed and dip into, or drizzle with, melted chocolate.

• Wash and chill pans before reusing for another batch.

1 Refrigerate ungreased rimless baking sheets to chill.

2 In large bowl, beat butter with icing sugar until fluffy; beat in egg yolk, vanilla, almond extract and salt. Stir in flour, then almonds. Spoon into cookie press; press out 1-inch (2.5 cm) diameter rosettes, about ½ inch (1 cm) apart, onto chilled pans.

3 Bake in centre of 350°F (180°C) oven for 8 to 10 minutes or until light golden on bottom. Let cool on pans on racks for 1 minute; transfer to racks set over sheets of waxed paper.

4 GLAZE: Stir together sugar, whipping cream and almond extract, adding more sugar or cream if necessary to make pourable. Drizzle over hot cookies. Immediately press silver dragée onto centre of each. Let cool. (MAKE-AHEAD: Layer between waxed paper in airtight container and store at room temperature for up to 5 days or freeze for up to 1 month.)

Makes about 90 cookies.

PER COOKIE, ABOUT:

cal	42	carb	4 g
pro	trace	fibre	trace
total fat	3 g	chol	9 mg
sat. fat	1 g	sodium	21 mg

PERCENTAGE RDI:

calcium	0%	vit. A	2%
iron	1%	vit. C	0%
folate	2%		

Shortbread Cookies

One of the world's finest cookies, shortbread is tempting in its simplicity and easy to vary with additions of chocolate, nuts, ginger — you name it — and to shape into bars, squares, rounds and mounds.

1 cup	butter, softened	250 mL
½ cup	instant dissolving (fruit/berry) sugar	125 mL
1 tsp	vanilla	5 mL
2 cups	all-purpose flour	500 mL
Pinch	salt	Pinch

1 In bowl, beat butter with sugar until light and fluffy. Stir in vanilla. Add flour and salt; stir until blended.

2 Between 2 sheets of waxed paper, roll out dough to ¼-inch (5 mm) thickness. Using 2-inch (5 cm) round or shaped cookie cutter, cut out cookies. Place on parchment paper–lined or ungreased rimless baking sheets. Prick each twice with fork. Freeze for 1 hour or until firm.

3 Bake in 300°F (150°C) oven for 30 to 35 minutes or until firm to the touch and slightly golden. (MAKE-AHEAD: Layer between waxed paper in airtight container and store at room temperature for up to 5 days or freeze for up to 2 weeks.)

TEST KITCHEN TIP: For chocolate shortbread, add 2 oz (60 g) bittersweet chocolate, melted and cooled, to butter mixture. For other variations, try these additions: 1 cup (250 mL) chopped toasted nuts; ½ cup (125 mL) mini chocolate chips; 1 tbsp (15 mL) grated orange rind.

Makes about 56 cookies.

PER COOKIE, ABOUT:

cal	52	carb	5 g
pro	1 g	fibre	trace
total fat	3 g	chol	9 mg
sat. fat	2 g	sodium	34 mg

PERCENTAGE RDI:

calcium	0%	vit. A	3%
iron	1%	vit. C	0%
folate	2%		

SHAPING VARIATIONS

Chocolate Mounds: Add 1 cup (250 mL) finely chopped milk chocolate bar to dough. Drop by rounded tablespoonfuls (15 mL) onto pans; form into mounds and press ½-inch (1 cm) chunk of bar into each mound. Freeze and bake as directed. Sieve icing sugar over cooled cookies. **Makes about 48 cookies.**

Slice and Bake: Turn out dough onto lightly floured work surface. Form into 4 bricks, each about 1 inch (2.5 cm) high and 1½ inches (4 cm) wide. Cover with plastic wrap and refrigerate for 2 hours or until firm. Cut into ¼-inch (5 mm) thick slices. Place on parchment paper–lined or ungreased rimless baking sheets. Prick each twice with fork. Bake as directed. **Makes about 56 cookies.**

Golden Shortbread Squares: Double butter, sugar, vanilla and flour; increase salt to ¼ tsp (1 mL). Press dough onto parchment paper–lined 17- x 11-inch (45 x 29 cm) rimmed baking sheet. With sharp knife, score into 50 bars. Prick each once with fork. Refrigerate for 1 hour or until firm. Bake in 300°F (150°C) oven for about 1 hour or until golden and firm to the touch. Cut into bars while warm. **Makes about 50 bars.**

Icebox Cookies

Shaping cookie dough into logs, ready to slice and bake, is an ideal way to have cookies ready to enjoy quickly — whenever you need them or crave them. Here's the basic butter- and sugar-rich dough with candied cherries, but you can add to it or dress it up as your whims dictate.

1 cup	butter, softened	250 mL
1 cup	granulated sugar	250 mL
1	egg	1
2 tsp	vanilla	10 mL
2⅔ cups	all-purpose flour	650 mL

½ tsp	baking powder	2 mL
¼ tsp	salt	1 mL
¾ cup	chopped candied red or green cherries	175 mL

TEST KITCHEN TIP: You can wrap and freeze logs of homemade cookie dough to present to busy friends. Be sure to include slice-and-bake instructions.

1 In large bowl, beat butter with sugar until light and fluffy; beat in egg and vanilla. In separate bowl, whisk together flour, baking powder and salt; stir into butter mixture in 2 additions. Stir in cherries.

2 Divide dough into thirds. Place, 1 at a time, on large piece of waxed paper; using paper as guide, roll into 8-inch (20 cm) long log. Remove paper; wrap in plastic wrap, twisting ends to seal. Refrigerate for at least 3 hours or until firm. (MAKE-AHEAD: Refrigerate for up to 3 days or freeze in airtight container for up to 3 weeks. Let stand at room temperature for 20 minutes.)

3 Cut into ¼-inch (5 mm) thick slices; place, about 2 inches (5 cm) apart, on parchment paper–lined or greased rimless baking sheets. Bake in 375°F (190°C) oven for 10 to 12 minutes or until lightly browned. Let cool on pans on racks for 5 minutes. Transfer to racks; let cool completely. (MAKE-AHEAD: Layer between waxed paper in airtight container and store at room temperature for up to 5 days or freeze for up to 2 weeks.)

VARIATIONS

Double Chocolate Cookies: Decrease flour to 2¼ cups (550 mL); add ½ cup (125 mL) cocoa powder to flour mixture. Substitute 5 oz (150 g) white chocolate, finely chopped, for the candied cherries. Bake for 10 to 15 minutes.

Fun Add-Ins: Omit candied cherries; add mini chocolate or butterscotch chips, toffee pieces, finely diced crystallized ginger, finely chopped pistachios, or finely chopped toasted pecans, almonds or hazelnuts.

Fun Dress-Ups: Before wrapping and refrigerating logs, roll in finely chopped nuts, coloured candy sprinkles, coarse coloured sugar or shredded coconut.

Makes about 84 cookies.

PER COOKIE, ABOUT:

cal 49	carb . . . . 7 g
pro . . . . 1 g	fibre . . . . trace
total fat . . . . . 2 g	chol . . . . 8 mg
sat. fat . . . . . . 1 g	sodium . . . 32 mg

PERCENTAGE RDI:

calcium 0%	vit. A 2%
iron 1%	vit. C 0%
folate 2%	

Speculaas

Traditionally moulded in carved wooden boards, these fragrantly spicy Dutch cookies are easier — and just as delicious — rolled out, cut into rectangles and baked with sliced almonds on top.

½ cup	butter, softened	125 mL
1 cup	packed brown sugar	250 mL
1	egg	1
1 cup	all-purpose flour	250 mL
¾ cup	whole wheat flour	175 mL
2 tsp	each cinnamon and ground ginger	10 mL
½ tsp	each baking powder, baking soda and ground allspice	2 mL
¼ tsp	each nutmeg and ground cardamom and cloves	1 mL
¼ tsp	each salt and pepper	1 mL
1 tbsp	milk	15 mL
½ cup	sliced almonds	125 mL

1 In large bowl, beat butter with sugar until fluffy; beat in egg. In separate bowl, whisk together all-purpose and whole wheat flours, cinnamon, ginger, baking powder, baking soda, allspice, nutmeg, cardamom, cloves, salt and pepper; stir into butter mixture in 2 additions. Turn out onto lightly floured surface; gather into ball and knead 10 times. Shape into disc. Wrap in plastic wrap; refrigerate for 30 minutes.

2 On lightly floured surface, roll out to ¼-inch (5 mm) thickness. With cookie cutter, cut into 3- x 2-inch (8 x 5 cm) rectangles or other desired shapes; place, ½ inch (1 cm) apart, on parchment paper–lined or greased rimless baking sheets. Brush with milk. Press almond slices into top of each in decorative pattern.

3 Bake in centre of 350°F (180°C) oven for 8 to 10 minutes or until edges are darkened slightly and tops are firm. Let cool on pans on racks for 5 minutes. Transfer to racks; let cool completely. (MAKE-AHEAD: Layer between waxed paper in airtight container and store at room temperature for up to 4 days or freeze for up to 2 weeks.)

Makes about 28 cookies.

PER COOKIE, ABOUT:

cal 101	carb .... 14 g
pro .... 2 g	fibre .... 1 g
total fat ..... 5 g	chol ...... 17 mg
sat. fat ...... 2 g	sodium ... 85 mg

PERCENTAGE RDI:

calcium 2%	vit. A 3%
iron 5%	vit. C 0%
folate 3%	

Sugar Cookies

No matter what the season, no matter what the celebration, there's a role for sugar cookies — trees for Christmas, dreidels for Hanukkah, hearts for Valentine's Day, chicks and eggs for Easter, and as for the rest of the year, animals or crinkle-edged rounds with or without icing.

¾ cup	butter, softened	175 mL		1 tsp	vanilla	5 mL
1 cup	granulated or packed light brown sugar	250 mL		2½ cups	all-purpose flour	625 mL
				½ tsp	baking powder	2 mL
1	egg	1		Pinch	salt	Pinch

1 In large bowl, beat butter until light and fluffy; beat in sugar in 3 additions. Beat in egg and vanilla. In separate bowl, whisk together flour, baking powder and salt; stir into butter mixture in 3 additions.

2 Divide dough in half; shape each into disc. Wrap in plastic wrap; refrigerate for at least 1 hour. (MAKE-AHEAD: Refrigerate for up to 24 hours.) Between 2 sheets of waxed paper or on lightly floured surface, roll out dough, 1 disc at a time, to ¼-inch (5 mm) thickness. With 3-inch (8 cm) cookie cutter, cut out shapes, rerolling scraps if necessary. With spatula, place cookies, 1 inch (2.5 cm) apart, on parchment paper–lined or greased rimless baking sheets.

3 Bake in centre of 375°F (190°C) oven for about 10 minutes or until light golden on bottoms and edges. Let cool for 1 minute on pans on racks. Transfer to racks; let cool completely. (MAKE-AHEAD: Layer between waxed paper in airtight container and store at room temperature for up to 5 days or freeze for up to 2 weeks.)

Makes about 36 cookies.

PER COOKIE, ABOUT:

cal	89	carb	12 g
pro	1 g	fibre	trace
total fat	4 g	chol	16 mg
sat. fat	2 g	sodium	45 mg

PERCENTAGE RDI:

calcium	0%	vit. A	4%
iron	3%	vit. C	0%
folate	5%		

DECORATING Sugar Cookies

ICING PAINT: In bowl, whisk 4 cups (1 L) icing sugar with ⅓ cup (75 mL) water, adding up to 2 tbsp (25 mL) more water if necessary to make spreadable; divide and, with liquid food colouring, tint as desired. With small paintbrushes or wooden craft sticks, paint base colour. While still wet, swirl in or dot with other tinted icing (wet on wet will give soft blurred edges), and press on or sprinkle with decorations such as coloured candy sprinkles, silver dragées or gold flakes if desired. Or let dry completely, then paint on contrasting-colour details.

PIPING ICING: In bowl, beat 2 tbsp (25 mL) meringue powder into ¼ cup (50 mL) water. Gradually beat in 2⅓ cups (575 mL) icing sugar until stiff, about 4 minutes. Divide and tint icing as desired. Spoon into piping bag fitted with plain tip; twist over icing. Holding bag at twist, squeeze out icing with slow even pressure, holding tip between thumb and forefinger to guide flow of icing. If desired, press sprinkles or candies into icing while still moist.

MAKE-AHEAD   CLASSIC

Rugalahs

The base of this festive horn-shaped crescent — probably the most popular Hanukkah cookie — is a cream cheese dough that's very easy to handle and so suitable for the sweet nut and fruit filling.

TEST KITCHEN TIP: If the jam you're using contains any large chunks, chop them into smaller pieces.

1	pkg (8 oz/250 g) cream cheese, softened	1
1 cup	butter, softened	250 mL
2 tbsp	granulated sugar	25 mL
2 cups	all-purpose flour	500 mL
FILLING:		
1 cup	coarsely chopped pecans, toasted	250 mL
½ cup	golden raisins (optional)	125 mL

¼ cup	each granulated sugar and packed brown sugar	50 mL
¾ tsp	cinnamon	4 mL
¾ cup	apricot jam	175 mL
TOPPING:		
1	egg	1
2 tbsp	coarse or granulated sugar	25 mL

1 In large bowl, beat cream cheese with butter until fluffy; beat in sugar. Stir in flour in 2 additions. Form into ball; cut into quarters and shape into discs. Wrap each in plastic wrap; refrigerate for at least 2 hours. (MAKE-AHEAD: Refrigerate for up to 24 hours.) Let stand at room temperature for 15 minutes before rolling.

2 FILLING: In small bowl, stir together pecans, raisins (if using), granulated and brown sugars and cinnamon. In separate bowl, stir jam with 1 tsp (5 mL) water until spreadable.

3 On lightly floured surface, roll out 1 disc into 11-inch (28 cm) circle. Spread 3 tbsp (50 mL) of the jam evenly over top; sprinkle with one-quarter of the nut mixture. Cut into 12 pie-shaped wedges.

4 Starting from wide end, roll up each wedge to form crescent; place, about 2 inches (5 cm) apart, on parchment paper– or foil-lined rimless baking sheets. Refrigerate for 30 minutes. Repeat with remaining dough and filling.

5 TOPPING: Beat egg lightly; brush over crescents. Sprinkle sugar over top.

6 Bake in 350°F (180°C) oven for about 25 minutes or until golden brown. Let cool on pans on racks for 5 minutes. Transfer to racks and let cool completely. (MAKE-AHEAD: Layer between waxed paper in airtight container and store at room temperature for up to 5 days or freeze for up to 2 weeks.)

Makes about 48 cookies.

PER COOKIE, ABOUT:

cal	113	carb	11 g
pro	1 g	fibre	trace
total fat	7 g	chol	21 mg
sat. fat	4 g	sodium	58 mg

PERCENTAGE RDI:

calcium	1%	vit. A	6%
iron	3%	vit. C	0%
folate	4%		

VARIATION

Chocolate Raspberry Rugalahs: Substitute chocolate chips for raisins and raspberry jam for apricot jam.

Glazed Apricot Blondies

Blondies are the golden version of dense, chewy brownies. It's easy to double this recipe when the occasion calls for lots of squares; just use a 13- x 9-inch (3.5 L) metal cake pan and bake for an extra 10 to 15 minutes.

½ cup	butter, softened	125 mL
1¼ cups	packed brown sugar	300 mL
2	eggs	2
2 tsp	vanilla	10 mL
1¼ cups	all-purpose flour	300 mL
¼ tsp	salt	1 mL

1 cup	chopped dried apricots	250 mL
½ cup	chopped pecans	125 mL
GLAZE:		
½ cup	icing sugar	125 mL
2 tbsp	butter, softened	25 mL
2 tsp	lemon juice	10 mL

1 Line 8-inch (2 L) square metal cake pan with parchment paper, leaving 1 inch (2.5 cm) extending over edges for handles. Set aside.

2 In large bowl, beat butter with sugar until fluffy; beat in eggs, 1 at a time. Beat in vanilla. In separate bowl, combine flour and salt; stir in apricots and pecans. Stir into butter mixture in 2 additions. Spread evenly in prepared pan.

3 Bake in centre of 325°F (160°C) oven for 40 to 50 minutes or until cake tester inserted in centre comes out clean. Let cool in pan on rack just until slightly warm.

4 GLAZE: In small bowl, stir together icing sugar, butter and lemon juice; spread over top. Let cool. Using parchment paper handles, lift out of pan. Peel off paper. Cut into squares. (MAKE-AHEAD: Cover and store at room temperature for up to 2 days or overwrap with heavy-duty foil and freeze for up to 2 weeks.)

TEST KITCHEN TIP: Make it easy to remove brownies, blondies and any squares or bars from a pan so that they can be cut neatly on a cutting board. Line pan with parchment paper, leaving 1 inch (2.5 cm) extending over edges for handles (you can line pan with foil, but foil needs to be greased after fitting into pan). Use handles to lift baked cooled brownies from pan. Peel off parchment paper and cut.

Makes 20 blondies.

PER BLONDIE, ABOUT:

cal	184	carb	27 g
pro	2 g	fibre	1 g
total fat	8 g	chol	37 mg
sat. fat	4 g	sodium	99 mg

PERCENTAGE RDI:

calcium	2%	vit. A	11%
iron	8%	vit. C	0%
folate	5%		

Oodles of Brownies

One delicious brownie can have so many flavour combinations and toppings, too. Use as a base for brownie sundaes.

	FLAVOURINGS	TOPPINGS
Nutty Caramel Brownies	¼ cup (50 mL) chopped toasted pecans or walnuts	½ cup (125 mL) toffee bits; ¼ cup (50 mL) chopped pecans or walnuts
White Chocolate Orange Brownies	½ cup (125 mL) white chocolate chips; 2 tbsp (25 mL) grated orange rind	1 cup (250 mL) white chocolate chips, spreading when melted
Peanut Butter Brownies	¼ cup (50 mL) crunchy or smooth peanut butter	1 cup (250 mL) peanut butter chips, spreading when melted
Mocha Brownies	4 tsp (20 mL) instant coffee granules dissolved in 1 tbsp (15 mL) hot water	1 cup (250 mL) chocolate chips, spreading when melted
Double Chocolate Brownies	½ cup (125 mL) chocolate chips	1 cup (250 mL) chocolate chips, spreading when melted

TEST KITCHEN TIPS

• To ease cleanup and removal from pan, line it with foil to extend 1 inch (2.5 cm) above opposite edges for handles; grease foil before adding batter. Or use parchment paper, omitting greasing.

• To make brownies ahead of time, wrap them in plastic wrap and store at room temperature for up to 3 days. Or overwrap with heavy-duty foil or place in airtight container and freeze for up to 2 weeks.

1 In saucepan over medium heat, melt together ⅓ cup (75 mL) butter, 4 oz (125 g) bittersweet or semisweet chocolate, chopped, and 2 oz (60 g) unsweet-ened chocolate, chopped. Let cool for 10 minutes.

2 Whisk in ¾ cup (175 mL) granulated sugar, 2 eggs, 1 at a time, 2 tsp (10 mL) vanilla and Flavourings in first column. Stir in ½ cup (125 mL) all-purpose flour and pinch salt.

3 Scrape into greased 8-inch (2 L) square metal cake pan; bake in centre of 350°F (180°C) oven for 25 to 30 minutes or until cake tester inserted in centre comes out with a few moist crumbs clinging to it. Sprinkle with Toppings in second column. Let cool in pan on rack. Cut into squares.

Makes 16 brownies.

Panforte

*A traditional treat in Sienna, Italy, this honey-sweetened "strong bread" tastes like a
blondie packed with nuts and candied fruit and with an elusive note of spice. You can
dust the top liberally with icing sugar.*

1 cup	hazelnuts	250 mL	¾ tsp	each cinnamon and white pepper	4 mL
1 cup	whole blanched almonds	250 mL	¼ tsp	each nutmeg and ground coriander	1 mL
¾ cup	chopped candied mixed peel	175 mL	Pinch	ground cloves	Pinch
¾ cup	chopped candied citron	175 mL	⅔ cup	granulated sugar	150 mL
½ cup	all-purpose flour	125 mL	⅔ cup	liquid honey	150 mL
1 tsp	each grated orange and lemon rind	5 mL			

TEST KITCHEN TIP: Be sure
to wrap panforte in foil;
plastic wrap will cause it to
soften.

1 Grease 8½-inch (2.25 L) springform pan. Line bottom and side with parchment paper; grease paper. Set aside.

2 Toast hazelnuts and almonds on rimmed baking sheet in 350°F (180°C) oven for 8 to 10 minutes or until fragrant. Transfer to tea towel; rub off as much of the hazelnut skins as possible.

3 Chop nuts coarsely and place in large bowl; stir in candied peel and citron, flour, orange and lemon rinds, cinnamon, pepper, nutmeg, coriander and cloves. Set aside.

4 In small heavy saucepan, stir sugar with honey. Bring to boil over medium heat; cook for about 3 minutes or until at hard-ball stage of 265°F (129°C) or until ½ tsp (2 mL) syrup dropped into cold water forms hard but pliable ball. Quickly stir into nut mixture, mixing well. Immediately spread in prepared pan.

5 Bake in centre of 325°F (160°C) oven for about 45 minutes or until slightly raised, golden brown and edge is firm. (Panforte will still be soft at centre.) Let cool in pan on rack for about 45 minutes or until centre is firm to the touch. Remove side of pan; invert onto second rack. Remove pan base; peel off paper. Invert back onto first rack; let cool completely. Wrap in foil; let stand for 24 hours. (MAKE-AHEAD: Store in airtight container for up to 2 weeks.)

VARIATION

Chocolate Panforte: Omit citron; increase mixed peel to 1 cup (250 mL) and add 2 oz (60 g) bittersweet chocolate, coarsely chopped, and 2 tbsp (25 mL) cocoa powder.

Makes 20 servings.

PER SERVING, ABOUT:

cal	211	carb	33 g
pro	3 g	fibre	2 g
total fat	9 g	chol	0 mg
sat. fat	1 g	sodium	25 mg

PERCENTAGE RDI:

calcium	4%	vit. A	0%
iron	6%	vit. C	0%
folate	5%		

Florentine Bars

These jewel-topped squares from author Pam Collacott are impressive for guests and are a good bet for best-sellers at bake sales.

1½ cups	all-purpose flour	375 mL
½ cup	icing sugar	125 mL
¼ tsp	salt	1 mL
¾ cup	cold butter	175 mL

FILLING:

3	eggs	3
¾ cup	packed brown sugar	175 mL
1 tsp	vanilla	5 mL

1 cup	mixed candied fruit	250 mL
½ cup	each red and green candied cherries, halved	125 mL
½ cup	candied mixed peel	125 mL
½ cup	candied pineapple, coarsely chopped	125 mL

TOPPING:

½ cup	semisweet chocolate chips	125 mL

1 Line 13- x 9-inch (3.5 L) metal cake pan with parchment paper, leaving 1 inch (2.5 cm) extending over long edges for handles. Set aside.

2 In bowl, stir together flour, icing sugar and salt; with pastry blender or 2 knives, cut in butter until mixture resembles coarse crumbs. Press evenly into prepared pan. Bake in centre of 350°F (180°C) oven for 15 minutes or until golden and firm to the touch.

3 FILLING: In bowl, whisk together eggs, brown sugar and vanilla until smooth; stir in candied fruit, red and green cherries, peel and pineapple. Pour over baked base, spreading evenly. Bake in centre of 350°F (180°C) oven for 30 to 35 minutes or until set. Let cool in pan on rack for 15 minutes.

4 TOPPING: Pour chocolate chips into bottom half of clean dry sturdy plastic bag; set flat in microwave and heat at Medium-Low (30%) for 3 to 7 minutes, checking every minute and removing bag from microwave as soon as chocolate is melted. Snip off tiny bottom corner of bag and use as piping bag to drizzle chocolate in thin closely spaced lines over baked filling. Let cool. Using parchment paper handles, lift out of pan. Peel off paper. Cut into bars. (MAKE-AHEAD: Cover and store at room temperature for up to 2 days.)

Makes 24 bars.

PER BAR, ABOUT:
cal .... 215 carb .... 36 g
pro .... 2 g fibre .... 1 g
total fat ..... 8 g chol ...... 42 mg
sat. fat ...... 4 g sodium ... 99 mg

PERCENTAGE RDI:
calcium ..... 2% vit. A 7%
iron .... 6% vit. C 8%
folate 5%

Simply Lovely Lemon Squares

As tart and refreshing as lemonade, this is a true classic, passing from one generation to the next and finding new fans. Cut into tiny bits and nestle into bonbon cups like after-dinner truffles, or cut more generous pieces when the occasion is casual.

¾ cup	butter, softened	175 mL
½ cup	granulated sugar	125 mL
¼ tsp	salt	1 mL
2 cups	all-purpose flour	500 mL
TOPPING:		
4	eggs	4
1½ cups	granulated sugar	375 mL

2 tbsp	finely grated lemon rind	25 mL
½ cup	lemon juice	125 mL
¼ cup	all-purpose flour	50 mL
1 tsp	baking powder	5 mL
2 tsp	icing sugar	10 mL

1 Line 13- x 9-inch (3.5 L) metal cake pan with parchment paper, leaving 1 inch (2.5 cm) extending over long edges for handles. Set aside.

2 In bowl, beat together butter, sugar and salt until light and fluffy; stir in flour in 2 additions. Press evenly into prepared pan. Bake in centre of 325°F (160°C) oven for about 35 minutes or until golden. Let cool in pan on rack.

3 TOPPING: Meanwhile, in bowl, beat eggs with sugar until pale and thickened; beat in lemon rind and juice, flour and baking powder. Pour over baked base, spreading evenly. Bake for 25 to 30 minutes or until golden brown and centre is set. Let cool in pan on rack. Dust with icing sugar. Using parchment paper handles, lift out of pan. Peel off paper. Cut into squares. (MAKE-AHEAD: **Refrigerate in airtight container for up to 4 days.**)

VARIATION

Lemon Almond Squares: Beat ¼ tsp (1 mL) almond extract into butter mixture; sprinkle top with 1½ cups (375 mL) sliced almonds before baking.

Makes 32 squares.

PER SQUARE, ABOUT:

cal	129	carb	20 g
pro	2 g	fibre	trace
total fat	5 g	chol	38 mg
sat. fat	3 g	sodium	78 mg

PERCENTAGE RDI:

calcium	1%	vit. A	5%
iron	4%	vit. C	3%
folate	5%		

Nanaimo Bars

While Canadians never seem to tire of this icon of our cooking heritage, three varia-
tions — with white chocolate, peanut butter and orange — add some variety. Since
Nanaimo Bars are so sweet, cut into truffle-size squares.

1 cup	butter, melted	250 mL
⅔ cup	cocoa powder	150 mL
½ cup	granulated sugar	125 mL
2	eggs, lightly beaten	2
3 cups	graham cracker crumbs	750 mL
2 cups	shredded coconut	500 mL
1 cup	finely chopped walnuts	250 mL

FILLING:		
⅓ cup	butter, melted	75 mL
¼ cup	milk	50 mL
2 tsp	vanilla	10 mL
4 cups	icing sugar	1 L

TOPPING:		
8 oz	semisweet chocolate	250 g
2 tbsp	butter	25 mL

1 Grease 13- x 9-inch (3.5 L) metal cake pan and line with parchment paper, leaving 1 inch (2.5 cm) extending over long edges for handles. Set aside.

2 In large bowl, whisk together butter, cocoa powder, sugar and eggs; stir in cracker crumbs, coconut and walnuts. Press evenly into prepared pan. Bake in centre of 350°F (180°C) oven for 10 minutes. Let cool in pan on rack.

3 FILLING: In large bowl, stir together butter, milk and vanilla; beat in sugar until thickened and smooth. Spread evenly over cooled base. Refrigerate for about 45 minutes or until firm.

4 TOPPING: Meanwhile, chop chocolate; in heatproof bowl over saucepan of hot (not boiling) water, melt chocolate with butter. Spread evenly over filling. Refrigerate until set. Using parchment paper handles, lift out of pan. Peel off paper. Cut into bars. (MAKE-AHEAD: Cover and store at room temperature for up to 2 days or overwrap with heavy-duty foil and freeze for up to 2 weeks.)

Makes 48 bars.

PER BAR, ABOUT:

cal	185	carb	22 g
pro	1 g	fibre	1 g
total fat	11 g	chol	24 mg
sat. fat	6 g	sodium	112 mg

PERCENTAGE RDI:

calcium	1%	vit. A	6%
iron	6%	vit. C	0%
folate	2%		

VARIATIONS

Topsy-Turvy Nanaimo Bars: For filling, decrease milk to 2 tbsp (25 mL) and icing sugar to 1⅓ cups (325 mL); add ⅔ cup (150 mL) cocoa powder. For topping, substitute 10 oz (300 g) white chocolate for semisweet chocolate.

Peanut Butter Nanaimo Bars: For filling, increase milk to ⅓ cup (75 mL) and decrease icing sugar to 1½ cups (375 mL); add 1 cup (250 mL) smooth peanut butter.

Orange Nanaimo Bars: For filling, substitute ¼ cup (50 mL) orange liqueur or orange juice concentrate for milk and add 1 tbsp (15 mL) grated orange rind.

Date Squares

These delicious date squares, with a thick, sweet date filling sandwiched between cinnamon-scented flaky oats, hail from the kitchen of the Hibernia drilling rig, off the coast of Newfoundland.

2½ cups	rolled oats	625 mL
1¼ cups	all-purpose flour	300 mL
1 cup	packed brown sugar	250 mL
1 tbsp	cinnamon	15 mL
¼ tsp	salt	1 mL
1 cup	butter, softened	250 mL

FILLING:

1	pkg (375 g) pitted dates	1
¾ cup	granulated sugar	175 mL
2 tbsp	each lemon juice and orange juice	25 mL

TEST KITCHEN TIP: For baking, always use large-flake rolled oats, either old-fashioned or quick-cooking. Avoid instant, which are specifically processed for hot cereal and are unsuitably sticky for baking.

1 FILLING: In heavy saucepan, stir together 2 cups (500 mL) water, dates, sugar and lemon and orange juices; let stand for 30 minutes. Bring to boil; reduce heat to medium and boil gently, stirring often, for about 10 minutes or until thick enough to mound on spoon. Let cool.

2 In large bowl, whisk together oats, flour, sugar, cinnamon and salt; with pastry blender or 2 knives, cut in butter until mixture resembles coarse crumbs. Press half evenly into greased 8-inch (2 L) square metal cake pan; spread evenly with date mixture. Top with remaining oat mixture, pressing down lightly.

3 Bake in centre of 350°F (180°C) oven for about 40 minutes or until light golden. Let stand in pan on rack for about 6 hours or until firm. Cut into squares. (MAKE-AHEAD: Cover and store at room temperature for up to 2 days or overwrap with heavy-duty foil and freeze for up to 2 weeks.)

Makes 24 squares.

RICE CRISP CEREAL Squares

In large saucepan, melt 3 tbsp (50 mL) butter over low heat; stir in 5 cups (1.25 L) miniature marshmallows until completely melted. Remove from heat. Stir in ½ tsp (2 mL) vanilla. Add 6 cups (1.5 L) rice crisp cereal; stir until well coated. With greased spatula, press evenly into greased 13- x 9-inch (3 L) glass baking dish. Cut into squares. **Makes 24 squares.**

PER SQUARE, ABOUT:

cal	227	carb	38 g
pro	2 g	fibre	3 g
total fat	8 g	chol	21 mg
sat. fat	5 g	sodium	106 mg

PERCENTAGE RDI:

calcium	2%	vit. A	7%
iron	8%	vit. C	2%
folate	5%		

Granola Bars

Wrap up one of these chewy no-nut bars and toss it into a school bag, backpack or purse — for a snack to see you through your day.

3½ cups	quick-cooking rolled oats	875 mL
⅓ cup	packed brown sugar	75 mL
⅓ cup	butter, melted	75 mL
⅓ cup	each corn syrup and liquid honey	75 mL
½ tsp	vanilla	2 mL

Pinch	salt	Pinch
¾ cup	dried cranberries or cherries	175 mL
¾ cup	chopped dried apricots	175 mL
½ cup	flaked coconut (optional)	125 mL

1 Line 9-inch (2.5 L) square metal cake pan with parchment paper, leaving 1 inch (2.5 cm) extending over 2 edges for handles; grease. Set aside.

2 In large bowl, stir together oats, sugar, butter, syrup, honey, vanilla and salt; stir in cranberries, apricots, and coconut (if using). Press into prepared pan.

3 Bake in centre of 350°F (180°C) oven for 50 to 60 minutes or until golden brown and firm to the touch. Let cool completely in pan on rack. Using parchment paper handles, lift out of pan. Peel off paper. Cut into bars. (MAKE-AHEAD: Cover and store at room temperature for up to 2 days or overwrap with heavy-duty foil and freeze for up to 2 weeks.)

Makes 15 bars.

PER BAR, ABOUT:

cal	202	carb	37 g
pro	3 g	fibre	3 g
total fat	5 g	chol	11 mg
sat. fat	3 g	sodium	54 mg

PERCENTAGE RDI:

calcium	2%	vit. A	8%
iron	9%	vit. C	2%
folate	2%		

No-Bake CHOW MEIN CRUNCHIES

In heatproof bowl over saucepan of hot (not boiling) water, melt together 1 cup (250 mL) each butterscotch and peanut butter chips and ½ cup (125 mL) each butter and smooth peanut butter, stirring often. Remove from heat; stir in 3 cups (750 mL) dry chow mein noodles and 1½ cups (375 mL) rice crisp cereal. Drop by heaping tablespoonfuls (15 mL) onto waxed paper–lined rimmed baking sheets; refrigerate until firm. (MAKE-AHEAD: Layer between waxed paper in airtight containers; refrigerate or freeze for up to 2 weeks.)

MAKE-AHEAD   FREEZABLE   CLASSIC

Chocolate Truffles

Not only are these a delightful treat to serve for special occasions, they are also a fun and easy homemade gift to make ahead for Christmas gift giving.

8 oz	semisweet or bittersweet chocolate, chopped	250 g
⅔ cup	whipping cream	150 mL
2 tbsp	cold butter	25 mL

COATING:		
8 oz	semisweet or bittersweet chocolate, chopped	250 g
½ cup	unsweetened cocoa powder	125 mL

1 Place chocolate in bowl. In small saucepan, heat cream with butter just until butter melts and bubbles form around edge of pan; pour into chocolate, whisking until smooth. Cover and refrigerate for 2 hours or until thickened and cold.

2 Using melon baller or small spoon, scoop rounded teaspoonfuls (5 mL), dropping onto waxed paper–lined baking sheet. Press scraps together; refrigerate for 30 minutes, then continue scooping until all scraps are used. (Press final bits into balls by hand.) Gently roll each ball between fingertips to round off completely. Freeze for about 1 hour or until hard and almost frozen.

3 COATING: In bowl over saucepan of hot (not boiling) water, melt chocolate, stirring occasionally. Let cool slightly. Sift cocoa into pie plate. Using 2 forks, dip each ball into chocolate, letting excess drip off. (If chocolate thickens, rewarm gently.) Place balls in cocoa.

4 Using 2 clean forks, roll truffles in cocoa; refrigerate on waxed paper–lined baking sheet until hardened. Place truffles in candy cups and refrigerate in airtight container until serving. (MAKE-AHEAD: Refrigerate for up to 1 week or freeze for up to 3 months.)

VARIATIONS

Hazelnut Truffles: Reduce cream to ½ cup (125 mL); add 3 tbsp (50 mL) hazelnut liqueur to melted chocolate filling. Omit cocoa. Dip frozen balls in chocolate; roll in 1½ cups (375 mL) finely chopped toasted hazelnuts.

Orange Truffles: Reduce cream to ½ cup (125 mL); add 3 tbsp (50 mL) orange liqueur to melted chocolate filling.

Peanut Butter Truffles: Omit butter. Add ¼ cup (50 mL) smooth peanut butter to melted chocolate filling.

Raspberry Truffles: Reduce cream to ⅓ cup (75 mL). Press 1 cup (250 mL) fresh or thawed unsweetened raspberries through fine sieve to remove seeds and make ½ cup (125 mL) purée; add to melted chocolate filling.

Makes about 24 truffles.

PER TRUFFLE, ABOUT:

cal	125	carb	13 g
pro	1 g	fibre	2 g
total fat	9 g	chol	11 mg
sat. fat	6 g	sodium	15 mg

PERCENTAGE RDI:

calcium	1%	vit. A	3%
iron	6%	vit. C	0%
folate	0%		

Preserves

15

Wild Blueberry Preserve 378

Pineapple Rhubarb Jam 379

Strawberry Jam 380

Summer Berry Jam 381

Peach Orange Conserve 382

Seville Orange Marmalade 383

Grape Jelly 384

Raspberry and Red Currant Jelly 385

Five-Spice Pears 386

Homemade Tomato Sauce 387

Peach Chutney 388

Chili Sauce 389

Peppy Salsa 390

Zucchini Pepper Relish 391

Golden Bread-and-Butter Pickles 392

Giardiniera 393

Wild Blueberry Preserve

Near Oxford, Nova Scotia, the blueberry capital of the world, innkeeper Donna Laceby makes batches of this softly set spread to serve with morning scones or as part of a home-baked dessert.

4 cups	fresh or frozen wild blueberries	1 L
4 cups	granulated sugar	1 L
1	pouch (85 mL) liquid fruit pectin	1
1 tsp	finely grated lemon rind	5 mL
2 tbsp	lemon juice	25 mL

1 In large Dutch oven, gently mash half of the blueberries to just break up. Stir in sugar and remaining blueberries. Heat over low heat, stirring often, until sugar dissolves.

2 Increase heat to high and bring to full rolling boil, stirring often. Stir in pectin and return to full rolling boil; boil for 1 minute. Stir in lemon rind and juice; return to boil. Remove from heat; skim off foam.

3 Pour into prepared 1-cup (250 mL) canning jars, leaving ¼-inch (5 mm) head-space. Seal with prepared discs and bands. Process in boiling water canner for 10 minutes. (See Step-by-Step Canner Basics, page 384.)

Makes about 4 cups (1 L).

PER 1 TBSP (15 mL), ABOUT:

cal	53	carb	14 g
pro	trace	fibre	trace
total fat	trace	chol	0 mg
sat. fat	0 g	sodium	1 mg

PERCENTAGE RDI:

calcium	0%	vit. A	0%
iron	0%	vit. C	2%
folate	0%		

Blueberries:
THE CANADIAN HARVEST

There are two kinds of blueberries: cultivated large high-bush berries and the smaller low-bush berries, known as wild blueberries. The wild blueberry bush is a natural seeding gift from birds who ingest the berries and excrete the seeds in their droppings; fields of bushes have sprung up on abandoned farm-land and burnt-over clearings. To keep these often hilly and rocky "fields" filling in and producing at optimum levels, the fields are managed through biannual cutting or burning, fertilizing and grass control. The tasty blueberries are picked, increasingly by mechanical harvester, throughout Atlantic Canada (especially Nova Scotia) and Quebec and are available fresh in season and frozen all year round. On a less commercial scale, berries are handpicked, often for personal use, all through northern Ontario east to Newfoundland.

Pineapple Rhubarb Jam

Rhubarb, grown from the Atlantic to the Pacific and popular with home gardeners everywhere, makes a fine jam, especially when its tartness is complemented by a sweet fruit such as pineapple.

4 cups	granulated sugar	1 L
1	pkg (57 g) light fruit pectin crystals	1
6 cups	chopped rhubarb (12 large stalks)	1.5 L

1 tbsp	lemon juice	15 mL
1	can (19 oz/540 mL) pineapple tidbits, drained	1

1 Combine ¼ cup (50 mL) of the sugar with pectin crystals; set aside. In large heavy stainless steel saucepan or Dutch oven, combine rhubarb, lemon juice and remaining sugar; cook, stirring, over medium heat until sugar dissolves. Bring to boil, stirring constantly; reduce heat and simmer for 5 minutes or until rhubarb is tender.

2 Stir in pineapple and pectin mixture; bring to boil, stirring constantly. Cook, stirring, for 1 minute at full rolling boil; remove from heat and skim off foam.

3 Pour into prepared 1-cup (250 mL) canning jars, leaving ¼-inch (5 mm) headspace. Seal with prepared discs and bands. Process in boiling water canner for 5 minutes. (See Step-by-Step Canner Basics, page 384.)

TEST KITCHEN TIP: Sugar helps the jelling process and keeps the fruit mixture from spoiling. Do not reduce the quantity of sugar specified in the recipe or the end product will not set properly. Jams and jellies set when the proper proportions of fruit, pectin, acid and sugar are present.

Makes about 7 cups (1.75 L).

PER 1 TBSP (15 mL), ABOUT:

cal	32	carb	8 g
pro	trace	fibre	trace
total fat	trace	chol	0 mg
sat. fat	0 g	sodium	0 mg

PERCENTAGE RDI:

calcium	1%	vit. A	0%
iron	0%	vit. C	2%
folate	0%		

Strawberry Jam

Strawberry jam, the number 1 choice for topping toast, is never more exquisite than when you capture the fresh taste of strawberries in your own jars. Boasting is allowed, even encouraged.

8 cups	strawberries, hulled (2 lb/1 kg)	2 L	4 cups	granulated sugar	1 L
			¼ cup	lemon juice	50 mL

1 In wide bowl, lightly crush about 1 cup (250 mL) of the berries at a time with potato masher; measure fruit to make 4 cups (1 L).

2 In large Dutch oven, combine crushed strawberries, sugar and lemon juice; stir over low heat until sugar dissolves. Increase heat to high and bring to full rolling boil, stirring often. Boil hard, uncovered and stirring often, for 10 minutes or until setting point is reached. (See Testing for Setting Point, page 381.)

3 Remove jam from heat. Let cool for 5 minutes, skimming off foam and stirring often. Pour into prepared 1-cup (250 mL) canning jars, leaving ¼-inch (5 mm) headspace. Seal with prepared discs and bands. Process in boiling water canner for 5 minutes. (See Step-by-Step Canner Basics, page 384.)

VARIATION

Strawberry Rhubarb Jam: Substitute 3 cups (750 mL) crushed strawberries and 2 cups (500 mL) thickly sliced rhubarb (12 oz/375 g) for the strawberries. Precook strawberries with rhubarb over medium-high heat for 10 minutes or until rhubarb is softened. Reduce sugar to 3 cups (750 mL). Boil hard for 8 minutes. **Makes about 5 cups (1.25 L).**

Makes about 5 cups (1.25 L).

PER 1 TBSP (15 mL), ABOUT:

cal	42	carb	11 g
pro	trace	fibre	trace
total fat	trace	chol	0 mg
sat. fat	0 g	sodium	0 mg

PERCENTAGE RDI:

calcium	0%	vit. A	0%
iron	1%	vit. C	12%
folate	1%		

Summer Berry Jam

This old-fashioned jam, often called jewel jam because of its rich ruby colour, is the kind of preserve you can't buy, and you may find yourself hoarding it to serve only to the special people in your life.

2½ cups	crushed stemmed red currants (1 lb/500 g)	625 mL		¾ cup	crushed raspberries (8 oz/250 g)	175 mL
1½ cups	chopped pitted sour cherries (12 oz/375 g)	375 mL		3½ cups	granulated sugar	875 mL
¾ cup	crushed strawberries (8 oz/250 g)	175 mL				

1 In large Dutch oven, combine currants, cherries, strawberries and raspberries. Bring to boil, stirring frequently. Reduce heat to medium-low and simmer, stirring occasionally, for 15 minutes. Remove from heat.

2 Stir in sugar and bring to boil, stirring. Boil vigorously, stirring constantly, for 12 to 15 minutes or until setting point is reached. (See Testing for Setting Point, below.)

3 Remove from heat; skim off foam. Pour into prepared 1-cup (250 mL) canning jars, leaving ¼-inch (5 mm) headspace. Seal with prepared discs and bands. Process in boiling water canner for 5 minutes. (See Step-by-Step Canner Basics, page 384.)

TEST KITCHEN TIP: As a general rule, you need to double the volume of whole berries, cherries and currants to obtain the amount of crushed fruit.

Makes about 5 cups (1.25 L).

PER 1 TBSP (15 mL), ABOUT:

cal	41	carb	10 g
pro	trace	fibre	1 g
total fat	trace	chol	0 mg
sat. fat	0 g	sodium	0 mg

PERCENTAGE RDI:

calcium	0%	vit. A	0%
iron	1%	vit. C	7%
folate	0%		

TESTING FOR Setting Point

CONSERVES, JAMS AND MARMALADES: Chill two small plates in freezer. Remove conserve/jam from heat. Drop ½ tsp (2 mL) onto one chilled plate and let cool. Tilt plate; the surface should wrinkle when pushed with fork. If too liquid, return to heat. Return plate to freezer. Repeat test every few minutes, using coldest plate, until desired consistency.

JELLY: Jelly sets at 218° to 220°F (103° to 104°C) on a jelly, candy or deep-fry thermometer. To test without thermometer, dip cold metal spoon into jelly, hold it horizontally well above steaming jelly and tip one side slightly to let liquid flow back into pan. When you first start testing, about four minutes after mixture has reached a rolling boil, liquid should run off spoon in two streams. As water evaporates, stream slows down and turns into drops. When two drops join in centre of spoon and hesitate, jelly is said to be "sheeting," which means it has reached jelling point or has set. Remove pan from heat and skim off any foam.

CHILI SAUCES, RELISHES AND SALSA: To test thickness, place 1 tbsp (15 mL) salsa on plate and tilt plate; salsa should flow slowly in one stream.

Peach Orange Conserve

A conserve differs from jam, not in the luscious effect it has spooned onto toast, bagels, English muffins or scones, but in its ingredients. There is always citrus to complement the main fruit, and sometimes even the luxury of additional dried fruit and nuts.

2	oranges, unpeeled	2	6 cups	granulated sugar	1.5 L
1 tbsp	coarsely grated lemon rind	15 mL	¼ cup	lemon juice	50 mL
¾ cup	water	175 mL	1	stick cinnamon (optional)	1
8 cups	coarsely chopped peeled peaches (4 lb/2 kg)	2 L	¾ cup	slivered blanched almonds (optional)	175 mL

1 Scrub oranges; cut out stem and blossom ends and any blemishes. Slice very thinly, then chop coarsely, discarding any seeds. In small saucepan, bring oranges, lemon rind and water to boil; reduce heat, cover and simmer for about 15 minutes or until rind is very tender (almost mushy).

2 In large Dutch oven, combine orange mixture, peaches, sugar, lemon juice, and cinnamon (if using); bring to boil over high heat. Reduce heat to medium-low and simmer, stirring frequently, for 55 minutes. Stir in almonds (if using); cook for 5 minutes or until setting point is reached. (See Testing for Setting Point, page 381.) Remove cinnamon.

3 Remove from heat; skim off any foam. Pour into prepared 1-cup (250 mL) canning jars, leaving ¼-inch (5 mm) headspace. Seal with prepared discs and bands. Process in boiling water canner for 10 minutes. (See Step-by-Step Canner Basics, page 384.)

VARIATIONS

Three-Berry Conserve: Substitute 3 cups (750 mL) each whole strawberries, raspberries and blueberries (9 cups/2.25 L total) for peaches. Reduce sugar to 5 cups (1.25 L). Omit cinnamon and almonds. Reduce cooking time to 20 minutes or until conserve is thickened. **Makes about 8 cups (2 L).**

Mixed Cherry Conserve: Substitute 1 lemon for oranges, and 4 cups (1 L) each Bing cherries and sour cherries (8 cups/2 L total) for the peaches. Precook cherries with ½ cup (125 mL) water for 10 minutes or until softened. Reduce sugar to 4 cups (1 L). Omit cinnamon. Reduce almonds to ½ cup (125 mL). Reduce cooking time to a total of 40 minutes or until conserve is thickened. **Makes about 6 cups (1.5 L).**

Makes about 12 cups (3 L).

PER 1 TBSP (15 mL), ABOUT:

cal	32	carb	8 g
pro	trace	fibre	trace
total fat	trace	chol	0 mg
sat. fat	trace	sodium	0 mg

PERCENTAGE RDI:

calcium	0%	vit. A	1%
iron	0%	vit. C	3%
folate	0%		

CLASSIC

Seville Orange Marmalade

Seville oranges make the finest marmalade and are the only oranges to produce a clear jelly around shreds of refreshingly bitter peel. Most thick-skinned, seedy Seville oranges now come from Arizona, usually starting in January.

8	Seville oranges, unpeeled (4 lb/2 kg)	8

2	lemons	2
15 cups	granulated sugar	3.75 L

TEST KITCHEN TIP: You can use a food processor to slice juiced orange and lemon halves; marmalade will be less clear.

1 Scrub oranges and lemons; cut out stem and blossom ends and any blemishes. Cut in half crosswise. With citrus juicer, squeeze out juice, dislodging all seeds. Strain through sieve into bowl; set juice aside.

2 Place seeds and any membranes on double thickness of 8-inch (20 cm) square of fine cheesecloth. Bring up sides; tie top with cotton string, enclosing seeds loosely. Place in large heavy Dutch oven. Pour in juice.

3 On cutting board, stack about 3 halves of oranges and lemons; cut into 3 parallel strips. Cut crosswise into slightly less than ¼-inch (5 mm) thick strips. Add to pan along with any accumulated juices. Repeat with remaining halves.

4 Add 16 cups (4 L) water; bring to simmer over medium heat. Simmer, stirring often, for 2½ to 3 hours or until peel turns to mush when pressed between fingers. Remove seed bag and let cool; squeeze juices into pan. Mixture should measure 15 cups (3.75 L); if not, add water to make up difference. Divide into 3 batches of 5 cups (1.25 L) each.

5 In clean Dutch oven, stir together 5 cups (1.25 L) of the sugar and 1 of the batches; bring to boil. Boil vigorously, stirring constantly, for 8 to 12 minutes or until free of foam, thickened and setting point is reached. (See Testing for Setting Point, page 381.)

6 Pour into prepared 1-cup (250 mL) canning jars, leaving ¼-inch (5 mm) headspace. Seal with prepared discs and bands. Process in boiling water canner for 10 minutes. (See Step-by-Step Canner Basics, page 384.) Repeat with remaining sugar and batches.

VARIATIONS

Orange Ginger Marmalade: Add ¼ cup (50 mL) chopped crystallized ginger along with sugar to 5-cup (1.25 L) batch.

Orange Brown Sugar Marmalade: Substitute 3 cups (750 mL) packed brown sugar for 3 cups (750 mL) granulated sugar in 5-cup (1.25 L) batch.

Makes about 18 cups (4.5 L).

PER 1 TBSP (15 mL), ABOUT:

cal	43	carb	11 g
pro	trace	fibre	trace
total fat	trace	chol	0 mg
sat. fat	0 g	sodium	1 mg

PERCENTAGE RDI:

calcium	0%	vit. A	0%
iron	1%	vit. C	8%
folate	0%		

Grape Jelly

Grape jelly is any kid's favourite, and it's so foolproof when pectin crystals are used. Blue labrusca grapes set the jelly standard because of their intense flavour and colour. Varieties to look for are Concord, Ferdonia and the marvellously seedless Coronation, a hybrid of labrusca and white seedless grapes.

10 cups	stemmed Concord or Coronation grapes (3¾ lb/1.875 kg)	2.5 L	1	pkg (57 g) fruit pectin crystals	1
			5 cups	granulated sugar	1.25 L

1 In large Dutch oven, crush grapes with potato masher. Add 1 cup (250 mL) water; bring to boil, stirring occasionally. Reduce heat, cover and simmer for 10 minutes.

2 Transfer to dampened jelly bag or colander lined with triple thickness of fine cheesecloth set over large bowl. Let drip, without squeezing bag, for about 2 hours or until juice measures 4 cups (1 L).

3 In large clean Dutch oven, bring juice and pectin to boil. Stir in sugar; bring to full rolling boil, stirring constantly. Boil vigorously, stirring, for 1 minute.

4 Remove from heat; skim off any foam. Pour into prepared 1-cup (250 mL) canning jars, leaving ¼-inch (5 mm) headspace. Seal with prepared discs and bands. Process in boiling water canner for 5 minutes. (See Step-by-Step Canner Basics, below.)

Makes about 7 cups (1.75 L).

PER 1 TBSP (15 mL), ABOUT:

cal	45	carb	12 g
pro	trace	fibre	trace
total fat	trace	chol	0 mg
sat. fat	trace	sodium	0 mg

PERCENTAGE RDI:

calcium	0%	vit. A	0%
iron	1%	vit. C	0%
folate	0%		

STEP-BY-STEP Canner Basics

🍃 Before starting to preserve, check that you have enough canning jars, often referred to as "Mason jars," and that they are free of cracks and nicks. It is fine to reuse real canning jars as long as they are in perfect condition, but do not reuse mayonnaise jars or jars that held commercial pickles, relishes, jams or spreads. Wash in hot, soapy water, rinse and air-dry.

🍃 Always use new lid discs. Five minutes before filling jars, immerse discs in boiling water for 5 minutes to soften the sealing compound. It is not necessary to boil the ring, or band, part of the lid.

🍃 Jars processed in a boiling water canner for less than 10 minutes need to be sterilized. To do so, fill boiling water canner about two-thirds full of hot water, letting water fill jars. Add wide-mouthed metal funnel and ½-cup (125 mL) metal measure for filling jars. Cover and bring to boil; boil for 10 minutes, timing so that jars are ready at same time as preserves. Lift rack and let rest on edge of canner.

🍃 Boil a kettle of water, ready to add to the boiling water canner when the

Raspberry and Red Currant Jelly

This raspberry and red currant combination is one you cannot buy and is definitely worth making, even if you have to grow or pick your own berries and currants.

3 cups	raspberries (12 oz/375 g)	750 mL	4 cups	granulated sugar	1 L
9 cups	stemmed red currants (3 lb/1.5 kg)	2.25 L			

1 In large Dutch oven, crush raspberries thoroughly with potato masher. Add currants in batches, crushing each addition. Bring to boil over medium heat, stirring occasionally. Reduce heat, cover and simmer for 10 minutes. Mash once more; simmer for 2 minutes.

2 Transfer to dampened jelly bag or colander lined with double thickness of fine cheesecloth set over large bowl. Let drip for 3 to 4 hours or until juice measures about 4 cups (1 L), squeezing bag occasionally.

3 Measure juice into large Dutch oven. Stir in sugar; mix well. Bring to full rolling boil over high heat; boil vigorously, stirring, for 5 to 8 minutes or until setting point is reached. (See Testing for Setting Point, page 381.)

4 Remove from heat; skim off any foam. Pour into prepared 1-cup (250 mL) canning jars, leaving ¼-inch (5 mm) headspace. Seal with prepared discs and bands. Process in boiling water canner for 5 minutes. (See Step-by-Step Canner Basics, page 384.)

filled jars are lowered into the water for processing.

🍂 When filling jars, use sterilized metal measure for ladling and sterilized funnel to prevent jar rims from getting splashed with food. Remove any air bubbles in chunky preserves by sliding a clean spatula between glass and food. If rims do get sticky, wipe with damp paper towel.

🍂 Leave headspace recommended in each recipe. Place prepared disc on jar; screw on bands firmly without forcing.

🍂 Place jars in canner rack. Lower rack. Avoiding jars, pour in enough boiling water to come 1 inch (2.5 cm) above

tops of jars. Bring back to vigorous boil. Time processing from the return to full boil.

🍂 Use canning tongs to remove jars from boiling water canner. They hold jars securely and safely as you transfer them from the canner to cooling racks.

🍂 Let jars cool on racks for 24 hours. Check seal; disc part of lid should be concave. Refrigerate any partially filled jars or unsealed jars (lids do not curve down after processing) and use within three weeks or time specified.

🍂 Wipe and label jars. Remove ring part of lids. Keep preserves in a cool, dark, dry place.

Makes about 4 cups (1 L).

PER 1 TBSP (15 mL), ABOUT:

cal	55	carb	14 g
pro	trace	fibre	0 g
total fat	trace	chol	0 mg
sat. fat	0 g	sodium	0 mg

PERCENTAGE RDI:

calcium	0%	vit. A	0%
iron	1%	vit. C	7%
folate	0%		

Five-Spice Pears

Tiny pears fragrant with spices and preserved in red wine will surprise even the most ardent preserver, making these a joy to give as well as to receive. Serve for dessert.

TEST KITCHEN TIP: When preserving pears, choose underripe ones so that they will keep their shape through the poaching and canning process.

SUBSTITUTION: For a nonalcoholic version, replace wine with apple juice; reduce sugar to 2 cups (500 mL) and boiling time for syrup to 5 to 8 minutes.

6 cups	water	1.5 L
½ cup	lemon juice	125 mL
4 lb	firm small pears (12 to 14)	2 kg
3 cups	granulated sugar	750 mL
1½ cups	dry red wine	375 mL
2	strips (2 x 1 inch/5 x 2.5 cm) lemon rind	2

4	slices gingerroot	4
2	sticks cinnamon, halved	2
4	whole star anise	4
½ tsp	each whole cloves and cardamom	2 mL
¼ tsp	black peppercorns	1 mL

1 In large bowl, combine water and half of the lemon juice. Peel, halve and core pears, adding to bowl as you work. Let stand for no longer than 20 minutes.

2 Meanwhile, in large Dutch oven, dissolve sugar in remaining lemon juice, wine and 3 cups (750 mL) water. Add lemon rind, ginger and cinnamon. In small square of cheesecloth, tie up star anise, cloves, cardamom and peppercorns; add to pan and bring to boil. Boil for 5 minutes.

3 Drain pears and add to pan; reduce heat and simmer, gently stirring occasionally, for 5 to 15 minutes or until pears are just tender but not mushy. With slotted spoon and letting excess liquid drip off, transfer pears to three 2-cup (500 mL) canning jars.

4 Bring syrup to rolling boil; boil, skimming off foam, for 10 to 12 minutes or until 3 cups (750 mL) remain. Strain over pears in jars, leaving ½-inch (1 cm) headspace. Discard lemon rind and ginger; divide cinnamon among jars. Untie cheesecloth bag; divide spices among jars. Run narrow spatula between pears and jar to release any air bubbles; add more liquid if necessary to re-establish headspace. Seal with prepared discs and bands. Process in boiling water canner for 10 minutes. (See Step-by-Step Canner Basics, page 384.)

Makes about 6 cups (1.5 L).

VARIATION

White Wine Pears: Replace red wine with a dry fruity white wine; a Riesling would serve beautifully. Omit ginger, star anise and peppercorns.

PER SERVING OF PEAR HALF PLUS
2 TBSP (25 mL) LIQUID, ABOUT:

cal	 146	carb . . . . 37 g
pro	. . . . trace	fibre . . . . 2 g
total fat	. . . trace	chol . . . . 0 mg
sat. fat	. . . . trace	sodium . . . . 2 mg

PERCENTAGE RDI:

calcium 1%	vit. A 0%
iron 2%	vit. C 5%
folate 1%	

Homemade Tomato Sauce

Making your own tomato sauce is a day-long process but definitely worth the effort when you taste the results.

10 lb	plum tomatoes (about 80)	4.5 kg
2½ cups	chopped onions	625 mL
3	cloves garlic, chopped	3
2	bay leaves	2
1 tbsp	granulated sugar	15 mL

1 tbsp	dried basil	15 mL
1 tbsp	dried marjoram	15 mL
2 tsp	salt	10 mL
1 tsp	pepper	5 mL
½ tsp	hot pepper flakes	2 mL

TEST KITCHEN TIP: If buying or picking your own tomatoes, allow a few days' ripening time to maximize their colour and flavour before preserving. To ripen, lay tomatoes in a single layer on newspapers or blankets in the basement or garage.

1 Wash and drain tomatoes; core and chop coarsely to make about 28 cups (7 L). In very large heavy Dutch oven, combine tomatoes, onions, garlic, bay leaves, sugar, basil, marjoram, salt, pepper and hot pepper flakes; bring to boil, stirring often to prevent scorching.

2 Reduce heat and simmer, stirring occasionally, for about 2 hours or until thick enough to stand wooden spoon in sauce. Discard bay leaves. Press through fine disc of food mill or large fine-mesh sieve to remove seeds and skins.

3 Let tomato mixture cool; ladle into freezer containers, leaving ½-inch (1 cm) headspace. Seal, label and freeze for up to 6 months.

Makes about 15 cups (3.75 L).

PER ¼ CUP (50 mL), ABOUT:

cal	18	carb	4 g
pro	1 g	fibre	1 g
total fat	trace	chol	0 mg
sat. fat	trace	sodium	83 mg

PERCENTAGE RDI:

calcium	1%	vit. A	8%
iron	3%	vit. C	18%
folate	3%		

Peach Chutney

A fruity sweet-and-sour relish adapted by the British in India, chutney is a piquant companion to cream cheese on a cracker, a grilled cheese sandwich, thin slices of firm cheeses, such as Gouda or Cheddar, and ham, pork or poultry, hot or cold.

1	seedless orange (unpeeled)	1	½ cup	raisins	125 mL
8 cups	chopped peeled peaches (4 lb/2 kg)	2 L	1 tbsp	mustard seeds	15 mL
2¾ cups	packed brown sugar	675 mL	1 tsp	salt	5 mL
2 cups	chopped onions	500 mL	1 tsp	each ground cloves, cinnamon, ginger and curry paste or powder	5 mL
2	cloves garlic, minced	2			
1 cup	diced sweet red pepper	250 mL	2 cups	cider vinegar	500 mL

1 Scrub orange; cut out stem and blossom end and any blemishes. Cut in half lengthwise; cut crosswise into thin slices, discarding any seeds. In large heavy Dutch oven, bring orange and 1 cup (250 mL) water to boil; reduce heat, cover and simmer for about 15 minutes or until rind is very soft (almost mushy) and water is almost evaporated.

2 Add peaches, sugar, onions, garlic, red pepper, raisins, mustard seeds, salt, cloves, cinnamon, ginger and curry paste to pot. Pour in vinegar; stir to combine. Bring to boil over high heat. Reduce heat to medium and simmer, stirring often, for about 1 hour or until reduced to 8 cups (2 L) and thick enough to mound on spoon.

3 Pour into prepared 1-cup (250 mL) canning jars, leaving ½-inch (1 cm) headspace. Seal with prepared discs and bands. Process in boiling water canner for 10 minutes. (See Step-by-Step Canner Basics, page 384.)

VARIATIONS

Pear Chutney: Substitute chopped peeled ripe firm pears for peaches.

Apple Plum Chutney: Omit peaches. Substitute 4 cups (1 L) coarsely chopped (unpeeled) red plums and 4 cups (1 L) coarsely chopped peeled cooking apples. Omit curry paste. Add ½ tsp (2 mL) ground coriander.

Makes about 8 cups (2 L).

PER 1 TBSP (15 mL), ABOUT:

cal	27	carb	7 g
pro	trace	fibre	trace
total fat	trace	chol	0 mg
sat. fat	trace	sodium	20 mg

PERCENTAGE RDI:

calcium	1%	vit. A	1%
iron	1%	vit. C	5%
folate	0%		

Chili Sauce

As Canadian as butter tarts and maple syrup, tangy sweet and chunky chili sauce is an icon of our culinary history. Star canner Phyllis Horne's winning recipe from the Royal Agricultural Winter Fair in Toronto proves that chili sauce can top more than burgers, macaroni and cheese and meat loaf.

22 cups	chopped peeled tomatoes (10 lb/4.5 kg)	5.5 L
6 cups	chopped onions (about 6 large)	1.5 L
2 cups	chopped sweet red peppers (about 2 large)	500 mL
2 cups	chopped sweet green peppers (about 2 large)	500 mL
1½ cups	chopped celery	375 mL

4 cups	granulated sugar	1 L
2½ cups	vinegar	625 mL
2 tbsp	pickling salt	25 mL
1 tsp	cinnamon	5 mL
¾ tsp	ground ginger	4 mL
½ tsp	each ground cloves, allspice and cayenne pepper	2 mL

1 In large heavy Dutch oven, combine tomatoes, onions, red and green peppers and celery. Stir in sugar, vinegar, salt, cinnamon, ginger, cloves, allspice and cayenne pepper; bring to boil. Reduce heat and simmer, stirring often, for about 2 hours or until tomatoes are broken down enough to make thick sauce.

2 Pour into prepared 1-cup (250 mL) canning jars, leaving ½-inch (1 cm) headspace. Seal with prepared discs and bands. Process in boiling water canner for 15 minutes. (See Step-by-Step Canner Basics, page 384.)

Makes about 16 cups (4 L).

PER 1 TBSP (15 mL), ABOUT:

cal 18	carb . . . . 5 g
pro . . . . trace	fibre . . . . trace
total fat . . . trace	chol . . . . 0 mg
sat. fat . . . . trace	sodium . . . 56 mg

PERCENTAGE RDI:

calcium 0%	vit. A 2%
iron 1%	vit. C 8%
folate 1%	

Peppy Salsa

Ever since we published our first salsa recipe in the early '90s, we've had requests for it every tomato season. And for good reason: with less sugar and a more adventure-some spiciness than ketchup or chili sauce, this salsa is in tune with our times.

8 oz	jalapeño peppers (about 6)	250 g	4	cloves garlic, minced	4
8 cups	coarsely chopped peeled tomatoes (about 4 lb/2 kg)	2 L	1	can (5½ oz/156 mL) tomato paste	1
3 cups	chopped Cubanelle, Anaheim or banana peppers (about 3 lb/1.5 kg)	750 mL	2 tbsp	granulated sugar	25 mL
			1 tbsp	salt	15 mL
2 cups	chopped onions	500 mL	2 tsp	paprika	10 mL
2 cups	cider vinegar	500 mL	1 tsp	dried oregano	5 mL
1 cup	each chopped sweet red and yellow peppers	250 mL	¼ cup	chopped fresh coriander	50 mL

1 On cutting board and wearing rubber gloves, cut jalapeño peppers in half; discard ribs and seeds. Chop finely to make 1 cup (250 mL).

2 In large heavy Dutch oven, combine jalapeños, tomatoes, Cubanelle peppers, onions, vinegar, red and yellow peppers, garlic, tomato paste, sugar, salt, paprika and oregano; bring to boil. Reduce heat to medium-low and simmer, stirring often, for 1 hour or until thickened. Add coriander; cook for 5 minutes.

3 Pour into prepared 1-cup (250 mL) canning jars, leaving ½-inch (1 cm) headspace. Seal with prepared discs and bands. Process in boiling water canner for 20 minutes. (See Step-by-Step Canner Basics, page 384.)

Makes about 11 cups (2.75 L).

PER 1 TBSP (15 mL), ABOUT:

cal	6	carb	1 g
pro	trace	fibre	trace
total fat	trace	chol	0 mg
sat. fat	trace	sodium	41 mg

PERCENTAGE RDI:

calcium	0%	vit. A	3%
iron	1%	vit. C	12%
folate	1%		

TIPS FOR Making Salsa SUCCESSFULLY

🌿 For a fiery-hot salsa, use small Scotch bonnet peppers or long thin red chili peppers instead of the jalapeños. For a milder version, substitute sweet peppers.

🌿 Wear rubber gloves when handling hot peppers.

🌿 To more easily peel a large quan-tity of tomatoes, place tomatoes in heatproof bowl or basin. Cover with boiling water and let stand for 30 to 60 seconds or until tomato skins loosen. Drain; chill in cold water to prevent cooking. Peel.

🌿 To test thickness of salsa, place 1 tbsp (15 mL) salsa on plate and tilt plate; salsa should flow slowly in one stream.

Zucchini Pepper Relish

For hotdogs or any kind of sausage, this is the tangy, golden relish of choice.

9	zucchini (3 lb/1.5 kg), finely chopped	9
3	onions, finely chopped	3
2	sweet red peppers, finely chopped	2
¼ cup	pickling salt	50 mL
2½ cups	granulated sugar	625 mL
1½ cups	vinegar	375 mL

1½ tsp	dry mustard	7 mL
1 tsp	celery seeds	5 mL
½ tsp	coarsely ground pepper	2 mL
½ tsp	turmeric	2 mL
1 tbsp	water	15 mL
2 tsp	cornstarch	10 mL

TEST KITCHEN TIP: Chop the zucchini and onions in batches in a food processor.

1 In large bowl, combine zucchini, onions and red peppers. Sprinkle with salt; stir to blend. Let stand for 1 hour, stirring occasionally. Drain in large sieve. Rinse thoroughly under cold running water; drain again, pressing out excess moisture.

2 In large heavy Dutch oven, combine sugar, vinegar, mustard, celery seeds, pepper and turmeric; bring to boil. Add drained vegetables; return to boil, stirring frequently. Reduce heat and simmer, stirring often, for 15 minutes or until vegetables are tender and liquid has thickened. Combine water with cornstarch; stir into relish. Cook, stirring, for 5 minutes or until liquid clears and thickens.

3 Pour into prepared 2-cup (500 mL) canning jars, leaving ½-inch (1 cm) headspace. Seal with prepared discs and bands. Process in boiling water canner for 15 minutes. (See Step-by-Step Canner Basics, page 384.)

VARIATION

Cucumber Pepper Relish: Substitute small scrubbed field cucumbers for zucchini.

Makes about 8 cups (2 L).

PER 1 TBSP (15 mL), ABOUT:

cal	19	carb ....5 g
pro	.......trace	fibre ....trace
total fat	...trace	chol ....0 mg
sat. fat	......0 g	sodium ....0 mg

PERCENTAGE RDI:

calcium 0%	vit. A 1%
iron 1%	vit. C 7%
folate 1%	

CLASSIC

Golden Bread-and-Butter Pickles

These are the very best pickles to serve on sandwiches. Use only small field cucumbers for this golden twist on an old favourite; scrub before slicing.

TEST KITCHEN TIP: Omit turmeric for traditional bread-and-butter pickles.

12 cups	thinly sliced (unpeeled) cucumbers (about 3½ lb/1.75 kg)	3 L	¼ cup	pickling salt	50 mL
2 cups	thinly sliced white onions	500 mL	3 cups	cider vinegar	750 mL
1 cup	thin sweet red pepper strips	250 mL	2 cups	granulated sugar	500 mL
1 cup	thin sweet yellow pepper strips	250 mL	4 tsp	mustard seeds	20 mL
			2 tsp	celery seeds	10 mL
			1 tsp	turmeric	5 mL

1 In large bowl, combine cucumbers, onions, red and yellow peppers and salt. Cover with 3-inch (8 cm) layer of ice cubes; let stand for 4 hours. Drain and rinse under cold water; drain well.

2 In large heavy Dutch oven, combine vinegar, sugar, mustard seeds, celery seeds and turmeric; bring to boil. Add cucumber mixture; return just to boil.

3 Pour into prepared 1-cup (250 mL) canning jars, leaving ½-inch (1 cm) headspace. Seal with prepared discs and bands. Process in boiling water canner for 10 minutes. (See Step-by-Step Canner Basics, page 384.)

Makes about 11 cups (2.75 L).

PER 3 PICKLES, ABOUT:

cal	15	carb	4 g
pro	trace	fibre	trace
total fat	trace	chol	0 mg
sat. fat	trace	sodium	191 mg

PERCENTAGE RDI:

calcium	0%	vit. A	1%
iron	1%	vit. C	7%
folate	1%		

Giardiniera

Count on this colourful Italian-style vegetable mix to adorn antipasto or relish trays and team up with cheese and cold meats.

4 cups	vinegar	1 L
2 cups	granulated sugar	500 mL
1 tbsp	pickling salt	15 mL
1 tbsp	celery seeds	15 mL
1 tbsp	mustard seeds	15 mL
1 tsp	peppercorns	5 mL
3	bay leaves	3

1 lb	green beans, cut in 2-inch (5 cm) lengths	500 g
2	zucchini, sliced	2
3 cups	cauliflower florets	750 mL
3 cups	pearl onions, peeled	750 mL
2 cups	thickly sliced carrots	500 mL

1 In large heavy Dutch oven, bring vinegar, sugar, salt, celery seeds, mustard seeds, peppercorns and bay leaves to boil; boil for 5 minutes. Add green beans, zucchini, cauliflower, onions and carrots; return to boil. Remove from heat. Discard bay leaves.

2 Fill prepared 2-cup (500 mL) canning jars with vegetables and liquid, leaving ½-inch (1 cm) headspace. Seal with prepared discs and bands. Process in boiling water canner for 10 minutes. (See Step-by-Step Canner Basics, page 384.)

HERB Vinegars

When fresh herbs are abundant, create unique vinegars to add a splash of summer to salads and sauces year-round.

⤷ Wash and thoroughly dry leaves and stems from your choice of herbs: mint, basil, tarragon, coriander, oregano and marjoram are ideal. Measure 1 cup (250 mL) firmly packed herbs into 4-cup (1 L) sterilized glass canning jar. Fill jar with about 4 cups (1 L) rice vinegar, white wine vinegar or cider vinegar. Close jar; let stand for 2 weeks.

⤷ Strain through coffee filter–lined funnel into dry sterilized jar; discard herbs. Close jar and store in cool, dark, dry place for up to 1 year.

⤷ To use, pour into sterilized bottles; add fresh herb sprigs and seal with new corks.

Makes about 12 cups (3 L).

PER ¼ CUP (50 mL), ABOUT:

cal	30	carb .... 8 g
pro	trace	fibre .... 1 g
total fat	trace	chol .... 0 mg
sat. fat	trace	sodium ... 90 mg

PERCENTAGE RDI:

calcium	1%	vit. A 12%
iron	1%	vit. C 8%
folate	4%	

CONTRIBUTORS

All recipes were developed by The Canadian Living Test Kitchen, with the exception of those by the following contributors:

Julie Aldis
Triple Pork Tenderloin with Mushroom Stuffing, 163
Julia Armstrong
Coconut Curry Fish, 186
Julian Armstrong
Tabbouleh Salad, 76
Elizabeth Baird
Black Bean Chicken Wings, 27
Caraway Pork Goulash, 159
Chicken Pesto Pasta, 235
Curried Lentil, Wild Rice and Orzo Salad, 79
Dutch Apple Pie, 329
Fatouche, 66
Fresh Blueberry Tart, 336
Glazed Almond Spritz Rosettes, 361
Golden Bread-and-Butter Pickles, 392
People's Choice Chili, 133
Honey Bran Muffins, 256
Icky Sticky Baked Date Pudding, 285
Jerk Roast Pork, 165
Lamb Shanks with Beans, 177
Lemon Sponge Pudding, 282
Panna Cotta with Raspberry Strawberry Sauce, 290
Pastitsio, 238
Pear Pandowdy, 334
Raspberry and Red Currant Jelly, 385
Red Curry Mussels, 189
Rib Eye on the Rotisserie, 152
Rich Brandied Fruitcake, 309
Roasted Pears in Port, 299
Sauerbraten Beef Stew, 131
Wild Blueberry Preserve, 378
Donna Bartolini
Flaky Phyllo Cups, 40
Bob Bermann and Barbara Gordon
Cornmeal "Blini" with Smoked Salmon, 33
Suzanne Bourret
Keeper Coleslaw, 71
Vicki Burns
Black Bean Soup, 55
Ginger Chicken and Green Onion Kabobs, 119
Vegetarian Moussaka, 224
Cinda Chavich
Glazed Sea Bass with Red Curry Sauce, 197
Spicy Thai Shrimp and Noodle Soup, 54

Diane Clement
Roast Chicken with Lemon and Garlic, 102
Pam Collacott
Breakfast Strudels, 216
Florentine Bars, 370
How to Adapt a Recipe for the Bread Machine, 267
Cynthia David
Jalapeño Corn Quesadilla Filling, 41
Riki Dixon
Breaded Lemon Chicken with Ricotta Leek Stuffing, 112
Carol Ferguson
Batter-Fried Fish, 193
Best-Ever Chocolate Chip Cookies, 353
Cod au Gratin, 194
Tomato French Dressing, 81
Margaret Fraser
Baked Brie with Tangy Cranberry Topping, 18
Maple-Glazed Peameal Bacon Dinner, 174
Kate Gammal
Five-Spice Pears, 386
Koftas with Cucumber Yogurt Salad, 143
Anne Hines
Very Berry Trifle, 292
Phyllis Horne
Chili Sauce, 389
Heather Howe
Lemon Oregano Pork Stew, 160
Peanut Butter Cookies, 359
Alice Jenner
Lentil Soup, 56
Sharol Josephson
Very Gingery Ginger Cake, 322
Lesleigh Landry
Warm Grilled Flank Steak Salad, 145
Anne Lindsay
Chutney-Glazed Ham with Mango Salsa, 167
Fruity Soda Bread, 260
Jennifer MacKenzie
Lavash, 272
Morning Sunshine Muffins, 255
Mushroom Lentil Burgers, 222
Dana McCauley
Cinnamon Toast Coffee Cake, 318
Beth Moffatt
Fresh Strawberry Pie, 337

Rose Murray
Deep-Dish Tourtière, 176
Deluxe Roasted Beef Tenderloin, 140
Glazed Apricot Blondies, 367
Herbed Rösti, 89
Hungarian Goulash Soup, 58
Old-Fashioned Cooked Salad Dressing, 82
Pepper Orange Pork Stew, 161
Cheryl Neely
Quick Orange Buns, 262
Ruth Phelan
Pecan Snowballs, 360
Daphna Rabinovitch
Beef and Broccoli Stir-Fry, 127
Blueberry Cheese Coffee Cake, 320
Charmoula Roast Turkey Breast, 108
Chocolate Blackout Cake, 303
Chocolate Caramel Macadamia Tart, 346
Frozen Peanut Butter Pie, 345
Layered Chorizo Bake, 215
Rugalahs, 366
Smoked Salmon Strata, 214
Emily Richards
Amaretti, 355
Brutti ma Buoni, 356
Steamed Lemongrass Mussels, 21
Mary Seldon
Golden Latkes, 89
Claire Stancer
Barbecued Tofu Sandwiches with Aïoli, 223
Linda Stephen
Banana Split Roll, 312
Coconut Cream Pie, 340
Bonnie Stern
Frozen Lemon Meringue Torte, 296
Roasted Arctic Char with Shrimp, 195
Strip Loin with Exotic Mushrooms and Shallots, 138
Anita Stewart
Date Squares, 373
Susan Van Hezewijk
Speculaas, 364
Stephen Wong
Chicken Hot Pot with Ginger, Green Onions and Mushrooms, 96
Joan Yoder and Dennis Helmuth
Saskatoon Berry Pie, 331
Joanne Yolles
Coconut Chiffon Cake, 311
Orange and Sour Cherry Buttermilk Cake, 306

GLOSSARY OF COOKING TERMS

Al dente: An Italian phrase meaning "to the tooth," which describes pasta, rice or vegetables cooked just until a slight resistance is felt when bitten.

Au gratin: A dish topped with cheese or moistened bread crumbs, crisped and browned in the oven or under the broiler.

Bain-marie: An oven and stove-top technique (double boiler) to provide a stable cooking temperature. A container of food such as custard is cooked in or over a larger container of hot water.

Bake: To cook by dry heat in an oven. Never crowd the oven; best results depend on free circulation of heat. Keep an oven thermometer in your oven to check for accuracy.

Bake blind: To bake a pastry shell before filling to prevent it from shrinking and/or blistering. Prick pastry shell with a fork, line with foil and fill with pie weights or dried beans to weigh down. Once heat sets the pastry, remove foil and weights and, depending on the recipe, bake crust a little longer.

Baste: To spoon or brush foods during cooking with liquids, butter or drippings.

Batter: Uncooked pourable mixture — thick or thin — usually containing eggs, milk and flour as for pancakes; may be used to coat food to be fried.

Beat: To mix rapidly with a spoon or electric mixer to make a mixture smooth and light by incorporating as much air as possible.

Blanch: To boil a food briefly in boiling water, then plunge it into cold water to stop cooking. Blanching loosens skins, sets colour, seals in juices and removes bitterness or saltiness.

Blend: To mix two or more ingredients together until smooth with wooden spoon, whisk, mixer or blender.

Boil: To heat liquid until bubbles vigorously break the surface (212°F/100°C).

Braise: A leisurely cooking method used to tenderize tough cuts of meat. Food is first browned in fat, then covered and cooked at low heat in a little liquid in oven or on top of stove.

Broil: To cook or brown foods directly under the broiler in an oven.

Brown: To cook quickly over high heat on top of the stove or in oven to provide colour and flavour. Pat food dry and avoid overcrowding the pan or food will release juices that reduce heat and cause it to steam rather than brown.

Butterfly: To cut food such as a chicken breast down the centre almost but not quite all the way through so the two halves can be opened flat like a book.

Caramelize: To heat sugar until it liquefies, becomes syrupy and darkens from golden to rich brown. Or to cook foods such as onions until their natural sugars rise to the surface and cause the food to brown.

Chiffonade: To cut food, especially leafy vegetables and herbs, into thin strips.

Chop: To cut food more coarsely than for cubing; makes pieces about ½-inch (1 cm) square.

Crimp: To press two pastry or dough edges together, sealing the dough and making a decorative edge. Crimping, or fluting, can be done with a single crust by folding excess dough underneath rim, then shaping the edge with fingers or the tines of fork.

Cube: To cut into cubes about ½ inch (1 cm) square (more uniform than chopping).

Cut in: To mix a solid cold fat such as butter or shortening into dry ingredients until mixture is crumbly with some larger pieces. Use pastry blender, two knives or food processor.

Deglaze: To pour a liquid, usually wine, stock or juice. into a pan where meat, poultry, seafood or vegetables have been browned. The liquid loosens and dissolves the browned bits, creating the base for sauce, gravy or "jus."

Degrease: To skim the grease from the top of a sauce, soup, stock or gravy with a spoon or skimmer; best done when the dish is cold and fat has solidified.

Dice: To cut food into small, equal-size cubes, about ¼ inch (5 mm).

Dough: A flour and water mixture, often incorporating other ingredients, stiff enough to knead or shape with your hands. Whereas batter is pourable, dough is too stiff to pour.

Dredge: To lightly coat a food with flour, bread crumbs, cornmeal, or grated hard cheese, for example.

Fillet: To remove bones from a piece of meat or fish. Also refers to piece of boneless flesh.

Flake: To break off small layers or pieces of fish with a fork to test for doneness.

Flambé: A dramatic technique used to set foods aflame by dousing them in some form of hard liquor, such as brandy, and then setting it on fire. Warming the alcohol first guarantees that it will catch fire.

Fold: A technique used to gently combine a light mixture such as beaten egg whites with a heavier mixture such as a batter by using a spatula to cut down vertically through the two mixtures to bottom of bowl, then bring some of the mixture up from the bottom to the top, constantly repeating this motion while rotating the bowl.

Fry: To pan-fry is to cook food in a skillet in just enough fat to coat the bottom of the pan and prevent the food from sticking. Deep-frying requires a deep heavy pan that can hold enough oil for the food to be submerged, usually about 1½ inches (4 cm). Stir-frying uses a little oil, high heat, small pieces of food and constant motion in a wok or deep skillet.

Ganache: A rich chocolate mixture used to fill truffles, to cover cakes or as a sauce. To make, pour boiling whipping cream over chopped chocolate; whisk until chocolate is melted and smooth.

Glaze: To coat food with liquid to give it shine or to brush pastry or bread with egg yolk before baking.

Grease: To coat a baking or cooking dish with unsalted butter, shortening or oil (using pastry brush), or with a fine oil spray, to prevent sticking.

Infuse: To steep herbs or spices, for example, in hot liquid to add flavour.

Julienne: To cut foods, often vegetables, into thin strips of varying sizes, most often matchstick-size.

Knead: To use hands or a machine to fold, push and turn dough until it is smooth and firm.

Lukewarm: Approximately body temperature.

Macerate: To let fruit stand in liquid, such as liqueur or juice, to tenderize or flavour it.

Marinate: To soak meats, poultry or vegetables in a highly seasoned liquid that also includes an acid, either to tenderize or to flavour or a combination of the two.

Mince: To chop into very fine pieces.

Mix: To combine two or more ingredients, either by stirring, whisking or beating.

Mold: To form into an attractive shape, either with your hands or by placing the mixture in a decoratively shaped container.

Mousse: An airy sweet or savoury mixture usually lightened with egg whites or whipping cream, sometimes set with gelatin.

Nap: To coat with sauce.

Parboil: To precook food, often vegetables, in boiling water to set colour, reduce raw flavour or make ahead.

Pickle: To preserve food in brine and/or vinegar solution.

Pinch: The very small amount of a seasoning you can pick up between your thumb and forefinger, about ⅛ tsp (0.5 mL).

Poach: To cook foods submerged or half submerged in simmering water.

Prick: To pierce foods, such as fruit and vegetable skins, to release air and moisture during cooking, or to pierce the bottom of an unbaked pie shell with the tines of a fork to prevent pastry from blistering or shrinking during baking (see bake blind).

Proof: To check that yeast is alive. To do so, sprinkle yeast over sweetened water; let stand for 10 minutes in warm place. If yeast bubbles, you have proof that your bread will, too. If the mixture does not bubble, start again with new yeast.

Purée: To mash finely using a food mill, blender or food processor until smooth.

Reduce: To boil down liquid, usually over high heat, in uncovered pan in order to evaporate liquid, concentrating both flavour and texture.

Refresh: To plunge hot cooked food into ice water to stop cooking process and set colour and flavour. Always remove food as soon as it is cold.

Roux: A mixture of melted fat and flour, classically in equal proportions, stirred together until well combined and cooked over medium heat long enough to cook off the rawness of the flour. This is the basis for classic white sauce, or béchamel.

Sauté: To cook, stirring, in a skillet over high heat.

Scald: To bring a liquid such as milk to just short of the boiling point; that is, until bubbles begin to gather around the edge of the saucepan.

Score: To make shallow incisions in the skin, flesh or fat of a food before cooking

to help maintain its shape, retain moisture or to tenderize. To score the top of bars delineates portion sizes either before or right after baking.

Sear: To brown meat or poultry very quickly in hot oven or in skillet over high heat.

Shuck: To remove the shells of shellfish such as clams, oysters or scallops, or to remove the outer husk from corn.

Sift: To pass dry ingredients such as flour or cocoa powder through a fine sieve in order to remove lumps.

Simmer: To heat so gently that the liquid barely reaches a bubble.

Skim: To spoon off fat, foam or other impurities from surface of simmering liquids.

Sliver: To cut into very fine, thin pieces.

Steam: To cook foods in a covered container over a small amount of boiling water.

Stew: To slow-cook foods submerged in a flavourful liquid either on top of the stove or in the oven.

Stir: To mix ingredients together with a spoon, whisk or spatula using a rotating motion.

Sweat: To cook vegetables in fat or sometimes a liquid over low heat, covered, until softened but not browned. Often the first step in making soup.

Temper: To prepare an ingredient, commonly beaten eggs, for combination with a much hotter ingredient by stirring a little of the hot ingredients into the eggs before combining them.

Tenderize: Pounding, marinating, scoring and slow cooking are all ways to turn a tough cut of meat into a more tender one by breaking down the tough connective tissue.

Truss: To tie poultry or meat into a compact form so that it cooks evenly and retains its shape.

Whip: To beat until soft peaks or stiff peaks form by using a whisk or an electric mixer.

INDEX

A

Almonds
  Almond Biscotti, 358
  Almond Cherry Crisp, 280
  Almond Snowballs or Crescents, 360
  Amaretti, 355
  Blueberry Orange Almond Loaf, 258
  Cherry Almond Biscotti, 358
  Glazed Almond Spritz Rosettes, 361
  Lemon Almond Squares, 371
Amaretti, 355
Anchovy Butter, 152
Angel Food Cake, Classic, 310
Antipasto, Grilled Vegetable, 31
Appetizers. See also recipe list, p. 17.
  Greek Salad, 72
  Risotto Milanese, 85
  Tabbouleh Salad, 76
  Two-Cheese Tomato Tart, 221
Apples
  Apple Chops, 158
  Apple Mustard–Glazed Trout Fillets, 202
  Apple Plum Chutney, 388
  Apple Spice Muffins, 254
  Best-Ever Apple Pie, 328
  Cranberry Apple Pie, 328
  Dutch Apple Pie, 329
  Maple Apple Beans, 87
  Pan-Seared Liver with Apple and
    Mustard, 128
  pan-seared onions and apples (tip), 163
  Spiced Plum Apple Crisp, 280
  Tarte Tatin, 330
Apricots
  Ginger Apricot Chicken Breasts, 110
  Glazed Apricot Blondies, 367
Arctic Char, Roasted with Shrimp, 195
Arrabbiata Pasta, 231
Artichokes
  Artichoke and Gorgonzola–Stuffed
    Baguette, 36
  Artichoke Pasta, 231
  Caramelized Onion Artichoke Quiche,
    212
  Penne Salad with Artichokes and
    Spinach, 78
  Prosciutto and Artichoke Quesadillas, 41
Asiago cheese, 236
Asian Burgers, Hot, 144
Asian Chops, 158
Asian Turkey Noodle Soup, 62
Asparagus, 49

Asparagus and Ham Omelette, 209
Asparagus Ham Strata, 214
Asparagus Miso Soup, 49
Cheese and Broccoli or Asparagus
  Soufflé, 218
Portobello Asparagus Strudels, 219
Smoked Salmon Asparagus Quiche,
  212
Versatile Crêpe with Ham, Brie and
  Asparagus Filling, The, 265
Avocados, 29
  Black Bean Chili with Avocado Salsa,
    226
  Layered Mexican Dip, 29
  Slow-Cooker Black Bean Chili with
    Avocado Salsa, 226

B

Bacon. See also Peameal bacon.
  Bacon Macaroni and Cheese, 234
  Baked Brie with Bacon and Sun-Dried
    Tomato Topping, 18
  Blue Cheese and Bacon Potato Salad, 75
  Pan-Seared Liver with Mushroom and
    Bacon, 128
  Roast Turkey with Bacon and Chestnut
    Stuffing, 104
Baking, 5, 7–8
Baklava, 344
Balsamic Mushroom Crostini, 35
Bananas, 259
  Banana Chocolate Chip Loaf, 259
  Banana Chocolate Chip Muffins, 259
  Banana Split Roll, 312
  Bananas in Caramel Sauce, 298
  Chocolaty Banana Muffins, 254
  Mini Banana Chocolate Chip Loaves,
    259
  Puffy Dutch Pancake with Bananas
    and Strawberries, 217
Bannock, 262
Barbecue sauces
  Southwestern Barbecue Sauce, 34
  Tangy Barbecue Sauce, 147
Barbecued. See also Grilled.
  Barbecue Chops, 158
  Barbecued Beef Ribs, 150
  Barbecued Pork Loin with Rosemary,
    168
  Barbecued Tofu Sandwiches with
    Aïoli, 223
  Barbecue-Roasted Turkey, 114

Bumbleberry Cobbler on the Barbecue,
  281
Rib Eye on the Rotisserie, 152
Salsa Barbecued Beef Brisket, 153
Saucy Barbecued Wings, 27
Slow and Easy Real Barbecued Ribs, 172
Barley, 59, 225
  Barley Pilaf, 83
  Barley Side Dish, 86
  Beef and Barley Soup, 59
  Turkey Mushroom Barley Soup, 62
Bars and squares. See also recipe list, p. 351.
  Golden Shortbread Squares, 362
  Morning Sunshine Bars, 255
  Rice Crisp Cereal Squares, 373
Basil, 70, 80
  Basil Parmesan Chicken Burgers, 120
  Buttermilk Basil Chicken Legs, 115
  Caprese Salad, 70
  Chicken Liver Pâté with Basil, 28
  Slow-Grilled Salmon with Garlic and
    Basil, 199
Beans, 226. See also Chickpeas; Lentils.
  Baked Beans, 87
  Bean Burgers with Coriander Cream,
    222
  Black Bean Chicken Wings, 27
  Black Bean Chili with Avocado Salsa,
    226
  Black Bean Ribs, 171
  Black Bean Soup, 55
  Lamb Shanks with Beans, 177
  Layered Mexican Dip, 29
  Maple Apple Beans, 87
  Pasta e Fagioli, 57
  Red Barn Corn and Bean Salad, 80
  Warm Garlic Bean Crostini, 35
Beef
  ground:
  about, 135
  Beef Moussaka, 178
  Best Burgers, 144
  Cabbage Rolls, 134
  Dutch Meatball Soup, 60
  Koftas with Cucumber Yogurt
    Salad, 143
  Meatloaf Many Ways, 136
  Party Meatballs, 34
  Pastitsio, 238
  Peking Hamburger Dumplings, 32
  People's Choice Chili, 133
  Picadillo Empanadas, 37

liver:
about, 128
Pan-Seared Liver, 128
ribs:
Barbecued Beef Ribs, 150
Mustard Devilled Ribs, 150
roast:
Classic Pot Roast with Vegetables, 142
Deluxe Roasted Beef Tenderloin, 140
Devilled Prime Rib with Roasted Garlic
    Gravy, 139
Easy Roast Beef with Onion Gravy, 137
Herbed Prime Rib Roast, 139
Onion Cranberry Brisket, 141
Rib Eye on the Rotisserie, 152
roasting chart, 9
Salsa Barbecued Beef Brisket, 153
Strip Loin with Exotic Mushrooms and
    Shallots, 138
short ribs:
Korean Beef Short Ribs, 149
steak:
Beef and Broccoli Stir-Fry, 127
Ginger Soy Beef Kabobs, 151
Grilled Beef Satays, 26
Herb and Onion Swiss Steak, 132
marinating, 148
Party Sirloin, 146
Red Wine and Oregano Grilled
    Marinating Steak, 148
Tender T-Bones, 147
Warm Grilled Flank Steak Salad, 145
stewing:
about, 130
Beef and Barley Soup, 59
Beef Bourguignonne with Noodles, 130
Big-Batch Beef Ragu, 232
Jamaican Beef Pepper Pot, 61
Old-Fashioned Beef Stew, 129
Sauerbraten Beef Stew, 131
stir-fry strips:
Steak and Vegetable Fajitas, 126
Beef Stock, 47
Beet and Vegetable Borscht, 46
Berries. See also individual berries.
Bumbleberry Cobbler, 281
Peach Berry Crisp, 280
Saskatoon Berry Pie, 331
Summer Berry Fools, 297
Summer Berry Jam, 381
Three-Berry Conserve, 382
Very Berry Trifle, 292
Biscotti, 358
Biscuits, Tea, 261
"Blini" with Smoked Salmon, Cornmeal, 33
Blue Cheese and Bacon Potato Salad, 75
Blueberries, 378
Blueberry Cheese Coffee Cake, 320
Blueberry Orange Almond Loaf, 258
Blueberry Pancakes, 263
Double-Crust Blueberry Pie, 332
Fresh Blueberry Tart, 336

Wild Blueberry Preserve, 378
Bok Choy, Braised Chicken and, 97
Borscht, Beet and Vegetable, 46
Bran Muffins, Honey, 256
Bread machine, 267
    Basic Bread: By Hand and Machine, 266
    Bread Machine Pizza Dough, 248
Breads. See also recipe list, p. 253.
    Bread Salad, 70
    Very Special Bread Pudding with
        Orange Crème Anglaise, 283
Breakfast Strudels, 216
Brie cheese, 18
    Baked Brie, 18
    Brie, Pear and Onion Strudel on a Bed
        of Greens, 39
    Pear and Brie Quesadillas, 41
    Versatile Crêpe with Ham, Brie and
        Asparagus Filling, The, 265
Broccoli
    Beef and Broccoli Stir-Fry, 127
    Broccoli Macaroni and Cheese, 234
    Cheese and Broccoli or Asparagus
        Soufflé, 218
    Orange Broccoli Chops, 158
Brownies, Oodles of, 368
Bruschetta. See also Crostini.
    Bruschetta, 35
    Bruschetta Quesadillas, 41
Brutti ma Buoni, 356
Buckwheat, 225
    Buckwheat Honey Pancakes, 263
Bulgur, 225
    Bulgur Pilaf, 83
    Tabbouleh Salad, 76
Bumbleberry Pie, Double-Crust, 332
Bundt Cake, Raspberry Chocolate Chip, 321
Buns
    Cinnamon Buns, 274
    Hot Cross Buns, 275
    Quick Orange Buns, 262
Burgers
    about, 144
    Bean Burgers with Coriander Cream, 222
    Best Burgers, 144
    Mushroom Lentil Burgers, 222
    Parmesan Chicken Burgers, 120
    Turkey Burgers, 120
Butter tarts, 342
Buttermilk
    Buttermilk Basil Chicken Legs, 115
    Buttermilk Cheddar Loaf, 268
    Buttermilk Loaf, 268
    Buttermilk Pancakes, 263
    Buttermilk Ranch Dressing, 82
    Buttermilk Rosemary Chicken Legs, 115
    Buttermilk Tea Biscuits, 261
    Orange and Sour Cherry Buttermilk
        Cake, 306
Butters, flavoured
    for fish, 201
    for grilled beef, 152

C
Cabbage
    Cabbage Rolls, 134
    Creamy Coleslaw, 71
    Keeper Coleslaw, 71
Caesar Salad, 69
Cajun Chicken Breasts, 110
Cajun Chicken Burgers, 120
Cajun Mayonnaise, Crab Cakes
    with, 20
Cajun Shrimp, 24
Cakes. See also recipe list, p. 301.
    cake-and-pastry flour, 311
    how to ice, 304, 321
    preparations before baking, 307
    testing for doneness, 308
Cantaloupe
    Cantaberry Sorbet, 294
Caprese Salad, 70
Caraway seeds
    Caraway Pork Goulash, 159
    Caraway Rye Bread, 270
Carrot Cake with Cream Cheese Icing,
    Canada's Best, 308
Casseroles. See also Stews.
    Creamy Shrimp Bake, 240
    Herbed Seafood Casserole, 196
    Lamb Moussaka, 178
    Layered Chorizo Bake, 215
    Luscious Mushroom Lasagna, 242
    Meatball and Rigatoni Bake, 241
    Old Favourite Lasagna, 244
    Old-Fashioned Chicken Pot Pie, 122
    Pastitsio, 238
    Spicy Sausage and Rigatoni
        Bake, 241
Cedar-Planked Salmon, 204
Challah, 277
Cheddar cheese
    Buttermilk Cheddar Loaf, 268
    Cheddar Burgers, 144
Cheese. See also individual cheeses.
    Blueberry Cheese Coffee Cake, 320
    Cheese and Broccoli or Asparagus
        Soufflé, 218
    Cheese Soufflé, 218
    Cheese Tea Biscuits, 261
    Raspberry Cheese Coffee Cake, 320
    Rolled Cheese Omelette, 209
    Spinach and Cheese Quesadillas, 41
    Two-Cheese Tomato Tart, 221
Cheesecake, Basic but Beautiful, 323
Cherries
    Almond Cherry Crisp, 280
    Cherry Almond Biscotti, 358
    Cherry Chocolate Baklava, 344
    Double-Crust Tart Cherry Pie, 332
    Mixed Cherry Conserve, 382
    Orange and Sour Cherry Buttermilk
        Cake, 306
Chicken
    about, 97

breasts:
Breaded Lemon Chicken with Ricotta Leek Stuffing, 112
Chicken Caesar Salad, 69
Chicken Pesto Pasta, 235
Chicken Phyllo Bundles with Herbed Sabayon, 113
Cordon Bleu Chicken Breasts, 118
Crispy Baked Chicken, 111
Ginger Chicken and Green Onion Kabobs, 119
Grilled Chicken Skewers with Dipping Sauce, 25
Grilled Stuffed Chicken Breasts Many Ways, 118
Grilled Teriyaki Ginger Chicken Satays, 26
Prosciutto-Stuffed Chicken Breasts, 118
Roasted Chicken Breasts Five Ways, 110
Sage and Lemon Chicken Breasts, 118
Sicilian Chicken, 98
Thai Green Curry Chicken, 100
cooked:
Barbecue Chicken Quesadillas, 41
ground:
Basil Parmesan Chicken Burgers, 120
Cajun Chicken Burgers, 120
Parmesan Chicken Burgers, 120
legs:
Buttermilk Basil Chicken Legs, 115
Buttermilk Rosemary Chicken Legs, 115
Chicken and Seafood Paella, 121
Chicken and Wild Rice Soup, 63
Chicken Noodle Soup, 63
Chipotle Mojo Chicken, 116
Mojo Chicken, 116
livers:
Chicken Liver Pâté with Basil, 28
thighs:
Big-Batch Cacciatore Sauce, 232
Braised Chicken and Bok Choy, 97
Chicken Adobo, 101
Chicken Hot Pot with Ginger, Green Onions and Mushrooms, 96
Old-Fashioned Chicken Pot Pie, 122
whole or cut up in pieces:
carving, 102
Piri Piri Chicken, 117
Portuguese Paprika Chicken, 117
Quick Chicken in Wine, 99
Roast Chicken, 102
roasting, 10
Spicy Chicken with Couscous Stuffing, 103
stuffing, 103
wings:
Black Bean Chicken Wings, 27
Honey Garlic Chicken Wings, 27
Saucy Barbecued Wings, 27
Chicken or Turkey Stock, 47
Chickpeas
Hummus, 30

Chili
Black Bean Chili with Avocado Salsa, 226
Chili Meat Loaf, 136
Make-Again Chili, 133
People's Choice Chili, 133
Slow-Cooker Black Bean Chili with Avocado Salsa, 226
Turkey Chili Soup, 62
Chili Sauce, 389
Chinoise Duck, 106
Chipotle peppers, 20
Chipotle Mojo Chicken, 116
Crab Cakes, with Chipotle Mayonnaise, 20
Chocolate
Banana Chocolate Chip Loaf, 259
Banana Chocolate Chip Muffins, 259
Best-Ever Chocolate Chip Cookies, 353
Bittersweet Chocolate Cream Pie, 341
Bittersweet Chocolate Crème Brûlée, 289
Cherry Chocolate Baklava, 344
Chewy Chocolate Chip Cookies, 353
Chocolate Angel Food Cake, 310
Chocolate Blackout Cake, 303
Chocolate Butter Tarts, 342
Chocolate Caramel Macadamia Tart, 346
Chocolate Chip Ice-Cream Sandwiches, 353
Chocolate Espresso Angel Food Cake, 310
Chocolate Fondue, 299
Chocolate Layer Cake, 302
Chocolate Mounds, 362
Chocolate Orange Pecan Oatmeal Cookies, 352
Chocolate Panforte, 369
Chocolate Peanut Butter Thumbprints, 359
Chocolate Pecan Pie, 343
Chocolate Raspberry Rugalahs, 366
Chocolate Sauce, 312
Chocolate Truffles, 375
Chocolaty Banana Muffins, 254
Double Chocolate Biscotti, 358
Double Chocolate Cookies, 363
Mini Banana Chocolate Chip Loaves, 259
Mocha Marjolaine, 314
Nanaimo Bars, 372
Oodles of Brownies, 368
Raspberry Chocolate Chip Bundt Cake, 321
storing, 302
Chocolate, white
Phyllo Fruit Cups with Orange White Chocolate Cream, 348
Reverse Chocolate Chip Cookies, 353
White Chocolate Crème Brûlée, 289
White Chocolate Lemon Tart, 347
White Chocolate Orange Brownies, 368

Chorizo, 215
Layered Chorizo Bake, 215
Choucroute Garnie, 175
Chowders
Corn Chowder, 45
Hearty Seafood Chowder, 53
Chutney
Apple Plum Chutney, 388
Baked Brie with Fruit Chutney Topping, 18
Chutney-Glazed Ham with Mango Salsa, 167
Crab Cakes, with Curried Mango Chutney Mayonnaise, 20
Peach Chutney, 388
Pear Chutney, 388
Ciabatta, 271
Cinnamon Buns, 274
Cinnamon Toast Coffee Cake, 318
Clams
Hearty Clam Chowder, 53
Hearty Fresh Clam Chowder, 53
Quick Clam Pasta Sauce, 230
Cobbler, Bumbleberry, 281
Coconut
Coconut Chiffon Cake, 311
Coconut Cream Pie, 340
Coconut Curry Fish, 186
Coconut Thai Rice Pilaf, 83
Cod au Gratin, 194
Coffee cakes
Blueberry Cheese Coffee Cake, 320
Cinnamon Toast Coffee Cake, 318
Raspberry Cheese Coffee Cake, 320
Coleslaw, 71
Compote, Rhubarb and Strawberry, 297
Conserves. See Preserves.
Cookies. See also recipe list, p. 351.
Almond Snowballs or Crescents, 360
baking, 357
cookie "greeting card," 353
No-Bake Chow Mein Crunchies, 374
Coq au vin, 99
Cordon Bleu Chicken Breasts, 118
Coriander
Bean Burgers with Coriander Cream, 222
Grilled Jumbo Shrimp Skewers with Coriander Dipping Sauce, 25
Lime Coriander Cream (tip), 55
Corn, 45
Corn Chowder, 45
Hearty Seafood and Corn Chowder, 53
Jalapeño Corn Quesadillas, 41
Red Barn Corn and Bean Salad, 80
Cornish Hens with Tuscan Touches, 107
Cornmeal "Blini" with Smoked Salmon, 33
Couscous, 225
Couscous Pilaf, 83
Couscous Side Dish, 86
Couscous Timbales, 181
Spicy Chicken with Couscous Stuffing, 103

Crab Cakes, 20
Cranberries
    Baked Brie with Tangy Cranberry
        Topping, 18
    Cranberry Apple Pie, 328
    Onion Cranberry Brisket, 141
    Pear Cranberry Crisp, 280
Crème Brûlée, 289
Crème Caramel, 288
Crêpe, The Versatile, 265
Crisps, Five Dessert, 280
Crostini, 35. *See also* Bruschetta.
Croutons, 69
Cuban Grilled Pork Sandwich, 170
Cucumbers, 50
    Creamy Cucumber Dressing, 82
    Cucumber Pepper Relish, 391
    Cucumber Raita, 188
    Cucumber Yogurt Salad, 143
Cumin and Lime Fish Kabobs, 200
Curry
    Coconut Curry Fish, 186
    Crab Cakes, with Curried Mango
        Chutney Mayonnaise, 20
    Curried Chops, 158
    Curried Lamb Phyllo Triangles, 40
    Curried Lentil, Wild Rice and Orzo
        Salad, 79
    Glazed Sea Bass with Red Curry
        Sauce, 197
    Party Meatballs with Curry Sauce, 34
    Red Curry Mussels, 189
    Thai Curry Shrimp, 24
    Thai Green Curry Chicken, 100

D
Dates
    Date Squares, 373
    Icky Sticky Baked Date Pudding, 285
    Oatmeal Date Sandwich Cookies, 352
Dessert Topping, Lower-Fat, 336
Desserts. *See recipe list, p. 279.*
Dill Sauce, 204
Dipping sauces
    Coriander Dipping Sauce, 25
    Dipping Sauce, 32
    Lemon Chive Dipping Sauce, 191
    Seafood Sauce, 25
    Thai Dipping Sauce, 25
Dips
    Hummus, 30
    Layered Mexican Dip, 29
Dressings. *See* Salad dressings.
Duck
    Chinoise Duck, 106
    Honey Rosemary Duck, 106
Dumplings
    Old-Fashioned Chicken Pot Pie, with
        Dumplings, 123
    Peking Hamburger Dumplings, 32
    Perogies, 227
    Potato Gnocchi, 245

Dutch Apple Pie, 329
Dutch Meatball Soup, 60
Dutch Pear Pie, 329

E
Eggplant
    Pesto and Roasted Eggplant Pizza, 251
Eggs. *See also recipe list, p. 207.*
    beating egg whites, 315
    hard-cooking, 211
    Microwave Scrambled Eggs for One or
        Two, 211
    poaching, 211
    soft-cooking, 211
Empanadas, 37
Equipment
    bakeware, 7–8
    grill pan, 41
    immersion blender, 48
    knives, 6
    measuring, 6
    meat loaf pan set, 136
    ovenware, 7
    stockpot, 61
    stove top, 6–7
    utensils and machines, 8
    woks, 156

F
Fajita Burgers, 144
Fajitas, Steak and Vegetable, 126
Fatouche, 66
Fennel
    Orange Fennel Rack of Pork, 164
    Sausage Fennel Pasta Sauce, 230
    Turkey Breast Stuffed with Fennel and
        Red Pepper, 109
Feta cheese
    Feta and Tomato Pizza, 249
    Greek Salad, 72
    Shrimp Braised in Tomato Sauce with
        Feta, 187
    Spinach and Feta Soufflé, 218
    Zucchini, Sweet Red Pepper and Feta
        Frittata, 208
Fettuccine Alfredo — The Classic, 237
Fish and seafood. *See also recipe list, p. 185;*
        individual fish and shellfish.
    Chicken and Seafood Paella, 121
    fish "en papillote," 194
    Fish Stock, 47
    Hearty Seafood Chowder, 53
    Mediterranean Seafood Soup with
        Rouille, 52
    Pan-Fried Fish, 193
    Seafood Sauce, 25
Five-Spice Marinade, 148
Florentine Bars, 370
Flour facts, 270
Flowers, candied edible, 296
Fondue, Chocolate, 299
Food Processor Pizza Dough, 248

Food safety, 4–5
Fools, 297
Freezable
    appetizers, 28, 32, 34, 36, 40
    beef dishes, 129–34, 144
    breads, 254–59, 261, 264–66, 268–70
    cakes, 302–05, 308, 310, 314, 318,
        321–323
    cookies, bars and squares, 352–54,
        357, 358–65, 367, 372–75
    desserts, 285, 286, 291, 294, 296
    egg, cheese and vegetarian dishes,
        216, 224, 227
    fish and seafood dishes, 196
    pasta and pizza, 230, 235, 238,
        240–42, 244, 245
    pies, tarts and pastry, 332, 340, 345
    pork and lamb dishes, 159, 161, 176, 178
    poultry dishes, 120
    soups, 55, 56, 60
French Toast, Basic, 213
Frittatas, Foolproof, 208
Fruit. *See also individual fruits.*
    buying guide, 12–13
    Double-Crust Fruit Pies, 332
    Dried Fruit and Lemon Tea Biscuits, 261
    Fresh Fruit Pavlova, 293
    Fruity Soda Bread, 260
    Phyllo Fruit Cups with Orange White
        Chocolate Cream, 348
Fruitcake, Rich Brandied, 309

G
Garlic
    Creamy Garlic Dressing, 82
    Devilled Prime Rib with Roasted Garlic
        Gravy, 139
    Garlic Roast Chicken, 102
    Honey Garlic Chicken Wings, 27
    Honey Garlic Ribs, 171
    Lemon Garlic Shrimp, 24
    Penne with Garlicky Rapini, 233
    Roast Chicken with Lemon and
        Garlic, 102
    Roasted Garlic Dressing, 74
    Slow-Grilled Salmon with Garlic and
        Basil, 199
    Warm Garlic Bean Crostini, 35
Gazpacho, 50
Giardiniera, 393
Ginger
    Chicken Hot Pot with Ginger, Green
        Onions and Mushrooms, 96
    Ginger Apricot Chicken Breasts, 110
    Ginger Brutti ma Buoni, 356
    Ginger Chicken and Green Onion
        Kabobs, 119
    Ginger Soy Beef Kabobs, 151
    Grilled Teriyaki Ginger Chicken
        Satays, 26
    Spicy Ginger Crinkle Cookies, 357
    Very Gingery Ginger Cake, 322

Goat cheese
    Baby Spinach and Goat Cheese
        Salad, 67
Gorgonzola–Stuffed Baguette, Artichoke
    and, 36
Goulash, Caraway Pork, 159
Grains, 225. *See also individual grains.*
    Grain and Pasta Side Dishes, 86
    Pick-a-Grain Pilaf, 83
Granola Bars, 374
Grape Jelly, 384
Gravy
    Onion Gravy, 137
    Roasted Garlic Gravy, 139
    Wild Mushroom Gravy, 105
Greek Salad, 72
Green onions
    Chicken Hot Pot with Ginger, Green
        Onions and Mushrooms, 96
    Ginger Chicken and Green Onion
        Kabobs, 119
Grilled. *See also* Barbecued.
    Cedar-Planked Salmon, 204
    Cuban Grilled Pork Sandwich, 170
    Grilled Beef Satays, 26
    Grilled Chicken Skewers with Dipping
        Sauce, 25
    Grilled Halibut with Tomato Salsa, 201
    Grilled Jumbo Shrimp Skewers with
        Dipping Sauce, 25
    Grilled Pork Satays, 26
    Grilled Salmon Fillets, 203
    Grilled Stuffed Chicken Breasts Many
        Ways, 118
    Grilled Teriyaki Ginger Chicken
        Satays, 26
    Grilled Trout Fillets with Tandoori
        Marinade, 202
    Grilled Vegetable Antipasto, 31
    Grilled Vegetable Pizza, 251
    Red Wine and Oregano Grilled
        Marinating Steak, 148
    Slow-Grilled Salmon with Garlic and
        Basil, 199
    vegetables, 93

H
Halibut
    Grilled Halibut with Tomato Salsa, 201
    Halibut Braised in Tomato Sauce, 187
Ham
    Asparagus and Ham Omelette, 209
    Asparagus Ham Strata, 214
    Chutney-Glazed Ham with Mango
        Salsa, 167
    Versatile Crêpe with Ham, Brie and
        Asparagus Filling, The, 265
Hamburgers. *See* Burgers.
Hazelnuts
    Baked Brie with Hazelnut Pear
        Topping, 18
    Hazelnut Pavlova, 293

Hazelnut Truffles, 375
Herbs. *See also individual herbs.*
    Chicken Phyllo Bundles with Herbed
        Sabayon, 113
    Eggs Benedict with Herbed Cream
        Sauce, 210
    as garnishes, 56
    Herb and Onion Swiss Steak, 132
    Herb Vinegars, 393
    Herbed Gazpacho, 50
    Herbed Hummus, 30
    Herbed Lamb Chops, 183
    Herbed Pizza Dough, 248
    Herbed Prime Rib Roast, 139
    Herbed Rösti, 89
    Herbed Seafood Casserole, 196
Hermits Galore, 354
Honey
    Honey Bran Muffins, 256
    Honey Dijon Vinaigrette, 81
    Honey Garlic Chicken Wings, 27
    Honey Garlic Ribs, 171
    Honey Mustard Chicken Breasts, 110
    Honey Rosemary Duck, 106
Horseradish Butter, 152
Horseradish Cream Sauce, Easy, 137
Hummus, 30
Hungarian Goulash Soup, 58

I
Ice cream
    about, 295
    Caramel-Baked Pear Sundaes, 298
    Chocolate Chip Ice-Cream Sandwiches,
        353
    Peach Ice Cream, 295
    Raspberry Ice Cream, 295
    Red Plum Ice Cream, 295
    Strawberry Ice Cream, 295
Icebox Cookies, 363
Icings and glazes
    Butter Icing, 304
    Chocolate Icing, 302
    Cream Cheese Icing, 308
    Lemon Glaze, 305
Italian Soufflé, 218

J
Jalapeño peppers, 19
    Jalapeño Corn Quesadillas, 41
    Stuffed Jalapeño Peppers, 19
Jamaican Beef Pepper Pot, 61
Jams and jellies. *See* Preserves.
Jerk Roast Pork, 165
Jerked Kabobs, Mild, 151
Jicamas, 73
    Peanut Jicama Salad, 73

K
Kabobs
    Classic Greek Kabobs, 151
    Cumin and Lime Fish Kabobs, 200

    Ginger Chicken and Green Onion
        Kabobs, 119
    Ginger Soy Beef Kabobs, 151
    Mild Jerked Kabobs, 151
    Provençal Beef Kabobs, 151
    skewers for, 119
Kasha Side Dish, 86
Kitchen equipment. *See* Equipment.
Koftas with Cucumber Yogurt Salad, 143
Korean Beef Short Ribs, 149
Korean Ribs, 171

L
Lamb
    Butterflied Leg of Lamb, 182
    Curried Lamb Phyllo Triangles, 40
    Herbed Lamb Chops, 183
    Lamb Moussaka, 178
    Lamb Shanks with Beans, 177
    Roast Leg of Lamb, 180
    Rosemary-Crusted Rack of Lamb, 181
Lasagna
    Luscious Mushroom Lasagna, 242
    Old Favourite Lasagna, 244
Latkes, Golden, 89
Lavash, 272
Leeks, 112
    Breaded Lemon Chicken with Ricotta
        Leek Stuffing, 112
    Smoked Salmon and Leek Frittata, 208
    Vichyssoise, 51
Lemongrass Mussels, 21
Lemons
    Breaded Lemon Chicken with Ricotta
        Leek Stuffing, 112
    Dried Fruit and Lemon Tea Biscuits, 261
    Frozen Lemon Meringue Torte, 296
    Lemon Almond Squares, 371
    Lemon Chive Dipping Sauce, 191
    Lemon Garlic Shrimp, 24
    Lemon Meringue Pie, 338
    Lemon Mint Chicken Breasts, 110
    Lemon Olive Pork Chops, 157
    Lemon Oregano Pork Stew, 160
    Lemon Poppy Seed Loaf, 257
    Lemon Sponge Pudding, 282
    Lemon-Glazed Pound Cake, 305
    Lemon-Lime Angel Food Cake, 310
    Port Lemon Crème Caramel, 288
    Raspberry Lemon Muffins, 254
    Roast Chicken with Lemon and
        Garlic, 102
    Sage and Lemon Chicken Breasts, 118
    Simply Lovely Lemon Squares, 371
    White Chocolate Lemon Tart, 347
Lentils
    Curried Lentil, Wild Rice and Orzo
        Salad, 79
    Lentil Soup, 56
    Mushroom Lentil Burgers, 222
Limes, 54
    Cumin and Lime Fish Kabobs, 200

Lemon-Lime Angel Food Cake, 310
Lime Coriander Cream (tip), 55
Liver and Onions, Pan-Seared, 128
Lobster, Boiled, 191

M
Macaroni and Cheese Five Ways, 234
Mandarin Sorbet, 294
Mangoes
    Chutney-Glazed Ham with Mango
        Salsa, 167
    Crab Cakes, with Curried Mango
        Chutney Mayonnaise, 20
Maple syrup
    Maple Apple Beans, 87
    Maple-Glazed Peameal Bacon Dinner,
        174
Marinades, tenderizing, 148
Marmalades, 383
Mascarpone, 291
Mayonnaises, 20
Measuring, 2
    equipment, 6
Meat cooking chart, 9–10
Meat doneness chart, 11
Meatballs
    about, 34
    Dutch Meatball Soup, 60
    Meatball and Rigatoni Bake, 241
    Party Meatballs, 34
Meatloaf Many Ways, 136
Mediterranean Burgers, 144
Mediterranean Quesadillas, 41
Mediterranean Seafood Soup with
        Rouille, 52
Mediterranean Vegetable Pie, 220
Mexican Dip, Layered, 29
Mexican Soufflé, 218
Millet, 225
Mint
    Baked Brie with Strawberry Mint
        Topping, 18
    Lemon Mint Chicken Breasts, 110
    Tomato and Mint Salad, 188
Miso, 49, 68
    Asparagus Miso Soup, 49
    Crunchy Iceberg Lettuce Salad with
        Miso Dressing, 68
Mocha Brownies, 368
Mocha Marjolaine, 314
Mojo Chicken, 116
Moroccan Marinade, 148
Moussaka
    Beef Moussaka, 178
    Lamb Moussaka, 178
    Vegetarian Moussaka, 224
Mozzarella cheese, 236
    Caprese Salad, 70
Muffins
    about, 256
    dress-ups, 254
    Easy-Mix Muffins, 254

Honey Bran Muffins, 256
Morning Sunshine Muffins, 255
Mushrooms, 44–45
    Balsamic Mushroom Crostini, 35
    Chicken Hot Pot with Ginger, Green
        Onions and Mushrooms, 96
    Chunky Mushroom Soup, 44
    Luscious Mushroom Lasagna, 242
    Mushroom Duxelles Omelette for
        Two, 209
    Mushroom Empanadas, 37
    Mushroom Lentil Burgers, 222
    Mushroom Pasta Sauce, 230
    Mushroom Pâté, 28
    Mushroom Pizza, 250
    Pan-Seared Liver with Mushroom and
        Bacon, 128
    Portobello Asparagus Strudels, 219
    Smoked Turkey and Mushroom
        Frittata, 208
    Strip Loin with Exotic Mushrooms and
        Shallots, 138
    Triple Pork Tenderloin with Mushroom
        Stuffing, 163
    Turkey Mushroom Barley Soup, 62
    Wild Mushroom Gravy, 105
Mussels, 189
    Chilled Lemongrass Mussels, 21
    Hearty Mussel Chowder, 53
    Mussel Sausage Simmer, 162
    Red Curry Mussels, 189
    Steamed Herbed Mussels in Wine, 21
    Steamed Lemongrass Mussels, 21
Mustard
    Apple Mustard–Glazed Trout
        Fillets, 202
    Devilled Prime Rib with Roasted
        Garlic Gravy, 139
    Honey Mustard Chicken Breasts, 110
    Mustard Devilled Ribs, 150
    Pan-Seared Liver with Apple and
        Mustard, 128
    Roast Chicken Dijonnaise, 102

N
Nanaimo Bars, 372
Noodles
    Asian Turkey Noodle Soup, 62
    Beef Bourguignonne with Noodles, 130
    Chicken Noodle Soup, 63
    Glazed Pork Tenderloin with Chinese
        Noodles, 166
    Pad Thai, 247
    rice, 247
    Singapore Noodles, 246
    Spicy Thai Shrimp and Noodle Soup, 54
Nori, 22, 68
Nuts, 355. See also individual nuts.
    Health Nut Oatmeal Cookies, 352
    Nutty Caramel Brownies, 368
    Other Nut Biscotti, 358
    toasting, 317

O
Oats, 225, 273
    Nova Scotia Oatmeal Rolls, 273
    Oat Tea Biscuits with Raisins, 261
    Oatmeal Cookies, 352
Olives
    Black Olive Hummus, 30
    Lemon Olive Pork Chops, 157
Omelettes, 209
One-pot meals. See Casseroles; Stews.
Onions
    Brie, Pear and Onion Strudel on a Bed
        of Greens, 39
    Caramelized Onion Artichoke Quiche,
        212
    Easy Roast Beef with Onion Gravy, 137
    French Onion Burgers, 144
    Herb and Onion Swiss Steak, 132
    Onion Cranberry Brisket, 141
    Pan-Seared Liver and Onions, 128
    pan-seared onions and apples (tip), 163
    peeling pearl, 160
Oranges
    Blueberry Orange Almond Loaf, 258
    Chocolate Orange Pecan Oatmeal
        Cookies, 352
    Orange and Sour Cherry Buttermilk
        Cake, 306
    Orange Broccoli Chops, 158
    Orange Brown Sugar Marmalade, 383
    Orange Caramel Custard, 288
    Orange Fennel Rack of Pork, 164
    Orange Ginger Marmalade, 383
    Orange Nanaimo Bars, 372
    Orange Panna Cotta with Orange
        Caramel Sauce, 290
    Orange Pecan Meringue Cake, 317
    Orange Truffles, 375
    Pepper Orange Pork Stew, 161
    Phyllo Fruit Cups with Orange White
        Chocolate Cream, 348
    Quick Orange Buns, 262
    Seville Orange Marmalade, 383
    White Chocolate Orange Brownies, 368
Orzo
    Curried Lentil, Wild Rice and Orzo
        Salad, 79

P
Pad Thai, 247
Paella, Chicken and Seafood, 121
Pancakes. See also Blini; Latkes; Rösti
    Classic Pancakes, 263
    Puffy Dutch Pancake with Bananas
        and Strawberries, 217
Pandowdy, Pear, 334
Panforte, 369
Panna Cotta, 290
Panzanella (Bread Salad), 70
Pappadams, shallow-frying, 188
Parmesan cheese, 236
    Basil Parmesan Chicken Burgers, 120

Parmesan Chicken Burgers, 120
Pasta. *See also recipe list, p. 229.*
  amount to cook, 243
  Arrabbiata Pasta, 231
  Artichoke Pasta, 231
  cheeses for, 236
  cooking, 233
  Curried Lentil, Wild Rice and Orzo
    Salad, 79
  Grain and Pasta Side Dishes, 86
  Pasta e Fagioli, 57
  Pasta Primavera, 237
  Pasta Primavera Frittata, 208
  Penne Salad with Artichokes and
    Spinach, 78
  types of, 239
Pastitsio, 238
Pastry. *See also recipe list, p. 325;*
    Puff pastry; Phyllo pastry.
  handling made easy, 327
  ingredients and techniques, 327
Pâtés, 28
Pavlova, 293
Peaches
  Double-Crust Peach Pie, 332
  Peach Berry Crisp, 280
  Peach Chutney, 388
  Peach Ice Cream, 295
  Peach Orange Conserve, 382
  Peachy Keen Sorbet, 294
Peameal bacon
  Maple-Glazed Peameal Bacon
    Dinner, 174
  Peameal Bacon Eggs Benedict, 210
  Peameal Bacon Roast, 174
Peanuts
  Chocolate Peanut Butter
    Thumbprints, 359
  Frozen Peanut Butter Pie, 345
  Peanut Butter Brownies, 368
  Peanut Butter Cookies, 359
  Peanut Butter Nanaimo Bars, 372
  Peanut Butter Truffles, 375
  Peanut Jicama Salad, 73
Pears
  Baked Brie with Hazelnut Pear
    Topping, 18
  Brie, Pear and Onion Strudel on a Bed
    of Greens, 39
  Caramel-Baked Pear Sundaes, 298
  Dutch Pear Pie, 329
  Five-Spice Pears, 386
  Pear and Brie Quesadillas, 41
  Pear Chutney, 388
  Pear Cranberry Crisp, 280
  Pear Pandowdy, 334
  Roasted Pears in Port, 299
  White Wine Pears, 386
Peas, Rice and, 186
Pecans, 343
  Chocolate Orange Pecan Oatmeal
    Cookies, 352

Chocolate Pecan Pie, 343
Orange Pecan Meringue Cake, 317
Pecan Kugelhopf, 276
Pecan Pie, 343
Pecan Snowballs, 360
Zucchini Pecan Raisin Muffins, 254
Pecorino Romano, 237
Pectin, 384
Peking Hamburger Dumplings, 32
Penne Salad with Artichokes and
    Spinach, 78
Penne with Garlicky Rapini, 233
Peppers, sweet, 50. *See also* Chipotle
    peppers; Jalapeño peppers;
    Scotch bonnet peppers
  Big-Batch Sausage and Pepper
    Sauce, 232
  Cucumber Pepper Relish, 391
  Gazpacho, 50
  Grilled Pepper and Sausage Pizza, 249
  Pepper Orange Pork Stew, 161
  Pork and Three-Pepper Teriyaki
    Stir-Fry, 156
  Red Pepper–Glazed Pork Loin, 164
  Roasted Red Pepper Hummus, 30
  Turkey Breast Stuffed with Fennel and
    Red Pepper, 109
  Zucchini Pepper Relish, 391
  Zucchini, Sweet Red Pepper and Feta
    Frittata, 208
Perogies, 227
Pesto
  Chicken Pesto Pasta, 235
  Pesto, 235
  Pesto and Roasted Eggplant Pizza, 251
  Pesto Potato Salad, 75
  Pesto Roll-Ups, 38
Phyllo pastry, 344
  Breakfast Strudels, 216
  Brie, Pear and Onion Strudel on a Bed
    of Greens, 39
  Cherry Chocolate Baklava, 344
  Chicken Phyllo Bundles with Herbed
    Sabayon, 113
  Classic Walnut Baklava, 344
  Curried Lamb Phyllo Triangles, 40
  phyllo cups (tip), 40
  Phyllo Fruit Cups with Orange White
    Chocolate Cream, 348
  Portobello Asparagus Strudels, 219
Picadillo Empanadas, 37
Pickles, Golden Bread-and-Butter, 392
Pies. *See also recipe list, p. 325.*
  apples for, 329
  assembling, 332
  Bittersweet Chocolate Cream Pie, 341
  Chocolate Pecan Pie, 343
  Cranberry Apple Pie, 328
  Dutch Pear Pie, 329
  freezing, 332
  glazing, 332
  Mediterranean Vegetable Pie, 220

Old-Fashioned Chicken Pot Pie, 122
  pastry for, 326
  weighing down shell before baking, 338
Pilafs
  Pick-a-Grain Pilaf, 83
  Spiced Shrimp and Rice Pilaf, 188
Piña Colada Muffins, 254
Pineapple Rhubarb Jam, 379
Piri Piri Chicken, 117
Pizza. *See also recipe list, p. 229.*
  At-Home Pizzeria, 250
  Feta and Tomato Pizza, 249
  Grilled Vegetable Pizza, 251
Plums
  Apple Plum Chutney, 388
  Double-Crust Plum Pie, 332
  Plum Galette, 333
  Plum Pudding, 286
  Red Plum Ice Cream, 295
  Spiced Plum Apple Crisp, 280
Polenta Side Dish, 86
Poppy seeds
  Lemon Poppy Seed Loaf, 257
  Poppy Seed Dressing, 82
Pork. *See also* Sausage.
  spice rubs for, 173
  chops:
  Five Speedy Pork Chop Suppers, 158
  Lemon Olive Pork Chops, 157
  Pork and Three-Pepper Teriyaki
    Stir-Fry, 156
  Singapore Noodles, 246
  ground:
  Deep-Dish Tourtière, 176
  rack of:
  Jerk Roast Pork, 165
  Orange Fennel Rack of Pork, 164
  Red Pepper–Glazed Pork Loin, 164
  ribs:
  Black Bean Ribs, 171
  Honey Garlic Ribs, 171
  Korean Ribs, 171
  Slow and Easy Real Barbecued
    Ribs, 172
  Thai Ribs, 171
  roast:
  Barbecued Pork Loin with
    Rosemary, 168
  Choucroute Garnie, 175
  Grilled Pork Satays, 26
  roasting chart, 10
  shoulder butt:
  Caraway Pork Goulash, 159
  Lemon Oregano Pork Stew, 160
  Pepper Orange Pork Stew, 161
  Pulled Pork on a Bun, 169
  tenderloin:
  Cuban Grilled Pork Sandwich, 170
  Glazed Pork Tenderloin with Chinese
    Noodles, 166
  Triple Pork Tenderloin with Mushroom
    Stuffing, 163

Port Lemon Crème Caramel, 288
Portuguese Paprika Chicken, 117
Potatoes, 75
    Boiled Potatoes, 88
    Golden Latkes, 89
    Herbed Rösti, 89
    Mashed Potatoes, 86
    Oven-Baked Fish and Chips, 198
    Oven-Roasted Potatoes, 88
    Potato Gnocchi, 245
    Potato Salad, 75
    Simply the Best Scalloped Potatoes, 88
    toppings for baked (tip), 37
    Vichyssoise, 51
Poultry. See Chicken; Duck; Turkey.
Pound Cake, Lemon-Glazed, 305
Preserves. See also recipe list, p. 377.
    Apple Plum Chutney, 388
    canner basics, 384–85
    Cucumber Pepper Relish, 391
    equipment for making, 385
    freezing fruit for, 382
    Mixed Cherry Conserve, 382
    Orange Brown Sugar Marmalade, 383
    Orange Ginger Marmalade, 383
    Pear Chutney, 388
    pectin and, 384
    processing method, 378
    sugar and, 379
    testing for setting point, 381
    Three-Berry Conserve, 382
    White Wine Pears, 386
Pressure Cooker Herb and Onion Swiss
    Steak, 132
Prosciutto
    Prosciutto and Artichoke
        Quesadillas, 41
    Prosciutto Roll-Ups, 38
    Prosciutto-Stuffed Chicken
        Breasts, 118
Provençal Beef Kabobs, 151
Provolone, 237
Puddings
    Icky Sticky Baked Date Pudding, 285
    Lemon Sponge Pudding, 282
    Plum Pudding, 286
    Very Special Bread Pudding with
        Orange Crème Anglaise, 283
Puff pastry
    Brie, Pear and Onion Strudel on a Bed
        of Greens, 39
    Prosciutto Roll-Ups, 38
Pumpkin
    Creamy Pumpkin Pie, 339
    Pumpkin Crème Brûlée, 289

Q
Quesadillas, 41
Quiches, 212
Quick breads. See recipe list, p. 253.
Quinoa, 225
    Quinoa Pilaf, 83

R
Ragus, 232
Raisins
    Oat Tea Biscuits with Raisins, 261
    Zucchini Pecan Raisin Muffins, 254
Rapini, Penne with Garlicky, 233
Raspberries
    Chocolate Raspberry Rugalahs, 366
    Double-Crust Raspberry Pie, 332
    Fuzzy Raspberry Sorbet, 294
    Panna Cotta with Raspberry
        Strawberry Sauce, 290
    Raspberry and Red Currant Jelly, 385
    Raspberry Cheese Coffee Cake, 320
    Raspberry Chocolate Chip Bundt
        Cake, 321
    Raspberry Cookies and Cream Torte,
        316
    Raspberry Crème Brûlée, 289
    Raspberry Ice Cream, 295
    Raspberry Lemon Muffins, 254
    Raspberry Truffles, 375
    Raspberry Vinaigrette, 81
    Really Raspberry Sorbet, 294
Ratatouille Pasta Sauce, 230
Red Currant Jelly, Raspberry and, 385
Red Wine and Oregano Grilled Marinating
    Steak, 148
Relish, Zucchini Pepper, 391
Rhubarb, 319
    Pineapple Rhubarb Jam, 379
    Rhubarb and Strawberry Compote, 297
    Rhubarb and Strawberry Fool, 297
    Rhubarb and Strawberry Frozen
        Yogurt, 297
    Rhubarb Upside-Down Cake, 319
    Strawberry Rhubarb Crisp, 280
    Strawberry Rhubarb Galette, 333
Rice, 84
    Chicken and Seafood Paella, 121
    Chicken and Wild Rice Soup, 63
    Coconut Thai Rice Pilaf, 83
    Curried Lentil, Wild Rice and Orzo
        Salad, 79
    No-Fail Rice, 84
    Pick-a-Grain Pilaf, 83
    Rice and Peas, 186
    saffron rice (tip), 190
    Spiced Shrimp and Rice Pilaf, 188
    Sushi Rice Salad, 77
    Turkey Rice Gumbo Soup, 62
Ricotta cheese, 237
    Breaded Lemon Chicken with Ricotta
        Leek Stuffing, 112
    Spinach Ricotta Macaroni and
        Cheese, 234
Risotto, 85
Roasted Pears in Port, 299
Roasted Red Pepper Hummus, 30
Roasted Roots Salad, 74
Roasted Vegetable Dress-Ups, 93
Rolls, Nova Scotia Oatmeal, 273

Rosemary
    Barbecued Pork Loin with Rosemary,
        168
    Buttermilk Rosemary Chicken Legs, 115
    Honey Rosemary Duck, 106
    Rosemary-Crusted Rack of Lamb, 181
Rösti, Herbed, 89
Rouille, 52
Rugalahs, 366
Rye Bread, Caraway, 270

S
Saffron rice (tip), 190
Sage and Lemon Chicken Breasts, 118
Salad dressings and vinaigrettes
    Buttermilk Ranch Dressing, 82
    Creamy Cucumber Dressing, 82
    Creamy Garlic Dressing, 82
    Creamy Light Yogurt Dressing, 82
    Creamy Poppy Seed Dressing, 82
    Ever-Ready House Dressing, 81
    Honey Dijon Vinaigrette, 81
    Miso Dressing, 68
    oils for, 76
    Old-Fashioned Cooked Salad
        Dressing, 82
    Peppercorn Ranch Dressing, 82
    Raspberry Vinaigrette, 81
    Roasted Garlic Dressing, 74
    Sun-Dried Tomato Vinaigrette, 81
    Thousand Island Dressing, 81
    Tomato French Dressing, 81
Salads. See also recipe list, p. 65; Salad
        dressings and vinaigrettes
    Cucumber Raita, 188
    Cucumber Yogurt Salad, 143
    Fresh Tuna Salade Niçoise, 205
    preparing greens, 66
    Tomato and Mint Salad, 188
    Warm Grilled Flank Steak Salad, 145
Salami Quesadillas, 41
Salmon
    Cedar-Planked Salmon, 204
    Crusty Salmon Cakes, 192
    Grilled Salmon Fillets, 203
    Poached Salmon with Beurre Blanc, 190
    Quarterdeck Planked Salmon, 204
    Slow-Grilled Salmon with Garlic and
        Basil, 199
Salmon, smoked
    Cornmeal "Blini" with Smoked
        Salmon, 33
    Salmon Eggs Benedict, 210
    Smoked Salmon and Leek Frittata, 208
    Smoked Salmon Asparagus Quiche, 212
    Smoked Salmon Roll-Ups, 38
    Smoked Salmon Strata, 214
    Smoked Salmon–Stuffed Baguette, 36
Salsa
    Avocado Salsa, 226
    Mango Salsa, 167
    Peppy Salsa, 390

Salsa Baked Beans, 87
Salsa Barbecued Beef Brisket, 153
Tomato Salsa, 201
Sandwiches. See also Spreads and
    toppings.
    Artichoke and Gorgonzola–Stuffed
        Baguette, 36
    Barbecued Tofu Sandwiches with
        Aïoli, 223
    Caprese sandwich (tip), 70
    Cuban Grilled Pork Sandwich, 170
    French Toast Sandwiches, 213
    Pulled Pork on a Bun, 169
    Smoked Salmon–Stuffed Baguette, 36
Saskatoon Berry Pie, 331
Satays, 26
Sauces, dipping. See Dipping sauces.
Sauces, dessert
    Apple Cranberry Sauce, 264
    Caramel Sauce, 298
    Cherry Berry Sauce, 264
    Chocolate Sauce, 312
    Orange Caramel Sauce, 290
    Orange Crème Anglaise, 283
    Orange Hard Sauce, 287
    Passion Fruit Sauce, 284
    Raspberry Sauce, 316
    Raspberry Strawberry Sauce, 290
    Strawberry Sauce, 312
    Toffee Sauce, 285
Sauces, savoury
    Big-Batch Beef Ragu, 232
    Big-Batch Cacciatore Sauce, 232
    Big-Batch Sausage and Pepper
        Sauce, 232
    Chili Sauce, 389
    Curry Sauce, 34
    Dill Sauce, 204
    Easy Horseradish Cream Sauce, 137
    Fine Tomato Pasta Sauce, A, 230
    Hollandaise Sauce, 210
    Homemade Tomato Sauce, 387
    Instant Tangy Sauce, 34
    Mushroom Butter Sauce, 245
    Mushroom Pasta Sauce, 230
    Peppy Salsa, 390
    Quick Clam Pasta Sauce, 230
    Ratatouille Pasta Sauce, 230
    Red Curry Sauce, 197
    Sage and Butter Sauce, 245
    Sausage Fennel Pasta Sauce, 230
    Southwestern Barbecue Sauce, 34
    Tangy Barbecue Sauce, 147
    tartar sauce (tip), 192
    Tofu Aïoli, 223
Sauerbraten Beef Stew, 131
Sauerkraut, 175
    Choucroute Garnie, 175
Sausage
    Big-Batch Sausage and Pepper Sauce,
        232
    Grilled Pepper and Sausage Pizza, 249

Layered Chorizo Bake, 215
Mussel Sausage Simmer, 162
Sausage Fennel Pasta Sauce, 230
Spicy Sausage and Rigatoni Bake, 241
Scotch bonnet peppers, 165
    Jerk Roast Pork, 165
Sea Bass, Glazed with Red Curry Sauce, 197
Seafood. See Fish and seafood.
Shallots
    Shallot Peppercorn Butter, 152
    Strip Loin with Exotic Mushrooms and
        Shallots, 138
Shortbread Cookies, 362
Shrimp
    about, 24, 25
    Cajun Shrimp, 24
    Creamy Shrimp Bake, 240
    Grilled Jumbo Shrimp Skewers with
        Dipping Sauce, 25
    Lemon Garlic Shrimp, 24
    Roasted Arctic Char with Shrimp, 195
    Shrimp Braised in Tomato Sauce with
        Feta, 187
    Shrimp Caesar Salad, 69
    Spiced Shrimp and Rice Pilaf, 188
    Spicy Thai Shrimp and Noodle Soup, 54
    Thai Curry Shrimp, 24
Sicilian Chicken, 98
Side dishes. See recipe list, p. 65.
Singapore Noodles, 246
Slow-Cooker Beef Bourguignonne, 130
Slow-Cooker Beef Stew, 129
Slow-Cooker Black Bean Chili with
    Avocado Salsa, 226
Slow-Cooker Chicken Noodle Soup, 63
Slow-Cooker Herb and Onion Swiss
    Steak, 132
Slow-Cooker Jamaican Beef Pepper Pot, 61
Slow-Cooker Sauerbraten Beef Stew, 131
Soda Bread, 260
Sorbets, 294
Soufflés
    Cheese Soufflé, 218
    Vanilla Soufflé with Passion Fruit
        Sauce, 284
Soups. See recipe list, p. 43.
Spaghetti Carbonara, 236
Speculaas, 364
Spinach
    Baby Spinach and Goat Cheese
        Salad, 67
    Eggs Florentine, 210
    Penne Salad with Artichokes and
        Spinach, 78
    Spinach and Cheese Quesadillas, 41
    Spinach and Feta Soufflé, 218
    Spinach Ricotta Macaroni and Cheese,
        234
Spreads and toppings
    Bacon and Sun-Dried Tomato
        Topping, 18
    Chicken Liver Pâté with Basil, 28

Fruit Chutney Topping, 18
Fruity Cream Cheese, 213
Hazelnut Pear Topping, 18
Mushroom Pâté, 28
Strawberry Mint Topping, 18
Tangy Cranberry Topping, 18
Squash Risotto, 85
Stews. See also Casseroles.
    Beef Bourguignonne with Noodles, 130
    Braised Chicken and Bok Choy, 97
    Caraway Pork Goulash, 159
    Chicken Adobo, 101
    Quick Chicken in Wine, 99
    Lemon Oregano Pork Stew, 160
    Mussel Sausage Simmer, 162
    Old-Fashioned Beef Stew, 129
    Old-Fashioned Chicken Pot Pie, with
        Dumplings, 123
    Pepper Orange Pork Stew, 161
    Thai Green Curry Chicken, 100
Stir-fried
    Beef and Broccoli Stir-Fry, 127
    Pork and Three-Pepper Teriyaki
        Stir-Fry, 156
Stocks, soup, 47
Stratas, 214
Strawberries
    Baked Brie with Strawberry Mint
        Topping, 18
    freezing for jam, 380
    Fresh Strawberry Pie, 337
    Panna Cotta with Raspberry
        Strawberry Sauce, 290
    Puffy Dutch Pancake with Bananas
        and Strawberries, 217
    Rhubarb and Strawberry Compote, 297
    Rhubarb and Strawberry Fool, 297
    Rhubarb and Strawberry Frozen
        Yogurt, 297
    Strawberry Ice Cream, 295
    Strawberry Jam, 380
    Strawberry Rhubarb Crisp, 280
    Strawberry Rhubarb Galette, 333
    Strawberry Rhubarb Jam, 380
    Strawberry Sauce, 312
    Strawberry Shortcake, 313
    strawberry shortcake with tea biscuits
        (tip), 261
    Versatile Crêpe with Strawberries
        Romanoff Filling, The, 265
Strudel
    Breakfast Strudels, 216
    Brie, Pear and Onion Strudel on a Bed
        of Greens, 39
    Portobello Asparagus Strudels, 219
Stuffing
    Bacon and Chestnut Stuffing, 104
    Bacon and Fresh Chestnut Stuffing, 104
    Couscous Stuffing, 103
    Italian Bread Stuffing, 104
    Mushroom Stuffing, 163
    Ricotta Leek Stuffing, 112

Substitutions, 2–4
Sugar Cookies, 365
Sumac spice, 66
Sundaes, 298
Sushi Platter, 22
Sushi Rice Salad, 77
Swiss Steak, Herb and Onion, 132

T
Tabbouleh Salad, 76
Tarte Tatin, 330
Tarts. *See also recipe list, p. 325.*
    Puckery Lemon Tart, 335
    Two-Cheese Tomato Tart, 221
Tea Biscuits, 261
Thai Curry Shrimp, 24
Thai Dipping Sauce, 25
Thai Green Curry Chicken, 100
Thai Ribs, 171
Tiramisu, 291
Tofu Sandwiches with Aïoli, Barbecued,
    223
Tomatoes, 387
    canned, 230
    Caprese Salad, 70
    Feta and Tomato Pizza, 249
    Fine Tomato Pasta Sauce, A, 230
    Gazpacho, 50
    Homemade Tomato Sauce, 387
    Tomato and Mint Salad, 188
    Tomato French Dressing, 81
    Tomato Macaroni and Cheese, 234
    Two-Cheese Tomato Tart, 221
Tomatoes, sun-dried
    Baked Brie with Bacon and Sun-Dried
        Tomato Topping, 18
    Sun-Dried Tomato Hummus, 30
    Sun-Dried Tomato Vinaigrette, 81
Tortes
    Frozen Lemon Meringue Torte, 296

Raspberry Cookies and Cream
    Torte, 316
Tortillas
    Quesadillas, 41
    Steak and Vegetable Fajitas, 126
    tortilla spirals (tip), 36
Tourtière, Deep-Dish, 176
Trifle, Very Berry, 292
Trout
    Apple Mustard–Glazed Trout Fillets,
        202
    Grilled Trout Fillets with Tandoori
        Marinade, 202
Tuna
    Fresh Tuna Salade Niçoise, 205
    Hearty Tuna Chowder, 53
Turkey
    Barbecue-Roasted Turkey, 114
    Charmoula Roast Turkey Breast, 108
    Chicken or Turkey Stock, 47
    Five Turkey Soups, 62
    Golden Roast Turkey, 105
    leftovers for soup, 47
    Roast Turkey with Bacon and Chestnut
        Stuffing, 104
    roasting, 10
    Smoked Turkey and Mushroom
        Frittata, 208
    stuffing, 105
    Turkey Breast Stuffed with Fennel and
        Red Pepper, 109
    Turkey Burgers, 120

V
Vanilla Soufflé with Passion Fruit Sauce,
    284
Vegetables. *See also individual vegetables.*
    Beet and Vegetable Borscht, 46
    boiling and steaming, 90–91
    buying, 12–15

Classic Pot Roast with Vegetables, 142
    Grilled Vegetable Antipasto, 31
    Grilled Vegetable Pizza, 251
    grilling, 93
    Mediterranean Vegetable Pie, 220
    microwaving, 91
    Roasted Roots Salad, 74
    Roasted Vegetable Dress-Ups, 93
    roasting, 92, 220
    Steak and Vegetable Fajitas, 126
    Turkey Vegetable Soup, 62
Vegetarian. *See recipe list, p. 207.*
Vichyssoise, 51
Vinegars
    Herb Vinegars, 393
    types of, 74

W
Waffles, 264
Watercress Vichyssoise, 51
Wheat berries, 225
    Wheat Berries Side Dish, 86
Whole Wheat or Multigrain Pizza
    Dough, 248

Y
Yeast breads. *See recipe list, p. 253.*
Yogurt
    Creamy Light Yogurt Dressing, 82
    Cucumber Raita, 188
    Cucumber Yogurt Salad, 143
    Rhubarb and Strawberry Frozen
        Yogurt, 297

Z
Zucchini
    Zucchini Pecan Raisin Muffins, 254
    Zucchini Pepper Relish, 391
    Zucchini, Sweet Red Pepper and Feta
        Frittata, 208